THE WELLCOME-MARSTON ARCHAEOLOGICAL RESEARCH EXPEDITION
TO THE NEAR EAST
VOLUME IV

LACHISH IV

(TELL ED-DUWEIR)

THE BRONZE AGE

TEXT

THE WELLCOME-MARSTON ARCHAEOLOGICAL RESEARCH EXPEDITION
TO THE NEAR EAST

LACHISH IV
(TELL ED-DUWEIR)

THE BRONZE AGE

BY

OLGA TUFNELL

D. F. W. BADEN-POWELL	DOROTHEA M. A. BATE	JAROSLAV ČERNÝ
DAVID DIRINGER	MADELEINE GILES	HANS HELBAEK
B. S. J. ISSERLIN	MARGARET A. MURRAY	BARBARA PARKER
EDITH PORADA	F. C. THOMPSON ERIC TODD	JOHN WAECHTER

TEXT

PUBLISHED FOR
THE TRUSTEES OF THE LATE SIR HENRY WELLCOME
BY THE
OXFORD UNIVERSITY PRESS
LONDON   NEW YORK   TORONTO
1958

PRINTED IN GREAT BRITAIN

DEDICATED

WITH GRATITUDE AND AFFECTION

TO THE ARAB STAFF AND WORKERS

WHOSE LOYALTY, SKILL AND ENTHUSIASM

WERE ESSENTIAL TO

THE SUCCESS OF OUR EFFORTS

AT TELL ED-DUWEIR

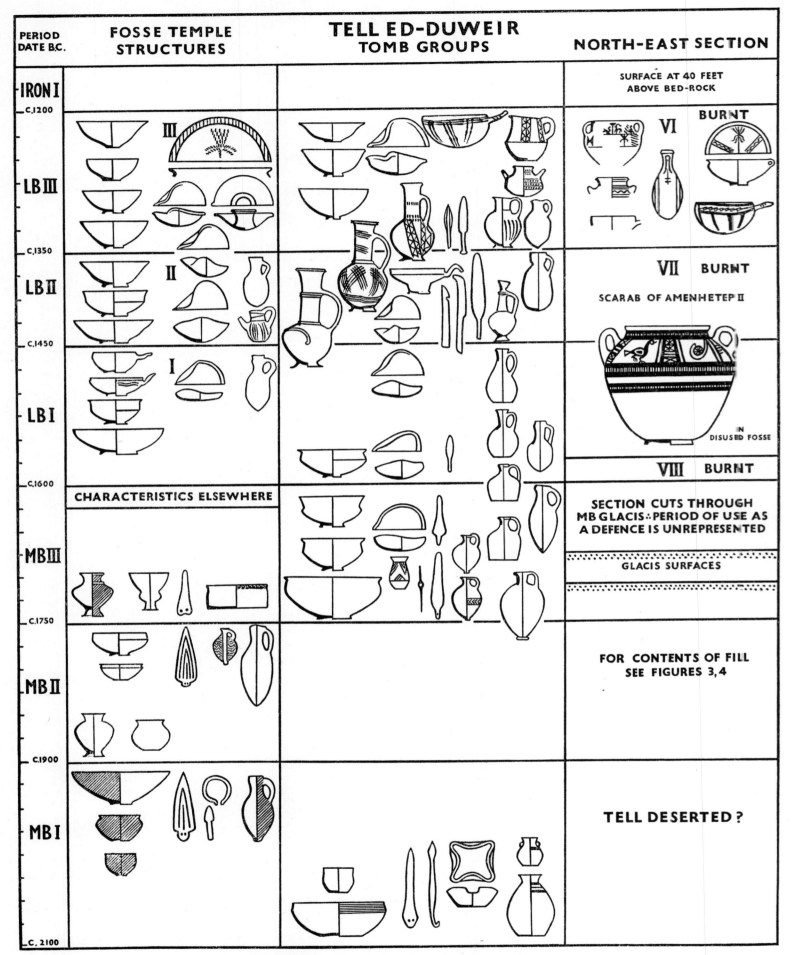

PERIOD DATE B.C.	FOSSE TEMPLE STRUCTURES	TELL ED-DUWEIR TOMB GROUPS	NORTH-EAST SECTION

MIDDLE AND LATE BRONZE AGE TYPES

PREFACE

IN this last of four volumes on Lachish, I have had invaluable help from many experts whose special knowledge has enabled me to present authoritative reports on material covering nearly two millennia, from before 3000 to just after 1200 B.C. Though the problems evoked are complex, they provide many new facts concerning the development of man's industry, especially with regard to his early experiments in the potter's craft, his surprising mastery of metallurgical processes, and the first efforts, as yet so imperfectly understood, towards the evolution of an alphabet.

The peoples of Palestine are already well known to us through the Old Testament, though no one can deny that the sequence and relative importance of events is still obscure, particularly in the formative period of the Patriarchs. Here, perhaps, the work at Lachish has a crucial contribution to make which cannot yet be fully assessed.

If the record proves of any value to future scholars, we have to thank those who sponsored the excavations as part of a broad scheme of research into the study of man. My own debt to them can only be partially repaid in a long task now ended, offered in homage to the living and the dead.

O. T.

1955

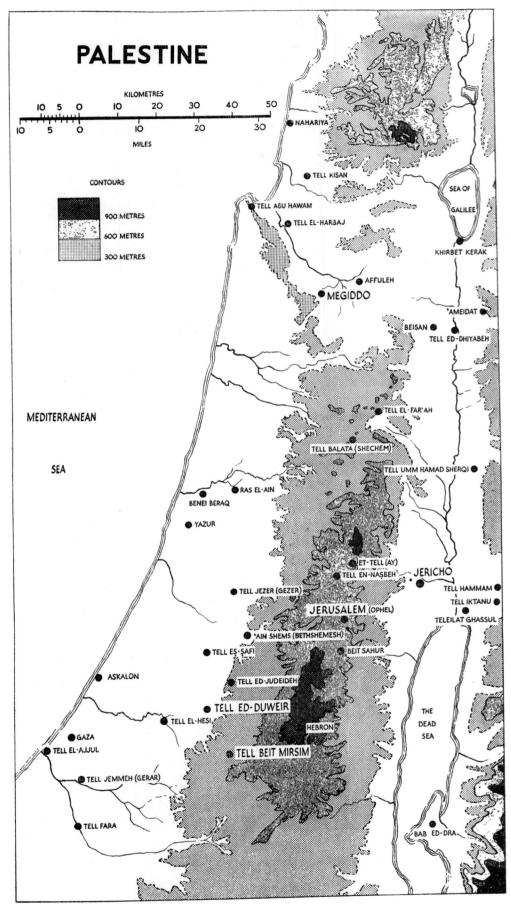

PALESTINE

KILOMETRES

10 5 0 10 20 30 40 50

10 5 0 10 20 30

MILES

CONTOURS

900 METRES
600 METRES
300 METRES

MEDITERRANEAN

SEA

● NAHARIYA

● TELL KISAN

SEA OF
GALILEE

● TELL ABU HAWAM
● TELL EL-HARBAJ

KHIRBET KERAK ●

● AFFULEH

● MEGIDDO

'AMEIDAT ●

BEISAN ●
TELL ED-DHIYABEH ●

● TELL EL-FAR'AH

TELL BALATA (SHECHEM)

TELL UMM HAMAD SHERQI ●

● RAS EL-AIN

BENEI BERAQ ●

● YAZUR

● ET-TELL (AY)
● TELL EN-NAṢBEH

JERICHO ●
TELL HAMMAM

TELL IKTANU

TELEILAT GHASSUL

● TELL JEZER (GEZER)

JERUSALEM (OPHEL)

● 'AIN SHEMS (BETHSHEMESH)

● TELL EṢ-ṢAFI
BEIT SAHUR

● ASKALON

TELL ED-JUDEIDEH

● TELL ED-DUWEIR

● TELL EL-HESI

THE
DEAD
SEA

HEBRON

● GAZA
● TELL EL-AJJUL

TELL BEIT MIRSIM

● TELL JEMMEH (GERAR)

● TELL FARA

BAB ED-DRA ●

MAP OF PALESTINE SHOWING SITES MENTIONED IN THIS BOOK

CONTRIBUTORS

FIELD WORK

In the first pages of *Lachish III* were recorded the names of the staff and visitors who took part in the varied duties of field excavation and supervision under the leadership of JAMES LESLIE STARKEY. This book is also the fruit of their labours, and those who shared in the task were:

G. L. HARDING, 1932–1936
R. RICHMOND BROWN, 1932–1937
C. H. INGE, 1932–1938
MISS O. TUFNELL, 1932–1938
W. B. K. SHAW, 1932–1935
H. W. PUMMELL, 1933–1938
DONALD BROWN, 1932–1935
MR. and MRS. H. DUNSCOMBE COLT, 1932–1933
H. H. McWILLIAMS, 1932–1933
L. UPTON WAY, 1932–1933
R. M. COX, 1933–1934
MISS E. DYOTT (Mrs. W. B. K. Shaw), 1934–1935
G. I. GOULDEN, 1934–1935

J. RICHMOND, 1934–1935
H. V. BONNEY, 1935–1938
A. LEWIS, 1935–1936
MISS L. McNAIR SCOTT (Mrs. Murray-Thriepland), 1935–1936
G. B. GARDINER, 1935–1936
MR. and MRS. E. F. WARREN HASTINGS, 1936–1938
J. S. KIRKMAN, 1936–1938
MISS B. H. PARKER, 1936–1937
MISS J. CROWFOOT (Mrs. Payne), 1936–1937
MISS M. V. SETON-WILLIAMS, 1937–1938
MISS NINA CUMING, 1937–1938
N. SHIAH, 1938

FIELD SURVEY, PLANS AND DRAWINGS

Based on the original survey made by MR. W. B. K. SHAW, which was continued by MR. G. I. GOULDEN, the main plans which appear in *Lachish IV* are largely the work of MR. H. V. BONNEY, who was in charge of the Survey for the last three seasons.

MR. G. LANKESTER HARDING made the field notes for the stratification of the North-East Section reproduced on Pl. 96, and the finished drawing, like most of the charts and figures in the text, is the work of MR. M. R. RICKETTS. Some pottery drawings were also made by MISS E. H. WEST; otherwise most of the finds were drawn in the field by Mr. Harding and myself, while DR. J. WAECHTER drew the flints on Pl. 19 and MR. J. B. HENNESSY drew the side types of scarabs on Pl. 41.

PHOTOGRAPHY

MR. RICHMOND BROWN was the Expedition's Photographer through five seasons until the final year, when MISS M. V. SETON-WILLIAMS took over the photographic records which he had begun. MR. SCHWEIG, Official Photographer to the then Government of Palestine, Department of Antiquities, was responsible for most of the views on Pl. 8.

In recent years, MR. M. B. COOKSON, Official Photographer to the Institute of Archaeology, has put all the resources of his Department at our disposal and, among many individual photographs throughout the book, the sherds on Pls. 11–13 are good examples of his skill. The magnified plant materials on the upper part of Pl. 15 are reproduced from the photographs of DR. HANS HELBAEK.

CONTRIBUTORS

REPAIR AND RECONSTRUCTION OF POTTERY

Miss Olive Starkey has again shown her deep and personal interest in the repair of the collection now housed in London, and Miss Ione Gedye and the students of their department at the Institute of Archaeology have assisted generously in many ways.

TEXT

In the assembly of comparative material as set out in Chapter 9, and in the assessment of the range of the Chalcolithic and Early Bronze Age groups described in Chapters 12 and 13, Dr. B. S. J. Isserlin supplied most valuable notes.

Once again, the list of Hieroglyphic and Ornamental Seals in Chapter 7 was compiled with the help and technical advice of Dr. M. A. Murray, while I am also indebted to Mr. Alan Rowe, whose readings of those scarabs now in Jerusalem first appeared in his *Catalogue of Egyptian Scarabs in the Palestine Archaeological Museum*.

Dr. E. Porada and Miss B. H. Parker are responsible between them for the notes on Cylinder Seals.

Opinions on the Canaanite inscriptions, discussed by many experts in the press and elsewhere since they were discovered, are summarized by Dr. David Diringer in the first part of Chapter 8. He also assembled notes concerning the etymology of the name Lachish to which Professor A. M. Honeyman has contributed his views.

In consultation with Sir Alan Gardiner, Professor Jaroslav Černý prepared the facsimile drawings and translations of the hieratic inscriptions on Pl. 44, in so far as the originals are decipherable.

Miss Linda Melton took a large and patient share in the preparation of the lists and the assembly of plates for three full years, and her place was taken in the final stages by Miss Patricia Wardle and Miss Rosalie Harper Ball.

The Staff of The Wellcome Foundation have given invaluable help in the preparation of the blocks, and they have co-operated throughout with the Printer and the Oxford University Press.

REPORTS AND APPENDICES

The value of this book is much enhanced by the reports on special subjects which are published as Appendices and elsewhere throughout the text.

Dr. Hans Helbaek of the National Museum, Copenhagen, has prepared an informative report on the Plant Economy of Ancient Lachish from most unpromising material.

Dr. I. G. Cunnison and Miss Madeleine Giles, under the supervision of Dr. J. C. Trevor of the University Museum of Archaeology and Anthropology, Cambridge, supplied the measurements and prepared the report on the human remains which date from the Bronze Age.

The late Miss D. M. A. Bate examined animal bones of the same period and Mr. D. F. W. Baden-Powell has identified and reported on shells from the Section and Tombs.

Dr. J. Waechter sorted the flint implements from surface and stratified deposits and his conclusions are the subject of Appendix C.

Metal analyses prepared by the staff of the National Physical Laboratory under the supervision of Dr. C. H. Desch will prove important in relation to results from other sites.

The metallurgical report on three daggers of different phases of the Bronze Age is perhaps the first comparative analysis on weapons from the same site to be made by the latest methods. It is due to the kind co-operation of Professor F. C. Thompson of the University of Manchester.

For many shorter reports and identifications which are incorporated throughout the text, The Wellcome Trust wish to express their thanks and gratitude to:

The Staff of the British Museum (Natural History) for various identifications of minerals.

10

CONTRIBUTORS

MR. H. C. BECK for the report on the gold bead, pp. 73 f.

MRS. G. M. CROWFOOT and MR. T. MIDGLEY for notes on textile and basket impressions, Pl. 13.

MR. G. C. GRIFFITHS for kiln tests on clay samples and for notes on the potter's methods and equipment, incorporated in Chapter 6.

DR. F. H. STUBBINGS for revision of the section on imported Mycenaean wares in Chapter 10.

MR. ERIC TODD for a most detailed examination of the bone object, Pl. 21.

PROFESSOR W. E. S. TURNER, University of Sheffield, for the report on the glass figurine from Tomb 4004, Pl. 27, and for examination of pottery crucibles, Type 71 on Pl. 57.

PROFESSOR F. E. ZEUNER and DR. I. W. CORNWALL kindly arranged for several analyses to be made of mineral substances.

To all those who have so kindly read sections of the proof, I offer my sincere thanks.

UNIVERSITY OF LONDON, INSTITUTE OF ARCHAEOLOGY

With the completion of the Lachish publications, the type specimens, photographs and records of the expedition will be presented to the Institute of Archaeology, where the material is available for study and the records may be seen.

PROFESSOR V. GORDON CHILDE, his Professorial, Administrative and Technical Staff have done all in their power to make these years of study in the Institute a happy and rewarding time.

CONTENTS

CONTENTS

14

LIST OF ILLUSTRATIONS

15

LIST OF ILLUSTRATIONS

LIST OF ILLUSTRATIONS

BIBLIOGRAPHY WITH ABBREVIATIONS

AAA   *Annals of Archaeology and Anthropology, University of Liverpool.* (Liverpool, 1908–1940.)

AASOR   *Annual of the American School of Oriental Research.* (New Haven, 1920–)

Abusir el Meleq   MÖLLERS, G., and SCHARFF, A.: *Archaeologischen Ergebnisse des Vorgeschichtenlichen Gräberfelds von Abusir el Meleq.* (Leipzig, 1926.)

ADAJ   *Annual of the Department of Antiquities of Jordan.* (Amman, 1951–)

Aegean Arch.   CASSON, S. (ed.): *Essays in Aegean Archaeology presented to Sir Arthur Evans.* (Oxford, 1927.)

AG I–IV   PETRIE, F.: *Ancient Gaza, I–IV.* BSAE LIII–LVI. (London, 1931–1934.)

AG V   PETRIE, F.: *City of Shepherd Kings,* and MACKAY, E. J. H., and MURRAY, M. A.: *Ancient Gaza, V* BSAE LXIV. (London, 1952.)

AJA   *American Journal of Archaeology, Archaeological Institute of America.* (Concord, 1885–)

AJSLL   *American Journal of Semitic Languages and Literatures.* (Chicago, 1897–).

Alalakh   WOOLLEY, SIR LEONARD: *Alalakh.* (Oxford, 1955.)

Alalakh Chron.   SMITH, S.: *Alalakh and Chronology.* (London, 1940.)

Alphabet   DIRINGER, D.: *The Alphabet: a key to the history of mankind.* (London, 1948.)

Amulets   PETRIE, F.: *Amulets.* (London, 1914.)

Ancient Records   BREASTED, J. H.: *Ancient Records of Egypt. Historical Documents from the earliest times to the Persian conquest, Vols. 1–5.* (Chicago, 1920–1923.)

Antiquity   *Antiquity.* (Gloucester, 1927–)

APEF   *Annual of the Palestine Exploration Fund.* (London, 1911–)

Arabah   GARSTANG, J.: *El Arabah.* BSAE VI. (London, 1900.)

Arch.   *Archaeologia.* Society of Antiquaries of London. (London 1849–)

Arch. Pal.   ALBRIGHT, W. F.: *The Archaeology of Palestine.* (Pelican Books, London, 1949.)

Armageddon   FISHER, C. S.: *The Excavation of Armageddon.* Oriental Institute of Chicago No. 4. (Chicago, 1929.)

AS   GRANT, E., and WRIGHT, G. E.: *Rumeileh, Ain Shems Excavations, Vols. I–V.* (Haverford, 1931–1939.)

Ay   MARQUET-KRAUSE, J.: *Les Fouilles d'Ay (et-Tell).* (Paris, 1949.)

B.I.   DUNAND, M.: *Fouilles de Byblos I.* (Paris, 1939.)

BASOR   *Bulletin of the American School of Oriental Research.* (Baltimore, 1919–)

BBSAJ   *Bulletin of the British School of Archaeology in Jerusalem.* (London, 1922–1925.)

BDS   PETRIE, F.: *Buttons and Design Scarabs.* BSAE XXXVIII. (London, 1925.)

BE   MONTET, P.: *Byblos et l'Egypte.* (Paris, 1928.)

Beck   BECK, H. C.: *The Classification and Nomenclature of Beads.* (*Arch. LXXXVII,* 1927; reprinted separately in 1928.)

Beni Hasan   NEWBERRY, P. E.: *Beni Hasan I.* (London, 1893.)

BM   BLISS, F. J., and MACALISTER, R. A. S.: *Excavations in Palestine.* (London, 1902.)

19

BIBLIOGRAPHY WITH ABBREVIATIONS

BMB   *Bulletin du Musée de Beyrouth.* (Paris, 1937–)

BMFA   *Bulletin of the Museum of Fine Arts, Boston.*

BP I   PETRIE, F., and TUFNELL, O.; *Beth-Pelet I.* BSAE XLVIII. (London, 1930.)

BP II   MACDONALD, E., STARKEY, J. L., and HARDING, L.: *Beth-Pelet II.* BSAE LII. (London, 1932.)

BS   GRANT, E.: *Beth-shemesh.* (Haverford, 1929.)

B-S   ROWE, A.: *Beth-Shan, Vols. I and II, Pt. I.* (Pennsylvania 1930, 1940). FITZGERALD, G. M.; *Vol. II, Pts. II and III.* (1930, 1931.)

BSAA   *Annual Report of the British School of Archaeology in Athens.* (London, 1918–)

CAH   *Cambridge Ancient History.* (Cambridge, 1928–)

Cemeteries II–III   PEET, T. E.: *The Cemeteries of Abydos II–III.* (London, 1913, 1914.)

Ch. Tombs   WACE, A. J. B.: *Chamber Tombs at Mycenae. Archaeologia LXXXII.* (London, 1932.)

CPP   DUNCAN, J. G.: *Corpus of Palestinian Pottery.* BSAE XLIX. (London, 1930.)

CTT   CARTER, H.: *The Tomb of Tutankhamen I, II.* (London, 1926.)

Dawn   CHILDE, V. G.: *The Dawn of European Civilisation.* (London, 1950.)

Deshasheh   PETRIE, F.: *Deshasheh.* (London, 1898.)

Dict. Géog.   GAUTHIER, H.: *Dictionnaire des noms géographiques contenus dans les textes hiéroglyphiques, Vols. I–VII.* (Cairo, 1925–1931.)

Egyptian Grammar   GARDINER, SIR ALAN: *Egyptian Grammar.* 2nd ed. (Oxford, 1950.)

Exc. Cyp.   MURRAY, A. S., SMITH, A. H., and WALTERS, H. B.: *Excavations in Cyprus.* (London, 1900.)

FFSV   PETRIE, F.: *Funeral Furniture of Egypt; Stone and Metal Vases.* BSAE LIX. (London, 1937.)

FGO   BLINKENBURG, C.: *Fibules Grecques et Orientales.* (Copenhagen, 1926.)

Furumark CMP   FURUMARK, A.: *The Chronology of Mycenaean Pottery.* (Stockholm, 1941.)

Furumark MP   FURUMARK, A.: *The Mycenaean Pottery.* (Stockholm, 1941.)

Gauthier   GAUTHIER, H.: *Le Livre des rois d'Egypte.* (Cairo, 1907.)

Gerar   PETRIE, F.: *Gerar.* BSAE XLIII. (London, 1928.)

Gezer   MACALISTER, R. A. S.: *The Excavation of Gezer. 1902–5 and 1907–9. Vols. I–III.* (London, 1912.)

GR   PETRIE, F.: *Gizeh and Rifeh.* BSAE XIII. (London, 1907.)

Great Tombs   EMERY, W. B.: *Great Tombs of the First Dynasty.* (London, 1949.)

Gurob   PETRIE, F.: *Gurob.* BSAE XLI. (London, 1927.)

Gurney   GURNEY, O. R.: *The Hittites.* (Pelican Books, London, 1952.)

Hall   HALL, H. R.: *Catalogue of Egyptian Scarabs, etc. in the British Museum.* (London, 1913.)

Harageh   ENGELBACH, R., and GUNN, B.: *Harageh.* BSAE XXVIII. (London, 1923.)

Hayes   HAYES, W.: *The Scepter of Egypt.* (New York, 1953.)

HE   PETRIE, F. and others: *A History of Egypt, Vols. I–VI.* (London, 1896–1905.)

HIC   PETRIE, F., and DUNCAN, J. G.: *Hyksos and Israelite Cities.* BSAE XII. (London, 1906.)

HNM   *Handbook to the Nicholson Museum, University of Sydney.* 2nd ed. (Sydney, 1948.)

HS   PETRIE, F.: *Historical Scarabs.* (London, 1889.)

IKG   PETRIE, F.: *Illahun, Kahun and Gurob.* (London, 1871.)

BIBLIOGRAPHY WITH ABBREVIATIONS

ILN   *Illustrated London News.*

Iraq   *Iraq, British School of Archaeology in Iraq.* (London, 1934–)

JAOS   *Journal of the American Oriental Society.* (New Haven, 1843–)

JPOS   *Journal of the Palestine Oriental Society.* (Jerusalem, 1923–1948)

JST   VINCENT, H.: *Jerusalem Sous Terre, Les Recentes Fouilles d'Ophel.* (London, 1911.)

L. I   TORCZYNER, H., HARDING, L., LEWIS, A., and STARKEY, J. L.: *The Lachish Letters.* (Oxford, 1938.)

L. II   TUFNELL, O., INGE, C. H., and HARDING, L.: *Lachish II: The Fosse Temple.* (Oxford, 1940).

L. III   TUFNELL, O.: *Lachish III: The Iron Age.* (Oxford, 1953.)

Leach   LEACH, BERNARD: *A Potter's Book.* (London, 1945.)

LGM   PETRIE, F.: *Labyrinth, Gerzeh and Mazghuneh.* BSAE XXI. (London, 1912.)

M. II   LOUD, GORDON: *Megiddo II.* (Chicago, 1948.)

Mélanges Syriens   *Mélanges Syriens offerts à M. Réné Dussaud.* (Paris, 1939.)

Mersin   GARSTANG, J.: *Prehistoric Mersin.* (Oxford, 1953.)

Missions en Chypre   SCHAEFFER, C. F. A.: *Missions en Chypre 1932–1935.* (Paris, 1936.)

MJ   *The Museum Journal of the Museum of the University of Pennsylvania.* (Philadelphia, 1917–)

MMC   BLISS, F. J.: *A Mound of Many Cities.* (London, 1894.)

Mound of the Jew   NAVILLE, E., and GRIFFITH, F. Ll.: *The Mound of the Jew and the City of Onias. Antiquities of Tell el Yahudiyeh.* (London, 1887, 1890.)

MPL   STUBBINGS, F. H.: *Mycenæan Pottery from the Levant.* (Cambridge, 1951.)

MRMC   MAY, HERBERT GORDON: *Material Remains of the Megiddo Cult.* (Chicago, 1935.)

MT   GUY, P. L. O., and ENGBERG, R. M.: *Megiddo Tombs.* (Chicago, 1938.)

Mutesellim   SCHUMACHER, G., and WATZINGER, C.: *Tell el-Mutesellim I, II.* (Leipzig, 1908–1929.)

New Light   CHILDE, V. G.: *New Light on the Most Ancient East.* (London, 1952.)

NS   NEWBERRY, P. E.: *Scarabs.* (London, 1906.)

ODU   PETRIE, F.: *Objects of Daily Use.* (London, 1927.)

OIP   SCHMIDT, E. F.: *The Alishar Hüyük. Seasons of 1928 and 1929, Part I.* University of Chicago Oriental Institute Publications, Volume XIX. (Chicago, 1932.)

PCBA   SJÖQVIST, ERIK: *Problems of the Late Cypriote Bronze Age.* The Swedish Cyprus Expedition. (Stockholm, 1940.)

PE   PETRIE, F.: *Prehistoric Egypt.* BSAE XXXI. (London, 1920.)

PEC   PETRIE, F.: *Corpus of Prehistoric Pottery.* BSAE XXXII. (London, 1921.)

Penn. Univ. Mus. Bull.   *Bulletin of the Museum of the University of Pennsylvania.* (Philadelphia, 1930–)

PEQ   *Palestine Exploration Fund Quarterly Statement.* (London, 1869–)

PPEB   WRIGHT, G. E.: *The Pottery of Palestine to the end of the Early Bronze Age.* (New Haven. 1937.)

Prosymna   BLEGEN, C. W.: *Prosymna.* (Cambridge, 1937.)

PSC   PETRIE, F.: *Scarabs and Cylinders.* BSAE XXIX. (London, 1917.)

PTW   PETRIE, F.: *Tools and Weapons.* BSAE XXX. (London, 1917.)

QB   BRUNTON, G.: *Qau and Badari I–III.* BSAE XLIV–XLVI. (London, 1927–1929.)

BIBLIOGRAPHY WITH ABBREVIATIONS

QDAP   *Quarterly of the Department of Antiquities, Palestine.* (Jerusalem, 1931–1946.)

Ranke   RANKE, H.: *Die Agyptischen Personennamen.* (Hamburg, 1935.)

RB   *Revue Biblique.* (Paris, 1932–.)

Rel. Chron.   EHRICH, R. W. (ed.): *Relative Chronologies in Old World Archeology.* (Chicago, 1953.)

RES   ROWE, ALAN: *A Catalogue of Egyptian Scarabs in the Palestine Archaeological Museum.* (Cairo, 1936.)

Risdon   RISDON, D. L.: *A Study of Cranial and other Human Remains from Palestine excavated at Tell ed-Duweir.* (*Biometrika 31*, London, 1939.)

RPP   INGHOLT, HARALD: *Rapport Préliminaire sur la Première Campagne des Fouilles de Hama.* (Copenhagen, 1934.)

RPS   INGHOLT, HARALD: *Rapport Préliminaire sur sept campagnes de Fouilles à Hama en Syrie.* (Copenhagen, 1940.)

RT   PETRIE, F.: *Royal Tombs of the First Dynasty, I and II.* Egyptian Exploration Fund 18th and 21st Memoir. (London, 1900, 1902.)

SAOC 10   Studies in Ancient Oriental Civilisation, No. 10. ENGBERG, R. M., and SHIPTON, G. M.: *Notes on the Chalcolithic and Early Bronze Age Pottery of Megiddo.* (Chicago, 1934.)

SAOC 17   Studies in Ancient Oriental Civilisation, No. 17. SHIPTON, G. M.: *Notes on the Megiddo Pottery of Strata VI–XX.* (Chicago, 1939.)

SAOC 18   Studies in Ancient Oriental Civilisation No. 18. ENGBERG, R. M.: *The Hyksos Reconsidered.* (Chicago, 1939.)

SCE   GJERSTAD, E., LINDROS, J., SJÖQVIST, E., and WESTHOLM, A.: *The Swedish Cyprus Expedition.* (Stockholm, 1934–.)

Seals Corpus   PORADA, E. (ed.): *Corpus of Ancient Near Eastern Seals in North American Collections. Vol. I: The Pierpont Morgan Library Collection.* (Washington, 1948.)

Sedment   PETRIE, F., and BRUNTON, G.: *Sedment I–II.* BSAE XXXIV–XXXV. (London, 1924.)

SPC   GJERSTAD, E.: *Studies in Prehistoric Cyprus.* (Uppsala, 1926.)

Stratigraphie   SCHAEFFER, C. F. A.: *Stratigraphie comparée et Chronologie de l'Asie Occidentale.* (London, 1948.)

STTN   BADÉ, W. F.: *Some Tombs of Tell en-Nasbeh discovered in 1929.* (Berkeley, 1931.)

SW   SELLIN, E., and WATZINGER, C.: *Jericho.* (Leipzig, 1913.)

Syria   *Syria, Revue d'Art et Archeologie.* (Paris, 1920–.)

Tanis II   PETRIE, F.: *Tanis II.* (London, 1888.)

Technology   SINGER, C., HOLMYARD, E. J., and HALL, A. R. (Editors): *A History of Technology, Vol. I.* (Oxford, 1954.)

TG I   MALLON, A., KOEPPEL, R., and NEUVILLE, R.: *Teleilat Ghassul I.* (Rome, 1934.)

TG II   KOEPPEL, R.: *Teleilat Ghassul II.* (Rome, 1940.)

TH   PETRIE, F.: *Tell el-Hesi* (Lachish). (London, 1891.)

TN I   McCOWN, C. C.: *Tell en-Nasbeh I.* (Berkeley, 1947.)

TN II   WAMPLER, J. C.: *Tell en-Nasbeh II: The Pottery.* (Berkeley, 1947.)

Tomb of Hemaka   EMERY, W. B.: Service des Antiquités de l'Egypte: *Saqqara: The Tomb of Hemaka.* (Cairo, 1938.)

Troy I–III   BLEGEN, C. W., CASKEY, J. L., and RAWSON, M.: *Troy I–III.* (Cincinnati, 1950–1953.)

BIBLIOGRAPHY WITH ABBREVIATIONS

Ugaritica II SCHAEFFER, C. F. A.: *Ugaritica II, Nouvelles études relatives aux découvertes de Ras Shamra.* (Paris, 1949.)

Ur I HALL, H. R., and WOOLLEY, C. L.: *Ur Excavations I: Al-Ubaid.* (London, 1927.)

Ur II WOOLLEY, C. L.: *Ur Excavations II: The Royal Cemetery.* (London, 1934.)

Weill WEILL, R.: *La Fin du Moyen Empire Egyptien, Vols. I–II.* (Paris, 1918.)

NOTES AND ABBREVIATIONS

THE excavations around the mound were divided into areas described as Cemetery Areas 100, 200, 500, 700, 1000, 4000, 6000 and 7000 (Pl. 88). Numbers not used in this series were to be allocated to intervening areas which either proved sterile or were not excavated in 1932–1938. Where area numbers are given as locus numbers in the Plate Descriptions, e.g. "500", it means that the object concerned was found on the surface in that area. The letters "D/X" indicate that the object concerned was found on the surface of the mound.

The pottery forms throughout the publication are numbered to correspond with the sequence 1–1025 on Pls. 56–87. An asterisk against the number in the group lists (Chapters 11–13) denotes that the vessel has been photographed and the appropriate plate number is given. The figures in brackets denote the number of specimens from a particular locus or of a particular type. The letters *L. II* and *L. III* prefacing a number on Pls. 68 ff. indicate that the drawing of the type in question has been reproduced from *Lachish II: The Fosse Temple* or *Lachish III: The Iron Age*.

The letters "PM" prefacing a number indicate that an example of the object concerned was acquired by the Department of Antiquities of the Government of Palestine under British Mandate, and is now in the Palestine Archaeological Museum, Jerusalem.

The letters "MMA" prefacing a number indicate that the object concerned is now in the Metropolitan Museum of Art, New York.

The name "Colt" indicates that an example of the object concerned was allocated to H. Dunscombe Colt in 1932–1933 and is now in the United States of America.

AE	bronze	EI	Early Iron Age	MC	Middle Cypriote
Ag	silver	EM	Early Minoan	misc.	miscellaneous
am.	amethyst	ex.	example	MM	Middle Minoan
Au	gold	ff.	following	mm.	millimetres
bf.	buff	Fig.	Figure	MMA	Metropolitan Museum of Art
bk.	black	frag.	fragment		
bl.	blue	ft.	feet	Mus.	Museum
bn.	brown	gar.	garnet	Myc.	Mycenaean
bur.	burnish	gn.	green	NE	North-East Section
c.	circa	gy.	grey	No.	Number
cf.	compare	H	hard fire	NK	not kept
Ch.	Chambre	haem.	haematite	NP	not published
Chalc.	Chalcolithic	hor.	horizontal	obv.	obverse
cm.	cream	I. of A.	Institute of Archaeology	out.	outside
cms.	centimetres	in.	inside	p.	page
cn.	carnelian	ins.	inches	pk.	pink
con.	concentric	irr.	irregular	Pl.	Plate
cu.	copper	LB	Late Bronze Age	PM	Palestine Museum
dec.	decoration	LC	Late Cypriote	qu.	quartz
diam.	diameter	LH	Late Helladic	rev.	reverse
dior.	diorite	lmst.	limestone	rd.	red
dk.	dark	lt.	light	ref.	reference
dyn.	dynasty	M	medium fire	S	soft fire
EB	Early Bronze Age	m.	metres	S. I, II, III	Structures I, II, III
e.g.	for example	MB	Middle Bronze Age	sard.	sardonyx

NOTES AND ABBREVIATIONS

S.D.	Sequence Date	T.	Tomb	WP	White Painted Ware
spi.	spiral	TBM	Tell Beit Mirsim	wt.	white
stea.	steatite	vert.	vertical		
Stra.	Stratum	wh.	wheel		

Place-names

Arabic place-names are transliterated freely with few diacritical marks, and are often given in abbreviated form. In order to distinguish between two well-known mounds of the same name, the northern *Tell el Far'ah* (near Nablus) is written in full, whereas *Tell Fara* denotes the site south of Gaza.

PART I
HISTORY AND ARCHAEOLOGY

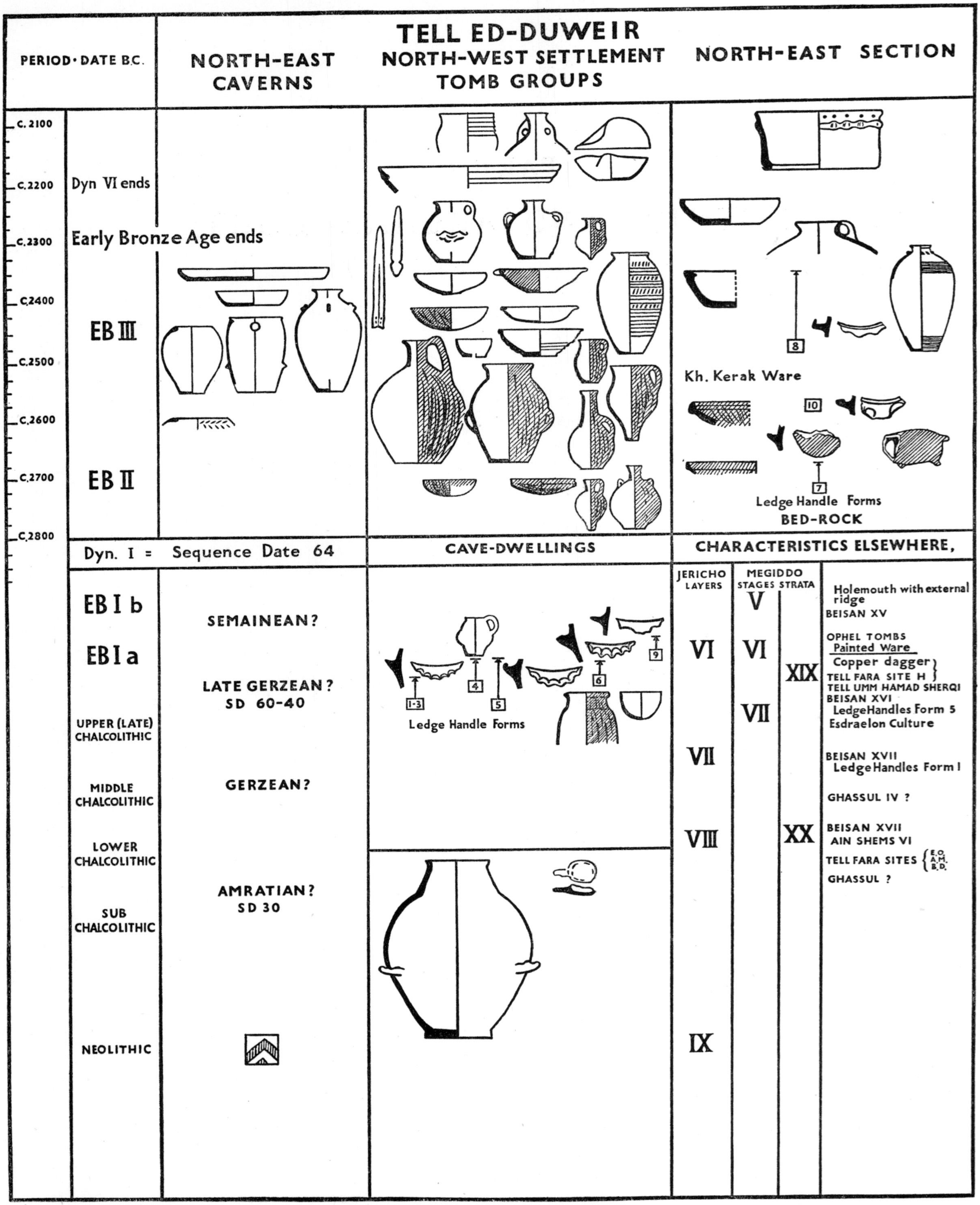

TELL ED-DUWEIR

PERIOD · DATE B.C.	NORTH-EAST CAVERNS	NORTH-WEST SETTLEMENT TOMB GROUPS	NORTH-EAST SECTION

C. 2100

C. 2200 Dyn VI ends

C. 2300 Early Bronze Age ends

C. 2400 EB III

C. 2500

Kh. Kerak Ware

C. 2600

C. 2700 EB II

Ledge Handle Forms
BED-ROCK

C. 2800

Dyn. I = Sequence Date 64	CAVE-DWELLINGS	CHARACTERISTICS ELSEWHERE,

EB I b SEMAINEAN?

EB I a

LATE GERZEAN?
SD 60-40

Ledge Handle Forms

UPPER (LATE) CHALCOLITHIC

MIDDLE CHALCOLITHIC GERZEAN?

LOWER CHALCOLITHIC

SUB CHALCOLITHIC AMRATIAN?
SD 30

NEOLITHIC

	JERICHO LAYERS	MEGIDDO STAGES	STRATA	
		V		Holemouth with external ridge BEISAN XV
	VI	VI	XIX	OPHEL TOMBS Painted Ware Copper dagger TELL FARA SITE H TELL UMM HAMAD SHERQI BEISAN XVI Ledge Handles Form 5 Esdraelon Culture
		VII		
	VII			BEISAN XVII Ledge Handles Form I
				GHASSUL IV ?
	VIII		XX	BEISAN XVII AIN SHEMS VI TELL FARA SITES {E.O. A.M. B.D.} GHASSUL ?
	IX			

FIG. 1. Chalcolithic and Early Bronze Age Types

28

CHAPTER I
SURVEY OF RESULTS

THE natural advantages of the site now known as Tell ed-Duweir were appreciated not only in the first and second millennia, as described in two previous volumes, but also in the more remote past, the cities of which lie buried deep in the heart of the unexcavated mound.

Since work ceased on the site in 1938, other excavations and scholarly studies have increased knowledge of man's activities in Palestine during the third to the fifth or even to the sixth millennium, and have indicated trade and cultural contacts with other peoples of the Fertile Crescent.

It is the purpose of this book to make the discoveries from Lachish available to those who can best interpret them, and it is proposed in this chapter to suggest their position in the cultural and chronological frame as it is known at present. Each year the background expands and changes in the light of research, and, if drastic adjustments are found necessary, as they have always been on each major site so far excavated, this contribution must still play an important part in a vast and complex problem which may never be fully solved.

The eloquence of material remains and of pottery in particular for the understanding of man's advance or regression, significant though it is, is balanced in importance by certain gaps and omissions in the sequence which are quite as valuable for the help they give in the isolation of types and in the general picture of primitive economy. As each phase becomes defined and distinct, it appears that the picture as a whole is more uniform and consistent than would have been thought possible only a few years ago. It is likely that the whole of the region from the south-east corner of the Mediterranean to the highlands of Moab, beyond the Jordan valley, can be regarded as a single cultural area in which only slight regional variations are discernible.

Early Settlements

Twenty-five miles to the south, near Tell Fara in the Wadi Ghuzzeh, lie some of the earliest pottery sites, preserved to us through natural aridity and the consequent absence of later settlements. Beyond the well-worn route of the Ghuzzeh valley lies Egypt, which at that time "appears as an isolated corner of the Near East" (*Rel. Chron.*, p. 3), though Egyptian villagers used imported wood and copper and the people of the Wadi Ghuzzeh knew handled cups and stone maceheads (BP II, p. 15). The Fara settlements provide several links with the cave-dwellings of the North-West Settlement at Duweir, and some contact is established with Teleilat Ghassul in the Jordan Valley to the east. The current date for the last phase of that site is estimated by Albright between 3800 and 3400 B.C. (*Rel. Chron.*, p. 29). More than 500 years before, by the same reckoning, the pottery Neolithic of Jericho IX is represented by a single sherd recovered from deep midden at the north-east corner of the mound (p. 44 and p. 300).

One Natufian flint end-scraper and this painted and burnished fragment suggest by their mere presence that the valley of the Wadi Ghafr, if not the mound itself, was occupied in Mesolithic and Neolithic times.

Flint blades of all periods from the Aurignacian onwards were found on the rock ridges north-west of the mound, and in Chalcolithic Ages family groups had made or enlarged natural caves in the soft limestone, where marks of their adzes can still be seen. The focal point in a settlement which ultimately covered 200 acres of ground appeared to be a megalith of a kind which has rarely survived west of the Jordan valley (p. 39). While the caves were inhabited in the Sub-, Lower and Middle Chalcolithic periods and onwards, few sherds can be expected to remain on the floors of any phase but the last period of use, and it is therefore late in the Chalcolithic Age when more substantial pottery deposits enable us to visualise to some degree the life of these troglodytes.

The cave-dwellers shared the same standards and used the same types of pottery as the people of Fara Site H, where most of the tools and weapons were made of flint. A copper dagger from that site can be matched in

Egypt at S.D. 61–62 (Fig. 1). It is now considered that Late Gerzean (Late Naqada II) ended at Sequence Date 64, and not at 78, so that objects which were thought to be Predynastic really belong to the Protodynastic period (see *A Provisional Chronological Table* by Alan Rowe, PEQ, 1955, p. 179, Note 1).

Working with Dr. Isserlin on comparative material, we have agreed to follow Shipton in the placing of Fara Site H and of the contemporary deposits at Duweir between Upper Chalcolithic and EB I, overlapping in part with each period and showing connexions with the Gerzean culture in Egypt.

The union of the kingdoms of the North and South under the strong rule of the First Dynasty coincides with the second phase of the Early Bronze Age in Palestine, where it may be marked by increased intercourse with the people of the Nile. The date of the foundation of the First Egyptian Dynasty is uncertain, ranging between the thirty-second and the twenty-ninth centuries B.C., as estimated by different scholars (op. cit., pp. 176–179). At the present time, the date proposed in *Relative Chronologies*, c. 3100 B.C. seems to allow too much time for the material which excavation has revealed, and the shorter chronology preferred by Scharff[1] and others, 2900–2850 B.C., is therefore adopted in this book (Fig. 1 and p. 68).

One significant surface find of a fragment of diorite, on which the edge of a finely engraved cartouche remains, is of a quality which was only mined in Nubia during the ist, iind and part of the iiird dynasties, p. 72. It is enough to show that products of the highest quality could reach Duweir, though there is otherwise little to represent the first phase of the Early Bronze Age—EB Ia—characterised elsewhere by pottery painted in bands of red and brown; EB Ib also lacks its most common forms at Duweir.

At the end of EB I or early in EB II the practical and aesthetic advantage of pottery treated with thick, non-porous and red-burnished slip was generally recognised, a phenomenon which was to recur in the first phases of the Middle Bronze and Iron Ages.

From Cave to City Life

The absence of a settlement datable to EB I on the north-west spurs and the scarcity of sherds belonging to these phases in the lowest 6 feet of the Section (Figs. 2–5, Pl. 96), suggest that the shift of a possibly reduced population to the mound itself did not assume an urban character before EB II. The disuse of warm and sheltered caves as dwelling-places may indicate a forced move, since it would have been impossible for a peaceful agricultural community, spread over a considerable space, to defend itself effectively in the event of attack. The threat or experience of war would encourage large-scale settlement on the isolated spur which now underlies the mound of Tell ed-Duweir, though nothing has so far been seen of a city wall belonging to any phase of the Early Bronze Age. A similar shift from caves to the rock surface is to be seen at Gezer (PPEB, p. 65). No city wall associated with the earliest occupation of Tell Beit Mirsim (AASOR XVII, p. 13) has come to light.

Meanwhile, the caves of the North-West Settlement were first used as burial-places, late in EB I or early in EB II, where successive burials were interred in Caves 1535, 1519, 1556 and 1513, which give an overlapping sequence between them to the end of the Early Bronze Age. The series coincides with Professor Garstang's Tomb A at Jericho to which he assigned a range of at least two centuries (AAA XIX, p. 42). It extends to the later Tomb 351 at that site, illustrating a stage known as EB IV by Wright (PPEB, p. 78). By that time 12 feet of deposit had accumulated on the north-east corner of the mound at Duweir, in which two living levels appear, where the amount of pottery suggests some density of population not only on the site which had become a *tell*, but also in the caverns of much greater age cut into the slopes below.

Meticulous study of carbonised seeds found in the Section and elsewhere at Lachish has enabled Dr. Hans Helbaek to present a picture of the plant economy which shows little change throughout the history of the site in diet and agriculture. Cereals and olives were abundant at all times, though the species of wheat was entirely Emmer or Eincorn in the Early Bronze Age, whereas Iron Age samples were composed of Club or Bread Wheat. The change may have occurred during the second millennium, for which period there is no relevant material from

---

[1] Agypten und Vorderasien in Altertum, Munich, 1950.

Duweir. Dr. Helbaek notes that additions to farinaceous food—leguminous seeds, grapes and olives—were the same in antiquity as they are for Near Eastern peoples today. (Appendix A.)

Invaders of the Caliciform Culture

No layer of ash or burning marks the end of the Early Bronze Age in the marginal area of the Section, where sherds were few and far between from 12 to 14 feet, in contrast to a violent destruction of Early Bronze Age Jericho (PEQ, 1952, p. 65).

Miss Kenyon has shown how those who destroyed the city introduced different burial customs and a primitive architecture much inferior to the buildings which had gone before. Though the pottery presents a very different appearance in technique, through increased use of the wheel, and is subject to decreased firing temperature in the pottery from burial groups, nevertheless, the forms are clearly based on EB traditions, retaining the characteristic flat base, some vestigial ledge handles and various details which are more akin to pottery of the first phases of EB than they are to that of EB III.

Comparing the sherds from Trench 1 at Jericho (PEQ, 1952, Fig. 6:36–45) and from Group 1529 at Duweir (Pl. 66:394–426), it is clear that the same well-developed phase of the Intermediate EB–MB or Caliciform Culture is represented at both sites, possibly preceding Stratum I at Tell Beit Mirsim in date.

It is perhaps these phases, all showing the same combination of hand-finished indented edges and wheel-made grooved and wavy lines, which best compare with the First Intermediate Period, dynasties vii–x in Egypt.

There can be no doubt that the people who were making this pottery were also those who overwhelmed Jericho and established themselves in the disused caves of the North-West Settlement at Duweir. It is already clear that several phases exist of this distinctive culture, the earliest being represented by Cemetery 1500 at Ajjul which may go back to Old Kingdom times. It overlaps with Cemetery 200 at the same site and is carried to a still later phase in Cemetery 2000 at Duweir, a development which must occupy two centuries or more (pp. 42 f.). Other chronological phases, or perhaps, as Miss Kenyon prefers, other ethnic groups, are represented at Jericho by different tomb-shapes and burial customs, which must still find their place in the picture of this intrusive people, who left no trace or influence on the products of the inhabitants of Palestine in the Middle Bronze Age.

The people of the Caliciform Culture share characteristics in common with the Beaker Folk who made their appearance in Europe soon after 2000 B.C. Both favoured beaker-shaped vessels, both decorated them with patterns arranged in zones and these patterns in each area were often executed with a sort of comb, though the method of application was different. In Europe, too, the ware is different from the wares current immediately before and after the Beaker episode. Both were also active in the practice of metallurgy (*Dawn*, pp. 218–224).

Though most authorities hold that the Beaker Folk spread from central Spain, Professor Childe has remarked on the possibility of some African elements. Now that more material of the Caliciform Culture is assembled from Palestine and will be available from Ingholt's excavations at Hama, it may be possible to establish further links between these people, both living at the same time on the same economic plane.

The first metal tools from Duweir cannot be ascribed to the Caliciform Culture, for there are daggers from earlier contexts in EB III–IV. Nevertheless, the people who were burying a few poorly-fired jars in Cemetery 2000 had also made or acquired copper daggers which represent a standard of form and technical achievement unsurpassed in all later periods in Palestine. They are described in detail by Professor F. C. Thompson in Appendix D.

It is uncertain if the people of the Caliciform Culture established a city on the mound or built a wall around it, since sherds were exceptionally rare at the point in the North-East Section where the pottery of this culture should occur.

These people certainly occupied the EB city site at Jericho and at Tell Beit Mirsim, p. 41; at Megiddo signs of their presence are less pronounced, though they occur in Strata XV and XIV. Different architectural plans and methods were introduced in Stratum XIV and pottery of the Caliciform Culture was also recovered above the site of the disused round altar, in a context attributed to Stratum XIII B (M II, Fig. 396; 4009 and Pl. 16: 8, 16–18, 21).

31

Egyptian, Syrian, and Aegean influence in the Middle Bronze Age, 2100–1750 B.C.

By the end of the third millennium the tentative and partial experiments in wheel-produced pottery, begun many centuries before and well illustrated in the products of the Caliciform Culture, gave place to pottery of different forms which was entirely wheel-made. All the characteristic details of EB tradition disappeared, red paint, rope mouldings and ledge handles among them—all of which require individual finish by hand.

In place of flat-based jars, storage vessels of ovoid form become ubiquitous. They appear suddenly, without obvious prototypes, and they were to survive until the desertion of the site. Though the new shape may mark the entry of a different ethnic group, there are nevertheless indications among the smaller forms (p. 189) that some underlying elements of EB tradition survived the impact of the Caliciform Culture and re-emerged in the second or third century of the Middle Bronze Age when Caliciform pottery had vanished without trace.

Duweir has little to offer from the first period, MB I, apart from a cache of jars and bowls left in Cave 1513. The site, however, was by no means deserted, judging from the sherds from the constructional core or fill of the later MB defences (pp. 55 ff.), the contents of which compare with Tell Beit Mirsim, Strata G–F: a phase of red-burnished bowls of metallic inspiration which can be equated with the latter part of the xiith dynasty in Egypt, c. 1850–1778 B.C., on the evidence of the Royal Tombs at Byblos (p. 179). The presence of shapes comparable to those in Tell Beit Mirsim Stratum G, without the burnish so typical of that stratum, suggests that the builders of the later MB terre pisée defence system at Duweir collected the fill for the embankment from city debris of a phase equivalent, perhaps, to the little-known Stratum F, p. 45. No city wall comparable to that of Strata G–F has yet been revealed at Tell ed-Duweir (AASOR XVII, p. 13), and at Megiddo the architects of a new town plan in the contemporary Stratum XII strengthened a wall of earlier times (M. II, p. 87).

Scarabs and Seals

The influx of scarabs, used to seal all manner of documents and pottery jars, noticeable in Strata XII–X at Megiddo and elsewhere, supports the suggestion that some sort of organised or administrative control was imposed by Egypt in the xiith dynasty, when intercourse between Egypt, Palestine and Syria reached a new level of intensity, greater than in the Early Bronze Age (Rel. Chron., p. 10). That it was widespread at the time is indicated by the number of scarabs with the name of Senusert I, c. 1991 B.C., from Palestinian sites (p. 94), with those of xiith dynasty officials holding Egyptian titles, though his successors are less well represented.

The elaborate scrolls which often surround the full and also the shortened versions of Senusert's name are largely confined in Egypt to the xiith and xiiith dynasties, and this early element in scarab design may be a foreign link in the chain of connexions between the Aegean and the Orient in the second millennium B.C. (p. 100). The numbers of skilfully designed scarabs from Palestinian sites and the fascinating variety of non-Egyptian motifs show high artistic capability among the craftsmen who made them. Judging from the pottery and weapons in the Duweir tombs, the main range for the MB scarab collection should fall within the last two centuries of that age, though allowance must be made for treasured pieces of earlier origin.

None of these well-executed scarabs from Duweir, with apparent names in cartouches, or with royal emblems forming part of the design, can be ascribed to any personage definitely placed on the King Lists of Egypt, though the same groups of signs occur on scarabs both in Egypt and Palestine (pp. 94–97). Since the King Lists are not complete or in chronological order, and since it is possible that hieroglyphs were used alphabetically for the transcription of non-Egyptian names, this is not disturbing, particularly at a time when attempts at invention of new scripts were being made in Palestine and particularly at Lachish (p. 127).

Even more important and instructive when they are fully understood will be the scarabs of decorative design, on which certain groups and motifs recur. They must surely reflect the personal tastes and preferences of the community in relation to their beliefs and their allegiance to the ruling power, if, as it appears, scarabs were issued from certain centres and had become commemorative rather than personal. It is perhaps possible to mark, for instance, through the introduction of royal emblems of both North and South, the celebration of the extension of "Hyksos" power over the two lands of Egypt (p. 98).

Ceramic Comparisons, MB II

Turning to the pottery evidence for the second period of the Middle Bronze Age, from *c.* 1900–1750 B.C., it is most striking that there are missing from Duweir all the distinctive forms associated with the necropolis at Jericho discovered in 1930–1936 by Professor Garstang, and with the slightly later Strata E–D at Tell Beit Mirsim. The lack of trefoil-mouth jugs, trumpet-foot goblets and other characteristic shapes is also apparent at Tell Fara, Tell el-Ajjul and, to a lesser extent, at Megiddo, where such forms are rare and are found with burials.

The use of burnish at these sites is also limited, being largely confined to piriform (pear-shaped) juglets, which are seen to occur at Duweir, Fara and Ajjul in contexts which may precede or be contemporary with the construction of the defences.

Pricked Tell el-Yehudiyeh ware, long considered to be type vessels of the "Hyksos" period, was certainly in use before the construction of the *terre pisée* embankments, as indicated by Albright (*Arch. Pal.*, pp. 93–95; for R. M. Engberg's useful list of the best-dated parallels see SAOC 18, pp. 26–27). It may well go back to the xiith dynasty, though the provenance of Egyptian parallels is still in question (*Rel. Chron.*, p. 12).

The pieces from Duweir (p. 189) and from the Courtyard Cemetery at Ajjul may belong to the end of that dynasty or the beginning of the next; they are poorly designed and executed in comparison with those from northern sites, while the juglets of piriform and cylindrical shape at Yehudiyeh itself exhibit the roughest decorations and are perhaps farthest from the source.

The ceramic repertory of the Jericho necropolis and of Tell Beit Mirsim E–D represents the output of a technically advanced community of great artistic sensibility, reproducing in pottery a tradition of metallic forms. The daggers and "togglepins" also include types which are lacking at Duweir, Fara and Ajjul (pp. 76–81).

"Hyksos" Communities, MB III

The contrast between the distinctive pottery of Jericho and Tell Beit Mirsim and that of the tomb groups of Tell Fara is most marked, and the cemeteries at that site provide a series of tomb shapes, which develop from a rounded bilobate or kidney-shaped chamber to one in which the outline is squared (BP I, Pls. XVII–XVIII). Tomb 153 is an early and unusual example of this type at Duweir, which is contemporary with Tomb 551 at Fara, while Tomb 550 at the same site may be a generation or two later in date. No new forms were introduced, though flared carinate bowls, Class A, are particularly fine early in the period. The traditional shapes of bowls, dippers and lamps survive in more clumsy style at both sites during the seventeenth century, and cylindrical juglets entirely replace those of piriform outline.

Retrogression is also apparent in the daggers at Tell Fara, which are small and debased in comparison with ribbed blades from Jericho (p. 77). They were finally replaced in the Fara tombs by tanged daggers which were functionally no more effective than knives. It is these which are dominant at Duweir and in the Structural Tombs at Megiddo. Apart from the faience kohl pots (p. 83), bone inlay incised with designs of birds and concentric circles (pp. 86 f.) and bronze "togglepins" (pp. 79 ff.), the tomb offerings found at Fara and Duweir are few in number and poorly designed in comparison with material from the Jericho necropolis and Strata E–D at Tell Beit Mirsim.

Fortifications of the Middle Bronze Age

The earliest system of defence which has so far come to light at Duweir is a relatively late construction which cannot have been made much before 1700 B.C. Partially exposed at points near the north-east and north-west corners of the mound, enough of the embankment has now been revealed to justify a tentative reconstruction of the appearance of this imposing ramp. The rectangular plan is so oriented that the sides correspond with the cardinal points of the compass, a phenomenon which is a feature of other constructions of this type (SAOC 18, p. 21). Packed against the sides of the mound, layers of debris were piled up to an even slope, rising from the base to a height of between 30 and 40 metres above the valley. This formidable glacis, or escarp—to use the correct military term—was faced with a coat of white lime plaster, which must have been frequently renewed. While the whole embankment was probably obsolete within a hundred years of construction, it has undoubtedly served in succeeding centuries to delay erosion of these slopes.

Embankments of this kind have elsewhere been crowned with a thin brick wall, and the whole is sometimes surrounded by a moat or fosse (BASOR 137, Feb. 1955, p. 26). The length and breadth of the fosse has been traced for nearly 140 metres on the west side of Duweir, but it was so shallow and the counterscarp was so low that it cannot have contributed materially to the strength of the defence.

Among many examples of this communal project, which must have required a considerable amount of work, are the defences of Tell Fara and Tell el-Ajjul. The sandy marl of the district south of Gaza was cut to a steep and uniform slope on those flanks of the two settlements which were unprotected by natural cliffs. At Duweir and Tell Beit Mirsim the limestone of the foothills could not be treated in the same way.

The *terre pisée* defences at Tell Beit Mirsim cannot be attributed to a particular phase of E (p. 47) and Professor Albright considered that they went out of use "before the end of D" (p. 48). The similar construction at Megiddo was attributed to Stratum XI, but it may post-date the city of that phase and be contemporary with Stratum X.

While the embankment was exposed and in effective use as a defence at Duweir, occupational debris presumably rose until it had reached the crest of the scarp (Level VIII) within the confine of the inner slope.

Last phase of the Middle Bronze Age city and its destruction

The sherds in Level VIII (p. 48) compare with those found in the context of one particular phase of construction at Tell Beit Mirsim, which lies between the remains of the East Gateway in period G–F and the foundations of the Iron Age cities A–D (AASOR XVII, § 38 and note).

The date of the destruction of Stratum D, representing one building phase, with two sub-phases near the palace, was discussed by Albright (AASOR XII, §§ 45–47; XIII, §§ 26, 39; XVII, § 67). In the final volume he was inclined to make D begin about 1600, ending *c.* 1560–1550 B.C., but the author himself was uncertain how wide the gap should be between Strata D and C (AASOR XVII, § 70).

The Middle Bronze character of Stratum D is not in doubt, and it shares most of the elements of Stratum E, from which it cannot be stratigraphically divided (AASOR XVII, § 35). It will be seen in the following chapters that the pottery of Strata E–D at Tell Beit Mirsim clearly represents a different phase from that of the bilobate tombs at Fara, City III at Ajjul, and the tombs at Duweir, see Chapter X. All the characteristic shapes of Strata E–D are missing at Duweir and are replaced by flared carinate bowls (Class A, p. 178, Type 23 K at Fara and Ajjul), which are themselves almost absent from Tell Beit Mirsim.

In considering the sequence of pottery forms, a certain lapse of time must be postulated for these developments, which are still purely MB in character. If it is right to associate the flared carinate bowls of Class A with the people who made the "Hyksos" defences, and if they were built in the seventeenth century, then the date proposed for the destruction of D as a whole is too late.

Introduction to the Late Bronze Age

All these groups clearly precede the introduction of pottery associated with the period of LB I, and in particular with the bichrome wares of Ajjul and Megiddo.

City III and Palace I at Ajjul, where the first bichrome sherds appear (AG II), were both destroyed by fire and shortly afterwards town and palace were rebuilt on different plans (p. 64). Though the older pottery forms tend to die out in City and Palace II and new ones are introduced, the change is gradually achieved and older traditions are retained. Severe though it was, the destruction did not finally break up the life of the city, and imports continued to arrive.

Indeed, no Palestinian site is richer than Ajjul in jewellery of wrought gold and bichrome pottery of excellent quality. No other site provides so many scarabs of known "Hyksos" names, and among them those of Apepa I are associated with bichrome ware in City II (p. 99).

Ajjul is, moreover, ideally situated to control both land and sea routes between Egypt and the north and it would be an essential base from which to launch an attack from the Asiatic side. Neither could it escape reprisals when, in due course, the "Hyksos", whose base it must have been, were expelled from Egypt. Perhaps it was then, *c.* 1567 B.C., that Palace I and City III were destroyed by the Egyptians in the campaign which culminated in a three-year siege of Sharuhen (CAH, p. 315), but other cities must also have suffered at that time, and the destruction of Level VIII at Duweir and Stratum D² at Tell Beit Mirsim may well be due to them.

The two centuries between 1600 and 1400 B.C. is perhaps represented at Duweir by part of the contents of Cave 4004, which appears to have been the result of a late xviiith dynasty clearance of a number of tombs in the vicinity, when the best of the gold would have been removed. Part of a gold head-band (Pl. 25:13 and p. 82), ear-rings (Pl. 25: 15–16) and many scarabs belong to this time, and one of Pepa (or Shesha) is identical in style with several from Ajjul (p. 96). In contrast to groups of the Middle Bronze Age, beads become common, and they include many made of glass, in which newly-introduced material there is also the figurine of a goddess, whose cult was to survive through many centuries (p. 83).

Foundation of the Fosse Temple

The following century, 1550–1450 B.C., is occupied by Structure I, but the town which the Fosse Temple served is not visible in the North-East Section, where few sherds were discovered between Levels VIII and VII (pp. 48, 64 f.).

There are no scarabs of the earlier Egyptian kings of the xviiith dynasty, and if Level VIII was destroyed in the campaign of Aahmes, when he expelled the "Hyksos", it does not appear that administrative Egyptian control was immediately imposed at Lachish. Nevertheless, a flow of trade between Syria and Egypt was encouraged by the campaigns of the first kings of the xviiith dynasty. Early imports of Base-Ring ware occurred in graves dated to that time in Egypt (p. 207), and at intermediate places like Megiddo Stratum IX and Ajjul City and Palace II.

Lachish under Egyptian suzerainty

The immediate cause of Thothmes III's Syrian campaign in the twenty-third year of his reign was a general revolt in the territory from Sharuhen to the Euphrates, conquered by his father (*Ancient Records, Egypt II*, § 408). Despite fighting in Sharuhen, that stronghold was too near the Egyptian border to make common cause with the rebels, and the same natural caution may have restrained the rulers of Lachish. Able therefore to ignore signs of unrest in the south, Thothmes made straight for Megiddo, where he overthrew a coalition of Syrian kings. The city surrendered after a siege, but the Annals do not suggest that it was burnt, and there is no evidence of conflagration on the mound. Thereafter the citadel, at least, seems to have been deserted for a century or more.

Increased security under Egyptian control initiated a new era of prosperity and trade at Lachish. The Fosse Temple was enlarged (Structure II), the city on the mound spread to the north-east corner (Level VII) and the tombs of the second half of the fifteenth century contained a varied assortment of imported wares. Scarabs bearing the names of Thothmes III and his son Amenhetep II are common in the tombs (p. 97), and a fine seal of Amenhetep from Level VII (p. 49) shows that the phase of the city in which it was found could not have been destroyed before his reign. Dating from the fifteenth-fourteenth centuries, a censer lid and Lachish Bowl No. 1 are inscribed in characters of the Early Canaanite script. They are discussed by Dr. Diringer on pp. 128 f.

The reign of Thothmes IV is likewise represented by scarabs, while that of Amenhetep III is commemorated more liberally than any other in the tombs and in Structures II–III of the Fosse Temple. The latter part of Amenhetep's lifetime and the reign of his successor Amenhetep IV, better known as Akhenaten, is covered by the Tell el-Amarna Letters. From them it is clear that a period of unrest had begun. The vassals and governors of the king's towns in Palestine and Syria were unable to pay the troops or to control the population, while appeals for supplies and reinforcements and the news of conspiracy and revolt met with no response from a monarch absorbed in religious and cultural matters. Notes on references in the Amarna Letters to Lachish will be found in *Lachish II*, pp. 26–27.

If there is an interval in the life of the city during the last years of the Amarna period (p. 66), it may coincide with the end of Structure II and the desertion of City Level VII. That Lachish maintained communication with Egypt is seen, not only in the Amarna Letters themselves, but also in typical beads of the period which are occasionally found in the tombs (p. 89), and more especially in the necklace of floral pendants which came from behind the altar of Structure III (L. II, Pl. XIV and pp. 74–76).

The last building of the Fosse Temple introduced no drastic change in plan, though the shrine itself was greatly developed, and two constructional phases were observed (L. II, p. 40).

The date of this reconstruction may be placed about the middle of the fourteenth century (p. 66), but the majority of the vessels and offerings necessarily belong to the phase when the building was last in use almost a century later.

Two tomb groups represent the interval between the building of Structure III and its destruction, and each contains one scarab of the two last kings of the xviiith dynasty, Ay and Horemheb (p. 97). The range of the larger Group 4013 must extend into the reign of Rameses II, for his name also appears on a scarab.

It is the last half-century of the Bronze Age, between 1250 and 1200 B.C., which is abundantly and richly represented in the pottery of Structure III and in that of Level VI (p. 53). At no other time in the history of the site was the pottery so elaborately decorated with designs of animals and plants. The Duweir Ewer, with a much discussed inscription (see p. 130), is an outstanding example of the thirteenth century.

Most of the common pottery forms of the time, which are known from the shrine and sanctuary of Structure III, are duplicated in the potter's workshop (Pl. 49 and p. 91), where those who visited the Fosse Temple probably bought bowls and dishes for their offerings, while the potter himself sat at his wheel by the mouth of the cave (Pl. 8). The simple tools and equipment of his trade and the materials which he used, like the trial pieces which he discarded, add greatly to our knowledge of the potter's craft towards the end of the Late Bronze Age.

Destruction by fire of the Bronze Age City

The historical evidence for the date of the burning of Structure III, which applies also to what is known of the contemporary city Level VI (pp. 49 f.), was discussed in L. II, pp. 22–24. Two dates were suggested: that of Merenptah's raid (c. 1223 B.C.) and one just before Rameses III's defeat of the invading northerners (c. 1190 B.C.). There are substantial arguments in favour of each of these dates, and within this very narrow margin it is unlikely that the matter will be solved.

As a final contribution to the problem, the inscriptions of the last years of the second and early centuries of the first millennium should be considered. They have been studied by Sir Alan Gardiner and Professor J. Černý.

The inscription on the anthropoid coffin (Pls. 45–46) is written in curious hieroglyphs, and all who have seen it are agreed that the writing is not that of an Egyptian scribe (pp. 131 f.). Bearded heads on the lids of the coffins are meant to portray the deceased and there are good reasons for identifying them with one of the bands which accompanied the Philistines, if not with the Philistines themselves. Besides the attempt at hieroglyphs, a wish to simulate Egyptian script and funerary practice is seen in the mourning figures of Isis and Nebthys. A date in the xxth dynasty during the reign of Rameses III is probable for Groups 570–571 in which the coffins occur (p. 249).

However, there were also practised scribes at Lachish, who wrote the cursive form of hieroglyphs with ease, and who labelled flared bowls (which had contained wheat samples) in hieratic script, and dated them by the Egyptian calendar (Pls. 44, 47).

In writing of the "king of Latish"—and there is no doubt that t was written—could the Egyptian tax-collector have been responsible for an aural or textual corruption of the place-name, which is unlikely to be one otherwise unknown? Professor A. M. Honeyman feels that "there is no ready answer to the puzzle from the Semitic side. A native mis-hearing of the name *Lakiš* is unlikely, for the sound shift $k \rangle t$ is not a Canaanite phenomenon, and a mis-writing of alphabetic *l-k-š* seems to be excluded by the dissimilarity of t (*taw*) and k (*kaph*) as well as by more general considerations."

More than a century later than the cuneiform transcriptions of the name Lachish, which appear in the Tell el Amarna correspondence of the fourteenth century under varying forms, e.g. *lakiša, lakiši*, Lachish Bowl No. 3 provides a version of the name written in hieratic. On epigraphic grounds, Sir Alan Gardiner considers "that the writing on the bowls (Nos. 3–5, p. 132) is clearly Ramesside, and I should think more probably dynasty xix than later" (letter dated 23/xi/54). Professor Černý feels that "the whole gives the impression of a text of about the reign of Merenptah, though one sign has a form used in Great Papyrus Harris, a document of Rameses IV of the xxth dynasty" (p. 133).

The latest royal scarab found on the burnt surface of the Bronze Age city bears the name of Rameses III (Pl. 39: 388 and L. III, pp. 46, 51), and once again the balance seems to fall for a date early in the xxth dynasty for the destruction of the Bronze Age city, pp. 97 f.

A scrap of pottery inscribed in black ink, which could belong to the debris from the city, probably dates from the twelfth or eleventh century B.C. In Dr. Diringer's opinion, it may be the first extant inscription in Early Hebrew script (Pl. 44: 7 and p. 131).

Burial Customs.

During most of the Bronze Age, when Tell-ed-Duweir was the site of successive cities, the dead were buried communally in large caves on the lower slopes, and on the surrounding spurs. Disorder was so great and the bones so fragmentary, that an impression emerged that in some cases, at least, the bodies and their offerings had been moved from an original burial-place, and dumped unceremoniously in any convenient cave.

No burials were exposed of the Chalcolithic period, and specially-cut graves or tombs containing Early Bronze Age interments were extremely rare.

When the people of the Caliciform Culture settled on the spurs to the north-west of the mound, these new-comers introduced single burial in rock-hewn cavities, among other material changes. It is a curious fact that in more than 120 tombs attributed to this period, no more than a few fragments of bone were found. The bodies, however, must have been buried in a flexed position, because the tombs were too small and cramped to admit them disposed in any other way (Pl. 93 and Fig. 13, p. 276).

These invaders left little if any trace of their culture on the people of the Middle Bronze Age, and it is no doubt significant that with the disappearance of the pottery characteristic of an intermediate phase or phases between the Early and Middle Bronze Age, the practice of communal burial returned.

Though an existing cave containing earlier deposits was often used for burials in MB II–III, certain tombs were specially cut. These chambers, of which Tomb 153 is bilobate or kidney-shaped, are illustrated on p. 61.

Tombs of the Late Bronze Age were frequently circular in plan (e.g. Tomb 216, p. 233), and the walls and floor were plastered, but it is not possible to be precise about the means of entry, where much is lost through denudation.

In her report on the crania recovered from the tombs, Miss Giles remarks on the high proportion of immature persons and the low average age of the adults. No valid comparison can therefore be made between this small series and a normal graveyard population. Nor does it provide sufficient reason to state that the people of Lachish changed in any major respect between the Bronze and Iron Ages.

Etymology of the place-name Lachish

According to some scholars, the place-name Lachish is of non-Semitic origin, but Professor A. M. Honeyman doubts whether it is wise to go far afield to find an explanation for the word. He writes, "It is apparently the same root that occurs in *lekeš* 'pine-wool', on which see Löw: *Flora der Juden III*, 45, and in Arabic *lakiš* 'recalcitrant'. The basic sense of the root, which is not a common one, would appear to be 'rough' or the like, but the evidence is rather scanty, and the possibility of a metathesis of the radicals opens up a wide range of possibilities. The Hebrew dictionaries are wise to refrain from offering an etymology."

Conclusion

As far as the shattered remains of successive burnt cities and of rifled tombs will permit, the history of Lachish and the cultural development of its people are sketched in the foregoing pages, while more detailed accounts of the discoveries appear in the chapters which follow. Inevitably, the picture as a whole lacks continuity and cohesion, but it gains in clarity when viewed in relation to other main centres of urban life.

In the study of comparative material, which forms the major part of this book, it will be seen that attention is largely focused on Jericho, Tell Beit Mirsim and Megiddo. The ceramic and structural evidence from these sites is most valuable, and has yet to be more fully sifted and explored, for the true synchronism between the phases represented at each site is still imperfectly achieved.

It is in the sphere of comparative material that the Middle and Late Bronze Age tomb series from Duweir is most helpful. In the first place, it provides a close sequence of MB pottery, which falls in the main after the contents of the 1930–1936 Necropolis at Jericho (p. 63) and Strata E–D at Tell Beit Mirsim, and between Strata XII–X at Megiddo, though the Duweir series overlaps in part with each site. The large tomb groups are contemporary with City III at Ajjul, and with the bilobate tombs at Tell Fara (p. 64) covering most of the seventeenth century, but the graves under the packing of the defence embankment belong to an earlier phase (p. 62), probably dating from the eighteenth century or the close of the xiith dynasty of Egypt.

No Palestinian site has yet produced a royal name or historic inscription in a securely stratified context to serve as a fixed point in the sequence of MB chronology, covering more than 500 years.

Neither can it be said on the Egyptian side that the order of succession and number of kings or the length of their reigns in partially concurrent dynasties is established beyond doubt. Until this is so, our results must be confined to integration of ceramic development at those sites where stratified city deposits and published reports are adequate.

At Megiddo, for instance, intervals occur between building periods on the mound when deserted zones were largely occupied by tombs (p. 66). It is beyond the scope of this book to deal with the subject of these gaps in the life of a great city, but it should be observed that the destruction of Stratum IX—usually attributed to the campaign of Thothmes III—led to a desertion of the site for a century or more. The conclusion is clear from a comparison between the pottery and scarabs from Tombs 216, 501 and 1003, covering the reigns of Thothmes III and his successors, and the material attributed to the same period at Megiddo from Stratum VIII.

With the establishment of the Egyptian Empire in the fifteenth century, we reach for the first time the firmer ground of historical record. The period is illustrated by a sequence of LB II–III tombs mentioned above, which provide between them an excellent collection of local and imported pottery, so far but poorly represented elsewhere. These groups and others of the fourteenth and thirteenth centuries supplement the contents of the superimposed Structures of the Fosse Temple (*Lachish II*), representing an era of material prosperity and communal growth.

The popularity of scarabs among the inhabitants of Lachish suggests that they had some knowledge of Egyptian hieroglyphs and their meaning, and at the same time quite ordinary bowls were occasionally inscribed in Early Canaanite script. Late in the thirteenth and early in the twelfth century practised scribes were using hieratic or the cursive form of hieroglyphs, while within the next century the first extant fragment of an inscription provides an unexpected link in the development of Early Hebrew writing.

The Bronze Age city and the Fosse Temple were destroyed by fire in a disaster which seems to have affected other cities at about that time. Tell el-Ḥesi and Tell Beit Mirsim, Tell ed-Duweir and ʿAin Shems, Megiddo and Tell Abu Hawam—to name only a few—all tell the same story. "Some new factor is clearly at work", wrote Inge in *Lachish II*, p. 23, "And unless the coming of the Israelites can be established in this period, the racial migrations recorded in the reigns of Merenptah and Rameses III, resulting in the settlement of the Philistines in the coastal plain, must be regarded as that factor."

CHAPTER 2

NORTH-WEST SETTLEMENT IN THE FOURTH AND THIRD MILLENNIUM

IN previous volumes attention has been focused on Tell ed-Duweir or its surrounding slopes. Though there may have been very early occupation in the vicinity, the great mound, as it exists today, began to develop comparatively late in the history of a site which owed its lasting importance to a good and abundant water supply easily obtainable from wells nearby in the Wadi Ghafr (Pl. 1: 1 and Pls. 88–89).

CHALCOLITHIC AND EARLY BRONZE AGES

The first settlement grew and expanded on the rock ridges north-west of the mound, where nearly 200 acres of ground show traces of man's presence. "So vast a centre of early life", wrote Starkey at the time of discovery, "is quite unknown anywhere in Palestine, and the only sites comparable are away to the east of the Dead Sea" (Field Report, Jan. 1934). In contrast with the reddish-brown tones of uncontaminated earth, the soil of the settlement (Pl. 4: 1), held in pockets between great patches of exposed rock, was grey or black, containing many fragments of pottery and charcoal.

The Dolmen

The central feature of the Chalcolithic Settlement was a megalith of a kind which is rare in districts west of Jordan (Pls. 2: 1; 89).

In 1934 it consisted of four or five blocks of limestone disposed in a rectangle with two outer blocks still upright on end. Local tradition maintained that some of the large blocks on the ground once spanned the two upright stones, but were allowed to fall a century ago when a villager of Qubeibeh dug the ground between them hoping to find a well. Lower down on the same spur to the west were other less massive ruins (not planned) surrounded by Chalcolithic pottery fragments.

Area 1500

When excavations began in 1934, the prefix "Area 1500" was applied to the ground enclosed by a modern stone wall, which defined the property of a family of Qubeibeh (Pls. 88–89). Only a small part was cleared and, at the northern tip of the same ridge, more excavations revealed a crowded burial-ground which is numbered Cemetery 2000.

The natural contours divide the land into an upper terrace of nari limestone and a terrace below, sampled only at the southern end, where the top nari layer has broken away to expose the softer quality howr. (For definitions of these terms see *Lachish III*, pp. 36–37.)

All along the edge of the upper terrace there were groups of tubular holes varying from 5 to 65 cms. in depth, and from 10 to 45 cms. in diameter; the greater number measured between 30 and 45 cms. in both dimensions. These holes are planned as "cup-marks" on Pls. 94–95 (see *inter alia* the floor of Cave 1513 and Loci 1522, 1543–1544). For a group of three holes linked to a fourth at a lower level, see Pl. 2: 3.

Similar holes were found in the rock at Gezer, some of which were "unquestionably connected with wine-presses and threshing-floors" (Gezer I, pp. 152–157). However, installations of this kind were used in recent times for crushing olives, and at present there is no better explanation of their purpose, nor can they be exactly dated.

Cave-Dwellings

1505, 1509, 1513, 1514, 1517, 1519, 1520, 1523 (Pl. 3: 1, 5), 1527, 1528, 1531, 1532, 1534, 1535 (Pl. 3: 2), 1537, 1538, 1540, 1553, 1556 (Pl. 3: 6), 1557 (Pl. 3: 4), 1558 (Pl. 3: 3 and Fig. 12).

Overlooking the easiest gradient where the modern pathway from the valley rises to the scarp, the earliest population had enlarged and used caverns in the soft limestone to make dwellings (Pls. 89, 94, 95). Nearly two dozen were excavated, and they were rather crowded near the path. Though these did not necessarily contain the earliest pottery, it is natural enough that the best and most accessible caves would be cleared out and re-occupied by later tenants in preference to the more remote and isolated caverns which appear to have retained the earlier and less contaminated groups.

Details of the best-preserved dwellings are photographed on Pl. 3: 1–5, and it will be seen how close they now are to the surface. The roof, long since collapsed, was most probably of the natural nari limestone, but there is also a possibility that it was composed of thatch (see p. 262). Sometimes the roof was supported by a wall of stones. Depressions in the floor were common, and pits neatly lined with squared blocks were a feature in Caves 1558 and 1535. The same carefully lined storage bins were also found in Cave 6005 near the north-east corner of the mound (p. 295). Homely utensils are to be seen in the hard stone mortar inset in the cave floor with the depression for the hearth beyond (Pl. 3: 5), and the same picture shows a characteristic stone quern. In one of the earliest caves, the stone threshold and door jambs, with the pivot for a door, are still in position (Pl. 3: 4).

Pottery sherds with a few utensils and implements of stone formed the main contents of these caves, and they are described in detail, according to period, under the appropriate headings in Chapters 9 and 12.

Date and Comparisons

Comparisons from other sites for the finds from the cave-dwellings range in date from Sub-Chalcolithic to EB IV, according to Wright's terminology (see PPEB). Within these extreme limits, the distribution is uneven, for few objects are attributable to the Sub- and Lower Chalcolithic periods and analogies with Middle Chalcolithic seem more pronounced. There are some associations with the Upper Chalcolithic of the Jordan Valley, but the outstanding connexions all through are those with southern Tell Fara Site H, to which the bulk of the finds would seem to belong.

The date of Fara H has been under dispute. Petrie (BP II, p. 15) originally drew attention to Predynastic Egyptian analogies for ledge handles from Fara at Sequence Date 40–60, and for a dagger at Sequence Date 61–62 (Fig. 1 and BP II, Pl. XXVI: 50). Vincent (RB XLIII) and Albright (BASOR 48, 1932, pp. 10–13) likewise regard this material as Chalcolithic or transitional to EB. However, Wright transferred Fara H from Chalcolithic to the Egyptian First Intermediate Period (PPEB, pp. 78 ff.), while Shipton came back to an early date through comparisons with Megiddo XIX (SAOC 17, pp. 43–44).

The evidence at Tell ed-Duweir would seem to support Shipton rather than Wright. A date at the transition between Chalcolithic and EB (ibid., p. 44) would agree with the general position in the earlier dwellings where there are objects which would otherwise belong to widely separated periods. In particular there are parallels for the jar (Pl. 11: 10) and the grooved handle (Pl. 13: 72) which would not be out of place in a context like Megiddo XIX. The grooved handle can also be matched in Egypt at S.D. 70, and there is another possible link in a Polished Red cylindrical jar (Pl. 12: 65 and Pl. 57: 74).

There are indeed difficulties with regard to the pushed-over ledge handles, which are nevertheless quite distinct from the envelope handles from Tell Beit Mirsim Stratum H and are also much thicker in section. On the other hand, Wright's comparisons between Fara H and the pottery of dynasties vii–x in Egypt (PPEB, pp. 79 ff.) seem to carry less weight in view of the distinct difference in ware and technique. Comparisons are indeed much closer between First Intermediate Period in Egypt and Group 1529 (Pls. 13, 66, and p. 42), where both indented edges and wavy line decoration appear.

If a date for Fara H at the transition between Chalcolithic and EB is accepted, then it is possible to arrange the cave-dwellings in a tentative series on the strength of the development of details such as ledge handles, and the result is tabulated on p. 145.

Mass Burials

With the shift of population to new ground, which was to become Tell ed-Duweir, during the second period of the Bronze Age, certain caves in the North-West Settlement were re-used for mass burials in that and the following phases (p. 62).

Among the pottery in the caves, the large groups from Caves 1535 (Pl. 58: 75–123), 1519 (Pl. 60) and 1513 (Pl. 59) form an interlapping sequence beginning in EB I and extending into the final phase of the period EB III and later. Burial 1556 in the filling of the Dwelling 1558 was a smaller group apparently associated with one body, which is photographed on Pls. 3: 6–7 and 14 and drawn completely on Pl. 61. It is none the less important for the link which it provides with the caverns in Area 6000 (p. 274) near the north-east corner of the mound. Compare Pl. 62: 303 with 296 on the same plate.

CALICIFORM CULTURE

Though the North-West Settlement was most thickly populated in the Early Bronze Age, the invaders who destroyed that established culture lived in some of the existing caves.

A name for these people and their distinctive products has not yet been generally established. When he found the cemeteries at Tell el-Ajjul, Petrie introduced the period as the "Copper Age" of Palestine (AG I, pp. 3–4). At the same time Albright was excavating contemporary city deposits at Tell Beit Mirsim (Strata I–H, see AASOR XII, XIII, XVII), which he attributed to the first phase of the Middle Bronze Age. Since then the pottery of the period has been found in quantity beyond the Jordan in eastern Palestine by Nelson Glueck (AASOR XVIII–XIX; XXV–XXVIII). In Syria at Ras Shamra certain tombs at the base of Level II, with contracted bodies and comparable weapons, have already been recognised by Schaeffer as akin to the Duweir cemetery (*Stratigraphie*, p. 188). Moreover, in 1952–1956, Miss K. M. Kenyon's excavations for the British School of Archaeology in Jerusalem provided fresh evidence at Jericho of the destruction inflicted by these newcomers on the Bronze Age city, and of their subsequent attempts to adopt an urban life (PEQ, 1952, p. 70). In accordance with the chronological position of these people between the inhabitants of the Early and Middle Bronze Ages, she favours the designation "Intermediate Early Bronze-Middle Bronze Age" for the period.

None of these terms is satisfactory, for it is already clear that there are several subdivisions within the period, either cultural or chronological, which will each require a name. It is therefore proposed to use "Caliciform Culture" for the phase or phases present at Duweir, derived from the shape of the beakers which are distinctive, though at other sites different pottery shapes may distinguish other factors in this complex culture. The term is used by Albright in relation to the pottery of Stratum H at Tell Beit Mirsim (*Rel. Chron.*, p. 31) and for a similar stage of development in Syria of which four phases were distinguished by Harald Ingholt at Hama (*Arch. Pal.*, pp. 80 ff.).

These settlements and the Cemeteries 1500 and 100–200 at Tell el-Ajjul (AG I, II) provide phases of the period which are in part contemporary with the tombs at Duweir. A few scattered sherds in and below the fill of the MB glacis in the North-East Section do not necessarily suggest that these people built a city on the mound (p. 45). It is indeed likely that they were content to use the deserted caves of the North-West Settlement and to live there, while it is possible that the surviving community of the Early Bronze Age still maintained a restricted existence on the mound and in the caverns near the north-east corner.

Group 1529 (Pl. 95, Grid XII F.18)

The best collection of pottery to illustrate the Caliciform beaker phase appears to be a dump of domestic crockery, for large parts of the vessels are reparable. The Group 1529 has therefore been taken as representative of the period, though other caves in the vicinity also contained similar wares (photographs on Pl. 13: 81–89, line drawings on Pl. 66: 394–424).

Besides the contacts with Strata I–H at Tell Beit Mirsim, the sherds from Group 1529 are closely connected with those of Trench 1 at Jericho (PEQ, 1952, Fig. 6: 36–45).

At Qau in Egypt, a general similarity of detail though not of form suggests that the same stage of evolution was in progress during the First Intermediate Period, where a hand-finished indented edge, wheel-made grooved and wavy lines, spouts and small vertical lugs were characteristic features (QB II, Pls. XCI–XCII). See also pp. 139 ff.

Though the main forms are based on Early Bronze Age tradition, greater mastery of the wheel and different methods of firing produced a repertory in which some shapes and certain decorations were introduced which were new and short-lived in the history of Palestinian ceramics, and which showed few if any contacts with the following periods.

In their early attempts to adjust themselves to a settled way of life, the invaders were probably the builders of the straggling house walls which remain on the denuded upper terrace of the North-West Settlement. Where the soil is deeper on the lower terrace, the foundation courses of a building were preserved, which had contained at least a dozen rooms (Pls. 2: 5; 95, Grid XII G. 18/19). Very little pottery was found in them, but a collection of flint implements in House 1551 shows a change in technique from that of the Early Bronze Age (see Appendix C).

Cemetery 2000 (Pl. 93, Grid VIII)

In clean, unused ground north of the cave-dwellings, these people of the Caliciform Culture or their descendants had cut 120 tombs in and under the exposed scarp (Pls. 4: 2; 88–89; 93). Few of these small chambers were intact owing to their position on the crumbling edge and to the operations of those who took stone for later buildings.

Side by side, or above one another on the slope, the cavities were apparently cut by a light metal adze of which the marks were sometimes visible (Pl. 4: 5). Many of the round or oval tombs were too small to take more than one tightly flexed body and in most of them all traces of human remains had disappeared. The average space from cave roof to floor was less than a metre, and the latter seldom exceeded 2 metres in diameter. Owing to the condition of the rock, few plans were completely preserved, and though a rough classification of tomb types may be made, it cannot be entirely conclusive (Fig. 13). The pottery is described in Chapter 9, pp. 275 ff.; the daggers are compared in Chapter 6, while the results of the analyses are given in Appendix D.

Date and Comparisons

At Tell el-Ajjul the dominant tomb shape of Cemetery 1500 (AG II, Pl. LIX) is rectangular and the grave goods include daggers—often the only offering—and jars with vestigial ledge handles (CPP Type 30 F).

In Cemeteries 100–200 (AG I, Pl. LV), on the other hand, the prevailing tomb outline is round both in shaft and chamber, daggers are rare and there were two javelins, one of which compares with those on Pl. 22: 1–3. The common jar of these cemeteries is type 30 G in CPP, and other forms include shallow bowls and cups (see AG I, II and a forthcoming review of the material by Miss Kenyon, ADAJ III.

The stone- or brick-lined tombs of Petrie's Type A (cf. Tombs 1516 and 1517 in AG II, Pl. LIII) are missing at Duweir, unless the empty stone-lined chamber Tomb 2122, occupying the highest point of the excavated area (Pl. 4: 6) was the focus near which later burials were made (Pl. 93, Grid VIII, 0·12).

The Duweir series includes one tomb shape having an unlined squared shaft and chamber (see Chapter 9, p. 276, Fig. 13, Shape 0). Rounded chambers with squared or rounded shafts certainly predominate at Duweir

(Shapes 1, 2), while round tomb plans apparently without shafts are also common (Shape 3). Besides those shapes which are denuded, there are eight tombs which approach the beginnings of the bilobate chamber, which becomes important in the Middle Bronze Age, cf. Tomb 153 (p. 63 and pp. 230 f.) It is perhaps significant that the tomb shape which is most akin to the two-lobed plan is at the outer fringe of the cemetery (Pl. 93, Grid VIII P. 11, 2100–2101). It will be seen that orientation appears to have no significance.

LATER GROUPS AND STRUCTURES

Middle and Late Bronze Age Burials (Pl. 94, Grid XII H/J.14)

Caves 1542, 1546, 1547, 1548 and 1552 contained communal burials covering most of the Middle Bronze Age, but only Tomb 1502 (Grid K.8 and p. 254) seems to have been cut specifically for a tomb. Compare the plan of Tomb 129 near the north-west corner of the mound, where there were other burials of the same period (L. III, Pl. 125).

A cache of pottery (Locus 1555, see pp. 60–61 and p. 273) is especially interesting since it contains imported wares belonging to the early part of the xviiith dynasty at the beginning of the Late Bronze Age, but apart from this evidence there are few if any signs of activity in the North-West Settlement at this period.

The Watch-tower and Roadway

The plan of the Settlement on Pl. 89 marks the route of an "ancient roadway", edged with stone blocks, which had led up presumably from the valley, though all signs of it on the lower slopes had disappeared (Pl. 2: 4). It follows the third ridge to an outlying spur and leads to a substantial square building. From this point (Pl. 2: 2) the upper fortifications and citadel of Lachish are visible and movements in the valley could be observed by the watchmen. Starkey thought that the site may have marked the position of an old outpost or watch-tower of the kind mentioned in the Old Testament, e.g. II Kings XVII: 9. The date of the building and of the road which led to it can only be established by excavation.

Post-Exilic and/or Medieval Graves (Pls. 94–95)

Clusters of single graves oriented east and west were dug along the scarp, of which the largest group is seen in Grid XII G.20 on Pl. 95. They compare with the post-exilic graves near the north-west corner (L. III, p. 174), and with the so-called Medieval graves on the mound (L. III, p. 146 and Pl. 122). Only a few bodies were undisturbed and most graves were without bones or offerings. The one exception of interest is the body of a child, buried in its mother's grave 1533, with a bright string of gold, glass, carnelian and onyx beads (p. 265).

CHAPTER 3
FOUNDATION AND GROWTH OF THE CITY

North-East Caverns (see pp. 156–71)

WHILE the main centre of the Chalcolithic era was on exposed ground north-west of Tell ed-Duweir, the lower slopes of that site near the north-east corner afforded better shelter and some large natural caves (Pl. 10: 1, Pls. 88–89 and L. III, Pls. 128–129). That man was established in the vicinity in earliest times is shown by the presence of a Natufian flint end-scraper (Group 4022, pp. 288 f. and Appendix C), deep in the midden at the base of the slopes, and nearby there was also a painted Neolithic sherd (pp. 29, 300) of the type associated with the latter part of Jericho IX (PPEB, pp. 8–9). Apart from a few sherds in the larger caves (e.g. Cave 6030) and a single flint implement in Cave 6029, the Chalcolithic period is poorly represented, though naturally the bulk of the pottery, with the earlier wares of EB, may have been cleared away to make room for the last phase of domestic occupation in EB III or IV. Shortly afterwards, some sherds in Cave 6013 were cleared out and left in a pile beside the entrance. Presumably that clearance was made for the crouched burials which were disposed around the cave, but none of them were supplied with offerings (for further details see Chapter 13).

While the caves were in use, a city was growing up on the rock outcrop above, of which traces were seen on the rock near the north-west corner, and which is known to exist near the site of the Great Shaft (L. III, Pl. 108).

North-East Section (see Chapter 4 and Pl. 96)

The basis for study of all phases of the Bronze Age is derived from the contents of a trench cut by the Expedition into the mound in two steps of 18 feet each, near the north-east corner where part of the Iron Age revetment had collapsed into the valley (L. III, Pl. 11: 1, Pl. 108, Grid T.8 and p. 71).

The stratification of these deposits is illustrated on Pl. 96 and the pottery is drawn on pp. 53–59 with relevant descriptions and comparisons on the opposite pages. From sloping bed-rock to modern ground surface the depth is some 40 feet, of which the lowest third to about 12 feet contains Early Bronze Age pottery fragments. For the equation of this region to the North-West Settlement and the North-East Caverns see pp. 41, 157 and 165.

Third Millennium Deposits

The earliest contacts are to be found with Tomb 1535, Megiddo Strata XIX–XVIII and Stages V–III, with Jericho Layers V–IV and with the 1952 British School of Archaeology excavations of the "second wall" at that site (PEQ, 1952, p. 78). There are, however, some intrusions at 6 feet and below. At 7 feet there is a concentration of stone perhaps belonging to a structure within the mound which had collapsed through decay and neglect. Besides connexions with Tomb 1535 at that point, there are the first links with Jericho Tomb A2–3 (p. 30) and a few parallels with Tell Beit Mirsim Stratum J.

At 8 feet there was a definite living level, where a potter had left lumps of prepared clay, unbaked sherds and part of an unfired holemouth jar (see pp. 57 and 90).

Though combed ware and pushed-up ledge handles had been found in earlier levels where they were probably intrusive, they became frequent from 7 feet to 11 feet and pieces of Khirbet Kerak pottery occur from 5 to 8 feet with two more fragments near bed-rock which may also be out of context. For the only rim profile in that ware see NE 7/284 on p. 57.

It is to the occupation between 7 and 11 feet, too, that the bulk of the sherds from Caves 6000 can be confidently assigned (Pls. 62–65), on account of the dominance of combed ware and the exclusive use of pushed-up ledge handles.

Though there are no clear-cut contacts for Tombs 1535 and 1556 with the Section above 9 feet, these two with Tombs 1519 and 1513, all provide some connexions with the upper levels of Tomb A at Jericho.

Decay and Desertion

Few sherds were found between 10 and 12 feet in the Section and the only sure trace of occupation is seen in the ruins of a poorly built wall at 10 feet, visible only in the north face. It may be among the attempts at settlement made by the incoming people of the Caliciform Culture (see also p. 42).

No signs of Early Bronze Age defence walls were exposed in the Section, but their foundations would most probably lie farther up the slope. Neither is there any evidence that the Bronze Age city was destroyed by fire; it appears rather to have suffered desertion and decay.

Second Millennium Deposits

There is no means of assessing the lapse of time represented by the meagre deposits in the Section between 12 and 14 feet. The cooking-pot fragments, with pierced holes, point to an equation with Tell Beit Mirsim Strata H–I or slightly earlier. No sherds of any kind were found at 14 feet and this sterile layer may mark the base of a new system of fortification, of which the core contained much earlier occupational debris.

Middle Bronze Age Defences (Pls. 1, 5, 6, 90, 96)

MB I–II Fill

Alternate layers of grey debris and brick wash were laid in the "sandwich" manner commonly used in the construction of earthworks at other sites, as described by General Y. Yadin in an instructive article on Hyksos fortifications (BASOR 137, Feb. 1955, p. 27). These layers would seem to be the inner core of a defensive slope, though their significance was not recognised in 1932–1933, when the plastered surface at the north-west corner had not been seen. Though the layers could have been laid in inverse chronological order, and though they could contain sherds of all periods up to the date of construction, there is a chance that the debris may have been taken from part of the mound unoccupied by the builders themselves (Figs. 3–4, pp. 55–57).

Between 15 and 19 feet sherds with Tell Beit Mirsim Strata G–F parallels become common and, at the same time, there are contacts with Megiddo Strata XV–XI. The wares are plain or wet-smoothed or self-burnished and few among them exhibit the red slip and burnish of Stratum G at Tell Beit Mirsim, suggesting that the fill was contemporary with the lesser-known period of Stratum F, when burnish was becoming less common. Among the few pieces with wide outside contacts is a sherd of White Painted IV type (No. 174 on p. 55), rarely found in Cyprus and best matched in single graves of Stratum XI at Megiddo, though it is lacking from the Structural Tombs (p. 198). At Ras Shamra jugs of similar ware are dated from 1900–1750 or 1700 (Ugaritica II, Fig. 131).

Fragments of storage jars covered with lime-wash and gaily decorated in bands of blue, red and black are to be found in the upper fill (p. 221). Found mostly in Strata G–F at Tell Beit Mirsim, this ware may be, on the excavator's authority, more precisely attributed to G (SAOC 18, p. 29, note 17). At Megiddo certain jars and stands similarly decorated occur in Strata XII–X, but they also are missing from the Structural Tombs. Occurrence of the painted ware at Byblos is mentioned by Engberg, while it was "the most recent to be observed in the filling of the Hyksos embankment" at Tell Kisan in the plain of Acre (op. cit., pp. 28–29).

Among other pottery forms in the MB fill, some rolled and bevelled rims, probably of round-based cooking pots, do not find ready comparisons elsewhere. Flat-based cooking-pots with raised bands edged with finger impressions are missing, like other characteristics of Strata E–D at Tell Beit Mirsim (AASOR XIII, pp. 83–86), though this is not surprising since they are lacking in the Duweir tombs. The only candidates for a date equivalent to Stratum D are some carinate bowls, and the plain or curved forms with inturned rim, which could equally well come from Stratum E in view of the variety of form and finish and the fragmentary nature of the material at both sites (AASOR XIII, p. 77).

MB III Plastered Surfaces

The fill is closed between 22 and 23 feet by a clearly defined white plaster surface, which extends outwards in the south face of the Section for some 8 feet in two very shallow steps. One foot below is another less clearly marked streak which may represent an earlier surface, and at 17 feet there are three further streaks which are either disused surfaces or layers of packing in the fill. The two topmost coats were both destroyed at the same point, leaving no clue as to the angle of slope. The height above sea level of the horizontal summit is about 244 metres, and the total height of city debris and constructional fill rises some 7 metres above bed-rock.

In 1933–1934, however, isolated patches of a lime-plastered surface were exposed near the north-west corner of the mound (PEQ, 1934, p. 167), which had been cut by the line of the Iron Age wall and buttresses. Judging by the angle of slope on surviving patches, which is 29° from ground level on the measured section (Pl. 90), the summit of the embankment may be estimated at about 260 metres above sea level. The two cuts separated by the width of the mound expose sections of the *terre pisée* defences on opposing slopes of the Tell periphery, and the difference in height between the two summits is largely due to the tilt of the underlying rock.

Close to the north-west corner, the underlying core of limestone chips and packed earth was excavated down to bed-rock (Pl. 5: 1–4). The core of the slope at this point shows a variation on the "sandwich" method of construction, consisting of a well-beaten thick layer of limestone chips on top of a cut-down fill of dark clay. The surface at the low points exposed is of smoothly surfaced lime plaster. Both methods belong, in Yadin's opinion, to an earlier and less developed type of glacis, preceding those built of stone blocks (BASOR 137, Feb. 1955, p. 27).

There are no sure traces of this later type of battered wall at Duweir, unless it is admitted that the revetment, which formed the base of the Iron Age wall resting against the outer side of the south face of the Section (Pl. 96), was originally of the earlier period (L. III, Pl. 11: 5–6 and p. 88).

Fosse (Pl. 90; L. II, Pl. LXXII; L. III, Pl. 125)

It will be seen on Pl. 90 that the sloping face of the glacis or escarp breaks off short of the shallow fosse, and that the angle of slope would have had to change sharply if the latter were to be of practical advantage.

The length and breadth of the fosse has been traced for nearly 140 metres on the west side of the mound (L. II, Pl. LXXII). That the water from it was conserved and utilised is suggested by the outlet to be seen in Grid Square C.13 (L. III, Pl. 125), which apparently conveyed the drainage from the southern slopes, where the fosse is no longer to be seen, into a circular cistern or pit (Grid B.13); for the ditch slopes in a gentle gradient from north to south with a drop of over a metre between the outlet just described and the ditch as seen below the Fosse Temple (L. II, Pl. LXIX). If the fosse turned towards the east at the north-west corner, the hard outcrop of limestone at that point has been so cut and quarried that any trace which may have existed below that projection has long since disappeared. Cavern 101 in Grid Square D.5 (L. III, Pl. 3: 1 and pp. 178 ff.) is probably also a quarry in origin, enlarged and re-used as occasion required. The sherds recorded from it are apparently no earlier than Late Bronze Age, and—if it had existed when the fosse was in use—all drainage would inevitably have poured into the cave.

The lower slopes along the north side of the mound were not examined, though the steep and even contour of that elevation suggests some inner retaining force (L. III, Pl. 106).

Neither are there any certain traces of the fosse at the north-east corner, or beyond it on the east side, where the course of the Wadi Ghafr now sweeps close to the slopes of the mound.

Only at the south-west corner, where the rock outcrop falls away from the ridge of Area 500, is there any possible trace. Cut into the side of an almost vertical face are the remains of two tombs (L. III, Pl. 126: Grid D.23, 24, Tombs 570 and 571, and p. 219) with shattered and disturbed deposits (pp. 248 f.), parts of which had fallen still farther down the slope. This vertical cut would line up well with the counterscarp of the fosse exposed below the Fosse Temple.

However, it is only to be expected that the plan of the defence system must have been interrupted near the south-west corner for the entrance ramp, which could hardly have been elsewhere on the circuit of the mound.

Date of Construction

In an attempt to fix the time of construction and duration of use for the "Hyksos" earthworks surrounding the mound at Duweir, which have been examined in the North-East Section and at the north-west corner, two main sources are available.

1. Sherds from the MB fill of the defence glacis discussed in some detail in Chapters 3 and 4 and above on p. 45, where connexions are noted with two main sites, Tell Beit Mirsim and Megiddo.

2. The pottery from Tombs 145, 157 and particularly of Grave 173 which is sealed under the core of the embankment at the north-west corner. On the whole, the contents are equivalent to part of Stratum E at Tell Beit Mirsim and part of Stratum XI at Megiddo, p. 62.

It is only the latest sherds within the fill, closed just under 23 feet above bed-rock by the topmost plaster surface, which are significant. They appear to equate with Tell Beit Mirsim Strata E–D and with Megiddo Stratum X, but as the four major and two minor phases of E are undefined and as the Megiddo building levels XII–X are interspersed with graves, which are rarely contemporary with the buildings, an exact equation with both these sites cannot be fixed.

Reviewing the evidence for the date of construction, it is seen that single black piriform and cylindrical juglets with pricked design come from Graves 145 and 157 under the MB fill, and that, except for a few sherds and two red burnished types, this distinctive Yehudiyeh ware was missing from the tombs (pp. 33 and 189 f.). The cylindrical juglet, Type 750, in particular allows an equation with the upper burial in Tomb 303 at Gaza (p. 190), for which M. Schaeffer fixes extreme limits between 1750–1650 B.C. (*Stratigraphie*, p. 154). A date in the early half of the period for the last burial in Tomb 157 would provide a *terminus ante quem* for the construction of the embankment *circa* 1700 B.C.

Duration of Use

Study of the Section illustrated on Pl. 96 will show that the contents belong to one of three main periods:

1. the original constructional fill which includes earlier material, from 12–20 feet;
2. a possible repair and surface renewal at 21–22 feet;
3. a period marked by burnt destruction between 23 and 24 feet, when occupation debris had risen to the summit of the bank (Level VIII).

The actual period when the glacis was in use is therefore unrepresented, and the length of time can only be measured by the fact that town debris had overflowed the limits of the inner embankment slope.

The problem must thus be approached more indirectly through negative and circumstantial evidence, bearing in mind, meanwhile, the acknowledged pitfalls.

Six seasons' intensive tomb work failed to produce the distinctive pottery and weapons which are characteristic of Tell Beit Mirsim Strata E–D and of the 1930–1936 Necropolis at Jericho, apart from the commonest forms of dippers, bowls, juglets and lamps, pp. 178 ff. If the builders of the *terre pisée* embankment owned pottery and weapons like those from Jericho and Tell Beit Mirsim, one would then expect to find them in profusion at Duweir.

The evidence seems to show that the MB town within its new defence did not begin to grow until the piriform juglet was passing out of use, which is missing in all but the earliest groups. This situation is matched at Tell Fara, where only a few small burials contained this shape (CPP Types, 60 M[4], M[5], N[4]), which was completely missing from the bilobate tombs, like all the distinctive forms of Strata E–D at Tell Beit Mirsim.

47

At Ajjul likewise, similar piriforms only occur in the Courtyard Cemetery (AG II, Pl. LVIII) and in the lower burial of Tomb 303 (AG III, Pl. XLIX) and Albright considers that these graves precede the construction of the "Hyksos" fosse (AJSLL LV, pp. 349–350).

Admitting a date of plus or minus 1700 B.C. for the glacis construction, one could then see, in the tombs beyond that defence, the burials of the people who were living at Duweir during most of the seventeenth century.

While the defence system was in use, the surface was presumably exposed and the good repair of the upper plaster face suggests that it, at least, could not have been open to the elements for long.

The fact that the debris of Level VIII above the crest of the defence was purely MB in character suggests that the glacis was obsolete by the time of the burning. The same situation seems to have existed at Tell Beit Mirsim, where Professor Albright considered that such fortifications were no longer in use by the end of Stratum D (AASOR XVII, p. 28).

Level VIII (c. 1567 B.C.)

Both the white plaster and the grey surfaces of the glacis or escarp below come to an abrupt end some 4 feet behind the backing of an 11-foot wall founded at 20 feet (Pl. 96), of which five courses of brick remain, built on poorly laid stone and backed by the same material. That the wall is constructionally later than the glacis is clear from the way it cuts into the plaster face, but it is doubtful if it represents a substantially later phase.

The glacis summit, as far as it was exposed, was covered with brickwash burnt red which, according to the drawn section, did not show signs of burning above the stump of the city wall. Over both wall and glacis, however, there was a well-defined layer of charcoal and red soil, suggesting that the city wall, which may have superseded the glacis late in MB III, was destroyed with the contents of the burnt brickwash at 24 feet (Level VIII). Alternatively, it could be associated with the unknown city of LB I, which presumably existed when Structure I of the Fosse Temple was in use.

Part of the stone footing and the major portion of the wall collapsed at the time of destruction or soon afterwards, and some of the stone which fell was retained in a pocket near bed-rock. It is against this deposit that the stone revetment was built, and for this reason no sherds which were later in date than the Middle Bronze Age were recovered from the fill behind the wall (L. III, p. 88). The revetment inevitably invites comparison with the battered construction of stone which superseded the *terre pisée* fortifications at Tell Beit Mirsim in Stratum D, but its exact date within the periods E^2 and D has still to be decided (AASOR XVII, p. 29).

The sherds of Level VIII, drawn on p. 55, consist of jar rims and bowls, including a large part of a burnished piece (No. 107). The finish may be compared with a bowl said to be characteristic of Stratum D at Tell Beit Mirsim, though the profile is not identical (AASOR XII, Pl. 44: 8 and § 35). The rim is flatter than similar forms found in Stratum E (AASOR XIII, Pl. 10: 2, 3 and § 34). Of jar rims in Level VIII, Nos. 108–109 are common in Strata E and D. It is perhaps Stratum D^2 which is equivalent to Level VIII.

Embedded in burnt brickwash and charcoal, the few sherds available from Level VIII only represent the last phase of a city, of which the main occupational debris must have gradually accumulated against the inner face of the glacis. It is perhaps the intensity of the burning, as much as the sherds themselves, which suggests an equation in time between this destruction and that of City III and Palace I at Ajjul, and of the last MB occupation of Tell Beit Mirsim. See, in particular, "typical D sherds" illustrated in AASOR XII, Pl. 46: 3, 6, 9–11, 13, 24. See also AASOR XVII, p. 30, Note 4a.

Whatever may have been the cause of the destruction at Ajjul, it does not seem to have been long before City and Palace II were rebuilt to a completely new plan. The same may have happened at Lachish, since the Fosse Temple was built to serve a local community, though there is little to represent the period of LB I in the North-East Section. The sherds at 25–26 feet could be contemporary, and No. 100 is a bowl rim which is among the most common types of Cities III and II at Ajjul.

Level VII (*c.* 1450–1370 or 1350 B.C)

At 28 feet, above the collapsed structure of the city wall, rough foundations were prepared for a new building, the outer wall of which is visible in both faces of the Section. The room of which it formed part had a plaster floor and that surface was extended to line part of a pit sunk in the room. The contents of this pit, sealed in below a layer of charcoal, represents the last phase of occupation in the house. Here, for the first time in the Section, Base-Ring ware is encountered in part of a jug with ridged neck, and a small piece of a lentoid flask, Nos. 92 and 93 on p. 53. There was also one sherd with white lines, in marked contrast to the quantities of such pieces associated with Stratum C at Tell Beit Mirsim. This neck with moulding is close to the Base-Ring jug type (L. II: 280), and the bowl rims, Nos. 64, 74 and 86, are like another form (L. II: 135) also exclusive to Structure II.

Found in the pit, which contained the latest sweepings of the house floor, a scarab bears the name of Amenhetep II, the son of Thothmes III, who reigned until *c.* 1425 B.C., but it can only establish that the house was not burnt before his accession. See No. 88, on p. 53.

The evidence on the whole seems to suggest that Level VII and Structure II ended at the same time.

Level VI (*c.* 1300–1225 or 1200 B.C.)

The last Bronze Age structure visible in the Section consisted of an outer wall, the true width of which is seen in the north face, though in the south face the Section has cut obliquely through a supporting pier or buttress.

The length of time which passed between the destruction of the house at Level VII and the building of this next structure at 32 feet cannot be established with any certainty. There are indeed one or two sherds which should equate with Structure II, e.g. NE 31/29 (L. II: 135) and NE 31/31 (L. II: 228), but both could derive from the building of Level VII.

Between 30–34 feet many of the sherds could be fitted together and there can be no doubt that these 5 feet represent one occupation level, though the ground below the floor was disturbed by destruction of that surface. The same can be said of 35–36 feet, where much ash and burnt brick indicates a new destruction by fire.

The domestic wares in this room are richer and more elaborate than anything from the contemporary burnt Level VI on the west side, but the number of Structure III bowl forms in both localities is a sound indication of the same period (L. III, pp. 74–76).

The sherds of Level VI in the Section can be compared with confidence to the contents of Structure III. All the characteristic elements are present and comparisons are noted in the inventory of Chapter 4, pp. 52–53; a double bowl NE 36/1; a krater with gazelle, tree and double axe motif NE 36/2; bowls with painted rims and one with zigzags and palmtree design NE 32/17, and an elaborate pilgrim flask NE 32/21, which is matched in Cave 4034.

The destruction of Level VI is roughly contemporary with that of Stratum C at Tell Beit Mirsim. Among decorative fragments it is not always possible to find exact parallels, but the photographs in AASOR XIII, Pls. 26–27, show all those same motifs as described above. The contents of Silo 6 (AASOR XII Pl. 29: 13 and Pl. 30), are attributed to the late eleventh or even the tenth century (op. cit., § 85), but in view of the palmette bowl, the pilgrim flask and the numerous painted storage jars it contains, a date in Stratum B before, rather than after, the Philistine dominion might be preferable. In that case an equation of C^2–B^1 for the occupation of Level VI might fit the facts.

The few comparisons for the pottery of Level VI seem closer to Stratum VII than to VI at Megiddo. The double bowl is common in Strata VII–VI, the gazelle and tree design of the krater is less conventional than on jugs attributed to Stratum VIII (M. II, Pl. 58: 1–2) which should belong to the period of Stratum VII, if it is accepted that the site was virtually unoccupied, except for burials, from the destruction of Stratum IX until the foundation of Stratum VII under Ramesside control. The opposed triangles or double axe motif on the krater are matched on the jugs belonging to that period (M. II, Pls. 63: 3, 66: 4). The check pattern on the sherd, NE 36/4, is found without the dots at Megiddo in Stratum VII (Pl. 67: 18, Pl. 69: 13), while the decorated pilgrim flask (cf. NE 32/21), though otherwise comparable, lacks a cream burnished surface (M. II, Pl. 70: 9).

Iron Age Level

Considerable denudation of the tell slopes removed most of this last Bronze Age building in the years which elapsed before the founding of a rather poor Iron Age wall of which only two courses were exposed in the west face of the trench.

CHAPTER 4
THE MOUND: CONTENTS OF NORTH-EAST SECTION

ON the following pages, drawings and descriptions are presented of significant pottery fragments found in the North-East Section. A process of selection was inevitable, particularly in view of the large quantity of Early Bronze Age sherds. It was decided to illustrate the earliest occurrence of a given form. For this reason, the prevalence of comb-faced sherds (p. 139), ledge handles, Form 8 (p. 153), and holemouth jars with bulbous rims (p. 164), between 5 and 10 ft. needs special emphasis.

In the list all sherds between 36 and 13 feet inclusive are wheel-made, and from 12 feet to bed-rock they are hand-made, unless stated to the contrary. All diameters are approximate. An asterisk* against a number on the illustrations denotes that the sherd so marked may be intrusive in the level at which it was found. Except where noted, drawings are reproduced at a scale of 1:5. The page numbers in brackets refer to Chapters 9 and 10. Where references to *Lachish II* are in italics, the relevant form is reproduced in *Lachish IV*.

Objects other than sherds include part of a calcite *tazza* (p. 86) in Level VI, datable from the reign of Thothmes IV to that of Rameses II, a scarab of Amenhetep II (pp. 49, 97), which provides a *terminus ante quem* for the burning of Level VII, and part of a stone vase (p. 85) of xiith dynasty inspiration found in or on the MB glacis fill.

From Early Bronze Age levels, limestone disks (p. 71) occur at 7 and 6 ft., there are beads at 6 and 3 ft. which resemble those from Cave 1535 (Pl. 29: 2), and a worn bone spatula (p. 73) was found at 2 ft. above bed-rock.

Carbonized plant samples collected from Early Bronze Age levels are examined by Dr. Helbaek (pp. 309–17). Shells of the same provenance are discussed by Mr. Baden-Powell (p. 324). It should be noted that plant and shell samples were missing from Middle and Late Bronze Age deposits, a lack which may be partly explained by the depth of constructional fill forming the Middle Bronze Age defences.

Flint implements are identified by Dr. Waechter (pp. 326–7), who notes that in spite of their scarcity, they are interesting because they cover the whole depth of the Section.

LEVEL VI. (NORTH-EAST SECTION, 36–30 ft.)

No.	WARE	REMARKS	FIELD No.
NE 36–34			
	Body, firing and surface		
1	Pk. gy. core, M, burnt	Double bowl, scraped bottom. 2 ex. Cf. L. II: 179–183; M. II, Pl. 67: 7–9, Stra. VIII–VII A. (See pp. 49, 183)	399
2	Pk. gy. core, S, pk. slip, traces bur.	Krater, dec. dk. rd. paint, palms, birds, antelopes, lines, zigzags. Cf. L. II: 250. (See p. 219)	400
3	Pk. gy. core, M, bf. surface	Storage jar, Class E, dec. dk. rd. paint. (See p. 224)	401
4	Pk. gy. core, M, bn. slip, bur.	Frag. dec. checks, spots dk. rd. paint. Cf. AASOR XIII, Pl. 26: 18, TBM Stra. C; *Ugaritica II*, Fig. 128: 4, *c*. 1365–1250. (See p. 50)	402
5	Pk. gy. core, grits1, M, rough worn surface	Krater or jar, cup depression on rim. (See p. 219)	403
6	Pk. M, rough surface	Curved bowl, Class H, diam. 20·5 cms. (See p. 181)	405
7	Pk. M, cm. surface in. and out.	Flared bowl, Class J, diam. 19 cms. (See p. 182)	406
8	Pk. M, bf. surface in. and out.	Krater rim? Rd. paint on rim. Diam. 22 cms. (See p. 219)	407
9	Pk. gy. core, M	Bowl rim, diam. 24 cms.	408
10	Pk. gy. core, M, wheelmarks in. and out.	Potstand. Cf. L. II: 330. (See p. 196)	404
11	Pk. grits1, M, cm. slip out.	Storage jar rim, Class E, diam. 12 cms. (See p. 224)	409
NE 33			
12	Pk. grits1, M, wheelmarks in. and out.	Flared bowl, Class J, diam. 19 cms. Cf. Pl. 72: *L. II*: 91. (See p. 182)	394
13	Pk. gy. core, M, cm. slip out.	Base of flask. Cf. Pl. 85: 977. (See p. 218)	395
14	Pk. gy. core, S, bf. surface	Krater rim. (See p. 219)	396
15	Bf. grits1, S, bf. surface	Krater rim.	397
16	Pk. gy. core, straw, M, bf. surface	Bowl, Class F, inverted rim with stump of handle. Cf. AASOR XII, Pl. 47: 12, TBM Stra. C. (See pp. 141, 180)	399
NE 32			
17	Pk. gy. core, straw, M, wheelmarks out. smoothed in.	Bowl, carinate B. Dec. dk. rd. paint, palm tree, lines, zigzags. Cf. Pl. 68: *L. II*: 125; AASOR XII, Pl. 29: 13; TBM Stra. B. (See pp. 49, 141, 179)	386
18	Pk. M, traces radial self bur. in.	Bowl misc., knob handle. Dec. dk. rd. paint on rim. Cf. Pl. 72: 630. (See pp. 141, 183)	387
19	Gy. M	White Slip II. Bn. paint. Cf. Pl. 79: 832; AASOR XII, Pl. 17: 18–46, TBM Stra. C. (See p. 202)	388
20	Rd. gy. core, M, self bur. out.	Imitation piriform, dec. dk. rd. lines, zigzags. Lug handles. (See p. 216)	389
21	Pk. gy. in. grits2, M, thick cm. slip	Pilgrim flask. Dec. dk. rd. con. circles, lines, zigzags. Cf. Pl. 84:956; M. II, Pl. 70 :9, Stra. VII A; AASOR XII, Pl. 30: 2, 4, 5, TBM Stra. B. (See pp. 49, 50, 217)	390
22	Pk. gy. in. M, vert. self bur.	Pilgrim flask. Dec. dk. rd. spi. on body. Cf. Pl. 84: 957. (See p. 217)	391
23	Pk. gy. core, H	Storage jar rim, Class D. 12 ex. Cf. L. II: 389. (See p. 224)	392
24	Calcite	Tazza. Cf. FFSV, Pl. XXXIII: 831 and p. 12, Thothmes IV–Rameses II. (See p. 86)	393
NE 31			
25	Rd. grits1, S, bf. surface	Flanged rim of small bowl, diam. 19 cms.	375
26	Pk. gy. core, M	Rim of small bowl or krater. Rd. paint on rim. Diam. 18·5 cms.	376
27	Pk. gy. core, grits1, M, bf. surface, wheelmarks in. and out.	Curved bowl, Class H. Diam. 22 cms. Rd. paint on rim. (See p. 181)	377
28	Pk. gy. core, grits1, M	Flared bowl, Class J. Diam. 20·5 cms. (See p. 182)	378
29	Bf. grits2, M	Curved bowl, inturned rim, Class H, Cf. L. II: 135. (See pp. 49, 181)	379
30	Pk. gy. in M, thick cm. slip	White Slip II bowl. Cf. Pl. 79: 833; L. II: 157; AASOR XII, Pl. 17: 18–46, TBM Stra. C; AAA XXI, Pl. XXXIV: 23, Jericho M III. b/c. (See p. 202)	380
31	Pk. gy. core, grits2, S, cm. slip out. vert. hand bur.	Goblet, dec. dk. rd. paint round rim, diagonal lines, zigzags. Cf. L. II: 228. (See pp. 49, 183)	381
32	Pk. grits1, M, wheelmarks in. and out.	Krater rim, side repaired by patch of lime plaster. Cf. L. II: 70. (See p. 219)	382
33	Pk. gy. core, M, wheelmarks in and out.	Krater rim, diam. 26 cms.	383
34	Pk. gy. core, M	Krater rim.	384
35	Bn. gy. core, M	Grooved lid? Diam. 16 cms.	385
NE 30			
36	Bn. M	Flanged rim of small bowl, diam. 20 cms.	365
37	Fine pk. M, hor. self bur. in. and out.	Imitation White Slip. Cf. Pl. 82: 913. (See p. 211)	367
38	Rd. pk. core, grits1, S	Monochrome bowl. PCBA Type 2. Cf. Pl. 79: *L. II*: 167; M. II, Pl. 54: 21, Stra. IX. (See p. 201)	366
39	Pk. M, wheelmarks in. and out.	Flared bowl, Class J. Dec. thick band rd. paint in. rim. (See p. 182)	368
40	Pk. gy. core, M, bf. slip in., hor. bur.	Flared bowl, Class J. Dec. band rd. paint on rim. Cf. Pl. 71: 619.	369
41	Pk. gy. core, M, hor. bur. in. and out.	Flared bowl, Class J. Dec. thick rd. band on rim.	370
42	Gy. H, bk. surface, shiny	Base-Ring II. Part of handle, inserted. Dec. 2 incised lines. Cf. Pl. 80: 845. (See p. 203)	371
43	Pk. grits1, S, bf. slip	Krater neck. (See p. 219)	372
44	Pk. M, wheelmarks out.	Neck of storage jar, diam. 10 cms.	373
45	Pk. gy. core, M, smoothed out.	Storage jar rim, Class D. Diam. 10 cms. Cf. Pl. 87: 1018; L. II: 389. (See p. 224)	374

LEVEL VII. (NORTH-EAST SECTION, 29–27 ft. and Pit A)

No.	WARE	REMARKS	FIELD No.
NE 29			
46	Bf. M, smoothed in., wheelmarks out.	Curved bowl, Class H, diam. 19 cms. (See p. 181)	350
47	Pk. gy. core, grits1, M, wheelmarks in. and out.	Curved bowl, Class H, diam. 22 cms. Cf. Pl. 71: *L. II*: 30.	351
48	Gy. grits1, M, bf. surface	Flared bowl, Class J. Diam. 22 cms. (See p. 182)	352
49	Bf. gy. core, M, smoothed in. and out. wheelmarks out.	Flared bowl (?), Class J.	349
50	Pk. gy. core, M, smoothed out.	Raised band around neck, diagonal notches	353
51	Lt. bn. grits1, S, smoothed in., wheelmarks out.	Bichrome "Bird and Fish" ware. Dec. faint rd. and bk. bands. Cf. M. II, Pl. 53: 1, 2, Stra. IX. (See p. 197)	354
52	Pk. grits1 and straw, M	Rim of storage jar, diam. 14 cms. Class D. 2 ex. (See p. 224)	355
53	Rd. gy. core, grits3, M	Storage jar rim, Class E, diam. 15 cms. Cf. AASOR XIII, Pls. 11: 3–5, 14: 5, TBM Stra. E, D. (See p. 224)	356
54	Pk. gy. core, S	Rim of jar or jug. diam. 7 cms.	357
55	Pk. gy. core, M, smoothed in. and out.	Bowl with handles, Class F, inverted rim. Cf. L. II: 135. (See p. 180)	358
56	Pk. gy. core, M, wheelmarks in. and out.	Neck of large jar	359
57	Bn. grits1, M, wheelmarks in. and out.	Storage jar rim, Class C. Diam. 16 cms. (See p. 221)	360
58	Pk. gy. core, M	Krater rim. (See p. 219)	361
59	Pk. gy. core, M	Krater rim.	362
60	Bf. grits1, M, bf. surface	Krater rim.	363
61	Pk. gy. core, M	Part of pedestal base	364
NE 28			
62	Pk. gy. core, M, smoothed in. wheelmarks out.	Curved bowl, Class H. (See p. 181)	331
63	Pk. gy. core, M, fine wheelmarks, edge charred	Plain bowl, Class G. (See p. 181)	333
64	Pk. gy. core, M, fine wheelmarks	Flared bowl, Class J, inturned rim. (See p. 182)	335
65	Pk. gy. core, M	Flared (?) bowl, Class J, thickened rim, diam. 21 cms.	337
66	Rd. gy. core, M, bf. slip in.	Curved bowl, Class H, thickened rim. (See p. 181)	332
67	Pk. gy. core, grits1, M, fine wheelmarks	Curved bowl, Class H.	334
68	Pk. gy. core, M, fine wheelmarks	Flared (?) bowl, Class J, thickened rim. (See p. 182)	336
69	Gy. grits3, M, bf. surface in. burnt out.	Cooking-pot rim. 3 ex. Cf. L. II: 364. (See p. 195)	338
70	Pk. gy. core, M	Storage jar rim, Class D. Diam. 10 cms. Cf. AASOR XIII, Pls. 7: 2–4, 6–9; 14: 4, TBM Stra. E, D. (See p. 224)	339
71	Pk. M	Storage jar rim, Class D. Diam. 10 cms. Cf. Pl. 87: 1018; L. II: 389.	340
72	Pk. gy. core, M	Storage jar rim, Class E. Cf. AASOR XIII, Pl. 11: 3–5; 14: 5, TBM Stra. E, D. (See p. 224)	341
73	Pk. gy. core, M	Krater rim. (See p. 219)	342
74	Pk. gy. core, M	Flared bowl, inturned rim. Class J. 2 ex. (See p. 182)	343
75	Pk. gy. core, M, smoothed in. scraped out.	Lamp?	347
76	Pk. bk. core, M	Frag. dec. krater, rd. lines, bk. zigzags. 6 ex. (See p. 219)	344
77	Pk. gy. core, M, bf. surface	Potstand rim. (See p. 196)	345
78	Pk. M.	Potstand?	346
NE 27			
79	Pk. gy. core, M, hor. self bur. in., wheelmarks out.	Plain bowl, inturned rim. Class G. Cf. Pl. 70: 584. (See p. 181)	324
80	Pk. grits1, M, hor. self bur. in., smoothed out.	Plain bowl, inturned rim. Class G.	325
81	Fine pk. gy. core, M, wheelmarks in. and out.	Carinate bowl, Class B. Cf. Pl. 68: 532. (See p. 179)	326
82	Bf. gy. core, M, fine wheelmarks in. and out.	Plain bowl, flat rim. Class G. (See p. 181)	327
83	Bn. large grits3, H, surface worn, burnt	Cooking-pot rim. Cf. L. II: 370; M. II, Pl. 55: 4, Stra. IX–VIII; AASOR XII, Pl. 47: 11, TBM Stra. C. (See p. 195)	328
84	Rd. gy. core, H, shiny gy. surface, slightly pocked	Base-Ring ware. Rim of jug. Cf. Pl. 80: 842. (See p. 203)	329
85	Pk. gy. core, M, smoothed in.	Disk base of large bowl, dec. in. circles rd. and bk. paint	330
NE 27–25 Pit A			
86	Pk. gy. core, S, smoothed in. rough out.	Flared bowl, inturned rim. Class J. Cf. L. II: 109. (See p. 182)	315
87	Pk. gy. core, grits1, M, smoothed in. and out.	Flared bowl, Class J.	314
88	Steatite	Scarab. Amenhetep II, with griffin and hieroglyphs. Side type near No. 37 on Pl. 41. (See pp. 49, 97)	316
89	Pk. M, smoothed out.	Storage jar neck, Class D. (See p. 224)	317
90	Bn. M, smoothed and bur? in. and out. burnt	Bowl frag. dec. dk. rd. lines, zigzags	318
91	Pk. gy. in., grits1, M	Storage jar neck, Class E, dec. alternate lines rd. and bk. (See p. 224)	319
92	Fine bn. gy. core, M, bk. surface, pocked and worn	Base-Ring ware. Jug neck, one ridge. Handmade. (See p. 203)	320
93	Fine bf. M, rd. slip and bur. out., pocked	Base-Ring ware. Part of lentoid flask. Handmade.	321
94	Coarse pk. grits2 and flint, M, rd. wash out.	Semi-ring base of large bowl	322
95	Bn. gy. core, grits and straw, M	Storage jar base, Class C. Cf. Pl. 87: 1014. (See p. 221)	323

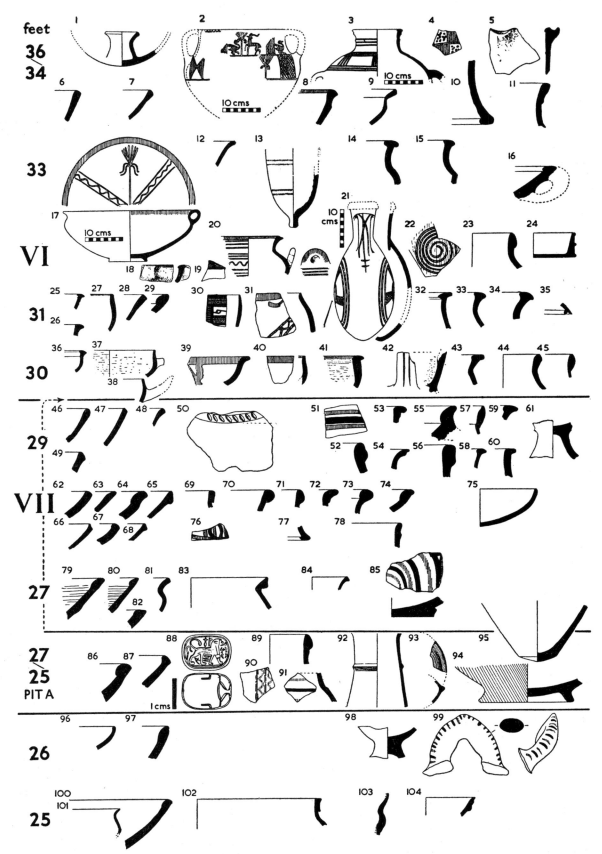

FIG. 2. North-East Section: Contents
Scale 1:5, except where otherwise stated

LEVEL VIII. (NORTH-EAST SECTION, 24 ft.)

No.	Ware	Remarks	Field No.
	Body, firing and surface		
105	Pk. M, bf. surface	Curved bowl, Class H, diam. 19 cms. Cf. Pl. 71: *L. II*: 30. (See p. 181)	297
106	Pk. gy. core, grits and straw[1], M	Curved bowl, Class H, diam. 23 cms.	298
107	Fine bf., M, rd. slip in. and out., squared bur. in., irr. out.	Flared bowl, Class J, diam. 39 cms. Cf. AASOR XIII, Pl. 10: 10, TBM Stra. E. (See pp. 48, 182)	299
108	Coarse rd. grits and flints[3], H	Rim of storage jar. Cf. AASOR XIII, Pl. 7: 2–4, 6–9, TBM Stra. E. (See p. 48)	300
109	Coarse bf. grits and flints[3], M, surface burnt gy.	Storage jar rim, Class E. Cf. AASOR XII, Pl. 46: 3, 9–11, 13, TBM Stra. D; XIII, Pl. 11: 3, TBM Stra. E. (See pp. 48, 224)	301
110	Coarse pk. grits[3], M	Cooking-pot rim. (See p. 195)	302
111	Coarse pk. grits[3] M	Cooking-pot rim.	303
112	Coarse rd. grits and flints[2], M	Krater rim. (See p. 219)	304
113	Pk. grits[3] and flint, M,	Krater rim, wheel-made (?), hand finish.	305

MB GLACIS FILL. (NORTH-EAST SECTION, 23–12 ft. approximately)

NE 23

No.	Ware	Remarks	Field No.
114	Fine pk. M, rd. paint cf. grain wash, partial hor. bur.	Rim of platter, wheel-made? Intrusive EB?	293
115	Coarse bn. grits and flint, M	Neck of jar	296
116	Fine pk. M, slip partly removed by wh., traces hor. bur.	Neck of jar	—
117	Coarse bn. grits and flint[3], M, surface worn	Storage jar base, Class C. Cf. Pl. 87: 1015; AASOR XIII, Pl. 6: 5, TBM Stra. E. See p. 221)	294
118	Shelly lmst., pk.	Frag. of stone vase, lug handle. Cf. FFSV, Pl. XV: 154. Dyn. xiii? (See p. 85)	295

NE 22

No.	Ware	Remarks	Field No.
119	Bn. grits[1], M, wheelmarks out. worn in.	Carinate bowl, Class A. Cf. Pl. 68: 512; M. II, Pl. 28: 15, Stra. XII. (See p. 178)	286
120	Bf. grits[1], M	Carinate bowl, Class C. Diam. 14 cms. (See p. 179)	287
121	Pk. gy. core, grits[3], M	Cooking-pot rim. (See p. !95)	288
122	Pk. gy. core, grits[3], M	Cooking-pot rim.	289
123	Coarse rd. grits[2] and flint, M	Cooking-pot rim.	290
124	Pk. grits[2] and flint, M	Part of raised band with incised hatching. QDAP XIV, Pl. VII: 2, 12, 13, 17, Nahariya MB II.	291
125	Bn. grits[2], M, wt. limewash out.	Frag. storage jar dec. bl./bk. bands outlined with rd. wavy line. 7 ex. See 133, 143. Cf. M. II, Pl. 43: 2 Stra. X; AASOR XIII, Pl. 22: 8–10, TBM Stra. G–F. (See p. 221)	292
126	Bn. M, worn in. scraped out.	Lamp, Class A? (See p. 185)	292a

NE 21

No.	Ware	Remarks	Field No.
127	Pk. gy. core, grits[1] S, bf. surface, radial self bur. in.	Curved bowl, inturned rim. Class H. (See p. 181)	279
128	Pk. gy. core, S, fine lines faint self bur. out.	Carinate bowl, Class C. Cf. M. II, Pl. 44: 15, Stra. X. (See p. 179)	280
129	Pk. grits[1], M, wheelmarks out. smoothed in.	Curved bowl, inturned rim, Class H. (See p. 181)	276
130	Pk. grits[1], M, wheelmarks in. and out.	Flared bowl, Class J. 4 ex. (See p. 182)	277
131	Pk. grits[1], S, bf. surface, hor. self bur.	Carinate bowl, Class B. (See p. 179)	278
132	Coarse rd. grits and flint[3], M, gy. surface out.	Cooking-pot rim, 2 ex. Cf. M. II, Pl. 46: 8, Stra. XIII–X. (See p 195)	281
133	Pk. M, wt. limewash out.	Frag. storage jar, dec. bands bl./bk. outlined in rd., wavy lines between. 2 ex. See 125, 143. (See p. 221)	282
134	Bn. grits[3], M	Ring base of small bowl	285
135	Pk. M, wheelmarks out., smoothed in.	Concave disk base of large bowl	284

NE 20

No.	Ware	Remarks	Field No.
136	Pk. bk. core, M, fine hor. bur. in.	Carinate bowl, Class D. (See p. 180)	264
137	Bf. S, smoothed out., wheelmarks in.	Carinate bowl, Class B. (See p. 179)	266
138	Coarse pk. gy. core, grits[2], M, bf. surface	Rim of bowl or krater	265
139	Coarse pk. grits[3], M	Flared bowl, inturned rim, Class J. (See p. 182)	267
140	Bf. sandy, M	Juglet neck, Class F. Cf. Pl. 77: 770; M. II, Pl. 23: 15, Stra. XII–X. (See p. 191)	268
141	Coarse pk. bn. core, grits and flint, M	Neck of large jar	275
142	Pk. grits[1], M	Grooved ring base of large bowl	270
143	Pk. grits[1], M, limewash out.	Frag. of storage jar with painted bands bl., outline rd. See 125, 133. (See p. 221)	269
144	Pk. gy. core, grits[2], M	Ring base of large bowl	271
145	Pk. M, smoothed out., wheelmarks in.	Concave base of small bowl	272
146	Pk. gy. core, S, smoothed out.	Concave base of small bowl	273
147	Gy. grits[3], M	Storage jar, Class B, oval section handle. Cf. Pl. 87: 1008; M. II, Pl. 43: 1, Stra. XII–X. (See p. 221)	274

NE 19

No.	Ware	Remarks	Field No.
148	Fine pk. H, cm. slip, close vert. bur. on neck, hor. on carination and in.	Carinate bowl, Class A. Cf. Pl. 66: 406; M. II, Pls. 19: 5; 28: 13, Stra. XIII A–XI. (See p. 178)	250
149	Fine bn. M	Plain bowl, Class G, inturned rim Cf. Pl. 70: 583; AASOR XIII, Pl. 10: 5, TBM Stra. E. (See p. 181)	247
150	Rd. gy. core, grits[2], M	Bowl or jug rim	248
151	Fine bf. M, pk. slip in., bur. in	Bowl, Class D? Cf. M. II, Pl. 14: 3, Stra. XIV–XIII. (See p. 180)	249
152	Rd. gy. core, grits[1], M, traces radial bur. in.	Plain bowl, Class G, inturned rim. Cf. M. II, Pl. 9: 6, Stra. XV–XII. (See p. 181)	244
153	Bn. grits[1], M	Curved bowl, Class H. (See p. 181)	245
154	Fine pk. grits[2], M, fine wheelmarks in. and out.	Curved bowl, Class H.	246
155	Coarse bn. M	Cooking-pot rim. (See p. 195)	252
156	Rough pk, gy. core, grits[3], H, burnt	Cooking-pot, bevelled rim	251
157	Fine rd. grits[1], H, rd. slip, vert. bur. out.	Neck of juglet, 2 bands rd. paint	253
158	Bn. grits[1], M	Neck of jar. See 170, 171	254
159	Pk. gy. core, grits[1] and flints, S, smoothed out., rough in.	Neck of jar. See 170, 171	255
160	Pk. grits[2], M, pk. slip out.	Neck of jar	256
161	Rough pk. gy. core, grits[2], M, thick limewash out.	Part of jar dec. bands brick rd. paint. (See p. 221)	257
162	Fine pk. grits[1], M	Dipper base, Class A. Cf. Pl. 78: 779. (See p. 193)	258
163	Bn. grits[1], M	Flat disk base turned	259
164	Fine bf. gy. core, M	Well-made ring base of jug, spi. finish	260
165	Fine pk. H	Concave foot base	261
166	Rd. gy. core, grits[2], M, smoothed out. worn in.	Storage jar, Class B, nearly flat base. See 167. (See p. 221)	262
167	Rd. gy. core, grits[2], M, smoothed out. worn in.	Storage jar, Class B, oval section handle. Part of 166. Cf. Pl. 87: 1009.	263

NE 18

No.	Ware	Remarks	Field No.
168	Fine gy. M	Carinate bowl, Class C, bevelled edge. Cf. Pl. 69: 552; AASOR XIII, Pl. 4: 1–3, Stra. G–F. (See p. 179)	238
169	Rough pk. M, wheel marks out. worn in.	Carinate bowl, Class C. Cf. AASOR XIII, Pl. 4: 8, TBM Stra. G–F.	231
170	Pk. grits and flint[2], M, smoothed in. and out.	Neck of jar. See 158, 159, 162	233
171	Fine pk. grits[1], M, smoothed in. and out.	Neck of jar. 5 ex.	232
172	Fine pk. M, smoothed in. and out.	Curved bowl, Class H. (See p. 181)	230
173	Rough pk. grits and flint, M, smoothed in. and out.	Jar. 2 grooves below rim	234
174	Fine pk. S, pk. slip, smooth bur. out., worn bf. surface in., lustrous paint	White Painted IV. Part of juglet, dec. dk. rd. hor. bands, diagonal criss-cross lines. Cf. M. II, Pl. 26: 15, Stra. XII; AASOR XIII, Pl. 22: 7, TBM Stra. G–F. (See pp. 45, 198)	235
175	Rough rd. grits and flint[3] M	Cooking-pot, bevelled rim	237
176	Rough bf. gy. core, M	Cooking-pot. Holes pierced from out. through rim, above raised band. Hand-made. Cf. AASOR XII, Pl. 3: 26–31, TBM Stra. I–F; AAA XXII, Pl. XXXII: 4, Jericho Layers IV–V. (See p. 195)	236
177	Fine bf. S, smooth bur. out.	Deep bowl? Cf. M. II, Pl. 36: 11, Stra. XI and in. rim	239
178	Lt. rd. grits[2], S	Neck of jar. Cf. M. II, Pl. 27: 6, Stra. XIV–XII	240
179	Pk. grits[2] and flint, M	Neck of jar	241
180	Rough gy. M	Concave disk base	243
181	Fine rd. grits[3], gy. core, H	Storage jar, Class B, oval section handle. (See p. 221)	242

NE 17

No.	Ware	Remarks	Field No.
182	Fine bf. S	Plain bowl, Class G, slightly inturned rim. (See p. 181)	217
183	Fine pk. H, bf. surface in.	Carinate bowl, Class C. Cf. Pl. 69: 545. (See p. 179)	216
184	Fine bf. H, fine wheelmarks in. and out.	Carinate bowl, Class B. Cf. Pl. 68: 527. (See p. 179)	215
185	Fine pk. M, pk. to bf. surface, self bur. in.	Curved bowl, Class H. (See p. 181)	214
186	Pk. M, smoothed in. and out. bf. surface out.	Rim of jar	218
187	Pk. grits[2], M, smoothed in. and out.	Rim of jar	219
188	Bf. grits[2], M, smoothed in. and out.	Rim of jar	220
189	Pk. grits[2] and flint, H	Cooking-pot, bevelled rim. (See p. 195)	221
190	Rd. gy. core, grits[1], M, matt rd. wash out.	Hand-made rim of jug	222
191	Rough rd. bk. core, grits[2], flints and straw, H, cm. surface, traces limewash out.	Pithos, hand-made (?), neck wh. finish. Cf. Pl. 62: 282. (See p. 165)	224
192	Pk. grits[1], M	Rim of jug?	225
193	Rough pk. bk. core, H, comb-faced under thick limewash	Raised band around neck, notched hand-made. (See p. 139)	223
194	Pk. M	Concave disk base	227
195	Pk. gy. core, grits[1], M	Flattened ring base	228
196	Pk. grits and flints[1], S	Ring base	229
197	Pk. grits[1], M	Shoulder of jar or jug with combed bands. See 302, 304. Cf. AASOR XII, Pl. 6: 22; 7: 14, TBM Stra. G	226

54

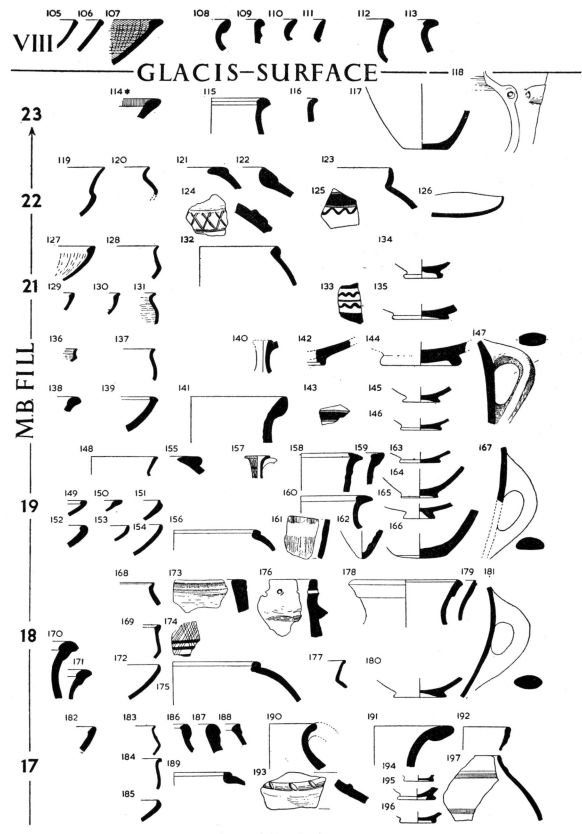

FIG. 3. North-East Section: Contents
Scale 1:5, except where otherwise stated

55

No.	WARE	REMARKS	FIELD No.

NE 16

Body, firing and surface

No.	Ware	Remarks	Field No.
198	Fine bn. S	Carinate bowl, Class C. (See p. 179)	207
199	Pk. gy. core, M, bf. surface in. and out.	Cup or beaker. Comb-faced out. Caliciform. (See p. 172)	208
200	Ik. grits[1] and flint, M, rd. wash in. and over rim, rd. matt stripes out.	Bowl rim. Cf. Pl. 64: 340 and see Bowls, string-cut, on p. 161	205
201	Fine pk. grits[1], M, pk. slip in., cm. surface out., hor. bur. in. and over rim	Bowl	206
202	Bf. grits[1], S, traces rd. wash in. and out.	Bowl, plain rim, or lamp, charred edge. Hand-made? (See p. 184)	203
203	Rough rd. grits[1] M, bf. surface in. and out.	Bowl, plain rim, finely comb-faced out. (See p. 300)	204
204	Rough rd. grits[3], H, combed surface	Row of vertical notches, potmark?	209
205	Fine pk. grits[1], M, rough in. and out., rd. wash in.	Sherd, band rd. paint out.	210
206	Bn. grits[3], M	Cooking-pot. (See p. 195)	211
207	Pk. grits[1], M	Storage jar, Class C. See 223. Cf. Pl. 87: 1016; AASOR XII, Pl. 46: 8; XIII, Pl. 22: 20–22, TBM Stra. G–F. (See p. 221)	212
208	Pk. grits[1], M, bf. slip out. rough in	Base of jug	213

NE 15

209	Fine pk. M, rd. wash out.	Platter or bowl. See 392	195
210	Bn. grits[1], M	Bowl? Wheel-made?	196
211	Rough rd. gy. core, grits[1] and straw, M, slip and traces bur. in. rough out.	Platter, upright rim wh. finished. Hand-made. (See p. 157)	194
212	Rough pk. gy. core, M	Cooking-pot. Holes pierced from out. through rim above raised band impressed thumb and finger. 4 ex. Hand-made. See 219–222, 226, 231, 256, 326. Cf. AASOR XII, Pl. 3: 26–31; XIII, Pl. 22: 11–15, TBM Stra. I–F; Megiddo SAOC 17, p. 35. (See pp. 45, 195)	197
213	Coarse bn. grits[3], M	Cooking-pot. AASOR XIII, Pl. 5: 2 for shape only, TBM Stra. G–F	201
214	Rough pk. grits[3], M	Rim of jar, wh. finish	198
215	Rough rd. gy. core, H.	Rim of jar, wh. finish. Cf. AASOR XII, Pl. 6: 10–12, TBM Stra. G	199
216	Pk. gy. core, grits[1], M	Rim of jar. Cf. AASOR XII, Pl. 6: 17 TBM Stra. G	200
217	Bf. M, worn in., rd. wash out.	Disk base, spi. wheelmarks out. Cf. AASOR XII, Pl. 4: 26, TBM Stra. H–I	202

NE 14 No finds

NE 13

218	Fine bf. S, limewash out.	Bowl, hand-made	187
219	Rough gy. M, rough surface in. and out., burnt	Cooking-pot. Hole pierced through rim from out. Hand-made. See 212. (See p. 195)	188
			188
220	Rough gy. M, rough burnt surface in. and out.	Cooking-pot. Holes pierced from both sides through rim. Hand-made. See 212.	191
221	Rough gy. M, rough bf. surface in. and out.	Cooking-pot. Holes pierced through. Hand-made. See 212.	190
222	Bn. bk. core, M, rough bf. surface in. and out.	Cooking-pot. Holes pierced through rim from out. Hand-made. See 212.	189
223	Pk. M, smoothed in. and out.	Storage jar, Class C. See 207. (See p. 221)	192
224	Fine gy. M	Jar?	193

NE 12

225	Bf. M, burnt gy.	Jar rim	181
226	Rough bf. gy. core, grits[1] M, rough surface in. and out.	Cooking-pot. Holes pierced from both sides through rim. See 212. (See p. 195)	183
227	Gy. M, gy. slip out. worn in.	Juglet, neck and oval section handle. Wheel-made.	184
228	Bn. gy. core, M, rough surface in. and out.	Flat base	185
229	Fine pk. gy. core, H, rd. slip out. to base, smooth bur.	Ring base of juglet, wheel-made. (See p. 190)	186

EB IV–III. (NORTH-EAST SECTION, 11–7 ft.)

NE 11

230	Coarse rd. gy. core, grits[3] S, bf. slip in., rough out.	Platter, plain rim, wh. finish in. and on rim. Cf. Pls. 63: 304, 320; 65: 370; Megiddo, SAOC 10, Chart Column 1c, Stages IV–I. (See p. 157)	178
231	Coarse gy. M, burnt through	Cooking-pot. Hole pierced from out. through rim. See 212. (See p. 195)	179
232	Pk. gy. core, M, traces limewash over hor. combing	Flat base	180

NE 10

233	Rough pk. grits[3], S, hor. combing, traces limewash out.	Incomplete potmark on Pl. 18:23	171
234	Pk. gy. core, grits[1], S,	Rim of holemouth	170
235	Rough pk. M, oblique combing under limewash out.	Raised band at base of neck, irr. obliquely notched. (See p. 139)	172
236	Rough, rd. gy. core, grits[3], M	Jug, ribbon-handle. Cf. Pl. 62: 288. Potmark on shoulder Pl. 18 38. (See pp. 142, 166)	173
237	Rd. gy. core, grits[1] and straw, M, traces limewash	Jar, rim wh. finished, or potstand	174
238	Fine bf. S	Jar rim. Dec. strokes rd. paint round rim, hor. band on neck. Wheel-made. Cf. M. II, Pl. 13: 5, Stra. XIV. (See p. 167)	175
239	Pk. grits[1], M, smoothed in., rough out.	Sherd, dec. bands rd. paint above and below carination. Wheel-made. Intrusive?	176
240	Bn. grits[1], M, burnt	Loop handle, oval section, on shoulder? (See p. 141)	177
241	Rough bn. gy. core, flint and straw, M, wt. limewash out. on hor. combing	Pithos, raised band obliquely notched at neck. Sherds in NE 9–10. Cf. Megiddo, SAOC 10, Chart Column 16A, Stages II–I. (See p. 139)	177a
242	Rough bn. grits[1], M	Carinate bowl, Class C, bevelled rim. Wheel-made. Intrusive. (See p. 179)	152
243	Bn. grits[3], M	Bowl or lamp, edge blackened. Wheel-made. Possibly string-cut (?). (See p. 160)	153

NE 9

No.	Ware	Remarks	Field No.
244	Rough bn. grits[3] and mica, M, rd. slip fired gy. in., hor. strokes hand bur. out.	Platter, inverted rim, wh. finished. (See p. 157)	151
245	Rough rd., M, rd. slip fired gy. in parts over rim, lattice bur. in., hor. strokes around rim	Platter, upright rim. Cf. Pl. 63: 322 (See p. 157)	150
246	Rough rd. grits[1], M	Holemouth, misc., wh. finish. Cf. M. II, Pl. 107: 7, Stra. XVII. (See p. 165)	155
247	Rough rd. grits[3], M, burnt	Holemouth, bulbous rim, wh. finish. (See p. 164)	154
248	Rough pk. gy. core, grits[1], S	Holemouth, bulbous rim, wh. finish. (See p. 164)	156
249	Rough pk. gy. core, grits[1], S, wt. limewash out.	Holemouth, misc., wh. finish. (See p. 165)	157
250	Rough pk. gy. core, grits[1], M, wt. limewash out. on hor. combing	Vat. (See p. 162)	158
251	Bf. gy. core, grits[1], M	Jug or jar, rim wh. finish. Cf. Pl. 63: 336. (See p. 166)	159
252	Rough rd. M, burnt gy.	Jug or jar, rim wh. finish. Cf. Pl. 63: 319. (See p. 164)	160
253	Bk. gy. core, M	Jug, ribbon-handle. Cf. Pl. 63: 316.	161
254	Rough pk. gy. core, M	Pithos rim, wh. finish. Cf. Pl. 62: 294. (See p. 165)	164
255	Rough pk. gy. core, M, traces wt. limewash out.	Raised hor. band, deep oblique notches. Cf. AASOR XII, Pl. 12: 12, TBM Stra. J. (See p. 139)	162
256	Fine bf. gy. core, M, surface burnt gy.	Cooking-pot. Hole pierced from out. through rim above raised band, thumb impressed. See 212. (See p. 195)	163
257	Rough pk. M	Part of oval section handle.	166
258	Gy. grits[1] and straw, M	Part of oval section handle.	165
259	Bn. gy. core, grits[3], S	Part of smooth cut raised base. Wheel-made.	167
260	Rough pk. gy. core, grits[3], M, rough surface in. and out.	Part of smooth cut raised base	168
261	Rough rd. gy. core, grits[3], M	Part of flat base	169

NE 8

262	Fine pk. M, rd. slip in. and over rim	Bowl, plain rim. Wheel-made. (See p. 159)	133
263	Bk. bn. grits[1], S, rd. wash in. and over rim	Bowl, plain rim, wh. finish. Scraped out. Cf. Pl. 63: 326. (See p. 159)	134
264	Fine pk. M, rd. slip in. and over rim	Platter, flanged rim, rounded top. Lime deposits in. Wheel-made. (See p. 157)	132
265	Rough bn. grits[2], M, gy. surface	Holemouth, bulbous rim, wh. finish. Incomplete potmark, edge ground smooth, Pl. 18: 13. Cf. Pls. 62: 289; 65: 387. (See p. 164)	135
266	Rough bn. grits[2], M, gy. surface	Incomplete potmark, Pl. 18: 12	136
267	Fine pk. gy. core, S, rd. slip in. rough out.	Sherd, circular hand bur. in.	144
268	Rough bn. gy. core, grits, M	Vat. (See p. 162)	140
269	Fine pk. gy. core, grits[1], S	Cooking-pot rim, wh. finish. (See p. 195)	143
270	Rough grits[3], S, bf. slip	Neck, wh. finish	137
271	Rough rd. large grits[3], M	Pithos rim (?), folded over, wh. finish. (See p. 165)	138
272	Bf. S, traces limewash out.	Spouted bowl, surface combed? Inserted tubular spout. Cf. Pl. 58: 108; TH, Pl. V: 13, "Amorite". (See p. 163)	139
273	Pk. M	Neck of jar, wheel-made	141
274	Rough rd. grits[3], M	Cooking-pot rim, wh. finish. (See p. 195)	142
275	Rough pk. gy. core, grits[1], M, traces limewash out.	Raised applied band, oblique notches, comb-finish. Cf. Megiddo SAOC 10, Chart Column 16A, Stages II–I. (See p. 139)	145
276	Gy. grits[3], M	Raised band, comb finish. (See p. 139)	146
277	Gy. grits[3], M	Plain handle, vert. pierced	147
278	Gy. grits[3], M	Part of ribbon handle	148
279	Bk. gy. core, S	Base of jar	149

NE 7

280	Fine pk. grits[1], M, rd. slip out. and over rim	Bowl. Small hor. ledge handle, 3 notches, See 285	113
281	Pk. gy. core, M, rd. slip in. and over rim, radial strokes bur. in., hor. out.	Bowl, plain rim. (See p. 159)	114
282	Fine bf. M, rd. slip in. and over rim, hor. out.	Bowl, plain rim. (See p. 159)	115
283	Pk. gy. core, grits[3], M, limewash out. and over rim	Bowl, upright rim. Wheel-made. (See p. 159)	116
284	Fine pk. in., gy. out. H, rd. slip in. and out.	Cup or bowl. Shiny bk. to bn. surface. Khirbet Kerak ware. (See p. 44)	106
285	Fine pk. M, rd. slip in. and over rim, irr. hand bur. in.	Bowl. See 280	107
286	Rough bf. gy. core, grits[1], M, slight self bur. radial strokes in., hor. on rim	Platter, flanged rim, rounded top. (See p. 157)	109
287	Fine pk. gy. core, M, rd. slip in. and over rim, radial strokes bur. in. hor. on rim	Platter, flanged rim, rounded top. Rim wh. finished. See 313. Cf. TH, Pl. VI: 73, "Amorite"	110
288	Fine pk. M, rd. slip in. and over rim, hor. hand bur. in.	Bowl, upright rim. Cf. Jericho PEQ, 1952, p. 77, Fig. 5: 14, Construction of 2nd wall; Megiddo, SAOC 10, Chart Column 22B, Stages IV–III. (See p. 159)	111
289	Fine bf. grits[1], M	Bowl, carinate, wheel-made. Intrusive. See 311	108
290	Bf. grits[2] and flint, M, rd. slip over rim	Platter, flanged rim, flattened top. Cf. Jericho, AAA XIX, Pl. IV: 23, Tomb A2; PEQ, 1952, p. 80, Fig. 6: 15, Midden against 3rd wall. (See p. 157)	112
291	Rough bn. M	Platter, inturned rim. Cf. Jericho AAA XIX, Pl. IV: 20, Tomb A3; AASOR XII, Pl. 1: 9, TBM Stra. J. (See p. 157)	104
292	Bf. oblique bur., hor. over rim	Platter, plain rim. (See p. 157)	105
293	Bf. grits[3], M	Holemouth, bulbous. (See p. 164)	117
294	Bf. grits[3] and mica, M	Holemouth, bulbous. (See p. 164)	118
295	Pk. gy. core, M	Jar rim, wh. finish	119
296	Pk. grits[3], M	Jar rim, wh. finish	120
297	Rough pk. grits[1] and flint M, thick limewash out.	Pithos rim, wh. finish. Cf. M. II, Pl. 4:5, Stra. XVIII for profile only. (See p. 165)	121
298	Rough pk. gy. core, M, limewash out.	Neck, wh. finish. Cf. Pl. 61: 255	122

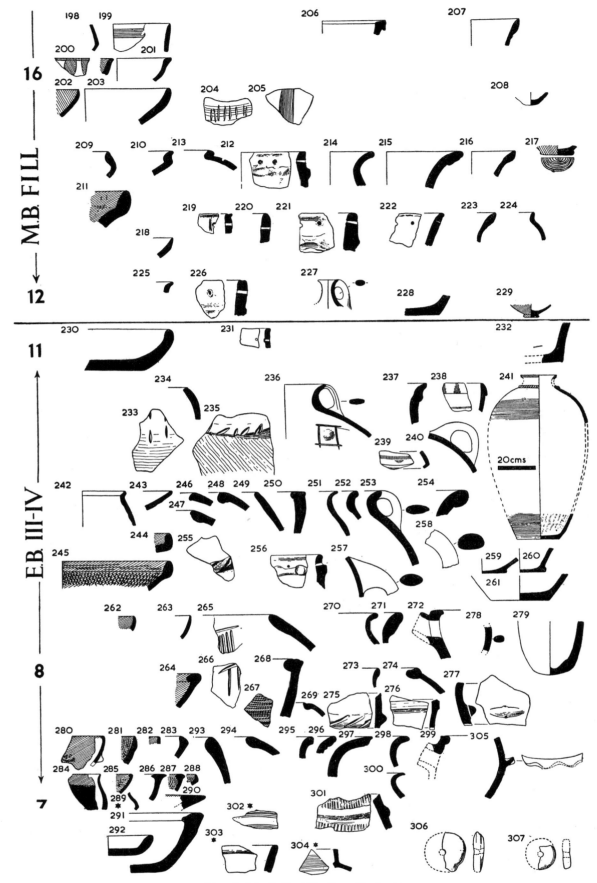

FIG. 4. North-East Section: Contents
Scale 1:5, except where otherwise stated

No.	WARE	REMARKS	FIELD NO.	No.	WARE	REMARKS	FIELD NO.
299	Rough pk. gy. core, grits³, M	Spouted bowl, rim wh. finish. Inserted side spout below inturned rim. Cf. Pl. 58: 108; Jericho, AAA XXII, Pl. XXXVIII: 3, Layer IV. (See p 163)	123	303	Fine bf. M	Irr. parallel lines incised, white filled. Wheel-made grooves out. Intrusive	126
				304	Pk. fine grits³, M	Neck of wheel-made jar. Band fine wheel-made grooves. Intrusive. See 197, 302	128
300	Bf. gy. core, grits³, M	Neck, wh. finish	124	305	Bf. M, rd. slip out. brush applied	Jar or jug, pushed-up ledge handle at widest diam. Edges worn. Cf. Pl. 64: 358. (See p. 153)	129
301	Pk. gy. core, grits¹, M	Jar, raised band around shoulder, vert. combing above and below	127	306	Howr lmst.	Half disk, pierced obliquely from opposite sides. (See p. 71)	130
302	Gy. M	Frag. of jar below neck, 2 bands wheel-made grooves. Intrusive. See 197, 304	125	307	Bn. M	Part of disk, pierced obliquely. (See p. 71)	131

NE 6

No.	WARE	REMARKS	FIELD No.
	Body, firing and surface		
308	Bf. gy. core, grits¹, M, rd. slip in., irr. hand bur. in., high polish	Bowl, plain rim, edge blackened. Cf. Pl. 65: 367. (See p. 159)	77
309	Rough pk. grits¹, S, rd. slip in.	Bowl, plain rim, edge blackened. Wheelmade. (See p. 159)	76
310	Gy. grits¹, M, smoothed	Bowl, band rd. paint in.	75
311	Fine bf. grits¹, M, smoothed out.	Carinate bowl. Intrusive. See 289	73
312	Fine pk. M, rd. hand bur. in. and on rim, high polish	Bowl, wheel-made	74
313	Fine bf. grits¹, M, pk. slip in. and on rim., hor. bur. on rim, radial bur. in.	Bowl, flanged rim, rounded top. Wheelmade. See 287. Cf. Pls. 58:92. (See pp. 157–159)	72
314	Rough pk. grits¹, M, rd. slip out. and over rim, hor. bur. out.	Bowl, surface pocked. Wheel-made	71
315	Bf. grits², S, smoothed out. rough in.	Bowl or cup	70
316	Bf. gy. core, grits² and straw, M, brownish slip in. and over rim, hor. hand bur. in. rim, obliquely widely spaced strokes	Platter, upright rim. Cf. Pl. 63: 323 for bur. only. (See p. 157)	69
317	Rough rd. gy. core, grits¹, M, smoothed	Cooking-pot. Wheel-made. Intrusive. (See p. 195)	78
318	Pk. gy. core, grits¹, M	Holemouth, bulbous rim, wh. finish. Cf. Pl. 64: 354. (See p. 164)	79
319	Rough bf. grits², M	Holemouth, bulbous rim, wh. finish. Cf. Pit 4022 on pp. 289 f.; Jericho, PEQ, 1952, p. 77, Fig. 5: 30, Upper midden against 2nd wall; TH, Pl. V: 51, "Amorite". (See p. 164)	80
320	Rough bn. grits¹, M, burnt gy.	Holemouth, misc. (See p. 165)	87
321	Bf. grits¹, S, rd. slip in., rough out., lattice bur. in.	Platter. Cf. M. II, Pl. 104: 12, Stra. XVIII.	83
322	Rough rd., M, rd. slip in., rough out., radial web bur. in.	Platter. Cf. M. II, Pl. 104: 11, Stra. XVIII.	84
323	Rough rd. grits² and mica, M, burnt gy.	Sherd, string impression out. Cf. Jericho, AAA XXII, Pl. XXXII: 20, Layers V–IV	86
324	Pk. gy. in., M, rd. slip out., rough in., fine strokes pattern bur. high polish out.	Sherd	85
325	Fine gy. H, smooth polished bk. surface in. and out.	Bowl? Dec. wt. bands, bk. wavy line over bk. surface in. and out.	88
326	Rough bf. grits¹ and flint, M	Cooking-pot. Holes pierced from each side through rim above applied band, thumb impressed. Intrusive? See 212. Cf. AASOR XII, Pl. 3: 27, TBM Stra. I; Jericho, AAA XXII, Pl. XXXII: 5, Layers V–IV; M. II, Pl. 107: 36, Stra. XVII; Pl. 108: 15, 17, Stra. XVI. (See p. 195)	81
327	Fine pk. gy. core, M, rd. slip out., hor. hand bur. out. high polish	Sherd	93
328	Pk. grits³, M, traces limewash?	Holemouth, misc. Cf. Jericho PEQ, 1952, p. 80, Fig. 6: 26, Layers of burnt material. (See p. 165)	82
329	Fine bf. H, bn. slip out.	Jar, dec. bk. and rd. bands on neck. Wheelmade. Intrusive	89
330	Fine pk. H, rd. slip in. or out.? spi. bur. high polish	Sherd	90
331	Fine rd. gy. in. grits¹, H, wt. limewash out.	Part of storage jar. Wheel-made. Intrusive	91
332	Rough bn. grits¹, S, rough in.	Mat impression on flat base out. Photograph on Pl. 13: 91 and see p. 72. Cf. M. II, Pls. 2: 16, 92: 15, Stra. XX	92
333	Pk. gy. core, grits², M, limewash out.	Pithos rim, wh. finish. (See p. 165)	94
334	Pk. gy. in. grits¹, M, rd. slip out., vert. hand bur.	Rudimentary lug handle unpierced	95
335	Bn. gy. core, grits¹, S	Pushed-up ledge handle, Form 8. (See p. 153)	96
336	Fine pk. M, rd. slip out., surface worn in. and out.	Part of double strand handle from jug. Intrusive. (See p. 142)	97
337	Rough pk. gy. core, grits², M, rd. slip out. traces bur.	Part of handle. Intrusive	98
338	Pk. gy. core, grits¹, M, cm. slip, slight hor. combing out.	Part of storage jar handle. Wheel-made. Intrusive	99
339	Howr lmst. S	Half disk, pierced obliquely from opposite sides. (See p. 71)	102
340	Rough rd. gy. core, M, mottled rd. and dk. bn. out. bur?	Part of smooth cut flat base	101
341	Pk. M	Bowl, wheel-made. Flat disk base. Intrusive?	100
342	Paste?	Bead as Pl. 29: 2	103a

NE 5

No.	WARE	REMARKS	FIELD No.
343	Bn. S, rd. slip in., traces bur.	Bowl, plain rim. (See p. 159)	55
344	Bf. grits¹, M, rd. slip in. and over rim out., burnt edge	Bowl, plain rim, wh. finish? Cf. Pl. 58: 75. (See p. 157)	56
345	Bf. M, rd. slip in. and over rim	Platter, flanged rim, rounded top, wh. finish. Cf. Jericho, PEQ, 1952, p. 77, Fig. 5: 37. Upper midden against 2nd wall. (See p. 157)	54
346	Bn. gy. core, grits² and straw, M, rd. slip in. with radial bur., hor. strokes around rim	Platter, upright rim. Rim wh. finish out., some hor. shaving. Cf. M. II, Pl. 104: 14, Stra. XVIII. (See p. 157)	53
347	Rough pk. grits³, M	Holemouth, misc., wh. finish. Cf. Pit 4022 on pp. 289 f. (See p. 165)	57
348	Gy. grits², M, hor. combed surface out., rough in.	Vat, wh. finish. Cf. Pl. 63: 311. (See p. 162)	58
349	Pk. gy. core, grits¹, M	Neck of jar	59
350	Pk. gy. core, grits¹, M	Neck of jar, wh. finish	60
351	Bf. grits², M	Pithos rim, folded, wh. finish. (See p. 165)	61
352	Bf. grits¹, M, smoothed	Loop handle. Cf. Pl. 56: 17. (See p. 140)	62
353	Comb-faced in vert. and hor. bands	Sherd. (See p. 139)	63

No.	WARE	REMARKS	FIELD No.
354	Rough pk. grits² and flint	Sherd, raised hor. band with pattern combing. (See p. 139)	64
355	Fine bf. gy. core, M, bn. slip in. and over rim, mottled patches, traces vert. bur. in.	Cup or bowl, wh. finish	65
356	Fine bf. M	Minute pushed-up ledge handle, Form 8, smoothed in. for application. Cf. Pls. 61: 250; 63: 331. (See p. 153)	66
357	Pk. grits¹, M, traces rd. slip	Body of animal, four stump legs and tail, part of neck with burnt edges. Cf. B.I., Pl. LXXVII: 4564, Bâtiment XVIII	67
358	Rough rd. gy. core, grits, M, limewash	Flat base, pattern combing alternating bands hor. and oblique strokes. Cf. Pl. 62: 296; M. II, Pl. 105: 4, Stra. XVIII. (See p. 139)	68

NE 4

No.	WARE	REMARKS	FIELD No.
359	Pk. M, rd. slip in. and over rim, burnt, oblique strokes bur. in.	Bowl, plain rim. (See p. 159)	42
360	Pk. M, rd. slip in. and over rim	Platter, upright rim. Cf. Pl. 63: 306; Jericho, PEQ, 1952, p. 80, Fig. 6: 7, Construction of 3rd wall. (See p. 157)	41
361	Pk. gy. core, grits², M, bn. slip in. and over rim, hor. bur. on rim. in. and out. oblique strokes in.	Platter, plain rim, wh. finish. Cf. Pl. 63: 321. (See p. 157)	40
362	Pk. grits³, M, burnt gy. smoothed in. and out.	Holemouth, bulbous rim. Incised potmark. Pl. 18: 74. (See p. 164)	44
363	Pk. grits², M, burnt gy.	Holemouth, bulbous rim. Cf. Jericho, PEQ, 1952, p. 77, Fig. 5: 29, Upper midden against 2nd wall. (See p. 164)	43
364	Gy. grits², M, bf. slip, wt. limewash out., hor. combing	Holemouth, misc. (See p. 165)	45
365	Pk. grits¹, S, wt. limewash out.	Holemouth, misc., wh. finish. (See p. 165	46
366	Rd. grits², M, wt. limewash out.	Jar neck	47
367	Pk. gy. core, M, thick wt. limewash out.	Jar neck	48
368	Bf. grits¹, S, smoothed in. and out.	Jar neck, rim wh. finish	51
369	Rd. fine grits¹, M, bf. thick wt. limewash	Part of side spout. Cf. AASOR XII, Pl. 2: 14, TBM Stra. J. (See p. 163)	49
370	Pk. gy. core, grits¹, M	Ledge handle, Form 10 (p. 154), "pinch lapped". Cf. Pl. 13: 67; M. II, Pl. 98: 25, Stra. XIX; Jericho AAA XXII, Pl. XXXV: 9, Layers V–IV	50
371	Bn. grits¹, S, rd. slip out.	Part of flat base, twist cut	52

NE 3

No.	WARE	REMARKS	FIELD No.
372	Pk. grits, S, bf.	Bowl, plain rim, wh. finish? (See p. 159)	30
373	Pk. grits, M, rd. slip, hor. hand bur.	Platter, flanged rim, rounded top. Rim wh. finish. (See p. 157)	31
374	Pk. grits³, flint and mica, H, rough	Holemouth, bulbous rim. Cf. Pl. 65: 387; Jericho, AAA XXII, Pl. XXVIII: 29, Layers V–III; Megiddo, SAOC 10, Chart Column 12b, Stages VII–III. (See p. 164)	32
375	Bf. grits¹, M, limewash out.	Holemouth, misc., rim wh. finish. (See p. 165)	33
376	Rd. gy. core, grits², M, cm. surface out.	Rim of pithos. (See p. 165)	34
377	Bf. M, rd. slip out., vert. hand bur. in.	Jar neck	35
378	Pk. grits and lime, M, bf.	Sherd. Hor. combing with oblique bands. (See p. 139)	36
379	Bf. grits, flint and lime, S, bn. slip, close vert. bur.	Ledge handle, pushed-up, Form 8. See 380. Intrusive? (See p. 153)	37
380	Bf. grits, flint and lime, M, burnt bk.	Ledge handle, pushed-up, Form 8. Cf. Pl. 61: 256; 63: 330; 64: 364; 65: 382. Intrusive? (See p. 153)	38
381	Pk. grits and flint, M, rd. slip out., rough in.	Flat base, twist cut	39
382	Paste?	Bead as Pl. 29: 2	39a

NE 2

No.	WARE	REMARKS	FIELD No.
383	Bf. grits¹, M, matt rd. wash in. and over rim	Bowl, plain rim, wh. finish. Cf. M. II, Pl. 6: 12, Stra. XIX–XVI. (See p. 159)	24
384	Bn. gy. core, grits¹, M	Bowl, plain rim, faint combing out., wh. finish. (See p. 159)	23
385	Bone, worn at both ends	Spatula. (See p. 73)	—
386	Pk. gy. core, grits, M, bf.	Holemouth, misc., wh. finish. (See p. 165)	25
387	Rd. bn. core, H, smoothed	Jar neck	26
388	Bf. M	Ledge handle, pushed-up, Form 8. See 379, 380. Intrusive? (See p. 153)	27
389	Rd. gy. core, grits and straw, M, traces rd. wash	Ledge handle, plain narrow, Form 7. Cf. M. II, Pls. 2: 27, 98: 11, Stra. XX, XIX, SAOC 10, Chart Column 14b, Stages V–III; Ay, Pl. LXXXVII: 1358 II, Fouille V, Ch. 108, assise 4	29

NE 1

No.	WARE	REMARKS	FIELD No.
390	Bf. S. hor. self bur. out.	Bowl, plain rim, wh. finish. (See p. 159)	6
391	Bf. M, rd. slip in. and over rim, lattice hand bur. in.	Bowl, plain rim. Cf. Pl. 58: 76; TH, Pl. VI: 91, "Amorite". (See p. 159)	5
392	Bf. S. rd. slip, hor. hand bur. out.	Platter, inverted rim. See 209. (See p. 157)	4
393	Pk. M, radial self bur. in.	Platter, flanged rim, rounded top. Traces rd. paint on rim. Wh. finish. Cf. AASOR XII, Pl. 1: 24, TBM Stra. J. (See p. 157)	3
394	Bf. M, rd. slip in. and over rim, lattice bur. in. hor. on rim	Platter, upright rim. Cf. Beisan, MJ XXIV, 1935, Pl. V: 20, Level XIV; Jericho AAA XXII, Pl. XXVIII: 36, Layers V–IV. (See p. 157)	2
395	Pk. gy. core, grits², M, rough out.	Platter, upright rim, wh. finish in. Cf. Jericho, PEQ 1952, p. 77, Fig. 5: 23, Occupation above 2nd wall. (See p. 157)	1
396	Pk. gy. core, grits², flint and straw, M, smoothed out. rough in.	Holemouth misc. Rim wh. finish. Thumb imprints. Cf. Jericho AAA XXII, Pl. XXVIII: 24, Layers V–IV. (See p. 165)	7
397	Pk. gy. core, grits² and mica, M	Holemouth, misc. Rim wh. finish. Raised band below rim. Traces dk. rd. paint out. Cf. Pit 4022 on pp. 289 f. (See p. 165)	8

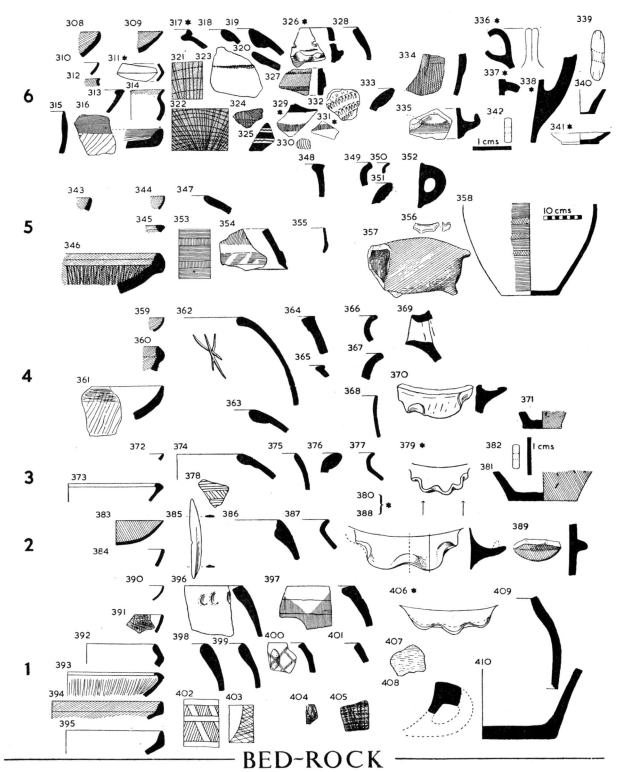

BED-ROCK

Fig. 5. North-East Section: Contents
Scale 1:5, except where otherwise stated

No.	Ware	Remarks	Field No.	No.	Ware	Remarks	Field No.
398	Pk. grits³, flint and mica, M, smoothed out. rough in.	Holemouth, bulbous rim. Cf. M. II, Pl. 97: 7, Stra. XIX; AASOR XII, Pl. 1: 18, TBM Stra. J; Jericho, SW Pl. 20a: 97, "Canaanite." (See p. 164)	9	404	Pk. grits², M, rd. slip in., hor. and diamond lattice bur. in.	Cf. Pl. 64: 342 for bur.	16
				405	Pk. gy. core, grits³ and straw, M, rd. slip in. rough out.	Square lattice bur. in.	17
399	Pk. grits³, M, rough in. and out.	Holemouth, bulbous rim, wh. finish. (See p. 164)	10	406	Pk. gy. core, M, bf.	Ledge handle, pushed-up, Form 8 (p. 153) Cf. Pl. 64: 364; AASOR XIII, Pt. 20: 21, TBM Stra. J. Intrusive?	19
400	Pk. gy. core, S, rough	Holemouth, misc., wh. finish on rim? Raised knob out. partly covered rd. paint. Cf. TH, Pl. V: 52, "Amorite", for rofile. (See p. 165)	11	407	Pk. grits², H, rough out.	Sherd, textile impression visible in parts over clearer impression of fine reed mat. Photograph on Pl. 13: 90 and see p. 72	20
401	Pk. S, smoothed out.	Holemouth, misc. Rim wh. finish. Cf. Jericho, PEQ, 1952, p. 77, Fig. 5: 15, occupation above 2nd wall. (See p. 165)	12	408	Pk. gy. core, grits³ and flint, M, radial self bur. in.	Bowl with part of loop handle. (See p. 140)	18
402	Gy.-pk. grits², H, bf.	Sherd, combed surface, reserved bands out. (See p. 139)	13	409	Pk. gy. core, grits³, H, rough in. and out.	Sherd	21
403	Pk. crushed lime, M, rd. slip, criss-cross bur. in.	Sherd	14	410	Pk. gy. core, grits³ and straw, H, rough in. and out.	Part of flat base	22

59

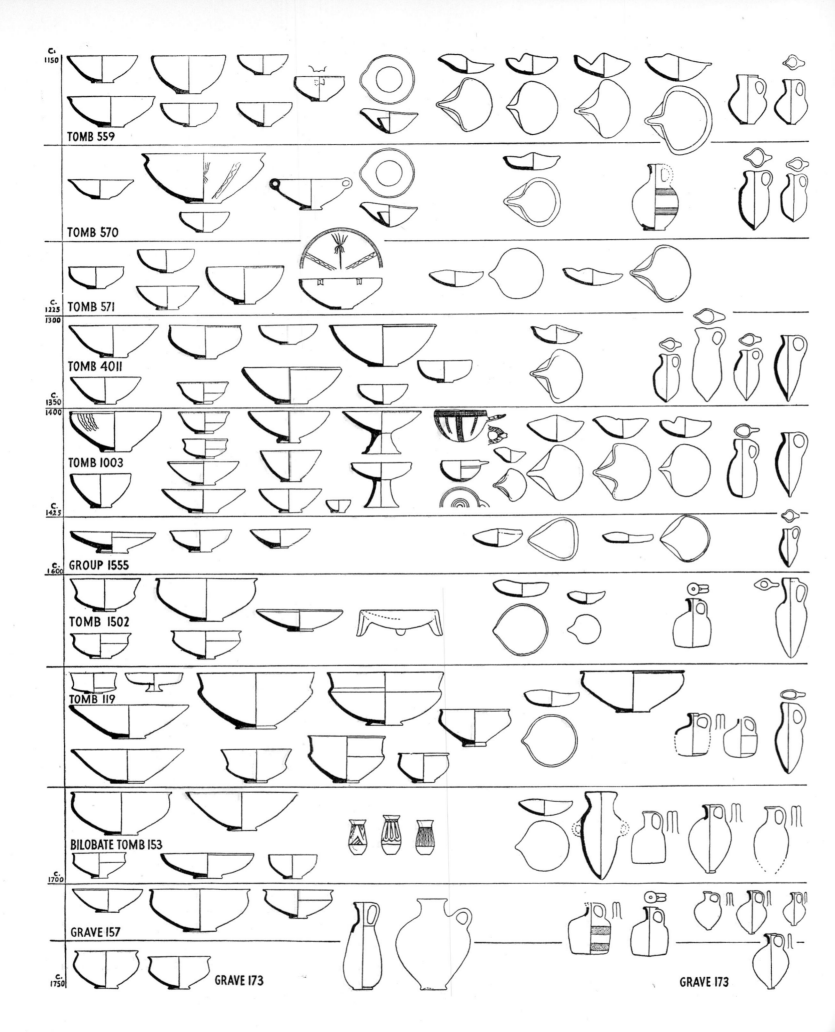

C. 1150

TOMB 559

TOMB 570

C. 1225 TOMB 571

1300

TOMB 4011

C. 1350
1400

TOMB 1003

C. 1425

GROUP 1555

C. 1600

TOMB 1502

TOMB 119

BILOBATE TOMB 153

C. 1700

GRAVE 157

C. 1750 GRAVE 173

GRAVE 173

FIG. 6. Some Middle and

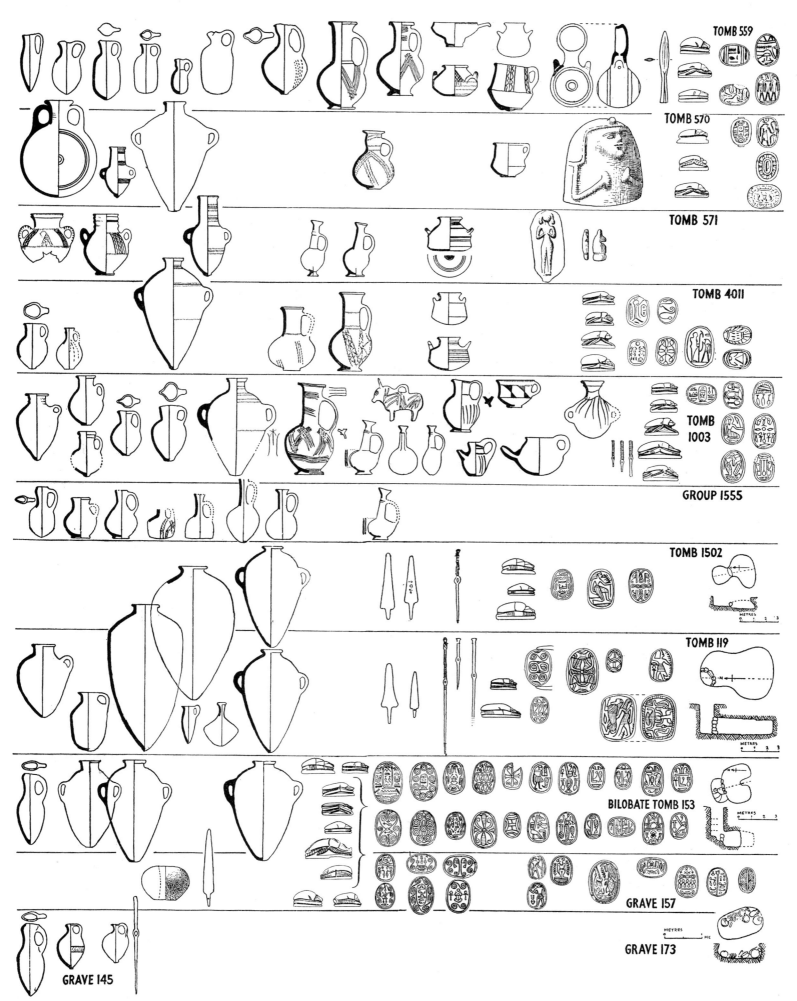

TOMB 559

TOMB 570

TOMB 571

TOMB 4011

TOMB 1003

GROUP 1555

TOMB 1502

TOMB 119

BILOBATE TOMB 153

GRAVE 157

GRAVE 173

GRAVE 145

Bronze Age Tomb Groups

CHAPTER 5

BURIALS OF THE MIDDLE AND LATE BRONZE AGE IN RELATION TO THE FOSSE TEMPLE

IN Chapters 3 and 4 deposits on the mound made during the second millennium were examined and divided into four main phases: Levels VI, VII, VIII and the fill of the MB glacis. The period before the construction of the MB defence system from the last occupation of the EB city is poorly represented in the North-East Section, though the deficiency is partially made good in the pottery of the Caliciform Culture in Cemetery 2000 (pp. 171–175). That phase (Intermediate EB–MB at Jericho) probably begins in the last centuries of the third millennium and extends, according to some authorities, to *c.* 1900 B.C. (Strata I–H at Tell Beit Mirsim), which is included in MB I (*Stratigraphie*, p. 129), but the basic affinity of the pottery to the earlier period is more suitable for discussion in Chapter 9.

It is therefore inevitable that the information gained from the pottery in the Section lacks continuity, as each phase may be separated from the other in time, but the gaps have been filled to some extent by the contents of the tombs, though here again use of the same cave for many burials makes precise dating difficult.

Burials in North-West Settlement (MB II–III, LB I, 1850–1450 B.C.)

Certain caves of the North-West Settlement were re-used for burials which took place quite early in the period under review (e.g. Tomb 1552), while others show a preponderance of later forms (e.g. Tombs 1546 and 1547 MB III, and also Locus 1555 LB I, for which see Chart on pp. 60f.). In that area only Tomb 1502, in which the inscribed dagger was found, may have been specially cut for the burials it contained.

Graves on the Mound (MB III, *c.* 1750 B.C.)

A valuable exception to many mass burials on the site is the child's Grave 173 (Pl. 5: 3, 4 and Pl. 20: 17–21), which was certainly sealed by the MB glacis, while Graves 145 and 157 were probably also below that packing (Pl. 90). The shoulder-handle jug, Type 672, corresponds with similar forms from Megiddo Stratum XI, though carinate bowls, like Type 537, range from Strata XIII to XI. The bag-shaped burnished jug (Type 669) finds a parallel in Stratum E at Tell Beit Mirsim, and the same form, unburnished, occurs in City C at Jericho (p. 187). The piriform juglet, Type 738, with thin red slip could also be contemporary (p. 190).

There should be no difficulty in assigning Graves 145 and 157 to the same phase in view of the preponderance of piriform over cylindrical juglets and the close relation of one of the former, with a band of pricked chevrons round the body, to a juglet of Stratum XI at Megiddo (p. 189 and M. II, Pl. 32: 32).

A cylindrical juglet, Type 750, is the only one from the site to have pricked decoration. It is comparable to a form from the uppermost of two burials at Tell el-Ajjul, Tomb 303, which is more fully discussed below on pp. 63, 190.

These three groups suggest that the embankment for the MB defence system was made after the occupation of Stratum XI had begun, and when Tell Beit Mirsim was passing through a late phase of the four major ones of Stratum E, p. 34.

Cemeteries around the Tell (MB II–III, *c.* 1800–1600 B.C.)

Close to the north-west corner of the mound in the western valley three communal tombs yielded the best groups, chiefly of MB III (Tombs 129, 119 and 153, for plan see L. III, Pl. 125). Within this range are other smaller groups disposed around the lower slopes of the mound.

Taking the contents of these cemeteries as a whole, it will be seen that they have forms of bowls, dippers and lamps in common with Megiddo Strata XII–X, Tell Beit Mirsim Strata E–D and the Jericho Necropolis of 1930–1936. But individual and distinctive shapes particularly common within that range at Jericho and Tell Beit Mirsim are missing at Duweir in the tombs and in the North-East Section, and they are also absent from the bilobate tombs at Tell Fara (BP I, Pls. XIV–XV; BP II, Pl. XC) and throughout the occupation of cities and palaces at Tell el-Ajjul (AG I, Pl. LXII: II, Pl. LV: III, Pls. LI, LII: IV, Pls. LXIX–LXX).

Comparisons

"Carinate vases with trumpet foot" are described by Albright as "so well-known that no discussion is needed" (AASOR XIII, p. 77). Their presence at Tell Beit Mirsim only eight miles from Duweir proves that their absence at our site is not due to local differences. The attribution of these vases to Stratum E is "not altogether satisfactory", though an early date is indicated on typological grounds (AASOR XIII, § 29). They are very common in the tombs at Jericho and in the Palace Storerooms (AAA XIX–XXI). They are less so at Megiddo, where only two examples occur in burials attributed to Strata X–IX (M. II, Pl. 44: 9 and Pl. 54: 19).

On the whole, it would appear that the Jericho tombs belong in the main to the century or half-century before the Duweir series, though they overlap in the upper and disturbed levels. Taking Tomb 5 as representative of them all, it will be seen in the useful chart (AAA XX, Pl. XXV) that the lowest and relatively undisturbed layers contain many trumpet-foot vases, though few of those published in AAA have a red-burnished slip, differing in this important respect from the vases of Tell Beit Mirsim E, which are in the red-slipped tradition of Stratum G. A cream slip or a plain wet-smoothed surface was the more usual finish in the Jericho tombs.

Among other significant forms missing from the Duweir series are the elegant chalices (AASOR XII, Pl. 43: 6 and XIII, Pl. 8: 13) and deep bowls on loop feet (AASOR XIII, Pl. 14: 3) from Tell Beit Mirsim Strata E–D, which are well matched at Jericho (AAA XXI, Pl. XXI: 2; XIX, Pls. XXXI–XXXIII), where the possibly earlier trefoil-mouthed jugs also appear.

With regard to the juglets, the lowest layers (f–g) of Tomb 5 contain an overwhelming number of piriforms (as Classes B–C), while cylindrical versions are rare, though they are in the ascendancy in the Duweir tombs (Classes E–F).

Class A juglets are Tell el-Yehudiyeh piriforms decorated with pricked designs, which are uncommon at Duweir, pp. 33 and 189. Professor Albright remarks that there were no complete examples in Stratum D ("standard black incised with double handle and button base") and that the sherds in question "may in part belong to the earlier phases of period D" (AASOR XII, p. 25). This fact favours an equation between an early phase of D, or possibly the end of E, and the beginning of the Duweir series, where a piriform of Class A came from Grave 145 below the packing of the MB defence.

Very similar juglets from the Courtyard Cemetery at Ajjul (AG II, Pl. XXXIV: 60 M⁵′, M⁶) are also earlier than the "Hyksos" embankment there, as observed by Albright (AJSLL, pp. 342–343). Superimposed burials at the same site are helpful (AG III, Pl. XLIX, Tomb 303, cf. Stratigraphie, Fig. 125), where the lower group contained a piriform juglet with a ribbed dagger of Type 25, which is not represented at Duweir (p.77), while the upper group provides a link with the only cylindrical form with pricked design (Pl. 77: 750), which came from Tomb 157 below the glacis fill at Duweir.

The first bilobate tombs at Tell Fara (BP I, Pls. XVII–XVIII) should perhaps date from this time, for Tomb 551 presents comparisons with the rare bilobate Tomb 153 at Duweir in the rounded nature of the chambers and in the resemblance of both pottery and scarabs. The continuity of the more angular Tomb 550 maintains close connexions with the Duweir pottery, but should perhaps be dated at least two generations later, taking into account the shape, which is closer to tombs of the xviiith dynasty, as well as the inferior quality and design of the scarabs (BP I, Pl. VII: 27–31).

63

Tombs in relation to the MB Glacis

While all the groups discussed above present a reasonable sequence, the question of their initial date and of the length of the series must rest on certain doubtful factors.

1. *The date of the pricked " Yehudiyeh" ware* is one of the most discussed problems of Palestinian archaeology. At the site in the Egyptian Delta which gave this ware its name, the majority of the published shapes are piriform (*Mound of the Jew*, pp. 9, 39, 40), and the same applied to the graves which Petrie dug later (HIC, Pls. VII and VIII). The design in all cases consists of chevrons very roughly incised, without the delimiting zones and bands which are to be found on the best examples from more northerly sites. Schaeffer points out that cylindrical juglets appear with the piriforms at Yehudiyeh, though they survive later, and the same overlap is to be seen at Duweir, p. 189. If a late xiith-dynasty date be accepted for the examples which are probably late in the sequence of development (cf. *Stratigraphie*, p. 154), then the three tombs below the MB defence at Duweir cannot have been filled much after *c.* 1750 B.C. and there is little against a date half a century earlier.

2. *The length of time between the date of the graves and the construction of the MB defences*, for which there is no material evidence. It is assumed that the tomb groups on the lower slopes of the mound were buried at a time when the MB defences were in course of construction and in effective use. If this is correct, then the resemblance which still exists between the common pottery forms of graves and tombs suggests an interval of no more than a few decades. It might also be possible to explain the isolated child-burial at the north-west corner, Grave 173, as a propitiatory offering before the ramp was begun.

Connexions with other sites

It should perhaps be noted as an additional point in favour of a separation between the pottery of Tell Beit Mirsim Strata E–D and that of the Duweir tombs that the carinate bowls of Class A are hardly represented at the former site, while at Duweir and, more especially, at Fara and Ajjul there are many forms of this class. CPP Type 23 K is dominant in City III ("xiith dynasty") at Ajjul and poorly represented in City II ("xvth dynasty"), and the same can be said for the cylindrical juglets Type 74 O (AG I, Pl. LXII). In City III dippers are still elongated, while in City II the squat form of LB I (CPP Type 53 A¹) and a possible White Shaved juglet (AG I, Type 51 P²′) appear. Single examples of CPP Type 89 A are found in Cities III and II, and this imported Whited Painted V juglet is also found in the horse burials at the same site. A version with less paint is found in Tomb 4004 at Duweir (Type 823, p. 201). Monochrome, present in City III, is well established by the time of City II. Common to Cities III and II are "fruit-stands" on tall pedestals (AG I, Pl. XXXVIII: Type 17 B), which are in the line of descent from more elaborate ones at Tell Beit Mirsim (AASOR XII, Pl. 44: 14 and § 42; XVII, § 32) of Strata G–F and of Megiddo X (M. II, Pl. 47: 10). Undecorated stands of the same general shape as those from City III at Ajjul (AG I, Type 17 B⁴′) are associated with plaster floors of buildings in Stratum X (M. II, Pl. 47: 14).

These few notes on a subject outside the scope of this work are perhaps enough to show that City III at Ajjul overlaps in part with the MB tombs at Duweir and carries on where they leave off, to cover the last quarter of the seventeenth century, extending perhaps to the date of the "Hyksos" expulsion, when it is likely that the frontier stronghold and port would be a major objective of the Egyptians. There is indeed a burnt layer between Cities III and II (AG I, p. 7), and ashes and erosion between Palaces I and II (AG II, p. 1), while no part of the first palace was re-used in the plan of the second.

Tombs and Fosse Temple: Structure I (LB I, 1600–1450 B.C.)

With the exception of Tell el-Ajjul and Megiddo, other Palestinian sites were hardly occupied during the first phase of the Late Bronze Age. Jericho and Tell Beit Mirsim were almost deserted, and Tell Fara showed no signs of the bichrome ware which is the hall-mark of the period.

At Megiddo bichrome jugs, mostly with shoulder handles, are only associated with burials in Stratum X, and M. II, Pl. 39: 5, 7 and 10 came from the last of the Structural Tombs, 3070. In Stratum IX, however, the handles of most jugs join at the rim, and some among them were found in rooms with plaster floors (M. II, Pl. 49: 3, 7), with decorated kraters (M. II, Pl. 53: 1, 2). The same rooms produced a chalice (M. II, Pl. 55: 14) of a form which is also seen in the Fosse Temple (L. II, Pl. XLVII).

The kraters are well matched by Type 256 (L. II, Pl. LVIII and pp. 79–80) of which two examples came from deposits north of the Fosse Temple at Duweir. The better piece can be no later than Structure I in date and may even precede that building.

An equation between the rooms of Stratum IX and the dumped rubbish in the fosse preceding or contemporary with Structure I is therefore reasonable. The upper half of a bichrome jug, L. II: 272, was found with the altar vessels of Structure I. Except for sherds from the temple area and part of a cylindrical juglet, Type 772 (Class G), from Group 1555, bichrome ware was otherwise lacking at Tell ed-Duweir.

Two main groups exist therefore for the study of the LB I period at Duweir: the contents of Structure I and the bulk of the pottery from Tomb 4004.

M. Schaeffer has remarked that the earliest material in the latter deposit goes back to the Middle Bronze Age (*Stratigraphie*, p. 186), a date which applies to many of the scarabs, though there are others which can be no earlier than the fourteenth century. The contents seem to be the result of a wholesale clearance of burials quite late in the xviiith dynasty, for the deposits were condensed into a layer of blackened earth only 30 centimetres in depth, spread evenly on the floors of three chambers of the cave, which may have been cut centuries before for industrial purposes.

Though the carinate bowls (Classes A and C) continue in a modified form, lamps with an inturned rim (Class B) are extremely common (p. 185). Cylindrical juglets (Classes E–F) are succeeded at this time by Black or Grey Lustrous ware (Class J), and transitional shapes showing characteristics of each (Classes G, H) are seen in the small Group 1555 (Pl. 51 and Chart on pp. 222 f.).

Black Lustrous ware was the earliest import of LC IA to reach Cyprus (p. 192). The transitional form with a long neck and cylindrical body (Class H—Type 773), and the prominence of the ware in Tomb 4004 (Class J—Types 777–778) may suggest that they represent a rare case of a Palestinian export, not for their own worth, perhaps, but for their contents. That Black Lustrous ware does not come from the same source as Base-Ring and allied pottery is certain, from the fact that it is wheel-made and that the handle is not inserted.

The only other significant group of the period is Grave 7011, which contained an imported Black Slip III juglet (Type 814, pp. 199 and 305). In much the same category are Monochrome bowls (pp. 201 f.) which precede the earliest Base-Ring, or are possibly cheaper contemporary goods. Both are represented in the Fosse Temple, Structure I (L. II, Pl. XLIV: 167–170) and in the tombs (Types 827–828).

The date of Structure I, *c.* 1475–1400 B.C., discussed in L. II, pp. 20–24, was adjusted by Schaeffer (*Stratigraphie*, p. 186) to *c.* 1600 (1550)–1450 B.C. This is certainly the maximum range for the occupation of the building, and it would be reasonable to place the pottery of Tomb 4004 at the beginning of the period, when Black Lustrous and lamps of Class B were most common, and to confine the use of Structure I to 1550–1450 B.C., when lamps of Class B (p. 185) were largely replaced by those of Classes C–D.

Tombs and Fosse Temple: Structure II (LB II, 1450–1370 or 1350 B.C.)

The contents of Tombs 216, 501 and 1003 follow the main phase of Tomb 4004 in a closely linked progression, and these groups together yield scarabs which cover the reigns of Thothmes III, Amenhetep II, Thothmes IV and Amenhetep III.

They provide the best material which has so far come to light for a study of the rich period when Egypt was in full control of her newly acquired empire. These groups contain most of the Base-Ring wares, with special emphasis on jugs and juglets decorated with firm lines of white paint, applied by a five-pointed brush, in imitation of the joins and seams required to make a rounded vessel from a flat skin or metal sheet (p. 205).

It is possible that Tell Beit Mirsim was reoccupied about this time, probably during the reign of Amenhetep III in the first half of the fourteenth century, when it appears that Tell Abu Hawam was also founded, but there is no clear evidence that either of these sites was inhabited by a large urban community in the fifteenth century.

Though the excavators were of the opinion that Megiddo was continuously occupied (M. II, p. 5), these tomb groups from Duweir go far to prove that the site was actually deserted after the destruction of Stratum IX. The scarcity of scarabs of Thothmes III and his successors would not be strong evidence alone, but further evidence is provided by the absence of all but the earliest Base-Ring wares, which were only found in burials of Strata IX–VIII (p. 207), except for one painted juglet which is out of context in a burial attributed to Stratum XII (M. II, Pl. 26: 11).

Base-Ring imports did not long survive the reign of Thothmes IV, for they are less common in Tomb 1003, which may date from the end of the fifteenth century (p. 251). Though certain late Base-Ring forms appear in fourteenth-century contexts at Duweir, the final history of Base-Ring production is best studied in Syria (p. 208).

The position of Structure II in the Consolidated Chart of Common Pottery Forms (pp. 222 f.) is immediately after Structure I and it will be seen that the contents of both buildings have much in common. The second structure was in use at the same time as the tombs noted above, and scarabs of Thothmes III, Amenhetep III and his wife Tiy also appear (L. II, Pl. XXXII: 2, 7, 8). The alteration proposed by Schaeffer for the dates of Structure II (*Stratigraphie*, p. 184) is quite acceptable, for the pit, originally ascribed to Structures I–II, which contained a Thothmes III scarab, could well belong to the later building (L. II, p. 69).

The maximum range for the building would therefore be 1450–1350 B.C., without an allowance for a possible interval towards the end of the Amarna period.

Tombs and Fosse Temple: Structure III (LB III, *c.* 1350–1225 or 1200 B.C.)

The tombs do not contain any scarabs of Amenhetep IV (Akhenaten) or of his immediate successors, a lack which in the opinion of M. Schaeffer may indicate an interval in the life of the city during the Amarna period (*Stratigraphie*, p. 187).

Tombs 4011 and 4013 (pp. 97, 286–287) contain scarabs of the usurper Ay and the general Horemheb, the last two kings of the xviiith dynasty, ending about 1320 B.C., while the two following decades are not represented by any inscriptions. A scarab of Rameses II extends the range of Tomb 4013 into that long reign which covers nearly three-quarters of the thirteenth century.

The potter's workshop in Cave 4034 was producing wares up to the time of the ruin of the town and Structure III of the Temple, though some Philistine and Iron Age sherds show that it was accessible in the twelfth–tenth centuries (p. 293).

The contents of Tombs 570 and 571 (pp. 248–250) and the less exotic groups in the same area near the city gate provide links with Structure III and Level VI, marked especially by palm and zigzag design and double bowls. These forms are missing from the Fosse Tombs at Tell Fara (BP II, Pl. LX, Cemetery 900) and from the later group of Philistine tombs in the plain (BP I, Pl. LXIV, Cemetery 500), though both series provide scarab comparisons, and the coffin lids of the Duweir Tomb 570 (Pls. 45 and 46) are nearest in style to those of Tombs 552 and 562 at Fara (BP I, Pl. XXIV).

Decorated vessels with gazelle and tree motif, of which a fine example is seen in Level VI (p. 53) and of which several pieces were found in Structure III (L. II, Pl. XLVIII), are rather poorly represented in the tombs (Types 991 and 999 are from small groups), though, in view of other comparisons with the tombs, their presence in the first two contexts suggests that the LB occupation of Duweir ended during the reign of Rameses II (BP II, p. 27).

Elsewhere there are connexions with Stratum C (AASOR XVII, p. 78) or even B[1] at Tell Beit Mirsim,

Tombs which have one or more periods of re-use have their numbers repeated in brackets.

PERIOD (SCHAEFFER) / DATE (SCHARFF)	EGYPTIAN KINGS & DYNASTIES	TELL ED-DUWEIR — GROUPS ON CONSOLIDATED CHART	SMALL TOMB GROUPS	N-E SECTION	JERICHO CITY	TOMBS	TELL BEIT MIRSIM	MEGIDDO STRATA	TELL EL AJJUL (GAZA)	CHARACTERISTICS ELSEWHERE
IRON I	RAMESES III DYN XX		523, 561				B¹	VI		TELL FARA FOSSE TOMBS CEM 900 / 'AIN SHEMS IVB - BURNT / TELL, ABU HAWAM IVA-BURNT / TELL EL-HESI IV / BEISAN VI
C.1200 / LB III	RAMESES II DYN XIX	[532] [570-1] [559] [4004] [4034] [4011] [4013] STRUCTURE III	537-8,556,557,4001,6001,6007, (6016) 502,503,508,7005,7008,7012 549,569,7017 539,4002-3 226 527, 536, 542,	BURNT VI 36 ... 32 feet	BURNT BUILDING M	T·13 a T·4 a-c	BURNT C²	VII / VIII	GOVERNORS TOMB PALACE IV	BEISAN VII / TELL EL-HESI SUB IV / Mycenaean Imports / BEISAN VIII
C.1350 / LB II	AMENHETEP III	STRUCTURE II [501] [1003] [216]	221,541,543,548,4019 524,528,554,555,556,4,1006 547, 567.	BURNT VII AMENHETEP II	BURNT CITY D	T·5 a-e	BURNT C¹	GAP	PALACE III	TELL EL-HESI III / 'AIN SHEMS IVA BURNT / TELL ABU HAWAM V / ALALAKH LEVEL IV / Base-Ring Ware
C.1450 / LB I	THOTMES III / DYN XVIII "HYKSOS"	[1555] STRUCTURE I [4004]	1005, 510, 4009,7011,7015,	26 / 25 feet / BURNT	GAP / PALACE & BURNT	GAP	GAP / BURNT	BURIALS ONLY IX LAST BURIALS IN STRUCTURAL TOMBS	PALACE & CITY II / HORSE BURIALS / BURNT	TELL EL-HESI II / Bichrome Ware / NAHARIYAH PHASE C / 'AIN SHEMS V ENDS / BEISAN NORTH CEM
C.1600 / MB III	EXPELLED / Second Intermediate	[129] [153] (4022 LAYER) [119] [1502] [1552] 145 [157] 173	III,511,1548,4008,6017,6028 1546,1547,6002,6027 (107)(1C8),115,121,1508,7014 1539, 1542 187	VIII GAP / MB GLACIS	CITY C / PALACE STORE ROOMS 18 30 36 / CITY C	T·19 T·22 T·4 b-e T·5 e T·9 a d	D² GAP / E-D	X CITY GAP / XI CITY	PALACE I / MB GLACIS / T·303 (UPPER)	TELL FARA CEM 500 / BILOBATE TOMBS / Daggers Type 27 / Lamps become common / Flared carinate bowls / Yehudiyeh Ware ends
C.1750 / MB II			7003		BURIALS TOWER AREA CITY B	T·5g T·9e	E E E F	BURIALS IN STRUCTURAL TOMBS XII CITY ?	CITY III / T·303 (LOWER)	NAHARIYAH PHASE B / Angular & rounded carinate bowls / Daggers Types 25-26 / BEISAN X-IX / 'AIN SHEMS VI
C.1900 / MB I	DYN XII SENUSERT I	(1513)	1504	FILL 14 12 feet / TELL DESERTED ?			BURNT G	XIII A / GAP	COURTYARD CEMETERY / GAP	RAS EL-AIN / NAHARIYAH PHASE A / Red Burnished Ware / Daggers Types 23-24 / Scarabs begin
C.2100	First Intermediate DYN VI ENDS	CEMETERY 2000	Houses 1512,1551 1510,1518,(1526)(1527), (1528) 1536, 1541,		LAYERS		H BURNT	XIV STAGES	CEMETERIES 100-200 / CEMETERY 1500	Caliciform pottery / Daggers Type 19 / Ledge Handles Form 12
EB IV / C.2400	Early Bronze Cities end	GROUP 1529	CAVERNS 6000	11 feet	I	T·351 A° A¹	I	O SHAFT TOMBS / XV / I		Ledge Handles Form 11 / EL-HUSN (EB IV-MB I) / BYBLOS BATIMENT XXVII / BAB ED-DRA / TELL EL-HESI "AMORITE"
EB III / C.2700		[1536] [1513] [1519]	(1538) 1501,(1514),1516, Kh Kerak Ware at 8-5 feet CAVERNS 6000		II CITY A III IV	A² A³ A⁴ (1952 excav) BURNT J. f3ʳᵈ Wall	J	XVI II / XVII III / GAP		AY LATE SANCTUARY / Ledge Handles Form 8 / Combed Ware / RAS EL-AIN / BEISAN XII-XI / TELL EL-FARAH DESTROYED
EB II / C.2900	DYN I	4022 LAYER 3 [1535]	(1538) (1553)	BED-ROCK	V VI	e.Upper Midden c.2' Wall		IV XVIII / V		Ledge Handles Form 10 / BEISAN XIII / AY EARLY SANCTUARY / TELL EL FARAH TOWN WALL / Upright rim bowls / Ledge Handles Form 7 / EL HUSN (EB II) / BEISAN XIV

CHRONOLOGICAL CHART

and with Stratum VII or, less closely, with VI at Megiddo. 'Ain Shems provides some particularly close parallels in Stratum IVb (AS V, p. 44). The tumuli graves at Tell Yehudiyeh present several comparable forms, which centre on the xxth dynasty, and pottery coffins are common at that site (*Mound of the Jew*, p. 48). Other less ornate groups of much the same period are Tombs 532 (Pl. 55) and 559 (p. 246). These and smaller groups in the vicinity may extend to the end of the thirteenth century and some were perhaps in use after the destruction of Level VI and Structure III.

PART II
INDUSTRIES, SEALS, INSCRIPTIONS

CHAPTER 6
UTENSILS, WEAPONS AND ORNAMENTS
FOURTH AND THIRD MILLENNIUM

Stone Implements and Vessels (Pls. 13: 97; 19; 21: 1–4; 26: 1–11)

THE only flint implements from the mound which can be certainly dated before the Early Bronze Age were recovered from the lower slopes at the north-east corner, where Pit 4022 produced an end-scraper which is undoubtedly Natufian, and Cave 6029 close by contained a Chalcolithic sickle-blade.

Surface deposits in the North-West Settlement produced quantities of sickle blades of all periods, but comparatively few were found in the actual caves. For Dr. Waechter's report see Appendix C and Pl. 19.

In connexion with the flints, it is perhaps worth noting that small lumps of pitch or bitumen, obtainable in the Dead Sea area, were found in Caves 1534, 1557 and 1556. On the analogy of Badarian and other sickles, composed of flint blades set firm in the holder by a bituminous filling, it seems probable that the pitch was needed for a similar purpose.

Worked and worn stones of uncertain use came from the surface and from caves. Among more distinctive pieces are large natural blocks of limestone, lightly pitted on the upper surface (Pl. 21: 2, 3). There were also squared rubbers about $9 \times 6 \times 4$ cms., well worn and polished from use.

Large rings of mizzi limestone, pierced and worn, were found in some numbers in Cave 4020, which may have been an olive press (Pl. 7: 4). Smaller rings of the same quality limestone, averaging 12–14 cms. in diameter, were found on all the Fara sites (BP II, Pl. XXVIII: 12 and p. 16), and the same shape recurs in the "Copper Age" tombs at Ajjul (AG II, Pl. XXII: 1 and p. 9).

Rings or disks of very soft howr limestone or pottery, between 4 and 6 cms. in diameter, occur at 6 and 7 feet in the Section (NE 7/306, 307 and NE 6/339 on pp. 57–59). These can be matched on the surface of Site O at Tell Fara (BP II, Pl. XXI and p. 17), and also in Site H, where they are said to be common at each level (BP II, Pl. XXIV and p. 19).

Basalt rings, well shaped and rounded, are also common throughout Site H (BP II, Pl. XXVI: 53 and p. 19) and they also occurred in the Duweir cave-dwellings (e.g. Pl. 13: 97). Other comparisons range from Strata XX–XVII at Megiddo.

Pebbles of crystalline stone with a worn central groove, both found in surface contexts, are shown on Pl. 21: 4 and Pl. 26: 11. A similar piece came from Fara Site H (BP II, Pl. XXVI: 55). Farther afield, Professor Mallowan found stones at Brak in contexts which leave no doubt that they had been used as bead polishing blocks (*Iraq* IX, 1947, Pl. XXIX: 3, 8). This practice goes back to the early third millennium in ancient Sind (see the article by Mr. Ernest Mackay in JAOS, Vol. 57, No. 1, pp. 1–15). In Europe, similar stones with a central groove are described as "arrow straighteners" (*Dawn*, pp. 221–222).

Of five stone maceheads, the first two illustrated on Pl. 26 came from Cave 1538, where the sherds are predominantly Upper Chalcolithic in date. These maces resemble the earliest pear-forms in Egypt, which appear at S.D. 42–43, for they are "widest at the base, short and almost globular" (PE, p. 22). Similar maceheads are found at Fara Site A (BP II, Pl. XXIII: 26 and XXVII: 81) and at Beisan Level XIII, EB II (MJ XXIV, Pl. 3: 27).

A developed pear-form macehead is drawn on Pl. 26: 3. It came from Cave 1519 and compares with those which Petrie attributed to the Protodynastic period (PE, p. 23 and Pl. XXVI). Nearby at Tell el-Ḥesi, pear-form maceheads were found in City I and Sub I. At Beisan an example came from Level XII, EB III, and another was found in an MB context (MJ XXIV, Pl. X: 23–24).

The mace illustrated on Pl. 26: 4 was found in Tomb 157, which was probably below the glacis fill. That shape is not among the Egyptian forms published by Petrie, and it is the latest example from Duweir, dating perhaps, if it is not an intrusion in the tomb, to MB II–III.

Pl. 26: 5 from a surface area probably belongs to the same period, for it compares in shape with a macehead attributed to Stratum D at Tell Beit Mirsim.

Among the usual collection of basalt and trachyte mortars of the shapes illustrated on Pl. 26: 6–7, a few fragments showed a decoration of incised triangles pendant from the rim, as illustrated on the shallow bowl, Pl. 26: 8, which came from surface debris. Similarly decorated mortars are typical of Teleilat Ghassul (TG I, p. 69 and Fig. 23: 2) and Garstang's Layer VIII at Jericho (AAA XXIII, Pl. XXXIII: 17). For general references see PPEB, p. 21.

The rim of a squat stone jar, drawn on Pl. 26: 10, suggests an affinity with vessels of Egyptian Predynastic times (PE, p. 35), while the small square palette is also reminiscent (Pl. 26: 9).

But by far the most tantalising discovery was a piece of Kephren diorite, about $6 \times 4 \times 1 \cdot 5$ cms., of a quality which was only obtained from a quarry due west of Toshka in Nubia, worked in the ist and iind and in part of the iiird dynasties, but no later. I am much indebted to Professor W. B. Emery for this information. The interior shows fine drill marks and on the highly polished outer surface there are lightly scratched lines, being part of the long side of a rectangle which was probably the edge of a cartouche. It might have solved many problems had it been complete and in a stratified position. For another likely contact with Egypt see p. 274.

Textiles and Basketry (Pl. 13: 90–94)

Neither cloth nor baskets could be expected to survive in caves so near the surface of a wind- and rain-swept plateau, but it is clear from the impressions of both materials on clay sherds that these crafts were known at the site in very early times.

Two parts of a cup or crucible have plain-weave textile impressions on the inner face, showing how this primitive form was fashioned on a core of woven material. The occurrence of a similar weave at Jericho (Tomb A 94) of Upper Chalcolithic date, suggests that the Duweir fragments may be at least as old. Mrs. G. M. Crowfoot very kindly made this comparison and provided the technical descriptions which appear opposite the photographs (Pl. 13: 93–94).

Close to bed-rock in the North-East Section (p. 59), another fragment bore the faint impression of a plain-weave textile over the clearer marks of a reed mat (NE 1/407). There was also the imprint of a coil basket (NE 6/332), while another fragment of the same kind was found in Cave-dwelling 1523 (Pl. 13: 90–92).

Mrs. G. M. Crowfoot's article on *Mat impressions on pot bases* published in 1938 (AAA XXV, pp. 3–11) assembled the examples from three main sites in Palestine, Jericho (Level VIII), Teleilat Ghassul and Tell Fara (Wady Ghuzzeh). Since the date of her study, mat impressions have been published from the earliest strata at Megiddo (M. II, Pl. 92: 15) and elsewhere. In Dr. Ben-Dor's words, they are "the characteristic feature of the chalcolithic base" (AAA XXIII, p. 87).

Bone (Pls. 13: 96; 21: 5)

Part of the metacarpal of an ox, with the knuckle ends sawn off leaving two holes at each end, is illustrated on Pl. 21: 5. Six holes were bored symmetrically near one end.

In order to discover if the bone could have been a primitive musical instrument, it was examined by Mr. Eric Todd of Leeds, who was good enough to make elaborate tests. As a result, he ruled out the possibility that the bone was

1. an aerophonic instrument of the tundun or bull-roarer type;
2. played by the vibration of the lips, as the *shofar*;
3. played with a cupped mouthpiece.

In considering the use of reed mouthpieces, he concluded that the resemblance of the bone to a double clarinet (*zamara*) was purely superficial, "for the entrance and exit holes lead to and from a central common chamber . . . partially divided by processes stretching from each end towards the middle", and, therefore, the bone was never a double tube instrument.

Finally he considered "the large class of Near Eastern instruments with two pipes connected to one double reed, the Egyptian oboe being a case in point". His experiments showed that, with a bassoon reed attached by a short length of tubing to one of the holes in the end opposite to the resonance holes, the other hole near the reed being closed by the thumb, the following notes (approximately) were obtained:

1. with thumb on hole—E;
2. with thumb removed—G sharp;
3. with thumb on hole (harmonic of 1 above)—G sharp.

These notes were true notes of the pipe and not notes of the reed. The six holes near the exit holes were presumed to be resonance holes as, when they were closed, the tone produced was slightly muffled. With a form of T-tube, made so that the vibrations from the reeds should communicate with the resonance chambers by means of both holes, notes 1 and 3 above were produced, without any appreciable difference in tone or pitch. Mr. Todd points out, however, that the fact that notes of musical pitch can be produced is no guarantee that the bone is a musical instrument.

Since these tests were made, many bones pierced with holes at one end have been found in the 1952–1955 tombs at Jericho, though in the majority the processes at the ends were intact, which would preclude their use as musical instruments.

The ox-bone just discussed came from Cave 1553 with pottery which is mostly Upper Chalcolithic in date. Comparable "amulets" found at Gezer (*Gezer* II, p. 449; III, Pl. XXVIII: 20) would, on Wright's revised chronology, date from EB I (PEQ, Jan. 1937, p. 73).

Several examples from Tomb A at Jericho (AAA XIX, Pl. XXIIa) extend the use of such bones to EB III, and it is assumed that the processes of these had been removed as they are described as "flutes".

Cave 1553 also produced part of a bone point (Pl. 13: 96). A thin bone spatula, 10 cms. long, was one of the few worked bones in the Section (NE 2/385 on p. 59).

Beads and Shells (Pl. 29)

The earliest group of importance comes from Cave 1535, which contains pottery dating from EB I–III with emphasis on the earlier range. It includes over a hundred beads, of which all but three are made of paste, many of them retaining a bluish-green glaze. Two of the three exceptions are in carnelian and steatite respectively (Pl. 29: 6, 7), while the third is a bead of solid gold. Mr. Beck prepared the following report in 1934 on this unique discovery from a Palestinian site.

Bicone bead from Cave 1535 (Pl. 29: 17)

Length: 0·27 ins. (0·60 cms.). Diameter: 0·24 ins. (0·50 cms.).
Weight: 1·42 grammes. Specific gravity: about 16.

This bead is a bicone in which the length is slightly greater than the diameter. It has on the external surface a series of marks made by an instrument with a curved end. . . . I think they were made intentionally, but whether they are intended for decoration or as an inscription I do not know.

It is difficult to state with absolute certainty how this bead was made, but it is evidently gold throughout and not gold on a base of bitumen or base metal. The specific gravity is somewhere near 16, which shows that it is purer than 18 carat gold, which is about 15. (Pure gold is 19·3 and the sovereign 17·7). A gold bead from Ur made entirely of pieces of wire twisted together and soldered has a weight of 1·237 grammes and a specific gravity of about 16.

I think the bead has been cast round a clay core. A careful examination shows that the perforation is slightly larger and much rougher in the centre. When it had been cleaned out with a feather it showed a slightly granulated surface with several cracks.

Part of the inner portion is level with the ends of the perforation, and here it is polished and looks exactly similar to the outside surface. . . . I can see no evidence of the bead having been made in two parts and soldered.

I cannot match this bead exactly from other countries. A number of gold beads of this shape have been discovered at Ur. There are two main varieties of these. One, the commonest, consists of a thin layer of gold sheet filled with a bituminous base. The second variety has a much thinner covering of gold on a base made of copper. There are also a few beads from Ur which I believe are solid gold, but without taking their specific gravity or cutting them in half it is difficult to be certain that they have not got a copper core. Beads of the last variety are not usually made in the bicone shape. The gold bead of A-an-i-padda, found at El Obaid, was also hollow. It was of a scaraboid shape, and had a cuneiform inscription on the curved surface. Gold bicone beads are found amongst Phoenician beads of the sixth to seventh centuries and among Cypriote beads of the Mycenaean and more recent periods, but so far as I know they are all made of sheet gold soldered together in the middle and are hollow. Egyptian gold beads are usually hollow and sometimes filled with bitumen. (See also a coiled wire bicone bead, Pl. 42: 3.)

Since Mr. Beck wrote his report, M. Dunand's excavations at Byblos have produced biconic moulds for beads from levels which equate with the Old Kingdom period in Egypt (B.I., Pl. CVI and *Stratigraphie*, Pl. XVIII and § 38). Comparable bicone beads in bronze are a feature of certain tombs at Ras Shamra, which are dated by the excavator between 2100–1900 B.C. (e.g. Tomb LXI, *Stratigraphie*, Pl. XII).

With the beads from Cave 1535, those from EB III–IV burials in Cave 1513, which are arbitrarily strung in the photograph on Pl. 17: 43, 44, should also be considered. Out of more than 500 beads, nearly 400 are paste or glaze, seventy-two are stone and two are of copper or bronze. Among them are a few disk beads of roughly cut quartz, one of which is photographed on Pl. 17: 45. They compare with those found at Brak (*Iraq* IX, 1947, Pl. XXVIII), which are in Professor Mallowan's opinion to be dated no later than 2400 B.C. in Iraq.

Schedule of Early Bronze Age Beads

Pl. 29:	1	2	6	7	9	16	17	21	23	25	44	45
1535	—	80	14	1	2	22	1	2	—	5	4	1
1513	3	73	173	—	—	34	—	148	10	13	81	—

Pl. 29: 44 and 45 represent shells which have been pierced for threading and suspension, and the popularity of the threaded shells is very marked in Cave 1513 (Pl. 17: 46). As the tops were rubbed away, the shell used is only tentatively identified as *Ancilla ovalis* derived from the Red Sea (see Appendix B, pp. 323 f.).

At Megiddo there are pierced shells from Stratum XVIII (M. II, Pl. 207: 1) which appear similar, and the beads in the same illustration compare with Pl. 29: 9. The faience beads from Strata XVII–XVI (M. II, Pl. 207: 5) resemble Pl. 29: 23.

Long barrel carnelian beads, Pl. 17: 44 and Pl. 29: 21, are especially common in Cave 1513 and they only recur thereafter in this stone in Tomb 4004 (7 examples) with single beads in Tombs 1552, 6027, 556 and 570. In Beck's classification it is not possible to subdivide these barrels, but the earlier ones are clearly distinguishable by their smooth and opaque surface and the whitish patination of the stone. Egyptian Old Kingdom comparisons for them from Qau are valid, as noted by Petrie when he found similar beads in the "Copper Age" cemetery 1500 at Ajjul (AG I, p. 3). The beads from Qau, at University College, London, and those from Ajjul at the Institute of Archaeology, are similar in appearance.

In general, the common beads from Caves 1535 and 1513 appear to be well matched with those from Jericho Tomb A (AAA XIX, Pl. XXIIb), where examples like Pl. 29: 2, 6, 16 and 25 can be distinguished.

No beads were found in Cemetery 2000 at Duweir.

Copper Weapons (Pls. 21: 6–15; 22: 1–10)

For analyses of some of the weapons discussed in the following sections see Appendix D, p. 328.

UTENSILS, WEAPONS AND ORNAMENTS

Castings

An important surface find in Grid Square G. 20 (Pl. 95) was a group of rough-cast implements in copper (Pl. 21: 11–15). At the time of discovery Starkey wrote: "two are probably from the same mould (Nos. 14, 15), while a third appears to be a long cutting edge for fastening to a fighting-stick (No. 12)", like Nos. 11 and 13, which are both incomplete.

While the castings cannot be dated on archaeological grounds, the analysis of Pl. 21: 14 would place this piece in the period of the Caliciform Culture rather than in the Early Bronze Age (Appendix D).

Daggers

Two daggers came from groups in which the pottery is mainly of the last phases in the Early Bronze Age. The fine blade shown on Pl. 14: 24 and on Pl. 22: 6 was found with a single male burial, though the bones were disturbed and the pottery lay apart at the same level (Pl. 3: 6, 7). A comparison comes from the top of Tomb 351 at Jericho (AAA XXII, Pl. XXXIV: 41).

Cave 1513 had contained many burials, and some were added early in the Middle Bronze Age. It is just possible, therefore, that the small dagger illustrated on Pl. 17: 41 and Pl. 22: 7 belongs to that horizon.

Both daggers belong to Type 18 with no midrib (see Mrs. Maxwell-Hyslop's classification in *Iraq* VIII, 1946, p. 21), and the best comparisons are to be found in Cemetery 1500 at Tell el-Ajjul, where similar daggers are found in stone-lined or rectangular graves which rarely contain pottery (Forms S, G and SL, AG II, Pl. LIX). The only parallel from Megiddo came from Tomb 1101B Lower, Stages 1–0 (SAOC 10, p. 54, Fig. 15), which was disturbed and burnt, and also contained tanged and socketed daggers.

As the first burials in Cemetery 1500 at Ajjul precede any from Cemetery 2000 at Duweir, it is not unreasonable to accept the daggers from Burial 1556 and Cave 1513 as the earliest from that site, for they certainly hold that position on typological grounds.

Points or Pins

Besides the round-sectioned point or pin found in Cave 1523 (for analysis see p. 328), there is a square-sectioned point (Pl. 22: 8) which was the only metal object from the North-East Caverns. It may be compared with the smaller point from a grave in Cemetery 2000 (Pl. 22: 10).

Weapons of the Caliciform Culture

Daggers of Type 18 are discussed above. In describing Type 19 (*Iraq* VIII, 1946, p. 21) Mrs. Maxwell-Hyslop remarks that it is an improvement on the previous type, "the tang is well-made with several rivets . . . the thickening down the centre of the blade found in Type 18 has become a carefully cast midrib and the blade is capable of being used as an efficient dagger".

The changeover from Type 18 to Type 19 would, in the nature of things, be gradual, and each type can be found in the same tomb, e.g. Jericho A 26 (PEQ, 1952, p. 75, Fig. 4, where No. 12 equals Type 18 and No. 13 has a full midrib like Type 19). Miss Kenyon described them as characteristic of Intermediate EB–MB at Jericho. So far, comparisons for Types 18 and 19 are confined to Palestine.

The dagger of Pls. 21: 8 and 22: 5 was submitted to Professor F. C. Thompson of Manchester as a typical specimen of the period for metallurgical examination and the results in relation to a Middle and Late Bronze Age dagger are given in Appendix D.

The dagger on Pl. 22: 4 from Tomb 2111, with three rivets and a slight midrib, is a variant of Type 19, and northern analogies are to be found for the javelin from the same tomb (Pl. 22: 1). They are photographed together on Pl. 21: 9, 10. With the javelin, two shorter ones should be considered from Tomb 2032 (Pl. 21: 7, drawn on Pl. 22: 2) and from Tomb 2100 (Pl. 22: 3).

75

Comparisons

More than twenty weapons of the same general kind have been published by Col. D. H. Gordon as part of the evidence for *The Chronology of the Third Cultural Period at Tepe Hissar* (*Iraq* XIII, 1951, Pt. I, pp. 49 ff.), see also my article on *The Shihan Warrior* (*Iraq* XV, 1953, Pt. II, pp. 161–166). The tomb which contained the dagger and the javelin had a rounded shaft and chamber (p. 276, Shape 2) and the two other javelins came from bilobate tombs (Shape 4). It is worth noting that of the two javelins from Tell el-Ajjul, one was also found in a bilobate tomb (AG I, Pl. XIX: 49).

Javelins or throwing spears were part of the normal equipment of the Sumerian army, and actual examples are found in graves at Ur in sets of four. They have wooden shafts, fitted with a notched butt to hold the throwing thong (*Ur* II, pp. 68–69 and Pl. 227). Associated with them are "poker-butt" spears (ibid., p. 303 and Pl. 227: 1), which are not found in Sargonid graves and are rare in the burials assigned by Woolley to the iind dynasty. According to some authorities the date of the earliest Royal Tombs at Ur falls between 2900–2700 B.C.

Wherever weapons of the same general kind are found elsewhere, they have a rather short history and they seem to coincide with destruction and drastic change. At Ras Shamra, Schaeffer found javelins but no "poker-butt" spears in the ashes of Level II, and on the surface of Level III but not in the tombs (*Stratigraphie*, p. 38, Fig. 55).

At Tell Kara Hassan (ibid., p. 81, Fig. 80) and Tell Ahmar or Barsib (ibid., p. 83, Fig. 82) both types were found in rectangular stone-lined cist graves under the houses. At Tepe Hissar (ibid., p. 448 and Fig. 239) both are associated with the wholesale destruction of the main occupation Level III B.

Among examples from the Caucasus, M. Schaeffer considers that the blades from Tiflis (ibid., p. 516, Fig. 293: 1, 2) date between 2200–2000 B.C., and it is these which most resemble the javelins from Duweir, which appear to represent the end of the series.

The only example of a "poker-butt" spear from Tell ed-Duweir (Pl. 21: 6 and Pl. 22: 9) came from a single oval grave, and from a similar burial there was a minute square-sectioned point (Pl. 22: 10).

Spindle-shaped points of copper or bronze are most numerous in Stratum II at Alishar Hüyük (OIP XIX, p. 152), and the Duweir point is comparable to one illustrated on Fig. 192: b. 1387, length 13·5 cms. Fig. 191 shows many much smaller points, among which b. 2797, length 3·5 cms., is close to Pl. 22: 10.

While the dates of all the comparisons are still debatable, and based largely on analogies with other sites, some authorities would place these weapons or implements between 2200–1900 B.C., or even later. The evidence from Palestine does suggest that javelins and "poker" spears or pikes were probably obsolete before 2000 B.C.

SECOND MILLENNIUM

Metal

Daggers and Knives

In the previous section it was seen that the daggers of the Caliciform Culture at Duweir belong to Type 19 (*Iraq* VIII, 1946, pp. 1–65). Types 20–21 and 24 in Mrs. Maxwell-Hyslop's classification are confined to Cyprus and North Syria and do not therefore concern us. Types 22 and 23 are found in those areas and in the shaft tombs at Megiddo (MT, Pls. 122: 8; 146: 5, 6). An example is also recorded from Ajjul (AG I, Pl. XVI: L. 5). A variety of Type 23, with two rivet holes extant and the third probably missing, was hammered at the riveted end to form a raised flange. It is illustrated on Pl. 23: 14 and Mrs. Maxwell-Hyslop has allotted it the Type No. 23b. It could also be considered as a primitive form of Type 32, because of the extension of the side flanges, an attribution which would suit its position in Tomb 555, which contained deposits belonging to the beginning and end of the Late Bronze Age.

MB II–III (Pls. 22: 11–20; 23: 1, 2)

Most of the weapons classed as daggers Type 27 and 27a should perhaps be described as knives, following Petrie and Albright (AASOR XVII, p. 52), for they have a tanged handle (usually without rivets) and a rounded blade.

Two examples of Type 27 retain one rivet in the tang, which is short in proportion to the blade. One of these came from Tomb 157 (Pl. 23: 2), while the other was recovered from Tomb 119 (Pl. 22: 17). In this last tomb there was also an unriveted blade of Type 27a (Pl. 22: 18).

Type 27a is well represented at Duweir, beginning, perhaps, typologically with the short rounded blades such as Pl. 22: 16 from Tomb 6002 or with Pl. 22: 12, 13, and carrying on with the slimmer No. 11, all from Tomb 1552. Pl. 22: 14 is comparable to the latter blade, and it was found in the same group as the inscribed "Lachish Dagger" No. 15, which has a longer tang in proportion to the blade. For Dr. Diringer's notes see p. 128.

Pl. 22: 18 is similar and came from Tomb 119 with the dagger, No. 17, of Type 27, which resembles Nos. 19 and 20 in form. Pl. 23: 1 completes the register of this type found in MB groups. The range probably extends into the following period as suggested by Pl. 23: 3 with its exceptionally long tang.

For Professor F. C. Thompson's metallurgical examination of the blade, Pl. 22: 12, submitted as a typical example of the MB period at Duweir, see Appendix D, p. 331.

Date and Comparisons

Having now surveyed the weapons available from Duweir, it will be seen that Types 17, 25 and 26 are altogether missing at our site. Type 17 is represented by examples from Tell Fara and Tell Beit Mirsim, attributed to the "Hyksos" period and Stratum D respectively. Examples are known in Crete from EM II–III and MM I (*Iraq* VIII, 1946, p. 20).

Type 25, with a finely ribbed surface, compares with blades attributed to the xith dynasty in Egypt (*Iraq* VIII, p. 26). Judging from the pottery found with the "technically advanced" Type 25, a date in the xiith or, at the latest, the xiiith dynasty would be suitable: see for instance the Ajjul Courtyard Cemetery Tomb 1417 (AG II, Pl. XIV: 74) and the slightly later Tomb 303 lower (AG III, Pl. XIX: 10), which both have daggers of Type 25. For these and other groups see *Stratigraphie*, Figs. 122–125.

An example from Megiddo with a long tang (M. II, Pl. 178: 3) attributed to Stratum XIII B was found alone and may not be in position stratigraphically. Other daggers of Type 25 came from Tomb 911 (MT, Pl. 118: 5; 122: 9); in each case they were associated with the "primitive" Type 22 (MT, Pl. 118: 9; 122: 8). A cylindrical juglet with pricked decoration is among the pottery (MT, Pl. 28: 40).

Type 26 is less elaborate, having a single wide rib down the centre and a tang with or without rivets. Examples came from layers e and c of Tomb 9 at Jericho (AAA XIX, Pl. XXXVII: 5, 6) and layer d yielded two long blades of Type 27a (ibid., Nos. 1, 2). The same association of types can be seen at Gezer (*Gezer* I, Fig. 160, Tomb 3; III, Pl. LX: 4, Tomb 1).

These groups have other contacts with the pottery and scarabs of the Duweir series which only begins when Types 27 and 27a have replaced Types 17, 25 and 26 late in MB II or early in MB III.

There are two main sources for comparisons: the bilobate tombs at Tell Fara, Cemetery 500, and the Structural Tombs at Megiddo, Strata XII–X.

The Fara tombs contain daggers of Types 17 (BP I, Pl. IX: 38, 46) Tombs 556, 559, and 17a (BP I, Pl. VI: 11) Tomb 551, while in Tomb 564 a dagger of Type 27a makes its appearance together with the previous Type 17 (BP I, Pl. XI: 75, 76). Tomb 569 is provided with a dagger of Type 27a (BP I, Pl. XI: 67) and so is Tomb 550 (BP I, Pl. VI: 14) and both these groups fall within the range of the Duweir MB III tombs.

To sum up, there is little to suggest a date much before 1750 or later than 1650 B.C. for Types 27 and 27a. Only in Tombs 1552 and 129, which cover a long range, do they occur with piriform juglets at Duweir, and the same may be said for Tomb 9 at Jericho.

There were no daggers in the bilobate Tomb 153 at Duweir, and in the more developed tombs of that shape at Tell Fara half the daggers are of Type 17 and half of Type 27a.

Daggers of Type 27 are associated with rectangular graves at Tell el-Ajjul (e.g. AG II, Pl. XIV: 70; IV, Pl. XXI: 214, Pl. XXVIII: 293) and at Tell Fara (BP II, Pl. XLIV: 60), except in the case of Tomb 364, which is a larger chamber. (AG III, Pl. XIX: 14).

LB I–III (Pl. 23: 3–21)

Pl. 23: 3–9 are all from Tomb 216 and the group is photographed on Pl. 54. No. 3 has a tang nearly a third of the total length, which is much longer than any example of Type 27a in the MB series. Typologically it probably falls between them and the nearest comparisons which are found at Megiddo in Strata VII–VI (e.g. M. II, Pl. 180: 45, 47 and Pl. 181: 48, 54).

Pl. 23: 4, 5, 6 are knives with a recurved tip. The implement was probably designed for use without a haft, and two out of three examples are finished with miniature representations of a hoof. On seeing the knives at the Institute of Archaeology, a former member of the Arab Legion at once identified them as a farrier's tools from their likeness to those in use today in Jordan.

Comparisons come from the J building level at Gerar, and knives with a horse's leg handle are well known in Egypt in the xviiith dynasty (PTW, Pl. XXVI: 145; Pl. XXIX: 231). See also the razors (?) with deer-footed handles from Megiddo (M. II, Pl. 180: 38, 44), attributed to Strata VIII and VII B.

Pl. 23: 7, 8 are "cutting-out" knives which are, according to Petrie, "usually before the xviiith dynasty", though they survive into the reign of Thothmes III (*Gerar*, p. 13 and PTW, Pl. LXII: 18; *Arabah*, Pl. XVI: E.10), a date which would suit the other contents of Tomb 216.

Pl. 23: 9 is a spearhead which completes the list of weapons found in Tomb 216.

Pl. 23: 10 is a small knife without tang or rivet holes which came from a cave roughly contemporary with Structure I and Tomb 4004.

Pl. 23: 11 is a spearhead from the latter group which was found above the main deposit and should therefore be contemporary with the use of Structure III and Level VI. Compare the closed socket and raised midrib with Pl. 23: 9 and 16. Examples from Bethshemesh and Megiddo Strata VIII–VII A could bring the spearhead No. 11 to the last century of the Bronze Age, and the context of No. 12 would favour a similar date.

Pl. 23: 13, 14 and 15 are all from Group 555, which contains deposits of both the beginning and the end of the Late Bronze Age. No. 13 is an incomplete spearhead or possibly a dagger. It is the only weapon from Duweir to show a fully developed midrib. If it were complete it might compare with the fine dagger with stop ridge from Tomb 1044 at Ajjul (AG II, Pl. XIV: 76, the only one of its kind among the flat blades of Type 28 in Mrs. Maxwell-Hyslop's classification), a tomb which contained Base-Ring wares, though they are not the earliest forms.

Pl. 23: 14 is perhaps transitional between Types 23 and 32 (p. 76). No. 15 is a version of Type 28, measuring about 19 cms. in length, with a plain, leaf-shaped blade and a stop-ridge. As the size of the weapons governs their classification, according to Macalister (*Gezer* II, p. 375) and Albright (AASOR XVII, p. 52), No. 15 should perhaps be included with the daggers.

A comparison with No. 15 is attributed to Stratum D at Tell Beit Mirsim, and this blade, though incomplete, appears to be about the same size. The xviii–xixth dynasty comparisons which are from Tell el-Ajjul and Gezer are all longer, and such blades are found in association with Base-Ring and Mycenaean wares, e.g. the Governor's Tomb (AG III, Pls. VI–XIII) and Tomb 1514 (AG II, Pl. XIV: 77), which also contained a Levanto-Mycenaean III B cylindrical cup dating from the thirteenth century (Furumark MP, Type 228, p. 623). It is significant that No. 15 came from Group 555, which contained a quantity of Mycenaean sherds, discussed in more detail on p. 213.

Pl. 23: 17 from Tomb 221 is incomplete, but it should perhaps be placed with the leaf-shaped daggers of Type 28a.

Pl. 23: 12, a spearhead, and Pl. 23: 18–21, knives and daggers, come from groups in Cemetery 500 which belong to the thirteenth or possibly the beginning of the twelfth century. The knife or dagger, Pl. 25: 68, probably comes from the same horizon. No. 12 is provided with an incipient midrib on both sides of the blade; cf. Nos. 9 and 11 on the same plate. No. 18 is a small and probably late version of Type 27a.

No. 19 is a knife with a missing end which may have been recurved, though the remaining part compares with blades of Thotmes III and Amenhetep II (PTW, Pl. XXIX: 235, 236).

Pl. 23: 20 from Tomb 538, which ends in a button stop, is best compared to Mrs. Maxwell-Hyslop's Type 53 (*Iraq* VIII, p. 59) used by the Philistines and their allies in the thirteenth and twelfth centuries B.C. No. 21 from the same group has a similar blade and section, though the handle is riveted and has a fish-tail end. For this detail only, compare a blade from Megiddo (M. II, Pl. 181: 55) attributed to Stratum VI.

Arrowheads (Pl. 25: 1–6, 17–22, 26, 27, 30, 32, 35, 36, 43, 47, 48, 52, 54–62, 66)

Leaf-shaped bronze arrowheads are illustrated with other small objects in individual groups on Pl. 25. All are corroded like the iron arrowheads of the first millennium (L. III, Pl. 60), but the outline of arrowheads before 1200 B.C. was long and slim in proportion to the width and the tang was not deliberately constricted.

Pl. 25: 1–6 illustrate a collection of arrowheads from Tomb 4004 of which No. 1 is unusual and No. 4 may belong to the late phase. Other groups which contained similar types were Tombs 555, 216, 501, 1003, 221, 542, 543, 547 and 4019, and it is perhaps not altogether fortuitous that these tombs are closely associated with the pottery of Structure II, both ending no later than the last half of the fourteenth century. A very small arrowhead (Pl. 25: 48) was associated with one of the blunt arrowheads described below.

Pl. 25: 27, 32 and 47 illustrate arrowheads with heavy blunt ends which are less common. They occur in groups attributed to the mid-fourteenth and mid-thirteenth centuries. Blunt arrowheads begin in Stratum VIII at Megiddo (M. II, Pl. 175: 30–34) and are found in Tomb 912B at the same site (MT, Pl. 126: 7–10). At Gaza they occur in Tomb 1044 with late Base-Ring forms, and at Fara they are clearly associated with a xixth dynasty tomb 936.

Pl. 25: 52 from Tomb 4013 shows a swelling at the base of the blade, which is normally an Iron Age peculiarity (L. III, p. 385), but which should probably be dated in this case to the last century of the Bronze Age.

Pl. 25: 58–62 are still more developed, with a pronounced midrib and more angular outline. These arrowheads come from Tomb 532, which belongs to the end of the thirteenth century if not to the beginning of the twelfth.

Personal Ornaments

"Togglepins" (Pl. 24)

The purpose and origin of these pins was lucidly discussed by Mrs. Henschel-Simon in her study of *The "Togglepins" in the Palestine Archaeological Museum* (QDAP VI, pp. 169–209). Her group divisions and type numbers are adopted here as they were also in the publication of Megiddo II (Pls. 219–223), except that the Greek letters which distinguish the subdivisions are translated in both publications.

"Togglepins" Group II A: without head. Types 3 and 7

Pl. 24: 1, 9 and 10 are the longest and possibly the earliest pins of Type 3. The first came from Tomb 145, while Nos. 9 and 10, where the hole is less centrally placed, are from Tombs 115 and 129. They can be matched in Strata XII–XI at Megiddo, and in most of the bilobate tombs at Tell Fara (see for instance BP I, Pls. VI–XI).

Pl. 24: 2 and 16 are much shorter, even allowing for loss of the point, and they came from Tombs 7014 and 4022, which are on the whole later in the series. They may be compared with pins from Tomb 5 at Jericho (AAA XX, p. 35, Fig. 10) and from Megiddo Strata IX–VIII.

Like No. 16, Nos. 23 and 28 are comparable in size to pins from the spread of rubbish in and below Structure I. The smaller size is also characteristic of the horse burials at Ajjul (e.g. AG I, Pl. XXI: 93, 94). No. 31 came from a denuded tomb of the xviii–xixth dynasties, though normally Type 3 does not survive far into the fifteenth century. See for instance a pin of Type 3 from Tell el-Ajjul, associated in Tomb 1055 with an early Base-Ring juglet (AG II, Pl. XVIII: 212 and AG I, Pl. L: 89 J).

Pl. 24: 11, 12 and 14 are of Type 7 with twisted shaft above the eyelet. Examples come from Tombs 129, 6027 and 1547 respectively and they are matched, almost equally with Type 3, in the bilobate tombs of Tell Fara.

The same combination can be seen in a large rectangular Tomb 1214 at Ajjul (AG IV, Pl. XXXIII: 435, 484), and bronze pins from that city would seem to be associated with the incomplete first building periods on the site which lay against the inner face of the grit bank (AG IV, p. 2). In any case they were well below the wall foundations of the LA building dating from the Late Bronze Age (AG IV, Pl. XXXIII: 430, 431, 433, 434).

Among several gold pins of Type 7 at Ajjul, one came from Tomb 1517 (AG IV, Pl. XVIII: 98), which also contained a bichrome jug (Type 68 K³) and a White Painted V juglet (Type 89 A, see AG III, Pl. XXXIX). The same horizon would also suit three "togglepins" from Megiddo found in tombs attributed to Strata X–VIII (M. II, Pls. 222: 53, 223: 64, 72).

"Togglepins" Group II B: with head.   Types 8 and 9

Pl. 24: 3, 7 and 8, Type 8a, are from Tombs 1542 and 119. Comparisons come from the bilobate tombs at Fara, Tombs 556 and 565 and particularly from Tomb 1021, where such pins are prevalent.

Type 8a is rare at Ajjul (AG IV, Pl. XXXIII: 496, Group 1702), where its main range probably preceded the expansion of city building, though other versions of Types 8 and 9 are common (see QDAP VI, pp. 196–204).

At Megiddo Type 8a occurs in Strata XIII B, XII, XI and IX, though of these only Pl. 221: 36 from Structural Tomb 3080, Stratum XI, is a closed group. Examples from Jericho come from Tombs 9c and 5g.

Pl. 24: 21, 25 and 30, Type 8b, are from Tombs 4004, 1003 and 221, which suggest a range from 1600–1350 B.C. The only example from Megiddo came from Tomb 5067, attributed to Stratum XII (M. II, Pl. 220: 27), but it is longer than any of this type from Duweir. A silver pin of Type 8b was associated with a Base-Ring jug, Type 89 H³, at Ajjul (AG I, Pl. L and II, Pl. III: 16, p. 7).

Type 8b is missing from Jericho and from Tell Beit Mirsim as both these sites were then unoccupied.

Pl. 24: 19, 22, 24, 26, 27 and 29 of Type 8c(a) are from Tombs 4004, 216, 501, 1003 and 221, covering the same range as Type 8b, 1600–1350 B.C. The only example from Megiddo came from Structural Tomb 3175, Stratum XI.

Pl. 24: 15, 18, 20 and 32, Type 8c(b), come from Tombs 1547, 4004 and 7013, ranging perhaps through the latter half of MB III and the earlier part of LB I. No. 18 is matched in a bilobate tomb at Tell Fara and No. 32 compares with a pin from a Fosse Tomb 902 of the xviiith dynasty and later. The type is missing from Jericho, Tell Beit Mirsim and Megiddo.

Pl. 24: 4 and 5, Type 8c(g), are represented in Tombs 1542 and 1502. The nearest parallel for No. 4 is from a peculiar double Tomb 1018 at Fara, which is akin to Tomb 1026 (BP II, Pl. XLV). Tomb 1018 also contained "togglepins" of Types 8a and 9a. At Jericho Type 8c(g) occurs in Tomb 9e, Tomb 13c, Tomb 19c and Tomb 31; it is also at Megiddo in Tomb 24 (QDAP VI, pp. 198–200).

Pl. 24: 6 is an example of Type 9b from Tomb 119, comparable to a pin from Tell Fara Tomb 569, and the same type, No. 13, occurs in Tomb 1547. These "togglepins" are common at Jericho, Tombs 9e, 19c, 30b, 31 and 31A (QDAP VI, pp. 202–203), though none are so long as No. 6.

Pl. 24: 17, of Type 9a, from Tomb 4004, is also well matched in Tomb 569 at Tell Fara, and there is a variant of this form in Tomb 1018 at that site (BP II, Pl. XLIII: 28). Type 9a is found in Tombs 9e and 19c at Jericho (QDAP VI, pp. 200–201).

Conclusions

Types 1 and 2 in Mrs. Henschel-Simon's classification are missing from, and earlier than, the range of the Duweir series, and the same seems to apply to Types 4, 5 and 6. See for instance the "togglepins" of Type 6c, *without head, spirally ribbed,* from Tomb 24 at Megiddo (QDAP VI, p. 194 and MT, Pl. 103: 19–21) found in a group which contained Yehudiyeh pricked ware juglets (MT, Pl. 23; and see Piriform Juglets, Class A on p. 189). All these should date no later than *c.* 1750 B.C.

Type 8c (g), *nail with flat head, spirally ribbed,* may be the earliest in the Duweir series, which soon becomes Type 8a, *nail with flat head, plain.* Type 8c (b), in which the flat head is *ribbed with rhythmical change,* begins in MB III and may continue into LB I.

Type 8b, *nail with flat head, incised,* follows, and can be found associated with Base-Ring ware like Type 8c (a and b). The full range may be from 1600–1350 B.C.

Type 9b, *knob head, vase-shaped,* is probably to be dated between 1750–1600 B.C., with No. 6 near the beginning and No. 13 near the end of the range. The same date may apply to Type 9a, *knob head, round and pointed.*

Type 3, *without head, plain*; the longest pin, No. 1, came from Grave 145 with a pricked ware juglet, so that the main range of this simple form seems to fall before the opening of the Duweir series. Type 3 is common in the bilobate tombs at Tell Fara, and is also to be found in association with Type 7 at Ajjul in the large rectangular Tomb 1214 (AG IV, Pl. XXXIII: 435, 484). Type 3 appears in the Courtyard Cemetery (AG II, Pl. XVIII: 204).

Type 7, *without head, twisted,* is also present in almost equal numbers with Type 3 in the bilobate tombs at Fara, and it is found associated with an early building phase after the construction of the grit bank at Ajjul. It is surely significant that Type 3 is rare at Jericho, only found in Tomb 5 (AAA XX, p. 35, Fig. 10), while the lack of Type 7 is indicative of a gap, as it is also at Tell Beit Mirsim.

In the final stages of their use, "togglepins" were reduced to a third of their original length.

Bracelets and Anklets (Pl. 25: 34, 37, 41, 42)

Pl. 25: 34, 37, 41 and 42 are all much-corroded bronze circles with an average diameter of 5 cms. If they were used as bracelets, they must have belonged to children, though the possibility that they were nose-rings cannot be excluded. The first two come from groups which centre on the mid-fourteenth century, and the last from tombs which were in use a century later. In any case, there is no evidence from Duweir that bracelets or anklets were used by the adult population until the Iron Age (L. III, pp. 389 ff.). On the other hand, it should be noted that the goddess Hathor-Astarte of the Qadesh type wears anklets and bracelets as sole ornaments (Pl. 49: 4 and p. 90).

Rings (Pl. 25: 8, 10, 28, 49, 50, 64)

Pl. 25: 8 and 10 of bronze and silver respectively are almost certainly finger-rings, and both come from Tomb 4004. No. 10, like No. 49 from Tomb 536, from which the scarab is missing, both show the method of winding the fine wire ends. Nos. 28 and 64 could have been used for various purposes, while No. 50 from Tomb 538, with its broad bezel, is most probably late in the thirteenth century.

For rings of the Iron Age, see L. III, pp. 390 ff.

Ear-rings (Pl. 25: 11, 12, 15, 16, 29, 31, 33, 38–40, 44, 46, 63)

Pl. 25: 11 and 12 are thin gold and bronze ear-rings, rather finer and more delicate than any of the Iron Age at Duweir (e.g. L. III, Pl. 54: 71, 72 and pp. 390–392). No. 15 from the same group, with a pendant composed of tiny gold balls, is of a type found in Stratum IX at Megiddo, which is especially common at

Tell el-Ajjul (see for instance AG IV, Pl. XX: 142, 143 and p. 8), and it survives into the Iron Age (L. III, Pl. 54: 73). No. 16, with paste bead pendant, from Tomb 555, is another variety which is popular at Ajjul, though the glass or paste pendants are missing.

Pl. 25: 29 from Tomb 501 is also seen in Stratum X at Megiddo. Nos. 31 and 44 both have metal pendants not closely matched elsewhere, and Nos. 33, 39, 40 and 46 are plain. No. 38, a finely made piece in gold, and No. 63 in the same metal from Tomb 570, are probably quite late products of the Bronze Age.

Head-band (Pl. 25: 13)

The end of a head-band in gold comes from Tomb 4004. For a more complete example with the same spiral-ended fastening, see AG IV, Pl. XVI: 42, Group 1203 and p. 7.

Amulets and Pendants (Pl. 25: 9, 14, 24, 65)

Pl. 25: 9, part of a pendant mount with traces of blue and red paste inlay from Tomb 4004, is another reminder of the fine workmanship displayed at Ajjul.

Nos. 14 and 65 are small examples from Tombs 4004 and 543 of the well-known crescent amulet, providing the protection of the moon god against evil eye and witchery (*Amulets*, p. 23). In Egypt it first appears in the xviiith dynasty, where it may not have originated, as it is found in earlier contexts elsewhere, e.g. from Megiddo Stratum X (M. II, Pl. 209: 25) and from deposits at Tell el-Ajjul (AG IV, Pl. XX: 168, 174 and p. 9).

No. 24 is a gold pendant from Tomb 216 which compares with one from the Temple Area. A reasonable parallel was found in the Governor's Tomb at Ajjul (AG III, Pl. VIII: 3), c. 1350–1250 B.C., and a larger version is associated with Stratum VII B at Megiddo (M. II, Pl. 213: 79).

Fibula (Pl. 25: 45)

The bronze fibula from Tomb 542 can be included amongst Blinkenberg's Cypriote types (FGO, pp. 230–253, Type XIII 5a), which are themselves derived from bow shapes characteristic of Mycenaean civilisation. He remarks that the earliest Forms 1–6 had not, up to the time that his study was written, been found in the island, and that with the Cypriote types he has included those of Asiatic origin. He suggests that it was late in the Mycenaean age when the fibula reached Cyprus. The type example which he shows comes from the cemetery of Deve Hüyük in Syria, centring on the fifth century B.C. (L. III, p. 394), where fibulae are reported to have a long range and the excavator refers to an example from a Middle Hittite grave (AAA VII, p. 123).

Toilet Articles (Pl. 25: 7, 23, 51, 53)

Pl. 25: 7 are tweezers from Tomb 4004, probably from the late deposit at the end of the Bronze Age, for these toilet aids are better attested after rather than before 1200 B.C. (L. III, Pl. 54: 27 and p. 395).

Pl. 25: 23 from Tomb 216 and Pl. 25: 53 from Tomb 559 may possibly be kohl sticks, in which case the same remarks would apply.

Pl. 25: 51 is a well-made bronze vase from Tomb 538 which also contained a good selection of bronze blades (Pl. 23: 18, 20, 21). With them, it probably dates from the thirteenth or early twelfth century.

God Reshef or Teshub (Pl. 25: 69)

Found in surface debris east of the palace (L. III, Pl. 116), the figure of Reshef is both corroded and incomplete. Analysis of the metal made by the kindness of the National Physical Laboratory proved it to be copper with a little tin, though it was not enough to constitute bronze. Compare the metal of the naked figure of a man which was made of bronze (L. II, p. 67 and Pl. XXVI: 33).

The arm of the figure, which was probably upraised, is now missing, while the left hand holds out some large object. The details of the conical head-dress and of the garb are obscured by corrosion, while the soles of the feet are dowelled to fit into a stand. Structure I produced a similar figure (L. II, Pl. XXVI: 31), which is itself well matched—except in the length of the kilt—by a figure, also from surface debris, at Megiddo, Strata IX–VII. Yet another example was found on the mound at Tell el-Ajjul (AG IV, Pl. XXI: 229), though its actual provenance is not clear.

For references to this northern god, see the general index of *Ugaritica I*.

Faience, Glass, Stone

Faience kohl pots (Pl. 26: 12–17)

Of the six kohl pots made of friable paste or composition originally overlaid by blue glaze decorated with designs in black, No. 12 reproduces the shape of the normal MB dipper at about half the size. The best comparison for it in shape comes from Tomb 1013 at Tell Fara with a twisted "togglepin" Type 7 (cf. Pl. 24: 14).

Five other pots, on which some of the decoration has been rubbed off, are of the shape which is generally associated with an MB context (AASOR XII, pp. 29–30). At Tell Beit Mirsim, one example with a net design is attributed to Stratum D (AASOR XII, Pl. 44: 15). Apart from the examples mentioned by Albright from Gezer, parallels were found at Tell Fara, as quoted by him and as noted in the plate descriptions opposite Pl. 26 in this book. It will be seen that they were found in bilobate tombs (e.g. BP I, Tombs 550, 556; BP II, Tomb 1021).

Pl. 26: 13, 14 were found in Tomb 1546 which was largely denuded, while Nos. 15–17 came from the rare bilobate Tomb 153 at Duweir. The average height of the first two was 8·4 cms., while the figure for those from Tomb 153 works out at 7·6 cms. Albright has noted that the average height for examples which he gives is 7·5 cms. (AASOR XII, p. 30).

It will be seen that the comparisons from Jericho are all from the deposit in Tomb 31, and Fig. 5: 4 (AAA XX, p. 14) is taller than the largest example from Duweir. Fig. 5: 2 is well matched by No. 16 from Tomb 153.

Glass Figurine and Spacers (Pl. 27: 2–3; Pl. 28: 23, 27)

Pl. 27: 2 from Tomb 4004, illustrated at double size, is a mould-pressed glass figurine of Astarte, a subject which is more commonly reproduced in pottery. A nude feminine figure in glass holding the breasts came from Level H, *c.* 1900–1750 B.C., at Hama (RPS, p. 105), though the excavator suggests that it is out of context.

Two figurines from Megiddo, which are described as made of faience are like the Duweir example. The first is an almost complete standing or recumbent figure, with hands clasping the breasts, from Schumacher's excavations, and the second is a fragment of the torso and arms in that position from a tomb of Stratum XII. Another close parallel came from Beisan "Thothmes III level". I am much indebted to Dr. D. B. Harden for drawing my attention to a figurine, acquired by Mr. Ray Winfield Smith in the Lebanon and now in his private collection, which is almost a duplicate, like an example in the Victoria and Albert Museum, Buckley Collection, c. 68–1936. Mrs. Ruth Amiran reminded me of several comparisons.

The date of No. 2, with its wide range of parallels, is more securely fixed by that of the glass spacer-beads found with it.

Pl. 27: 3 illustrates three bead spacers, of which two are drawn on Pl. 28: 23, 27. These are graded in width, one section is curved, and all are pierced for longitudinal threading.

The best comparisons come from Megiddo, where a small grave in Stratum IX contained a skeleton on which similar spacers (of faience?) were found around the neck (M. II, Fig. 343, T. 2010). The pottery includes rather late bichrome ware (Pl. 48: 4), and the same can be said for two other groups in which such spacers were found (M. II, Pls. 210: 39; 211: 47). Later examples from the same site are small and poorly made.

The Astarte figurine and the spacers should both date from LB I, probably in the reign of Thothmes III, no later than *c.* 1450 B.C.

In view of the interest in the early history of glass, fragments from the base of the Astarte figurine and chips from one of the spacers were submitted to Emeritus Professor W. E. S. Turner, F.R.S., University of Sheffield, who kindly made the following report on the composition of the glass figurine, Pl. 27: 2 from Tomb 4004:

"The specimen consisted almost entirely of the weathering products resulting from the slow attack of moisture during many centuries.

"A small example of the outer shell of the specimen was removed for examination and then some of the weathering product within the outer shell. A tiny piece of what appeared to be residual glass was extracted and also submitted to spectrographic analysis. The general results are as follows:

"1. *Outer layer*. The chief constituent was silica followed next in order by calcium oxide. Other oxides clearly present were antimony oxide, ferric oxide, alumina, tin oxide (SnO_2), copper oxide (CuO) and magnesium oxide. Traces of lead, nickel, silver, manganese, zinc and sodium were found.

"2. *Intermediate layer*. The dominant constituent was again silica, and the constituents next in order were lime, iron oxide, tin oxide and copper oxide. Following next were antimony oxide and alumina. The other constituents found in the outer shell were also present in very small amounts.

"3. *Residual glass*. The glass composition was also marked by the dominant presence of silica, next in order being lime, magnesia, iron oxide, copper oxide and nickel oxide.

"*Conclusions*

"It is quite clear first that the original glass is of the soda-lime-magnesia-alumina-silica type, with a marked quantity of iron oxide present, of the kind which is common to all the Egyptian xviiith dynasty glasses, and also some glasses from Knossos of about 1400 B.C. and some fragments from Nimrud of the eighth to sixth centuries B.C. There are also colouring elements which are of the type generally found in glasses of those dates, copper being the chief. There is also evidence that antimony oxide was present in distinctive amount—a constituent found in the glasses from Nimrud, although it is not found to the same degree in some of the Egyptian glasses."

Mortars and Pestles (Pl. 26: 18, 19, 21–23, 33, 38, 45)

The only groups to produce these utensils in coarse basalt were Tombs 1502 and 129, and in the latter the pestles were found with them. Comparisons came from Tell Beit Mirsim, of which two are certainly from Stratum E, while a third may belong to either E or D (AASOR XVII, Pl. 38: 39–40 and § 65). Another early comparison comes from Megiddo Stratum XIII A (M. II, Pl. 262: 9), though these mortars in less bold and smaller shapes also appear in later contexts.

Jericho Tomb 9c produced a larger pestle and mortar, which resembles No. 23 in shape though it is as large as No. 18.

Among numerous mortars from Tell el-Ajjul (e.g. AG III, Pl. XXVII: 93, 94 and IV, Pl. XL: 88–94) which are taller and narrower than those from Duweir, Nos. 89 and 93 appear to come from below the LA building level in Room E (AG IV, Pl. LXI), while No. 94 was found in the curious splayed bilobate Tomb 1502, which contained a group including a cylindrical juglet, calcite vases, bone inlay and a "togglepin" of Type 7.

No mortars were found in the bilobate tombs of Tell Fara, but there is a comparison for Pl. 26: 18 from Tomb 1006, which also contained a dagger of Type 27.

It would seem therefore that basalt tripod mortars should date in the main before rather than after 1750 B.C., though they do not seem to go back to the beginning of MB I. A range between 1950–1750 B.C., with small versions continuing even later, seems possible.

Pl. 26: 33 is a small tripod bowl or mortar in limestone from Locus 564. The feet were originally joined by cross-bars, a detail which is reminiscent of the basalt mortars from the burnt "Achan" group at Gaza (AG II, Pl. IV and Pl. XXIII: 46, 47).

Pl. 26: 38 illustrates a basalt bowl on a pedestal foot from Tomb 216, which may date to LB I or II.

Hones (Pl. 26: 24, 42)

Oblong stones, roughly squared and polished and pierced for suspension at one end, came from Tomb 6027 and Pit 556. There were beads in both groups and these pendants may have been either worn as amulets or used as hones for domestic use. Comparisons are to be found at most sites (e.g. M. II, Pl. 213: 67, Stratum VIII and Pl. 216: 116, Stratum VI).

Calcite and other Stone Vases (NE 23/118 on p. 55; Pl. 26: 20, 25–31, 34–37, 41, 46–48; Pl. 27: 1)

Part of a large globular vessel of shelly limestone came from the MB fill of the glacis slope. The shape and detail of the pierced lug handle are of xiith dynasty inspiration (see FFSV, Pl. XV: 154).

With few exceptions all the stone vases from the tombs are of banded calcite (calcium carbonate) of Egyptian provenance, which is to be distinguished from the local Palestinian variety which is really gypsum (calcium sulphate). As Dr. I. Ben-Dor has remarked in his article on *Palestinian Alabaster Vases*, the term "alabaster" is in fact loosely applied to two distinct minerals (QDAP XI, pp. 94–95). He also notes that the Egyptian vessels which have a baggy outline identical with those found in Palestine are mostly circular in plan. He suggests that an oval shape was more convenient for export packing (op. cit., p. 101).

Pl. 26: 20 and 28 are vases with rounded profiles from Tombs 129 and 4004. In Egypt a form like No. 20 is illustrated among those of the xiith dynasty (FFSV, Pl. XXIX: 655). No. 28 is more baggy, but both forms are circular in plan, unlike the comparable vases from Sedment, which are oval in plan.

Professor Albright discusses alabastra from Tell Beit Mirsim Stratum D which are, in comparison, coarse in outline and less precisely finished at neck and base (AASOR XII, Pl. 43: 2 and pp. 28–29). He compares them with Egyptian vessels, including those from Sedment (*Sedment* I, Pl. XLI) attributed to the xvith dynasty. In each case the plan is oval rather than round.

Pl. 26: 25, 26 and 27 from Tombs 1552 and 4004 are three cylindrical vases which are matched in Strata E–D at Tell Beit Mirsim and at Ajjul. Like the Tell Beit Mirsim parallels, Nos. 25–27 are oval in plan, which is also characteristic of examples from Group 27 at Gurob (*Gurob*, Pl. XXII) where several scarabs date from the Second Intermediate Period, though the pottery includes Base-Ring juglets like Type 857 and both Red and Black Lustrous ware (*Gurob*, p. 10). A date in M.B. III would suit the Duweir specimens.

Pl. 26: 29 is a kohl tube with the top in the form of a palm column. The material is limestone, burnt black, and nearly all the lower tube is missing. A duplicate made in ebony is published by Petrie (ODU, Pl. XXII: 23 and p. 27) and dated by him to the xviiith dynasty.

Pl. 26: 30 and 31 are somewhat unusual pieces, both from Tomb 4004 like No. 29. Parallels have not been traced in excavation reports.

Pl. 26: 34–37 are from Tomb 216 and Group 555. No. 34 is not closely matched among Egyptian forms. No. 35 of soft worn calcite is dowelled on the base to fit into a stand, which was found with it. A similar base and stand, but with tall neck, belongs to the last half of the xviiith dynasty in Egypt. No. 36 is incomplete. No. 37 represents a well-known form of Egyptian kohl pot, matched in Egypt from the xiith dynasty. A parallel comes from Grave 3 at Tell el-Yehudiyeh, with pricked ware, and there is another good match in a xvith dynasty grave at Sedment. No. 37 is, however, not out of place in an early xviiith dynasty context (see the brick vaulted tomb D. 114 from *Cemeteries of Abydos III*, pp. 29–31 and Pl. X: 6), where these forms are represented by three examples found in company with a cylindrical pot like Pl. 26: 27 and a *tazza* like No. 39, to be discussed below. The tomb is well provided with Base-Ring juglets of early Types 857 and 859 and with Red Lustrous flasks; it is further dated by scarabs of Thothmes III. No. 37 contained black oily matter which proved on analysis to contain manganese dioxide, one of many ingredients to be found in kohl.

Pl. 26: 41, also from Tomb 216, has a baggy body not unlike the forms of MB II–III, though it is elongated in outline and was originally provided with a loop handle.

Pl. 26: 46, 47 both came from tombs in Cemetery 500 which were used up to the end of the thirteenth century. While the former is not exactly matched, No. 47 is well attested in Egypt as a xixth dynasty form (FFSV, Pl. XXXVI: 918). In Palestine it can also be found in Stratum IVb at 'Ain Shems.

No. 48 is a fragment of good-quality calcite from the tell surface, incised with a design of lotus petals originally filled in with blue. It may be compared with a tubular vase from Egypt (FFSV, Pl. XXXIII: 842 and pp. 12–13). Petrie considered that such decoration dates from the end of the xviiith dynasty.

Pl. 27: 1 illustrates part of a large collection of calcite fragments from Tomb 108, probably dating from the late fourteenth or thirteenth centuries (see L. III, p. 188). Such pieces were rather common among the burnt debris of Level VI on the mound. Also in Tomb 108 were fragments of other stone vases made of marble or serpentine (NP) which are also in the Palestine Archaeological Museum (PM. 34: 111).

Tazze (Pl. 26: 32, 39; NE 32/24 on p. 53)

Of two *tazze* or goblets from the tombs, No. 39 with plain sides from Tomb 216 is the earlier form. An excellent parallel comes from D. 114 at Abydos (*Cemeteries* II, Pl. X: 6), which has already provided comparisons for the kohl pot No. 37 from the same group. A date no later than the reign of Thothmes III, *c.* 1450 B.C., is therefore appropriate.

In his discussion of these forms, Petrie goes on to remark that the midrib on the side of the *tazza* made its appearance about the reign of Thothmes IV, continuing under those of Amenhetep III and Rameses II (FFSV, p. 12), a conclusion which is in keeping with the Duweir evidence.

The minute *tazza* No. 32 (diameter 5 cms.) from Locus 554 about midway in this range shows an incipient midrib and a rounded base. The advanced form is illustrated from the Section Level VI (No. 24 on p. 53). Other fragments of this type with a disk base were recovered from Tomb 547 (NP). Small *tazze* on stands made in pottery were found in Tomb 532 (Pl. 72: 640–641).

The rim section of a goblet or *tazza* came from the west section in disturbed debris of Level III (L. III, pp. 75–76).

These *tazze* are fully discussed by Dr. I. Ben-Dor in QDAP XI, pp. 105–106. Both in material and shape, the Duweir examples prove to be imported from Egypt, and the site has not produced any *tazze* of his Type IV, which are without exception of local Palestinian gypsum.

Double Spoon (Pl. 26: 43)

Part of a double spoon with handle comes from Tomb 556. Open single spoons of the same general character are dated to the xviiith dynasty in Egypt (FFSV, Pl. XXXV: 886–895). No. 43 may belong to the end of that period or to the early xixth dynasty.

Stopper (Pl. 26: 44)

A pyramidal stopper from Tomb 1006 is the only one from Duweir, though it is closely matched from an unspecified context at Ajjul.

Bone and Shell

Inlay (Pl. 28: 1–4, 8, 10–12, 17, 18)

Pl. 28: 1 illustrates a group of thin bone slips from Tomb 6028, among which the Egyptian *zed* sign and stylized birds are prominent. Other pieces incised with dot and circle and with lines came from Tombs 119, 555 and 121 (Pl. 28: 2–4, 17), which cover late MB II or III, while plain pieces without incisions of any kind are found in LB contexts (Pl. 28: 8, 10–12).

It has long been known that such inlays were set in wooden caskets, and a complete example with sliding lids was found at Lahun in a group of the early xviiith dynasty (*Sedment* II, Pl. XLVIII: 6), while at Sedment itself bone slips were found in graves of the xvith dynasty (*Sedment* I, register on Pl. XLVI).

There is no reason to propose an Egyptian origin for this inlay, for it is to be found on most Palestinian sites. At Gezer, for instance (*Gezer* II, pp. 247 ff., Fig. 398 and Pls. XXXIV, CXCV), Macalister considered that it ranged throughout the history of the site, but see Albright (AASOR XVII, § 56). At Ajjul (AG I, Pl.

XXIII; II, Pl. XXIV; III, Pl. XXIX; IV, Pl. XXXVII) bone inlay was especially common, which should be contemporary with or later than the construction of the fosse in the seventeenth century.

That some mutual influence exists between the makers of these boxes and the bichrome pottery is suggested by the decoration of a jar from Tomb 1517 at Ajjul, which also contained a "togglepin" of Type 7 (p. 80) (AG IV, Pl. XLIV: 9). It shows very similar birds with the eyes represented by a dot and circle in metopes of opposed diagonal hatching. The eyes are so marked on most of the birds on these inlays at Ajjul, and the same may be said of Megiddo, where inlays are confined to Strata XII–IX. It is important to note that they are almost always associated with burials and in Strata XII–X about half the examples illustrated came from Structural Tombs (M. II, Pls. 192–194). The lack of eyes on the birds from Duweir suggests degeneration and the best comparison for Pl. 28: 1 is found in Stratum IX (M. II, Pl. 195: 15). In the tombs at Megiddo, these inlays are introduced in MB II (MT, p. 186 and Pls. 108–109, 111, 113: 18), and the same technique and tradition continues into LB I (MT, Pls. 145: 2 and 152: 14). It is perhaps significant that the best collections (MT, Pls. 108–109) both came from Tomb 42, which is a bilobate chamber (MT, Fig. 50 on p. 50). The pottery in the group includes a White Painted V jug (MT, Pl. 24: 3) suggesting a date very close to LB I.

Fragments of inlay are to be found in the bilobate tombs at Tell Fara (BP I, Pl. XI) and from those of Cemetery 1000 at that site (BP, Pl. XLIV).

At Tell Beit Mirsim quantities of bone inlay, mostly decorated with simple rectilinear designs, were found in Strata E–D, but from the notes on the subject it seems that pieces from certain D provenances were in the majority, though the excavator suggests that "most of the pieces in clear D context come from boxes which had been handed down for . . . generations" (AASOR XVII, §§ 56–58). However, Professor Albright equates bone inlay referred to phase D¹ "with high probability" and pieces found on native marl at Ajjul (AJSLL, p. 349). There are no birds shown among these fragments, a lack which is matched by the absence of bichrome ware at Tell Beit Mirsim (see above, pp. 64 f.).

All our evidence goes to show that these boxes came into use no earlier than MB III, say about 1700 B.C., and they were still being made up to the early reigns of the xviiith dynasty, but no later.

There are also comparisons from Asia Minor; for a summary of the use of the dotted circle as a decorative motif with widespread distribution in the Near East and a broad chronological range see *Troy* II, pp. 16 ff.

The reappearance of this motif is to be seen in Iron Age deposits at Duweir and elsewhere (L. III, pp. 381–383).

Spacers

Pl. 28: 5 and 6 are pierced plaques of bone which may be spacers for bead necklaces or possibly belt fasteners, as Petrie has suggested, for one example was in position on the hip bone of a body (AG IV, p. 11 and AG III, Pl. XLIX, Grave 305). See also the same shape, undecorated, at Gezer (*Gezer* III, Pl. CXXXII: 13, 23).

Wands or Spindles

Pl. 28: 7, 13, 14 and 15 are all parts of wands or spindles, which were a feature of Structure III of the Fosse Temple (L. II, Pl. XX: 23–28 and p. 62). They differ only in the ends, which have incised bands and no cross hatching, which may be a thirteenth- rather than a fourteenth-century detail, to which the examples from Tombs 216 and 501 probably belong. This point is emphasized by the similar material from Megiddo, mostly from Strata VIII–VI, which is more highly decorated than the Duweir examples (M. II, Pl. 197; MT, Pl. 84 and p. 171, Fig. 175).

Comb

Pl. 28: 16 is the greater part of a comb, which happens to be the only one recovered from Duweir. It may stand midway between such combs as those from Sedment (*Sedment* I, Pl. XLII: 2; II, Pl. LX: 28, 48) of the xvith and xviiith dynasties, and similar combs which belong to the xixth dynasty (ODU, Pl. XX: 8).

Whorls and Ring

Pl. 28: 9 is a whorl or more probably a button, from the small size of the hole. Comparisons are numerous elsewhere, especially in the LB II tombs at Megiddo (MT, Pl. 84: 3–6 and *passim*), where the use of two such whorls in a spindle is clearly shown (op. cit., Pl. 84: 1). Petrie suggests that they could have been used as buttons (AG I, Pl. XXIII: 13 and p. 8). A whorl of a different shape is made of stone (Pl. 26: 40).

Pl. 28: 19 is a cushion-shaped whorl, pierced, while Nos. 20–21 are of the same shape though unpierced. No. 21 is finished with a bronze rivet and both are decorated. All three came from Tomb 538. It has been suggested that similar pieces from Megiddo were furniture inlay (MT, Pl. 130: 6–7), but this explanation could not apply to some unpierced whorls from Gezer which are decorated on both sides (*Gezer* III, Pl. CXXXII: 44–48). With Nos. 19–21 there was a shell ring (Pl. 28: 22), for which there are Iron Age parallels at Duweir (L. III, p. 240 and Pl. 57: 43).

Ivory (Pl. 48: 4, 6)

Pl. 48: 4 is a carved leopard's head with truncated neck, pierced through below the chin, perhaps part of a piece of furniture or a box. It is a less common motif than the duck's head, Pl. 48: 6. The latter will have belonged to an ivory spoon like those illustrated in L. II, Pl. XX: 21–22, and a similar head came from Structure III (L. II, Pl. XVII: 10 and p. 61). Spoons with this terminal are common in Egyptian wall paintings of the xviiith dynasty and the example here illustrated should date to about 1400 B.C.

Beads and Shells (Pl. 29)

Middle and Late Bronze Age

Apart from the deposit in Cave 1513 (EB III–IV and later), there are no pottery groups which can be placed entirely in the first phase of the Middle Bronze Age, which includes at least part of the xiith dynasty, when beads were varied and popular in Egypt, and when links with Palestine and Syria were strong (p. 32).

In fact, less than thirty beads were recovered from all MB tombs prior to Tomb 4004, and of these half came from Tomb 6027, which is also late in the series. Pl. 29: 2, 5, 6, 15 and 21 were the only forms.

Tomb 4004 (Pl. 27: 4–9) presents the largest and most varied collection of beads. Besides seven well-polished long-barrel carnelians, there are others (Pl. 29: 5) which are only roughly cut, and the proportion of these becomes much greater in the succeeding Tomb 216 (Pl. 29: 6 and Pl. 54: 9), while the size tends to become smaller in Tomb 1003. A few pale amethyst beads in Tomb 4004 are reminders of the xiith-dynasty popularity of this material, well matched in the Second Intermediate period, 1785–1580 B.C. (QB III, Tomb 7578, beads NP. Department of Egyptology, University College, London).

Outnumbering stone beads by five to one, paste is the most common material, and new and distinctive shapes are notched and gadrooned (Pl. 29: 32–41). Examples of No. 41 were found in the Maket tomb at Kahun, dated to the reign of Thothmes III, and the same group produced oblate disks like Pl. 29:1 (IKG, Pl. XXVI: 16, 17). Glass beads appear in Tomb 4004; they are either light blue in colour like the figurine (Pl. 27: 2) or they are mottled black and white in imitation of stone. Glass eye-beads are found in Egypt during the xviiith dynasty (Beck, Fig. 56).

Large and small multiple segmented beads in light glass (?) and paste are found in the interlapping series of Tombs 4004, 555, 216, 1003, 4002, and 4013 (Pl. 29: 27–28), fifteenth to thirteenth centuries. They also occur in all three structures of the Fosse Temple (L. II, Pl. XXXV: 67–68). In their paper on the British and European faience beads Dr. J. F. S. Stone and the late Horace Beck discussed the similarity of the beads from Tomb 555 with those from Europe (*Arch.* LXXXV, 1936, p. 225). On seeing the beads from the other groups, Dr. Stone confirmed that they differed in perforation from the beads in Tomb 555.

With Base-Ring and Mycenaean imports and their imitations, gadrooned disks (Pl. 29: 42) in red, yellow and blue glaze are found in Cave 4002. They compare with Tell el-Amarna beads (cf. L. II, Pl. XXXV: 47 and Pl. XIV) and they include the typical lotus-seed vessel of the period (Pl. 29: 43). The last groups in the series to contain beads in any quantity are Tombs 556, 538, 559 and 508 (Pl. 55: 16). The beads are made of poor-quality paste or stone, and carnelian is rare.

Mr. Baden-Powell tentatively identified a tropical shell, *Mitra oniscina* and individuals of *Pectunculus*, *Planaxis*, *Potamides* and *Conus* Sp. among shells buried as ornaments in LB tombs. Some species prove derivation from the Red Sea area, while a few cowries, probably *Cypraea annulus*, are almost certainly from the south, like the same species which become popular in the Iron Age (L. III, p. 400). For Mr. Baden-Powell's report, see Appendix B.

Amulets

Plate 29:

Debased hand: 51	*Thoth*: 63	*Taurt*: 58, 66
Aegis of Bast: 59	*Fish*: 60, 61	*Head*: 64
Ptah Sokar: 52, 54, 55, 62, 65	*Uzat*: 56, 57, 67, 68	*Bes*: 53

Apart from the debased hand (or fly?) amulet in Tomb 1552, which could be as early as the ixth dynasty in Egypt, no amulets were found before the occupation of Tomb 4004, and it is probable that the pair of red glaze sacred eyes and the small figure of Taurt belonged to late burials. The Ptah-Sokar and Bes amulets in Cave 4002 could have belonged to Iron Age burials (L. III, pp. 239 ff.). For Dr. M. A. Murray's identification of amulets, see L. III, pp. 379–381 and Pls. 34–36.

Clay Figurines and Objects

Anthropomorphic Jar (Pl. 48: 5, 7–9; Pl. 86: 1005)

The fragments of this unique vessel were found scattered over a wide area (7013) with many other burnished and painted sherds of the Late Bronze Age, and two Iron Age forms (L. III, pp. 62–63 and 254).

The body is wheel-made in two sections, of which the upper part represents the tapering neck, to which a mask of hand-modelled clay was affixed. The beard or cravat in the centre was another addition.

The ware is pink, softly fired with a black core in parts, containing much lime grits and straw. The buff surface is vertically pared and burnished.

The eyebrows and lashes were incised and painted black, and the same paint was used to emphasise the pupils and lower lids and to indicate a thin moustache. The jowl was painted red, like the remaining part of the cravat, and there were traces of black and red bands around the neck. Low on the body there was a further design of a zigzag between red bands.

Holes were provided where the shoulders should be and extra clay was then added to simulate them, though there is nothing to show how they were finished.

With regard to the racial type portrayed, it is interesting to recall that Sir Arthur Keith in his article on *The Men of Lachish* (PEQ, 1940, pp. 7–12) made a racial diagnosis from his personal observation of the population of the Delta and the neighbouring part of Palestine at the time at which he wrote. Among them he observed individuals "who represented a type which was of smaller build, with less decided features, and of a darker, almost black complexion; and this type is narrow-headed". He went on to suggest that it might represent a remnant of the Philistines and the people who inhabited Lachish. Two characters were noted by Mr. Risdon in the Lachish people (*Biometrika* XXXI, Parts I, II, July 1939) which Sir Arthur observed are non-Egyptian, "namely narrowness and prominence of the bridge of the nose and the curvature of the cheekbones".

These features are outstanding in the modelling of the head under discussion. The small moustache and the thick eyebrows meeting on the bridge of the nose are also characteristic of individuals who were living in south Palestine until 1947.

Rattles (Pl. 28: 24–26)

Pl. 28: 24 and 25 show two jug-shaped rattles both from Tomb 1003 and therefore probably not later than 1400 B.C. A rattle like No. 24 is included with White Painted V ware in Cyprus (SPC, pp. 173–174), which comes to an end at the same time. A reasonable comparison for No. 26 came from Tell Zakariya (BM, Pl. 45: 8), though it had no handle. There is little to show that rattles became common in the Bronze Age, and the shape is not standardised, though several varieties appear to concentrate in the thirteenth century or later (cf. M. II, Pl. 255: 5, Stratum VI A). For other references see MRMC, pp. 25–26. For Iron Age rattles see L. III, Pls. 27–28 and p. 376.

Mould and Figurines (Pls. 48: 1–3; 49: 1–5)

Pl. 48: 1 is part of a mould from a surface area of the head and shoulders of a goddess. Nos. 2–3 show impressions from the mould, full face and profile. The nose is prominent and the lips are pursed above a receding chin. The arms are apparently bent to support the breasts, but at this point the mould breaks off. The head-dress and ornaments are more elaborately shown than is usual on such mould-pressed figurines. The lady wears a bandeau with a central medallion, while the hair is dressed in tight curls, though a loose ringlet or ribbon hangs to one side. Hathor horns are shown rising from the head with a plume or ornament between, and there is a necklace round the neck with pendent streamers. The mould should represent a much Semitised version of the goddess Hathor-Astarte, for which close parallels are hard to find in published material.

Pl. 49: 1 is a mould-pressed nude figurine of more orthodox Astarte type from Tomb 571. It seems to have been spoilt in the making, for both face and breasts are flattened and anklets are the only visible details.

Pl. 49: 2–5 illustrate an important group from the potter's workshop, Cave 4034, for they show that such figurines were made on the premises. No. 2 is part of a mould, No. 3 is the lower half of an unbaked figurine, the details of which did not turn out too plainly from the mould, and the same may be said for the baked figure No. 5.

Pl. 49: 4 is far more successful, comparing most favourably in style and delicacy with other figurines of the Qadesh class, of which the best parallels come from Tell Beit Mirsim Stratum C (see *Mélanges Syriens* I, pp. 116–118 and Figs. A: 1, B: 2–4). Some of them wear anklets, like No. 4, though it should be noted that they do not hold such long-stalked flowers or emblems in their hands. Unlike Nos. 1, 3 and 5, which are rounded or oval in section, the plaque No. 4 is well finished and knife-pared on the flat back and sides, which are 1·6 cms. in depth.

Such clay and terra-cotta figurines cannot here be discussed in detail, in view of the amount that has been written on the subject. References to earlier studies are to be found in Professor Albright's article in *Mélanges Syriens* quoted above, and Iron Age material is summarised in *Material Remains of the Megiddo Cult* by H. G. May. For Iron Age figurines from Duweir, see L. III, pp. 374–375.

Potters' Tools and Equipment

The existence of a local pottery industry at Tell ed-Duweir from at least Chalcolithic times is supported by the discovery of the Kiln 1525 (p. 263 and Fig. 11).

In the last phases of the Early Bronze Age on the mound itself, there was a definite living level at 8 feet in the Section where a potter had worked (pp. 44, 57).

Not far from the city gate, in a popular industrial quarter (L. III, Pl. 126, Grid A. 26. Pit 563 on p. 247), there were the remains of a kiln or oven where a basalt socket, Pl. 21: 1, was found. The upper surface is flat and polished from rotary use, and the conical cup in the centre is also shiny. The proportions of the stone and socket are complementary to those of the tenon stone from Cave 4034 (Pl. 49: 12) to be discussed below, though there can of course be no actual connexion between them. The hemispherical underside is pitted with the even marks of the tool used in its construction and the maximum depth is 10·8 cms. The date of the pit and its few

UTENSILS, WEAPONS AND ORNAMENTS

contents cannot be fixed precisely within the limits of MB–LB, though one towards the end of the period is more likely.

Cave 4034: tools and equipment of the thirteenth century B.C.

The layout of Cave 4034 and the range of its occupation as a potter's workshop are discussed on pp. 291–293, illustrated on Pl. 92. A cave is a sensible and usual location for the craft in eastern climates to this day, for a lower temperature, permitting slower drying, is more easily maintained, and the same conditions were certainly required in antiquity. For a comparable cave, used as a potter's workshop towards the end of the first millennium, see C. S. Fisher, *The Excavation of Armageddon*, p. 49.

It remains to describe the materials, tools and equipment which were left *in situ*. Of the potter's raw materials there were heaps of prepared clay and of crushed lime and shell. Scattered about the cave and especially in Pit A there were lumps of red and yellow substance (p. 140) and sherds on which the colours had been ground (Pl. 49: 10).

In Pit A, between 1 and 2 metres from the top (Pl. 92, Section E–F), two stones were found which are photographed on Pl. 49: 12–13. One is of basalt, the other of mizzi limestone. The upper surface of each is highly polished and has a raised knob in the centre, though the underside is only roughly hewn. They appear to have been bearings for two separate foot-operated fly-wheels, and each would be the upper of the two parts of the lower bearing, with the tenon pointing down. In neither case has the socketed member been preserved, which was set in the ground, and the nature of the overhang in Pit A shows that the upper bearings could not have been worked in the position where they were found. For an account of the potter's wheel in the ancient east, see *Technology*, pp. 195–204.

Stone sockets and tenons of the same hard stones are to be found on other sites, notably at Tell el-Ajjul (AG I, Pl. LII: 10 and p. 11 and AG V, Pl. XX: 48, 49) and at Megiddo, where an early example is recorded from Stratum XV (M. II, Pl. 268: 3). They are also found in the tomb area, though it appears significant that in every case the location is actually a large irregularly shaped cave, bearing features in common with the Duweir workshop as to holes and depressions and even to deep pits approached by stairs (e.g. MT, Pl. 153: 11 (2 ex.) T.4 and p. 101; Pl. 154: 13, T.26 and p. 103; Pl. 157: 17, T.59A and pp. 106–108). The layout of Cave 63 is especially instructive (MT, pp. 108–111 and Fig. 132) and the scarcity of bones, together with such contents as the tournette (?) (MT, Pl. 158: 19) and the "feluccas" (Pl. 158: 1 and *passim*) discussed in the Introduction, p. 7, make it very likely that these large caves were used for pottery making. For similar worn templates from Cave 4034, see three pieces illustrated on Pl. 49: 15. Iron Age equivalents with pierced central holes are shown in L. III (Pl. 41: 12, 14; Pl. 58: 2) from Cave 6024, p. 250, where it was suggested that they were used in weaving. They would be practical adjuncts in either industry.

Pit A also produced a small mortar used for grinding red ochre (Pl. 49: 14), and set at the foot of the stairs in Pit B there was a stone mortar or trough about 50 cms. in diameter.

Pl. 49: 15 includes a selection of small tools, pebbles and shells, well worn and polished from use, and a bone point, probably used as an incising tool or for the removal of irregular clay from pieces on the wheel; all of which were obvious assets in a potter's kit. There were also a great number of sherds irregularly shaped and worn about the edge.

Mr. G. C. Griffiths, who has examined pottery from both the Fosse Temple and the workshop, observed ample evidence in the centre of the bowls of some hard material "used as a 'rib' to regularize interior centre shaping and the numerous shaped sherds and shells suggest that the potter used them on account of the coarse nature of the clay and the abundance of lime and shell particles (grit), which would be very rough on the hands". Notes on these and other tools used in pot-making are to be found in *Technology*, p. 390.

91

CHAPTER 7

HIEROGLYPHIC AND ORNAMENTAL SEALS

SCARABS

General Notes

COMPARISONS for the scarabs and seals have been sought in the main works on the subject, Newberry's *Scarabs* and Petrie's *Hyksos and Israelite Cities*, both published in 1906. These studies were followed by Hall's *Catalogue of Egyptian Scarabs in the British Museum* (1913), Petrie's *Scarabs and Cylinders with Names* (1917) and his *Buttons and Design Scarabs* (1925) and Rowe's *Catalogue of Egyptian Scarabs in the Palestine Archaeological Museum* (1936). This last work reproduces the scarabs from Duweir, which were chosen by the Department of Antiquities before the date of publication. See RES numbers in the list of plate descriptions beginning on p. 113.

An analytical study of Egyptian and Palestinian scarabs is to be found in *La Fin du Moyen Empire Egyptien* by Raymond Weill (1918). He divides "Hyksos" scarabs into four well-differentiated periods, though each is closely linked to the next (Weill II, p. 729).

Dr. M. A. Murray has written on Palestinian scarabs in PEQ, 1948–1949, pp. 95 ff., and proposes a reading for the group of signs which Weill read as "Anra" and placed in the first period of "Hyksos" scarabs (Weill I, pp. 191 ff. and II, p. 785).

Also of value for comparative purposes are the seals and sealings from Uronarti, discovered by Reisner and published in the *Bulletin of the Museum of Fine Arts, Boston*, XXVIII (1930), pp. 47–55, which date from the early part of the xiiith dynasty.

For advice in the preparation of the plate descriptions, this work is much indebted to the generous help of Dr. M. A. Murray and of Mr. Alan Rowe. Notes on the Cylinder Seals, pp. 111 f., Nos. 163–165 and 323, are the work of Dr. Edith Porada and Miss Barbara Parker.

Among nearly 400 engraved scarabs from Duweir, more than half came from large groups which, on the evidence of the pottery and other objects, date from the latter part of MB II and from MB III, say between 1800–1600 B.C. and also from LB I–II.

That time was one of change and resettlement in Palestine; the earlier kings of the xiith dynasty of Egypt, whose names are widespread on scarabs and other monuments in Syria and Palestine, had given place to a period of divided control under lesser monarchs of the xiiith and xivth dynasties.

About 1700 B.C. an incoming Asiatic or "Hyksos" power occupied southern Palestine, using it most probably as a base from which they subdued the Delta region, as a preliminary to the conquest of Egypt and the establishment of rule under their own kings of the xvth dynasty. Revival of Theban initiative less than a century later ultimately secured the expulsion of the foreigners by the founder of the xviiith dynasty. From that point onwards Palestine formed part of the Egyptian empire and the degree of control can be readily traced from the royal names to be discussed below.

The earlier centuries which most concern us here still present a complex and unresolved problem, summarised below according to present opinion on the interrelation of dynasties and dates as given by W. Hayes in *The Scepter of Egypt* (1953). They are referred to the phases of the Middle and Late Bronze Age period in Palestine, as defined by Schaeffer and adopted in the present volume.

The condition of the burials precludes any stratigraphic record of the contents; Tomb 4004, for instance, contained over 150 scarabs, ranging from the xiiith to the xixth dynasties, compressed within a black layer only 30 cms. in depth (Fig. 14 on p. 282).

Pls. 30–40 present the scarabs and seals in line drawing and, whenever possible, in photograph; relevant descriptions follow at the end of this section. The side types are drawn on Pl. 41 and the comparable numbers in Rowe's catalogue are noted opposite the plate. The scarabs from each tomb are shown together in a group, while the order of the larger tombs, as established by the pottery in them, is to be seen on the Consolidated Chart, pp. 222 f., and the position of the smaller tombs is related to them on p. 67.

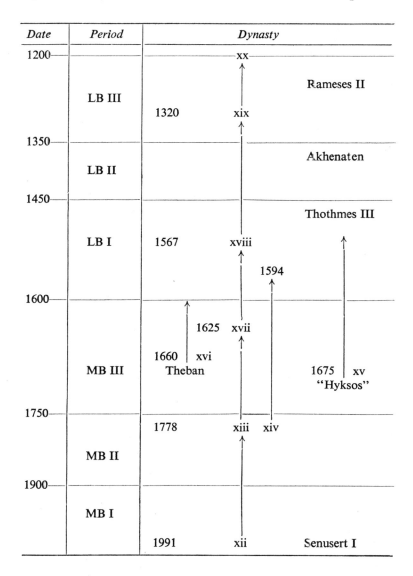

In the notes which follow, the subdivisions have been made according to motif and style, except for such obvious headings as the first on Royal Names. The only group containing scarabs which may perhaps be isolated stratigraphically is in Tomb 157, which appears to have been deposited in a rock cavity once covered by the MB glacis, though at the time of discovery most of that fill had fallen into the fosse below. The inventory of those scarabs is more fully described under Date and Comparisons. In cases where scarabs have names and one or more outstanding motifs, the number is listed under each relevant head.

Royal Names and Official Titles

Dynasties		Dynasties	
xii	126, 347	xv–xvi	63, 64, 90, 91, 101, 104, 105, 134, 139–141, 196, 267
xiii–xv	3, 5, 23, 26, 35–37, 135, 251	xiv–early xviii	1, 2, 4, 83, 93, 106, 117, 123, 142, 145, 186, 188, 189, 327

Scarabs bearing royal or pseudo-royal names enclosed in a cartouche or accompanied by royal emblems belonging to the period before the xviiith dynasty, present many problems in the interpretation of the hieroglyphs, and few among them have been satisfactorily read or identified. If they are copies of misunderstood signs, which appears unlikely from the excellence of the work, then they may represent the use of hieroglyphs by a non-Egyptian people for the transcription of their own language.

Dynasty xii

The earliest royal scarab from Duweir presents the sun name of Senusert I, second king of the xiith dynasty. No. 126 may be of Egyptian rather than local make, if Weill's suggestion is accepted that the terminal of the *kā* arms is open on the former and closed to a circle in "Hyksos" type scarabs (e.g. Nos. 23, 26, 104, etc., and Weill II, p. 730), but compare the arm terminals of scarabs of Senusert I in Egypt, which are more usually closed than open (PSC, Pl. XII).

The presence of Senusert's name at Gaza (Level III), Megiddo (Stratum X) and Beisan (Level IX or XI A), and as far north as Ras Shamra (RS II) has already been noted by Schaeffer and he includes in his list a scarab of Senusert I from Tell Beit Mirsim (Strata G–F), but this has not been traced in AASOR publications (*Stratigraphie*, p. 188).

Unfortunately, neither No. 126 nor No. 347 with the same name were found in a good context at Duweir. No. 126 came from a quarry and No. 347 was found in a burial pit where most of the contents date to the late xviiith dynasty. The question of re-use of xiith dynasty names by kings of the "Hyksos" period is discussed below and on p. 110.

Dynasties xiii–xv

No. 3 is encased in gold; Rowe described it as follows (RES 109):

"This case is made in two pieces, one with a small turned up rim, covering the base portion, and the other covering the back and the upper part of the sides. The foil was lightly beaten or pressed over the scarab itself so as to take the impression of the latter. In about the centre of the wings is a vertical bow-shaped hole for a green-stone inlay, made both through the casing and in the surface of the steatite below. *c.* xivth dyn."

Incised in the scarab and impressed in the gold casing among other signs are the titles "King of Upper and Lower Egypt". Rowe compares a title *ne Nekhen* ("he who belongs to Hieraconpolis") of Amenemhat III, but this was questioned by Newberry in a personal communication.

No. 5—*Rā-men-ka*, cf. Gauthier II, p. 116. An earlier king of the same name appears in op. cit. I, p. 181. Following the name on the scarab is an inverted *nesew* ("king of Upper Egypt" see RES 58 for comparisons). The side type 53 is a usual one for a harder quality of stone than the normal light steatite.

No. 23 (RES 26) and No. 26 (RES 30) may, in Rowe's opinion, bear variants of the sun name (*Rā-khā-ka*) of Neferhetep II. The side types 11 and 16 of these two scarabs tend to place them in the middle rather than in the early range of the Duweir series, contemporary perhaps with the occupation of Tomb 153. Weill suggests that the desert princes found it expedient as Kings of Upper Egypt to adopt sun names of their Egyptian predecessors; among the names of obscure kings which he records at that period is one Khakare (Weill II, p. 535). See also the three-column arrangement of hieroglyphs on scarabs of Khyan and Anther (Ontha) (PSC, Pl. XXI: 15. 1, 15. 3 and Weill II, p. 825).

Nos. 35, 36 and 37 are all from Tomb 129, which may have received burials over a long period. Nos. 35 and 36, however, present the best examples of the scroll border from the site. The name in the cartouche on No. 35 resembles Canaanite rather than hieroglyphic script; it should be compared for the scroll border with a scarab

94

of the same style, which reads *Ka-kheper-Rā* in the cartouche (Weill II, p. 745: 19), a name which Weill finds in Egypt and in Palestine, and which he would attribute to a "Hyksos" king rather than to Senusert I of the xiith dynasty. No. 36 is also comparable for the scrolls and for the signs within the upper loop, replaced on No. 35 by two *nefer* signs. These also appear within the cartouche on No. 36. Cf. also No. 142. For the use of two *nefer* signs to represent *Rā* in scarabs of Senusert I, see RES 149 and PSC, p. 19; the scarabs shown in the latter work, Pl. XII: 16–18, bear the hooked scroll as found in xiiith dynasty contexts at Uronarti (BMFA XXVIII, 1930, pp. 47–55).

No. 37 is a partially broken scarab, which can be restored to read "priest who has admittance to Nekhebet, Iew-ef-ne the Venerable" (RES 50). Rowe lists other persons named Iew-ef-ne of the xii–xivth dynasties.

No. 135 from the slopes of the north-east corner of the mound gives the sun name of Sebekhetep VI (dyn. xiii?), for which a parallel exists in Stratum XI at Megiddo. See Petrie, HE I, p. 219, Fig. 130 and HS No. 322; Newberry, NS, Pl. x: 16 for other scarabs of this king.

No. 251 from Tomb 4004 appears to be of xiiith dynasty origin from the delicate cutting of the hieroglyphs (cf. PSC, Pl. XVI: AJ, AV). The following translation and notes are due to the courtesy of Mr. Alan Rowe; the scarab was found after the publication of his catalogue and is therefore not included there.

"Overseer of the provisions (*dfa*) of the Temple of Ḥāpy (Nile-God), Khemem the Venerable." For the temple cf. "Temple of Ḥāpy of the South", Gauthier, *Dict. Géog.* IV, p. 100. Khemem is found as a Middle Kingdom name in H. Ranke, *Die Ägyptischen Personennamen*, 1935, p. 269.

Dynasties xv-xvi

Nos. 63 and 64 are both from Tomb 4022 which, on the evidence of the pottery, seems to be placed about the time of the construction of the MB defences. Associated with them was No. 65 bearing the royal emblems of South and North.

No. 63 bears a name enclosed in a cartouche which Rowe would read as *Rā-khā-kheper*, a late form of the name of Senusert II (cf. RES 10). If so, it is not in its true archaeological context, but the writing of the first sign (or signs?) is by no means clear.

No. 64 is of exceptional interest. The central figure sits on a high-backed chair. The head is seen in profile, but the shoulders are presented front view; the right arm is bent and raised to shoulder level. The dress apparently consists of a long bordered garment reaching below the knee, and it is attached at or draped over the left shoulder. Around the figure are seven signs, of which the three behind the chair are read by Rowe as *it neter* "father of the god" (a priest). For the equivalent of the sign used with *neter* see RES, p. x. Immediately above these three signs is the *uas* sceptre. In front of the figure is a sign, *khā* (?), below the arm is a *nefer* and under the chair is a *Rā* sign.

There are numerous parallels for the wrapped garment: BDS, Pl. XV: 985, attributed by Petrie to the Middle Kingdom period, shows a large standing figure, dressed in a garment of this kind confronted by a kneeling suppliant, cf. the figure on No. 72 from Duweir.

Figures similarly dressed associated with *uraei* (AG IV, Pl. XI: 395; V, Pl. IX: 35, 36), or with *nefer* signs (AG V, Pl. IX: 37) are found at Tell el-Ajjul, and Tomb 569 at Tell Fara (BP I, Pl. XII: 20) which contained close pottery links with our series.

A specially fine figure with quasi-alphabetical signs came from Jericho Tomb 13 layer c (AAA XX, Pl. XXVI: 6, also p. 37, Fig. 11 and RES 154).

Petrie considered that these figures portrayed the Hittite overlords of the "Hyksos" rulers (AG V, p. 7), and Rowe queried whether the Jericho scarab represented a Canaanite king. It is also worth considering whether these figures do not portray the "Hyksos" rulers themselves. In any case, these wrapped garments would be the kind of dress which might be effectively secured at the shoulder by a "toggle-pin" (pp. 79 ff.).

Nos. 90, 91 and 101 are all from Tomb 157, before the construction of the MB defences. No. 90 (RES 168) might be a corruption of a royal name, *Rā-āa-ḥetep*, but Newberry in correspondence was unable to accept this reading. For a continuous scroll and an oval enclosure of the signs see Weill II, p. 750. The signs themselves belong to his Anra period, in which several groups are preceded by *hetep* (Weill I, p. 192). No. 91 (RES 179) gives the title "treasurer of the King of Lower Egypt, Neferewy-āa". Less possibly the name might read *Rā-āa*, cf. RES No. 15 of Preface, item (10), and No. 90 above. No. 101 (RES 153) may perhaps contain the name of *Rā-āa-khā*.

Nos. 104 and 105 are from the bilobate tomb 153 at Duweir, which belongs, in the pottery sequence, to about the time of the construction of the MB defences.

No. 104 (RES 21) contains a name in the cartouche which Rowe suggests may be a version of that of Sebek-hetep III of the xiiith dynasty. On the other hand, he points out that Gauthier (II, p. 97, No. 4) also mentions a supposed later king of this name, *Rā-ne-khā-neferewy*, whose name is the same as that on the scarab, and a context later than the xiiith dynasty would be more consistent with the pottery in the group and with side type 11. Repeated on each side of the cartouche are signs which may possibly read "treasurer of the work of the spelt".

No. 105 (RES 215) like the majority of scarabs in Tomb 153 conforms to side type 11. Both Rowe and Murray agree that the signs in the cartouche are a variant of the *Rā-ne-Rā* or "Anra" group.

Nos. 134 and 139, with side types 8 and 7, are from open areas. No. 134 should date from the xvith dynasty on the analogy of the concentric circles (cf. No. 105), while No. 139, with the name *Rā-āa-hetep*, enclosed in a rather poor hook-scroll border, can be attributed to the xv–xvith dynasties. Weill places a king of that name in Group I, comprising names of the second "Hyksos" period (Weill II, p. 868: 14).

No. 140, from Tomb 4004, introduces a name which is also well matched in the style of the unconnected hook-scroll border at other sites, notably at Gaza. Weill mentions more than twenty examples, and he assigns the name somewhat tentatively to his "Anra" group. He places scarabs of *Pepy* (or *Sheshi*) in Group K with or just after those of the second period (Group I–J) of "Hyksos" scarabs (Weill I, pp. 193 ff.; II, p. 878). Both Petrie and Rowe attribute similar scarabs to the xvith dynasty. The reading *Pepa* is preferred by Petrie (PSC, Pl. XXI: 16. c heading) to *Shesha* or *Sheshi* (RES 204–207). Unfortunately the scarab cannot be attributed with any certainty to either of the three personages who are considered to have borne this name (CAH I, p. 313). Note the similarity of the hook-scroll border to a scarab of Khyan (NS, Pl. XXII: 26). Cf. also No. 267 below.

No. 141, the upper part of the group within an inferior hook-scroll border, reads: *Hetep-khā-hetep*, followed by *āa-em-neter*. Weill doubts whether scarabs with these and similar signs represent a royal name (Weill II, pp. 759 and 789 ff.). Rowe, on the other hand, would attribute them to a king of about the xvth dynasty (RES 166–176). No. 196, a cowroid, includes similar elements to No. 141.

No. 267 (cf. No. 140), with side type 37, may belong to a late bearer of the name *Pepy* or possibly *Sheshi*. In writing of a duplicate of this scarab from Tomb 491 at Gaza (AG IV, Pl. V: 17), Schaeffer (*Stratigraphie*, p. 165) notes that it was attributed by Otto to Apepa II and by Rowe to a successor, *Sheshi* (RES 205).

Dynasties xiv–early xviii, doubtful names

In addition to possible royal names listed above, there are certain defective or simplified versions of the sun name, which may represent a king or more possibly a good-wish motto. Nos. 1 and 2 (with the sun circle included in the border), 4 and 93 could read *Rā-kheper* (RES 158 and Weill II, p. 857: 16). Nos. 83, 117 and 145 could read *Rā-nefer* (RES 119 and Weill II, p. 855: 12) though a simple translation of this last would be "Happy Day". See also the scarab of Thothmes III, No. 286, where these signs appear in the field. No. 102 is read *Rā-wah* by Rowe and No. 327 contains a possible name *Wah-nefer-Rā* (RES 32).

Other variations are Nos. 186 and 188, both of which include *Rā-ka* as central signs; while No. 189 reads *ka-kheper-ka*. Nos. 188 and 189 are both cowroids, the backs of which compare with PSC, Pl. LXXI: 30, a type which bears the *Rā-kā* signs on the face. It is dated from the time of Apepa I (PSC, Pl. XX: AL, AM, AN; XXI: 15. 5. 12, 13), extending to the reign of Hatshepsut (op. cit., Pl. XXVI: 18. 5, 31) of the early xviiith dynasty.

Nos. 106 and 142 are similar. For the use of two *nefer* signs on the latter, see No. 35 and below.

No. 123 from Tomb 153 is allocated by Rowe to dynasty xiv on a reading of *Kheper-neb*, which he suggests may stand for *Rā-kheper-neb* (or *nebew*), Intef V, the *Rā* being represented by two *nefer* signs. See also under Royal Emblems.

From the perusal of over thirty scarabs, it will be seen that none can be attributed to a known historical figure, with the exception of Senusert I, subject to the reservations discussed below (p. 110).

Nevertheless, these many uncertainties may be due to our ignorance of the period and of the names and succession of the kings and petty princes who ruled in Lower Egypt and in Southern Palestine between the xiiith and the early xviiith dynasties.

Dynasty xviii	*Dynasties xix–xx*
Thothmes III: 173, 281–286, 298, 299, 300, 301, 352	Rameses II: 358, 389
Amenhetep II: 287, 295, 317; N.E. Section, No. 88 on p. 53.	Rameses II contractions?: 243, 372, 380
Thothmes IV: 288, 300, 324, 344	Rameses III: 388
Amenhetep III: 128, 171, 208, 247, 289–294, 303, 304, 313, 314, 322, 338	Ramesside emblems: 343, 368
Ay: 351	Re-issues?: 266, 359, 379, 382
Horemheb: 357	Unknown: 127, 384

Dynasty xviii

There are no contemporary scarabs at Duweir of any xviiith dynasty king before those of the great conqueror of Syria, Thothmes III, though the founder of the dynasty, Aahmes I, is honoured by a Ramesside re-issue, No. 359. Thothmes did not launch his Syrian campaign until the last years of his reign in the mid-fifteenth century, and the prosperity and Syrian trade which that conquest brought to South Palestine should date from the latter half of the century. His scarabs occur in Tombs 4004 and 216, contemporary with his reign, while the last, No. 352, may commemorate his name. Those of his successors, Amenhetep II and Thothmes IV, are also represented, while scarabs of Amenhetep III are plentiful in Tomb 4004; they occur also in Tombs 216 and 501, and they are found in the last Structure of the Fosse Temple (L. II, Pl. XXXII).

However, Schaeffer has rightly observed a break in the deposits of Tomb 4004 between a Middle Bronze period and a Late Bronze Age reoccupation (*Stratigraphie*, p. 186), and, though this cannot have been long, a further interval during the fourteenth century would be consistent with the pottery.

The same author notes (op. cit., p. 137) that after the prosperous reign of Amenhetep III there were no scarabs of his immediate successors in Tomb 4004, and actually those same names are altogether missing from the cemeteries. It does not appear, however, that all contacts with Egypt were lost during the Amarna period, 1375–1360 B.C., cf. for instance the necklace which survived in Structure III (L. II, Pl. XIV).

A royal name to fill the following decade is that of Amen-Onkhs (L. II, Pl. XXXII: 10) on a scarab found in a pit of Structure III. It was presumably this queen who, on the death of Tutankhamen, appealed to the Hittite king to send her one of his sons as a consort, rather than marry an Egyptian commoner (Gurney, *The Hittites*, p. 31).

No. 351 from Tomb 4011 is a scarab of Ay and No. 357 from Tomb 4013 is of Horemheb, the general who, though not known to be of royal blood, gained the throne at the end of the xviiith dynasty. The reigns of these two kings extend from *c.* 1350–1320 B.C.

Unidentified possible names are No. 127, with highly decorated back, found with a scarab of Amenhetep III, and No. 384 in a gold mount.

Dynasties xix–xx

The reign of Seti I, who recovered Palestine and Jordan for the Empire, is not represented among the scarabs at Duweir, and the long reign of Rameses II, *c.* 1292–1225 B.C., is only marked by a scarab from Tomb 4013,

No. 358, and by another scarab from a surface area on the Tell (p. 132), No. 389, while there are certain contractions from smaller groups which are probably of his name, Nos. 372, 380.

Also in the vicinity of No. 389 was a scarab of Rameses III, No. 388; both were affected by the fire which destroyed the last Bronze Age city on the mound.

Quite the most common side types (on Pl. 41) for all these royal names were Nos. 22–23. Some re-issues can perhaps be detected by late side types, e.g. Nos. 266, 359 and 382 with side types 36, 38, 37.

Besides the scarabs there are several plaques bearing royal names and titles. No. 317 naming Amenhetep II is worthy of mention, though it does not come from a stratified context, for the detail of the designs which are inscribed on all four sides. It should be compared with a scarab of the same king from Pit A in the North-East Section, which provides a *terminus ante quem* for the destruction of the house level at 29 feet (p. 53, No. 88).

No. 295, a rectangular block of soft paste, bears the name of Amenhetep II and is especially important on account of the inscription on the opposite face, written in characters which may be allied to Early Canaanite script (p. 128).

Royal Emblems

King of the South and North

Dynasties xii–xiv or early xv	*Dynasties xv or xvi*
Nesew (Lower Egypt or North): 12, 17, 50, 85, 92, 94, 102, 109, 126, 200, 201, 204	*Nesew-bit* and Union (Upper and Lower Egypt): 29, 52, 65, 77, 79, 80, 123, 229, 347

A number of scarabs include beneficent hieroglyphs and give prominence to the emblems of royalty, and it is worth considering how far they reflect the political situation of Palestine in relation to divided or united power in Egypt.

The respective emblems can be divided into two groups. In the first there are three scarabs from Tomb 157, before the construction of the MB defences, which show *nesew* signs opposed in the design, Nos. 92, 94 and 102. An exception from Tomb 157 is No. 91 of the "Treasurer of the King of Lower Egypt" which is personal rather than commemorative. Similar pairs of *nesew* signs on scarabs rather more finely cut are to be seen on Nos. 17 and 50 from Tombs 1552 and 129, which would also seem to belong to the same or a slightly earlier period, and there is one occurrence in the bilobate Tomb 153, No. 109. Juxtaposition of *nesew* signs between flanking crowns is seen on a scarab of Senusert I (PSC, Pl. XII: 12), and with a continuous scroll border on a scarab of Senusert III (PSC, Pl. XIII: 12. 5. 12).

Some features in the design of No. 204 agree with BDS, Nos. 377–378, which Petrie attributed to the xith or xiith dynasty (BDS, p. 18). Emblems of Lower Egypt also figure on Nos. 200–201 from Tomb 4004, for which compare Weill II, p. 757, Figs. 50–53.

In the second group, in contexts which appear contemporary with or later than the construction of the MB fosse and glacis, there are the scarabs in which the royal emblems of South and North figure prominently. At the same time, the *sma* or sign of union between the South and North of Egypt appears on the plaque No. 29 from Tomb 119. No. 52 and No. 123 are attributed by Rowe to dynasty xiv.

An important comparison for Nos. 65, 79 and 80 is to be found in the cutting of these signs over a cartouche of Apepa I (PSC, Pl. XXI: 15. 5. 9). Others in the same style ascribed by Rowe to the "xiiith dynasty or later" are RES 34, 39.

It may be, as Weill has suggested, that the title King of the North was used by the Apepa family before the extension of their power in the South (Weill I, p. 199) and that the influx of both titles marked in our later tombs reflects that event. Weill is inclined to regard the Apepa family as contemporary with the predecessors of

Aahmes, and he considers that Aahmes himself in his conquest of the Delta destroyed the remains of their power (Weill I, p. 201). This would tally with the position at Ajjul, where scarabs of these kings are common, and are to be found in City II (AG I, Pl. XIII: 2, 44).

Red Crown (of Lower Egypt)

Dynasties xv–xix

15, 16, 24, 33, 48, 53, 55, 58, 75, 76, 78, 115–122, 124, 125, 138, 188, 210–214, 312, 329, 337, 341, 350

A common factor in many of the scarabs from Duweir is the red crown of the North (Lower Egypt). It may be worn by Horus, the Falcon, or by the cobra (uraeus). In other cases, it is placed on or above the *neb* sign, and it often fills the side space of the scarab in a conventional form. See Weill II, pp. 757 ff. for analogous designs.

This emblem is lacking on the scarabs of Tomb 157, while it is most common in the bilobate Tomb 153, where it is also seen with *sma* sign of union, e.g. No. 121. All the scarabs of this class from Tomb 153 have side type 11, with the exception of No. 120, side type 14. The sudden appearance of the red crown on scarabs in Palestine may mark the beginning of "Hyksos" control in Egypt. See also Structural Tomb 3080 at Megiddo (M. II, Pl. 149: 67–74).

While it is seen that the red crown figures in various ways to form the largest group among the decorative items at Duweir, it is surprisingly rare at Tell Fara (see No. 33 and a similar example from a rectangular Tomb 574). A red crown flanking two *nefer* signs figures on a scarab with plant sign from Tomb 551 (BP I, Pl. VII: 13), and crowned uraei are shown in Tomb 545 (BP I, Pl. VII: 48), Tomb 556 (Pl. X: 73) and, somewhat debased, in Tomb 569 (Pl. XII: 121). It is even less common in Cemetery 1000, where there is a single crowned figure with lotus on a scarab with decorated back (BP II, Pl. XLIII: 9).

The red crown does not figure in the design of any scarabs from the Fosse Temple, and during the Late Bronze Age at Duweir this symbol only appears on a few scarabs from the tombs. The poor style, back and side types of these scarabs may indicate that they belong to late xviiith or early xixth dynasty revivals.

Patterns

Scroll border

Dynasties xii–xiv or early xv	*Dynasties xv–xvi*
4–7, 23, 35, 36, 41, 106, 109, 133, 136, 142, 347	90, 91, 139, 141
Dynasties xvi–early xviii	*Partial scroll, hooked*
Mixed scrolls: 364	67, 101, 140, 143

The best designs are to be seen on Nos. 35 and 36 from Tomb 129, and No. 91 from Tomb 157. The latter is ascribed by Rowe to dynasty xv, though scroll and hieroglyphs seem to be in an earlier tradition. They compare with borders from Stratum XII at Megiddo (M. II, Pl. 149: 22, 32, 47) when scarabs were introduced in quantity. The date of the design is well attested in the scarabs of Senusert I of the xiith dynasty (PSC, Pl. XII: 12. 2. 3 and 16–17), and it is also commonly associated with private names at that time, of which No. 41 is an example.

The borders with three scrolls on each side and a single connecting loop above are of the Middle Kingdom period; they figure in the xiiith dynasty collection from Uronarti (BMFA XXVIII, 1930, Fig. 4), and a scarab of Semqen (PSC, Pl. XXI: 15. 2) may bring this version of the scroll border to the early part of the "Hyksos" period.

Nos. 23 and 90 (see under *Royal Names* and *Formulas*) most probably illustrate the next development, represented by one scarab from Uronarti (BMFA XXVIII, 1930, Fig. 4: 19), with the scroll continuing unchanged at the top; cf. a scarab from Stratum XI at Megiddo which also shows a version of the *rn* or Anra formula within the border (M. II, Pl. 150: 87).

Nos. 4, 5, 6, 7 and 109 are all smaller and show a less bold pattern. That the design could occur as late as the xixth dynasty is shown by a scarab of Rameses II (PSC, Pl. XLI: 45).

No. 133 contains apparently stylised hieroglyphs. No. 136 is a scarab impression with part of a scroll design, which has left the mark of the ring bezel on the jar handle to which it was applied, when the clay was leather hard. Many examples were found at Gezer, where Macalister noted that they were "almost always xiith dynasty or Hyksos" (*Gezer* II, p. 176). For Nos. 139 and 141 see under *Royal Names*.

Among incomplete scrolls, such as Nos. 67, 101 and 143, No. 140 with side scrolls only is interesting. It bears the name Pepy or Sheshi (see under *Royal Names*). The same name and title (PSC, Pl. XXI: C. Pepa), surrounded by concentric circles, suggests that both designs are contemporary, but at least three personages are known to have borne this name, among the predecessors of the xviiith dynasty (Weill II, pp. 147, 167 ff.).

No. 142 may be compared with No. 106 (see under *Royal Names*) for some elements in the design.

No. 364, with an unusual border of mixed scrolls, and side type 2, embodies a wish of political or personal significance, "May the union last".

Scrolls, linked

Dynasties xii–xvii

8, 9, 27, 38, 39, 62, 107, 110, 144–151, 305, 331, 370

Round linked scrolls covering the whole field of the scarab with few if any hieroglyphs are beautifully planned in the variety and balance of the scrolls (BDS, p. 12). They begin in the xiith dynasty at the same time as the oval side-scrolls (BDS, p. 14), probably so shaped to make more room for the central inscription. See *Quadruple Spirals* in Dr. Kantor's discussion on *The Aegean and the Orient in the Second Millennium* B.C. (AJA LI, 1947, pp. 23 ff.), where she attributes the sources of the xiith dynasty examples to Cretan prototypes.

While none of those from the Duweir tombs need be earlier than dynasty xiii, side types 2, 3, 5 and 6 are usual, and the later types, 15 and 46 (cf hard stone) do not seem to carry the linked design far into the xvth dynasty. Nos. 305, 331 and 370 betray an origin perhaps as late as the xviiith dynasty, taking into account the date of the groups which contained them as well as poor execution and late side type.

At Megiddo, linked scrolls are represented in Stratum XI and in Stratum XII and they are missing from Stratum X. In Stratum IX there is a comparison for No. 331 from Tomb 2117, which dates from LB I.

S-Scrolls

Dynasties xiii-xvii

28, 68, 93–95, 320

Dynasty early xviii

Some with plant: 153–157, 209, 355

Linked S-scrolls are included with the round scrolls, linked, above. The same scroll, separate on the field, with other signs and symbols, is distinctive and the better examples, Nos. 93–95, come from Tomb 157, probably before the construction of the MB defences. Nos. 28 and 68 from Tombs 119 and 6027 are inferior in detail, while the seal No. 320 from the area of the Great Shaft (L. III, Pl. 108) is the only one to compare in shape with seal No. 167 from Tomb 4004.

On the whole, it may be said that the S-scroll, which is uncommon at Duweir, may precede the main period of our tombs, where the debased versions are more usual.

The debased versions, with plant, like Nos. 153–157 and 209, are dated by Petrie to the early xviiith dynasty (BDS, p. 15) and No. 355 provided an example from the end of that period.

The S-scroll separate on the field is a common motif among the scarabs of the "foundation jar" from the Temple Area at Byblos (cf. under *Concentric Circles* below), and here again the introduction of a lotus provides further links with the smaller scarabs of Tomb 4004 (BE, Pl. LXV).

The same motif occurs on scarabs from Megiddo, Tomb 24 (MT, Pl. 105: 7) and from Strata XIII A–XI (M II, Pl. 149: 5, 8; 150: 88). Tomb 556 at Tell Fara (BP I, Pl. X: 70, 71) and with plants in Tomb 563 (BP I, Pl. XII: 131, 132).

Looped cords and twists

Dynasties xiii–xvii
19, 22, 24, 83, 102, 181–186, 190, 202

Looped cords originate, as Petrie observed, after the scroll patterns (BDS, p. 14), a conclusion which is fully in keeping with the Duweir evidence. The motif also occurs with a twisted cord or guilloche, which sometimes forms a separate element in the design, or a dividing band.

The design is first seen in Tomb 1552 with a rope border, No. 19, with which looped cords but rarely occur. The same tomb produced No. 22 which is worse than others of the class at Tell Fara. Rather similar in conception to No. 19 is No. 102 from Tomb 157, before the construction of the MB defences (see under *Royal Names*, p. 96).

No. 24 from Tomb 1502 introduces red crowns in each corner, and No. 83 is a square design of twists surrounding the signs *nefer-Rā* (see under *Royal Names*).

The rest, Nos. 181–186, 190 and 202, came from Tomb 4004, and they are all somewhat degraded versions with some late side types, i.e. 36 and 37.

The simple twist in the centre of the design is to be seen at Megiddo in Stratum XI (Pl. 150: 81, 86) and in VII B (M II, Pl. 152: 176, 179). It would be possible to assign all the scarabs with twist design from Tomb 4004 to the re-use of the cave at the end of the Bronze Age, though, if so, one would expect to find it in the Ramesside tombs at Tell Fara, where it does not occur.

Rope Borders

Dynasties xiii–early xviii	Dynasties xix–xx
7, 19, 20, 29, 45, 49, 96, 137, 158, 194, 210, 238	132, 227, 272, 369, 386, 387

Most of the scarabs under this heading are also included in other sections. The rope border is best seen on the fine plaque, No. 29, and on the large scarabs, Nos. 96 and 158, showing a similar style of deep cutting. It occurs in conjunction with debased scrolls on No. 7, it surrounds looped cords and twists on No. 19, and on Nos. 20 and 45 it is seen with hieroglyphic formulas (pp. 103–104).

The rope border begins on private scarabs of the xiiith dynasty (PSC, Pl. XVI: H–Q). It occurs in uncertain contexts of the xivth dynasty (PSC, Pl. XX: P, U). Thereafter, it is rarely found on royal scarabs, but see PSC, Pl. XXI: 5. 5, Apepa I, dynasty xv, and Pl. XXIV: 17 for Amenhetep I, early xviiith dynasty, which spans the proposed range for this border at Duweir.

There was a revival of the design under Seti I (PSC, Pl. XXXIX: 35) and Rameses II (Pl. XLI: 52), which is fully in keeping with the scarabs attributed here to the xixth dynasty, for which there are also good parallels in the Ramesside tombs at Tell Fara.

101

Palm Pattern

Dynasties xv–xviii

81, 84, 100, 199, 263

These small scarabs, in which the field is occupied by a ribbed pattern which may have originally represented a palm, can be matched at Tell Fara. No. 100 from Tomb 157 is paralleled in Shaft Tomb 570 (BP I, Pl. VII: 9), in Tomb 593 (BP I, Pl. XII: 119) and in 1007 (BP II, Pl. XLIV: 74). No. 263 from Tomb 4004 appears in a Fara bilobate Tomb 1021, but otherwise rather different versions of these patterns are confined to Tomb 6027, Nos. 81 and 84, and No. 199 from Tomb 4004 is a very small cowroid, bringing a reminiscence of the design down to the early xviiith dynasty.

The best examples seem, therefore, to belong to contexts contemporary with Tomb 157, and they are more common in burials other than bilobate tombs at Tell Fara. Petrie relates the ribbed pattern (e.g. BDS, Pl. VIII: 231) to the designs on button seals, and he considers that "they are mostly before the xiith dynasty" (BDS, p. 15). Rowe, on the other hand, attributes No. 100 to the "Hyksos" period.

Concentric Circles

Dynasties xiii–xvi

1, 10, 40, 69, 105, 108, 134, 175, 176

The concentric circle is a well-known degradation of the spiral, according to Petrie (BDS, p. 15) and examples of the name Pepy or Sheshi date the change, so far as Egypt is concerned, to the time of one of the three personages to bear the name (see under *Royal Names* above, and NS, Pl. XLIII: 18 and PSC, Pl. XXI, where the name is associated with partial hook scrolls [16. c. 1–5] and with concentric circles [16. c. 6]).

The best examples of circles are from Tombs 1552, 129 and 153, Nos. 1 (with a lotus on the back), 10, 40 (with linked concentric circles nearest to the spiral), 105, 108 and 134, all associated with side types between 5 and 14, while the small and poor versions from Tombs 6027 and 4004, Nos. 69, 175, 176, have side types 37, 19 and 25. Nos. 1, 105 and 134 are also included under *Royal Names*, though none is fully readable.

It is possible that the change from the scroll to concentric circles is seen slightly earlier in Palestine than in Egypt, though its main period occurs from the xvth or xvith to xviiith dynasties. A loose circle ornament on scarabs of Thothmes III, Amenhetep II and even Rameses II is very different from the more compact and uniform circles from Duweir (PSC, Pl. XXVIII: 94, 95; Pl. XXX: 31; Pl. XLI: 46–51).

No. 108 shows the beginning of the cross pattern (q.v.) for which there is a parallel in Tomb 24 at Megiddo (MT, Pl. 105: 4) and in Stratum XII (M II, Pl. 149: 42).

Scarabs with concentric circles are seen in the contents of the "foundation jar" at Byblos (BE, Pl. LXV); cf. for instance the second and fourth scarabs from the right in the seventh row, with Nos. 176 and 175, both from Tomb 4004 at Duweir.

Cross Pattern

Dynasties xiii–xviii   *Dynasties xvi–xviii*

Curled ends: 10, 107, 111, 112, 168, 169, 179, 180, 306, 354   Looped uraei: 191–193, 297, 362

No. 10 with a combination of the cross pattern and concentric circles (q.v.) is from Tomb 1552, and should date from about the xiv–xvth dynasties.

The cross pattern with curled diagonals on No. 107 is unusually elaborate and may be earlier, especially when seen in relation to the back and side type 6. Nos. 111 and 112, both with side type 11, are more normal examples of the type, which Petrie dates from the middle of the xiith to the xvith dynasty (BDS, p. 16). All three came from the bilobate Tomb 153. No. 111 is comparable to a scarab from Structure II (L. II, Pl. XXXII: 21) and is matched in Tomb 551 at Tell Fara, in Tombs 24 and 3110 at Megiddo, and in Tomb 9 at Jericho.

Nos. 168, 169, 179 and 180 from Tomb 4004 take the design from the xvith dynasty or earlier (BDS, p. 16) to perhaps the early xviiith dynasty, especially when seen in relation to the cowroids with looped uraei, Nos. 191–193. For xviiith dynasty degradations see Nos. 297, 306, 354 and 362.

Cord Patterns

Dynasties xv–early xviii

31, 32, 61, 82, 113, 177, 178, 194

Nos. 31, 82, 177 and 178 are elaborately designed cord patterns, while Nos. 32, 61, 113, and 194 are rather simple. Petrie would place these patterns between the xiiith and xviith dynasties, and in no case are they to be associated with the xiith dynasty. A scarab similar to No. 61 ''with a curious modification of the cross pattern'' is probably near dynasty xviii (BDS, pp. 14–15).

The more elaborate designs find comparisons in Megiddo Tombs, No. 177 in Tomb 24 and No. 178 in Tomb 37. In fact, the comparisons from the tell at Megiddo came respectively from a Structural Tomb of Stratum XII (No. 61) and from a locus below the floor of Stratum X (No. 177), both of which should perhaps belong within the period of Stratum XI (for an explanation of the use of brackets to enclose a locus number, as T. 3055, see M. II, Text p. 1).

The cord pattern is not to be seen in Tomb 157 (before the construction of the MB defences), and only the simple design, No. 113, came from the bilobate Tomb 153. It is the simple pattern which is typical of the bilobate tombs at Tell Fara, and it is also matched at Tell Beit Mirsim in Stratum D. The cowroid shape, No. 194, ranges between the xvith and early xviiith dynasties.

Two scarabs with cord designs are attributed to Structures II and III respectively (L. II, Pl. XXXII: 13, 14).

Figures and Signs

Figures with Emblems

Dynasties xiv–xviii	Dynasties xv–xix

Human figures with emblems

(a) Palm and lotus	(b) Uraei (cobra)	(c) Signs, etc.
25, 29, 30, 97, 130, 231–233, 236–238, 308, 311, 316, 325, 326	45, 72, 114, 366	235, 237, 239, 332

Dynasties xiv–xviii

Falcon-headed gods:

46, 98, 129, 137, 234, 239, 245

This design may perhaps be seen at its best in the human figures which commonly hold a lotus or a palm. The man wears a wound and bordered loin cloth with an end apparently tucked in at the waist. The torso seems to be bare, though in the fine examples, Nos. 29 and 45 for instance, an elaborate necklace is worn. The head with flowing hair or wig and the legs are shown in profile, while the torso is seen front view. The arms are seldom raised more than is necessary to hold the emblem. Exceptions are No. 30 in the attitude of Reshef, for which cf. L. II, Pl. XXXII: 1 from Structure I, and No. 236 with the arm raised in greeting. The men stand or stride; other figures, some of which may be female, are kneeling, see Nos. 25, 72, 325, 326 and 366. A parallel for the figure on No. 72 is discussed under *Royal Names*, No. 64.

Dr. Murray has described many comparable scarabs in PEQ, 1948–1949, pp. 93–95, and has shown how the palm and lotus transmute into the cobra, e.g. in No. 45, while the human figure becomes a falcon-headed god, representing Horus or Rā (cf. examples from Structures II and III of the Fosse Temple, L. II, Pl. XXXII: 6, 25). Nos. 97 and 98 show human and falcon-headed figures; they both came from Tomb 157, before the construction of the MB defences, and a similar type to No. 97 is attributed by Petrie to the xiii–xvth dynasties (BDS, p. 25). The best collection of these figures is to be found in Cemetery 1000 at Tell Fara (BP II, Pl. XLIV and p. 22), which may precede rather than follow the bilobate tombs at that site (BP I, Pls. VII–XII).

Nos. 114 from Tomb 153 and 130 from Group 511 illustrate the transition from man to falcon-headed figure (No. 129), and the same change is seen in Nos. 239 and 234. Compare No. 234 with BDS, Pl. XV: 1001 and p. 27, where Petrie attributes this type of scarab to the xiv–xvth dynasties.

No. 137 is a scarab impression found between buttresses of the Iron Age wall (Pl. 90). It represents a falcon-headed god with hawk and *kheper*, and the style and rope border suggest it is early in the series, not far removed in time from Nos. 29 and 45. These represent quite the most detailed figures in the series and, if style is a criterion, they should be the earliest.

Nos. 239, 245 are debased examples belonging to the xviiith dynasty or later, though falcon-headed gods were to revive in favour during the xixth–xxth dynasties (see under *Gods and Pharaoh*, p. 108).

Hathor-Astarte

Dynasties xiii–xv	*Dynasties xvi–xviii*
11, 47, 99	15, 162, 167, 174, 250, 307, 319

Nos. 11 and 99 from Tombs 552 and 157 show the great goddess of earlier times nude, standing full face, with prominent cow ears, between palms. There are comparisons from bilobate Tombs 565 and 545 at Tell Fara. No. 47 from Tomb 129 is rather similar, though the head is seen in profile. Nos. 15 and 162 show the Hathor head only, with horns and well-marked ears. There is a parallel for No. 162 from a room of Stratum XII at Megiddo. All these should be no later than the xvth dynasty.

No. 167 is a beautifully made round seal, carved on the back with eight small scarabs disposed round a central rosette. The back is matched in a xvith-dynasty group at Sedment. No. 174, with a uraeus on the back, shows a poorly drawn Hathor head and could be slightly later. No. 250, on the other hand, is finely cut and ranks among the best of this type, with No. 307 from Tomb 216. A parallel on a round seal for the upper group on No. 307 is dated by Petrie to the reign of Thothmes III (BDS, Pl. XI: 551 and p. 19) which agrees with the main occupation of Tomb 4004 at Duweir. The plaque No. 319 is dated by the style of the Hathor head and sistrum from the reigns of Thothmes III to Thothmes IV, i.e. from c. 1450–1400 B.C. (BDS, Pl. X: 550 and p. 19).

Formulas and Hieroglyphs in Columns (or between lines)

Dynasties xv–xvi

20, 21, 34, 51, 54, 55, 60, 70, 87, 88, 103, 105, 138, 158–161, 207, 232

Various combinations of recurring hieroglyphic signs are described in detail by Weill (I, pp. 191 ff. and II, p. 785) and Murray (PEQ, 1948–1949, pp. 92–97). Weill places the group which he describes as "Anra" in the first of four periods of "Hyksos" scarabs (p. 96) and Dr. Murray suggests a reading for one of the recurrent formulas, of which there are several variants. Petrie recognises them as the *rā-en-rā* group, probably a blunder for "Rā gave", a frequent theophonic name in the Middle Kingdom (BDS, p. 17).

Divisions of the inscriptions into three vertical columns separated by lines can be seen on scarabs of Anther (Ontha) and Khyan, both of whom bear the title Prince of the Desert (PSC, Pl. XXI: 15. 1, 15. 3 and Weill II,

p. 825). A similar arrangement occurs on No. 26; see under *Royal Names*, Nos. 54 and 70 and 161, though all but the first merely delineate hieroglyphic formulas.

No. 138, divided into horizontal zones by a *nub* sign and outstretched wings, is divided vertically by crowns between which there are three signs, the first being the unusual determinative for town or village (*niwt*). The group is matched by Weill (II, p. 744: 16 and p. 860). This scarab was found in a room of Level III on the city mound (see L. III, p. 125). The early side type helps to confirm that it was not there in its true context. It is also like No. 60 in the arrangement of the signs.

Nos. 55, for which cf. Weill I, p. 235: 2, 138, 160–161, are the only scarabs of "Anra" type to include the red crown though it is much debased on No. 160. For the group of signs enclosed in a pseudo-cartouche on No. 160, compare our Nos. 87 and 207. No. 161 has a good comparison for the vertical lines ending in red crowns in Stratum XII at Megiddo (M II, Pl. 149: 197).

Stylised Hieroglyphs

Dynasties xiii–xiv	*Dynasties xv–xviii*	*Dynasties xviii–xix*
18, 49, 73, 152, 203	56, 57, 59, 74, 89, 92, 103, 109, 131, 168, 195	132, 205, 206, 252, 254–259, 296, 315, 327, 330, 375, 376, 386, 390

The scarabs under this heading show more or less conventional groups of Egyptian hieroglyphs and symbols allied to a variety of side types.

Nos. 18 and 203 show a similar disposition of signs. No. 49 can be compared for back and style of cutting with No. 17; see p. 98.

The arrangement of the snakes on No. 73 from Tomb 6027 finds parallels at Yehudiyeh and Tell Fara, and in a scarab attributed to Antef V (BDS, Pl. XXIV: 11. 7–9). The design as a whole is more closely matched at Ajjul and at Megiddo Stratum X. For the same symbols with a rope border see No. 132. Compare also No. 386 from Tomb 570, which shows a revival of the style in the xviii–xixth dynasties at Duweir and in the Ramesside tombs at Tell Fara.

No. 74 displays the plant emblem of the Delta with other signs, like No. 124 from Tomb 153 (see under *Red Crown*, p. 99), and both should perhaps belong to the xvth or xvith dynasty. No. 89 is distinguished for its well-cut signs.

Nos. 56, 57 and 59 are all from Tomb 129. They are small and somewhat debased and may date from the early part of the xvth dynasty.

No. 109 from the bilobate Tomb 153 is already noted under *Scroll Borders*. The central hieroglyphs include opposed *nesew* signs, very poorly made, as befits their last appearance in our series.

No. 131 compares with a scarab of Stratum E or D at Tell Beit Mirsim.

No. 152, with careful hatching, is probably the most interesting of the stylised pieces from Tomb 4004. No. 168 is already noted for its design on the obverse under *Cross Pattern, Curled Ends*, pp. 102 f. The reverse shows a conventional group ending in uraei, which also figure on the cowroid No. 195.

No. 205 may be compared to No. 296 for a different treatment of the same subject. The remainder of the scarabs from Tomb 4004 are undistinguished, and the same may be said of No. 315 from the area of the Great Shaft (L. III, Pl. 108), Nos. 327 (see under *Royal Names, doubtful*) and 330 from Tomb 1003, and Nos. 375 and 376. No. 390 from the casemate fill of Palace A (L. III, p. 116) is marked as Ramesside in date from the detail of the back.

Animals

Most of the scarabs on which animals figure prominently are executed in a distinctive and bold style, with the outlines deeply cut and the bodies filled in with hatchings. Other groups cut in a similar way are the

Hathor-Astarte and the human figures holding palms or lotus flowers, also the earlier versions of the red crowns. Perhaps all these should be described as Canaanite in origin, for the style they display is not Egyptian.

Taking the chief animals in the chronological order of popularity, the first and most important is from Tomb 157, dating before the construction of the MB defences.

Crocodiles

Dynasties xiii–xvi

12, 96, 129, 166

No. 96 shows a brilliantly executed group comprising the crocodile of the Fayum, the vulture of El Kab and the fish of Oxyrhynkhos. These animals together probably commemorate the extension of Theban dominion at the beginning of the xiiith dynasty when, despite the fact that the feudal prince of El Kab still retained his independent title, the Theban king penetrated south and at the same time left his mark in the Fayum (Weill II, p. 532). As an illustration of the commemorative purpose of some scarabs and as a confirmation of history, No. 96 is of special value.

No. 12 from Tomb 1552 also shows a crocodile, probably referring to Sebek (BDS, p. 25), with the *nesew* emblem of the North (q.v.), and a poorly cut piece, No. 129, presents the animal with a falcon-headed figure (q.v.) in a design which finds a parallel at Jericho Tomb 43 and at Tell Fara Tomb 1026.

No. 166 is exceptional for the fact that the successful design of two crocodiles on either side of a palm tree is repeated on the reverse without change. From its large size the plaque can hardly have been mounted in a ring.

Lions and Heraldic Beasts

Dynasties xiii–xx

29, 42, 43, 71, 215–222, 317, 343, 345, 349, 368, 378

No. 29 resembles No. 166 in size and style. The obverse shows a standing figure (p. 103) beside a sphinx couchant (or overthrown?). On the reverse the sign of Union appears, standing on *nubti*, which is the epithet of Setekh, god of the South, flanked by the cobra-goddesses of the North. The whole is enclosed in a rope border like No. 96. This fine piece seems to mark a commemoration of the conquest and union of Upper and Lower Egypt.

No. 42, with Nos. 215 and 216 from Tombs 129 and 400A, show an active and vigorous lion; one animal is in combat with two figures, both of whom wear belted tunics with crossed-over front, rather different in style from the kilts of the Canaanite figures. The backs of Nos. 42 and 215 are elaborately decorated and neither is well matched after the xiii–xivth dynasties.

Petrie observes that the lion on scarabs was familiar from the xiiith to xv–xvith dynasties (BDS, p. 24).

Nos. 43 and 71 from Tombs 129 and 6027, with No. 345 from Tomb 542, are clearly less well observed in detail, and the same may be said for Nos. 217–219, some of which, with the mythical animals on Nos. 220–222, may belong to the late xviiith or xixth dynasty. Compare in this connexion the vigour of the beast on No. 317, bearing the name of Amenhetep II.

Nos. 343 and 368 from Tombs 559 and 4002 are different versions of the same type of composition. Both show a couchant sphinx with winged uraeus behind; the detail of No. 343 is duplicated on the reverse of a plaque inscribed with the name of Rameses III (PSC, Pl. XLV: 20. 1. 12).

No. 349 is a winged creature of the Ramesside period.

No. 378, an eye-backed seal (see under *Horus Eyes*), is a better version of an amuletic seal with lion and Rā circle, which can be found as late as the xxvith dynasty (BDS, Pl. XIV: 889 and p. 24).

Deer

Dynasties xiii–xviii

44, 149, 223–226

No. 44 may represent the oryx from its resemblance to a scarab published in BDS (Pl. XIV: 867) and the same can be said for No. 225 (op. cit., Pl. XVIII: 1400). Both comparisons are attributed to the xvth dynasty by Petrie (BDS, p. 24). Nos. 223, 224 and 226 are other less careful versions of the same theme from Tomb 4004, which from the side types could be xviiith dynasty or later.

No. 149 is of amethyst and, though this material was in common use in Middle Kingdom times, such scarabs are rarely inscribed.

Fish

Dynasty xviii

170, 230, 318, 328, 356

The fish backs of No. 170 from Tomb 4004 and No. 356 from Tomb 4011 illustrate very clearly the degradation in style of the later version, belonging to the end of the xviiith if not the xixth dynasty.

No. 230 shows a fish occupying all the space available, while No. 318 presents it in much more detail.

No. 328 from Tomb 1003 with a fish between a *nefer* and an *ānkh* sign should be dated to the middle of the xviiith dynasty.

Frogs

Dynasty xviii

333, 334

No. 333 from Tomb 547 has a frog back with *ānkh* on the reverse, while No. 334 from the same group also shows that animal incised on a lion-backed seal.

Beetle

Dynasties xviii–xix

249

The face of No. 249 is entirely occupied by a deeply incised *kheper* sign, which is rarely figured in that position. Cf. RES 638 of unknown provenance and NS, Pl. XXV: 27.

Cattle

Dynasty xix

227, 228, 381

Nos. 227, 228, both from Tomb 4004, appear to represent the Hathor cow (cf. BDS, Pl. XIII: 853 and p. 24). They are probably xixth dynasty in date, and the use of a rope border on No. 227 is a revival from Ramesside times. Of much the same period is No. 381 with two bulls rampant.

Horus Eyes (uzat)

Dynasties xiv–xv	*Dynasties xvi–xix*
52, 92	66, 86, 172, 246–248, 260, 261, 310, 335, 341, 350, 378, 383

As an element in a rather crowded design, a pair of Horus eyes is to be found in scarabs of about the xivth dynasty (PSC, Pl. XX: AJ, AR, AU, AZ). Similar designs are attributed by Weill to the Hyksos period (Weill II, pp. 754–755). The only comparable examples from Duweir are No. 52 from Tomb 129 (RES 108) and No. 92 from Tomb 157 (RES 269).

No. 66, on the other hand, introduces a single eye more prominently displayed, and it comes from Tomb 4022 together with Nos. 64 and 65 with emblems of Upper and Lower Egypt. They are contemporary with or later than the MB defence system. No. 86 is of about the same period, and Nos. 260–261 show degradations from Tomb 4004. The latter may fall within the xviiith dynasty, like No. 310 from Tomb 216.

From the early part of the xviiith dynasty eye-backed amulets become common (BDS, p. 16), and Nos. 172 and 246–248 should belong to that time, while Nos. 335, 341, 378 and 383 are late xviiith or even xixth dynasty in date.

Amen-Rā

Dynasties xviii–xix

248, 268–275, 302, 313, 321, 340, 346, 348, 361, 373, 374, 377

Inscribed on an eye- and a duck-backed seal and on seven scarabs from Tomb 4004 is the name of Amen-Rā, variously abbreviated and debased, with other signs to fill in and balance the composition.

Apart from No. 302, the name is missing from subsequent Tombs 216, 501 and 1003, which suggests that it only became popular towards the end of the xviiith dynasty with the restoration to power of the Theban gods after the fall of the Amarna regime.

The scarabs and seals from Tomb 4004, together with Nos. 340, 346, 348, 361, 373, 374 and 377 would therefore belong to the end of the xviiith and the xixth dynasty, a conclusion which fits the evidence from Tell Fara, where such scarabs occur in the Ramesside tombs. At Ajjul they are to be found in Tomb 1057 (AG II, Pl. VII: 28, 30).

For Petrie's remarks on possible readings of this common class of inscription, see BDS, p. 21.

Gods and Pharaoh

Dynasties xviii–xx

240–245, 309, 317, 339, 353, 360, 365, 367, 371, 385, 391

Nos. 295 and 317 (see under *Royal Names*) are each dated by the name of Amenhetep II (*c.* 1447–1420 B.C.). No. 295 shows single figures of gods with signs which probably describe them (p. 128). The reverse of No. 317 depicts the king and gods, a group which became popular on scarabs of the Ramesside period, e.g. No. 365 from Tomb 4002.

The Pharaoh smites his enemies on No. 243 from Tomb 4004 and No. 391 found in a late context on the mound. These should belong to the reign of Rameses II (e.g. PSC, Pl. XL: 19. 3, 24, 25 and BDS, Pl. XV: 996 and p. 27), and all are well matched in the Ramesside tombs at Tell Fara.

Three gods, probably Amen, Rā (?) and Horus (cf. BDS, Pl. XV: 1044 and p. 28), figure on No. 240 from Tomb 4004, No. 339 from Tomb 559 and No. 371 from Tomb 538, and similar groups occur at Megiddo in Stratum VII and in the Ramesside tombs at Tell Fara.

Ptah is the principal figure on No. 244 from Tomb 4004; he is seen with Rā on No. 353 from Tomb 4011 and with a crowned uraeus on No. 360 from Tomb 4013. The name is written on the reverse of No. 377. Ptah with the goddess Maāt is seen on a scarab from Structure III (L. II, Pl. XXXII: 20).

No. 242 shows Setekh with symbols. Petrie states that figures of this god begin in the xixth dynasty (BDS, p. 27) and it should therefore belong to the last phase of use in Tomb 4004.

No. 245 may represent Rā, while Nos. 309, 367 and 385 show later stages in the process of change from a lotus-carrying figure to one in which the limbs merge into a cobra, already discussed on pp. 103 f. These versions may be late xviiith dynasty, though it is more likely that they belong to the xixth dynasty, when there are many comparisons for them in the Ramesside tombs at Tell Fara.

Dates and Comparisons

The contents of Tomb 157 appear to have been deposited before the construction of the MB defences, and it is therefore the only group containing scarabs which can be isolated stratigraphically. It may be dated perhaps between 1750–1700 B.C., just before the beginning of the xvth dynasty, to which most of the scarabs from it are assigned by Rowe.

The motifs are found to include full scroll borders, Nos. 90–91 not of the earliest kind; S-scrolls Nos. 93–95 which are otherwise uncommon at the site, while royal emblems on Nos. 92 and 94 and 102 only include those of the North or Lower Egypt. No. 91, with the finest work and an early side type, is an exception of personal rather than commemorative interest. No. 96 is unique for the lifelike presentation of the animals, a piece which may celebrate the extension of Theban power in Egypt early in the xiiith dynasty (p. 106).

Nos. 97 and 98 show a human and a falcon-headed figure holding the lotus, and both are somewhat better in execution than others of the type at Duweir. These standing figures with flowers are not found in Cemetery 500 at Tell Fara, but they are the most usual motif in Cemetery 1000 at that site (BP II, Pls. XLIII–XLIV).

No. 99 is matched for motif in a shaft tomb at Tell Fara, Tomb 545, and in the bilobate Tomb 565, and both show early characteristics. Like the figures on Nos. 29 and 96, the Astarte on No. 99 wears a necklace of pendent drops.

No. 100 is a conventional palm branch, which appears more common in burials other than bilobate tombs at Tell Fara.

It will be seen that elements in common between Group 157 and the tombs at Tell Fara are largely confined to the earlier groups in that series, including motifs which are typical of Cemetery 1000 (BP II). At Ajjul two scarabs from the Courtyard Cemetery are comparable: a figure kneeling with lotus and a design of S-scrolls (AG II, Pl. VII: 103, 104).

Turning to the scarabs from the only bilobate Tomb 153 at Duweir, a different situation prevails.

Nos. 104–105 have unreadable signs in the cartouches, but the backs, like the elaborate ones on Nos. 107–108, are comparable to those attributed by Newberry to the reign of Amenemhat III and later (NS, p. 71 and Figs. 61–62). Nos. 105 and 108 show concentric circles, and it is remarkable that there are no good scarabs of the kind from the bilobate tombs at Fara. Nos. 106–107 and 109 show scrolls, which should be compared with those from Group 157. No. 110 presents a fine linked scroll, typical of xiiith-dynasty scarabs. Nos. 111–112 introduce the cross pattern with curled ends, matched in bilobate Tomb 551 at Tell Fara, while the cord pattern (No. 113) appears in Tombs 1021 and 559.

But the outstanding difference between our Tomb 153 and 157 is that Nos. 115–125, mostly with side type 11 (Pl. 41) are all concerned with designs which include the red crown (of the North or Lower Egypt); and the sign of union between South and North also appears. It seems likely therefore that this tomb represents the point in time when the incoming "Hyksos" were celebrating the extension of their power over the whole Egyptian

Kingdom. The red crown is curiously rare in the bilobate tombs at Tell Fara, being confined to Tomb 551 (BP I, Pl. VII: 13) and it is altogether missing from Cemetery 1000. Another tomb which should be considered for parallel material is Tomb 24 at Megiddo (MT, Pls. 105–106), which on the pottery contents should precede and overlap with Tombs 157 and 153.

Apart from Tomb 157, and to a lesser extent the bilobate Tomb 153, both containing pottery which is closely contemporary, other groups of scarabs must be considered on their own merits. In that case two major problems arise: the definition of "Hyksos" type scarabs and their place in the Egyptian dynastic progression.

1. The definition of "Hyksos" type scarabs presents difficulties, particularly where references have been made to works by different authors using different chronologies over a space of fifty years.

Gauthier, for instance, divided the "Hyksos" rule in two: the first chiefs who had not yet assimilated Egyptian culture forming the xvth dynasty, while those whose monuments were found throughout the Nile Valley constitute dynasty xvi (Gauthier II, p. 134).

Weill places "Hyksos" type scarabs in two groups: Group F includes the formulas of the "Anra" or first period and Group I includes scarabs of the Khyan and Apepa families in the second period (Weill II, p. 819). While his statement about the rare occurrence of the name Khyan in Palestine remains true, excavations at Ajjul have produced some examples of the Apepa kings, and of the name *Pepa* or *Shesha*, allocated by him to dynasty xvii (Weill II, pp. 762–765).

2. In placing the first group of "Hyksos" type scarabs in relation to those of Egyptian provenance, Weill discussed two possibilities. Either "Hyksos" kings had adopted names of predecessors of the xiith dynasty, such as *Ka-kheper-Rā* (see under *Royal Names*), or scarabs with these names were contemporary with the xiith-dynasty monarchs themselves.

While he inclined to the first solution (Weill I, pp. 243–244), more recent material may show that the scarabs bearing royal names known from xiith-dynasty records may belong to that period.

Although the patterns on the scarabs from Duweir are all to be matched in Egypt and are certainly as good in execution as the Egyptian examples, the deeply cut scarabs with fine hatching which show formulas, figures with emblems, Hathor-Astarte, lions and deer are in a different tradition.

The vigour and realism of the best pieces, Nos. 25, 29, 45, 96 and 231, have no equal in Egypt and they are outstanding among the more normal products at Tell ed-Duweir. In this connexion the scarabs of Stratum D at Tell Beit Mirsim are instructive (AASOR XVII, Pls. 28–29), for they include several of the best quality, and the formulas of the first "Hyksos" period are characteristic. Moreover, there is the fine piece, which Albright has

Dynasties	Royal emblems	Patterns	Figures and signs
xii–xv	King of the North (Lower Egypt)	Scroll borders, scrolls, linked S-scrolls, looped cords, twists, rope borders, palms	Figures with emblems Hathor-Astarte Formulas Stylised hieroglyphs (*kheper* and snakes) Animals: crocodiles, lions
xv	King of the South and North, Apepa I Red Crown (Lower Egypt) Pepa or Shesha, Son of Rā	Scroll border, partial Concentric circles Cross pattern, cord pattern	
xviii	Thothmes III Amenhetep II } Lord of Upper and Thothmes IV } Lower Egypt	Cross pattern, looped uraei	Animals: deer, frogs, fish, beetle Horus eyes Amen-Rā
xix		Revivals: Rope borders Concentric circles	Gods and Pharaoh Stylised hieroglyphs (*kheper* and snakes)

compared with a scarab of the xii–xiiith dynasties (AASOR XII, p. 34, Fig. 6). The crowded design includes two sets of opposed *nesew* signs and a pair of well-drawn red crowns, emblems of the North (Lower Egypt). The side type is even better than the first in the Duweir series (Pl. 41: 1). The general aspect of the scarabs from Stratum D would suggest that it would be preferable to bring at least the first phase of that Stratum (D¹) to an end about a century earlier than the excavator has proposed (pp. 33 f.).

Finally, in an attempt to formulate some order in a complex subject, which in the light of further research may undergo more change, the emblems and patterns discussed in this chapter are tabulated on p. 110.

CYLINDER SEALS

Four cylinder seals were found in the Late Bronze Age tombs, of which three come from Tomb 4004 and one from Pit 557 of the Ramesside period. The first three were included by Miss Barbara Parker in her article on the Palestinian cylinder seals (*Iraq* XI, 1949, pp. 1–43). Miss Parker's descriptions and comments are here incorporated with some added remarks and comparisons by Dr. Edith Porada.

No. 163 (*Iraq* XI, Pl. XXII: 149)

The principal figure of the scene is a man standing with both arms upraised. Beside him is a large dagger, beyond are a bull and an antelope set at right angles to the ground. Two drillings are in the field.

The spidery linear carving on the soft serpentine or steatite of this seal is also found on a cylinder from Tomb 19 at the Late Bronze Age site of Bamboula in Cyprus (AJA, LII, Pl. XI: 46, p. 193), where the seal is referred to as from Kourion and dated to LC III A. Moreover, the animals on this and another Cypriote seal (op. cit., Pl. XI: 45, from the Cesnola collection) are also turned at right angles to the ground. The same is the case on a cylinder found at Megiddo (MT, Pl. 148: 1, also reproduced by Miss Parker, *Iraq* XI, Pl. XXII: 148) and on another from Gaza (AG IV, Pl. XII: 7).

In view of the analogies from Cyprus, the cylinders from Tell ed-Duweir, Megiddo and Gaza should probably be regarded as imports from that island.

No. 164 (*Iraq* XI, Pl. XXIII: 151)

The cylinder shows a walking male figure with a short oblique line above his head, possibly intended for a feather. Beside or behind the man are a bull and a winged creature. Above the bull's back is a scorpion.

The scene can be interpreted as a procession of three figures or, alternatively, as the man standing between the bull and the winged creature. The latter resembles the griffin of a related seal in the Morgan Library (*Corpus of Ancient Near Eastern Seals in North American Collections*, Vol. I, 1948, No. 1004) in the beak-like head and the feather with a recurved tip—and may therefore be similarly interpreted. The combination of a bull and griffin in No. 164 could derive from the ancient Mesopotamian motif of a monster attacking an animal.

This cylinder is one of the few objects to be found above the main deposits in Tomb 4004 (q.v.), which implies a date of about 1400 B.C. or later for the piece. Such a date can also be supported by that of a related cylinder from Abu Hawam (QDAP IV, Pl. XXVI: 413; *Iraq* XI, Pl. XXII: 153) which was found in Level V, 1400–1200 B.C. This seal so closely resembles the cylinder from Duweir in the spacing of the figures and the rendering of the bodies that both may have been made by the same engraver. This engraver could have been active in Palestine after about 1400 B.C., since his seals lack the traditional features of earlier styles. The old motif of the attack by a griffin on a bull, for example, seems to have been transformed on the Duweir cylinder into a peaceful walk. Despite the crude linear rendering, moreover, the forms of the figures are quite naturalistic, contrasting with the traditional schematic treatment of Mitannian design.

No. 165 (*Iraq* XI, Pl. XXIII: 150)

The scene consists of three men standing front-face, each with one arm raised. The line which marks the body is extended between their legs to the line border. This may be a simplified and partly misunderstood rendering of the end of the garment or girdle hanging between the legs of men on Mitannian sealings (cf. *Seal Impressions of Nuzi*, AASOR XXIV, Pl. XX: 404, 408).

For the row of men Miss Parker referred to Mitannian examples (*Iraq* XI, Pl. V: 32), noting, however, that one raised arm is typical of figures on Cypriote seals (like *Iraq* XI, Pl. XX 134).

Mitannian designs show the hands clasped or with one hand resting on the next man's shoulder. The raised arm is also found on some of the Iron Age scaraboids (e.g. L. III, Pl. 44: 72, 73).

The difference probably implies another meaning, since the Mitannian examples (cf. AASOR XXIV, Pls. XIX–XX) usually show long rows of more than three figures, suggesting marching men, while the Cypriote example and the Duweir cylinder could represent worshippers. It is possible, however, that both designs show dancers, in the attitude of their respective dances.

The mixture of Mitannian and Cypriote motifs and the simplified linear execution on the Duweir cylinder suggest that it was made after the more carefully done Nuzi type designs, of which a number were found in the Fosse Temple (L. II, Pl. XXXIII: 40, 41, 43, 45, 46, 48–51).

No. 323

The design is divided into two registers and framed above and below by bands of cross hatching. From left to right in the upper register there are two long-robed figures grasping a standard between them; a figure in a knee-length garment follows, facing left with one arm raised, the other extended, between two oblique crosses; a third long-robed figure standing front-face grasps a staff or sword with one hand and raises a staff or mace with the other. At the left of the lower register a large star is held (?) by a figure in a knee-length garment; while the rest of the field is filled by a standard, placed on a hill or stand and flanked by sitting winged antelopes.

Some of these motifs can be traced to Mitannian designs on seal impressions from Nuzi. The two men with the standard, for example, may represent a simplified version of such designs as Nuzi 2, 4, 7, 20; the man and star in the lower register of the Duweir cylinder may be compared to a figure on the imprint, Nuzi 903, of which the original also seems to have been cut in a cursory manner, but not as lightly as on the glass piece. The winged animals flanking the standard on a hill can be related to Nuzi 847 and 926, where the hill is shown by drillings, which are omitted in the Duweir seal. This indicates that the latter should be later than the more carefully made Nuzi examples.

Conclusions

Two of the four cylinders show the disintegration of the Mitannian style of engraving which had prevailed in Syria and Palestine in the fifteenth and fourteenth centuries. Cylinder 164 belongs to a style for which no earlier examples are known and which may be a local product of fourteenth- or thirteenth-century date. Cylinder 163 can be dated to the end of the Bronze Age owing to the Cypriote parallels cited above. Cylinder 165 shows a mixture of Mitannian and Cypriote motifs and is later in style than the Nuzi-type cylinders associated with Structure III of the Fosse Temple; it should therefore be dated quite late in the thirteenth century. About the same date during the Ramesside period would be suitable for the glass cylinder, Pl. 38: 323, in agreement with the associated pottery.

Thus it can be said that the four cylinders can be placed between the Mitannian (Nuzi-style) glyptic of the Fosse Temple and the scarabs and scaraboids of the Iron Age layers. They therefore represent important evidence for the history of glyptic art in the fourteenth–thirteenth centuries, by showing the final stages of the traditional style and the appearance of rather crude local groups, shortly before cylinder seals became obsolete in Palestine and in all other areas outside Mesopotamia, their country of origin.

Scarabs and Seals: Description of Plates 30–40

Scale 1:1. All scarabs are made of steatite unless otherwise stated under Remarks. Scarabs are approximately dated through comparison of style and design to those of Egyptian and Palestinian provenance, estimated in the works detailed on p. 92, according to the Royal dynasties of Egypt.

Plate 30 (Photographs on Pl. 31)

No.	Locus	Side Type Plate 41	Remarks	Field No. Museum No.
1	1552	5	R^c-ḫpr in concentric circles. Lotus-flower on back. Dyn. xiv (?). Cf. PSC XI: 11A for style of beetle and XIII: 12.4,4. Senusert II.	2203
2	1552	25	Ḫpr in twist border. R^c-ḫpr (?). Dyn. xiv–xvi. Cf. 202; AG IV, VII: 230, G. 935.	2215
3	1552	2	Nśw bit, nb Nḫn, "King of Upper and Lower Egypt, Lord of Hieraconpolis", between ʿnḫ signs with nub below. Encased with gold sheet. c. Dyn. xiv. RES 109; BP I, VII: 39, Tomb 582.	2212
4	1552	6	R^c-ḫpr in continuous hook-scroll. Dyn. xiv (?)	2217
5	1552	53	R^c-mn-kʿ᾽ in continuous hook-scroll above inverted nescw(?) Dyn. xiii/Hyksos. RES 58.	2218
6	1552	3	Nśw (?) -nb-nfr in continuous hook-scroll. Partly broken. Dyn. xiii–xiv.	2220
7	1552	6	ʿp(p)? ḫʿ, possibly "Apep appears", in continuous hook-scroll with rope border. Rowe reads variant of R^c-᾽ꜣ-ḫʿ cf. RES 142–152; Gauthier II, p. 404. Dyn. xv.	2219
8	1552	3	Scrolls, linked, round. Dyn. xiii. BDS VII: 31; BP I, VII: 35, Tomb 568; NS XVIII: 20.	2207
9	1552	hidden by setting	Scrolls, linked, round. In Au setting. Dyn. xiii.	2209
10	1552	14	Cross pattern with concentric circles. BDS VIII: 254. Dyn. xiv–xv.	2208
11	1552	39	Hathor between palms. Cf. BP I, X: 103, Tomb 565; BDS XV: 1054. Dyn. xv.	2202
12	1552	14	Sbk-ʿnḫ (?) with nśw. Crocodile. Dyn. xiii–xiv (?)	2211
13	1552	44	Amethyst, Au setting. Uninscribed. Dyn. xii–xiii.	2223
14	1552	44	Amethyst. Uninscribed. Dyn. xii–xiii.	2222
15	1552	14	Red-crowned falcon and Hathor on nb. Dyn. xv–xvi.	2205
16	1552	11	Red-crowned falcon and feather-crowned uraeus on nb. Dyn. xv–xvi.	2213
17	1552	3	Stylised hieroglyphs. Nub-nfrw in centre. Dyn. xiii–xiv (?).	2210
18	1552	19	Dd-nb-ʿnḫ. Dyn. xiii (?).	2206
19	1552	8	Looped cords and twists in rope border. Dyn. xiv (?). Cf. BDS VIII: 131 for cord pattern.	2204
20	1552	33	Formulas in palm and rope border. Cf. AAA XX, XXVI: 1, Tomb 19. Dyn. xv.	2214
21	1552	—	Stylised hieroglyphs, rn-rn. Three scarabs on back. Dyn. xv.	2221
22	1552	37	Twist pattern debased. Dyn. xiii–xvi. Cf. BP I, XII: 135, Tomb 564, 138, Tomb 554.	2216
23	1502	11	R^c-kꜣ-ḫʿ, (Neferhetep II) in continuous hook-scrolls. c. Dyn. xiii. Gauthier II, p. 39, No. 24. RES 26.	1723 PM 34.2788
24	1502	8	Central twist with duplicate pattern of twist between red crowns, inverted above. Hyksos. RES 418.	1724 PM 34.2789
25	1502	14	Kneeling man, wearing knee-length loin-cloth and wig, holding palm. Nb below. Hyksos. RES 282. Cf. M. II, 150: 73, T. 3080 Stra. XI; BP I, X: 88, Tomb 594.	1722 PM 34.2787
26	1542	16	Between vertical lines kꜣ-n-ḫʿ-R^c-n-mn-R^c-n, possibly Neferhetep II. Dyn. xiii. RES 30. BDS X: 470.	2090 PM 34.3094
27	119	—	Scrolls, linked, round. BDS VII: 56; HIC VIII: 42, Yehudiyeh Grave 37. Dyn. xiii.	638 MMA 34.126.6

No.	Locus	Side Type Plate 41	Remarks	Field No. Museum No.
28	119	—	Three S-scrolls, the centre one enclosed in oblong. Dyn. xv.	634 MMA 34.126.7
29	119	—	Plaque in AE ring. Obv.: standing man in wig and kilt and couchant sphinx; rev.: sign of union on *nub* between uraei within rope border. Dyn. xv–xvi (?).	641
30	119	15	In AE ring. Kilted figure holding branch, right arm raised. *Ḥ'(?)-'nḫ* in field. Dyn. xv–xvi (?).	635
31	119	—	In AE ring. Cord pattern (?) hatched. Dyn. xv–xvi (?).	636 MMA 34.126.9
32	119	37	Cord pattern. BP I, XXII: 215, Tomb 580; AASOR XVII, 28: 12, Stra. D; AG IV, IX: 280, Tomb 1545. Dyn. xvi.	639
33	6002	19	Red crown on *nb* above uraeus, flanked by *ḥm* (Murray) or *s'* (Rowe) and *nfr* signs. BP I, XXII: 213, Tomb 574; AG II, VII: 106, Tomb 1410B. Dyn. xv–xvi.	6507
34	6002	39	*Dy-n-R'-n-R'* between vertical lines and hatching. Dyn. xv.	6506
35	129	5	*rdi-n-R'* (?) in cartouche, above, *nfrwy*; surrounded by continuous oval scroll. Dyn. xiii–xiv.	730
36	129	—	Name (?), *K'-nfrwy* or *Ḥ'-nfrwy* (Rowe) in cartouche; *ḥtp* above, *nub* below; all surrounded by continuous hook-scroll. NS XXIV: 21. Dyn. xiii–xiv.	725 MMA 34.126.21
37	129	20	Upper part broken. Restored reading: *w'b 'q n Nḫbt, Iw-f-n, nb imȝḫy*: "priest who has admittance to Nekhebet, Iew-ef-ne, the venerable". Dyn. xiii. RES 50. Name translates "He is mine" (Murray)	727 PM 33.1954
38	129	—	*Nb-nfr* enclosed in scrolls linked. Cf. HIC, VII: 1 for scroll. Dyn. xiii–xiv.	738 MMA 34.126.22
39	129	—	Scrolls linked with signs in spaces. Cf. M. II, 149: 48, Stra. XII, T. 5106. Dyn. xiii–xiv.	744 MMA 34.126.28
40	129	11	Mounted in AE ring. *Nfr* in linked concentric circles. Dyn. xiv–xvi.	729
41	129	38	*Iri-mr*, a private name, in continuous hook-scroll. Dyn. xiii/Hyksos. RES 61.	740 PM 33.1956
42	129	—	Lion facing uraeus. Dyn. xiii–xiv.	724 MMA 34.126.20
43	129	25	Lion with two *nb* signs in field. BP I, X: 69, Tomb 556. Dyn. xv–xvi.	726
44	129	—	Deer with uraeus and palms in field. Dyn. xv. BP I, X: 92, Tomb 596; BDS XIV: 867.	735 MMA 34.126.25
45	129	39	Man with emblem, with signs in field, surrounded by rope border. Dyn. xv.	723
46	129	—	Falcon-headed god holding uraeus on *nb*. Uraeus in front (below). BP I, VII: 46, Tomb 545. Dyn. xv–xvi.	732 MMA 34.126.26
47	129	14	Hathor with palms, head in profile. Dyn. xv.	742
48	129	—	*Nub-nfr* and other signs, flanked by red crowns. Dyn. xv–xvi.	733 MMA 34.126.24
49	129	8	Jumbled signs with *nub* below and reversed above; all within rope border. Dyn. xiv (?).	736
50	129	15	Signs, possibly *wȝḥ-k'-nb* (Rowe), flanked by *nśw-ḫpr*. Dyn. xv.	739
51	129	—	Hieroglyphs in three vertical rows. Dyn. xv.	737 MMA 34.126.23
52	129	2	*Nśw bit, R'-nb*, "King of Upper and Lower Egypt, Ra-neb"; with flanking hieroglyphs. Dyn. xiv. RES 108.	728 PM 33.1955
53	129	11	*Nfr-nub* flanked by *ḥm* (Murray) or *s'* (Rowe) and red crowns. Dyn. xv–xvi.	734
54	129	1	In AE ring, partly broken. Signs between vertical lines. Dyn. xv.	741
55	129	14	Stylised signs *Rn Rȝ* between red crowns. Dyn. xv–xvi.	746

Plate 30 (*cont.*)

No.	Locus	Side Type Plate 41	Remarks	Field No. Museum No.
56	129	—	Stylised signs. Dyn. xv.	731 MMA 34.126.29
57	129	—	Stylised hieroglyphs. Dyn. xv.	743 MMA 34.126.27
58	129	11	*Ḥm Nt*, "Servant of Neith" (Red Crown) (Murray) or *S'-Nt*, "Prophet of Neith" (Rowe). Dyn. xv–xvi.	745
59	129	—	*Ḥm Ḥr*, "Servant of Horus, or *S' Ḥr*, "Protection of Horus". Stylised hieroglyphs. Dyn. xv.	747 MMA 34.126.30
60	6028	15	Variant of *R'-'ꜣ-ḫ'*, between uraei. Wings in centre, uraei reversed above. Dyn. xv–xvi (?).	6673 PM 38.755
61	6028	33	Cord pattern. BP I, XXII: 215, Tomb 580; AASOR XVII, 28: 12, Stra. D; M. II, 149: 27, T. 3095, Stra. XII; BDS VIII: 252. Dyn. xv–xvii.	6675
62	6028	3	Scrolls, linked, round. Cf. M. II, 150: 92, T. 3085, Stra. XI; AAA XIX, XXXVIII: 7, Tomb 22. Dyn. xv.	6674
63	4022	11	*R'-ḫ'-ḫpr* in cartouche, surrounded by hieroglyphs. Cf. RES 10. Dyn. xv–xvi.	6065
64	4022	2	Man wearing wrapped garment, seated on high-backed chair. Name (?) and other signs in field. (See p. 95.) Dyn. xv–xvi.	6063
65	4022	25	*Nśw-bit*; *'nḫ* flanking *nub* below. Cf. BP I, X: 80, Tomb 59; AG IV, VII: 193, TAD 860. See No. 79. Dyn. xv–xvi.	6066
66	4022	14	Horus eye and other signs. Dyn. xvi.	6064

Plate 32 (Photographs on Pl. 33)

No.	Locus	Side Type Plate 41	Remarks	Field No. Museum No.
67	6027	25	*Nfr* in hook-scroll above. *Dd* between *nfr* signs below. Gauthier II, p. 50, No. 51. Dyn. xv.	6634
68	6027	26	S-scroll between lines and *nfr* signs. AASOR XVII, 29: 14, Stra. E–D. Dyn. xv–xvii.	6636
69	6027	37	Concentric circles. Cf. M. II, 150: 78, Stra. XI, T. 3110; Jericho, 1953, Tomb A. 34.110. Dyn. xv–xvi.	6651
70	6027	8	*'nḫ* signs between vertical lines, with *ḥm* (Murray) or *s'* (Rowe) and *šn* signs flanking. Dyn. xv–xvi.	6653 PM 38.754
71	6027	5	Lion with *'nḫ*, *nb* and plant in field. Dyn. xv.	6632
72	6027	38	Figure kneeling with uraeus. Dyn. xv–xvi.	6645
73	6027	27	*Ḫpr* below two uraei facing. M. II, 151: 114, Stra. X, N. 14; AG I, XIII: 73, DK 652; AG II, VIII: 119, MB 116; cf. for similar cutting and snakes, BP I, VII: 34, Tomb 568; HIC VII: 28, Yehudiyeh Grave 5. Dyn. xiv.	6633
74	6027	14	*Nfr* between *ḥm* (Murray) or *s'* (Rowe); *nb* below; plant emblem of the Delta above. Cf. M. II, 150: 68, T. 3080, Stra. XI. Dyn. xv–xvi.	7276
75	6027	11	Uraeus with *mꜣ't* feather and red-crowned hawk on *nb*. Dyn. xv–xvi.	6637
76	6027	19	Red-crowned uraeus on *nb*; *ḥm* (Murray) or *s'* (Rowe) signs flanking. Dyn. xv–xvi.	6641
77	6027	3	*Nśw-bit* above *dd-'nḫ* on *nb*. Dyn. xv–xvi.	6649
78	6027	25	*Nub* and *ḫ'* (reversed) between red crowns reversed. Dyn. xv–xvi.	6639
79	6027	7	*Nśw-bit*; *'nḫ* flanking; *nub* below. Cf. RES, p. 10 and No. 34. BP I, X: 80, Tomb 559. Dyn. xv–xvi.	6640
80	6027	25	*Nśw-bit*; *nfr* flanking; two *nb* signs below. Dyn. xv–xvi.	6638
81	6027	—	Zig-zag or palm pattern, worn and burnt. Dyn. xvi.	6652

No.	Locus	Side Type Plate 41	Remarks	Field No. Museum No.
82	6027	39	Cord pattern, hatched. BP I, XII: 123, Tomb 569. Cf. BP II, XLIII: 7, Tomb 1021. Dyn. xv–xvii.	6647
83	6027	—	*Rˤ-nfr* in square, flanked by *ḥm* (Murray) or *sꜣ* (Rowe) signs or twists. Dyn. xv–xvi.	6646
84	6027	—	Palm pattern. Dyn. xv–xvi.	6635
85	6027	25	*Ḥm-ḫpr* flanked by *nśw* and *nfr* signs. For *ḥm* (Murray), Rowe reads *wꜣḥ* or *sꜣ*. Dyn. xiv or later.	6644
86	6027	25	Horus eye below plant on *nb* sign, and *ḫpr*. Dyn. xvi.	6648
87	6027	37	*rn* formula (? *rdi-n-Rˤ*). Dyn. xv–xvi.	6650
88	6027	35	*rn* formula. Dyn. xv–xvi.	6643
89	6027	37	Stylised hieroglyphs, two *ḫˤ* signs with *nb* flanking. Dyn. xv–xvi.	6642
90	157	2	*Ḥtp-ˤ(ꜣ)-ḥtp-Rˤ*, in ellipse. Surrounded by hook-scroll. Dyn. xv. RES 168.	2657 PM 34.2996
91	157	2	*Sdꜣwty* (?) *bity, Nfrwy-ˤꜣ*, "treasurer of the King of Lower Egypt, Nefer-ewyāa". Enclosed in hook-scroll. Dyn. xv. RES 179.	2651 PM 34.2990
92	157	11	Stylised hieroglyphs: *dꜣy-ˤiˤrt*, "stretches-forth-the-arm the uraeus". Below: two Horus eyes. *Nśw* and *ˤꜣḥ* repeated. Hyksos. RES 269.	2656 PM 34.2995
93	157	27	*Rˤ-ḫpr* flanked by *ˤnḫ* signs; S-scroll above and below. Dyn. xv. RES 158.	2653 PM 34.2992
94	157	27	*Nfr* between *nśw* signs, *nub* below; S-scroll flanking; Dyn. xiii or later. RES 41.	2647 PM 34.2986
95	157	6	Plant design, curled ends. S-scrolls flanking. Hyksos. RES 397.	2650 PM 34.2989
96	157	15	Vulture, fish and crocodile with plant. Rope border. Dyn. xiii/Hyksos. RES 68.	2652 PM 34.2991
97	157	33	Man smelling flower. *Nfr* in field. Hyksos. RES 289. BDS XIV: 941.	2649 PM 34.2988
98	157	27	Falcon-headed god holding lotus. Hyksos. RES 292.	2648 PM 34.2987
99	157	24	Hathor with palms on *nb*. Hyksos. RES 273. Cf. BP I, VII: 47, Tomb 545, T. 565.	2654 PM 34.2993
100	157	13	Palm branch. See Pl. 38: 263. RES 376; BP I, VII: 9, Tomb 570, XII: 119, Tomb 593. Dyn. xv.	2655 PM 34.2994
101	157	24	*Mn-Rˤ* (?), *mn-ḫpr-ꜣ-ḫˤ*, perhaps king Rā-āa-khā; *nub* below; partial hook-scroll. Dyn. xv. RES 153.	2658 PM 34.2997
102	157	11	*Nśw wꜣḥ-Rˤ*, "king of Lower Egypt, Rā-waḥ". Below: twist, looped cord and *nub* sign. Dyn. xiii or later. RES 32. M.A.M. reads *nśw-šn-Rˤ*.	2659 PM 34.2998
103	157	24	Stylised hieroglyphs, divided by flower-bud on long stalk. Possible reading: *Rˤ-ˤꜣ-ḫˤ. c.* Dyn. xv. RES 152.	2660 PM 34.2999
104	153	11	*Rˤ-n-ḫˤ-nfrwy, n nb* in cartouche; flanked by signs arranged symmetrically. Possibly Sebekhetep III or later. Dyn. xiii. RES 21. Gauthier II, p. 31: 23.	2603 PM 34.2951
105	153	11	Reversed writing of *di-n-Rˤ* in cartouche. Concentric circles surrounding. Dyn. xvi. RES 215. Cf. PSC XII: 20 for circles.	2604 PM 34.2952
106	153	11	*Dd-ḫpr-nub* in hook-scroll. Dyn. xiv. RES 107. Cf. 142.	2616 PM 34.2964
107	153	6	Scroll design or cross pattern with lotus flowers, *nfr* repeated in centre. Dyn. xiii–xiv. RES 97.	2602 PM 34.2949
108	153	6	Concentric circles. Dyn. xiii/Hyksos. RES 76. AAA XX, p. 9, Fig. 3, 5 Tomb 31; BDS VIII: 207; M. II, 149: 42, Stra. XII, T. 4107; MT 105: 4, Tomb 24.	2609 PM 34.2957

No.	Locus	Side Type Plate 41	Remarks	Field No. Museum No.
109	153	24	Stylised hieroglyphs with *nśw*, surrounded by hook-scroll. Dyn. xv. RES 200. BP I, X: 65, Tomb 556 (for hook-scroll only).	2619 PM 34.2967
110	153	6	Three rows of scrolls linked. Hyksos. RES 400. Cf. BDS VII: 59.	2610 PM 34.2958
111	153	11	Cross pattern, curled ends. Hyksos. RES 370; M. II, 150: 77, Stra. XI, T. 3110; MT, 105: 6, Tomb 24; AAA XIX, XXXVII: 11, Tomb 9; BP I, VII: 14, Tomb 551. Cf. BDS VIII: 262.	2608 PM 34.2956
112	153	11	Cross pattern, curled ends. Hyksos. RES 369. BP I, XLIII: 503, Tomb 238. Cf. BDS VIII: 262–264.	2606 PM 34.2954
113	153	37	Cord pattern. Hyksos. RES 414. BP I, X: 87, Tomb 559; BP II, XLIII: 16, 21, Tomb 1021; AG IV, IX: 342, T. 850. Cf. BDS VIII: 253. Dyn. xv–xvii.	2620 PM 34.2968
114	153	27	Man holding uraeus (?), another below. RES 279. Cf. BP I, VII: 46, Tomb 545. Dyn. xiv–xv.	2617 PM 34.2965
115	153	11	Falcon wearing red crown with uraeus on *nb*. Plant and Horus eye above. Hyksos. RES 336. Cf. AG IV, IV: 91; RES 176.	2613 PM 34.2691
116	153	11	Red crown, *ḥm* and *ʿnḫ* above; *śʾ* between two *nfr* signs below. Hyksos. RES 349.	2611 PM 34.2959
117	153	11	Uraeus wearing red crown, on *nb*. *Rʿ-nfr* to left; *ḥm* repeated on right. Dyn. xiv/Hyksos. RES 119. Cf. AAA XX, XXVI: Tomb 4, No. 5.	2615 PM 34.2963
118	153	11	Red crown and *ḥm* (Murray) or *śʾ* (Rowe) in centre; *di* (?) above and *nb* below. Hyksos. RES 345.	2607 PM 34.2955
119	153	11	Red crown on *nb* with *ḥm* (Murray) or *śʾ* (Rowe) in centre; *nb* inverted above. Hyksos. RES 346.	2623 PM 34.2971
120	153	14	Red crown on *nb* in centre, flanked by *ḥm* (Murray) or *śʾ* (Rowe). *Ḥtp* above. Hyksos. RES 252. M. II, 150: 68, T. 3080, Stra. XI; *Gurob*, XXII: 15, Group 27, Amenhetep I or earlier.	2605 PM 34.2953
121	153	11	Traces of AE ring. Plant emblems representing union of Upper and Lower Egypt, flanked by red crowns, one inverted. Hyksos. RES 366.	2621 PM 34.2969
122	153	11	Two uraei facing with *śʾ* between in centre; red crown above and below. Hyksos. RES 328.	2614 PM 34.2962
123	153	2	*Nśw-bit*. Below: *ḫpr-nub*, *nb-nfr* on each side. Dyn. xiv. RES 106.	2612 PM 34.2960
124	153	11	Plant emblem of the Delta above. Red crown, *ʿnḫ* and *nfr* with *nb* below. Hyksos. RES 350.	2618 PM 34.2966
125	153	11	Falcon wearing red crown, with *nfr*, *nb* below. Hyksos. RES 340. Cf. M. II, 150: 69, T. 3080, Stra. XI.	2622 PM 34.2970
126	168	6	*Ḫpr-kʾ-Rʿ* (Senusert I), flanked by *nśw* and *ʿnḫ* signs. Dyn. xii. RES 5.	2679 PM 34.3003
127	543	37	*Ḫpr-ʿnḫ-Rʿ* repeated on each side of *ʿnḫ* and *dd* (?) signs.	3738 PM 36.1820
128	543	22	*Nb-mʿʿt-Rʿ* (Amenhetep III) in cartouche. To left: *ymn-tyt* "Image of Amen". Dyn. xviii.	4349 PM 36.1484
129	511	27	Falcon-headed god with crocodile on *nb*. Cf. RES 276 (Jericho, Tomb 43). BP II, XLIV: 70, Tomb 1026. Dyn. xv.	3468
130	511	6	Man holding lotus with *nfr* on *nb*. Dyn. xiv.	3467
131	511	11	Stylised hieroglyphs on *nb* with plant signs. AASOR XVII, 29: 1, Stra. E–D. Dyn. xv–xvi.	3470 PM 36.1813
132	511	22	Uraei facing; *ḫpr* in centre; surrounded by rope border. Dyn. xviii or later.	3469
133	K.18	7	Stylised hieroglyphs in hook-scroll. Dyn. xii–xiv.	7229

Plate 32 (cont.)

No.	Locus	Side Type Plate 41	Remarks	Field No. Museum No.
134	D/X	8	Royal name (?) in cartouche; concentric circles surrounding. Dyn. xv–xvi.	5356
135	6000	8	Ḫꜥ-ḥtp-Rꜥ (Sebekhetep VI) with title "good ḥmi of all lands" between vertical lines. Crown, uraeus and other signs flanking. Gauthier II, p. 42, No. 26.	7259
136	D/X	—	Seal impression on jar handle. Two signs and partially preserved scroll.	7346
137	NW corner	—	Seal impression on jar handle. Falcon-headed god standing with hawk and ḫpr in field. Rope border. Dyn. xv.	7160 PM 39.822
138	K.17: 1089	14	Formula. Nb above with ḫpr flanked by kꜣ signs. Wings in centre. Below: name (?) between red crowns. See L. III, pp. 124–125. Dyn. xv–xvi.	7160 PM 39.822
139	D/X	7	Ntr-nfr, ꜥꜣ-ḥtp-Rꜥ, ꜥnḫ-ḏt, "the good god, Aa-Hetep Rā, gifted with life" in hook-scroll. Cf. RES 166. Dyn. xv.	6100

Plate 34 (Photographs on Pl. 35)

No.	Locus	Side Type Plate 41	Remarks	Field No. Museum No.
140	4004	5	Sꜣ-Rꜥ-ppy (Pepy or Sheshi); in cartouche. ꜥnḫ ḏt "Living eternally" below. Hook-scroll, sides unconnected. Dyn. early xvi. AG III, III: 9. Cf. RES 206. AT 690; AG IV, IX: 274; PSC XXI, xvi c: 1–4.	5712
141	4004	2	ḥtp-ḫꜥ-ḥtp,-ꜣ-m-ntr in hook-scroll. Cf. 196; RES 169–175. Dyn. xv.	5687
142	4004	22	Ḫpr in circle with ḏd above and nfrwy below; surrounded by scroll. Possibly reading ḏd-ḫpr-Rꜥ. Gauthier II, p. 101, No. 35. Cf. 106. Dyn. xiv.	5661
143	4004	42	Partial scroll, hooked, with signs. Dyn. xv–xvi.	5677
144	4004	15	Scrolls linked, with two crosses in central spaces. Cf. BDS VII: 28. Dyn. xiii–xiv.	5734
145	4004	5	Hrw-nfr (or nfr-Rꜥ) in linked scroll border. Dyn. xv. BDS VII: 52; PSC XX: X. Cf. BP I, X: 101, Tomb 565.	5735
146	4004	2	Scrolls linked. NS XVIII: 24. Dyn. xiii–xviii.	5645
147	4004	2	Scrolls linked. MT 113: 17. Dyn. xiii–xviii.	5708
148	4004	2	Scrolls linked. Dyn. xiii–xviii.	5736
149	4004	46	Amethyst. Deer couchant in hook-scroll. Dyn. xiii–xiv.	5775 PM 38.68
150	4004	hidden by setting	Au mount with Ag ring. Scroll design with signs in field. Cf. BDS VII: 84. Dyn. xvi.	5773
151	4004	46	Debased form of linked scrolls with nfr. Dyn. xvi.	5668
152	4004	20	Stylised hieroglyphs, hatched. Dyn. xiii–xiv.	5680
153	4004	37	S-scroll in centre with plant. Cf. BDS VIII: 179 and p. 15. Dyn. early xviii.	5743
154	4004	19	Scroll and plant with uraeus and nfr. Cf. BDS VIII: 185 and p. 15. Dyn. xvi–early xviii.	5751
155	4004	27	Scroll and plant with ꜥnḫ. Dyn. early xviii.	5764
156	4004	37	S-scroll in centre, with plants. BDS VIII: 187 and p. 15; BP I, XII. 131, Tomb 564. Cf. M. II, 150: 88, Stra. XI, T. 4055. Dyn. early xviii.	5639
157	4004	37	Scroll and plant with nfr in centre. AG I, XIII: 4, Level II. Dyn. early xviii.	5766
158	4004	4	rn formula between vertical and horizontal lines in rope border. Dyn. xv.	5673
159	4004	2	rn formula in three vertical lines; central line enclosed in imitation cartouches. AAA XX, XXVI: 7, Tomb 5.e. Dyn. xv.	5681
160	4004	21	rn formula divided into imitation cartouches, flanked by crowned falcons and ꜥnḫ signs. Cf, AASOR XVII, 28: 13, Stra. D. Dyn. xv–xvi.	5679

Plate 34 (*cont.*)

No.	Locus	Side Type Plate 41	Remarks	Field No. Museum No.
161	4004	8	*rn* formula between vertical lines, flanked by *nfr* signs above and red crowns below. Dyn. xv.	5746 PM 38.66
162	4004	19	Hathor head with palm branch between lines. Cf. NS XXV: 14, 15; M. II, 149: 11, Stra. XII, 2139. Dyn. xvi.	5706
163	4004	—	Cylinder seal, dark steatite. Man with arms raised, followed by quadrupeds (see p. 111).	5665 PM 38.56
164	4004	—	Cylinder seal, dark steatite. Man followed by bovine and winged quadrupeds. Scorpion in field. MT 95: 34, Tomb 877 Bl (see p. 111).	5664 PM 38.55
165	4004	—	Cylinder seal. Stylised human figures (see p. 111).	5656 PM 38.54
166	4004	—	Plaque with same design on both sides. Crocodiles with palm tree in centre. Cf. NS XXV: 23. Dyn. xv–xvi.	5631
167	4004	—	Seal, with eight small scarabs disposed round central rosette on back. Reverse inscribed with Hathor head and two falcons on *nb* sign. Dyn. xvi. *Sedment I*, XLIII: 50, Group 1300.	5663
168	4004	—	Plaque. Obv.: cross pattern, curled ends. Rev.: design with *sm'* central, flanked by *m''t* feathers and uraei. Dyn. xvi–xviii.	5651
169	4004	—	Plaque with same design on both sides. Cross pattern, curled ends. Dyn. xvi–xviii.	5703
170	4004	—	Fish-backed seal with plant and *nb* signs on face. Cf. RES s. 50 for fish. Dyn. xviii.	5676
171	4004	—	Plaque. Obv.: *nb-m''t-R'* (Amenhetep III). Rev.: *Ymn-ḥtp-ḥq'-w'st* "Amenhetep, ruler of Thebes". Dyn. xviii.	5720
172	4004	—	Plaque. Obv.: Horus eye. Reverse surface worn. Dyn. xviii.	5771
173	4004	—	Plaque. Obv.: *Mn-ḫpr-R'*, *ntr-nfr* (Thothmes III). Rev.: *Ymn-R'* with *nb* signs. Dyn. xviii.	5652
174	4004	—	Plaque with uraeus on back. Hathor head on face. Dyn. xvi or later.	5772 PM 38.67
175	4004	19	Concentric circles joined. Cf. BDS VIII: 207; M. II, 151: 124, Stra. X, T. 3070. Dyn. xv–xvi.	5658
176	4004	25	Concentric circles joined. BDS VIII: 210. Cf. AAA XIX, XXXVII: 10, Tomb 9. Dyn. xv–xvi.	5688
177	4004	15	Cord pattern. BDS VIII: 158; MT 105: 5, Tomb 24; M. II, 151: 131, Stra. X, T. 3055; AG III, III: 3 AT 653. Dyn. xv–xvii.	5671
178	4004	23	Cord pattern. MT 137: 1, Tomb 37; BDS VIII: 150; B.I, CXXX: 1420, Levels I–II; AG V, X: 155, DS 830. Dyn. xv–xvii.	5657
179	4004	27	Cross pattern, curled ends with central knot. Cf. BDS VIII: 245, 246. Dyn. xvi–xviii.	5693
180	4004	22	Cross pattern with lotus flower in corners. Dyn. xvii–xviii.	5650
181	4004	37	Central twist with *'nḫ* and *nb* signs flanking. Cf. BDS VIII: 225; NS XIX: 2; M. II, 150: 86, T. 4055; Stra. XI. Dyn. xvi–xvii.	5754
182	4004	36	Central twist with debased *nb* signs. BP I, XII: 134, Tomb 564; AG V, X: 163, 3/2 level 863; HIC, VIII: 46, Yehudiyeh Grave 37. Dyn. xiii–xvi.	5812
183	4004	19	*Ḫ'* sign above looped cords. Dyn. xvi–xvii.	5682
184	4004	37	Central twist with flanking lotus flowers. Cf. AASOR XVII, 29: 9, Stra. E. Dyn. xvi–xvii.	5752
185	4004	37	*Ḫ'* sign above looped cords. Dyn. xvi–xvii.	5632
186	4004	14	*K'-R'* above looped cords. Cf. BDS VIII: 199. Dyn. xvi–xvii.	5747
187	4004	30	Lotus flowers reversed between lines. Dyn. xvi–xvii.	5695
188	4004	—	Cowroid. *K'-R'* in imitation cartouche, flanked by debased red crowns on four sides. Dyn. xv–xviii.	5726 PM 38.61

Plate 34 (*cent.*)

No.	Locus	Side Type Plate 41	Remarks	Field No. Museum No.
189	4004	—	Cowroid. *K'-ḫpr-k'* in centre. Plant emblem of the Delta above and below. Dyn. xvi–xviii.	5727 PM 38.62
190	4004	—	Cowroid. Looped cord and *nub* sign with plant emblems of the Delta at top and reversed at bottom. Cf NS XX: 33. Dyn. xvi–xvii.	5674 PM 38.58
191	4004	—	Cowroid. Cross pattern and uraei. Dyn. xviii.	5731
192	4004	—	Cowroid. Cross pattern and uraei. Dyn. xviii.	5729
193	4004	—	Cowroid. Cross pattern and uraei. Dyn. xviii.	5730
194	4004	—	Cowroid. Cord pattern in rope border. Cf. BDS VIII: 252, without rope border. Dyn. xvi.	5669
195	4004	—	Cowroid. Stylised hieroglyphs: *dd* sign flanked by *'nḫ* signs and uraei; *nb* below. Dyn. xv or later.	5813
196	4004	—	Cowroid. Name (?). Cf. 141. Dyn. xv?	5733
197	4004	—	Cowroid. Faint traces of hieroglyphs.	5732
198	4004	—	Cowroid. Upper half missing.	5774
199	4004	—	Cowroid. Palms and lines. Dyn. xviii.	5763

Plate 36 (Nos. 200–230 photographed or Pl. 35, Nos. 231–249 on Pl. 37)

No.	Locus	Side Type Plate 41	Remarks	Field No. Museum No.
200	4004	19	*dd* sign flanked by *nśw* and *'nḫ*. Nub below. Cf. BP I, XXII: 228, Area 800. Dyn. xiii or later.	5749
201	4004	16	*W'd* sign flanked by *nśw*. Three *nfr* signs and *nub* below. Dyn. xiii or later.	5738
202	4004	16	Looped cords, debased; *nub* sign below, within rope border. Cf. 2. Dyn. xiv–xvi.	5678
203	4004	40	Stylised hieroglyphs: *ḫpr* on side above *nub* sign flanked by *'nḫ* signs. BP II, LXXIII: 47, F/X. Cf. HIC IX: 125, Yehudiyeh. Dyn. xiii–xiv.	5750
204	4004	27	*Nśw-'nḫ* above Horus eyes; *ḫpr* in centre flanked by *'nḫ* signs; *nub* below. Dyn. xiii–xiv.	5744
205	4004	—	Stylised design, plant emblem of the Delta on *nb*. Dyn. xviii.	5691
206	4004	5	Stylised hieroglyphs: winged sun above uraeus and *'nḫ* sign; *nb* below. Dyn. xviii.	5636
207	4004	11	Formula, with large *nb* sign. Dyn. xv.	5742
208	4004	38	Stylised hieroglyphs uraeus and maāt feather above *nb*. Dyn. xviii.	5660
209	4004	6	Scroll and plant on *nb*; *nub* sign above. Dyn. xviii.	5808
210	4004	26	Red-crowned falcon with mixed signs in rope border. Dyn. xv–xvi.	5741 PM 38.65
211	4004	37	Red crown, debased, and plant on *nb*; *ḫtp* sign above. Dyn. xviii.	5698
212	4004	23	Red crowns, debased. Dyn. xviii.	5753
213	4004	11	Red crown and *nfr* (?) sign. Plant emblem of the Delta above. Dyn. xv–xvi.	5709
214	4004	36	Debased red crown with *'nḫ* sign. Dyn. xviii.	5769
215	4004	6	Lion smiting two men. Dyn. xiii–xv.	5654
216	4004	6	Lion with uraei in field. Dyn. xv–xvi.	5810
217	4004	27	Lion, walking. Dyn. xv–xvi.	5757
218	4004	37	Lion couchant. Cf. AASOR XVII, 29: 4, TBM Stra. E. Dyn. xv.	5761
219	4004	38	Sphinx trampling man. Dyn. xix.	5707
220	4004	23	Sphinx or lion. Dyn. xviii–xix.	5646
221	4004	24	Sphinx or lion. Dyn. xviii–xix.	5758
222	4004	—	Glass. Winged animal. Dyn. xviii.	5648

Plate 36 (*cont.*)

No.	Locus	Side Type Plate 41	Remarks	Field No. Museum No.
223	4004	19	Deer, head turned. Dyn. xviii.	5705
224	4004	37	Deer with plant. AG V, X: 118, FL 869. Dyn. xviii.	5759
225	4004	35	Deer couchant with plant. Cf. BDS XVIII: 1400. Dyn. xv.	5655
226	4004	43	Deer, running. Dyn. xviii.	5760
227	4004	37	Hathor cow with *nfr* in field, in rope border. Dyn. xix.	5689
228	4004	50	Hathor cow. Dyn. xix.	5686
229	4004	19	*Nśw-bit* debased. Dyn. xv–xvi.	5770
230	4004	37	Fish. Dyn. xviii.	5653
231	4004	39	In AE ring. Man holding lotus with uraeus in field on *nb*. Dyn. xv–xvi.	5666
232	4004	39	Man holding lotus with hieroglyphs below reading: *di-n-Rˁ*, "gift of Ra". Dyn. xv–xvi.	5672
233	4004	39	Man holding plant on *nb*. Dyn. xiv–xv.	5692
234	4004	14	Falcon-headed god with two uraei on *nb*. BP I, VII: 46, Tomb 545; AG III, IV: 137. Dyn. xiv–xv.	5697
235	4004	14	Man with signs in field. Dyn. xv–xvi.	5739 PM 38.64
236	4004	44	Obsidian (?). Man, arm raised, with plants. Dyn. xv–xvi.	5635
237	4004	13	Man holding palm branch with *nfr* signs in field. Dyn. xv–xvi.	5659
238	4004	19	Kneeling figure with palm in triple rope border. Dyn. xvi–xvii.	5737
239	4004	—	Cowroid. Kneeling figure with *hs* vase. Dyn. xviii.	5728 PM 38.63
240	4004	24	Three gods hand in hand. See Pl. 39: 339, 371. M. II, 152: 188, E = 2092, Stra. VII. Cf. BP I, XXXI: 305, Tomb 641. Dyn. xix.	5756
241	4004	37	Falcon-headed god with uraei. BP I, VII: 46, Tomb 545. Dyn. xix.	5809
242	4004	38	Setekh with *wˁś* sceptre. Dyn. xix.	5634
243	4004	23	Pharaoh slaying enemy. In field: *Wsr-mˁˁt-Rˁ* (Rameses II). Cf. RES 671. BP II, LII: 136, Tomb 934. Dyn. xix.	5662
244	4004	36	Ptah with sceptre and *nfr* sign. Dyn. xix. Cf. BP I, XII: 172, Tomb 902.	5748
245	4004	22	Ra (?) with sceptre, debased and worn. Dyn. xviii or later.	5816
246	4004	—	Eye-backed seal. Reading *Rnwtt* (?) on face. Dyn. xviii.	5724 PM 38.60
247	4004	—	Blue glaze with white inlay. Eye-backed seal with *nb-mˁˁt-Rˁ* in cartouche on face (Amenhetep III). Dyn. xviii.	5723
248	4004	—	Eye-backed seal with *Ymn-Rˁ* on face. Dyn. xviii.	5762
249	4004	23	Large *ḫpr*. Dyn. xviii–xix.	5683

Plate 38 (Photographs on Pl. 37)

No.	Locus	Side Type Plate 41	Remarks	Field No. Museum No.
250	4004	hidden by setting	In Au setting. Hathor head with *nfr* above, flanked by uraei, *wˁḏ* and *wˁḥ* signs. Dyn. xvi.	5649 PM 38.53
251	4004	4	*Ht-ntr, ḥmm ḏfȝ* (?) *Ḥˁp(y) nb imȝḥ*. Rowe translates: "Overseer of the provisions (*ḏfa*) of the Temple of Ḥāpy (Nile-God), Khemem, the Venerable." Dyn. xiii. p. 95.	5670 PM 38.57
252	4004	hidden by setting	In Au setting. Stylised hieroglyphs above and below central bar. Dyn. xix.	5745
253	4004	38	Debased uraei joined, facing out, under wings. Dyn. xix.	5765
254	4004	9	Stylised hieroglyphs. Dyn. xviii–xix.	5694

No.	Locus	Side Type Plate 41	Remarks	Field No. Museum No.
255	4004	38	Stylised hieroglyphs: *ḫpr* and uraeus, lines on right. Dyn. xix.	5684
256	4004	13	Stylised hieroglyphs: *dd* flanked by *ʿnḫ* signs above; group repeated below. Dyn. xviii–xix.	5740
257	4004	37	Debased signs including *nfr.* and *nsw.* Dyn. xviii–xix.	5638
258	4004	14	Stylised hieroglyphs: *dd* in centre, *ʿnḫ* on right, left side broken. Dyn. xviii.	5699
259	4004	29	Glass. Debased signs. Scarab made in a mould. Dyn. xviii–xix.	5685
260	4004	37	Debased signs—*nfr* and Horus eye. Dyn. xviii–xix.	5768
261	4004	38	Glass (?). Horus eye. Debased and worn. Dyn. xviii–xix.	5702
262	4004	—	Broken scarab. Signs incomplete.	5711
263	4004	37	Palm pattern. See Pl. 32: 100. BP I, XII: 119, Tomb 593; BP II, XLIII: 22, Tomb 1021. Dyn. xv.	5767
264	4004	38	Glass (?). *ʿnḫ* sign.	5710
265	4004	38	Glass (?). Signs worn.	5814
266	4004	36	*Sꜣ-Ymn*, *nfr.* Dyn. xviii–xix.	5643
267	4004	37	*Sꜣ-Rʿ-ppy* (Pepy or Sheshi) *di-ʿnḫ.* AG IV, V: 17, Tomb 491. Dyn. xv–xvii.	5675
268	4004	—	Duck-backed seal. *Ymn-Rʿ* between two *nb* signs on face. Cf. NS, p. 87, Figs. 91–92. Reign of Amenhetep III. Dyn. xviii.	5641
269	4004	30	*Ymn-Rʿ* and plant design. Dyn. xviii–xix.	5690
270	4004	31	*Ymn-Rʿ* and other signs. Dyn. xviii–xix. BP II, XLVIII: 3, Tomb 905, Dyn. xix–xx.	5642
271	4004	35	*Ymn-Rʿ* with lotus bud. Dyn. xviii–xix BP II, LVII: 351, Tomb 982; BDS XII: 661; AG II, VII: 28, Tomb 1057, 40, Tomb 1073.	5696
272	4004	hidden by setting	In Au setting. *Ymn-Rʿ* in rope border. Dyn. xix.	5815
273	4004	22	*Ymn-Rʿ*, worn. Cf. AG II, VII: 30, Tomb 1057. Dyn. xviii.	5667
274	4004	23	*Ymn-Rʿ*, chipped. Dyn. xviii.	5637
275	4004	38	Red glass (?). *Ymn-Rʿ*, worn. Dyn. xix.	5633
276	4004	38	Black glaze or glass. Debased signs. Dyn. xviii–xix.	5700
277	4004	—	Blue glaze. Debased signs.	5701
278	4004	41	Paste. Debased signs.	5704
279	4004	41	Quartz. Uninscribed.	5784
280	4004	41	Amethyst. Uninscribed.	5777
281	4004	22	*Mn-ḫpr-Rʿ* (Thothmes III) in cartouche with kneeling figure of king holding *ḥqꜣ* sceptre. Dyn. xviii.	5713
282	4004	22	*Mn-ḫpr-Rʿ* (Thothmes III) in central cartouche, flanked by two pairs of uraei, winged sun above and *nub* below. Dyn. xviii.	5811
283	4004	22	*Mn-ḫpr-Rʿ* (Thothmes III) in central cartouche, flanked by *mꜣʿt* feathers and uraei. Dyn. xviii.	5717
284	4004	22	*Mn-ḫpr-Rʿ* (Thothmes III) in central cartouche, flanked by signs. Dyn. xviii.	5714
285	4004	22	*Mn-ḫpr-Rʿ* (Thothmes III) in small cartouche each side of knot design ending in uraei. *Nb-tꜣwi* above, *ntr-nfr* below. Dyn. xviii.	5715
286	4004	23	*Mn-ḫpr-Rʿ* (Thothmes III), protected by winged uraeus. *Hrw-nfr, hrw-nb* in field. Dyn. xviii.	5715
287	4004	22	*ʿ-ḫprw-Rʿ* (Amenhetep II) in cartouche with *mꜣʿt* and *nfr* signs to right. *Nb* sign above inverted, repeated below. Dyn. xviii.	5640
288	4004	22	*Mn-ḫprw-Rʿ* (Thothmes IV) in cartouche with protecting falcons on either side. Dyn. xviii.	5718 PM 38.59
289	4004	22	*Nb-mꜣʿt-Rʿ* (Amenhetep III) in central cartouche with uraei flanking, winged sun above and *nub* sign below. Dyn. xviii.	5719
290	4004	22	*Nb-mꜣʿt-Rʿ* (Amenhetep III) in central cartouche, flanked by uraei. Dyn. xviii.	5725

Plate 38 (*cont.*)

No.	Locus	Side Type Plate 41	Remarks	Field No. Museum No.
291	4004	23	*Nb-mᶜᵗ-Rᶜ* (Amenhetep III). Dyn. xviii.	5647
292	4004	22	*Nb-mᶜᵗ-Rᶜ* (Amenhetep III). Dyn. xviii.	5722
293	4004	38	*Nb-mᶜᵗ-Rᶜ* (Amenhetep III). Dyn. xviii.	5721
294	4004	22	*Nb-mᶜᵗ-Rᶜ* (Amenhetep III). Dyn. xviii.	5755
295	555	—	Very soft paste. Oblong seal, pierced vertically, each face inscribed. 1, 2, 3 see p. 128; 4: *ᶜ-ḫpr-Rᶜ* (Amenhetep II) flanked by *mᶜᵗ* feathers with *nb-tᶜwï-ntr-nfr* below. Dyn. xviii.	3846 PM 36.1825
296	555	23	Stylised design. Plant emblem of the Delta on *nb* with *ḫᶜ* above. Dyn. xviii–xix.	4346
297	555	22	Cross pattern, looped uraei. Cf. BP I, XII: 130, Tomb 564. Dyn. xviii.	3844 PM 36.1823
298	216	16	*Mn-ḫpr-Rᶜ* (?) (Thothmes III) debased signs in cartouche, flanked by *mᶜᵗ* feathers. *Nb tᶜwï ntr nfr* above; *nb* below. Dyn. xviii or later.	4677
299	216	22	*Mn-ḫpr-Rᶜ ntr nfr* (Thothmes III). Dyn. xviii.	4668
300	216	—	Faience plaque. Obv.: *mn-ḫprw-Rᶜ* (Thothmes IV) in cartouche with *Ymn-tyt* to left. Rev.: *mn-ḫpr-Rᶜ* in small central cartouche with winged scarab flanked by uraei. (Thothmes III). Dyn. xviii.	4673
301	216	22	*Mn-ḫpr-Rᶜ* (Thothmes III) in small cartouche with couchant sphinx and winged uraeus. Dyn. xviii.	4672
302	216	23	Glazed. Plant emblem of the Delta above *Ymn-Rᶜ*. Dyn. xviii–xix.	4666
303	216	22	Glazed paste. *Nb-mᶜᵗ-Rᶜ* (Amenhetep III). Dyn. xviii.	4663
304	216	22	Glazed. *Nb-mᶜᵗ-Rᶜ* (Amenhetep III). Dyn. xviii.	4664
305	216	19	Scrolls, linked in two rows of three. RES X: 401 (Beisan—Room 1234, "Thothmes III" level); BDS, VII: 103.	4665
306	216	52	Cross pattern, curled ends. Dyn. xviii.	4670
307	216	16	Hathor head above, flanked by cats. Kneeling figures below supporting *wᶜḏ* sign. Cf. BDS XI: 551 for upper motif. Dyn. xviii.	4676
308	216	41	Glass. Man holding lotus, with uraeus below. Made in a mould (?). Dyn. xviii.	4669
309	216	14	Falcon-headed god holding lotus with uraeus below. Worn. Dyn. xviii.	4667
310	216	19	Horus eye. Dyn. xviii.	4671
311	501	10	Man holding lotus; *ᶜnḫ* below. Dyn. xviii.	3408
312	501	30	Red-crowned, winged uraeus with signs in field. *Nub* below. Dyn. xviii.	3409
313	501	—	Eye-backed seal. *Ymn-ḥtp ḥqᶜ- wᶜst* reading "Amenhetep, ruler of Thebes" on face.	3407
314	501	—	Semi-cylindrical seal. Rounded face: *nb-mᶜᵗ-Rᶜ* (Amenhetep III) in cartouche, flanked by *mᶜᵗ* feathers. Flat face: *Ymn-Rᶜ nfr-ḥst*, cf. No. 318. Dyn. xviii.	3406
315	P.17	30	Stylised hieroglyphs. Seated figure holding *wᶜst* sceptre with *mᶜᵗ* feather and *ᶜnḫ* sign.	7244
316	P.17	19	Standing figures facing, holding flower with long stem; *nb* below. Cf. BDS XIV: 947. Dyn. xv–xvi (?).	7243
317	D/X	—	Plaque inscribed on four sides. 1. *ᶜ-ḫprw-Rᶜ* (Amenhetep II) in cartouche, which is repeated above sphinx trampling on man. 2 and 4, standing gods. 3, group of King and gods. Dyn. xviii. Cf. *Sedment II*, LVIII: 41, T. 1810.	6147
318	100	—	Plaque. Obv.: *Ymn-Rᶜ nfr-ḥst*. Rev.: fish. Dyn. xviii.	7288
319	D/X	—	Plaque. Obv.: falcon and *nfr* with winged sun and uraeus. Rev.: Hathor head with uraei. Dyn. xvi–xviii.	6108
320	P.17	—	Button seal. Rosette back. Face inscribed with S-scroll and *nb* signs. Dyn. xv–xvii.	7245

Plate 38 (*cont.*)

No.	Locus	Side Type Plate 41	Remarks	Field No. Museum No.
321	100	—	Clay impression on jar sealing. *Ymn-Rˤ*. Dyn. xviii–xix.	5371
322	D/X	—	Semi-cylindrical seal. Flat face inscribed *Ymn* debased. Rounded face: *Nb-mˤˤt-Rˤ* (Amenhetep III) in cartouche surrounded by *mˤt* feathers. Dyn. xviii.	3051 PM 34.3089
323	557	—	Glass cylinder seal. Stylised men and animals in two registers within cross-hatched border (see p. 112).	3872

Plate 39 (Photographs on Pl. 40)

No.	Locus	Side Type Plate 41	Remarks	Field No. Museum No.
324	1003	22	*Mn-ḫprw-Rˤ* (Thothmes IV) in central cartouche. *Ḥˤ-ḫˤśt-nbt, nb-tʾwi*. Dyn. xviii.	3983
325	1003	37	Two kneeling figures facing on *nb* sign. Cf. AASOR XVII, 29: 6, TBM Stra. D. Dyn. xviii.	3979
326	1003	37	Kneeling figure holding lotus on *nb* sign. Dyn. xviii.	3981
327	1003	5	Stylised hieroglyphs: *wʾh-nfr-Rˤ* with flanking signs. Dyn. xviii.	3980
328	1003	34	Fish with *nfr* and *ˤnḫ* signs. Dyn. xviii.	3984
329	1003	20	*Nfr* sign with red crowns flanking. *Nb* sign above and below. Dyn. xviii or earlier.	7284
330	1003	37	Stylised hieroglyphs: *Ḥˤ-nfrw*. Dyn. xviii.	3982
331	547	19	Linked S-scrolls with *ˤnḫ* signs in spaces. M. II, 151: 139, Stra. IX, T. 2117. Dyn. xviii.	3753
332	547	30	Blue paste. Man holding shield or bow. Dyn. xviii or later.	3756
333	547	—	Blue glaze. Frog-backed seal with *ˤnḫ*. Dyn. xviii.	3755
334	547	—	Lion-backed seal with frog incised on obv. Dyn. xviii.	3754
335	547	—	Glass plaque with Horus eye. Dyn. xviii.	3757
336	547	30	Glass (?). Uraeus on *nb* sign with *ˤnḫ*. Faint and worn.	3758
337	502	16	Red-crowned falcon with uraeus on *nb*. *Nfr-Rˤ* in field. Dyn. xix.	3422
338	4019	22	Blue glaze. *Nb-mˤˤt-Rˤ* (Amenhetep III). Dyn. xviii.	6033
339	559	16	Three gods hand in hand. See Pl. 35: 240 and 39: 372. M. II, 152: 188, E = 2092, Stra. VII. Dyn. xix.	4220
340	559	12	*Ymn-Rˤ* between lines. Dyn. xix.	4224
341	559	33	Debased Horus eye joined to uraeus and other signs. Cf. BP I, XXXIII: 331, Tomb 528. Dyn. xviii.	4221
342	559	hidden by setting	Glass in Au setting. Design worn.	4223
343	559	16	Couchant sphinx crowned with double plume and uraei. *Mˤˤt* figure seated with winged uraeus behind. M. II, 152: 175, N = 2131, Stra. VII B; *Gerar*, XVII: 26; BP II, LII: 141–144, 146–147, Tomb 934; L: 52–55, Tomb 922; LIII: 229, Tomb 935. Cf. PSC XLV: 20.1.12, Rameses III, Dyn. xx.	4222
344	542	22	*Mn-ḫprw-Rˤ* (Thothmes IV) in horizontal cartouche above *tyt-Ymn*. See L. III, pp. 361 ff. Dyn. xviii.	3727
345	542	14	Lion and ibex (?) with *ntr-nfr* and uraeus in field. Dyn. xviii.	7281
346	542	38	*Ymn-Rˤ* with *nb*. Dyn. xviii–xix.	7280
347	556	hidden by setting	In Au setting. *Ḫpr-kʾ-Rˤ* (Senusert I), flanked by *nśw, nb* and *nfr* signs. Large *bit* above, *nub* below. The whole surrounded by hook-scroll. Cf. M. II, 151: 129, Stra. X. Dyn. xii or later.	4348

No.	Locus	Side Type Plate 41	Remarks	Field No. Museum No.
348	556	11	*Ymn-Rʿ* flanked by *nb* signs. Dyn. xviii–xix.	3864
349	556	38	Debased winged animal. Dyn. xix.	4348a
350	556	38	Debased eye and red crown with other signs. BP I, XLIII: 523, Tomb 212; BP II, L: 49, Tomb 921. Dyn. xviii–xix.	3865
351	4011	22	*Ḫpr-ḫprw-Rʿ* (Ay). Dyn. xviii.	5923 PM 38.81
352	4011	23	*Mn-ḫpr-Rʿ* (?) in small imitation cartouche, with kneeling figure. Dyn. xviii.	5924 PM 38.82
353	4011	19	Ptah and Rā. BP II, LII: 165, Tomb 934. Dyn. xviii–xix.	5925 PM 38.83
354	4011	27	Cross pattern, debased. Dyn. xviii.	5926 PM 38.84
355	4011	23	Scroll and plant. Cf. BDS VII: 113. Dyn. xviii.	5927 PM 38.85
356	4011	—	Fish-backed seal with debased signs on obv. Dyn. xviii.	5927a PM 38.122
357	4013	25	*Ḏsr-ḫprw-Rʿ* (Horemheb) with *ḥqʾ* and *mꜣʿt* signs. Dyn. xviii.	6002 PM 38.119
358	4013	16	*Wsr-mꜣʿt-Rʿ, stp-n-Rʿ* (Rameses II) in cartouche with titles, left: *nṯr-nfr-nb-tꜣwï*; right: *mry-Ymn-nb-wʾst.* Dyn. xix.	6001 PM 38.118
359	4013	38	*Nb-pḥty-Rʿ* (Aahmes). Late re-issue of first king of Dyn. xviii. Cf. BP I, XII: 173, Tomb 902.	6003 PM 38.120
360	4013	41	Ptah and crowned uraeus. Dyn. xviii–xix.	5998 PM 38.138
361	4013	38	*Ymn-Rʿ.* BP II, LIII: 185, Tomb 934. Dyn. xviii–xx.	6004 PM 38.121
362	4013	7	In AE ring. Cross pattern with buds. Dyn. xviii.	6000 PM 38.117
363	4013	—	Plaque. Debased design, worn.	5999 PM 38.139
364	4002	2	*Ḏd-smꜣ* (May the union last) in hook- and S-scrolls. Dyn. xvi–xviii.	6948a
365	4002	16	Pharaoh hand in hand with two gods. Wings above, *nb* below. Cf. BP II, XLIX: Tomb 978, LII: 137, Tomb 934. Dyn. xviii–xix.	6945
366	4002	27	Kneeling man with arm raised between uraei facing. Cf. BP II, LII: 161, Tomb 934. Dyn. xviii–xix.	6947
367	4002	38	Falcon-headed god holding uraeus, with *nb* signs below. Cf. BP II, LII: 162, Tomb 934. Dyn. xviii–xx.	6944
368	4002	22	Ramesside emblems: sphinx with winged uraeus and other wings in field. Dyn. xix.	6948
369	4002	32	Crowned uraeus with *nfr* sign on *nb* in rope border. For rope border cf. BDS XI: 57; BP II, LII: 179, Tomb 934. Dyn. xx.	6946
370	538	hidden by setting	In Au setting. Linked scrolls.	3686
371	538	22	Three gods hand in hand on *nb* sign. See Pl. 36: 240 and 39: 339. BP I, XXII: 191, Tomb 552. Dyn. xviii–xix.	3684
372	538	22	*Wsr-mꜣʿt-Rʿ, stp-Ymn-Rʿ*, contraction for Rameses II.	3685
373	508	38	*Ymn-Rʿ.* Palindrome. Dyn. xviii–xix.	3461
374	508	5	*Ymn-Rʿ* between *nb* signs. Dyn. xviii–xix.	3460
375	508	37	Stylised hieroglyphs: *ḥtp-mꜣʿt-Rʿ-ʿnḫ.* Dyn. xviii–xix.	3462
376	221	36	Faience or glass (?). Stylised hieroglyphs: *Ptḥ-nfr-ḥr* (?). Dyn. xviii–xix.	4890 PM 36.1506

Plate 39 (*cont.*)

No.	Locus	Side Type Plate 41	Remarks	Field No. Museum No.
377	221	—	Green jasper plaque. Obv.: *Ymn-Rʿ*. Rev.: *Ptḥ-nb-mʿʿt*. Dyn. xviii–xix.	4891 PM 36.2269
378	500	—	Blue glaze. Eye-backed seal. Lion on obv. Dyn. xviii or later.	4085
379	7017	17	In Au setting. *Mn-ḫpr-Rʿ* (Thothmes III) in central cartouche with *mʿʿt* feathers above. Bound captives on either side. Re-issue.	6716
380	7017	5	*Wśr-mʿʿt-Rʿ*, *śtp-mn*, contraction for Rameses II.	6717
381	7017	22	Two bulls rampant. Dyn. xix.	6718
382	4034	37	*Mn-ḫpr-Rʿ* (Thothmes III) in imitation cartouche with standing figure left. Dyn. xviii or later. Re-issue.	7000 PM 39.808
383	4034	—	Debased eye-backed seal with falcon, *mʿʿt* feather and uraeus on obv. Dyn. xviii–xix.	7001 PM 39.809
384	570	hidden by setting	In Au setting. Royal name (?) unread, in cartouche with *ḫpr* and uraei on each side.	6737
385	570	38	Ra with uraei. BP II, LII: 159, Tomb 934. Dyn. xix–xx.	6738
386	570	16	Blue glaze. *Ḫpr* in centre with uraei on each side in rope border. BP I, XXII: 207, Tomb 562. Dyn. xix.	6739
387	570	18	Blue glaze. *Mʿʿt* feather in rope border. BP II, LVII: 394, Tomb 984. Dyn. xix.	6740
388	J.15	22	*Wśr-mʿʿt-Rʿ*, *mry-Ymn* (Rameses III). Dyn. xx. See L III, p. 51. M. II, 152: 195, Stra. VII A. Cf. PSC XLV: 20.1.6.	7228
389	J.15	22	Carnelian. *Wśr-mʿʿt-Rʿ*, *śtp-n-Rʿ*, *mry-Ymn* (Rameses II). Dyn. xix. PSC XLI: 36. See L. III, p. 51.	7227 PM 39.829
390	K.11 1053	5	Stylised hieroglyphs. See L. III, p. 116. Dyn. xix.	6769
391	L.12 1058	28	Pharaoh, probably Rameses II, slaying captive. BP II, LVII: 376, Tomb 984. See L. III, p. 117. Dyn. xix.	6778

For description of bronze feather, Pl. 40: 392, see under Houses 6001, p. 294, Scale 1:1; and for scarab in granulated gold mount, Pl. 40: 393, see under Tomb 570, p. 248, Scale 5:1.

CHAPTER 8

INSCRIPTIONS

A. EARLY CANAANITE

By DAVID DIRINGER, D.LITT.

AMONG the rare inscriptions of the Bronze Age in Palestine, those from Tell ed-Duweir are of cardinal importance, both for the origins of the alphabet and the study of North Semitic epigraphy in general. While the Early Hebrew writings discussed in the previous volume (L. III, p. 67) are extremely valuable, the inscriptions of the Bronze Age may prove to be even more so.

The Duweir Ewer and Lachish Bowl No. 2 were discussed by Dr. T. H. Gaster in *Lachish II* (pp. 49–57). In his opinion, the script of these documents is an important "missing link" in the history of our own alphabet, representing the long-sought intermediate stage between Palaeo-Sinaitic and the earliest known North-Semitic letters. This statement would confirm Sir Alan Gardiner's Sinaitic theory, current since 1915, that the Palaeo-Sinaitic inscriptions represent a stage of writing intermediate between Egyptian hieroglyphics and the Semitic alphabet, but Gardiner's reading of the name of the goddess Baʿalat is the only probable one which is generally accepted, amongst all the earlier decipherments of these inscriptions.

In a more recent tentative decipherment (*The Early Alphabetic Inscriptions from Sinai and their Decipherment*, BASOR 100, April 1948, pp. 6–22), Professor W. F. Albright identifies nineteen out of a total twenty-five to twenty-seven Sinaitic signs. Although he pays homage to Gardiner's "decisive step toward the solution of the puzzle", and affirms that it "must remain basic to any system", Albright regards "the Proto-Sinaitic script as normal alphabetic Canaanite from the early fifteenth century B.C.", and its language as a "vulgar Canaanite" dialect.

The essential difference between Albright and Gardiner is of a chronological nature. Gardiner would date the Palaeo-Sinaitic inscriptions to the end of the xiith dynasty (*c.* 1800 B.C.), while Albright, following Petrie, would attribute them to the early fifteenth century. This date would shift the suggested place of origin of the alphabet from Sinai to Palestine, where several Middle and Late Bronze Age inscriptions have been discovered recently, about half of them coming from Tell ed-Duweir.

In a still more recent article (*The Evolution of the Proto-Canaanite Alphabet*, BASOR 134, April 1954, pp. 15–24) F. M. Cross, Jr., in full agreement with Albright's theory, regards the Palaeo-Sinaitic inscriptions as written in "Proto-Canaanite alphabetic symbols" and Syria/Palestine as the place of origin of the alphabet, though he traces the development of this script from Palaeo-Sinaitic rather than from Early Canaanite. Even if it were agreed that the Early Canaanite Late Bronze Age specimens represent "a bridge thrown across the gap between the proto-Sinaitic inscriptions and those of the Early Iron Age" (Albright), and that their characters "stood midway between the much-discussed semi-hieroglyphic Sinai script and the later Phoenician alphabet" (Gardiner), there still remains the fact that the Early Canaanite Middle Bronze Age inscriptions are two centuries earlier than the Palaeo-Sinaitic. Thus the latter script cannot be regarded as the great Mother-alphabet of all the alphabetic scripts.

The Canaanite Middle Bronze Age inscriptions are: the Gezer Potsherd, found in 1929, the Shechem Stone Plaque, found in 1934, and the Lachish Dagger which will be discussed below. More numerous are the Late Bronze Age inscriptions, five of which come from Tell ed-Duweir. See F. M. Cross, Jr., BASOR 134.

MIDDLE BRONZE AGE

Lachish Dagger (Pl. 22: 15, and Pl. 42: 2; from Tomb 1502, p. 77).

The contents of Tomb 1502 belong to the third phase of the Middle Bronze Age; taking all the objects into consideration, the extreme limits for the range of the group may extend from 1700–1600 B.C. (p. 254), a conclusion which agrees with Starkey's statement that it "can be assigned quite definitely to a date perhaps before, but not later than, 1600 B.C."

Assuming therefore that this inscription is alphabetic, as all scholars agree, it should be considered with the Gezer Potsherd and the Shechem Plaque as one of the three extant *incunabula* or earliest attempts at alphabetic writing.

Inscription

The cleaning of the dagger in December 1936 by the laboratory staff of the Palestine Museum brought to light a vertical inscription of four signs, which is by general agreement to be read downwards (Pl. 42: 2). Suggested readings are set out below, but so far no effort at decipherment has seemed remotely plausible.

1. *b* (Böhl); *d* or *ṣ* (Gardiner); *d* (Obermann); *b* or *p* (Maisler [now Mazar], Yeivin).
2. *r* (reading agreed by all).
3. *n* (Böhl, Gardiner, Gaster); *l* or *n* (Maisler); *m–n* (Obermann); *l* (Yeivin).
4. *s* (Böhl, Gaster, Yeivin); *t* (Gardiner); *z–s* (Obermann).

Sign 2, the pictographic outline of a human head, is the only one on which agreement has been reached; on an acrophonic basis, the first letter of *rôš* "head" should constitute the alphabetic symbol for *r*. However, it must be remarked that the human-head sign is to be found in the Cretan pictographic script and, among others, in Egyptian and Hittite hieroglyphs. Moreover, it is not absolutely certain that Semitic is the language of the inscription.

LATE BRONZE AGE

Oblong Seal (Pl. 38: 295; from Tomb 555, p. 98).

This seal, recovered early in 1935, is made of whitish paste, which is now very soft. It is engraved on all four sides and is pierced through the plain ends. One face is inscribed in good hieroglyphs with the name of Amen-hetep II, *c.* 1450–1425 B.C. The three remaining sides each bear a figure. From right to left on the drawing (Pl. 38: 295), Amen is recognisable by his head-dress, and traces of the name are visible in the top corner; the next god is clearly Ptah, while the third figure holding a staff is very poorly preserved.

It is the inscription describing the figure of Ptah which is especially interesting, for it appears to be written in characters which are somewhat allied to the Early Canaanite script. Most of the signs have the form of North Semitic letters (*'ayin, gimel, taw, zayin* (?)), but on the whole the inscription is undecipherable. These signs may have some connexion with the symbols of the inscriptions found at Kahun and in other Egyptian sites (Diringer, *The Alphabet*, p. 207). For a similar inscription see A. Goetze, BASOR 129, Feb. 1953, pp. 8 ff.

Censer Lid (Pl. 44: 1; photographs on Pl. 45: 4 and Pl. 53; from Tomb 216, pp. 232 f.).

Tomb 216 contained most of the so-called Base-Ring wares, which came into use in the last years of the reign of Thothmes III, *c.* 1500–1450 B.C. The full chronological range of the group is extended by later royal scarabs to at least 1375 B.C. Tomb 216 was therefore more or less contemporary with the occupation of Structure II, and the main deposits were made before 1350 B.C.

Inscription

Only three letters, written in red paint, have been preserved, though Grimme and Obermann have suggested that there are remains of two other letters. Assuming that the inscription runs from right to left, the three signs have been read as follows:

1. *b* (Obermann); *g* (Stawell); *w* (Gaster); *k* (Yeivin); *l* (Grimme).
2. *g* (Böhl, Gaster, Grimme); *'ayin* (Obermann).
3. *h* (Grimme); *z* (Böhl, Gaster, Obermann Stawell).

Dr. Yeivin, in contrast to the other scholars, reads the inscription upside down, but he takes into consideration only one sign, i.e. sign 3 of the other readings. If he has adopted the right method, then his decipherment would also be correct and the sign could be a North-Semitic *kaph*.

Lachish Bowl No. 1 (Pl. 43 and Pl. 44: 2; from Tomb 527, p. 239)

This bowl, found in 1935, compares in shape with L. II: 14 exclusive to Structure II, but the other objects of the small group of pottery, particularly the imitations of imported wares, appear to be contemporary with the rise of Structure III of the Fosse Temple. Thus the bowl may be attributed to the very end of Structure II or the beginning of Structure III. Miss Tufnell accepts the date *c.* 1375 B.C. or later for the end of Structure II and *c.* 1350 B.C. (about the time of Amen-Onkhs) for the beginning of Structure III. Thus the bowl may be dated approximately to the second quarter of the fourteenth century B.C.

Inscription

The inscription, painted with a brush in white lime, consists of eleven signs. The sixth seems to be a word-dividing stroke or dash, which divides the inscription into two parts (p. 140).

Part one. The direction of the line seems to be from right to left, beginning near the base of the vessel. The five letters are neat, and their reading is agreed on by most scholars:

$$b-\check{s}-l-\check{s}-t,$$

i.e. the preposition *b* combined with a form of the numerical "three". Albright and Cross agree with this interpretation, though they read *bṯlṯt*. Albright propounds the theory that the North Semitic *š* derived from the Proto-Canaanite symbol, represented by a "composite bow", which had the original Semitic phoneme *ṯ* (th), pronounced *s* in South Canaanite. In Late Bronze Age Canaanite the phonemes *ṯ* and *š* fell together, and, with the standardisation of the North Semitic alphabet the phonemes *š*, *ś* and *ṯ* fell together and became the letter *š*.

Yet the first sign has been read by Grimme as *p*, and by Obermann and Stawell as *d*. Indeed, while most scholars read the inscription from right to left, Obermann and Stawell read from left to right. Moreover, Stawell reads the inscription from the position occupied by the bowl while standing on its base, i.e. upside down in comparison with the other readings.

Part two (letters 7–11) is more keenly debated. Several suggestions have been advanced, the following being the most important:

7. *k* or *y* (Gaster, Harding); *k* (Burrows, Stawell); *y* (Bauer, Grimme, Dussaud, Maisler [now Mazar], Yeivin).
8. *m* (Bauer, Dussaud, Maisler, Yeivin); *'ayin* (Grimme); *p* (Stawell); *š* (Harding).
9. *y* (Bauer, Dussaud, Grimme, Harding); *k* (Stawell); *g* (Maisler, Yeivin).
10. *'aleph* (Grimme); *w* (Stawell); *r* (Bauer, Dussaud, Maisler, Yeivin).
11. *z* (Stawell); *z* or *ṣ* (Yeivin); *ḥ* (Bauer, Dussaud, Grimme, Harding); *ṣ* (Maisler).

In conclusion, the decipherment of part two seems a hopeless task.

Duweir Ewer (Structure III, third quarter of the thirteenth century B.C.)

This inscription has been dealt with by Dr. T. H. Gaster in *Lachish II*, pp. 49–54. Since then, it has been discussed by other scholars, including Albright and particularly by F. M. Cross, Jr.

Cross accepts the following points:

(*a*) The inscription reads from left to right (see *Lachish II*, p. 49 and *passim*).

(*b*) The first word (letters 1–3 in *Lachish II*) to be read *m-t-n* (*mattan*).

(*c*) The last three letters (9–11 in *Lachish II*) to be read *'aleph, lamed, taw*; the interpretation "Elath" (the goddess Elath).

(*d*) The theory, previously suggested by some scholars (Albright, Eisler, Grimme, Maisler, Obermann, Yeivin), that the three vertical dots following the first word indicate a word-divider and not the number "three".

(*e*) As to the letter 4, Cross accepts the reading *š*, but he agrees with Albright that the phoneme of the symbol is still *ṭ* or *ś* (see p. 129).

(*f*) For the letter 7, he accepts the value *t*.

Cross disagrees with other scholars in the decipherment of the letters 5 and 8, which he regards as *yodh*. He completes letter 6 as *lamedh*, and restores the *lacuna* between letters 6 and 7 with the letters *r b*. Cross's reading is therefore as follows:

$$m \; t \; n. \;\; \underline{t}/\acute{s} \; y \;\; (l) \;\; (rb)ty \; 'lt$$

His interpretation differs from all previous ones. Although he admits that the first word ("Mattan") may mean, as is generally accepted, "a gift", he prefers to see in this word a personal name "Mattan". For the second word he prefers the interpretation "a tribute", though he does not exclude the possibility of Albright's theory "a sheep". The word *r b t y* (probably *rabbotay* or, perhaps, *rabbatiya*) would mean "my lady". Thus the whole inscription, according to Cross, would read "Mattan. A tribute to my Lady 'Elat."

However, both reading and interpretation are still an open problem.

Lachish Bowl No. 2 (L. II, Pl. XXIX: 12; from Temple Area)

The fragment cannot be attributed to a particular structure, therefore its chronological range could fall anywhere between *c.* 1580 and the final destruction of the temple in the thirteenth century B.C.

Inscription

The inscription, written in carbon ink, consists of eleven signs, of which the first and last do not seem to be letters, though Grimme and Obermann regarded them as traces. No agreement has been reached as to the reading of any sign. Indeed, it is impossible to determine whether the inscription should be read horizontally from left to right or right to left, or vertically either up or down. At first, the inscription was regarded as a foreign copy of Egyptian hieratic script.

This inscription has been discussed by Dr. T. H. Gaster in *Lachish II*, pp. 55–57.

Lachish Sherds No. 6 (Pl. 47: 5; from Tomb 571, pp. 249 f.)

A few bowl fragments of which some are reproduced on Pl. 47 were once inscribed in dark-red paint. They came from Tomb 571 adjacent to Tomb 570 which had contained the anthropoid coffin painted with hieroglyphic signs. The contents of both tombs are closely contemporary and should be dated to the last century of the Late Bronze Age. No interpretation of the signs is possible.

INSCRIPTIONS

TRANSITION PERIOD (LATE BRONZE—EARLY IRON)

Lachish Sherd No. 7 (Pl. 44: 7 and L. III, p. 116; from L. 12: 1057)

This small piece of pottery, which does not appear from the wheelmarks on the reverse to have been part of a bowl, came from the casemate fill of Palace A (L. III, Pl. 110). It is therefore earlier than the construction of that building in the late tenth or early ninth century and, though it could on archaeological grounds belong to debris from the last Bronze Age city, Level VI, Miss Tufnell was thus able to confirm my first and immediate impression that the script itself would warrant a date in the eleventh century.

Inscription

There are three letters written in black ink, of which the first is partly erased and the second and third are incomplete. Beyond the first letter there is part of a vertical stroke bending towards the broken edge.

Reading from right to left, the letters are perhaps 'ayin, waw, taw in North Semitic script. The rather angular shape of the 'ayin and the curved form of the waw can be explained by the difficulties of inscribing on a curved surface.

Taking all uncertainties on date and reading into consideration, this little scrap may be the first extant Early Hebrew inscription, preceding the Gezer Calendar by about a century.

Though the interpretation is no less hypothetical than the reading, it is possible and indeed probable that the remainder of the letter which precedes 'ayin is a lamed, in which case, assuming that the word is complete, the whole inscription would read:

la'ûth

Curiously enough, this word appears once only in the Bible and is not certainly translated, though according to some scholars it would mean "to support, to comfort (the weary)". If this sherd is part of a votive inscription, then its use would be consistent with its meaning in the passage from Isaiah l. 4:

'Adonay YHWH nathan li leshôn limmûdîm lada'ath la'ûth 'eth-yaeph dabhar ("The Lord God hath given me the tongue of the learned, that I should know how to comfort him that is weary.")

B. PSEUDO-EGYPTIAN HIEROGLYPHS

Anthropoid Coffin (Pl. 45: 3, Pl. 46; from Tomb 570, p. 249).

Among many fragments from Tomb 570, some of which showed faint traces of coloured decoration, were about a hundred pieces which formed the cylindrical front and sides of a slipper coffin. The central part had been carefully burnished to take an inscription, written in thick red paint and enclosed on both sides and at the bottom by a line. All the signs are perfectly clear, though some are incomplete through cracks and missing pieces of pottery.

Five bands of red paint at shoulder level are preserved above the side panels, which show figures of Isis and Nebthys mourning and holding lotus flowers. If these bands continue across the front of the coffin, the small strip of red paint preserved above the arm sign may be part of the first band, and the inscription which we have would be complete.

Inge, however, thought that

"the inscription appears to be only the latter half, because the foot of the coffin joins on quite close to the bottom of the wording, which is terminated by a straight line. If one estimates that the inscription began somewhere on a line with the chest, the part that remains would not come much higher than the knees, if the coffin were made for an adult. On the original there is actually the faintest trace of a sign above the hand. Another point which suggests that the inscription is not complete is that the line ruled on the bottom is quite close to the final sign, and it would be reasonable to expect a line at the same distance from the top."

At the time of discovery in 1938, photographs of the inscription were submitted to Sir Alan Gardiner,

131

Dr. M. A. Murray and Mr. Alan Rowe, and their tentative decipherments are tabulated on Pl. 46. All are agreed, however, that the inscription is very curious, and that the writing is not that of an Egyptian scribe.

"To me", wrote Sir Alan, "this little hieroglyphic legend seems absolute gibberish as it stands. Was it the writing of a Palestinian scribe who knew a number of Egyptian words and strung them together to give the impression of a genuine hieroglyphic sentence? For example, no Egyptian would ever start on the left with a downward stroke for the water ripple sign (N. 35)[1]. . . . The last example on the coffin is as un-Egyptian as it could be but does, on the other hand, resemble the 'Sinai' script. Against this, the word for Amentet is excellently written, though the irrigation canal sign (N.23) like ḥm (U.36) further on is in hieratic. . . . I can guarantee, however, that there is no personal name."

Though anthropoid pottery coffins are not uncommon in the xviii–xxth dynasties and survive in different forms up to Roman times, this is the first example from Palestine which is inscribed. (For full discussion see Albright, AJA 2nd Series, Vol. XXXVI, 1932, pp. 295–306, and for further examples see Rowe, RES, pp. xxxv–xxxvi, footnote 1.)

There are, however, inscribed coffins of this type from Egypt, and, significantly enough, one of the best comes from Tell Yehudiyeh (HIC, pp. 16 ff. and Pls. XIV, XV). Albright has already referred to the painted hieroglyphs on coffins found by Naville and Griffiths at the same site and he accepts Naville's reading for one coffin bearing a personal name of foreign origin, "written in the syllabic orthography employed by the Egyptians for the spelling of foreign words and names" (AJA op. cit., p. 304).

Provisional transliteration

1 *di*	4 *mw*	7 *ḥm*
2 (?)	5 *imntt*	8 *n*
3 *k*	6 *n*	9 (?) *k*

C. EGYPTIAN HIERATIC

Lachish Bowl No. 3 (Pls. 44:3,4 and 47:1,2; from Tell, Grid Square K.16:1031)

Lachish Bowl No. 4 (Pls. 44:5 and 47:4; from Tell, Grid Square J.15:1038)

Lachish Bowl No. 5 (Pls. 44:6 and 47:3; from Tell, Grid Square J.15:1037)

The hieratic bowl, No. 3, and the fragments, Nos. 4 and 5, were all found to the south-east of the Palace-Fort (L. III, Pl. 115 and pp. 112, 114). The easterly end of this building (Palace B–C) stood high on a mass of dumped rubbish, cut from some region of the Late Bronze Age city to the north. This method of work was demonstrated by a sectional cut which showed a distinct tilt from north to south. Fragments Nos. 4 and 5 came from an upper layer of dumped scree over the ramp.

The pieces of Bowl No. 3 were strewn over some hundred square feet lower down the slope and were only recovered after most careful search. The quality of the pottery is like that of Bowl No. 1 and the profile is even more flared than the common bowls of Structure III (L. II, Pl. XL: 90–91). At the time of discovery, Starkey felt no doubt that in form, quality and technique, the bowl belonged to the middle of the thirteenth century.

In the same horizon of dumped material, a well-cut carnelian scarab much damaged by fire was found, bearing the name of Rameses II (Scarab No. 389) and nearby was a steatite scarab which may perhaps be attributed to Rameses III (Scarab No. 388). Among significant pieces from the same area are the burnt fragments of the octopus krater and pieces of a chariot vase (Pl. 83: 949, 951 and p. 213). Many scraps of gold foil and fragments of fine quality alabaster vases all testify to the wealth of the Ramesside city and to its destruction by fire.

---

[1] References are to Gardiner's Sign List in his *Egyptian Grammar*.

Report on Inscriptions

By Professor J. Černý.

The fragments of Lachish bowls Nos. 4 and 5 inscribed in Egyptian hieratic writing are too small to allow of any dating except for a quite vague assignation to the Ramesside period. No. 4 yields no translatable text, while the text of No. 5 runs "*that day*" which was almost certainly preceded by a date.

The text of No. 3, though longer, has nevertheless lost about one-third of its extent and the ink is very pale. The writing is rather cursive and contains few characteristic signs datable with certainty. The whole gives the impression of a text of about the reign of Merenptah (xixth dynasty), but the sign *b3* in line 1 has a form used in Great Papyrus Harris, a document of Rameses IV of the xxth dynasty. There is considerable uncertainty as to the reading of a number of signs.

Lachish Bowl No. 3

Transcription

Translation

Inside:

1. "Year 4, fourth month of the Inundation season, day 26. That which - - - . . . 2. That which - - - bread (?).
2. - - - king (of) Latish (?) Y - - -, wheat (of the country) - - pu, total 1000+100x out of (the) harvest tax of the - - -."

Outside:

1. "In the year 4, second month of Summer season, day - - -, wheat - - - - 420, [total (?)] 1000x - - -.
2. - - - ? year 4, fourth month of Summer season, day 1. Wheat - - - - 300+10x+3 - - - 900."

PART III
POTTERY

GENERAL NOTES

THE pottery described in *Lachish II* and *Lachish III* covered in each case a mere three centuries, whereas the task of the present study is more formidable, ranging from some time in the fourth to the end of the second millennium.

Sources

The vessels to be discussed came from four main areas:
1. Cave dwellings of the North-West Settlement, Area 1500 (pp. 144–155).
2. Burials in the deserted caves, Area 1500, and in the Cemetery 2000 (Caliciform Culture, pp. 156–175).
3. Accumulated city rubbish on the mound, from bed-rock upwards to 36 feet in the North-East Section (Chapter 4, pp. 51–59).
4. Tombs, caves and pits in and around the lower slopes of the mound, Areas 100–200, 500, 1000, 4000, 6000, 7000 (pp. 176–224).

System of Numbering

For the methods of field recording used in the excavations see *Lachish III*, pp. 257 ff.

Classification and Notes on the Plate Descriptions

In the following study, the photographs and drawings of pottery are necessarily subdivided:

Pls. 11–13 with Pls. 56 and 57 illustrate the sherds of the cave-dwellings in the North-West Settlement.

Pls. 14 and 16 with Pls. 58–61 show complete tomb groups from the deserted caves.

Pls. 15 and 62–65 chiefly contain incomplete platters and jars from the North-East Caverns.

Pl. 13 with Pls. 66 and 67 show a representative selection from deposits and tombs of the Caliciform Culture.

Pls. 49–55 present selected tomb groups of the Middle and Late Bronze Age.

Pls. 68–87 are devoted to Middle and Late Bronze Age pottery forms arranged in classes according to the function and shape of the vessel. Method of manufacture and decorative finish have also been considered as subsidiary aids to classification. The characteristics are described in detail in the following pages, and comparisons with similar vessels from other sites are noted. Where several varieties of form are grouped under one head, it has been done to avoid too many subdivisions.

The classification was arranged on the same general lines as in the previous books (L. II, p. 78 and L. III, pp. 258–259), subject to necessary modifications. In order to assess the contact between the tombs and the three Structures of the Fosse Temple, those forms which appear in both tombs and Temple are reproduced here under the original type numbers of *Lachish II*.

The ware of the type specimens is described in general for Pls. 56, 57, 80 and 81: 868–875, and in detail for the remaining plates. Limestone temper in small or large quantities is a common factor which is taken for granted. "Straw" temper in the description means finely chopped vegetable matter; I am indebted to Dr. Hans Helbaek for the suggestion that it may in fact be derived from animal dung. For the degree of kiln firing expressed by H = hard, M = medium, S = soft, see L. III, p. 260. The wares of other examples compared with the form of the type specimen may differ in detail from its description.

When one or more examples of a type were found elsewhere on the site, the appropriate locus number or numbers are given. If a duplicate example is also drawn with the contents of the Early Bronze Age caves (Pls. 56 and 57), the locus number is followed by the plate reference.

Diagonal hatching from top right to bottom left indicates a surface covered with a dark-red slip. Where visible, the lines of burnishing are shown. In the converse direction, top left to bottom right, the hatching denotes a matt red surface, possibly brush-applied and not always fired, which is reminiscent of "grain-wash" and is described in this book as "red wash". These conventions apply only to Pls. 56–68. Comb-facing (see below) on large jars is drawn in accordance with the pattern.

For the Middle and Late Bronze Age pottery (Pls. 68–87), slip and burnish, where they occur, are described under "Remarks". Red paint is indicated throughout as vertical hatching.

All pot drawings are published at a scale of 1:5, except Pls. 62, 67 and 87, which are at 1:10.

Methods of Manufacture

The greater part of the notes on this subject published in L. III, pp. 259–260, are also applicable to the pottery of the Middle and Late Bronze Age periods, especially in so far as they apply to the ordinary domestic local wares.

With regard to the hand-made pottery of the Chalcolithic Age, general notes on the wares are given at the head of Pls. 11–13. For notes on the pottery of the Caliciform Culture, see p. 171.

Clay and Firing

Limited, if not haphazard, methods of firing necessitated considerable tempering of the natural fatty iron-bearing clays with pulverised shell and lime grits and grog, permitting a rapid exclusion of moisture which avoids shattering and cracks due to sudden exposure to heat, a difficulty with which the potter was familiar (pp. 140, 177).

While the flame temperatures in the kiln were relatively high, due to the probably quick-burning nature of the fuel, it is improbable that the firing was of considerable duration. The actual baking, apart from drying and cooling, probably took less than two hours.

Mr. G. C. Griffiths considers that this is borne out by the coloured 2-millimetre skin of heat-penetrated biscuit on inner and outer surfaces and the relatively unfired inner darkened core. The firing did little more than achieve a superficial hardening and coloration of exterior surfaces.

Slip and Burnish

For Kelso and Thorley's definition of "slip" as opposed to "wash" see AASOR XXI–XXII, § 100 and L. III, p. 260.

On Pls. 56–68 (and cf. pp. 159–160) it will be seen that slip is shown schematically by fine diagonal lines from top right to bottom left, while the direction of the strokes of burnishing has also been indicated as far as possible (i.e. NE 6/321, 322, 324 on p. 59).

Application of a matt red coating, which in some cases may be a true wash, is indicated by fine diagonal lines sloping from top left to bottom right. This distinctive finish is to be found on bowls from the North-East Caverns. See under Bowls, p. 159.

With the end of the Early Bronze Age and the intrusion of the Caliciform Culture, the deep red slip and finely patterned burnish which had strengthened and beautified the pottery of the third millennium underwent a change, which cannot be followed at Duweir, for the phases when it was most apparent at Tell Beit Mirsim (Strata G, F) are only poorly represented. In the glacis fill which is contemporary with these strata there are few burnished sherds, and when the MB II–III tombs came into use red slips had largely disappeared. Even self wheel-burnish was rare and the technique is best seen on the bowls from Grave 173 (Pl. 20: 17, 18).

Towards the end of the Bronze Age a light brown slip rather smoothly burnished came into use. Besides the Duweir Ewer (see L. II, frontispiece), examples of this finish are to be seen on the inscribed coffin and censer lid (Pl. 45: 3, 4). It seems likely, therefore, that a specially smooth surface was prepared before painted signs or decoration were applied.

Comb-facing

The term used by both Petrie and Albright is also employed in this publication to describe both a coarse and finely ribbed pottery surface, which may be patterned in vertical and horizontal zones or plain. It is often confined to the upper part of the vessel.

In practice, it has been shown that a surface of this kind can be obtained without the aid of an implement, and it is commonly and inadvertently achieved by an inexperienced potter (I am indebted to Dr. B. S. J. Isserlin for this observation).

It suggests that comb-facing is, in fact, a sign of early experiment in the change over from hand- to wheel-made pottery, and with increased mastery of the technique it tended to die out.

A few comb-faced sherds are to be found in the Section from bed-rock to 4 feet. From 5–10 feet they are plentiful and nearly all are coated with lime-wash. These six feet cover the last phases of the Early Bronze Age. They are not entirely equivalent to Stratum J at Tell Beit Mirsim, where combed sherds are common, because those of J are nearly always painted in reddish-brown, which is a rare finish at Duweir (p. 156).

Comb-facing is typical of the pottery from the North-East Caverns, Area 6000 (Pls. 62–65), and an occasional piece came from the North-West Settlement; see in particular Pl. 62: 296, p. 165. The likeness between these sherds and those of the "Amorite" city at Tell el-Hesi (TH, Pl. V) is especially striking.

Combed ware and its relation with Egypt is the subject of an article by M. W. Prausnitz in PEQ, 1954, pp. 91–96. In it the author questions the alleged contemporaneity in Egypt of stump-based, flat-based pitchers and combed-ware, on which the chronology for Megiddo was mainly based. A comb-finished jar first occurred at that site in Stage IV (SAOC 10, No. 10, Fig. 8E) which, in Mr. Shipton's words, "helps to substantiate the equation of Stratum XVIII to part of Stage IV as well as Stage III" (SAOC 17, p. 40).

While sherds with comb-facing are still to be seen in the MB glacis fill from 15–21 feet, it should be noted that this finish is lacking on pottery of the Caliciform Culture.

The pottery of this phase had achieved a free technique known as "wheel" or "band" combed decoration, consisting of horizontal and wavy bands of combing, together with oblique, vertical and horizontal rows of notches. These styles are found in Group 1529 especially (Pl. 66), and to a lesser degree in Cemetery 2000 (Pl. 67). At Tell Beit Mirsim, equivalents were found in Strata H–F (AASOR XII, p. 8).

Plain fine combing is a characteristic of early MB, increasing in popularity at Tell Beit Mirsim "until it attains its maximum in the D stratum, after which it dies out rapidly" (AASOR XII, p. 11). It is perhaps significant that fine combing is rarely found in pottery from the tombs or Section at Duweir.

Decoration

Plastic Bands and Notches

Developed from finger dents left unsmoothed on the surface, for instance on crucibles (Pl. 56f: 34, 52 and 54), the potter reacted to the plastic quality of the clay by strengthening and ornamenting the edge by indents and added bands.

This special feature of Chalcolithic pottery (PPEB, p. 81) is rare on pottery attributed to the Early Bronze Age at Duweir (Fig. 15: 10, 14), but very neat, smooth, indented edges are to be found on jar Types 420 and 421 (Early Caliciform Culture), and plastic indented bands are common on the coarse hand-made flat-based cooking-pots which bridge the change from EB to developed MB II in Palestine (e.g. Pl. 57: 69 and Pl. 66: 415).

Rope moulding in a variety of styles is produced by notching a raised band obliquely; at the stage when it was in common use, EB III–IV, the large jars which are so frequently finished with a rope band at the neck were partially wheel-made (Pl. 62). Diagonal or herring-bone notches, most of which reproduced string-marks round the neck, were in contemporary use, and they continued to appear on some jars and jugs of the Caliciform Culture (Pl. 67).

When the wheel came into full use, and men largely replaced women in the making of pottery, hand-finished details, like ledge handles, disappeared (p. 155), and plastic bands were only retained on the flat-based cooking-pots which were presumably still made by women.

Paint

Painted decoration is to be seen on the Types 44 and 48 on Pl. 57 and Cup 191 on Pl. 60 and in the striped rims of Types 339, 340 and 369 on Pls. 64–65. They are of Upper Chalcolithic and Early Bronze Age date and it is clear that painted ware of EB Ia is hardly represented at Duweir. No pottery of the Caliciform Culture is painted, possibly due to the unsuitable nature of the surface. But this reason could not apply to the smooth-finished pottery of the Middle Bronze Age, and again no painted decoration is found, apart from such pieces as Pl. 79: 813, which is a recognised import (White Painted IV) and a few fragments of painted storage jars from the glacis fill. The bichrome wares, which were an outstanding feature of Megiddo Strata X–IX, are missing from the tombs, and are confined to a few vessels from Structure I of the Fosse Temple.

The fact remains that at Duweir, at least, little painted ornament appears before the fifteenth century. Skeuomorphic design is ubiquitous on Base-Ring and White Slip wares, and, here again, they are imported.

It is only in the late xviiith and early xixth dynasties that painted design becomes less restrained. Even then motifs are conventional lines and zigzags, or panels of criss-cross lines and triangles, executed in black and red, or in red alone. The gazelle and tree group only appears on two vessels, Types 991 and 999, and on Type 990 there is a single lotus.

Various tests were made on lumps of red substance, which had been rubbed down, probably to provide the colour required to decorate these pots. As clay minerals are difficult to distinguish by chemical tests alone, Professor F. E. Zeuner kindly arranged for an X-ray examination to be carried out by Mr. Bannister of the British Museum (Natural History):

"He found that beside approximately 5% Quartz and about 15% Haematite, the substance is made up of Kaolinite ($Al_2O_3 . 2 SiO_2 H_2O$), a crystalline mineral of the clay family. . . . Apart from some haematite which provides the colour, a clay-mineral is the chief constituent (which) seems . . . to suggest an interesting conclusion. The powder mixed with water forms a perfect emulsion which can be painted on pots with a brush. During the firing process, however, the clay-component will fuse with the clay of the paste beneath, so that the pattern on the finished pot will be more or less waterproof."

A white substance was frequently used to repair cracks in firing which commonly occurred in the bowl bases (pp. 138, 177, and L. II, Pl. XXX: 42, 43 and p. 82). The inscription on the bowl illustrated on Pl. 43 was painted on with a brushful of similar material, which proved on analysis to be calcium carbonate with a trace of iron and siliceous matter (p. 129).

For the use of lime-wash in an EB context at Duweir, see pp. 156 and 165. It was also common in the Section from 5 to 10 feet (p. 139) and crushed lime was also found in the potter's workshop (pp. 91, 292).

Handles

On Bowls and Beakers

Loop handles with thickened attachment come from Cave 1534 (Pl. 12: 35 and Pl. 56: 17) and from near bed-rock in the Section (NE. 1/408, 5/352, p. 59). Both could have Upper Chalcolithic affinities.

Rudimentary loop handles on crucibles (or bowls) from Caves 1503 and 1553 (Pl. 56: 29 and Pl. 57: 66 [Pl. 12: 54]) seem to date from EB I, like a little highly polished cup (Pl. 58: 104).

Evolution from a single pierced lug or string hole on bowls with EB II connexions in Cave 1535 (Pl. 58: 88, 89) is seen to degrade to unpierced lug projections in groups which come down to EB III (Pl. 59: 154–155; Pl. 60: 195, 197 and Pl. 61: 244). The North-East Caverns provide examples of much the same period (Pls. 64: 345 and 65: 374).

It is interesting to see that single pierced lug or string holes are also a feature on Caliciform beakers (Pl. 66:

403 [Pl. 13: 84]; 409, 416) and on a bowl (Pl. 66: 428) from Group 1529, suggesting that these and other details of this wheel-made pottery are more akin to the tradition of EB II than EB III.

Two loop handles on bowls of MB and LB provenance are rare at Duweir, and those recovered are grouped together on Pl. 69. See Bowls, Class F, on p. 180, and Pl. 72: L. II: 66. Also of this group are NE. 33/16, 17 with connexions at Tell Beit Mirsim, Strata C–B (p. 53).

Rudimentary bar or knob handles have already been recorded from the Fosse Temple (L. II, Pls. XLII: 142; XLIII: 158, 164) and they also occur in tombs of the thirteenth century (Pl. 72: 627, 629, 630 and p. 183). They present another link with the Section Level VI (NE 32/18 on p. 53).

Wish-bone handles occur on Monochrome, White Slip II (Pl. 79: 831–835) and Base-Ring bowls (Pl. 81: 868–871) except for a few poor imitations (Pl. 82: 906–907 and 909–913). A decorated handle in this tradition came from the Section between Levels VII and VIII (NE 26/99 on p. 53).

On jars

Two-lug handles

Lug handles attached to the jar at the junction with neck and shoulder and then apparently pierced with a stick are to be seen on Pl. 56: 4 (Pl. 11: 4), Pl. 56: 11, Pl. 57: 49 and Pl. 59: 167. These have Chalcolithic and EB I affinities.

This technique is missing from Duweir in EB II–III, but it occurs again in groups of the Caliciform Culture, both on jars (Pl. 66: 417–419, 423; Pl. 67: 481–483, 488–498) and on "teapots" (Pl. 66: 452 and Pl. 67: 486–487). The same kind of handle, unpierced, is seen on Pl. 67: 483–484. A further variety foreign to Palestinian tradition are horned handles which are also pierced with a stick (Pl. 66: 411–412).

On Amphoriskoi

The lug handles of this class are mostly pierced. They are probably EB I–II in date and the forms are listed and discussed more fully on p. 168.

Four-lug (or ear) handles

In the first and possibly the earliest jar with four handles in this series, the handles are pierced (Pl. 56: 21), but in other cases, all from Cave 1535, the handles made of small rolls of clay were separately attached (Pl. 58: 118, 120, 124). The range for them at Duweir is EB I–II.

Pierced handles

Handles at the widest diameter of the jar were pierced in the thickened wall, and were not separately attached. Those illustrated on Pl. 12: 51, 60, 61 have Middle-Upper Chalcolithic affinities and are the probable forerunners of loop handles which begin at much the same time.

Two-loop handles

It is assumed that there were originally two handles on the jars illustrated on Pl. 11: 20 and Pl. 56: 3, and in both cases the loops were separately attached. These examples are probably Upper Chalcolithic in date.

Otherwise, these somewhat protruding handles belong to EB III, and are set at the widest diameter on red-burnished pots in Cave 1519 (Pl. 60: 217, 222, 223), while the same position is maintained on an unburnished form in Cave 1513 (Pl. 59: 171). Other loop handles are set from rim to shoulder (Pl. 60: 218–219), while the introduction of shoulder handles in Caves 1556 (Pl. 61: 254) and 1513 (Pl. 59: 168–170) and 1516 (Pl. 61: 254) and in the Section (NE 10/240, p. 57) may foreshadow the popularity of the kind in the early Middle Bronze Age.

On Jugs and Juglets

Grooved and multiple-strand handles of Chalcolithic-EB I affinity are discussed under Special Features of the Fourth and Third Millennium on p. 155.

Ribbon handles on jugs and juglets are rare before the Early Bronze Age; for a possible exception see Pl. 11: 24 from Cave 1538.

From EB I onwards they are very common in the groups illustrated on Pls. 58–61, and the forms cn which such handles occur are listed with references on pp. 166–171.

Several handles on jugs from Caves 6000 are very crudely attached, which may signify a date in EB III–IV (Pl. 63: 316, 319; Pl. 65: 385, 388, 391, 391A).

Loop handles on jugs from rim to shoulder, associated with ledge handles at the greatest width of the body, are to be found in Caves 1519 and 1556 (Pls. 60: 226; 61: 251) and in Cave 1513 (Pl. 59: 172, 176, 177). They also occur in Caverns 6000 on jugs which are probably of this type, see Pl. 62: 285–286, while a complete example is seen on Pl. 62: 288. Comparable fragments occur in the Section (NE 10/236 on p. 57).

All these loops were associated with pushed-up ledge handles, and the development of the various significant forms of the latter is discussed on pp. 148–154 with a text illustration, Fig. 7.

Classification of jugs from groups of the MB–LB periods is largely based on the shape and position of the handles, with those formed of double-strands treated as the earliest class (see Jugs, Classes A–E on Pls. 74–76 and pp. 187–189). For an example in the Section, see NE 6/336, which is possibly intrusive.

Both piriform and cylindrical juglets have double-strand and plain ribbon handles, and though there is little difference in their range at Duweir, the ribbon handles on cylindrical juglets may survive into the fifteenth century (see Juglets, Classes A–J, on Pl. 77 and pp. 189–192).

On Dippers (Pl. 78)

Dipper handles are attached either below rim level in MB and early LB contexts, rising to rim level at the turn of the fifteenth–fourteenth century. The handle is never poked through at the shoulder, which distinguishes these local dippers from imported wares (e.g. Pl. 79: 817–826).

On Base-Ring Wares (Pls. 80, 81)

The same characteristic of a poked-through handle distinguishes the jugs and juglets of Base-Ring ware, whereas this feature does not occur on imitations.

On Mugs

Base-Ring mugs (Pl. 80: 850, 852–853) have a projection above the handle which is missing from Pl. 80: 851.

Among the mugs in local ware reproduced on Pl. 84, only one, Type 964, has this feature. Most of the rest have very roughly attached handles, an indication of their late origin in the thirteenth or possibly the early twelfth century.

On Mycenaean Imported Wares and Imitations (Pl. 82: 914–930, 940–944; Pl. 83: 945–947)

Horizontal loop handles on cylindrical and squat pyxoid jars are usually two in number, placed opposite each other, which "is of a specifically Helladic character" according to Furumark (MP, pp. 83, 89, 42). The only exceptions are three symmetrically placed handles on Types 918 and 919 which, with a concave neck and horizontal lip, are "evidently taken over from the pithoid jars" (Furumark, MP, p. 42, note 2).

It will be seen that both three and two handles are featured on the piriform jars from Duweir in imported (Types 945–946) and imitation quality (Types 940–944), and they should therefore be datable close to the point of reduction from three to two handles, when the smaller number becomes a typical feature of Myc. III C (Furumark, MP, p. 43), 1230–1100 B.C.

GENERAL NOTES

On Pilgrim Flasks (Pl. 84)

The handles of pilgrim flasks spring archwise from the point of attachment to the neck, a feature which is considered characteristic of Stratum C at Tell Beit Mirsim; the only exception (Pl. 84: 953), in which the handle joins the neck at right angles, is probably an import (AASOR XII § 57).

On Storage Jars (Pl. 87)

Storage-jar handles in the Section (NE 6/337–338) are probably intrusive. Loop handles set low on the body occur in the MB glacis fill (Nos. 147, 167 and 181 on p. 55). All show an oval section which is characteristic also of all jars on Pl. 87. Those in Class E have handles decorated in red.

CHAPTER 9
FOURTH AND THIRD MILLENNIUM

THE pottery under this main chronological heading is divided into three groups:

A. Chalcolithic and Early Bronze Age. Pottery of the cave-dwellings in the North-West Settlement (Area 1500), including those later groups elsewhere on the site in which ledge handles occur (pp. 151–159).

B. Early Bronze Age. Pottery from burial groups in the deserted cave-dwellings, from caverns below the north-east slopes (Area 6000) and from contemporary city deposits on the mound above (pp. 55–59), from EB I onwards, though chiefly of EB III date.

C. Caliciform Culture. Pottery brought by newcomers at the end of the Early Bronze Age (Group 1529 and Cemetery 2000). For the distinctive wares and shapes imported at this time the term Caliciform Culture is adopted (see pp. 31, 41). The time range of the people of this culture may precede or overrun the arbitrary date of 2000 B.C. for the junction of the Early and Middle Bronze Ages by a century or more.

In this account, the dates proposed by Dr. G. E. Wright in *The Pottery of Palestine from the Earliest Times to the End of the Early Bronze Age* will be followed, with those few adjustments which seem called for by the new material which has come to light since he prepared his study in 1937. *Relative Chronologies in Old World Archeology*, edited by Robert W. Ehrich, provides a summary of expert opinion up to 1954.

A. CHALCOLITHIC AND EARLY BRONZE AGE

Sources

The pottery to be discussed was found in caves of the North-West Settlement (Area 1500), situated on the edge of a wide plateau overlooking the valley which separates it from the mound of Tell ed-Duweir (Pls. 1: 1, 2–3, 94–95). Natural caves were enlarged and the soft substratum of rock was excavated to make dwelling-places. The sherds illustrated on Pls. 11–13, 56 and 57 are a selection from material which belongs to this period of domestic use, in the fourth and early third millennium B.C.

System of Numbering (For general notes see L. III, pp. 257 ff.)

The cave numbers listed below in very approximate chronological order range from 1525, containing a form which has Lower Chalcolithic associations, to 1520, covering Upper Chalcolithic and extending to an advanced stage of EB development.

The chart which follows includes relevant contacts with Tomb 1535, the North-East Section, Cemetery 6000, Group 1529, and Cemetery 2000, in order to follow the ledge handles to the final phases of degradation. The occurrence of crucibles and jars is noted with reference to special features and, in particular, to ledge handles. Each column heading is separately discussed with references to comparisons elsewhere.

For the list of contents in each cave, see under the appropriate number in Chapter 12, where burial groups in caves of the late third millennium, EB III–IV, and the pottery of the Caliciform Culture are also discussed.

Pottery in Cave-Dwellings (North-West Settlement, etc.)

Group	Crucibles	Jars: Sloping necked	Holemouth Thin	Holemouth Bulbous	Basins	Indented edge	Ledge handles 1–3	4	5	6	7	8	9	10	11	12	Multiple-strand handles	Culture
Cemetery 2000																× ×		CALICIFORM CULTURE
1529						×									×			
Cemetery 6000	×			× × ×								× × ×						←EARLY BRONZE→
NE 0–12 ft.				× × ×							×	× × ×		×				
1535											×	× × ×		×				
1520	× ×		×					×	×	×			×				×	CHALCOLITHIC
1503	× ×	×			×				×	×		×					×	
1509	×		×	×		×		×	×	×				×				
1553	× ×		×			×		×	×		×							
1523	× × ×		×			×	×	×	×	×		×					×	
1514		×																
1534	× ×	× ×		× ×	×	×	× ×	×	× × ×	×		×					× ×	
1557					×		×		× × ×									
1558	×		×	×	×													
1532																		
1517	×		×			×	×		× ×									
1527/8	× ×																	
1550	× ×	×					×		×									
1538	× × ×	×	×			×	× ×		×		×						×	
1540	× ×	×																
1537	×	×	×			×	×		×									
1531						×	×											
1525	×	×	×			×												

Crucibles

Photographs	Types, Pls. 56–57, 60
Pl. 11: 11, 12, 19, 21, 22; Pl. 12: 54, 57, 58; Pl. 13: 93, 94	1, 12, 14, 15, 23, 31–35, 42, 43, 45, 46, 50–58, 65–67, 71

Crude hand-made hemispherical cups with an average diameter of 9 to 12 cms. can perhaps be best described as crucibles. They are the most common form in the cave-dwellings and are made of a buff or pinkish ware containing grits and straw temper. An occasional example is stained (or painted?) red on the rim. For a general account of similar crucibles from Predynastic Egypt see *Technology*, Fig. 400 on p. 608.

Fingermarks are often visible outside (e.g. Types 34, 52 and 54) and many show cracks and charring on the base, though the rim is less frequently affected. For this reason they do not seem to have been used as lamps, and they are too small for practical cooking pots. Sherds of Types 35 and 58 were numerous in and around the site of Kiln 1525, where many of these cups may have been made (Fig. 11 on p. 263). The majority appear too thin to stand the heat of molten metal, and there were indeed no signs of metal slag inside. On the other hand, the inner surface often presented an even creamy-grey appearance up to a point just below the rim.

A more pronounced lining or wash distinguished two nozzled crucibles of thicker ware, found in surface deposits not far from the rough castings illustrated on Pl. 21: 11–15, and they were submitted for analysis in order to determine whether they had been used for melting metal.

Report on Crucibles, Pl. 57: 71, by Emeritus Professor W. E. S. Turner, F.R.S.

The spectrographic analyses were carried out in the Admiralty Laboratory, Sheffield.

The crucible, grey-fawn in colour, was somewhat sandy, friable and vesicular in character and the body contained some hard particles. The shape was circular, being that of a bowl or deep saucer, about 4½ inches in diameter and 1½ inches in internal depth.

A pouring nozzle had the entrance to its channel only a little above the bottom of the crucible so that the capacity of the latter would be very limited unless, as may well have been the case, the exit of the nozzle was temporarily plugged during a fusion. The circular entrance to the nozzle from inside the crucible was about three-eighths of an inch in diameter, the exit thirteen-sixteenths. A thin lining or wash of apparently different substance from the body of the pot, whitish in appearance, had been applied to the interior of the crucible and spout. In one crucible only the bottom and part of the interior walls were covered with this wash, but in another crucible the whole of the interior up to the rim was so coated.

1. Composition of the Body

The analysis showed that the major constituents were silica, calcium oxide and iron oxide; whilst alumina, sodium oxide and titania were also present in substantial amounts. Magnesium oxide was present to the extent of probably between 1% and 2%. Minor constituents (a small fraction of a per cent) were copper, nickel and manganese. Traces of several other elements were found, including lead, silver, tin, cobalt, vanadium and chromium.

2. The Thin Lining or Film

The most marked constituent was lime, and then followed alumina and silica.

It is quite possible that the silica content was substantially more than revealed by the spectrographic examination. In the lining were found also small amounts of iron oxide, copper oxide and magnesia. Most of the trace elements found in the body were also present in the lining.

The application of a protecting film or lining containing a high percentage of lime was known to Egyptian 18th-dynasty glass makers. Cylindrical crucibles found at Tell el Amarna with such protective lining have been described by me in the *Journal of the Society of Glass Technology, Transactions*, 1954, 38, 436–440, where chemical analyses are recorded. These spouted crucibles were more likely used for metal than for glassmaking.

Conclusion

On submitting the analysis to Professor F. C. Thompson, Department of Metallurgy, Manchester, he expressed the opinion that it is highly probable that the two vessels in question were crucibles in which metal was melted. "They correspond fairly closely in shape to those which are known", he wrote, "and even the wash . . . is quite reasonable. A lime-wash to prevent absorption of the metal by the porous crucible seems to have been quite a common practice."

From the list of references below, the crude cups without nozzles would seem to date from the transitional period between Chalcolithic and EB I (pp. 40 f.). The best parallels for them come from the southern Tell Fara, Site H, which produced a primitive metal dagger (BP II, Pl. XXVI: 50, Pl. XXVIII: 1 and p. 12) and quantities of copper ore and haematite.

The two nozzled crucibles cannot be dated from their archaeological context, but their advanced shape and appearance suggests a later date, contemporary, perhaps, with the metal workers of the Caliciform Culture.

Plate	Comparisons	
11: 21	Tell Fara (I. of A. ref.: E. IV. 2048) Site H, Pit XI	
12: 54	Tell Hammam (TG I, Pl. 61: 5)	EB I
12: 57, 58	Tell Fara (I. of A. ref.: E. IV. 2025) Site H, D. 1, 4–5 ft.?	
56: 14	Et-Tell (Ay, Pl. LXX: 666) Tomb C	EB II?
57: 43	Tell Fara (BP II, Pl. XL: 43) Site H	
57: 46	Tell Fara (BP II, Pl. XL: 49) Site H	
57: 50	El Husn (APEF VI, Fig. 1: 4)	EB I
57: 53	Megiddo (MT, Pl. 3: 2) Tomb 903 Upper	Stages VII–IV
	Jericho (AAA XXIII, Pl. XXXVI: 13)	Layer VII
57: 65	Tell Fara (I. of A. ref.: E. IV. 2026) Site H, Pit XI	

Jars

Sloping necked

Photographs

Pl. 11: 8; Pl. 12: 52

Types, Pls. 56–58

26, 59, 60, 132

Made of light brown or reddish ware with a somewhat lumpy surface, these jar rims range from 15 to 43 cms. in diameter. Two reconstructed jars are drawn in Types 26 and 59.

Plate	Comparisons	
12: 52	Tell Fara (I. of A. ref.: E. III. 2045) Site A	
	Beisan (MJ XXIV, 1935, Pl. I: 25 with raised band)	Level XVIII
56: 26	Tell Fara (BP II, Pl. XL: 47) Site H, 6·5–7 ft.	
57: 59	Teleilat Ghassul (TC II, Pl. 77: 7)	Niveau IV

Holemouth, thin rims

Photographs   Types, Pls. 56–57, 63,

Pl. 11: 1, 7, 10, 16; Pl. 12: 63;   5, 38, 63, 315, 318

Pl. 13: 78

Holemouth jar rims which have not been turned in to make a thickened edge are usual in the cave dwellings and only some sherds from Caves 1534 and 1558 were folded to strengthen the rim, presenting the bulbous appearance which was common in the deposits of the North-East Section (see pp. 57–59, 164).

The thin, hand-made rims had been kiln-fired (or subsequently charred) to a dull even grey, and the body contained much crushed flint and limestone, with occasional addition of crystalline particles.

Indents on the rim occur (Pls. 11: 7, 10 and 13: 78) and the fragment on Pl. 12: 63 is decorated with a thumb-impressed band. These are characteristic of the Tell Fara sites, see refs. on p. 268.

Plate	Comparisons	
12: 63	Jericho (AAA XXII, Pl. XXXII: 1) Strip 3, 11·34 m.	Layers V–IV
	Et-Tell (*Ay*, Pl. LXXXII: 2197) Fouille H, Ch. 116, parquet B	EB II?
56: 5	Megiddo (SAOC 10, Chart Column 12B)	Stages VII–III
	Affuleh (PEQ, July 1936, pp. 150 ff. Pl. I: 9)	Late Chalc.
57: 38	Tell el Far'ah (RB LV, 1948, p. 561, Fig. 6: 6)	EB I
57: 63	Megiddo (M. II, Pl. 102: 5)	Stratum XVIII
	Beisan (MJ XXIV, 1935, Pl. IV: 4)	Level XIV
	Tell el Far'ah (RB LIV, 1947, p. 411, Fig. 3: 5)	EB I
	Teleilat Ghassul (TG II, Pl. 82: 19)	Niveau IV A

Basins

Photographs   Types, Pls. 56-57

Pl. 12: 36, 37, 59, 62   25, 28, 73

Fragments of a deep open bowl or basin, irregularly hand-burnished both inside and out, were found in those groups which contained material of the transition from Chalcolithic to EB. Similar pieces came from Tell Fara Site H (BP II, Pl. XXXVI: 2) confirming their position in the sequence (pp. 40 f.).

At Fara, these sherds mark the introduction of burnished wares, though they formed but a small proportion of the pottery (BP II, p. 12).

Elsewhere it is not easy to match the shape, unless they are related to the Egyptian Protodynastic basins, of which a rather similar and early form is published in QB I (Pl. XIII: $3N_2$ and p. 15). It was found with a vessel with tilted spout (ibid., Pl. XVI: $99X_2$), which is a feature foreign to Egypt (*Rel. Chron.*, p. 4), introduced in the Gerzean period in Egypt, equivalent to late Chalcolithic—EB I in Palestine.

Type 73 from Pit 171 is perhaps a very late descendant which is unburnished; similar forms occur at Megiddo Stages IV–I (SAOC 10, Chart Column 1), see also PPEB Form III, and below p. 158.

Plate	Comparisons
12: 36	Tell Fara (I. of A. ref.: E. IV. 2048) Site H, D. 2, 6·5–7 ft.
12: 59, 62	Tell Fara (BP II, Pl. XXXVI: 2) Site H
56: 25	Tell Fara (I. of A. ref.: E. IV. 2078) Site H, 6–7 ft.

POTTERY

SPECIAL FEATURES

Indented edge on Bowl, Pl. 56: 2 (Pl. 11: 3)   on Jar, cf. Pl. 57: 61 (Pl. 12: 44)
       on Bowl, cf. Pl. 56: 2 (Pl. 12: 40)   on Jar (Pl. 11: 23)
       on Bowl, Pl. 56: 9

Forms with an indented or wavy edge, caused by the impression of thumb or fingers, occur in the earliest groups of the series, with Upper Chalcolithic connexions.

This characteristic detail is missing from all subsequent groups of EB, and does not recur until it becomes prominent again on jars of the Caliciform Culture, when the decoration is much smoother and more regular (see Types 420, 421, 449). Compare this finish also with pottery of the First Intermediate period in Egypt (QB II, Pls. XCI, XCII).

Plate	Comparisons	
11: 3	Tell Fara (BP II, Pl. XXXV: 6th row from top, 2nd on right) Site O	
	Tell en-Naṣbeh (TN II, Pl. 85: 4th row middle)	EB
	Tell el Farʿah (RB LIV, Pl. XIV: 12)	Énéolithique Moyen B
	Tell Umm Hamad Sherqi (AASOR XXV–XXVIII, Pt. II, Pl. 104: 4)	Upper Chalcolithic
11: 23	Tell Fara (BP II, Pl. XL: 67) Site H	
	Jericho (AAA XXII, Pl. XLIII: 17) Tomb 355	
	Tell Fara (BP II, Pl. XXXIII: 4th row, middle) Site B	
	(BP II, Pl. XXXV: 7th row, right) Site O	
	(BP II, Pl. XXXVII: 4th row, middle) Site H	
	ʿAin Shems (AS IV, Pl. XXIII: 16)	Stratum VI
	Teleilat Ghassul (TG II, Pl. 86: 20, 21)	Niveau IV B
12: 40	Tell el Farʿah (RB LIV, 1947, p. 409, Fig. 2: 4)	Énéolithique Supérieur
	Tell Fara (BP II, Pl. XXXV: 7th row, right) Site O	
	(BP II, Pl. XXXVII: 4th row, 3rd from right) Site H	
	Tell Hammam (TG I, p. 102, Fig. 52: 6)	Niveau IV
56: 9	Tell Fara (BP II, Pl. XXXII: top middle) Site E	
	(BP II, Pl. XXXV: 3rd on right) Site O	
	Jericho (AAA XXII, Pl. XXXV: 5) Strip 3, 9·62 m.	Layers VII–VI
	Megiddo (SAOC 10, Chart Column 14G)	Stages VII–IV
	Megiddo (M. II, Pl. 98: 23)	Stratum XIX
	Tell el Farʿah (RB LIV, 1947, Fig. 2: 18 and p. 401)	Énéolithique Supérieur
57: 61	Tell en-Naṣbeh (TN II, Pl. 85: 3rd row left)	EB
	Jericho (AAA XXIII, Pl. XXXII: 23B)	Layer VIII

Ledge Handles

Special acknowledgement is due to Engberg and Shipton for the classification of ledge handles published in SAOC 10 and amplified in SAOC 17, to Wright's notes in *The Pottery of Palestine* (abbreviation: PPEB) and to Glueck's *Explorations in Eastern Palestine* (AASOR XV, XVIII–XIX, XXV–XXVIII). The range chart for ledge handles from Jericho is published in AAA XXII, Pl. XXXV. There is also a note on the subject by Macalister (BM, p. 83).

As knowledge of these significant details increases, the problem of suitable names for the different forms of ledge handles becomes more involved. In this study it is therefore proposed to give each form a number, followed by notes on how the handle was made. It is clear that in the period under review most ledge handles were separately made from a wedge or roll of clay of roughly a hand's breadth. The wedge was pinched out, and, to begin with, finger-marks on the edge would naturally occur in the process of attaching the handle to the pot.

In the following headings, the drawings on Pls. 56–67 and photographs on Pls. 11–13 on which ledge handles of Forms 1–12 occur are listed in the right-hand column, while comparable forms in the studies of Messrs. Engberg and Shipton and Dr. G. E. Wright are given on the left.

148

FOURTH AND THIRD MILLENNIUM

Forms 1, 2, 3

SAOC 10, 14ɢ, p. 13.
PPEB, Form 1a, p. 103.

Form 1: Pl. 56: 7 (Pl. 11: 5)
Form 2: Pl. 56: 9; Photographs: Pl. 11: 30–32
Form 3: Photograph: Pl. 11: 13

In fixing the wedge of clay on to the vessel the potter pressed against the projecting edges to secure a good join, leaving finger-marks in so doing; the join was then made good by smoothing the underside obliquely with the thumb. The indentations are either lightly pressed as on Pl. 11: 5 (Form 1), or more pronounced as on Pl. 11: 31–32 (Form 2). Form 3 has twin ledge handles (Pl. 11: 13) of which examples occur in Caves 1517 and 1557. These are "scalloped thumb-indented" handles, though perhaps four digits were normally used.

Plate	Comparisons	
11: 5	Beisan (MJ XXIV, 1935, Pl. II: 2 and pp. 10–12)	Levels XVI–XIV
	Megiddo (M. II, Pl. 103: 20)	Stratum XVIII
	'Ain Shems (AS IV, Pl. XXIII: 7)	Stratum VI
11: 31	Megiddo (M. II, Pl. 98: 23)	Stratum XIX
	Tell Umm Hamad Sherqi (AASOR XXV–XXVIII, Pt. II, Pl. 102: 9)	Upper Chalcolithic
	Beisan (MJ XXIV, 1935, Pl. II: 8)	Level XVII
	Tell el Far'ah (RB LIV, 1947, p. 409, Fig. 2: 18)	Énéolithique Supérieur
	Tell Fara (BP II, Pl. XXXVI: top left) Site H, D. 2	
11: 32	Beisan (MJ XXIV, 1935, Pl. II: 3 and p. 12)	Levels XVI–XIV
	Jericho (PEQ, 1952, p. 77, Fig. 5: 4) Below 1st town wall	EB Ib?
	Megiddo (SAOC 10, Chart Column 14ɢ)	Stages VII–IV
	Jerusalem (JST, Pl. VII: 13) Galerie III	

Form 4

SAOC 10, 14c (?) not illustrated, p. 13

Photographs
Pl. 12: 47, 56; Pl. 13: 69

Types:
Pl. 57: 41, 44

Very small ledge handles between 3 and 4 cms. in length appear on hand-made bowls (?) or jugs (?). They may compare with Class 14c at Megiddo and like them they are made of light-brown ware with a dark red or reddish-brown wash. The handle from Cave 1553 (Pl. 12: 56) is finely nail-indented. That on Type 41 is a very neat version close in the amount of tilt to Form 5.

Plate	Comparisons	
13: 69	Tell el Far'ah (RB LIV, 1947, p. 415, Fig. 5: 26)	EB I
	(RB LIV, 1947, p. 419, Fig. 7: 25)	EB I

Form 5

SAOC 17, Pl. 17: 15, p. 43

Photographs
Pl. 11: 14, 15, 28, 29; Pl. 12: 49, 50, 55; Pl. 13: 66, 79

Types:
Pl. 56: 6 (Pl. 11: 6), 26; Pl. 62: 280

Handles of Form 5 were the most common in the early caves. They were made in the same way as Forms 1–3, but the pressure was increased to tilt up the edge of the clay. They differ from the so-called "pushed-up" ledge handles in that the fingers were kept together in the process, and the wedge used was still essentially triangular. This form is perhaps equivalent to SAOC 17, Pl. 17: 15, though the upward tilt is not pronounced in the example illustrated. It can also be compared with Albright's "pushed-up scalloped" ledge handle, as illustrated by

149

FIG. 7. Ledge Handles

Scale 1:2

Form	Locus	Remarks	Field No.
1	1517	(Pl. 11: 5) Also Type 7	1844g[1]
2	1531	Also Type 9	1978a
3	1537	(Pl. 11: 13)	2047i
4	1534	(Pl. 12: 47)	1982Ax
5	1517	(Pl. 11: 6) Also Type 6	1844g[2]
6	1503	(Pl. 13: 71)	1735f
7	NE 2	No. 389 on p. 58	29
8	6030	Also Type 330	6681m
9	1520	(Pl. 13: 77)	1949Ad
10	NE 4	No. 370 on p. 58	50
10A	1535	—	2041i
11	1529	Also Type 412A	1977a
12	2120	Also Type 458	2503

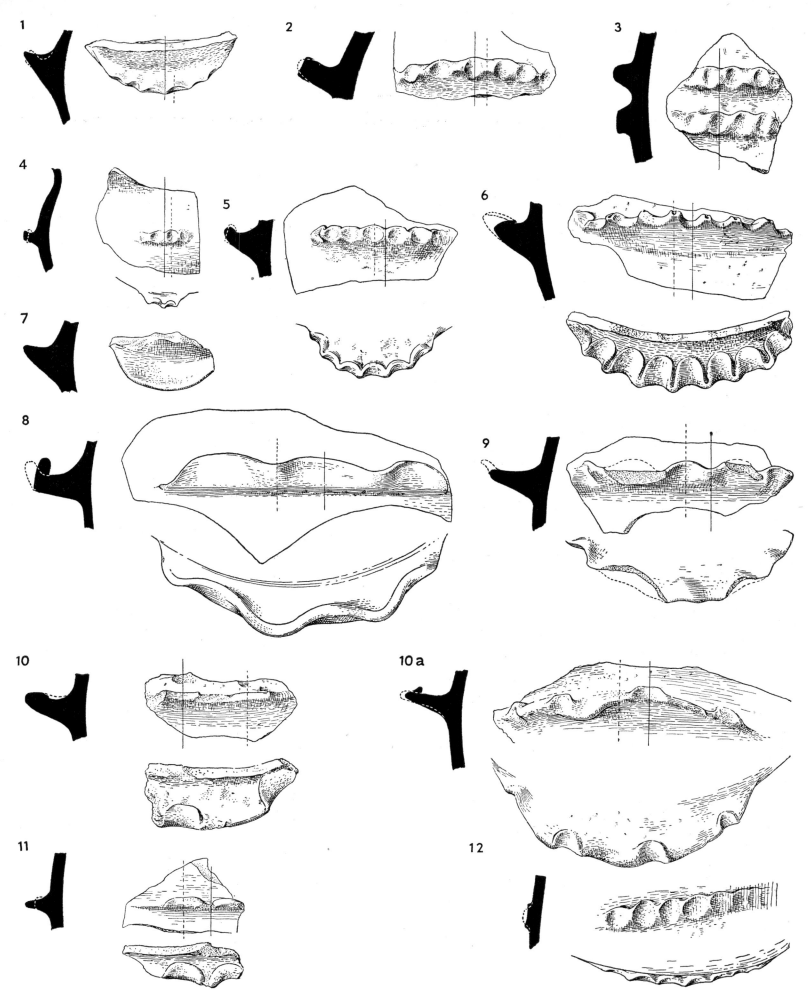

FIG. 7. Ledge Handles

Glueck (AASOR XVIII–XIX, p. 54, Fig. 29) which he assigns to EB IV A and to the transition between it and MB I (ibid., p. 255).

Plate	Comparisons	
11: 6	Beisan (MJ XXIV, 1935, Pl. IX: 22)	Level XII
	Tell en-Naṣbeh (TN II, Pl. 11: 181) Room 17	Level II
	Tell Fara (I. of A. ref.: E. IV. 2068) Site H, D. 1, 5–6 ft.	
	Et-Tell (Ay, Pl. XLVII: 2480a) Tombe 12	EB II?
11: 28	Et-Tell (Ay, Pl. LXXXVI: 1445) Fouille H, Ch. 138	EB I–II?
	Eastern Palestine (AASOR XVIII–XIX, p. 54, Fig. 29)	EB IV A
12: 49	Tell Fara (I. of A. ref.: E. IV. 2069) Site H, Pit 8	
	Tell en-Naṣbeh (TN II, Pl. 11: 179) City Wall, V layer	
	Jericho (AAA XXII, Pl. XXXV: 5) Strip 3, 9·62 m.	Layers VII–VI
12: 50	Tell Umm Hamad Sherqi (AASOR XXV–XXVIII, Pt. II, Pl. 102: 5)	Upper Chalcolithic
13: 66	Megiddo (SAOC 10, Chart Column 14B)	Stages IV–I
	Tell Fara (I. of A. ref.: E. IV. 2069) Site H, Pit 8	
	Et-Tell (Ay, Pl. XLVII: 2240) Fouille H, Ch. 116, sous parquet B	EB I–II?

Form 6

Photographs	Types:
Pl. 13: 68, 71	Pl. 56: 24; Pl. 57: 48 (Pl. 13: 74)

There are few published comparisons for these handles, which are exceptionally good. Like Forms 1–5, the indents are closely spaced and might come next in order before Forms 7 and 8. Each of the eight scallops was strongly pinched out separately between finger and thumb, turned over and well pressed down, leaving a clear indent. The nearest things to them are perhaps the incomplete handles which Albright and Glueck have designated "pushed-up, pinch-lapped" (AASOR XVIII–XIX, p. 254, Pl. 1: 10, 11). These particular forms Glueck also compares to "folded" handles of Stratum I at Tell Beit Mirsim.

The handles of Form 6 come from caves which contain pottery of developed Early Bronze Age affinity.

Plate	Comparisons	
13: 68	Tell eṣ-Ṣafi (BM, Pl. 26: 12)	"Early Pre-Israelite"
13: 71	Gezer (Gezer III, Pl. XXII: 19) Cave 15 I	EB I

Form 7

	Photograph	Types:
SAOC 10, 14D, E, p. 13	Pl. 11: 27	Pl. 58: 107; Pl. 62: 290 (Pl. 15: 4)
PPEB, Form 1c, p. 103		N.-E. Section p 59: NE 2/389

Plain, narrow ledge handles came from Cave 1538 (Pl. 11: 27), from Cave 1553, from NE 2/389, and a specially broad version is seen on the vat from Cave 6013. A small plain handle on a spouted vessel, Type 107, may be compared with the pushed-up handle of Type 108 from the same group.

Plain handles thus occupy a position midway in the Duweir series, which conforms with their place between "the wavy and thumb-indented types of the Chalcolithic strata and the pushed-up variety typical of the Early Bronze period" at Megiddo (SAOC 10, p. 15).

Typologically I do not feel that these plain handles are out of place in chronological position, for the naturally imposed finger-prints of Forms 1–5 have been smoothed out, and in the forms which follow this has to be done before the wide and open waves of the pushed-up Form 8 can be achieved. For Wright's conclusions see PPEB, p. 93, for Glueck's see AASOR XVIII–XIX, p. 252.

Plate	Comparisons	
11: 27	Megiddo (SAOC 10, Chart Column 14D)	Stages V–III
	'Ameidat (AASOR XVIII–XIX, Pl. 1: 2)	EB I–II
	Beisan (MJ XXIV, 1935, Pl. VI: 8)	Level XIII
	Jericho (AAA XXII, Pl. XXV: 12) Strip 3, 9·67 m.	Layers VII–VI
	Affuleh (JPOS XXI, 1948, Pl. VII: 15) Pit A–B, surface	
	Tell el Far'ah (RB LIV, 1947, p. 407, Fig. 1: 31)	Énéolithique Moyen
	(RB LIV, 1947, p. 409, Fig. 2: 21)	Énéolithique Supérieur
	Tell ed-Dhiyabeh (AASOR XXV–XXVIII, Pt. II, Pl. 57: 4)	EB I
NE 2/389	Megiddo (M. II, Pls. 2: 27, 98: 11)	Strata XX, XIX
	Megiddo (SAOC 10, Chart Column 14D)	Stages V–III
	Et-Tell (Ay, Pl. LXXXVII: 1358) Fouille V, Ch. 108, assise 4	

Form 8

SAOC 10, 14B, p. 13
PPEB, Form Ie, pp. 94, 104

Types:

Pl. 58: 108, 121, 122; Pl. 59: 172 (Pl. 17: 34), 174–176 (Pl. 17: 36–38), 178 (Pl. 17: 40), 179; Pl. 60: 226 (Pl. 16: 44); Pl. 61: 250–252 (Pl. 14: 16–18), 255 (Pl. 14: 22), 256 (Pl. 14: 25), 264; Pl. 62: 288 (Pl. 15: 3); Pl. 63: 330, 331; Pl. 64: 358, 364; Pl. 65: 382
N.-E. Section, pp. 57–59: NE 6/335; 5/356; 3/379, 380; 2/388; 1/406

The most common forms of handles, both in the North-East Section and in the Cave 6000 (p. 166), are so-called "pushed-up" ledge handles. They differ from Forms 1–5 and 7 in three ways. The wedge was rolled out thin, not much thicker perhaps than the wall of the pot, making the handle wider. Both the trough and the crest of the wave are pushed-up, unlike Form 9, where only the crest is so. Wright notes the first occurrences in Megiddo, Stage IV, Jericho Layer V and at Beisan XIV, though no clear examples are actually published from this level. Especially common in EB III, Wright considers that the "pushed-up" handle is typical of the last phase. It cannot be said that the range of such handles from Eastern Palestine is similar in effect to those from Duweir, though the principle of construction appears to be the same. (Cf. AASOR XXV–XXVIII, Pt. II, Pl. 148.)

Plate	Comparisons	
13: 79; 63; 330	Megiddo (SAOC 10, Chart Column 14B)	Stages IV–I
NE 1/406	Tell Beit Mirsim (AASOR XIII, Pl. 20: 21)	Stratum J

Form 9

SAOC 10, 14H, p. 14
PPEB, Form Ib, pp. 93, 103

Photograph
Pl. 13: 77

Wright has noted that the earliest appearance of the "wavy" handle at Megiddo in Stage VII is still later than the earliest appearance of the "scalloped (thumb-indented)" form in Level XVII at Beisan (our Form 1).

He also considers that such handles are confined entirely to the Maritime Plain and to the Plain of Esdraelon. The one handle which approximates to a true wavy ledge handle is Form 9 (Pl. 13: 77), the near exception which may prove the rule.

Engberg and Shipton (SAOC 10, p. 14) have described how they were "impressed alternately from above and below by thumb and forefinger action". This method produces a freer, more open wave, quite unlike the close indents of Forms 1–6.

Mme Marquet-Krause also records the appearance of "wavy" handles after the thumb-indented forms at Ay (*Ay*, p. 20). Here, again, this seems quite logical in view of the way in which they were made.

*Forms 10, 10*A

SAOC 17, Pl. 17: 16	Photograph	Types:
PPEB, Form Id, pp. 93, 104	Pl. 13: 67	N.-E. Section, p. 59: NE 4/370

"Pinch-lapped" is a useful descriptive term for this kind of handle, and the number of pinched folds on an otherwise plain handle may range from one to four. The indents are made by pinching each one separately between finger and thumb at intervals along the plain ledge handle. They are uncommon at Duweir; one example came from Cave 1509 (Pl. 13: 67), while another, NE 4/370, was found in the North-East Section.

These handles are characteristic of the early sanctuary at Ay; they are associated with Layers V–IV and with the upper midden accumulation against the Second Wall of Miss Kenyon's 1952 excavations at Jericho. They occur in Stratum XIX at Megiddo, and are found as late as Level XII at Beisan. There are two possible examples of this class from eastern Palestine (AASOR XVIII–XIX, p. 254 and Pl. 12: 2, 3).

Plate	Comparisons	
13: 67	Megiddo (M. II, Pl. 98: 25)	Stratum XIX
	Jericho (AAA XXII, Pl. XXXV: 7) Strip 4, 10·80 m.	Layers V–IV
	Jericho (PEQ, 1952, p. 77, Fig. 5: 33–35) Upper midden against 2nd wall	EB II?
	Et-Tell (*Ay*, Pl. XLVII: 1766) Fouille V.2, Ch. 198	EB II–III
	Beisan (MJ XXIV, 1935, Pl. IX: 21)	Level XII

Form 11

SAOC 10, 14A, p. 103	Type:
PPEB, Form If, pp. 94, 106	Pl. 66: 412A

This form of handle is only represented by a fragment on a wheel-made pot from Group 1529 (Pl. 66: 412A). Two folds remain which are closely pressed down and present a fat and puffy effect, like some handles from Site H at Tell Fara (BP II, Pl. XXXVI: middle row). The fragment is near Albright's "folded wavy ledge handle" (which is equal to Guy's "envelope") handle though he has personally confirmed, on seeing the piece in question, that it is not identical. At Tell Beit Mirsim, the "folded" handle is typical of Stratum I (cf. Pl. 66: 412A and AASOR XII, Pl. 3: 40).

Form 12

	Types:
	Pl. 59: 180 (Pl. 17: 42); Pl. 67: 456, 458, 459, 460 (Pl 20: 4), 461

Reproductions of the ledge handle persist on a jar from Cave 1513 (Type 180) and vessels from Cemetery 2000. In each case, all that remains is a slight finger-marked projection, placed rather low on the circumference of the jar.

The best comparisons for these vestigial ledge handles are to be found in Cemetery 1500 at Tell el-Ajjul (AG II, Pl. XXIX), while there are apparently only two examples in the slightly later Cemeteries 100–200 (AG I, Pl. XLI).

Conclusions

Forms 1–6 all display closely spaced finger indents along the handle edge. From the size of the marks it seems that the potter was frequently a woman, and it is usual to find two sets of the four digits side by side. On the strength of comparative material, Forms 1–6 range from Upper Chalcolithic or earlier to EB I, if it is agreed that Fara Site H should be placed in the transition from Chalcolithic to EB I (p. 30).

Form 7, the plain ledge without indents, is uncommon at Duweir, like Form 10 which is also a plain handle with one or more indents upon it.

Form 8, the pushed-up ledge handle, must be considered in relation to Form 9, for both are constructed in the same way, though Form 9 has closer affinities with the true wavy handle, which Wright has suggested was the result of reciprocal Egyptian influence (PPEB, p. 93). The earliest extant ledge-handled jar from that country, which begins the series at S.D. 40, is a plain flat-based vessel with a small sloping neck made by hand in one with the body (PEC, Pl. XXVIII: 1). The handles are attached below the widest circumference and the general outline is not unlike Type 461, though in that case the neck is partly wheel-made and therefore more angular, and the handles are more debased. Both jars are about the same height, 37–39 cms., and few of those which follow in the Egyptian series are as close to the Palestinian form.

While the place of origin of the ledge handle and its diffusional contacts are still obscure, many experts consider that it may have begun in Lower Egypt, though little is known of the prehistoric pottery of the Nile Delta (AASOR XII, §§ 1–5). If this could be proved, it might account for the sudden emergence of the "pushed-up" ledge handle, which seems to lack immediate predecessors in the Palestine sequence. It is, for instance, difficult to believe that Forms 8 and 9 develop directly from Forms 1–6, with only Forms 7 and 10 as intermediate.

Forms 11 and 12 would follow on far more reasonably from the earlier series with the closely spaced indents which they show. Both are associated with Caliciform flat-based jars and both die out during the period of their use. The folded ledge handle is, in any case, restricted to Stratum I at Tell Beit Mirsim (AASOR XIII, § 6) and vestigial remains are also to be seen in Strata H–I (ibid., Pl. 20: 1).

Multiple-strand Handles

Photographs
Pl. 11: 25; Pl. 21: 42, 43; Pl. 13: 72

Types:
Pl. 57: 41, 44

Loop handles composed of two, three or more strands occur on small jugs, of which Types 41 and 44 are complete examples. In the earliest one from Cave 1538 (Pl. 11: 25), the strands are separately rolled and then stuck together, but in the handles from 1534 (Pl. 12: 42, 43) the effect is produced by scored grooves.

Especially important is the handle, Pl. 13: 72, which compares very closely with that on a jar found at Gerzeh with ledge handles on the body which are unfortunately broken. The detail of the groove is not visible in the published drawing and the original vessel at University College, London, should be seen. On Egyptian evidence, that Palestinian import dates between S.D. 43–70.

Plate	Comparisons	
11: 25	Et-Tell (*Ay*, Pl. LVIII: centre) Fouille Z, ch. 207, Niveau II	
12: 42	Tell Fara (BP II, Pl. XXXI: bottom middle) Site H, 7–7·5 ft.	
	Jericho (AAA XXII, Pl. XXXVI: 15) Strip 2, 9·21 m.	Layers VII–VI
12: 43	Tell Fara (BP II, Pl. XXXVII: 3rd from bottom, right) Site H, 6–7 ft.	
13: 72	Megiddo (SAOC 10, Chart Column 9E)	Stage III
	Jericho (AAA XXII, Pl. XXXVI: 20) Strip 2, 9·11 m.	Layers VII–VI
	Gezer (*Gezer* II, p. 153, Fig. 316: 19 and p. 154) Cave 2 I	EB I
	For date see PEQ, Jan. 1937, p. 73	
	Gezer (*Gezer* III, Pl. 19: 5) Cave 11 II	EB I
	Tell Fara (BP II, Pl. XXXVII: bottom right) Site H, surface	
	Tell Fara (I. of A. ref.: E. IV. 2079) Site H, Pit 1	
	Gerzeh (LGM, Pl. XI: 2c and PEC, Pl. XXVIII: 1)	S.D. 43–70

B. EARLY BRONZE AGE I–IV

In the first centuries of the third millennium, the rock surface now covered by Tell ed-Duweir became the main living centre, and the deserted caves of the North-West Settlement were speedily reused as burial-places.

Burial Groups

The sherds of Chalcolithic and Early Bronze I–II living phases are discussed in the previous sections, pp.144–155, while the burial groups in the same caves take over at a slightly later phase, and continue through the Early Bronze Age; the contents are listed and analysed below. Descriptive notes on each cave are to be found in Chapter 12.

Group	Illustrations	Date
1513	Pls. 17 and 59	EB III–IV and later
1556	Pls. 14 and 61: 234–257	EB III
1519	Pls. 16 and 60	EB II–III
1516	Pls. 60: 233 and 61: 258–261	EB II–III
1501	Pl. 58: 124–130	EB II–III
1538	Pl. 61: 262–272	EB II–III
1535	Pl. 58: 75–123	EB I–III

North-East Section, 0–12 feet

At the same time it is necessary to consider the contemporary pottery from the North-East Section, which is drawn and described on pp. 57–59.

North-East Caverns

In the lower slopes of the mound at least four large partly natural caves had been used and enlarged by man for industrial and domestic purposes.

For this reason, perhaps, the repertory of form is somewhat restricted, and it shows only rare links with the contemporary tomb groups in the North-West Settlement. The best contacts are to be found in the domestic rubbish of the city above, especially between 7 and 12 feet in the North-East Section.

The general quality of the pottery is consistent and distinctive. It presents a reddish-brown lumpy surface with a dark, almost black core, containing crushed flint and limestone. It is usually comb-faced and often covered by a lime-wash. In these respects it compares with Tell Beit Mirsim Stratum J, but there is no painting in reddish-brown bands, which is particularly common at Tell Beit Mirsim (AASOR XII, p. 5) and is a feature in Tomb A at Jericho (AAA XIX, Pl. VIII). For that decoration on lime-wash surface, see the sherds from Cave 1520 on Pl. 13: 73, 74 and 80. Pattern-burnished red slip was largely confined to the interior of platters and bowls in the pottery of the North-East Caverns.

The caverns were themselves in use for a considerable time and each contains some sherds from an early horizon, though the majority date from EB III or even from that lesser known period EB IV. It is not yet clear whether the repertory of form which distinguishes certain deposits grouped under this head is due to the difference between domestic and burial pottery, or whether it marks a later chronological phase.

Potmarks (Pl. 18)

Numbers of potmarks were a distinctive feature of the North-East Caverns and a few examples were recovered from the North-East Section and from burials in the North-West Settlement. The more complete marks are illustrated on Pl. 18; they were incised before firing, and the majority came from vats or holemouth jars. Most of the signs are simple linear groups, and it has been suggested that they indicate the number of measures of grain contained in the vessels (MT, p. 12 and Fig. 7). These Megiddo examples were found in the lower deposits of a cave which, in the excavators' opinion, represents a dwelling rather than a tomb, and they equate the sherds with Megiddo, Stages VII–V (MT, p. 9).

Whenever sizeable collections of these potmarks are found they are seen to be from town debris or domestic deposits. At Tell el-Hesi, Bliss found potmarks most comparable to those from Duweir in the earliest "Amorite" strata (MMC, pp. 21–25), and many more were found there in 1898 (BM, Pl. 29). At Gezer a few signs of the same kind range from First to Fourth Semitic, though potmarks were most common in the Second period (*Gezer* II, p. 176 and III, Pl. CXC). For the approximate date of this phase, *c.* 1800–1400 B.C., see Albright, *Arch. Pal.*, pp. 31–32. Thus comparable marks with raised dabs and linear incisions were ascribed at Megiddo to the Chalcolithic period, while at Hesi and Gezer the dates proposed are on other evidence perhaps too late.

In discussing the potmarks from Tell el-Hesi, Bliss drew comparisons for them from Egypt (BM, p. 82, note), but despite the numbers of such marks, in the ist dynasty especially, the connexion is not close (RT I, Pls. XLIV–LVIII). Somewhat nearer in effect are potmarks of the ivth-xith dynasties (QB I, Pl. XXXIV, especially Nos. 4, 7, 12).

The proposed equations between the North-East Caverns and the city deposits in the Section are set out below.

Cave	Illustrations	N.-E. Section	Date
6031	Pls. 62; 65: 365–391	7–9 ft.	EB III
6030	Pls. 62; 63: 320–336	6–9 ft.	EB III
6013	Pls. 62; 64: 337–364	4–9 ft.	EB I–III
6005	Pls. 62; 63: 304–319	0–7 ft.	EB I–II (and later ?)

Platters

Rims	Surface		
	Burnished	Slip or wash	Plain
Inverted	NE 1/392 Type 344	NE 15/209	—
Upright	NE 1/394; 5/346; 6/316; 9/244, 245; 15/211 Types 306, 322	NE 4/360	NE 1/395
Flanged, concave top	—	—	Types 309, 350, 379
Flanged, rounded top	NE 1/393; 3/373; 5/345; 7/286, 287 Types 307, 376	NE 8/264 Types 308, 348, 375	Types 325, 327, 377
Flanged, flattened top	Type 378	NE 7/290	Type 347
Inturned	Type 349	Type 373	NE 7/291 Type 324
Plain	NE 4/361; 7/292 Types 321, 323	—	NE 11/230 Types 277, 278, 304, 320, 341, 370

The term describes a wide and shallow vessel of coarse buff or reddish ware with a flat or rounded base and a rim diameter between 30 and 60 cms. The best criterion for the study of platters will eventually be found in the subtle changes of the rim (PEQ, 1952, pp. 81–82). In the recent excavations at Jericho, Miss Kenyon has shown that the short inverted rim "somewhat triangular in section" is common to all levels associated with the Second Wall (cf. Nos. 394 and 395 at 1 ft., p. 59, which appear more upright in rim section). In the period of the Third Wall at Jericho, the angle and lip become more rounded, and there is a distinct hollow beneath the angle (cf. PEQ, 1952, p. 80, Fig. 6: 7, 15, with No. 360 at 4ft. and No. 290 at 7 ft. in the North-East Section). A large portion of a plain-rimmed platter, unburnished (No. 230), at 11 feet equates with those of the North-East Caverns.

Nearly all the platters were pattern-burnished inside, the trend moving from a widely spaced lattice or criss-cross to radial or oblique strokes, usually completed with a band of horizontal burnish near the rim. The outside was often left rough, and many pieces show traces of grass-wiping or knife-paring.

In the large caves below the north-east corner of the mound (Area 6000) platters were very common, and, owing to the long occupation of these sheltered homes, many kinds of rim were present.

Inverted rims are rare, but represent the earliest kind of platter in our series. They are closely followed by those with an *upright* profile.

Of platters with a *flanged* rim, Types 309, 350 and 379 with a concave top are distinctive. They compare with more elaborate rims at Tell el-Hesi from the "Amorite" city (TH, Pl. VI: 55–61). It would appear that the groove was designed to take a lid. The nearest parallel in the stratified deposits at Jericho comes from Layer V (AAA XXIII, Pl. XXXVIII: 23).

Platters with rounded top, flanged inside and out, occur at Jericho. At Megiddo the same forms come from Strata XVIII–XVI. Platters with a *plain, unthickened* rim are also common, but they equate more probably with Strata XVII–XVI. These unburnished platters are especially typical of Tomb 351 at Jericho (AAA XXII, Pl. XXXIV: 31–36) which Wright dates to EB IV, and they are exclusive to the North-East Caverns at Duweir, though one large sherd was recovered from the North-East Section at 11 feet.

There were no true platters from the North-West Settlement burials, and their absence may emphasise their function as domestic or industrial ware. The nearest approach in size and appearance is seen in Types 90–92 from Tomb 1535 and in Types 195 and 198 from Tomb 1519. Of these, Type 91 is slipped and burnished all over, the strokes being radial inside and irregular out. Where the others are not too worn, they show radial strokes inside, though the outer surface is unslipped and there is no overspill around the rim. A rim of this kind occurred at 6 feet in the Section (No. 313 on p. 59).

The comparisons listed below will show the distribution of platter rims in the North-East Section and in the caves of Area 6000. The only platter from another source at Duweir is illustrated on Pl. 57: 73, though it is perhaps too deep to be so classified (p. 147).

Comparisons

Platter, upright rim

NE 1/394	Beisan (MJ XXIV, 1935, Pl. V: 20 and p. 16)	Levels XIV and XII
	Jericho (AAA XXII, Pl. XXVIII: 36) Strip 2, 11·53 m.	Layers V–IV
NE 1/395	Jericho (PEQ, 1952, p. 77, Fig. 5: 23) Occupation above 2nd wall	EB II
NE 4/360	Jericho (PEQ, 1952, p. 80, Fig. 6: 7) Construction of 3rd wall	EB III?
NE 5/346	Megiddo (M. II, Pl. 104: 14) E = 4033	Stratum XVIII
Pl. 63: 306	Beisan (MJ XXIV, 1935, Pl. V: 20 and p. 16)	Levels XIII, XII
	Et-Tell (*Ay*, Pl. LXXXI: 1177 II) Fouille V, Ch. 78, assise 3	EB I
Pl. 63: 322	(*Ay*, Pl. LXXVII: 2023) Fouille H, Ch. 116, parquet A	EB III
	Tell el-Hesi (TH, Pl. VI: 66)	"Amorite"

Platter, flanged rim, rounded top

NE 1/393	Tell Beit Mirsim (AASOR XII, Pl. 1: 24)	Stratum J
NE 7/287	Tell el-Hesi (TH, Pl. VI: 73) 270 NE	"Amorite"
Pl. 64: 348	Jericho (PEQ, 1952, p. 77, Fig. 5: 39) Upper midden against 2nd wall	EB II?

Platter, flanged rim, flattened top

NE 7/290	Jericho (AAA XIX, Pl. IV: 23) Tomb A2.40	EB III
	Jericho (PEQ, 1952, p. 80, Fig. 6: 15) Midden against 3rd wall	EB III?
Pl. 65: 378	Jericho (AAA XIX, Pl. IV: 23) Tomb A2.40	EB III
Pl. 65: 379	Et-Tell (*Ay*, Pl. LXXXI: 1437) Fouille H, Ch. 125, assise 2 du mur nord	

Platter, inturned rim

NE 7/291	Jericho (AAA XIX, Pl. IV: 20) Tomb A3.12a	EB III
	Tell Beit Mirsim (AASOR XIII, Pl. 1: 9)	Stratum J
Pl. 63: 324	Megiddo (SAOC 10, Chart Column 1D)	Stages IV–I
	Megiddo (M. II, Pl. 102: 37) = 4045	Stratum XVIII

Platter, plain rim

NE 11/230	Megiddo (SAOC 10, Chart Column 1C)	Stages IV–I
Pl. 62: 277	Megiddo (M. II, Pl. 5: 19) 5203	Stratum XVII
Pl. 62: 278	Megiddo (M. II, Pl. 5: 18) N = 5203	Stratum XVII
Pl. 63: 321	Megiddo (M. II, Pl. 102: 27) E = 4033	Stratum XVIII
Pl. 63: 323	Et-Tell (*Ay*, Pl. LXXVII: 2004) Fouille H, Ch. 116, parquet A	EB III

Bowls

Rim	Surface		
	Burnished slip	*Slip or wash*	*Plain*
Upright	NE 7/288 Types 198, 260	NE 7/283	—
Inturned	Types 83, 196	—	—
Flanged	NE 6/313 Types 87, 90, 91, 92	Types 86, 142	Types 310, 346
Plain	NE 1/390, 391; 4/359; 5/343; 6/308; 7/281, 282 Types 75, 76, 78, 79, 84, 194, 242, 259, 342, 367, 368, 371, 372	NE 2/383; 4/344; 6/309; 8/262, 263; NE 16: 202 Types 135, 145, 189, 238, 243, 258, 326, 332, 337, 343, 366	NE 2/384; 3/372; NE 16: 203 Types 77, 80, 136–138, 141, 143, 144, 146–149, 234–237, 329, 365
Special features *With lugs*	Types 88, 89, 155, 195, 244	Type 154	Types 197, 345, 374
String-cut *striped rim*	— NE 16: 200	Types 151, 153 Types 305, 339, 340, 369	Types 85, 150, 152, 241, 328, 338 —

It is by no means easy to distinguish some of the larger bowl fragments from platters, and a few could find a place in either group. Generally the bowls are between 15 and 30 cms. in diameter, and the greater number have a plain, unthickened rim. Complete sections from rim to base are rare, and classification must depend on rim shape and surface treatment alone. In this respect, it is useful to divide the bowls which show slip and burnish inside from those which have a matt red slip or wash unevenly applied. A sherd count in the Section shows that, except for isolated examples, bowls with good pattern burnish inside, highly polished, did not appear above 6 feet, and in any case the fragments were small and infrequent. Lattice burnish has an early trend on bowls as well as on platters, and this finish is followed by radial or oblique strokes inside, bounded by horizontal lines of burnish near the rim. Matt red bowl fragments were present from bed-rock upwards, but they were numerous from 4 to 10 feet. These bowls are rare in Caves 6005 and 6013, but quite common in the later Caves 6030 and 6031. The "Red wash" bowls at Megiddo (SAOC 10, Chart Column 20) extend from Stages VII–IV. They seem smaller and deeper than those in the Section and the walls are thicker and the rims turn in more, but many examples from both sites show traces of charring. A matt red wash bowl occurs at Tell el-Hesi (TH, Pl. VI: 90).

Comparison of the Charts for platters and for bowls (p. 157 and p. 159) will show that the same kinds of rim occur in both.

The upright rim is poorly represented, despite the long range attributed to a similar "inturned" rim at Megiddo from 3000 B.C. to the end of the Early Bronze Age (SAOC 17, p. 38, § 6). In the same work, Bowl No. 21 with that rim is said to be confined to Stratum XVIII (p. 41, § 140).

Bowls Classified According to Base

Cave	Round	Flattened	Flat	String-cut
1513	3	10	2	4
1556	2	4	2	1
1519	4	8	3	15
1516	1	1	1	1
1535	11	3	4	2

In the burials of the North-West Settlement, where the pottery is less broken, it will be seen that the bowls, ranging in diameter from 11·5 to 18 cms. and having a perfectly round base, are predominant in Tomb 1535.

Bowls with a wider diameter and a flattened base, which may still appear round from some angles, achieve ascendancy in the later groups. A really flat base is rare, though it occurs throughout the period on bowls of better quality and finish.

In Tombs 1535, 1516, 1519 and 1556 few bowls are without some traces of slip and burnish, but only in Tomb 1535 is the whole surface so covered. One bowl was lattice burnished inside, though the others in the group were all irregularly finished inside and out.

The next stage, when the slip covers the inside of the bowl and extends only over the rim, is found in Tombs 1535, 1516 and 1519. Radial strokes inside are characteristic of the earlier pieces in Tomb 1535 and in the later tombs are some examples which are spirally finished in the centre.

In Tomb 1513, the last big group of this series, only three bowls out of more than a score had slip and burnish, while some others retained traces of a matt red slip or wash which is very common on the string-cut bowls. The development in technique which led to the production of string-cut bowls is seen in Types 80, 147, 235, 236 and 329, which show marks of string-cutting on a more or less rounded base.

Bowls, string-cut

Types:
Pls. 58–65: 85, 150–153, 241, 328, 338
Striped rim: 305, 339, 340, 369

The term is adopted from that used at Megiddo, where the same form of bowl is found from Stages IV to I (SAOC 10, Chart Column 2) and in Strata XVIII–XVI (SAOC 17, p. 39). These bowls are "characterized by undulating wheel marks on the exterior" (SAOC 10, p. 7). They are in fact among the potter's first attempts to throw a wholly wheel-made form.

There are no clear examples of a string-cut bowl in the Section; No. 243 at 9 feet may belong to that category.

These bowls are made of a light clay containing limestone grits, fired rather softly throughout to pink or buff. The inner surface is well smoothed and is often coated with a thin, unburnished red, pink or buff slip or wash. The wheel-marks on the outside are usually well pronounced and, once the technique is perfected, the bowl stands on a sharply defined flat base.

The string-cut bowl makes its appearance in the North-West Settlement burials; there are fifteen examples in Tomb 1519 and the type is still represented in Tomb 1513.

Al these groups have close contacts with Tomb A at Jericho, and it is therefore somewhat surprising that the string-cut bowl does not appear there, though one example comes from the late Tomb 351.

Related to the string-cut bowl and made of similar wares, are bowls with a more thickened rim which is decorated with bands of red colour like the inside surface of the bowl. In published reports, this variety only appears at Jericho in Layers V–IV, and those pieces compare closely with the fragments, Types 305, 339, 340 and 369, of which the first types come from the earliest caverns 6005 and 6013. For the same decoration see No. 200 from the MB fill in the North-East Section, p. 57.

Comparisons

Bowls, upright rim

NE 7/288	Jericho (PEQ, 1952, p. 77, Fig. 5: 14) Construction of 2nd wall	EB II?
	Megiddo (SAOC 10, Chart Column 22B)	Stages IV–III
Pl. 60: 198	Affuleh (JPOS XXI, Pl. VI: 40) Pit E	
Pl. 61: 260	Jericho (AAA XXII, Pl. XXX: 19) Room 129, 10·87 m	EB II
	Megiddo (SAOC 10, Chart Column 22B)	Stages IV–III
	El Husn (APEF VI, 1953, Fig. 1: 6)	EB II
	Ras el-Ain (QDAP V, p. 121, Fig. 66)	EB
	Beisan (MJ XXIV, 1935, Pl. V: 21 and p. 14)	Levels XIV and XII
	Megiddo (SAOC 17, Pl. 13: 8 and Chart XVIII: 21)	Strata XVI–XVII
	Et-Tell (*Ay*, Pl. LXXVI: 1739) Fouille Z, Ch. 151	

Bowls, inturned rim

NE 5/345	Jericho (PEQ, 1952, p. 77, Fig. 5: 37) Upper midden against 2nd wall	EB II?

Bowls, flanged rim, rounded top

Pl. 58: 86	Jericho (AAA XXII, Pl. XXX: 14) Room 126, 10·74 m.	Layers V–IV
Pl. 58: 90	Jericho (AAA XIX, Pl. IV: 23) Tomb A2.40	EB III
Pl. 58: 91	Jericho (AAA XIX, Pl. IV: 18) Tomb A2.35	EB III
	Megiddo (MT, Pl. 4: 5) Tomb 910A, fill	Stages IV–III
Pl. 64: 346	Jericho (AAA XXII, Pl. XXVIII: 38) Strip 2, 11·53 m.	Layers V–IV
	Tell el Far'ah (RB LIV, 1947, p. 405, Fig. 5: 2)	EB I

Bowls, plain rim

NE 1/391	Tell el-Hesi (TH, Pl. VI: 91) 280 SE: 1600, 270, NE: 1500, 285 NE: 1200	"Amorite"
NE 2/383	Megiddo (M. II, Pl. 6: 12)	Strata XIX–XVI
Pl. 58 75	Jericho (AAA XXII, Pl. XXXI: 28) Room 129, 10·77 m.	Layers V–IV
Pl. 58 77	Jericho (AAA XXIII, Pl. XXXVI: 8)	Layer VI
	Et-Tell (*Ay*, Pl. LXXIX: 773) Tombe G	EB II
Pl. 58 79	Byblos (B.I, p. 369, Fig. 288: 5403) Bâtiment XXVII, Salle C, see also	EB I
	Byblos (RB LIX, 1952, Pl. III: 3rd row, centre)	EB I
Pl. 59 135	Byblos (B.I, p. 369, Fig. 288: 5405) Bâtiment XXVII, Salle C	
Pl. 59: 141	Jericho (AAA XIX, Pl. III: 3) Tomb A1.17c	EB III
Pl. 59: 146	Et-Tell (*Ay*, Pl. LXXV: 1390) Fouille H, Ch. 122	
Pl. 61: 258	Jericho (AAA XIX, Pl. III: 1) Tomb A2.18g	EB III
	Jericho (AAA XXII, Pl. XXXI: 28) Strip 1, 10·77 m.	Layers V–IV
	Megiddo (M. II, Pl. 6: 12)	Stratum XVI
Pl. 65: 365	Jericho (AAA XXII, Pl. XXVII: 9) Strip 2, 11·53 m.	Layers V–IV

Bowls, with lugs

Pl. 58: 88	Et-Tell (*Ay*, Pl. LXXXV: 1569 row 4) Fouille H, Ch. 144, assise 2	
	(*Ay*, Pl. LXVII: 22.635) Tombe C	EB II?

Bowls, with Lugs (cont.)	*Comparisons* (cont.)	
Pl. 58: 88	Beisan (MJ XXIV, 1935, Pl. V: 18 and p. 16)	Levels XIII and XII
	Tell el Farʿah (RB LIV, 1947, p. 417, Fig. 6: 2 and p. 419, Fig. 7: 36)	EB II
	Jericho (PEQ, 1952, p. 77, Fig. 5: 36) Upper midden against 2nd wall	EB II?
Pl. 58: 89	Jericho (AAA XXII, Pl. XXX: 20 without lugs, cf. AAA XXIII, p. 93) Room 126, 10·74 m.	Layers V–III
	Jericho (AAA XXIII, Pl. XXXVII: 10)	Layer III
	Ras el-Ain (QDAP V, Pl. LXIV: 11)	EB III
	Jericho (PEQ, 1952, p. 77, Fig. 5: 36) Upper midden against 2nd wall	EB II?
Pl. 61: 244	Et-Tell (*Ay*, Pl. LXXVII: 2013) Fouille H, Ch. 116	EB II?

Bowls, string-cut

Pl. 58: 85	Megiddo (SAOC 10, Chart Column 2)	Stages IV–I
Pl. 59: 152	Megiddo (MT, Pl. 5: 16) Tomb 1128 Fill	Stages IV–I
	Et-Tell (*Ay*, Pl. LXV: 9.1525 and 13.893) Fouille H, Ch. 116	EB II–III

Bowls, string-cut, striped rim

Pl. 63: 305	Jericho (AAA XXII, Pl. XXVIII: 34 for stripes on rim) Strip 2, 11·53 m.	Layers V–IV
	Jericho (AAA XXII, Pl. XXXIII: 14) Strip 3, 11·53 m.	Layers V–IV

Crucibles, Cups and Funnels

Crucibles	*Cups*	*Funnels*
Types: Pl. 60: 181 (Pl. 16: 1), 182, 183 (Pl. 16: 2), 184	Types: Pl. 58: 81, 82; Pl. 59: 139–140 (Pl. 17: 5, 6); Pl. 60: 190–193 (Pl. 16: 9–12); Pl. 61: 239 (Pl. 14: 6), 263; Pl. 65: 392, 393	Types: Pl. 60: 185–188 (Pl. 16: 3–6)

Survivals of the crucibles which were so common in the fifth to fourth millennium were found with Group 1519, but otherwise they were lacking in the third millennium. In their place are largely wheel-made cups, well smoothed and finished, which continue at least until the end of EB III. Confined to Group 1519 are similar cups or funnels which are pierced through the base.

Comparisons

Crucibles

Pl. 60: 184	Et-Tell (*Ay*, Pl. LXXVIII: 2566) Fouille H, Ch. 116	EB II or III

Cups

Pl. 59: 140	Bab ed-Dra (BASOR 95, 1944, Pl. I: 42)	EB
Pl. 65: 393	Et-Tell (*Ay*, Pl. LXV: 8.1528) Fouille H, Ch. 133, près de l'autel	EB II

Funnels

Pl. 60: 186	Jericho (AAA XIX, Pl. VII: 15) Tomb A3.7c	EB III
	Ras el-Ain (QDAP V, p. 120, Fig. 20)	EB
Pl. 60: 187	Jericho (AAA XIX, Pl. IV: 6) Tomb A3.28b	EB III
	Megiddo (MT, Pl. 6: 22) Tomb 1101B, lower	Stages I–O

Vats

	Types:
N.-E. Section, pp. 57–59	Pl. 62: 273–276, 290 (Pl. 15: 4);
NE 5/348; 8/268; 9/250	Pl. 63: 311, 313; Pl. 64: 353

Type 290 is among the first drawings to be published of a vessel which can best be described as a vat or bin. It stands on a flat base to over 60 cms. in height, and has a wide, open mouth with an inturned rim which may have been covered with a wooden (?) lid, unless the so-called platters were actually used for the purpose. A tubular spout just below the rim is so placed that it would be practically impossible to tip the heavy vat to pour liquid from it once the level of the contents had begun to fall. It would seem more likely that the spout was an air vent, for liquid in process of fermentation or for grain in store.

The vats are made of pink, red, brown or buff ware, and the grey core contains flint and limestone. The lumpy surface is often greyish-green, a point which the vats share in common with the spouted bowls. The rims, at least, show wheel finish and the outer surface is frequently horizontally combed. The incomplete vat, Type 290, has small plain ledge handles placed very low (Form 7 on p. 150), and Type 275 has a series of small knobs round the rim.

Pieces of similar vats are a feature of the "Amorite" city at Tell el-Hesi.

For general remarks on spouts, see the next section.

Comparisons

Pl. 62: 290	Et-Tell (*Ay*, Pl. LXXVII: 2082) Fouille V¹, Ch. 229	EB III?
	Tell el-Hesi (MMC, Pl. 3: 85) City I and Sub I	"Amorite"

Spouted Bowls

Types:

N.-E. Section, pp. 57–59   Pl. 58: 106–108; Pl. 61: 250 (Pl. 14:
NE 4/369; 7/299; 8/272   16), 252 (Pl. 14: 17), 264; Pl. 63:
                                  331, 333, 335; Pl. 64: 351, 358;
                                  Pl. 65: 381

The position of spouted bowls in the Section appears to be limited from 4 to 8 feet, but, owing to the nature of the fragments, which are extremely small, it is perhaps necessary to include the sherd NE 5/348 and the small ledge handle, NE 5/356, which resembles that on a spouted bowl 250. If sherds NE 1/396, 397 and 400 could be shown to belong to such vessels, the range would cover our whole period and, if not, they might belong to the great vats which are described above.

The spouted bowl can be described as a smaller version of the vat; it has an inturned anti-splash rim and a tubular spout in common, and is often provided with two ledge handles.

The fragments in the Section are made of a greenish-grey ware with an oatmeally surface and are horizontally combed on the outside. Pieces in the caves of Area 6000 present a similar appearance, and the rim is always finished on the wheel, a point which was noted by Petrie as characteristic of the "Amorite" comb-faced pottery at Tell el-Hesi (TH, Pl. V: 13 and p. 41).

In the burials of the North-West Settlement, this tradition is maintained in Types 107 and 108, though the same Tomb 1535 provides another spouted bowl, Type 106, covered with a thick red slip, vertically hand burnished. A better version in the same ware came from Tomb 1556, Type 252, while Type 264 from a burial in Cave 1538 is similarly finished. Spouted bowls do not appear in Tombs 1519 and 1513.

The forms, Pl. 64: 358 and 65: 381 may also have had spouts, though much of the rim circumference is missing.

Two spouted bowls from Jericho, Tomb A, layers 2 and 3 respectively, are published in AAA XIX, Pl. VIII: 5 and 4; they have painted decoration and no pronounced thickening at the rim.

Spouts were introduced at Beisan in Level XIV (MJ XXIV, Pl. V: 2–4) continuing through Level XIII, where they are common, to Level XII, but the rims do not find close comparisons at Tell ed-Duweir.

Albright has remarked on the popularity of the side-spout all over the ancient Orient in the third millennium (AASOR XII, pp. 6–7) and he notes its presence in Canaanite Jericho (SW, J 101, E 12), and in Stratum J at Tell Beit Mirsim.

Heavy bowl-spouts extend from Stages VI to III at Megiddo (SAOC 10, Chart Column 27) and are present in Strata XVII–XVI (M. II, Pl. 106: 9; Pl. 109: 8). Parallels exist at Jericho in Layers V–IV for the rims and spouts of the North-East Section.

Though these heavy spouts undoubtedly have their origins in deposits elsewhere which are earlier than the occupation of the mound at Tell ed-Duweir, the evidence collected above suggests that they were at their commonest phase in the "Amorite" city at Tell el-Hesi, Stratum J at Tell Beit Mirsim, Stratum XIII at Beisan, Layers V–IV at Jericho and Stages VI–III at Megiddo, and that they did not long survive in quantity. The tradition was nevertheless retained in the spouted jars found in the cemeteries of the Caliciform Culture, and a similar functional use may perhaps be expressed in the spouted jars of the vi–viiith dynasties in Egypt (p. 174).

Comparisons

NE 4/369	Tell Beit Mirsim (AASOR XII, Pl. 2: 14)	Stratum J
NE 7/299	Jericho (AAA XXII, Pl. XXXVIII: 3) Strip 4 169, 7·70 m.	Layer IV
NE 8/272	Tell el-Hesi (TH, Pl. V: 13) 270 NE	"Amorite"
Pl. 58: 108	Tell Beit Mirsim (AASOR XII, Pl. 2: 14 and p. 6)	Stratum J
	Gezer (*Gezer* I, p. 91, Fig. 31) Cave 15 I	
Pl. 64: 358	Megiddo (MT, Pl. 6: 29) Tomb 1101B lower	Stages O–I

Holemouth Jars

Bulbous rims   Types

N.-E. Section, pp. 57–59   Pl. 62: 289 (Pl. 15: 5); Pl. 64: 354;
NE 1/398, 399; 3/374; 4/362, 363; 6/318, 319; 7/293, 294; 8/265; 9/247, 248   Pl. 65: 387, 390

Fragments of holemouth jars with bulbous rims are common in the Section from bed-rock up to 10 feet, and between 6 feet and 10 feet they are especially numerous. Such fragments appear sporadically thereafter in Middle Bronze Age levels. The fragments present a very uniform appearance; the ware is consistently buff or brown, containing flint, limestone and some straw and is well and evenly fired.

No holemouth jars were found in the burials of the North-West Settlement, but this domestic vessel was extremely common in Caves 6000 and all the rims were of the bulbous variety. Standing intact upon the rock floor of Cave 6013, Type 289 is one of the few complete specimens of a shape which seems to be found throughout the Early Bronze Age period (see PPEB, Form VIIIb). It should be noted that the holemouth rim with ridge (op. cit., Form VIIIa), representative of EB Ib, does not occur in any context at Tell ed-Duweir, and the inverted rim bowl with which it is contemporary is also extremely rare. For Jars, holemouth, thin rim, see p. 147.

Comparisons

NE 1/398	Megiddo (M. II, Pl. 97: 7)	Stratum XIX
	Tell Beit Mirsim (AASOR XII, Pl. 1: 18)	Stratum J
	Jericho (SW, Pl. 20A: 97)	Canaanite
NE 3/374	Jericho (AAA XXII, Pl. XXVIII: 29) Strip 2, 11·53 m.	Layers V–III
	Megiddo (SAOC 10, Chart Column 12D)	Stages VII–III
NE 4/363	Jericho (PEQ, 1952, p. 77, Fig. 5: 30) Upper midden against 2nd wall	EB II?
NE 6/319	Tell el-Hesi (TH, Pl. V: 51) 280 SE	"Amorite"
NE 9/246	Megiddo (M. II, Pl. 107: 7)	Stratum XVII
Pl. 62: 289	Et-Tell (*Ay*, Pl. LXXVIII: 2543) Fouille H, Ch. 116, sous parquet B	EB I?
	(*Ay*, Pl. LXXXIV: 619) Fouille D, Ch. 34	
Pl. 64: 354	Jericho (PEQ, 1952, p. 77, Fig. 5: 11) Construction of 2nd wall	EB II?
Pl. 65: 387	Et-Tell (*Ay*, Pl. LXXXIV: 226) Fouille G, Ch. 3	EB III
Pl. 65: 390	Megiddo (SAOC 10, Chart Column 12D)	Stages VII–III
	Megiddo (M. II, Pl. 97: 7) S = 4047	Stratum XIX
	Jericho (AAA XXII, Pl. XXVIII: 28) Strip 2, 11·53 m.	Layers IV–III
	Tell Beit Mirsim (AASOR XII, Pl. 1: 18)	Stratum J
	Tell el Far'ah (RB LIV, 1947, p. 419, Fig. 7: 12)	EB II
	Et-Tell (*Ay*, Pl. LXXXIV: 357 row 4) Fouille G, Ch. 3	EB III?

Miscellaneous   Types, Pls. 63–65:
N.-E. Section, pp. 57–59   315, 318, 355,
NE 1/396, 397, 400, 401; 2/386; 3/375; 4/364, 365; 5/347; 6/320, 328;   356, 384, 388
  9/246, 249

Thin-walled holemouth vessels with little or no thickening at the rim are largely confined to the earliest cave-dwellings (see pp. 146 f), and a few pieces can be found to match them from the Section.

Fine pattern combing is seen on Type 315, and notches disposed herring-bone fashion or in lines occur on Types 356 and 384 around the rim. All these came from Caves 6000.

The square-cut rims, NE 1/396 and 397 (PPEB, Form D–VIIIb), may belong to holemouth jars, vats, or spouted bowls. The same applies to NE 1/400, 401. They are rare in the Section and Caves 6000, but Wright would give them a long range extending into MB I, and they occur at Megiddo in Stages IV–I. Square-cut rims, with and without the slight ridge at the rim, are found in all phases of EB wall construction at Jericho (PEQ, 1952, pp. 62–82, Figs. 5: 3, 15; 6: 13, 26).

Comparisons

NE 1/396	Jericho (AAA XXII, Pl. XXVIII: 24) Strip 2, 11·53 m.	Layers V–IV
NE 1/400	Tell el-Hesi (TH, Pl. V: 52) 280 SE	"Amorite"
NE 1/401	Jericho (PEQ, 1952, p. 77, Fig. 5: 15) Occupation above 2nd wall surface	EB II?
NE 6/328	Jericho (PEQ, 1952, p. 80, Fig. 6:26) Layers of burnt material	EB III

Pithoi

N.-E. Section, pp. 55–59   Types, Pl. 62:
NE 3/376; 5/351; 6/333; 7/297; 8–10/241, 254, 271, NE 17/191   281–284, 291–295, 296 (Pl. 14: 23),
                                                                 297–302, 303 (Pl. 15: 1–2)

The first pithos sherd appears at 3 feet in the Section, but those below 7 feet are probably intrusive. On the potter's floor at 9–10 feet was the greater part of a large combed vessel, comparable to jars from Megiddo, which are rare in Stage II and numerous enough to be typical of Stage I (SAOC 10, Chart Column 16A). The jar from the Section differs from those in Caves 6000 in that it has a ridged rim, while the rope moulding around the neck is more pronounced.

Pithoi are ubiquitous in all four caves. Type 303 is a complete example, standing about 90 cms. high on a flat base. The ware is consistently red with a bluish-grey core containing flint, limestone and some straw. A cream or buff surface is fairly frequent, which is coarse and lumpy outside, if it is not finished with pattern combing. Types 299 and 301 have traces of a lime-wash (p. 139).

Large pithoi do not normally find a place in funerary deposits, but one had been used, broken in half, to contain or cover the body of a man in Burial 1556. It is Type 296; the neck is wider and less flared than anything seen in the caves. Surface combing is restricted to the shoulder and the lug handles on it are not pierced.

The equation of the jar at 9–10 feet with Megiddo Stages II–I, prompts us to place the narrower flaring necks, which are common in Caves 6005 and 6013, contemporary with the possible occupational gap between 6 and 7 feet in the Section.

Comparisons

NE 7/297	Megiddo (M. II, Pl. 4: 5 for profile only)	Stratum XVIII
NE 10/241	Megiddo (SAOC 10, Chart Column 16A)	Stages II–I
Pl. 62: 296	Abydos (RT II, Pl. V: 18, incised drawing on stone fragment)	ist dynasty?
	Megiddo (M. II, Pl. 6: 7 for lugs)	Stratum XVI
	Gezer (*Gezer* II, p. 138, Fig. 308 for outline) Crematorium	EB I
	See PEQ, 1937, p. 70	
Pl. 62: 303	Et-Tell (*Ay*, Pl. XLIX: 2)	EB III

Jars or Jugs

Notched Decorations

The interest of Type 389 lies in its similarity to a common class of jar neck at Megiddo (SAOC 10, Chart Column 10) which was in vogue from Stages IV–I. It is uncommon at Duweir and fragments come only from two caves, 6013 and 6030. Sherds are recorded from Tell Beit Mirsim, Stra. J (AASOR XIII, Pl. 20: 28, 30–31).

The jars are made of light buff or red ware, containing some grits; while the body appears to be hand-made, the neck was clearly wheel-finished, and the decoration below it consisted of two rows of oblique notches. Type 386 is a variant which conserves the tradition of a raised band with notches, as seen on the pithoi.

Comparisons

Pl. 64: 361	Megiddo (M. II, Pl. 101: 31)	Stratum XVIII
Pl. 65: 389	Tell en-Naṣbeh (TN II, Pl. 10: 151) Tomb 61	
	Megiddo (SAOC 10, Chart Column 10)	Stages IV–I

Ledge-Handled

Jars: Types: Pl. 58: 121; Pl. 59: 174–175 (Pl. 17: 36, 37), 178 (Pl. 17: 40), 179; Pl. 61: 255–256 (Pl. 14: 22, 25)

Jugs: Types: Pl. 59: 172 (Pl. 17: 34), 176–177 (Pl. 17: 38, 39); Pl. 60: 226 (Pl. 16: 44); Pl. 61: 251 (Pl. 14: 18); Pl. 62: 285, 286, 288 (Pl. 15: 3); Pl. 65: 385

Jars and jugs with ledge handles are not easily distinguishable in the Section, and some, at least, of the rim fragments which occur in the EB levels would belong to this form. There is a good example, NE 10/236, with a ribbon handle and a potmark, and others are NE 9/251–253, see p. 57. Both jars and jugs are certainly present in Caves 6000, and among many well-made pushed-up ledge handles (Type 364), some may have belonged to these forms.

It will be seen at a glance that the jugs and jars from the burials in the North-West Settlement have small and rather poor ledge handles (Form 8), where they are not too broken to classify.

The ware is normally pink or buff, imperfectly fired, and it presents a lumpy surface which is sometimes covered with a lime-wash. An exception is Type 251, beautifully hand-burnished, and it matches in quality the spouted bowl 252 from the same group. The size of ledge-handled jars ranges from vessels over 30 cms. high to miniature versions.

Comparisons

Pl. 60: 226	Jericho (SW, Pl. 21: C. 1)	Canaanite
Pl. 61: 251	Jericho (AAA XIX, Pl. VI: 13 with wider neck) Tomb A1.22c	EB III
Pl. 62: 288	Tell el-Judeideh (BM, Pl. 23: 2J)	"Early Pre-Israelite"
	Et-Tell (Ay, Pl. LXV: 11.1565) Fouille H, Ch. 141, sanctuaire, cf. Syria XVI, 1935, Pl. LVI	EB III?

Loop-Handled

Handles to rim:
Types: Pl. 60: 218, 219 (Pl. 16: 38, 39)

Handles on shoulder or body:
Types: Pl. 58: 118, 124; Pl. 59: 171 (Pl. 17: 33); Pl. 60: 217, 222, 223 (Pl. 16: 36, 37)

Despite some latitude in the kind of handle and its position of attachment, these jars are usually made of soft buff ware, carefully slipped and burnished. The bodies are well formed, and in some cases the flared neck is wheel-made and possibly luted (see p. 171 for this method on jars of the Caliciform Culture). All these varieties are typical of Tomb 1519.

Comparisons

Pl. 58: 124	Lebe'a (BMB I, 1937, Fig. 10: 2nd row, right) Tomb 6	2400–2100 B.C.
Pl. 60: 222	Jericho (AAA XIX, Pl. VI: 17) Tomb A1. 16f	EB III
	Et-Tell (*Ay*, Pl. LXVII: 20. 691 for outline only) Tombe C	
Pl. 60: 223	Megiddo (SAOC 10, Chart Column 11C for form only: Megiddo example is metallic ware, Duweir example has red bur)	Stages III–I

Narrow-Necked

Types:
Pl. 59: 168–170 (Pl. 17: 30–32);
Pl. 61: 254 (Pl. 14: 19)

Narrow-necked jars with loop handles on the shoulder are uncommon everywhere and confined at Duweir to Burials 1556 and 1513. They are made of buff ware with few grits and are covered with a cream slip.

Comparisons

Pl. 59: 170	Tell Beit Mirsim (AASOR XIII, Pl. 20: 25)	Stratum J
	Et-Tell (*Ay*, Pl. LXXV: 1282) Fouille V, Ch. 93	EB I ?
Pl. 61: 254	Tell el-Hesi (MMC, Pl. 3: 84) City I or Sub I	"Amorite"

Plain or with Lugs

Types:
N.-E. Section, p. 57   Pl. 59: 173 (Pl. 17: 35); Pl. 60:
NE 11/238   220–221 (Pl. 16: 40, 41), 225 (Pl.
16: 43), 227 (Pl. 16: 45), 229–233
(Pl. 16: 47–51); Pl. 61: 257 (Pl. 14:
21); Pl. 78: 802–805

The plain jars come from Tombs 1519 and 1513, and they are especially interesting for they are among the few forms which appear to originate in EB III–IV and which carry on into the Middle Bronze Age. Types 229–233 from the earlier tomb are made of a buff or orange ware and two among them are finished with a red slip and vertical hand-burnish. Though the bodies are hand-made, the necks show clear signs of wheel-finish. In Tomb 1513, the whole pot is made on the wheel, of buff or orange ware, and the surface in two examples is covered with a buff slip. Faint traces of combing are to be seen on Type 803, and this finish is a link with painted jars at Megiddo (e.g. M. II, Pl. 8: 8, 9, 13: 5), Strata XV–XIV for which cf. rim NE 11/238.

Comparisons

NE 11/238	Megiddo (M. II, Pl. 13: 5)	Stratum XIV
Pl. 60: 220	Jericho (AAA XIX, Pl. VIII: 17) Tomb A2.16f	EB III
Pl. 60: 221	Tell Beit Mirsim (AASOR XIII, Pl. 1: 8)	"probably Stratum J"
Pl. 60: 230–231	Megiddo (SAOC 10, Chart Column 5B and p. 8, Fig. 3, with trickle paint)	Stages III–I
Pl. 60: 233	Lebe'a (BMB I, 1937, Fig. 10: bottom left) Tomb 6	2400–2100 B.C.

Amphoriskoi, Jug and Juglets

Cave	Amphoriskoi	Juglets			
		Narrow neck	Wide neck	Pointed	Pointed miniature
1513	—	—	2	2	4
1556	1	—	—	3	1
1519	—	3	5	5	2
1501	2	2	—	—	1
1538	3	1	4	—	—
1535	10	4	5	2	2
TOTALS	16	10	13	12	10

Strong general similarities of ware and the fact that both amphoriskoi and juglets were being made at a time when the change over from hand to wheel technique was only partially accomplished suggest that these forms should be discussed together.

Amphoriskoi

Types:

Pl. 58: 110–117, 127, 130, 134; Pl. 61: 245 (Pl. 14: 11), 265–267

Lug-handled juglets are found chiefly in Tomb 1535, with others in smaller groups of the same period. Of a pinkish-buff ware, all but the crudest showed some trace of slip and burnish and were turned on a slow wheel.

None of them had the painted decoration which belongs to the earlier specimens of this class in EB I (PPEB, Form VI) and they are more at home with the decadent versions (see p. 141).

Comparisons

Pl. 58: 113	Abusir el-Meleq (*Abusir el-Meleq*, Pl. 13: 59 for shape only)	
Pl. 58: 115	Tell en-Naṣbeh (TN I, p. 73; II, Pl. 12: 209) Tomb 67	EB I–II
Pl. 58: 116	Gezer (PEQ, January 1935, Pl. IV: top row, 2nd from right)	EB I–II
Pl. 58: 127	Jericho (AAA XXIII, Pl. XXXV: 3)	Layer VI
Pl. 58: 134	Tell en-Naṣbeh (TN II, Pl. 12: 213) Tomb 66	EB I–III
	Et-Tell (*Ay*, Pl. LXXI: 774) Tombe G	EB I–III

Jug and juglets, narrow-necked

Types:

Jug: Pl. 60: 228 (Pl. 16: 46)
Juglets: Pl. 58: 93, 98–100, 125, 129, 133; Pl. 60: 204 (Pl. 16: 23), 206 (Pl. 16: 25); Pl. 61: 272

The jug, Type 228, is twice the average height of the juglets, but in form and ware is clearly a larger size of the same standard pattern. It is the only example of a widespread type (PPEB, Form B–IVd) which is found at Megiddo, Stages III–I, and in Stratum XVIII (SAOC 17, p. 40). On that evidence, Shipton notes a rough synchronism between Stratum XVIII, Jericho EB II (Layers IV–III) and Beisan Stratum XIII, and his comparisons extend to the Syrian jugs from First Dynasty tombs in Egypt. A pitcher of the same date found by Professor W. B. Emery (*Tomb of Hemaka*, Pl. XXVI and Pl. XXVII: Type 12) is closely matched from Caananite Jericho (SW, Pl. 21: e. i).

Like the jug, the juglets are made of pinkish-buff ware, fired soft to medium, and all but one show signs of slip and burnish. About half the total number were hand-made and they varied in height between 8 and 16 cms., with a miniature version at 4·5 cms.

Comparisons

Pl. 58: 100	Tell el Farʿah (RB LVI, 1949, p. 120, Fig. 6: 34) Tomb 2	EB I
Pl. 60: 204	Jericho (AAA XXII, Pl. XXXI: 8) Strip 5, 10·31 m.	Layers V–IV
	Gezer (*Gezer* II, p. 139, Fig. 309: 2nd left) Cave II 28. See PEQ, 1937, p. 74, note 35	EB II
Pl. 60: 228	Jericho (AAA XIX, Pl. VIII: 16) Tomb A1.28g	EB III
	Saqqara (*Tomb of Hemaka*, Pl. XXVI and Pl. XXVII: Type 12)	ist dynasty
	Tell el Farʿah (RB LIV, 1947, p. 419, Fig. 7: 29)	EB II

Juglets, wide-necked

Types:

Pl. 56: 18; Pl. 58: 94–97, 131; Pl. 59: 161, 162 (Pl. 17: 22); Pl. 60: 200–203 (Pl. 16: 19–22); Pl. 61: 268–271; Pl. 63: 312; Pl. 65: 391A

Juglets with a wider neck appear to have a slightly later trend than the previous class. The ware is brown, pink or buff with an orange tone, fired soft to medium. All examples are slipped and vertically hand-burnished, but in later cave groups there are some plain or crudely finished pieces. The juglets range in height from 6 to 16 cms.

Wright suggests that the type (PPEB, p. 97, Form IVe (G)) derives from pitchers like those in Stages III–I at Megiddo (SAOC 10, Chart Column 3), though it is also possible that they have common origins with the unclassified Type 215, p. 170. He dates Tomb 351 at Jericho in EB IV, which may well apply to the latest of these forms, like Type 312.

Comparisons

Pl. 58: 94	Jericho (AAA XIX, Pl. VI: 5) Tomb A2.28c	EB III
Pl. 58: 96	Jericho (AAA XIX, p. 39, Fig. 8: 10) Tomb 24	EB I
Pl. 59: 162	Jericho (AAA XIX, Pl. V: 12) Tomb A0.4m.	EB III
Pl. 63: 312	Jericho (AAA XXII, Pl. XXXIV: 4) Tomb 351	EB IV
	Beisan (MJ XXIV, 1935, Pl. X: 12)	Level XII
	Gezer (*Gezer* II, p. 139, Fig. 309) Cave II 28. See PEQ, 1937, p. 74, note 35	EB II

Pointed juglets and miniature versions

Pointed: Types: Pl. 58: 101; Pl. 59: 166 (Pl. 17: 26); Pl. 60: 205 (Pl. 16: 24), 207 (Pl. 16: 26), 212–214 (Pl. 16: 32–34); Pl. 61: 247–249 (Pl. 14: 13–15)

Miniature: Types: Pl. 58: 102, 103, 126; Pl. 59: 158–160 (Pl. 17: 20, 21, 28); Pl. 60: 209 (Pl. 16: 28), 216 (Pl. 16: 29); Pl. 61: 246 (Pl. 14: 12); Pl. 65: 383

Juglets with pointed bases and a ribbon handle from rim to shoulder, and miniature versions of this form, are to be found in each of the Groups 1535, 1519, 1556 and 1513. They are all made of a pinkish-orange ware, fired soft to medium, and most examples are covered with a reddish-orange slip, rather well and smoothly burnished. About half the total number were hand-made, and half had been thrown on a slow wheel.

The juglets ranged in height from 10 to 16 cms. and the smaller and cruder ones among them came from Burial 1556.

The same juglets in miniature size, ranging from 4 to 9 cms., usually show some traces of red or orange slip and burnish. There are examples from Groups 1535, 1556, 1519 and 1513, so it is clear that they were in contemporary use with the larger versions.

Pointed juglets (PPEB, Forms B, G and D–IVb) are discussed by Wright as decadent and less graceful descendants of the stump-based pitcher, being confined to EB II–III, except for some debased types in EB IV.

POTTERY

Comparisons

Pl. 58: 101	Jericho (AAA XIX, Pl. V: 1) Tomb A2.8f	EB III
	Jericho (SW, Pl. 21: E 3)	Canaanite
Pl. 58: 102	Jericho (AAA XIX, Pl. II: 5) Tomb A2.22b	EB III
	Tell Beit Mirsim (AASOR XIII, Pl. 1: 10)	Stratum J
Pl. 58: 103	Jericho (AAA XIX, Pl. II: 7) Tomb A3. 31a	EB III
Pl. 59: 159	Jericho (AAA XIX, Pl. II: 18) Tomb A0.5e	EB III
Pl. 60: 205	Jericho (AAA XIX, Pl. V: 1) Tomb A2.8f	EB III
	Jericho (AAA XXII, Pl. XXXI: 22) Room 129, 11·15 m.	Layers V–IV
Pl. 60: 209	Megiddo (M. II, Pl. 5:2)	Stratum XVII
Pl. 60: 216	Jericho (AAA XIX, Pl. III: 16) Tomb A1.6d	EB III
Pl. 65: 383	Jericho (AAA XIX, Pl. III: 15) Tomb A2	EB III

Unclassified

Plate	Remarks and Comparisons	
56: 24	Bowl, two ledge handles, Form 6 (pp. 150, 256)	
29	Bowl with loop handle (p. 254)	
30	Bowl (pp. 254, 262, 263)	
57: 40	Vase (p. 262)	
58: 104	Cup	
105	Pot, 4 small holes below rim; Qau and Badari (QB II, Pl. LXXXIX: 15B) Tomb 1746	ixth dyn.
109	Spouted jug, see p. 216	
119	Vase, vestigial ledge handles	
120	Vase, four loop handles	
	Vase with ledge handle, misshapen; Tell en-Naṣbeh (TN II, Pl. 9: 143) Cave 193c	EB I–II
123	Jar neck, small loop handle on shoulder. Megiddo (M. II, Pl. 3: 2)	Stratum XIX
	Beisan (MJ XXIV, 1935, Pl. IV: 14)	Level XIV
128	Jug	
59: 156	Jug (photograph on Pl. 17: 16)	
157	Miniature jar (photograph on Pl. 17: 17)	
163	Jug (photograph on Pl. 17: 24)	
164	Stump-based jug (photograph on Pl. 17: 25). Cf. PPEB, Form G–IVb	EB III
	Megiddo (SAOC 10, Chart Column 8B)	Stage II
165	Juglet with pointed base (photograph on Pl. 17: 23, 27)	
167	Wide-mouthed jar with lug handles (photograph on Pl. 17: 29). Cf. Types 496–498	
	Lebe'a (BMB I, 1937, Fig. 10: top left, inset) Tomb 6	2400–2100 B.C.
60: 199	Juglet, round based (photograph on Pl. 16: 18)	
	Beisan (MJ XXIV, 1935, Pl. X: 16 (near), and p. 17)	Levels XII and XI
208	Jug (photograph on Pl. 16: 27)	
	Jericho (AAA XIX, Pl. XXVII: 12) Tomb A4. m. 1)	EB III
210	Juglet with pointed base (photograph on Pl. 16: 30)	
211	Juglet with pointed base (photograph on Pl. 16: 31)	
215	Jug with stump base (photograph on Pl. 16: 35), see p. 169	
	Jericho (AAA XIX, Pl. XXVII: 13) Tomb A4.y3	EB III
224	Jug (photograph on Pl. 16: 42)	
61: 240	Round pot (photograph on Pl. 14: 7)	
253	Jar, degraded lug handles (photograph on Pl. 14: 20)	
261	Pot	
62: 279	Large jar with applied band, thumb impressed	
280	Jar with two ledge handles, Form 5 on pp. 149 f.	
287	Jar with flat base	
63: 314	Jar or jug neck; Jericho (AAA XXII, Pl. XXVIII: 3) Strip 2, 11·53 m.	Layers V–IV
316	Jug neck. Cf. NE 9/253 on p. 57	
317	Jar neck	

Plate (cont.)		*Remarks and Comparisons*	
63: 319	Jug neck. Cf. NE 9/252 on p. 57	64: 362	Jar neck
336	Jar neck	363	Pot, row of oblique notches below neck and two pierced lug handles
64: 352	Part of raised band with herring-bone notches		
357	Jar neck	65: 380	Jar neck
64: 359	Jug neck	385	Jug, ledge-handled (?)
360	Jar neck, Et-Tell (*Ay*, Pl. LXXXIV: 457) Fouille D, Ch. 25	391	Jug neck

C. CALICIFORM CULTURE

Under this head there are two qualities of ware to be discussed, coming respectively from domestic debris (pp. 42, 178 f., 264), and from tombs (pp. 275–279).

Group 1529

In comparison with the pottery of the Early Bronze Age, Caliciform Culture pottery is thin, well-smoothed and levigated, containing fewer and smaller grits of even size. In section, the ware has fired buff, pink or even orange, and it often retains a grey core. The surface may or may not be treated with a slip, which is usually greenish-buff in colour.

The decoration consists of combed lines, both straight and wavy, wheel applied, though occasional indented rims and raised indented bands are recollections of an earlier tradition.

Both domestic and burial vessels share the characteristic flat base on every shape; while, with increasing use of the wheel, necks become more flared and spouts and ledge handles tend to disappear. Small pierced handles at the neck are also common to both phases (Pl. 66: 417–419 and Pl. 67: 488–498).

Apparently confined to the domestic wares are the horned lug handles (Pl. 66: 411–412) and the string-hole projections on Caliciform cups (Types 403, 409, 416 and 422).

For an incomplete ledge handle from the group see Form 11 on p. 150, Type 412 A.

Especially significant is the flat-based lamp (Pl. 66: 399) which is photographed on Pl. 13: 89 to show its base, which is characteristically rough like all the bases of jars and bowls of this period, and of the four-spouted lamps which occur in the tombs, Type 448.

Types 406 and 407, of exceptional quality, are links, like the lamp, with the pottery of the Middle Bronze Age, the earliest phase of which is poorly represented at Duweir.

Cemetery 2000

Like the pottery of Group 1529, the wares are buff, orange or brick-red in section, with some limestone grits, and the surface is often a greenish-buff. The walls are thin and the shapes are aesthetically pleasing, but the whole effect on both small and large pieces is marred by sagging and distortion in the kiln. All the jars are now extremely friable and soft, but perhaps that is partially due to the same conditions of humidity and exposure which may have affected the human remains.

It is possibly worth mentioning that a noticeable proportion have a neat round hole in the side, a peculiarity which can also be observed in contemporary vessels from Tell el-Ajjul, Megiddo and Yazur.

The jars illustrated on Pl. 67 were all built up initially by hand on a flat circular disk. Necks were wheel-made and luted on, when the shoulders were then finished with one or more bands of fine wheel-made grooves, p. 139. Imitation of basketry nets is to be seen in the diagonal lines around the neck of Types 455 and 459, and an indication of cord binding at the base of the neck is reproduced by incised notches (e.g. Types 455, 456, 458). In general, the size of the jars is reduced in the later tombs.

Debased reproductions of ledge handles on Types 456, 458–461 (see Form 12 on p 150) seem to imply that the cemetery groups belong to a later phase of the Caliciform Culture than Group 1529, and that the latter

171

should find its place between Stratum I at Tell Beit Mirsim, where envelope handles are characteristic, and Stratum H, where all traces have disappeared. Wright's statement on the lack of ledge handles in Cemetery 2000 at Duweir was based on seeing the comparatively small selection of jars in the Palestine Museum (BASOR 71, p. 33).

In further support of a chronological progression between the domestic and burial groups, compare the crude versions of beakers or cups (Types 438–445) with those of Group 1529, and note the degradation of the carinate bowls from Types 394 and 400 to Types 427, 429–436.

There was little room for pottery in the tombs, and one large jar was often the only offering. The largest groups, which may represent the grave goods of two people, did not exceed nine pieces. It would therefore be impractical to publish the pottery group by group, but the significant ones are shown together in Fig. 13 in relation to their tomb shapes, and the pottery is listed on pp. 277–279.

The sherds from Group 1529 are too fragmentary for classification, but are mentioned for their special features in the General Notes on Pottery, pp. 139–141; for a note on the cooking-pot, Pl. 66: 415, see p. 195. Sherds which may belong to the Caliciform Culture are rare in the Section, e.g. NE 17/197, NE 16/199 on pp. 55 f., though there are intrusions at 7 ft.

Bowls

Combed and carinate

Types, Pl. 66:

427, 428 (Pl. 20: 2), 429, 430 (Pl. 20: 5), 431, 432 (Pl. 20: 15), 433–435, 436, 437 (Pl. 20: 6)

Bowls are found in tombs of each shape; it can only be said that the larger ones, Types 430 and 437, occur in tombs of Shapes 1–2, that Types 431, 432 and 436 are associated with Shapes 2–3 and that Types 433–435 are only found in tombs of Shapes 3–4 (p. 276).

Plate	Comparisons	
66: 428	Tell el-Ajjul (AG I, Pl. XXXVII: 6R) Tomb 115	Copper Age
66: 430	Tell el-Ajjul (AG I, Pl. XXXIX: 24F for profile) Tomb 160	Copper Age
	Tell Beit Mirsim (AASOR XIII, Pl. 3: 7)	Stratum H

Beakers, Cups and Funnels

Types, Pl. 66:

438, 439 (Pl. 20: 7), 440, 441 (Pl. 20: 8), 442–447, 450, 451

The cups of this series are far removed in quality and form from the Caliciform types from which they are derived, though a relationship is clear from comparison of Types 396 and 441. The largest, Type 439, comes from a Shape 1 tomb, the others seem to be distributed evenly throughout.

Both funnels come from Shape 2 tombs and they are reminiscent of Types 185–188, which were only found in Tomb 1519. They could be used to strain liquids which were poured into the large jars, and would fit easily on to most necks.

Plate	Comparisons	
66: 440	Tell el-Ajjul (AG I, Pl. XL: 29 Z⁵ for form) Tomb 258	Copper Age
	El Husn (APEF VI, Fig. 1: 2 for outline only)	EB IV–MB I
66: 441	Megiddo (MT, Pl. 22: 12) Tomb 112CA	MB I
	Megiddo (SAOC 17, p. 34 and Pl. 10: 21)	Stratum XV
	Tell Beit Mirsim (AASOR XIII, Pl. 3 9)	Stratum H
66: 445	Megiddo (M. II, Pl. 15: 7 for outline)	Stratum XIV

172

FOURTH AND THIRD MILLENNIUM

Lamps

Type, Pl. 66:

448 (Pl. 20: 16)

Only three examples of four-spouted lamps were found, each one in a tomb of different shape. They cannot, therefore, be considered typical of the particular phase of the Caliciform Culture exhibited at Duweir. They are uncommon at Tell Beit Mirsim, where a sherd is illustrated from Stratum J, and they appear to be missing altogether from both cemeteries at Ajjul. At Megiddo the two examples published from the mound are both from open areas, and only one four-spouted lamp came from Ay. At Jericho they are, however, really common, where in twenty-two tombs a four-spouted lamp was placed in a niche in nearly every one (PEQ, 1953, pp. 92–93, Pl. XL: 2).

An example which appears to be found in an earlier context comes from a deposit in Bâtiment XXVII at Byblos, where plain-rimmed, pattern-burnished bowls are numerous, and there is also a jug of the same family as Type 215 (see p. 170, Unclassified). As the excavator, M. Dunand, has remarked, these types would be equivalent to Tomb A at Jericho (B. I, p. 371). For Schaeffer's equation of Bâtiment XXVII with the vith dynasty in Egypt, c. 2300 B.C., see *Stratigraphie*, Fig. 71 and Pl. XVIII. Five- or six-spouted lamps were found at Sedment in Egypt (*Sedment* I, Pl. XXX: 38a, b) which were dated to the ix–xth dynasty.

Plate	Comparisons	
66: 448	Tell Beit Mirsim (AASOR XIII, Pl. 20: 27)	Stratum J
	Yazur (QDAP X, 1944, Pl. XIV: 3)	EB–MB transition
	Megiddo (MT, Pl. 10: 28) Tomb 217в	MB I
	Megiddo (M. II, Pl. 9: 20, Pl. 15: 22)	Strata XV, XIV
	Beisan (B–S I, Pl. 15: 1) Grave 203	c. 2000 B.C.
	El Husn (APEF VI, Fig. 1: 1)	EB IV–MB I
	Ras Shamra (*Ugaritica II*, Fig. 71: 13)	Date uncertain
	Byblos (B. I, Pl. CLII: 5411 and pp. 369–370) Bâtiment XXVII, Salle C	
	Hama (RPS, p. 36)	Niveau J
	Ay (*Syria XVI*, p. 343) Nécropole	Fin d'Ancien Bronze

Jars

Jars, flaring-necked

Types, Pl. 67:

460 (Pl. 20: 4), 464–471, 472 (Pl. 20: 11), 473, 474 (Pl. 20: 12), 475, 476, 477 (Pl. 20: 10), 478, 479 (Pl. 20: 9), 480 (see also Pl 59: 180).

The characteristic jar of Cemetery 2000 has a tall ovate body made by hand and a well-flared neck, made on the wheel and often finished with one or more bands of combing on the shoulder. Bernard Leach writes in *A Potter's Book*, "The most difficult form to throw is that which has a large belly and a narrow neck. . . . For this reason the neck is often thrown separately and luted and thrown on when both it and the body have stiffened a little" (p. 75). There is evidence to suggest that this method was employed on jars of this class (cf. p. 171).

All that can be said about the distribution in relation to tomb types is that Type 469 is strong in Shape 2, and that the much smaller Type 476 is numerous in Shape 3 tombs.

Plate	Comparisons	
67: 464	Tell el-Ajjul (AG I, Pl. XLI: 30 G⁴) Tombs 119, 173, 177, 236, 258	Copper Age
67: 465	Beit Sahur (BASOR 71, p. 31, Fig. 2: 1)	MB I
67: 466	Tell Beit Mirsim (AASOR XIII, Pl. 2: 3 for knob on shoulder)	Stratum H
67: 476	Tell el-Ajjul (AG I, Pl. XLI: 30 G⁵) Tombs 117, 274	Copper Age

173

Jars, flaring-necked, with handles or lugs

Types, Pl. 67:

481, 482 (Pl. 20: 13), 483, 484

None of these jars occur in Tombs of Shape 1. Types 482 and 483 are both strong in Shape 2 tombs, while Type 484 is exclusive to Shape 3. Types 481 and 482 survive in Shape 4 tombs and both have pierced handles. It is especially interesting to note that a comparison for Type 481 comes from the bilobate tomb at Ajjul which contained the javelin.

Plate	Comparisons	
67: 481	Tell el-Ajjul (AG I, Pl. XLIV: 33 M⁹ for outline only) Tombs 240 280	Copper Age
67: 484	Tell Beit Mirsim (AASOR XIII, Pl. 2: 7)	Stratum H

Jars, squat with pierced handles

Types, Pl. 67:

488–498

Types 492, with notches and bands, and 494 came from Shape 1 tombs, while Type 490, similarly decorated, and Type 491, with herring-bone incisions, are from Shape 2 tombs. Types 488–489 and the small version 493 extend into the bilobate tombs Shape 4.

Though we may note a general resemblance to the series of squat jars from El-Husn, where they are the commonest form, the effect as a whole is very different, for the El Husn jars appear to be entirely hand-made, and therefore they have no bands of wheel-combing, which are a more common decoration than string-notches at Duweir.

Wright has proposed a derivation for these forms from the ear-handled juglets of EB (PPEB, p. 98, Form VI) and he considers that the wide-mouthed type (D–IVc) becomes one of the most characteristic forms of MB I, after which it disappears entirely.

Plate	Comparisons	
67: 488	El Husn (APEF VI, Fig. 3: 46)	EB IV–MB I
67: 490	Beit Sahur (BASOR 71, p. 31, Fig. 2: 2)	MB I
67: 491	Tell el-Ajjul (AG II, Pl. XXXV: 69 L² for herring-bone ornament only Tomb 1564	Copper Age
	El Husn (APEF VI, Fig. 2: 42)	EB IV–MB I
67: 493	Tell el-Ajjul (AG I, Pl. XLIV: 33 M⁷) Tomb 200	
	Tell el-Harbaj (BBSAJ, No. 4, 1924, Pl. IV: 10) Cave-Tomb 1.	
67: 497	Tell Beit Mirsim (AASOR XIII, Pl. 3: 10 and p. 65)	Stratum H

Jars, collar-necked

Types, Pl. 67:

455 (Pl. 20: 1), 456–463

Of the jars with collar-neck, Types 455–457 also have spouts and the inspiration for that detail can perhaps be linked to spouted jars of the vi–viiith dynasties in Egypt (QB II, p. 6 and Pl. LXXXVIII: 92c). See p. 164.

It is on the collar-neck jars that vestiges survive of ledge handles (Form 2, p. 150); the only exception being Type 460 with its incipient flared rim. Indeed, collar-necked jars are but rarely associated with those with flared rim and, when they are found together, Type 468 is the usual form.

The only close comparisons for collar-necked jars come from Tell el-Ajjul, Cemetery 1500, where they were found in rectangular pits or in tombs with a square shaft cutting (see AG II, p. 2, Tomb Types A and B). They all have degraded ledge handles, and in B tombs one in six jars has a spout. The forms in common with this early Ajjul cemetery are Types 455, 456 with spout, 458 and 461. In the Tell el-Ajjul Cemetery 100–200, published in AG I, Pls. XLI–XLIII, containing later burials, forms in common are Types 457 and 459. In this

174

cemetery we find only two ledge-handled jars and spouted jars are rare (Pl. XLIII). The later trend is shown perhaps in Types 30 J¹ and J⁴, where the former has a flared neck and the latter shows wheel-made combing on the shoulder.

Both these features bring the Ajjul Cemetery 100–200 close to the Duweir Cemetery 2000 in time, though a comparison of Pls. XLI–XLIII with Pl. 67 in this book will show that combed lines below the neck are more frequent at Duweir, perhaps illustrating increasing familiarity with the wheel.

Plate	Comparisons	
67: 455	Tell el-Ajjul (AG II, Pl. XXIX: 30 J⁷ for decoration) Tomb 1522	Copper Age
67: 456	Tell el-Ajjul (AG II, Pl. XXIX: 30 J⁹) Tomb 1559	Copper Age
67: 458	Tell el-Ajjul (AG II, Pl. XXIX: 30 F⁸) Tombs 1540, 1545, 1553, 1569	Copper Age
67: 459	Tell el-Ajjul (AG I, Pl. XLI: 30 F⁶ for form and ledge handles only) Tomb 248	Copper Age
67: 461	Tell el-Ajjul (AG II, Pl. XXIX: 30 F⁴) Tombs 1548, 1554, 1556	Copper Age
67: 463	Tell el-Ajjul (AG II, Pl. XXIX: 30 F¹⁰ for outline only) Tomb 1549	Copper Age

"Teapots"

Types, Pls. 66–67:

452, 453, 454 (Pl. 20: 3), 485–487

Two kinds of spouted vessels are sometimes described as "teapots" and they are not to be confused with the collar-necked jars which also have spouts.

Types 452–454 and 485 are copies of stone or metal prototypes. They have a somewhat baggy body, with small lug projections opposite the spouts, which are broken in two out of four examples. Type 454 is comparable at Ajjul, where examples come from a rectangular shaft and a round pit.

In the north, general comparisons may be noted with the "teapots" of Type 1 assembled by Col. D. H. Gordon as a part of the evidence for *The Chronology of Tepe Hissar III* (*Iraq XIII*, pp. 42–44), in which he demonstrates the eastward trend of the type towards the end of the third millennium B.C.

Type 486, with a bridge from rim to spout, was found near the surface in Cemetery 2000 and was unconnected with a tomb. It is one of the typical forms of the Shaft Tombs at Megiddo.

Plate	Comparisons	
67: 454	Tell el-Ajjul (AG I, Pl. XLII: 30 J³) Tomb 234	Copper Age
67: 486	Megiddo (MT, Pl. 10: 25) Tomb 217	MB I
	Megiddo (MT, Pl. 12: 2) Tomb 877A2	MB I
	Megiddo (MT, Pl. 20: 15) Tomb 878A	MB I
	Megiddo (MT, Pl. 21: 4) Tomb 1098 Shaft	MB I
	Tell Harbaj (BBSAJ, No. 4, 1924, Pl. IV: 7) Cave-Tomb 1	

CHAPTER 10

SECOND MILLENNIUM

Classes and Totals

A MINIMUM number of 1,983 more or less complete vessels has been examined and classified. It consists of the following classes:

Bowls	716	Imported Wares	77
Chalices	7	Base-Ring Wares	171
Goblets	3	Imitation Base-Ring	70
Lamps	282	Imitation Imported	47
Jugs	89	Spouted Vessels	9
Juglets	197	Pilgrim Flasks	16
Dippers	155	Mugs	19
Cooking-Pot	1	Miniature Pithoi	24
Plain Jars	4	Kraters	9
Potter's Jars	5	Miscellaneous	18
Potstand	1	Storage Jars	63

The method of presentation adopted in *Lachish III* is followed as far as possible in the following classifications. The pottery forms reproduced from *Lachish II* and *III* are shown as drawn in those volumes. Their original numbers are retained, preceded by L. II and L. III respectively. In this way it is possible to correlate the contents of the three Structures of the Fosse Temple with the tombs, and to note some small similarities with Iron Age forms.

Owing to the amount of comparative material from other sites of the Middle and Late Bronze Ages, it has been found necessary to confine exhaustive search for parallels to three main sites, Jericho, Tell Beit Mirsim, and Megiddo. Outstanding comparisons from other sites are quoted whenever possible.

BOWLS

The outline of the development of bowl shapes during the sixteenth to thirteenth centuries, which was presented in *Lachish II*, is confirmed and extended in this book. Using the characteristic forms of the bowls found in the three superimposed and stratified buildings of the Fosse Temple as a primary guide, it has been possible to place each tomb group in position on that scale at the period when they were most in use.

Analysis of the bowls found in the Fosse Temple showed that they could be divided into four main classes, which lead through carinate and plain bowls to a majority of curved forms in Structure III.

	Structures						
	I		II		III		
Bowls	No.	%	No.	%	No.	%	Total
Carinate	34	3	42	4	30	3	106
Plain	25	2	26	3	30	3	81
Flared	11	3	76	8	147	15	234
Curved	29	1	165	17	376	38	570
Total	99	9	309	32	583	59	991

The same method was then applied to the bowls from each tomb or deposit and it was then extended to other main pottery types, as described above on p. 137.

176

The tomb groups which precede the foundation of Structure I provide a high percentage of carinate bowls, which have also been subdivided under various headings where they will be studied in detail.

It will be seen that the best and most satisfying shapes, never to be surpassed in the history of bowl production in Palestine, are the Flared and Rounded Carinate Bowls, Classes A and B. Angular Carinates, Class C, tend to be smaller, at least in their early phase, and the series ends with many debased versions, Class E straggling on to the end of the Bronze Age.

From the evidence at Lachish, it is not possible to say which of the three main types of carinate bowls is the earliest, nor can the correct order be established with certainty. All three may be found in the same group, though it appears likely that the angular forms from a metal prototype were going out, in favour of the flared forms, which have much in common with carinate vases and chalices so characteristic of certain tombs at Jericho and of Tell Beit Mirsim E–D. The lack of these forms at Lachish warns us against too close a synchronisation of date within the period defined by these strata, for it would be strange, if the tombs at Lachish were exactly contemporary, to find nothing but one "trumpet foot" base in so large a collection of pottery (p. 63.)

The two well-made bowls of Class D may belong to a phase, between EB IV and MB I, which is likewise poorly represented at our site.

Plain bowls with straight rather than curved sides, and an inturned rim, Class G, are uncommon in MB tombs and the Section, though a small version with unthickened rim carries through into the period of Structure III.

The steady rise of bowls with curved sides, Class H, from Structure I onwards, reached a climax with 38 per cent. in Structure III, though by that time the incidence of bowls with flared sides, Class J, had risen sharply from 3 to 15 per cent.

Viewing the production of bowls from the nineteenth to the thirteenth centuries as a whole, it is clear that towards the end of the period production was speeded in all details at the expense of craftsmanship. It will be seen from the figures given below that the earlier Carinate and Plain bowls show between 23 and 45 per cent. of Semi-Ring or Ring bases, which need considerable finish, while the later Curved and Flared bowls show between 43 and 52 per cent. of disk bases, which were carelessly and quickly removed from the wheel. For a selection of bases from the Section in the MB fill, see p. 55.

Bases	Carinate %	Plain %	Curved %	Flared %
Flat . .	—	12	1	2
Foot . .	10	7	1	—
Ring . .	45	23	16	15
Semi-Ring .	45	42	30	31
Disk . .	—	16	52	43
Odd . .	—	—	—	9

N.B. The figures given are approximate percentages.

Definitions: *Flat* as L. II, Types 11–14; *Foot* or pedestal, as L. II, Types 6, 57 and Pl. XXX: 40; *Semi-Ring* as L. II, Types 7–9; it retains a bevelled section on the inner side; *Ring*—there are a few neat and well-turned rings as L. II: 4; the majority are rounded in section, crudely and clumsily finished.

A technical reason for the change over from a form of ring to a disk must also be considered. While examining the bowls from the Fosse Temple, it was seen that many bases were cracked in kiln firing and the fissures had been filled in by dabs of white lime, p. 140 (L. II, Pl. XXX: 42–43 and p. 82). A more detailed investigation showed that 25 per cent. of those with ring bases were cracked or repaired. This percentage was halved in the case of those with disk bases, and the improvement suggests that at least one factor in the change was the need to overcome this technical difficulty (pp. 138, 140).

Carinate

Bowls, Class A	N.-E. Section, p. 55	Types, Pls. 66, 68:
Compare	MB Fill: 119, 143	499, 500 (Pl. 51: 7), 501 (Pl. 51: 8),
L. II Flared Bowls, Classes 2, 6		502–508, 509 (Pl. 51: 24 and Fig.
L. III B. 5		15: I), 510 (Pl. 50: 1), 511, 512
		(Pl. 51: 6), 513 (Pl. 51: 5), 514
		(Pl. 51: 1), 515 (Pl. 51: 3), 516–
		522; *L. II*: 114; *L. III*: 9

Made of a thin and finely levigated pink, brown or buff ware, and often covered by a burnished slip produced by hand and wheel, bowls Types 499–507 are highly competent technical productions; they are among the best forms to reach Palestine during the Bronze Age or indeed at any time. Though the origins of the class are obscure and were not necessarily indigenous, there is no doubt that the potters who made the bowls which have survived had fully mastered the art, and this knowledge is well expressed in the fine detail of the rim and base.

The earliest piece of a flared carinate bowl occurred in Group 1529 (Pl. 66: 406), containing pottery which is equivalent to Strata H–I at Tell Beit Mirsim; the fragment is also matched at Duweir in the glacis fill at NE 19/148, p. 55. A comparison comes from a burial under the lime floor of a house in Stratum XIII A at Megiddo, and the same bowl, Type 101, persists in sealed burials under the walls and floors of Stratum XI. The Megiddo bowl Type 101 from T. 2141 is not well sealed in Stratum X and most of the forms with it are duplicated in Stratum XII.

Though the origins of the flared carinate bowls cannot be traced at present in Palestinian sites, they were introduced at Megiddo probably in Stratum XIII, and they survived in tombs of Stratum X. The presence of small bowls, like Types 499–507, is well attested in the lower layers of Tombs 19, 13, 9 and 4 at Jericho, and in Stratum E at Tell Beit Mirsim.

With them in Tombs 129, 1552, and 119 are larger flared carinate bowls, which are competent though less well finished, e.g. Types 512–519. Comparisons are lacking from Tell Beit Mirsim and from the 1930–1936 Necropolis at Jericho, though similar large bowls are common in the bilobate tombs at Tell Fara and in cities III–II at Ajjul (CPP Type 23 K). At Megiddo, these bowls came from various small groups attributed to Strata XII–XI (Pl. 28: 14, 15, 18, 20; 36: 22; 37: 6) but the type appears to be reliably connected with the buildings of Stratum X (M. II, Pl. 44: 22; 53: 18, 19).

The main phase of the large flared carinate therefore seems to lie in the seventeenth and early sixteenth centuries B.C., and certain versions appear in Structure I of the Fosse Temple. (See L. II 129, 130, and Megiddo comparisons listed below).

The degradation of the smaller bowls sets in with Types 508–510, 521–522 and can still be seen perhaps in some Iron Age forms.

406	Megiddo (M. II, Pl. 19: 5)	Strata XIII A–XI
499	Jericho (AAA XX, Pl. V: 2) Tomb 13c.5	
500	Jericho (AAA XIX, Pl. XXXVI: 2) Tomb 9d.4 bis	
	Jericho (AAA XX, Pl. XV: 9) Tomb 4c.69	
501	Tell Beit Mirsim (AASOR XIII, Pl. 8: 16)	Stratum E
505	Megiddo (M. II, Pl. 21: 12)	Strata XIII–XI
506	Tell Beit Mirsim (AASOR XIII, Pl. 8: 14)	Stratum E
507	Jericho (AAA XIX, Pl. XXXII: 5) Tomb 9c.38	
	Jericho (AAA XXI, Pl. XVIII: 2) Tower Area J. 31, Spot 4	City B, MB I
	Jericho (AAA XX, Pl. III: 4) Tomb 19c.6	
517	Tell Fara (BP I, Pl. XV: 23 K[12]) Tomb 550	MB II
L. II: 129	Megiddo (M. II, Pl. 44: 21)	Strata X–IX
L. II: 130	Megiddo (M. II, Pl. 61: 8)	Strata VIII-VII

Bowls, Class B

Compare

L. II. In-curving bowls, Classes 1, 3

N.-E. Section, pp. 53–55

Level VI: 17

Level VII: 81

MB Fill: 131, 137, 184

Types, Pl. 68:

523 (Pl. 50: 8), 524 (Pl. 20: 18),

525, 526 (Pl. 51: 4), 527 (Pl. 51:2),

528–536; *L. II*: 125

Bowls in this class have a full well-rounded keel and a slightly everted rim; they tend to be deeper in proportion to their width. The ware is like that of the larger flared carinates.

Closely allied to Class A, the origin of the rounded carinate bowl is equally obscure; that it may be similar is indicated by a well-burnished fragment from the same Group 1529 (Pl. 66: 407) which produced the fragment of a flared carinate bowl. There are no bowls of this class with the same smooth finish from the Section or the tombs. The ware of those few pieces from the Section is buff with faint wheelmarks or a self burnish outside, for which compare the surface of Type 524 (photograph on Pl. 20: 18).

The series may be considered to extend into the Late Bronze Age with derivations such as Types 533–536, and it may include fragments from Levels VI and VII which are like the palm bowl, L. II: 125, a form which is exclusive to Structure III.

There is little comparable material for the rounded carinate bowl elsewhere. The fragment from Group 1529 finds its nearest parallel at Megiddo in Stratum XI (M. II, Pl. 36: 14). Type 532 provides a link with Tell Beit Mirsim Stratum E, where a rounded outline is characteristic (AASOR XIII, Pl. 8), and there are besides a few comparisons from Jericho.

525 Jericho (AAA XIX, Pl. XXXVI: 9) Tomb 9e.77	
528 Jericho (AAA XXI, Pl. XXII: 2) Palace Store-room 36.5	City C, MB II
532 Jericho (AAA XXI, Pl. XVIII: 5) Tower Area J. 31, Spot 4	City B, MB I
Tell Beit Mirsim (AASOR XIII, Pl. 8: 3)	Stratum E
536 Tell Beit Mirsim (AASOR XII, Pl. 47: 7)	Stratum B or C

Bowls, Class C

Compare

L. II Flared bowls, Class 5

L. III B. 6

N.-E. Section, pp. 53–57

Level VIII: 101

MB Fill: 120, 128, 168, 169, 183, 198

EB III–IV: 242

Types, Pl. 69:

537 (Pl. 20: 17), 538, 539 (Pl. 50: 6), 540–553, 554 (Pl. 52:29), 555, 556; *L. II*: 139

The earliest forms of the angular carinates, Class C, are Types 550–553 from Caves 1504 and 1513, some of which retain the red burnished slip and the bevelled rim which is their characteristic in the tombs of Stratum XIV at Megiddo, and in Strata G–F at Tell Beit Mirsim. Albright does not consider it impossible that they were imported into Palestine even earlier (AASOR XII, p. 14). Metal prototypes for these angular carinate bowls, with objects datable to the xiith Egyptian dynasty were found at Byblos (e.g. BE, p. 125, no. 605, Pl. LXXI; B I, p. 147, no. 2171, Pl. LXVI).

There are none of these bowls, burnished on dark-red slip, in the MB glacis fill within the Section, though the bevelled edge is to be seen at NE 9/242, probably slightly below its true context. The forms from the glacis fill are equivalent in shape though not in ware with bowls from Stratum G at Tell Beit Mirsim (AASOR XIII, Pl. 4: 1–8).

Angular carinate bowls without burnish occur at Megiddo in tombs of Strata XIII–XII, though they are rare in those of Strata XI–X. Contacts for the later versions, which are wide in proportion to their height, are closer to bowls from Cemetery 500 at Tell Fara reproduced in CPP.

Certain versions are present in the Fosse Temple (i.e. L. II, Pl. XLIII: 127 and 139), but they are mostly from pits, and only one can be directly associated with the sanctuary of Structure I.

537 Tell Fara (BP I, Pl. XV: 23 J⁴) Tomb 550	MB II
Megiddo (M. II, Pl. 28: 6)	Strata XIII–XII
Tell Beit Mirsim (AASOR XIII, Pl. 12: 3)	Stratum D

540	Tell Beit Mirsim (AASOR XII, Pl. 41: 8)	Stratum E
	Tell Fara (BP I, Pl. XV: 18 J⁴) Tomb 550	MB II
543	Tell Fara (BP I, Pl. XV: 23 E³) Tomb 550	MB II
554	Tell Fara (BP I, Pl. XV: 23 K⁹) Tomb 569	MB II
546	Jericho (AAA XIX, Pl. XXXVI: 10) Tomb 9d.48	
550	Megiddo (M. II, Pl. 9: 9)	Stratum XV
551	Tell Beit Mirsim (AASOR XII, Pl. 41: 3)	Stratum G
	Jericho (AAA XIX, Pl. XXXVI: 7) Tomb 9e.1 bis	
552	Megiddo (M. II, Pl. 16: 14)	Stratum XIII B
553	Jericho (AAA XX, Pl. V: 5) Tomb 13c.33	

Bowls, Class D	N.-E. Section p. 55	Types, Pl. 69:
	MB Fill: 136, 151 (?)	557, 558

Both bowls of Class D come from Cave 1513 and are made of buff ware with buff or red slip. Type 558 shows a good radial burnish inside, which suggests an early horizon for these bowls. No close comparisons are available, though it is worth noting the pieces from the Section and the outline of a bowl from Strata XIV–XIII at Megiddo which resembles Sherd 151 (M. II, Pl. 14: 3).

Bowls, Class E		Types, Pl. 69:
Compare		559–564, 565 (Pl. 52: 20), 566
L. II Flared bowls, Class 2		(Pl. 52: 23), 567–575, 576 (Pl. 55:
L. III B. 7		18), 577 (Pl. 55: 17); *L. III*: 56

Among the small bowls of Class E are those which, for poor quality of form and ware, can be considered debased. It is seldom possible to assign them to either of the first three carinate classes, though they retain the elements of the form.

Made of coarse pink or light-brown ware, such bowls appear in ones and twos in half a dozen tombs which are largely of the seventeenth century, and there are only single specimens in Tomb 4004 and Structure I, which chiefly represent the sixteenth and early fifteenth centuries. In Tombs 216, 501 and 1003 and in Structures II and III they are more common, though they are a mere survival and always remain subsidiary to the curved and flared bowls of that period. A glance at the Iron Age small bowls in Class 7 (L. III, Types 37–40, 56) shows that the form lingers on.

563	Tell Beit Mirsim (AASOR XII, Pl. 42: 6)	Stratum D
	Tell Fara (BP I, Pl. XV: 18 J⁸) Tomb 550	MB II
572	Jericho (AAA XX, Pl. V: 3) Tomb 13b.34	

Bowls, Class F	N.-E. Section, p. 53	Types, Pl. 69:
Compare	Level VI: 16	578 (Pl. 50: 9), 579 (Pl. 50: 10),
L. II In-curving bowls, Class 8	Level VII: 55	580–582

All bowls, whether carinate or curved, which are provided with loop handles are included in this class. They are mostly larger than average, with diameters of 35–40 cms.

The ware is brown, pink or buff, and the surface is often plain without slip or burnish, as befits their probably domestic function. For this reason and their size, handled bowls are rare in tombs and more common in Structures I–III of the Fosse Temple. Many of the sherds from the upper feet of the North-East Section may have belonged to bowls of this class.

Types 578–580 represent the Middle Bronze Age version of the form with inturned rim, which is matched at Tell Beit Mirsim. The type continues through the LB Stratum C, though, as Albright remarks, the technique is very different. The Level VI fragment compares with a bowl from Stratum C found in a room which also contained part of an Imitation Base-Ring jug (AASOR XII, Pl. 47: 12, 10 and pp. 23, 39).

578	Megiddo (M. II, Pl. 46: 2)	Strata X–IX
	Jericho (AAA XIX, Pl. XXXV: 7) Tomb 9d.4	
580	Tell Beit Mirsim (AASOR XIII, Pl. 10: 6)	Stratum E

Plain

Bowls, Class G	N.-E. Section, p. 53	Types, Pl. 70:
Compare	Level VII: 63, 79, 80, 82	583, 584 (Pl. 51: 9, 10), 585 (Pl. 51:
L. II Bowls without flare, Class 1	MB Fill: 149, 152, 182	11), 586 (Pl. 51: 31), 587, 588, 589
		(Pl. 52: 26), 590, 591 (Pl. 51: 53),
		592; *L. II*: 2, 3, 7, 10, 12, 13, 15,
		25, 29, 35

It is hard to distinguish bowls with a straight side from those with a slightly curved outline, and it is especially so when only part of the profile is preserved; some latitude must therefore be allowed between Classes G and H.

The inturned rim, already referred to under Class F and recurring also in Class J, is an early feature on wide and shallow bowls in both classes, which is seen from 17 feet upwards in the Section, and in Types 583, 584 and 587 from the tombs. It is still traceable in such types as L. II: 35 from Structures I–II.

The ware is more often pink than buff and the broken section shows a grey or black core. The general range of the straight-sided bowl may cover all phases of MB II–III, equal perhaps to Strata XIII–IX at Megiddo, but towards the end of the period the soft buff wares give way to the more typical LB pink fabric with a grey core, and this change can be seen in the last occurrence of the bowl in Stratum IX. Those from the Palace Store-rooms at Jericho appear to be of the later fabric, like most of the comparisons which are found in Structures I–III. Though plain bowls are only fitfully represented in the seventeenth century at Duweir, they are represented also in Structure I and maintain their numbers to the end of the Fosse Temple, though by then the total is insignificant compared with curved and flared bowls, and the average diameter of the plain bowl has much decreased (p. 176).

583	Tell Beit Mirsim (AASOR XIII, Pl. 10: 5)	Stratum E
584	Tell Fara (BP I, Pl. XV: 6 C³ Tomb 550	MB II
587	Tell Fara (BP I, Pl. XV: 6 C⁴) Tomb 569	MB II
588	Megiddo (M. II, Pl. 54: 7)	Strata XIII–IX
L. II: 3	Jericho (AAA XXI, Pl. XXVI: 24) Palace Store-room 73.37	City D, MB II
L. II: 7	Jericho (AAA XXI, Pl. XIX: 14) Palace Store-room 17.1	City C, MB II
L. II: 15	Jericho (AAA XXI, Pl. XX: 12) Palace Store-room 29.1	City C, MB II

Curved ✶

Bowls, Class H	N.-E. Section, pp. 53–55	Types, Pls. 70–71:
Compare	Level VI: 6, 27, 29	593–602, 603 (Pl. 52: 24), 604–609,
L. II Bowls without flare, Classes 1–4	Level VII: 46, 47, 62, 66, 67	610 (Pl. 55: 31); *L. II*: 14, 19, 20,
In-curving bowls, Class 1	Level VIII: 97, 105, 106	21, 24, 30, 36, 37, 38, 41, 45, 46, 48,
	MB Fill: 127, 129, 153, 154,	50, 51, 52, 137, 143, 144, 145, 146;
	172, 185	*L. III*: 8, 20, 21, 25

The same reservations about the comparisons of Class G also apply to Class H. Types 593–601 are brown, buff or pinkish-red and are often finished with a slip. The same variety of ware and finish is seen in the Section within the glacis fill. In the Fosse Temple the wares are more consistently pink, and by the period of Structure II the bowls had become smaller and deeper in proportion to their width and were paramount in numbers.

The wide and shallow curved bowls have general comparisons in Strata XII–XI at Megiddo and Stratum E at Tell Beit Mirsim. Parallels for the smaller curved bowls occur in the lowest level at Tell Abu Hawam, and in Stratum VII at Megiddo (M. II, Pl. 68: 12–16); they are rare in Strata IX–VIII, where the excavated areas of the site were occupied by burials.

593	Jericho (AAA XX, Pl. III: 15) Tomb 19c.29	
594	Tell Fara (BP I, Pl. XV: 21 B¹) Tomb 550	MB II
601	Megiddo (M. II, Pl. 29: 15)	Strata XII–XI
606	Tell Beit Mirsim (AASOR XIII, Pl. 16: 9)	Stratum C
L. II: 20	Tell Abu Hawam (QDAP IV, p. 36: 224)	Stratum V
L. II: 48	Megiddo (M. II, Pl. 68: 15)	Stratum VII

Flared

Bowls, Class J	N.-E. Section, pp. 53–55	Types, Pls. 71–72:
Compare	Level VI: 7, 12, 28, 39, 40, 41	611 (Pl. 50: 11), 612, 613 (Pl. 51:
L. II Flared Bowls, Classes 3, 4, 5	Level VII: 48, 49 (?), 54, 65 (?),	30), 614, 615 (Pl. 52: 31), 616
	68 (?), 74, 86, 87	(Pl. 52: 27), 617–619, 620 (Pl. 55:
	Level VIII: 100, 107	19), 621 (Pl. 55: 28), 622 (Pl. 55:
	MB Fill: 130, 139	26), 623; *L. II*: 4, 28, 30, 42, 78,
		81, 82, 83, 90, 91, 93, 94, 95, 118,
		120

There is little to choose in ware and finish between the later bowls of Class H and those of Class J.

The earliest fragments to show even a slight flare confined entirely to the rim are seen in the glacis fill. In the burning of Level VIII there is a well-burnished fragment which shows the centripetal strokes and flaring rim common at Tell Beit Mirsim Stratum D (AASOR XII, § 35), while the shape is also matched in Stratum E (AASOR XIII, Pl. 10: 10).

These bowls are, however, much larger and better made than the bowls with slightly flared sides which come into their own in Level VII and which are such a feature of Structures II and III. Comparisons are to be found in the earliest settlement at Tell Abu Hawam, and in Tomb 4 at Jericho.

611	Megiddo (M. II, Pl. 37: 19)	Stratum XI
617	Tell Beit Mirsim (AASOR XIII, Pl. 12: 16)	Stratum D
621	Tell Beit Mirsim (AASOR XII, Pl. 45: 20)	Stratum C2
L. II: 4	Tell Abu Hawam (QDAP IV, p. 43: 264)	Stratum V
L. II: 93	Jericho (AAA XX, Pl. XII: 2; Pl. XIV: 5) Tomb 4a.18; 4c.51	
L. II: 95	Tell Abu Hawam (QDAP IV, p. 48: 293)	Stratum V

Miscellaneous

Compare	Type, Pl. 72:
L. III B. 6	624 (Pl. 52: 19)

The only bowl with a round base came from Tomb 216, but in general shape and ware it is not unlike Type 625.

At Megiddo and at Duweir round-based bowls and platters, which were common enough in the Early Bronze Age, are almost completely lacking in MB contexts, and the nearest parallel in the following period, apart from Cypriote imports and their imitations, cannot be closely dated (M. II, Pl. 72: 4).

Types, Pl. 72:
625, 627, 628

The round bowl, Type 625, with an omphalos base, appears to be the earliest of three which, on the analogy of medieval and modern Arab "Fear cups", may have had a therapeutic value (JPOS XVI, p. 81, Fig. 1).

Compare	N.-E. Section, p. 53	Type, Pl. 72:
L. II Pl. XLIV: 179–183	Level VI: 1	626
L. III Pl. 81: 116		

The double bowl differs from those in Structures II and III in having a central cup which is lower than the rim. If it were not so often broken, the height of the inner rim in relation to the outer edge might prove important chronologically.

Though there is one "cup and saucer" or double bowl attributed to Stratum VIII at Megiddo, its true range would seem to be in Strata VII–VI (M. II, Pl. 62: 10; Pl. 67: 7–9).

Compare		Types, Pl. 72:
L. II, Pl. XLIII: 158	N.-E. Section, p. 53	629, 630
L. III Pl. 81	Level VI: 18	

Like Type 627 above, Types 629 and 630 are decorated with red paint and all three have rudimentary bar handles. They come from three of the latest tomb groups. Though there are no close parallels to the bowls themselves, the handles are to be found on bowls associated with Structures II–III, and the decoration of palm and zigzags on Type 630 is characteristic of those buildings (L. II: 117, 125, 142). Besides the parallels quoted in L. III, p. 265, from Tell Beit Mirsim B2, 1150–1100 B.C., there are others from Megiddo Strata VII–VI dating to the same period (M. II, Pl. 69: 6 and Pl. 78: 8).

Compare	Types, Pl. 72:
L. II Pl. XLII: 132	631, 632
L. III Pl. 79: 31–34; Pl. 81: 106–7	

The miniature bowls come from Tomb 1003 and from the potter's workshop. Similar bowls occur sporadically during the Bronze and Iron Ages and they may well be children's toys.

Compare	Type, Pl. 72:
L. II Pl. XXXIX: 66	*L. II*: 66
L. III Pl. 81: 115	

This special round-bottomed bowl with loop handles and a bent-up side was exclusive to Structure III and other examples came from the potter's workshop where they were made. None were found in the tombs. At Megiddo, bent bowls were exclusive to Stratum VII; see M. II, Pl. 66: 6 for a good comparison.

Compare	N.-E. Section, p. 53	Types, Pl. 72:
L. II, Pl. XLVI	Level VI: 31	633 (Pl. 53: 27), 634, 635, 636 (Pl.
L. II, Pl. XLVII		51: 55), 637–639, 640 (Pl. 55: 50),
		641 (Pl. 55: 48)

The Duweir Censer, Type 633, is remarkable for its decorated lid bearing three characters on the underside which are discussed by Dr. Diringer on pp. 128 f. The shape, with its pierced lugs reproduced on the flat-fitting lid, can only be matched in Structure III (L. II: 217) and the surface is smoothly burnished on a brown slip. At Tell Abu Hawam there is a small vessel of the same shape from Stratum V (QDAP IV, Pl. 44: 272).

The chalices, Types 634–638, are open bowls attached to a splayed and hollow foot, which are called *Bowls on Stands* in *Lachish II* (Pl. XLVI). The ware is usually pink with added grits and straw, covered with a pinkish-buff slip showing some burnish. Type 635 stands out for the use of a thick white slip under red painted bands.

A red rim or concentric bands inside the bowl are the normal decoration of these bowls in Structure II, and the same may be said of Types 634–637.

The sherd from Level VI belongs to a globular goblet of a form exclusively found in Structure II (L. II: 228–231), and it provides evidence that the north-east corner of the mound was occupied at that time though the last house of Level VI may not then have been built.

Type 639 is the only fragment of a goblet comparable to those of Structure III (L. II: 232–236). It was found above the main deposit of Tomb 4004.

Types 640–641 belong to a different tradition, shared most probably with the calcite *tazze* and reproductions of the form (p. 86), discussed by Dr. Ben-Dor and dated by him to the fourteenth and thirteenth centuries (QDAP XI, pp. 105 ff.).

With regard to comparisons elsewhere for chalices on stands, they seem to begin as bowls with a short base in Tomb 3095, Stratum XII, at Megiddo, and a closer approach to the Duweir forms is seen in Strata X–IX, where the unusual white wash of Type 636 is matched (M. II, Pl. 44: 29). They are characteristic of the Structural Tombs. (M. II, Pl. 29: 29, 30; 38: 5, 8, 9; 45: 11–15).

The tall and elegant splayed chalice which also begins in Tombs of Stratum XII at Megiddo (e.g. M. II, Pl. 29: 5) is missing from both tombs and Section at Duweir, and it is a far cry to the probable derivations which are a feature of Structure III (L. II: 232–235) and are only represented in the tombs by Type 639.

For the development of chalices in the Iron Age see L. III, Pl. 83: 154–164.

LAMPS

In the Early Bronze Age levels of the North-East Section there were many fragments of plain round-based bowls which may have been used as lamps, for they almost invariably showed a charred and blackened rim. There were few distinctive lamp sherds from Middle and Late Bronze Age levels, so that the evolution from plain bowls to saucer lamps with pinched lip is traced in the tombs alone through seven successive stages.

It may be that the south Palestinian potter was not in the vanguard of development, for a much more advanced type of lamp than any found with the burials comes from Group 1529 (Pl. 13: 89 and Pl. 66: 399). With the four-spouted lamp of Cemetery 2000 (Pl. 66: 448), it has the characteristic rough base common to all jars of the period and it is therefore not intrusive.

In setting aside these flat-based lamps as advanced and non-indigenous products at Duweir, Types 645–646 may also be considered. Flat-based lamps occur at Jericho side by side with round-based forms (e.g. in Tomb 9 AAA XIX, Pl. XXXII: 6–11), and the same can be said for Megiddo, though there they appear less common. In Syria the flat-based lamps are ubiquitous from the eighteenth century onwards, and those few examples which reached sites in Palestine probably did so as the result of trade contact with the north. Apart from such exceptions there is little to show that this detail was assimilated in south Palestine before the Iron Age (L. III, p. 282).

Lamps in Classes A–D were of buff or light-brown clay, which fired to a greenish surface. Slip was rarely applied and lamps were never burnished. From about 1450 B.C. onwards the ware was more often fired to a pinkish-red surface with a grey core, which was certainly typical of lamps in Structures II–III.

It will be seen that there are lamps of Class A at Jericho and Megiddo, but not at Tell Beit Mirsim. Though lamps of Class B are found in Stratum D, those of Classes C–D are missing, corresponding perhaps to the gap between the destruction of Stratum D and the reoccupation of Stratum C, where the later lamps of Classes E–G appear.

The parallel for a lamp of Class D at Jericho came from the last phase of the Palace Store-rooms, and Classes E–F are completely missing. This supports Garstang in his observation that Tomb 13 "was not re-used until a relatively late phase in the Late Bronze Age" (AAA XX, p. 15). That reoccupation is marked by the appearance of lamps in Class G from M building and from the topmost layer of Tomb 13.

Lamps, Class A	N.-E. Section, p. 55	Types, Pl. 72:
	MB Fill: 126	642, 643, 644 (Pl. 51: 12), 645–647

The slight pinched spout of Class A is an early step in the development of saucer lamps, and for this affinity the two flat-based types, 645–6, mentioned above, are included. Type 647, with a nearly flat base, is comparable to the earliest lamp type at Jericho, and Garstang notes that a flat base is not a distinctive feature (AAA XXI, pp. 114 f., Fig. 1: Type 5).

Lamps of Class A are not found at Tell Beit Mirsim.

642	Jericho (AAA XX, Pl. III: 16) Tomb 19b.2	
643	Megiddo (M. II, Pl. 16: 20)	Stratum XIII B
644	Jericho (AAA XIX, Pl. XXXII: 7) Tomb 9b.11	
646	Megiddo (M. II, Pl. 19: 18)	Strata XIII A–XI

Lamps, Class B	Types, Pl. 73:
	648, 649 (Pl. 51: 25), 650–653

Later, perhaps as an anti-splash device, the bowl rim was turned in, and this tended to produce a more elongated spout. These lamps are most numerous in Tomb 4004, though they must belong to a phase before the foundation of Structure I, where they are uncommon.

Besides the comparisons from Jericho tombs noted below, a lamp like Type 650 was found in the drain which passed over the foundations of the MB palace "presumably from a floor level that had disappeared" (AAA XXI, p. 106 and p. 114, Fig. 1: Type 3). Another example of Type 3 from under the wall of Room 76 "gives a clue to the date of its reconstruction" (AAA XXI, p. 126). The Jericho Type 4 can also be included in Class B, for it compares with Type 653.

648	Tell Fara (BP I, Pl. XV: 91 A[1]) Tombs 550, 551, 569	MB II
649	Tell Beit Mirsim (AASOR XIII, Pl. 10: 12)	Stratum E
	Tell Beit Mirsim (AASOR XII, Pl. 43: 3)	Stratum D
650	Megiddo (M. II, Pl. 55: 9)	Strata IX–VIII
	Jericho (AAA XIX, Pl. XXXII: 6) Tomb 9c.29	
	Jericho (AAA XX, Pl. XVII: 10) Tomb 4e.18	
	Jericho (AAA XX, Pl. XXIV: 12) Tomb 5e.60	
651	Tell Beit Mirsim (AASOR XII, Pl. 43: 4)	Stratum D
652	Tell Beit Mirsim (AASOR XIII, Pl. 15: 18–20)	Stratum D
	Megiddo (M. II, Pl. 15: 20)	Strata XIV–IX
653	Jericho (AAA XX, Pl. VI: 4) Tomb 13c.45	

Lamps, Class C	Types, Pl. 73:
Compare	654 (Pl. 51: 36), 655–659
L. II, Pl. XLV: 184–187	

In Class C attention is fixed on the high-prowed spout, and in some examples there are early signs of a flattened rim. These very shallow lamps are more numerous in Structure I than in Structure II; though they occur in some tombs with lamps of Class D, their range is slightly earlier, and they were perhaps most common between 1500 and 1450 B.C.

654	Megiddo (M. II, Pl. 38: 21)	Strata XI–X
	Jericho (AAA XX, Pl. XIV: 10) Tomb 4c.78	
658	Jericho (AAA XXI, p. 114, Type 2) M building	LB I

Lamps, Class D	
Compare	Types, Pl. 73:
L. II, Pl. XLV	660, 661, 662; *L. II*: 192, 193

Lamps in Class D are deeper with a wide, open spout. The centre of the profile view is usually higher than the spout or back. With the exception of the miniature MB Type 660, these lamps are chiefly in use during the occupation of Structures I–II, and there are none from any later context. The range lies between say 1500 and 1400 B.C. Only Jericho produces a comparison, for Megiddo and Tell Beit Mirsim were then unoccupied.

L. II: 192	Jericho (AAA XXI, Pl. XIX: 10) Palace Store-rooms 17.4	City C, MB II

Lamps, Class E

Compare
L. II, Pl. XLV

Types, Pl. 73:
663; *L. II*: 195, 197, 199, 202

Class E is the predominant form in both Structures II and III. The spout is well pinched and flanged, while the back is often plain. The dip of the spout is clearly marked in profile.

Lamps of Class E mark the reoccupation of Tell Beit Mirsim C and the earliest settlement of Tell Abu Hawam. Those which are attributed to Stratum VIII at Megiddo are most probably closer to Stratum VII in date. There were no lamps of this class in Structure I, so they must begin during the occupation of Structure II and continue into the period of Structure III, though not necessarily to the final phase of use. The range may cover the fourteenth century at Duweir.

L. II: 195	Tell Abu Hawam (QDAP IV, p. 36: 227)	Stratum V
	Tell Beit Mirsim (AASOR XII, Pl. 48: 8)	Stratum C
	Megiddo (M. II, Pl. 66: 11)	Strata VIII–VII B
L. II: 197	Tell Abu Hawam (QDAP IV, p. 49: 300)	Stratum V
	Tell Beit Mirsim (AASOR XII, Pl. 48: 3; XIII, Pl. 18: 9)	Stratum C
L. II: 202	Tell Beit Mirsim (AASOR XIII, Pl. 18: 7)	Stratum C^1
	Megiddo (M. II, Pl. 62: 4)	Stratum VIII

Lamps, Class F

Compare
L. II, Pl. XLV
L. III, Pl. 83

Types, Pl. 73:
664; *L. II*: 200, 203; *L. III*: 144

The characteristics of the previous class are much enhanced in these lamps, which remain secondary to Class E throughout the occupation of Structure III, though their later tendency is shown in the tombs. The heavy flanged rim at the back of the last types in the class tends to tip the spout up, producing a change in the angle which becomes more marked in Class G. Both classes should belong to the thirteenth century, though F may be more common in the earlier half.

664	Tell Beit Mirsim (AASOR XII, Pl. 48: 1)	Stratum C
	Megiddo (M. II, Pl. 66: 9)	Strata VIII–VI A
L. II: 203	Tell Abu Hawam (QDAP IV, p. 30: 163)	Stratum IV

Lamps, Class G

Compare
L. II, Pl. XLV
L. III, Pl. 83.

Types, Pl. 73:
665 (Pl. 55: 37), 666–668; *L. II*: 204

A broad flat rim inside and a deeply pinched spout are salient points in Class G. The marked outer flange appears to have developed late in Structure III, and it was to become more common in the Iron Age (L. III, p. 282).

Comparisons from elsewhere show that the last form of Class F and the types of Class G can extend into Stratum IV at Abu Hawam, Stratum B at Tell Beit Mirsim and Stratum VI at Megiddo.

668	Jericho (AAA XX, Pl. IV: 8) Tomb 13a.3	
	Jericho (AAA XX, Pl. XIV: 13) Tomb 4c.49	
	Jericho (AAA XXI, p. 114, Type 1) M building	LB I
L. II: 204	Megiddo (M. II, Pl. 72: 6)	Strata VII–VI
	Tell Beit Mirsim (AASOR XII, Pl. 50: 6)	Stratum B

JUGS

The classification of the jugs is based on the nature and position of the handle rather than on the shape of the body, which remains ovoid during nearly the whole period under review.

The paucity of jugs from the tombs does not allow a close definition of the range of each class, but certain general observations may be useful. Class A, with a double-strand handle attached at or near the rim, does not much survive Stratum XII at Megiddo. Class B, with shoulder handle, is almost ubiquitous in Stratum XI, while it will be seen that the bichrome jugs which are so varied and frequent at that site in Strata X–IX are altogether lacking in the tombs at Duweir.

In Classes C–E it will be seen, by reference to individual types and their comparisons, which are the MB and LB varieties. The development as a whole is not inconsistent with the order in which the classes are arranged.

The ware is usually buff, pink or brown with a self-coloured or pink slip. Both grits and straw are mixed in with the clay. Only jugs of Classes D and E show signs of irregular burnish.

Jugs, Class A	Types, Pl. 74:
Double-strand handle, ring base	669 (Pl. 20: 20), 670 (Pl. 50: 23), 671

A double-strand handle is the feature which links the three jugs in Class A to both the piriform and cylindrical juglets of the same period. That the multiple handle reflects Chalcolithic–EB I tradition is suggested by the small jugs (Pl. 57: 41, 44) with three-strand and two-strand handles respectively (pp. 141, 155).

Type 669 from Grave 173 below the fill of the MB glacis is a complete jug of a kind which is rare in south Palestine. The nearest comparisons include an incomplete vase covered with creamy-buff slip and burnished both vertically and horizontally from Stratum E at Tell Beit Mirsim, and a jug of plain drab ware from an early room of the Palace Stores at Jericho. There can be little doubt from the fine detail of rim and base that our jug derives from a form popular at Ras Shamra between 1900–1750 B.C., though there appear to be no examples from that site with a baggy body (*Ugaritica II*, Fig. 129).

Types 670–671 have double-strand handles attached to the rim and a ring base. Though there are no close parallels from Megiddo, these jugs should fall between Strata XIV–XIII, where burnished jugs with flat bases were the rule, and Stratum XI, when shoulder handles on jugs had become ubiquitous.

669	Jericho (AAA XXI, Pl. XIX: 16) Palace Store-rooms 18.1	City C, MB II
	Tell Beit Mirsim (AASOR XIII, Pl. 10: 13)	Stratum E
	Tell el Ajjul (AG I, Pl. XLIX: 65 Y¹)	City II

Jugs, Class B	Types, Pl. 74:
Shoulder handle; moulded rim, round mouth, all kinds of base represented.	672 (Pl. 20: 21), 673, 674 (Pl. 51: 21), 675–677, 678 (Pl. 51: 45), 679,
Compare	680 (Pl. 52: 35), 681 (Pl. 52: 34),
L. II, Pl. LI: 286	682 (Pl. 52: 37), 683–687

The only shoulder-handle jug with a ring base, Type 672, which in itself compares with Types 670–671, is equal to Stratum XI at Megiddo. It comes from the single Grave 173 below the glacis fill, and it helps to fix that burial rather close in time to the introduction of the new defence system. The tradition which inspired that type must have survived to produce such obvious descendants as Types 678–679, which occur in the tombs containing the first examples of Base-Ring ware.

The loop handle attached to the shoulder moves up nearer the neck on the later jugs; compare Types 674 and 676 from MB groups with Types 682 and 686 of about 1400 B.C.

672	Megiddo (M. II, Pl. 31: 2)	Stratum XI
674	Tell Fara (BP I, Pl. XV: 38 B²) Tomb 550	MB II
675	Megiddo (M. II, Pl. 17: 25)	Strata XIII A–X
676	Tell Beit Mirsim (AASOR XII, Pl. 8: 1)	Stratum D

Jugs, Class C

Handle from ridged neck to shoulder

Compare

L. II, Pl. LI: 278

Types, Pl. 75:
688–690, 691 (Pl. 52: 33), 692, 693 (Pl. 55: 55), 694 (Pl. 55: 63)

The handle is attached to a ridged neck just below the rim, which soon develops a pronounced moulding. The body is wide above, tapering at first to a flattened base, which later becomes a small knob.

Type 688 from Cave 1513 may compare with a fragment of undoubted H provenance from Tell Beit Mirsim. Albright remarks that it is "the first appearance of a wide-mouthed jug with pinched lip which later (in MB II) becomes common" (AASOR XII, § 19). Types 689 and 690 are from the same group, p. 257.

688	Tell Beit Mirsim (AASOR XII, Pl. 5: 19)	Stratum H–MB II
	Megiddo (M. II, Pl. 20: 3; Pl. 25: 9)	Strata XIII–XII

Jugs, Class D

Handle rim to shoulder or below rim; mostly with pinched mouth; round, convex, flattened or knob base.

Compare

L. II, Pl. LI: 277

Types, Pl. 75–76:
695–699, 700 (Pl. 52: 32), 701 (Pl. 52: 41), 702–704, 705 (Pl. 51: 57), 706 (Pl. 51: 58), 707–711, 712 (Pl. 55: 14), 713, 714 (Pl. 55: 51), 715

Jugs with the handle attached directly to the rim are rare before the Late Bronze Age at Duweir. Those which are clearly earlier, Types 695–696, have rounded bodies and little or no flattening to the base. Designed most probably for domestic use, these large jugs would perhaps be more common in town deposits.

Types 701–703 and 710–712 with decoration in red owe something to Imitation Base-Ring ware. The last three come appropriately enough from the latest tombs in the series. Type 711 compares with a jug from the Ramesside Fosse tombs at Tell Fara.

696	Megiddo (M. II, Pl. 25: 6)	Strata XII–X
	Jericho (AAA XXI, Pl. XVII: 15) J. 31, city burials 2	City B, MB II
697	Minet el-Beida (*Ugaritica II*, Fig. 52: 32) Depot 213	1450–1365 B.C.
709	Megiddo (M. II, Pl. 59: 4)	Stratum VIII
711	Tell Fara (BP II, Pl. LXXXVII: 68 N⁴) Tomb 927	XXth dyn.

Jugs, Class E

Handle from or below rim to shoulder; mostly pinched or trefoil mouth; foot, ring or disk base.

Types, Pl. 76:
716, 717, 718 (Pl. 51: 46), 719, 720 (Pl. 53: 21), 721–726

Type 716 standing on a well-turned foot is the most satisfying, as it is also probably the earliest form. The same profile less sensitively reproduced is seen on Type 717, which is matched in Stratum D at Tell Beit Mirsim. The tradition is almost lost by the beginning of the Late Bronze Age, unless the decorated jug, Type 720, can be counted a descendant.

Ring, or more rarely disk, bases are characteristic, and it is this feature only which appears to distinguish the large jugs 724 and 719 from the jugs of Class D.

The series ends with Types 722–723, 725–726 which probably derive from Imitation Base-Ring, though the handle is attached at or near the rim, and vertical lines of decoration are replaced by horizontal bands. Type 725 with a chalky white slip under red and black bands finds near comparisons at Tell Fara, and the surface has the same appearance as Philistine ware.

717	Tell Beit Mirsim (AASOR XII, Pl. 42: 10)	Stratum D
725	Tell Fara (BP II, CPP type 59 T) Tombs 543, 552	xviii–xixth dynasties

JUGLETS

The piriform juglet appears to be the natural successor of the pointed juglets of the last phases of the Early Bronze Age (e.g. Pl. 58: 101–103). The succession is seen at Tell Beit Mirsim, beginning with a pointed juglet in Stratum J (cf. Type 126), and followed in Stratum H by a well-defined piriform among the very different vessels which are characteristic of the Caliciform Culture (AASOR XIII, Pls. 1: 10; 3: 13); one of the few complete pieces ascribed to Stratum F is also piriform (AASOR XII, Pl. 41: 7). With Stratum E, contacts with Duweir are resumed and they continue in Stratum D.

The charts of tomb deposits at Jericho, e.g. Tomb 5 (AAA XX, Pl. XXV), make it quite clear that, on the whole, piriform juglets have an earlier range than the cylindrical forms, though they are often found together and they share the same details of two-strand handles, fixed with an imitation rivet. Garstang notes that this "button" is a late detail, like the flat base on cylindrical forms (AAA XIX, p. 44).

At Duweir, the piriform juglets are described under Classes A–C, while the cylindrical forms comprise Classes D–F. The transitional Classes G–H are allied to Bichrome and Black Lustrous wares respectively.

Both piriform and cylindrical juglets are usually made of pinkish-buff ware with a marked orange tinge, containing few grits. In most cases slip was applied which fired grey, cream or pink, but many have lost their original surface.

Piriform Class A	Types, Pl. 77:
Pricked decoration; two-strand handle	727, 728 (Pl. 50: 15), 729 (Pl. 50: 17)

Type 728 is burnished to a smooth and shiny surface on which defined segments of pricked chevrons filled with white lime give a pleasing appearance. Types 727 and 729 are much worn and the design is not well executed; on Type 727 it is confined to one herring-bone band. Of these examples, Type 727 came from Grave 145, which was probably covered by the glacis fill. The others were both from Tomb 1552 which continued in use during most of the MB period. The three examples take a fairly early place in the series of juglets illustrated on Pl. 77, while the pricked bands mark a connexion with the cylindrical form, Type 750.

At Tell Beit Mirsim, Albright notes the introduction of this ware in Strata G–F, though it did not become abundant till Stratum E; by the time of Stratum D it was nearly extinct (AASOR XIII, §§ 31–32, 45).

Of six juglets in burials attributed to Strata XIV–XI at Megiddo, two were sealed in below the floors of Stratum X (M. II, Pl. 24: 31, T. 4099 and Pl. 32: 32 from T. 3110), giving an equation which is especially useful for Type 727.

It is clear, however, from the scarcity of these Tell el-Yehudiyeh pricked juglets at Duweir, that their main phase had passed before the MB defence system was built, and before the majority of the tombs were occupied (pp. 33, 63, 197).

727	Megiddo (M. II, Pl. 32: 32) Tomb 3110	Stratum XI
	Jericho (AAA XX, Pl. XVII: 4) Tomb 4d.32	MB II

Piriform Class B	Types, Pl. 77:
Two-strand handle	730, 731 (Pl. 50: 14), 732–735, 736
	(Pl. 51: 28), 737

Type 731 is small and squat in comparison with most of the juglets in Class B. It has also retained a thick

189

highly polished red slip which is reminiscent of Early Bronze Age technique (e.g. Pl. 61: 251–252). In this connexion see also the finely burnished concave button base from the Section, NE 12/229 on p. 57, which is of better quality than the general standard of the Duweir series The bases seldom have a finished ring and they end more often in a flat or rounded knob, but a long series would be required to achieve a reliable sequence. It does appear, however, that some juglets in Classes A and B were partly made by hand, though neck and shoulder were finished on the wheel.

730	Jericho (AAA XIX, Pl. XXXIV: 10) Tomb 9d.5	
732	Megiddo (M. II, Pl. 24: 18)	Strata XII–X
	Jericho (AAA XX, Pl. VII: 9) Tomb 13c.16	MB II
733	Tell Beit Mirsim (AASOR XIII, Pl. 9: 6)	Stratum E
735	Jericho (AAA XX, Pl. XX: 1) Tomb 5g.32	

Piriform Class C	Types, Pl. 77:
Ribbon-handle	738 (Pl. 20: 19), 739, 740, 741 (Pl. 50: 16), 742–749

Nearly all the juglets in this class have traces of burnish over a reddish slip. The bodies show the same variety of form as in the previous classes, but it seems that they were wheel-made down to the button base, which tended to be flat or convex.

The distinctive detail is a plain, smooth ribbon-handle; though it becomes prominent in Stratum XII at Megiddo, the best comparisons for our types come from Strata XI–X and by Stratum IX piriform juglets were almost extinct.

738	Megiddo (M. II, Pl. 41: 5)	Strata XI–X
744	Megiddo (M. II, Pl. 33: 4)	Stratum XI
	Jericho (AAA XXI, Pl. XIX: 17) Palace Store-rooms 18.3	City C, MB II
747	Jericho (AAA XXI, Pl. XVII: 18) J. 31 City Burials 3	City B, MB I

Cylindrical Class D	Type, Pl. 77:
Pricked decoration, two-strand handle	750

This cylindrical juglet is 15·6 cms. in height, which is above the average for those which follow in Class E. The decoration of pricked bands around the body is more formal than that on the same form at Tell el-Yehudiyeh (HIC, Pls. VII and VIII). Found in Grave 157, it provides a link with the uppermost of two burials at Tell el-Ajjul discussed by Albright (AJSLL, 1938, p. 344). See pp 23, 189 and Schaeffer (*Stratigraphie*, p. 154).

750   Tell el-Ajjul (AG III, Pl. XXXIX: 74 0^{15′}) Tomb 303A

Cylindrical Class E	Types, Pl. 77:
Two-strand handle	751–762, 763 (Pl. 51: 13)

The juglets of Class E are entirely wheel-made, except for the attachment of the two-strand handle. Type 754 is very angular; the finely grooved rim, so characteristic of Base-Ring I types (e.g. Pl. 80: 842–844), foreshadows that technique, and may indicate some mutual influence.

Among twenty examples of Type 753, some retain a rather sharp angle at the shoulder and a flat base. They are well fired, with a grey slip, vertically hand-burnished from neck to base, which was also covered in irregular strokes. On the whole, less burnish was applied on juglets of this class, and they have a pinkish-buff rather than a reddish-grey surface.

Type 759 from Groups 1547 and 6028 is an interesting variant, with the handle attached almost at the rim and the body widening to a flat base, which, as Garstang has observed, is a late detail (p. 189). Compare also Type 773, transitional to Black Lustrous ware.

The average height of juglets in Class E ranges from 15–13 cms. and there is a smaller size at 9 cms., represented by Types 756 and 761.

Comparisons come from Tell Beit Mirsim, Strata E–D, and from the tombs at Jericho. The parallels at Megiddo are less clear. Five out of eight cylindrical juglets attributed to Stratum XII come from the earliest structural tomb, T. 3095, which is certainly later than that house level. A similar case for the three other examples could be made, suggesting that this class as a whole is no earlier than Stratum XI. Four out of six juglets from Stratum D at Tell Beit Mirsim have double-strand handles and in one case that feature is vestigial, indicated by an incised line lengthwise (AASOR XIII, § 45 and Pl. 15).

751	Tell Beit Mirsim (AASOR XIII, Pl. 9: 5)	Stratum E
	Jericho (AAA XX, Pl. VII: 1) Tomb 13a. 15	MB II
	Jericho (AAA XX, Pl. XX: 2) Tomb 5e. 13	MB II
753	Tell Beit Mirsim (AASOR XIII, Pl. 9: 2)	Stratum E
	Tell Beit Mirsim (AASOR XIII, Pl. 15: 6)	Stratum D
754	Jericho (AAA XXI, Pl. XXI: 10) Palace Store-room 30.6	City C, MB II
	Tell Fara (BP I, Pl. XV: 74 0¹) Tomb 551	MB II
755	Jericho (AAA XIX, Pl. XXX: 10) Tomb 9a. 5	MB II
756	Tell Fara (BP I, Pl. XV: 74 0³) Tomb 550	MB II
	Megiddo (M. II, Pl. 50: 3)	Strata XII–IX
758	Jericho (AAA XIX, Pl. XXX: 9) Tomb 9c.37	MB II
	Jericho (AAA XX, Pl. XVI: 2) Tomb 4c.2	MB II
760	Jericho (AAA XX, Pl. XVII: 2) Tomb 4e.1	MB II

Cylindrical Class F	N.-E. Section, p. 55	Types, Pl. 77:
Ribbon-handle	MB Fill: 140	764–771
Compare		
L. II, Pl. LII: 288		

The two-strand handle of Class E is replaced in Class F by a plain ribbon-handle, attached more closely to the rim. The largest examples are 14 cms. in height and they range downwards to 9 cms. Where traces of a slip are visible, the surface colour is cream or brown and there are no grey examples. The only cylindrical juglet in the Fosse Temple comes from Structure I.

Where comparative material is concerned, the remarks on cylindrical juglets from Megiddo in Class E are equally applicable to the ribbon-handle juglets of Class F, which are even slightly later in date. Ribbon-handles appear rare in Stratum D at Tell Beit Mirsim in relation to those with double-strand, and, from the illustrations, only the smallest, as Type 767, seems to have a plain handle.

764	Megiddo (M. II, Pl. 23: 15)	Strata XII–X
766	Jericho (AAA XX, Pl. VII: 8) Tomb 13b.28	MB II
767	Tell Beit Mirsim (AASOR XIII, Pl. 15: 5)	Stratum D
	Megiddo (M. II, Pl. 40: 16)	Stratum X
770	Tell Fara (BP I, Pl. XV: 74 0¹⁶) Tomb 569	MB II
771	Megiddo (M. II, Pl. 23: 13)	Strata XII–XI

Cylindrical Class G	Type, Pl. 77:
Painted decoration, handle missing	772 (Pl. 51: 37)

Underneath a cream slip, the ware of Type 772 from Group 1555 does not differ from that of other cylindrical juglets, but its decoration of crossed diagonal bands bordered in black is close to the bichrome design of Megiddo IX. The comparison from that site, attributed to Stratum VIII, is from a burial which also contains a Black Lustrous juglet (Class J) and beads which are comparable to those in Tomb 4004. It must belong to the first phase of the Late Bronze Age.

772	Megiddo (M. II, Pl. 59: 6) T. 3004	Stratum VIII

Cylindrical Class H	Type, Pl. 77:
Two-strand handle	773 (Pl. 51: 38)

Type 773, also from Group 1555, combines the body of a cylindrical juglet with the much longer, more elegant neck and smooth finish of Black Lustrous ware (Class J).

Black or Grey Lustrous Class J	Types, Pl. 77:
Ribbon-handle	774, 775 (Pl. 51: 41), 776
Compare L. II, Pl. LI: 276	(Pl. 51: 40), 777, 778

These are Black Lustrous wheel-made juglets, described by Gjerstad as "typical Middle Canaanite" (SPC, pp. 201, 208) and by Sjöqvist, who notes that they are closely allied to black punctured, so-called Tell el-Yehudiyeh ware, and that the whole group is of non-Cypriote origin (PCBA, p. 86). Black Lustrous ware was the first import to Cyprus of Late Cypriote IA (op. cit., p. 103).

The range of Class J is very limited; the forms are found in Graves 7011 with a Black Slip III juglet, in 1555 with White Shaved and early Base-Ring wares, in 1005 and in Structure I (L. II: 276), but they were the most common class of all in Tomb 4004.

The links between these juglets and their predecessors are strengthened by the material from Duweir. It is seen that both piriform and cylindrical juglets were exposed to the influence of punctured design, and transitional shapes are found in Types 773 and 775.

Black Lustrous juglets are the last expression of a long tradition which may well be native to Syria and Palestine. Unlike the Base-Ring ware and White Shaved dippers with which they are contemporary, Black Lustrous juglets are always wheel-made, and the lower end of the handle is never inserted through the wall of the pot.

There are no comparisons from Tell Beit Mirsim and Jericho, which were both unoccupied when these juglets were in use. At Megiddo they are attributed to Strata IX–VIII, but there is no evidence at that site or elsewhere that they survived much beyond the first half of the fifteenth century. Black Lustrous juglets were also found in early xviiith dynasty burials at sites in and near the Fayum in Egypt, and at Tell el-Yehudiyeh.

774	Megiddo (M. II, Pl. 59: 5)	Strata IX–VIII
776	Gurob (*Gurob*, Pl. XXI: 91q) Tomb 293	Early xviiith dynasty
	Sedment (*Sedment* II, Pl. LXIII) Tomb 273	Early xviiith dynasty
777	Harageh (*Harageh*, Pl. XLV: 91n) Tomb 670	xviiith dynasty
	Gurob (*Gurob*, Pl. XXII: 25) Tomb 27	Amenhetep I
	Yehudiyeh (HIC, Pl. VIIIB; 107–108) Grave 406	xviiith dynasty
	Ras Shamra (*Ugaritica II*, Fig. 75: 14)	1450–1365 B.C.
778	Gurob (*Gurob*, Pl. XXII: 26) Tomb 27	Amenhetep I

DIPPERS

Dippers are, perhaps, the most characteristic form of the Middle Bronze Age, when they were larger and better made than at any later time. With the piriform and cylindrical juglets, they appear in the earliest MB tombs at Duweir, when their development is already far advanced.

Drastic change is unlikely in a shape which was in constant domestic use, and the transition is very gradual from the skilfully burnished dippers with truncated or knob base seen elsewhere (e.g. at Megiddo Strata XV–XII), through the elongated buff forms with a pointed base, carefully smoothed and finished on the wheel, to the squat or baggy versions of the Late Bronze Age which are fired a brickish-red.

The attachment of the handle below or rising just above rim level is a useful minor criterion in the divisions between Classes A and B. While rim and handle show some variations in Class C, the body is always rounded at the base and is sometimes definitely baggy.

Two dippers fall outside the normal repertory of the site, Type 783 and Pl. 86: 995. Both have trefoil mouths and a small truncated base, and both have red slip, features which suggest affinity with Tell Beit Mirsim Strata G–F and Megiddo Strata XV–XII. These large and elegant dippers are much more at home at Ugarit, where there is a good parallel for Type 783 (see under Class B) dated between 1900–1750 B.C.

Though the elements of Class A were preserved in the common dipper of Structure I (L. II: 304), the more elegant forms dominant in the Middle Bronze Age also survived (L. II: 297–298), and the last version, where the handle joins the rim, is seen in a pit of Structure II (L. II: 303). After the relative importance of dippers in both buildings, Class A was extinct by the time of Structure III, and only six dippers of later forms were found there among over 500 bowls. Bowls had, in fact, almost completely displaced dippers in performance of the temple rites by the middle of the fourteenth century. Albright has noted the disappearance of dippers in LB I, and considers that they were replaced by a type superficially the same, but showing vertical paring with a knife from rim to base (AASOR XII, § 32). These are probably the local imitations (Class B) of White Shaved ware, without the characteristic method of poking the handle through the wall. Though they may have been more common in the north, the original imports do not seem to have reached Duweir in great quantity. For further discussion, see under Imported Wares, p. 200.

Dippers, Class A	N.-E. Section, p. 55	Types, Pl. 78:
Mouth chiefly ovoid, handle below rim to shoulder, elongated body becoming squat, pointed base.	MB Fill: 162	779 (Pl. 50: 29), 780, 781 (Pl. 51: 17), 782 (Pl. 51: 42); L. II: 290, 292, 295
Compare L. II, Pl. LII		

The commonest dippers in MB tomb groups at Duweir are Types 780 and 781. Made of a medium-fired, pink or brown ware, Type 780 has an average height of 22·4 cms. and Type 781 of 19·3 cms. There are comparisons from Tombs 9 and 4 at Jericho, and from Megiddo Strata XII–X, but the flattened or knob base which sometimes occurs on dippers at those sites and farther north is not found at Duweir.

Albright has noted the curious lack of these dippers in Stratum E at Tell Beit Mirsim (AASOR XIII, § 46) and all our contacts are therefore with Stratum D, though it must be admitted that otherwise the main forms of the period are lacking at Duweir.

Contemporary with the introduction of Black Lustrous, and Base-Ring wares and imported White Shaved dippers, the elongated body of Types 780–781 is replaced by that of Type 782, which can be closely matched in the dippers of Structure I and Tomb 4004 (L. II: 290, 292, 295, etc.). The common form in that building is L. II: 304, which is among the few dippers with pointed base to survive in Structure II. The elongated body like that of Types 780–781 also survives there in a late version, where the handle is joined at rim level (L. II: 303).

780	Tell Beit Mirsim (AASOR XII, Pl. 42: 12)	Stratum D
	Jericho (AAA XXI, Pl. XVIII: 11) Tower J. 31, Spot 4	City B, MB II
	Jericho (AAA XIX, Pl. XXXV: 10) Tomb 9e.41	
	Tell Fara (BP I, Pl. XV: 51 G⁷) Tombs 551, 569	MB II
781	Tell Beit Mirsim (AASOR XII, Pl. 42: 9)	Stratum D
	Tell Beit Mirsim (AASOR XIII, Pl. 15: 7)	Stratum D
	Tell Fara (BP I, Pl. XV: 51 G⁴″) Tomb 550	MB II
	Megiddo (M. II, Pl. 41: 12)	Strata XII–X
	Jericho (AAA XIX, Pls. XXXII: 2; XXXV: 11) Tombs 9a.2; 9e.27	
	Jericho (AAA XX, Pl. XVII: 6) Tomb 4d.12	
L. II: 292	Megiddo (M. II, Pl. 58: 5)	Strata IX–VIII

Dippers, Class B	Types, Pl. 78:
Pinched mouth, handle rising above rim, shorter body, shaved to pointed base.	783–785, 786 (Pl. 53: 22), 787–793, 794 (Pl. 55: 39)
Compare L. II, Pl. LII	

Apart from Type 783, which is discussed on pp. 192 f., the earliest dipper in this class comes from Structure I (L. II: 294); others from the tombs which may have an early history are Types 784–786.

Types 787–794 all belong to tombs which are among the latest in the Duweir series. The ware is a fairly hard reddish-brown, and the body is often shaved with a knife. This treatment is applied to asymmetrical shapes, which could not easily be finished on the wheel, for example the high handle of these dippers and the spout of the LB lamps (L. II, Pl. XLV). The resemblance in form of Types 784–786 to White Shaved ware is marked, but, on the whole, dippers of Class B should perhaps be counted as the local products of the time rather than deliberate imitations. Like the imported White Shaved dippers, which have a long life in Cyprus from 1550–1200 (PCBA, p. 77), Class B may cover much the same range, with special importance in the period of Late Cypriote II B or from 1350–1275 B.C., a date which would be consistent with that of the named scarabs of Ay and Horemheb from Tombs 4011 and 4013 respectively where dippers of Class B are common.

These forms begin in Megiddo VIII, though the date for some burials in this Stratum should perhaps be placed no earlier than 1350 B.C. For the buff or drab dippers of Tell Abu Hawam, with vertically shaved bodies, which were "exceedingly common" throughout LB levels, see Tell Abu Hawam (QDAP IV, p. 47: 287–288).

783	Ras Shamra (*Ugaritica II*, Fig. 106: 12)	Ugarit Moyen II 1900–1750
788	Megiddo (M. II, Pl. 63: 4)	Strata VIII–VII
789	Megiddo (M. II, Pl. 67: 16)	Strata VII B–VI A
790	Megiddo (M. II, Pl. 71: 8)	Strata VII–VI

Dippers, Class C
Mouth ovoid or pinched, handle rim to shoulder, round base.
Compare L. II, Pl. LII

Types, Pl. 78:
795–797
L. II: 306, 311
L. III: 282, 288, 300

The dippers of Class C are distinguished from their predecessors in having a round instead of a pointed base. Except for L. II: 306 from Structure II and Type 797 from contemporary groups, the handle is attached at rim level, a feature which was to become, like the round base, invariable in the Iron Age (L. III, Pl. 88 and pp. 294–296).

Dippers with a round base were found in Tombs 216, 501, 1003 and in Structures II–III. The bodies are often clumsy and misshapen, so that the form is no advance on previous achievement, though it was to continue with little change into the Iron Age with great improvement in surface treatment.

Lamon and Shipton note that their "jug type 142"—with a pinched mouth— "is obviously a Stratum V carry-over from Stratum VI and LB traditions" (M. I, p. 165, § 27). An acknowledged short break in time between Strata VI and V (M. I, pp. 3–7), and the few dippers in Structure III do nothing to increase our view. All that can be said is that Class C with Class D began before the end of Structure II and continued to appear in the last tombs of the series.

Dippers, Class D
Ovoid mouth, everted profile, handle rim to shoulder, various bodies, round base
Compare L. II, Pl. LII

Types, Pl. 78:
798 (Pl. 52: 11), 799 (Pl. 53: 8), 800
L. II: 308, 309
L. III: 301, 302

Dippers of Class D represent the dregs of the series; they are found in much the same groups as the dippers of Class C, beginning before the end of Structure II and continuing to the last tombs, though they total but half the number of Class C. One would expect to find comparisons for these dippers in the Fosse Tombs at Tell Fara, but examination of them in the Institute of Archaeology collection yields little more than a general resemblance.

798 Tell Fara (BP I, Pl. XXV: 4th row) Group 542   *c.* 1320 B.C.

COOKING-POTS

With bands and holes, straight sides, flat base

N.-E. Section, pp. 55–59

MB Fill: 176, 212, 219–222, 226

Early Bronze: 231, 256, 326

Types:

Pls. 57: 69; 66: 415

The only complete flat-based pot from the site was a surface find, Pl. 57: 69, but it compares for the moulded band and the pierced holes above with most of the similar sherds from the Section between 9 and 13 feet. The ware in all cases is coarse brown, buff or grey, but flint and lime grits are not so frequent as in cooking-pot wares of later days. A sherd from Group 1529 (Pl. 66: 415) suggests that this kind of cooking-pot was in use during the period of the Caliciform Culture.

The lowest sherd in the Section, at 6 feet, is possibly intrusive, though parallels from contemporary EB I–II layers are recorded from Jericho besides those noted below (AAA XXII, Pl. XXXII: 3, 11).

At Megiddo these vessels begin in Strata XVII–XVI and continue with modifications till Stratum XII. In Shipton's first study of the pottery, he equates Strata XIV–XIII with Tell Beit Mirsim G–F on the change which occurs from fully pierced to punched holes in the rim (SAOC 17, p. 35). This point is somewhat disturbed by the group of pots attributed to Stratum XVI with and without punched holes (M. II, Pl. 7: 9–12).

At Tell Beit Mirsim the flat-based pot with fully pierced holes spanned Strata I–F and was replaced in E–D by a form without holes and with finger impressions on the rim (AASOR XII, Pl. 44: 10–13, etc., and § 36). The lack of cooking-pots of the latter kind at Duweir adds to the evidence that the main phases of E and part of D at Tell Beit Mirsim are unrepresented, both in the Section and the tombs.

NE 18/176	Jericho (AAA XXII, Pl. XXXII: 4) Strip 5, 10·01 m.	Layers IV–V
NE 15/212	Tell Beit Mirsim (AASOR XII, Pl. 3: 26–31)	Strata I–F
	Tell Beit Mirsim (AASOR XIII, Pl. 22: 11–15)	Stratum G
NE 6/326	Tell Beit Mirsim (AASOR XII, Pl. 3: 27)	Stratum I
	Jericho (AAA XXII, Pl. XXXII: 5) Strip 5?, 10·76 m.	Layers IV–V
	Megiddo (M. II, Pl. 107: 36)	Stratum XVII
	(M. II, Pl. 108: 15, 17)	Stratum XVI

Roll rim, etc.

N.-E. Section, pp. 55–59

MB Fill: 121–123, 132, 155, 156, 175, 189, 213

Early Bronze: 269, 274, 317

Profiled rim

N.-E. Section, pp. 53–55

Level VII: 69, 83, 102, 110, 111

MB Fill: 206

Compare L. II, Pls. LV, LVI

Type, Pl. 78:

801 (Pl. 55: 27)

With the introduction of a round base, there is a corresponding change in the quality of the ware, which mostly fires pink or red and contains a high proportion of flint and lime grits. There are no complete vessels from Duweir, but sherds with varied roll and bevelled rims occur in the glacis fill between 15 and 22 feet. Similar rims occur at Tell Beit Mirsim G–F and at Megiddo Strata XIII–X, though at the latter site the first complete round-based pot is later than the wall of Stratum XII (M. II, Pl. 30: 3, Tomb in wall 3182).

A rather different rim is expressed in NE 22/123, for which compare an intrusive (?) cooking-pot from Cave 1520 (Pl. 57: 39).

The profiled rim occurs once in the glacis fill, though it is mainly found above it in Level VII, with parallels in Structures II–III of the Fosse Temple and with Stratum C at Tell Beit Mirsim, where Albright considers that the collared or otherwise profiled rim appears about the fifteenth century (AASOR XII, p. 40, § 55).

Parallels for Structure I forms are missing from the Section but occur at Tell Beit Mirsim Strata D and C¹ (L. II: 357 and AASOR XIII, Pl. 17: 2; L. II: 356 and Pl. 17: 5), where a Structure II–III vessel is also matched in Stratum C¹ (L. II: 367 and AASOR II, Pl. 47: 11).

Apart from Type 801 in a thirteenth-century burial, the scarcity of cooking-pots is no less acute in MB and LB tombs than in Iron Age groups (L. III, p. 309).

NE 27/83	Tell Beit Mirsim (AASOR XII, Pl. 47: 11)	Stratum C
	Megiddo (M. II, Pl. 55: 4)	Strata IX–VIII
NE 21/132	Megiddo (M. II, Pl. 46: 8)	Strata XIII–X
NE 15/213	Tell Beit Mirsim (AASOR XIII, Pl. 5: 2 for shape only)	Strata G–F

JARS

Types, Pl. 78:
802–805

Plain

For reasons of space these jars could not be included on Pl. 59, which presents the bulk of the deposits from Tomb 1513. For description see under Jars, plain or with lugs, p. 167.

Types, Pl. 79:
807–810, 811 (Pl. 49: 6)

Potter's

The beaker-shaped jar decorated with red and black bands from Group 1005 may date from LB I; other jars were found in the potter's workshop 4034. Possibly they were made for his own use to hold water near the wheel. Compare the vessels from the Iron Age workshop 6024 (L. III, Pl. 90: 393, 394).

POTSTANDS

Compare	N.-E. Section, p 53	Type, Pl. 79:
L. II, Pl. LIII	Level VI: 10	812
L. III, Pl. 90	Level VII: 77	

Potstands are rarely present in Bronze or Iron Age burials, and the grooved example from Tomb 129 is by no means complete. The potter's workshop contained a stand which was compared to one from Structure III (L. II: 330), and several of the storage jars of which fragments remain would have been large enough to fit it.

The tall Bronze Age stands gave place in the Iron Age to lower rings of thick and heavy ware (L. III, p. 304) and their weight assured stability and compensated for the loss of height.

IMPORTED WARES AND IMITATIONS

The pottery grouped under this general heading is that which conforms to various classes common in the ceramic repertory of Cyprus, though they do not necessarily originate from that island. The names adopted are those which are used in the works of the Swedish Cyprus Expedition (q.v.).

It will be seen that the earliest distinctive imports in this category are a juglet of White Painted IV ware from a tomb and a sherd from the fill of the MB glacis. They provide a much needed link with the dumped debris in the workmen's town at Kahun, xii–xiiith dynasty, where other sherds foreign to Egypt included piriform juglets, Class A, with pricked design, and MM II B Kamares ware (IKG, Pl. I and pp. 9 f.). The date for comparisons in Cyprus is dependent on this evidence from Egypt, but White Painted IV is said to appear towards the end of MC II, and it replaces WP III completely in MC III, when the later kind with unslipped surface and broad bands of paint, White Painted V, comes in. This last is more typical of LC I (HNM, pp. 143–146).

Black Slip III ware and analogous forms in Red-on-Black ware are but poorly represented in the Fosse Temple (L. II, Pls. LI: 274, LXIV: 3). A juglet, Type 814, and a bowl, Type 816, are useful additions from Grave 7011 and Tomb 4004. Red-on-Black ware is not well stratified at Megiddo, where a jug attributed to Stratum XII and a bowl from Stratum XI both come from disturbed and broken areas (M. II, Pls. 26: 14, 38: 16). It is common at Tell el-Ajjul II, with the bichrome wares which are a special feature of Strata X–IX at Megiddo (M. II, Pls. 39, 49), and it is probably to that horizon rather than to XII–XI that the Red-on-Black from Megiddo should belong.

Albright has noted that Bichrome ware is wholly missing at Tell Beit Mirsim "unquestionably because of a gap at that site between the Egyptian destruction about 1550 B.C. and the reoccupation of Stratum C some generations later" (*Arch. Pal.*, p. 96). To a lesser degree, the same explanation may be valid at Duweir, for no Bichrome was found in the tombs (but see Type 772, cylindrical juglet, Class G), and the one piece in the Section NE 29/51 on p. 53, was far above its true context. The two decorated kraters (L. II: 256 and Pl. LVIII: 1, 2) both come from dumped rubbish in the Fosse, and they provide an important *terminus ad quem* for the disuse of that defence. Both pieces are attributed to the "Ajjul Vase Painter" by W. A. Heurtley (QDAP VIII, Pls. XIV: k and XIV B, p. 28, Notes). From different parts of the same deposit came the neck and handle of a Bichrome jug (L. II: 272), a sherd (L. II, Pl. LXI: 3), and a much debased krater (L. II: 253). The Black Slip III jug (L. II: 274) mentioned above and a Black Lustrous juglet (L. II: 276) came from the same horizon as the early Base-Ring sherds, including the bowl and krater (L. II: 169, 170). In a nearby pit was one of two White Slip I bowls (L. II: 154), while the other was with the altar group of Structure I (L. II: 155). Monochrome bowls were found in the same contexts (L II: 167, 168).

Wares described in the last paragraphs are dated by Schaeffer to LB I (*Stratigraphie*, p. 184) and are found in Tomb 10 at Milia (QDAP VIII, pp. 1–20), attributed largely to LC I A, with the important addition of Black Pricked ware (Piriform Juglets, Class A), though it is not possible to see how far the design is degraded.

Apart from these isolated imports, the great bulk consisted of Base-Ring wares, beginning with the finest quality in Structure I, which gave place in Tombs 216, 501 and 1003 to a progressive series which did not long survive the disuse of these tombs. Only sherds of the common forms were found in Structure III and the latest survivals are perhaps the debased juglets in Tomb 571.

Quite late in the series and closely allied to Base-Ring II ware is a hand-made jug with fluted belly, generally described as Bucchero ware. In Cyprus it appears in LC II A, where Monochrome and White Shaved wares continue (HNM, p. 160).

White Painted IV juglet	N.-E. Section, p. 55	Type, Pl. 79:
(SPC, pp. 169–171)	MB fill: 174	813

The ware is pinkish-buff, once covered by a buff slip, which is now worn. Three broad brown bands were painted round the neck and the body was covered with fine vertical lines and zigzags. The lower end of the handle was inserted through the wall.

Since Gjerstad's study of 1926, it has become clear that White Painted IV ware is not indigenous to Cyprus, where it is not common, and there is no very close parallel in the publications to Type 813.

Schaeffer has reviewed, like Gjerstad before him, the known occurrences of White Painted IV ware in Palestine and Egypt, and he shows how only the neck and handle of a juglet found with other wares foreign to Egypt in the workmen's town at Kahun can be certainly dated to the xiith dynasty (IKG, Pl. I: 18 and p. 10, *Stratigraphie*, p. 351 and SPC pp. 304 f.).

In assessing the development of White Painted wares Schaeffer agrees with Gjerstad that a place apart should be reserved for White Painted IV, though its period of use overlaps that of White Painted II and III

Imported Wares, Types, Pl. 79

Locus	White Painted IV Black Slip III Red Lustrous	White Shaved	White Painted V	Monochrome	Bucchero	White Slip II	Total
532	—	820, 822	—	—	—	835	3
4013	—	—	—	—	830	—	1
4011	—	820	—	—	—	—	1
S. III	—	—	—	—	L. II: 285	L. II: 157(2) 165(7) 166(3)	13
221	—	—	826	—	—	—	1
536	—	821, 822	—	—	830	—	3
542	—	820	—	—	—	—	1
547	—	—	825	—	830	831, 835	4
1006	—	—	—	—	—	831	1
4019	—	—	—	—	830	—	1
1003	—	820	825	—	830(2)	831	5
528	—	—	—	—	—	835	1
555	815	—	825(2)	828	—	—	4
564	—	—	825	827	—	—	2
501	—	820	825	828	—	833(2)	5
216	— —	817, 818, 819(2), 820(2), 821	824, 825(4), 826	828(2), 829	—	831(2), 832, 833, 834	21
S. II	—	—	L. II: 282(4)	L. II: 167(2)	—	L. II: 156(3), 157(3), 161(3), 165(2), 166(6)	23
S. I	L. II: 273, 274	—	—	L. II: 167(2), 168	—	L. II: 156(3), 165(3)	11
4004	816	819	823, 825	827(2), L. II: 167, 168	830(2)	—	10
7011	814	—	—	—	—	—	1
1555	—	821	—	—	—	—	1
129	813	—	—	—	—	—	1
Total	6	17	19	15	9	48	114

(*Stratigraphie*, p. 352). His observations at Ras Shamra, where all categories of White Painted ware are numerous in the tombs and houses, leads him to doubt their Cypriote origin (op. cit., p. 353).

However, the publication of Megiddo II brings out fresh evidence; jugs and juglets of White Painted IV are found in Strata XII–X. Further study of the single burials which contain examples of these wares suggests that they centre in Stratum XI and are certainly slightly later than the buildings of XII. Three burials in particular (T. 5243, 4109 and 3076) yield useful material including plain or curved bowls with inturned rim, a Cypriote import of White Painted ware (Pl. 34: 16), of which another example is attributed to Stratum X (Pl. 41: 30) being found in conjunction with a lime-wash storage jar (Pl. 43: 2), see p. 221. It should be noted that no White Painted IV ware was found in the structural tombs of Stratum XI which contain the latest repertory of MB forms.

The interest of the unique juglet from Duweir is that it comes from Tomb 129, containing a full range of plain MB wares, and no other distinctive imports.

Among the sherds from the fill of the MB glacis was part of the body of a White Painted IV juglet decorated with wide bands and narrow crossed diagonals (NE 18/174). A similar piece is attributed to Stratum G at Tell Beit Mirsim (AASOR XIII, Pl. 22: 7) and compared by Albright to a vase from Ugarit (AASOR XIII, § 25 and *Stratigraphie*, p. 124). The relative sequence between the decorative patterns of crossed diagonals and finely painted vertical lines with wavy strokes between still has to be worked out.

813　　Megiddo (M. II, Pl. 26: 13)　　　　　　　　　　　　　　　　　　　　Stratum **XII**
　　　　Ras Shamra (*Ugaritica II*, Fig. 131: 8) Ugarit Moyen 2 ou début 3　　*c.* 1750–1675 B.C.
　　　　Qrayé (BMB III, Pl. XIIb and p. 59) The flask from a cave-tomb of mass burials is placed by
　　　　Schaeffer in the first period of use between 1900–1750 B.C. (*Stratigraphie*, p. 76)

　　　　　　　　　　　　　　　　　　　　　　　　　　　　　　　　　　　Types, Pl. 79:
Black Slip III juglet (SPC, pp. 145–148)　　　　　　　　　　　　　　　814
Red-on-Black or Black Slip III bowl (SPC, p. 178: 1)　　　　　　　　　816

　　The buff body of Type 814 is covered by a thick matt slip; the decoration consists of two incised bands around it with irregular zigzags in between; the incisions are unfilled.

　　Though indigenous to Cyprus, Gjerstad states that Black Slip III ware is "to a great extent influenced by the advanced Late Cypriote types, both native and foreign" and he notes the resemblance of the flask to corresponding Base-Ring types. At Ajios Jakovos he found a flask like Type 814 associated with a central layer of mass burials dated to the beginning of Late Cypriote I— "some MC wares still survive . . . but the main feature of the group is the introduction of Base-Ring I ware. The imported vases are Plain White and Black Lustrous" (SCE I, p. 334). It is the same situation at Duweir in the large groups, but the phase is well isolated in Grave 7011, where, with Type 814, there were two Black Lustrous (Class J) juglets and a dipper (Class A) like those from Structure I (L. II: 290, 292, 295) and Tomb 4004, which are also found at Megiddo in Strata IX–VIII.

　　Type 816 is an open-spouted bowl, of buff ware covered by a dark slip, fired black outside and reddish-brown in. From the state of the surface it is not certain if the bowl was originally painted. Schaeffer considers that Red-on-Black ware, which does not appear until towards the end of Ugarit Moyen 2 (1900–1750 B.C.), remained in use until an advanced phase of the following period, that is to say up to 1650 B.C. in round figures. (*Stratigraphie*, p. 27.)

816　Ras Shamra (*Syria* XIX, 1938, p. 236 and Fig. 31) Caveau LXI

Red Lustrous III Ware　　　　　　　　　　　　　　　　　　　　　　　Type, Pl. 79:
(SPC, p. 201; PCBA, p. 53, bottles 1a, 1b)　　　　　　　　　　　　　　815
Compare L. II, Pl. LI: 273

　　There are two spindle-shaped flasks or bottles, with neck and handle missing, in this ware. Both are wheel-made.

　　The flask from the altar group of Structure I (L. II: 273) was once covered by a highly burnished red slip, which is now worn to reveal an orange-buff surface below. The tall and slender body of the flask from Group 555 (with part of another, both in the Palestine Museum) is also vertically burnished on red slip.

　　The position of the flask near the altar of Structure I supports Sjöqvist's suggestion that this peculiar shape served a ceremonial purpose.

　　Both Gjerstad (SPC, p. 200, *Syrian Ware*) and Sjöqvist (PCBA, pp. 52, 85) are agreed that Red Lustrous ware is non-Cypriote in origin. It is said not to appear in Cyprus before LC II A or 1400 B.C. (HNM, pp. 149, 151), but this ware is found in an earlier context in the Fosse Temple, probably no later than the reign of Thothmes III.

　　Bottles like Type 815 were found in Egyptian graves of precisely that period, and shorter, sturdy flasks like L. II: 273 occurred in a grave attributed to the reign of Amenhetep I.

　　The origin of the ware is not yet determined, but, in view of the numbers found at Ras Shamra and Atchana, Sjöqvist is inclined towards a Syrian origin (PCBA, p. 86).

815　　　　　Rifeh (GR, Pl. XXVIII: 315) Tombs 157, 158　　　　　　　　Thothmes III
　　　　　　　Harageh (*Harageh*, Pl. XLV: 92e) Tomb 608　　　　　　　　Thothmes III
L. II: 273　Gurob (*Gurob*, Pl. XXII: 28) Tomb 27　　　　　　　　　　　Amenhetep I
　　　　　　　Rifeh (GR, Pl. XXVIII: 314) Tomb 1　　　　　　　　　　　　Thothmes III

Red-on-Black or Black Slip III bowl
See under 814

White Shaved dippers
(SPC, p. 181; PCBA, p. 32, jug 1b)

Type, Pl. 79:
816

Types, Pl. 79:
817 (Pl. 53: 10), 818, 819 (Pl. 53: 6),
820–821, 822 (Pl. 55: 40)

All these hand-made dippers are of soft pink or buff ware, the body is shaved with a knife to a pointed base, the handle rises above the rim and the lower end is inserted through the wall. Compare the dippers, Class B, on p. 194.

The earliest among them is probably Type 821, of which an example came from Group 1555 which is unlikely to be later than c. 1450 B.C. The type is also rare in LC I in Cyprus (HNM, p. 153). Types 819–820 are found in later contexts, well on in the fourteenth century, a result which is in keeping with the distribution of these dippers elsewhere.

Gjerstad considers that they are imitations of the "Syrian" jugs with pinched rims and pointed base (SPC, pp. 181, 201, 208) in which category he includes all non-Cypriote wares. Sjöqvist also believes that "the priority of the type on Syro-Palestinian ground is . . . beyond doubt" (PCBA, p. 77). In his opinion, the statistics favour a Cypriote origin for the ware, and the common type persists from the beginning of LC I to the end of LC II. "During LC II B" (1350–1275 B.C.), he writes, "they constitute about 10% of all vases found in the tombs excavated by the Swedish expedition at Ajios Jakovos and Enkomi."

Sjöqvist remarks on the technical peculiarity of these dippers, and in particular on the paring of the body with a knife. This process is not unknown in Palestine, as he suggests, but is reserved for asymmetrical shapes which could not be finished on the wheel. (See under Dippers, Class B, p. 194.) It is the rise of the handle above the rim level which suggests the necessity for this technique.

Insertion of the lower end of the handle into the body is the old method of Cyprus and, for this reason, Sjöqvist considers that White Shaved is certainly of Cypriote manufacture (PCBA, p. 78). While agreeing that this "procedure is entirely absent on Syro-Palestinian ground", except in the case of recognised imports, the feature is to be seen in the low levels of Trench X at Mersin (Mersin, Fig. 127: 10, 12).

The statistics of finds in Cyprus show that the majority of these juglets came from the east coast sites and in particular from Enkomi (PCBA, p. 78). Their relative chronology in Cyprus is indeterminate, but they are found in groups covering LC I and II, with special importance between 1350 and 1275 B.C. (PCBA, p. 167), which is in keeping with the situation at Duweir, though most examples come from Tomb 216.

Admitting the priority of the type in Syria-Palestine, one must suppose that the Cypriote potters reproduced it in their own tradition for the foreign market, exporting these containers for a prized product of the island to buyers on the mainland.

819 Enkomi (*Missions en Chypre*, p. 78, Fig. 32: 43) Tombe 3, couche inf. Cf. PCBA, p. 105 — XV–XIVth century
    Megiddo (M. II, Pl. 71: 12) — Stratum VII
    Tell Abu Hawam (QDAP IV, p. 47: 288) — Stratum V
820 Megiddo (M. II, Pl. 58: 9) — Stratum VIII
821 Megiddo (M. II, Pl. 58: 8) — Stratum VIII

White Painted V Ware (SPC, p. 171)
Compare L. II, Pl. LI: 282

Types, Pl. 79:
823, 824 (Pl. 53: 9), 825, 826
(Pl. 53: 15)

This unslipped buff ware with crude black decoration is clearly derived from White Painted IV. The paste and shaved body also provide a link with White Shaved ware, as Gjerstad has remarked (SPC, p. 181). The decoration on the four types from Duweir is limited to plain black or brown vertical and horizontal bands, representing the last phase of a more elaborate and varied style of decoration which can be seen at Ras Shamra. M. Schaeffer attributes the best examples to a date centring on 1750 B.C., with more debased examples slightly later. He goes on to say that no juglets of White Painted V have been found in the numerous tombs of Ras Shamra covering the period 1600–1450 B.C. (*Stratigraphie*, pp. 354–355) or to the following phase 1450–1365 B.C. However, there were few finds at Ras Shamra between 1750–1550, according to Schaeffer's chart (*Stratigraphie*, p. 39), and his work has indeed produced comparisons with Duweir juglets in contexts which appear consistent with a sixteenth–fifteenth century date, but see Schaeffer's own explanation of their presence in these groups (*Stratigraphie*, p. 354).

Taking them on face evidence, certain groups with these later forms from Ras Shamra are consistent with the conclusion from Duweir that the White Painted V shovel-mouth juglet (Type 823) can occur in a sixteenth–fifteenth century context with the "teapot", Type 825, a late version of which is exclusive to Structure II (L. II: 282). Cf. Grave 613 at Tell Fara (BP I, Pl. LXX and CPP types 89A and 64 F²).

Comparisons for Types 823 and 825 occur in the tombs at Milia (QDAP VIII, pp. 1–20), all of which were occupied in LC I A, while Tomb 10 was probably re-used in LC I B. Certain pieces in Tomb 10 attributed to White Painted V could perhaps be included in White Painted IV (e.g. Pl. V: 72, 73).

On considerations of style and technique, it seems difficult to divide White Painted V from White Shaved wares, and at Duweir, at least, they appear to be contemporary, though White Shaved continued well into the thirteenth century B.C.

823	Abydos (*Cemeteries II*, Pl. XXIX) S. chamber x.52	2nd intermediate
	Deshasheh (*Deshasheh*, Pl. XXXIII: 25) Grave 44	
	Enkomi (SCE I, Pl. CIX: 6) T. 19. 43	LC I–mid LC II
	Milia (QDAP VIII, Pl. I: 69–71) Tomb 10	LC I A and I B
	Ras Shamra (*Syria XIX*, 1938, p. 223 and Fig. 19 K) Caveau LIV, couche sup.	XVIII–XVth centuries
	Megiddo (M. II, Pl. 51: 5) T. 3017	Stratum IX
824	Enkomi (SCE I, Pl. CIX: 8) T. 19. 81	LC I–mid LC II
825	Megiddo (MT, Pl. 24: 3) T. 42	MB II
	Megiddo (M. II, Pl. 59: 10) T. 3005	Stratum VIII
	Enkomi (*Missions en Chypre*, p. 78, Fig. 32: 36, cf. PCBA, p. 105) Tombe 3, couche inf.	XV–XIVth centuries
	Ajios Jakovos (SCE I, Pl. CIX: 7) T. 14. 20	LC I A
	Ras Shamra (*Ugaritica II*, Fig. 104: 5)	1450–1365 B.C.
	Ras Shamra (*Syria XX*, 1939, p. 282, Fig. 4E) Caveau LXXV	XVI–mid XIVth centuries

Monochrome bowls and jug (SPC, pp. 181–185)	N.-E. Section, p. 53 Level VI: 38	Types, Pl. 79: 827 (PCBA, p. 32, bowl 1) 828 („ „ bowl 2b) 829 („ „ jug 2) (Pl. 53: 40) *L. II*: 167 („ „ bowl 2a), 168

The bowls are all made of brown ware, covered by a brush-applied slip which has fired unevenly to reddish-brown. The only jug, Type 829, had a hard even grey body, and the surface was covered with a shiny black slip; there was incised decoration on the handle.

On Sjöqvist's classification, the earliest bowl, Type 827, came from Tomb 4004, while the common form with a plain rim, *L. II*: 167, was also present and persisted into Structures I–II. Type 828, which is similar, came from Tomb 216, Group 555 and Tomb 501, representing the last occurrence of Monochrome at Duweir.

The jug, Type 829, is rare in Cyprus, but it should be closely allied to Base-Ring I and Bucchero wares; cf. for instance, Types 838 and 829. Sjöqvist considers that Monochrome is well founded on MC pottery tradition, but its relative chronology in the island is indeterminate, though maximum quantities were found in LC II A–B, 1400–1275 B.C.

There is apparently no Monochrome ware in published reports from Egypt, and its occurrence is rare in Palestine, being confined to those sites with LB I deposits. Duweir provides nearly the full range of the Cypriote repertory, and Monochrome ceased to be imported to the site early in the fourteenth century. The only sherd from the North-East Section was found between Levels VI and VII at 30 feet.

827	Enkomi (SCE I, p. 489: 2, 5–7) Tomb 4	LC I A
	Megiddo (M. II, Pl. 61: 20)	Strata IX–VIII
828	Megiddo (M. II, Pl. 54: 21)	Stratum IX
	Enkomi (*Missions en Chypre*, p. 78, Fig. 32: 12) Tomb 3	XV–XIVth centuries
	Milia (QDAP VIII, p. 11, 17–18) Tomb 11, bottom layer	LC I A
	Minet el-Beida (*Ugaritica II*, Fig. 52: 25) Depot 213	1450–1365 B.C.
	Minet el-Beida (*Syria XVII*, 1936, p. 123, Fig. 14: S)	XIVth century
	Ras Shamra (*Syria XIX*, 1938, p. 226, Fig. 21 G) Caveau LIV, couche sup.	XVIII–XVth centuries

Bucchero jug
(SPC pp. 193 ff.)
Compare L. II, Pl. LI: 285

Type, Pl. 79:
830 (PCBA, p. 35, jug 1b)

There are eight jugs in this ware; all of the same type, which equates with Sjöqvist's Jug 1b. The ware is thin brown, often with a grey core, covered by a dark-grey slip, fired red in parts, with a shiny surface.

These hand-made jugs do not occur in Structures I–II and the only one attributed to the period of Structure III comes from 100 Houses (L. II: 285).

The evidence from the tombs is more conclusive. One of the two Bucchero jugs from Tomb 4004 was among the topmost vessels in the western chamber; the others on the chart, p. 198, are closely contemporary with Tomb 1003. The last example, also hand-made, came from Tomb 4013.

The few comparisons from mainland sites and the close alliance of Bucchero and Base-Ring II ware in Cyprus suggest a common origin, and the date of the jugs at Duweir seems to fall after the import of Base-Ring had reached a peak, early in the fourteenth century (PCBA, p. 84). Cf. the charts on p. 198 and p. 204.

830	Megiddo (MT, Pl. 14: 21) Tomb 877 C 1	LB
	Minet el-Beida (*Syria XIII*, 1932, Pl. VI: 1, top row) Depot 213	1450–1365 B.C.
	Tell el-Ajjul (AG II, Pl. XXXIV: 59 A 2) Tomb 1053	

White Slip bowls
(SPC, pp. 194–200)
Compare L. II,
Pl. XLIII: 156, 157, 165, 166

N.-E. Section, p. 53
Level VI: 19, 30

Types, Pl. 79:
831 (PCBA p. 45, bowl 2a) (Pl. 53: 4)
832 (,, ,, ,, ,,) (Pl. 53: 3)
833 (,, ,, ,, 2b)
834 (Pl. 53: 5)
835 (Pl. 55: 54)

There are no White Slip I bowls from the tomb series and those from the Fosse Temple are all confined to Structure I (L. II: 153–155).

White Slip II ware does, however, occur in the first Structure and it continues through to Structure III, though the bowls are mostly in fragments.

White Slip II bowls in the tombs are made of a pinkish-brown clay, fired grey in section, with a thick white slip all over. The decoration is rather crude in dark-brown paint. The common form is Type 831, equivalent to L. II: 165, the only type which covers the range of all three Structures. Types 832 and 834 are confined to Tomb 216, while Type 833 makes one further appearance in Tomb 501. It is these common bowls which are a feature of Tell Beit Mirsim, Stratum C (AASOR XII, Pls. 17, 18), while they are altogether lacking in Megiddo VIII and there are two comparisons from Stratum VII B. The latest crude version, Type 835, is well placed in the Ramesside tombs at Tell Fara.

White Slip II sherds appear in the Section at 31–32 feet and they are therefore in Level VI rather than VII.

831	Ras Shamra (*Ugaritica II*, Fig. 121: 15, 16, 17)	1450–1250 B.C.
	Megiddo (M. II, Pl. 72: 5)	Stratum VII
	Megiddo (MT, Pl. 60: 1) Tomb 48	LB II
832	Tell Abu Hawam (QDAP IV, Pl. XVI: 221–222)	Stratum V, last phase
834	Megiddo (M. II, Pl. 65: 26)	Stratum VII B
	Enkomi (*Missions en Chypre*, p. 78, Fig. 32) Tombe 3, couche sup.	XV–XIVth centuries
835	Minet el-Beida (*Ugaritica II*, Fig. 57: 22) Grande Tombe 4	1450–1365 B.C. or later
	Tell Fara (BP I, Pl. XII: 152) Tomb 902	xix–xxth dyn.
	Tell Fara (BP II, Pl. LXXXII: 19 P⁶) Tomb 949	xix–xxth dyn.
	Megiddo (MT, Pl. 62: 9) Tomb 63 E	LB II

Base-Ring

Base-Ring Ware	N.-E, Section, p. 53	Types
(SPC, pp. 185 ff.; PCBA, pp. 34–40)	Level VI: 42	Pls. 80, 81
Compare L. II, Pls. XLIV, LI, LII	Level VII: 84, 92, 93	Fig. 8

The name "Base-Ring" is used to describe a distinctive ware by all those who have written on the subject since Sir J. L. Myres first coined the term. It has long been recognised that there are many forms which have no separately made foot or ring base, but, nevertheless, it is too late to change a name which denotes vessels made in a standard repertory of shapes in a very thin grey or reddish-brown ware, and most commonly found in Cyprus, Syria, Palestine and Egypt in groups of the fifteenth to thirteenth centuries.

Important questions of origin and quality have been discussed by Erik Sjöqvist in *Problems of the Late Cypriote Bronze Age*, published in 1940. This admirable study summarised and analysed all the material of known provenance up to the outbreak of World War II. Since then, abundant material has been published from Ras Shamra, and the series from Duweir includes all the usual forms of the Cypriote repertory.

Sjöqvist defines varying qualities of ware, divided into two main groups of chronological significance, Base-Ring I and Base-Ring II. Certain vessels can be assigned without doubt to the first or second class, but other examples in the slow process of degradation are not so easily classified, and already the author's attributions have been challenged in some respects (see J. F. Daniels in AJA, 1942, pp. 286–293).

For that reason the pictorial presentation of the material from Tell ed-Duweir is primarily arranged on form, while the attribution to Base-Ring I or II is given tentatively opposite the plate. It is doubtful whether the division can be firmly maintained, based—as it must be—on very slight variations.

Despite the common use of the wheel in all areas where Base-Ring vessels are found, they were not wheel-made. Examination suggests that they were perhaps built up or constructed of four or more sections, and then joined when leather-hard. In view of the extremely thin walls of many vessels in Base-Ring I ware, it is worth considering whether they were not cast in sections and then joined. The ridges at the base of the neck would represent the natural thickening at the junction of two parts, and in some cases the join was made good by paring the surface with a knife. The ribbon handle is invariably poked through the wall of the neck and body. The upper attachment is cut off and smoothed over, but the potter could not easily reach the lower join at the shoulder, and a protruding end is seen whenever the pot is broken. The ring base, which gives its name to the ware, was perhaps separately made and then attached to the rounded bottom.

Two qualities are distinguishable in Base-Ring I ware and they are as described by Sjöqvist:

"The thin ware is made of a very well-silted clay of gray—seldom buff—colour. It contains no foreign particles as binder, and therefore the surface has a tendency to flake off, especially on the finer vases. It is hard-baked and very light, giving off an almost 'metallic' or glass-like clink, and is very water-tight. The surface is covered with a thin lustrous slip, usually dark-grey in colour. . . .

Locus	Base-Ring Ware			Total
	I	*I–II*	*II*	
6001	—	—	845	1
571	—	858	867	2
4013	—	—	875	1
S. III	—	L. II: 176(2), 313(2)	L. II: 279, 283(3), 312, 314	10
221	—	871	—	1
527	—	—	866	1
536	—	871	—	1
541	—	865	—	1
542	—	865	—	1
543	—	—	845	1
547	869	842, 865, 871	845, 866, 874	7
1006	—	841, 871	844, 845	4
1003	857, 859(2), 869	855	840, 844, 845(2), 847, 866, 867, 873	13
524	869	842, 865	—	3
528	—	865	845	2
548	869	—	844	2
554	859, 869(2)	842(2), 871	—	6
555	857(7), 860(3), 869	839, 849(4), 865(2), 871	844, 875	21
564	850, 861	842	—	3
501	857(3), 861(2)	842, 849, 865, 871	844(5), 845(2), 847, 853, 870, 873, 874(3), 875	24
216	838, 848, 850, 852, 856, 857(11), 859(2), 860, 861, 862, 863(2), 868, 872(2)	839, 842(5), 843, 849, 851, 858(2), 865(2), 871	836, 844(8), 845(6), 846, 853, 854, 864(2), 867(4), 870, 873(2)	67
S. II	L. II: 173(2), 301(3), 302(2)	L. II: 174(3), 176(4), 280(2)	L. II: 279(4), 339(2)	22
S. I	L. II: 169(3), 170	L. II: 174, 176(2)	—	7
4004	837, 857, 862, 863(3)	865(2)	—	8
1555	860	—	—	1
Total	72	62	76	210

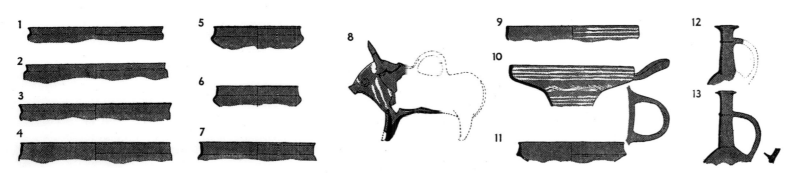

FIG. 8 Base-Ring Fragments. Scale 1: 5

Nos. 1–2, Pit 254 (L. II, p. 91); 3 Grid D.8–10; 4–7 Area 100; 8 Tomb 501; 9 Area 100; 10 Locus 564; 11 Area 100; 12 Tomb 4004; 13 Locus 564

"The thick ware is made of coarse gray or light-brown clay mixed with sand and grains of quartz and chalk. . . . It is well baked and of a hard consistency. Sometimes the core is gray or dark-brown and the surface slightly more reddish. It is covered by a brown, sometimes reddish, thin slip that is generally quite matt but occasionally shows a slight lustre" (PCBA, p. 34).

Both qualities of ware are found at Tell ed-Duweir, the thin variety being typical of many Base-Ring sherds from the Fosse Temple (see Fig. 8, and L. II, Pl. XLIV: 169, 170) and elsewhere, and of most of the jugs from Tomb 216. The thick ware is less common and the best-preserved example is jug 837 from Tomb 4004.

Single fragments of Base-Ring pottery are found in the North-East Section between 27 and 32 feet, comprising Level VII and the earlier part of Level VI. Only those pieces showing some shape are illustrated on p. 53.

It will be seen from the Base-Ring chart, p. 204, that the largest and richest selection is found in Tomb 216, and that in the group the balance between Base-Ring I and II is about equal.

Base-Ring II ware is coarse and thick in comparison with either quality of Base-Ring I. The section is usually a brownish-red, and the surface exhibits a colour range from brown to red with grey patches. It is usually pocked, due to the admixture of grits which have sometimes "blown" near the surface, and the general effect is reminiscent of the Iron Age Black-on-Red III juglets (see L. III, p. 297).

Decoration

The decoration is of two kinds:

(a) Raised ribs or ridges on the neck at the junction with the pegged handle and, at the point where the neck and body join, there are spirals or half hoops on the body. In the best examples the ridges are diagonally incised.

(b) Painted white lines, applied in groups of three or four, horizontally on the neck and diagonally or vertically on the body. From the spacing of the lines it is clear that they were made by four brushes or points tied together, cf. similar method of application on Red-on-Black ware as noted by Petrie (AG I, p. 10).

The careful and elaborate decoration of Type 841 reproduces the seams and stitches of the prototype in a way which suggests leather rather than metal work. Both kinds of decoration, whether detailed or debased, represent the tucks and seams needed to make a globular vessel from a flat sheet. Sjöqvist favours the use of metal for the original jug type 3a in his classification (PCBA, p. 37), but the bronze jug, on which he bases his conclusion, is plain and gives no sign of skeuomorphic design (Murray, *Excavations in Cyprus*, 1900, p. 16, Fig. 29). If all the prototypes for the standard Base-Ring shapes were made of metal, it seems strange indeed that the metal rivets were so rarely reproduced (see the only example from Duweir, jug 836, which is attributed to Base-Ring II).

Shape

The Base-Ring pottery from Tell ed-Duweir comprises nearly all the forms of the Cypriote repertory with some additions. Jug 836 (Pl. 53: 42; PCBA, p. 39, type 4) is only rarely found on the mainland, the examples mentioned by Sjöqvist coming from Gaza (AG I, Pl. L: 89 H³, Tomb 808; II, Pl. XXXVI: 89 H¹¹⁻¹³, Tomb 1166), are not comparable (PCBA, p. 173). Jug 837 is perhaps intermediate in shape between PCBA, p. 36, type 4, and a jug with a shorter neck from the Minet el-Beida deposit. The form of jug 837 is comparable to that of a jug in Monochrome ware from Stephania Tomb 5 to be published by Mr. J. B. Hennessy.

Jug 838 (Pl. 53: 41) is not illustrated in the Cypriote repertory though the neck ridges are reminiscent of the earliest Bucchero jug (PCBA, p. 53, type 1a). There is indeed little to choose between hand-made Bucchero ware and Base-Ring fabrics, p. 202. Jug 841 (Pl. 51: 51) is a magnificent specimen, and though the rim and part of the neck are missing it probably had the shovel mouth of a similar piece published by Sjöqvist (PCBA, p. 36, jug type 3a) and classified as Base-Ring I. Gjerstad records the type as Base-Ring II (SCE I, Pl. CXIII: 9, E.3.280).

Type 842 (PCBA, p. 39, jug 1a) retains some raised moulding, and Sjöqvist considers that the form is transitional from Base-Ring I. Jugs 843 (Pl. 53: 73), 844, 845, 846 (Pl. 53: 79) and 847 (PCBA, p. 39, jugs 2b, 2c, 2d) are the common types in Tombs 216, 501 and 1003, while it is only in the last two that jug 847 with its constricted neck makes an appearance. It is an easy step from jug 847 to juglets 865–866.

The bulls, Fig. 8: 8 and Types 840 and 839 (Pl. 53: 34), are of a class which is well known. In the case of the Base-Ring I bull, the legs are pinched out from the body clay though the horns are poked through. Both horns and legs are poked through in the Base-Ring II bulls, 839 and 840.

Bottles 848 (Pl. 53: 36) and 849 appear to have an early trend in keeping with the quality of the ware, which is the thick variety of Base-Ring I. For shape cf. Red Lustrous ware, Type 815 and p. 199.

Mugs 850–853 (Pl. 53: 69–72) are chiefly associated with Tomb 216, the two first having a ridged neck.

Juglet 854 is comparable perhaps to the large jug 837. It is made of unusually thick ware somewhat pocked on the surface. Juglets 855 and 856 (Pl. 53: 44) have a ridged neck with shovel mouth and a small trumpet base; the difference in size and its position in Tomb 1003 suggests Type 855 as the later piece. Cf. the shovel-mouth juglets at Ras Shamra (Ugaritica II, Fig. 112: 1–7) which all have a low wide base.

Juglets 857 and 858 (Pl. 53: 45, 56; PCBA, p. 32, jug 2a) with trumpet foot are among the most widespread forms. They are seldom decorated with white lines. For a rare example which has lost the ridges at the neck see Type 863 (Pl. 53: 47, 55). Juglets 859 (Pl. 53: 50, 53), 860 (Pl. 51: 44) and 861 have a wider base, and the first two types show two raised vertical ridges on the body. The occurrence of Type 860 in burials of Strata IX–VIII at Megiddo suggests that it is contemporary with Type 857.

Juglets 862 (Pl. 53: 59), 864 (Pl. 53: 63), 865 (PCBA, p. 39, jug 3), 866 and 867 are all late and clumsy versions. Sjöqvist has remarked on the scarcity of the form like 865 (jug type 3) in Cyprus, and points out its frequency in Egypt, Palestine and Syria. He goes on to suggest that these examples were made in one or more colonies or emporia of Cypriote settlers on the Syrian coast (PCBA, pp. 80–81).

Bowl 868 (Pl. 53: 39; also L. II: 174) is possibly a fraction earlier than the more angular-sided bowl type 2a (PCBA, p. 39). Bowl 869 is quite close in this respect to bowl type 1a, and it compares with sherds from Structure II (L. II: 173). Bowl 870 is not exactly matched in the Cypriote repertory. Bowl 871 (cf. L. II: 176) is the last of the series, as bowl type 2b, which it resembles, is in Cyprus, though the form goes back to Structure I.

Sjöqvist has remarked on the clear development of these bowls for which he provides a metal prototype (PCBA, p. 41). In varying qualities of ware, they range from the beginning of Structure I to the occupation of Structure III, and a comparison for Type 871 can be found as late as Megiddo Stratum VII.

Lentoid flasks, Types 872 (Pl. 53: 31, 37), 873–875, may have a late trend. They are not provided with string holes like the Cypriote Base-Ring I lentoid (PCBA, p. 36, type 3) and the form is not illustrated there in a Base-Ring II context.

Internal evidence for the progression of form is seen on the Base-Ring chart on p. 204.

Dates and Comparisons

The diffusion of Base-Ring wares in coastal regions of the eastern Mediterranean and on trade routes which serve those ports presents the best common denominator for chronological synchronism in the fifteenth and fourteenth centuries. Nevertheless, the finer points of detail and particularly the grading of the ware leave many problems to be solved. Frequency of occurrence of certain standard shapes is also important, and at Duweir the largest collection of Base-Ring types so far recovered from Palestine can make some useful contributions.

The finest quality ware is to be found in or around Structure I of the Fosse Temple in those same deposits which contained the Bichrome ware (p. 197). Besides the Base-Ring I bowl and krater, L. II: 169, 170, there were many sherds of which a selection has been drawn on Fig. 8. It is only of recent years that wares of this eggshell thinness have come to light, notably at Alalakh, Niqme-pa's palace, Level IV (sherds in I. of A. collection) and at Bamboula in Cyprus (Penn. Univ. Mus. Bull., Vol. VIII, pp. 3–14). Unfortunately this book is too far advanced to make full use of Sir Leonard Woolley's Alalakh which has recently appeared, and the Bamboula collection is not yet published.

With the fine Base-Ring wares in Structure I are Monochrome bowls which may precede them in date, if they are not coarser contemporary products. There are no Base-Ring jugs and few juglets in Structure I, where bowl fragments without white lines predominate. The bowls so decorated (Fig. 8: 9, 10) are exceptions.

At Tell Beit Mirsim only two pieces of Base-Ring ware were found in Stratum D, and the two fragments illustrated bear firm well-painted lines, which are more typical of Stratum C (AASOR XII, Pl. 13: 3, 5, p. 25 and Pls. 16–17). These and other anachronistic Base-Ring sherds from Palestinian deposits are discussed by Mr. J. R. Stewart, and he makes the point that there is no reason to believe that Base-Ring ware of any kind was reaching Palestine before c. 1550 B.C., or before the time of Megiddo IX and Tell el-Ajjul II, a conclusion with which Albright agrees (BASOR 138, April 1955, p. 49), and which is in line with the evidence from Duweir.

In Egypt juglets like Type 857 are found in graves which belong to the early xviiith dynasty, though there is little to suggest that they were imported before the reign of Thothmes III. There is indeed ample confirmation that this juglet, with its trumpet foot, was widely exported in the course of Thothmes' Syrian campaigns. At Duweir it appears in those tombs where scarabs of Thothmes III and his immediate successors are most numerous, and the latest example comes from Tomb 1003, in use during the last quarter of the fifteenth century. Strong corroborative evidence for the range of the form is provided by the pottery from Niqme-pa's palace at Alalakh, Level IV.

Among the more usual Base-Ring I forms is jug type 2a in Sjöqvist's classification (Alalakh, p. 356) which is like the Duweir juglet Type 857. Jug type 1a (our Type 842) is admittedly transitional to Base-Ring II in Sjöqvist's view, and it is the favourite form of Base-Ring ware in Niqme-pa's palace (op. cit., pp. 357 and 361). Jug type 2a is almost equally popular, though it lacks white-line decoration, which appears to be rare though not unknown in that building.

Various chronologies proposed for Alalakh are discussed by Sir Leonard in Chapter XIII. Professor Sidney Smith has shown that Niqme-pa of Alalakh, King of Mukish, was a vassal of Saushshatar of Mitanni, who wrested the suzerainty of Syria from Amenhetep II about the third year of that Pharaoh's reign (Alalakh and Chronology, pp. 39 f.). His successor, Thothmes IV, conducted a Syrian campaign which met with little success and it is precisely at this time that we see the last of such early Base-Ring forms as Types 857 and 842. Since the absolute chronology of Egypt is uncertain, within half a century, the duration of the standard Base-Ring I Type 857 and the transitional jug 842 should extend, say, from Thothmes III's conquest of Syria, which brought Base-Ring wares to Palestine in quantity, to some time in the reign of Thothmes IV.

This would accord well with the date of destruction of Niqme-pa's palace now proposed by Sir Leonard (Alalakh, p. 130), c. 1415 B.C. Since the documents recovered from that building postulate about fifty years of occupation (p. 392), the date of its foundation would necessarily be earlier than 1435 B.C. as he proposes in his time framework for the levels on p. 389. Level IV is said to start with the building of Niqme-pa's palace (p. 388). A date for the beginning of Level IV "after 1483–after 1459" as proposed by Smith (p. 384) would be preferable on the evidence now available from Duweir.

It is significant that Type 857, with trumpet foot, Type 860 with wider foot and raised rib, Type 842 and the flask 849 are the only Base-Ring forms which are paralleled in city deposits at Megiddo, where they occur in the burials of Strata IX–VIII, which were presumably made after the Egyptian conquest, when the buildings of Stratum IX were destroyed or abandoned. The fine bowls of Structure I may precede Thothmes' conquest by a few decades.

The main tombs which contain Base-Ring ware, i.e. Tombs 4004, 216 and 501, all contain scarabs of Amenhetep III. As there is no Base-Ring II in the earliest of these groups and few of those forms which go with it, we must assume a gap in the deposits as already remarked by M. Schaeffer (Stratigraphie, p. 186). Though white-painted decoration is not exclusively a late sign, there is no doubt that the bulk of the jugs and other forms which are so decorated fall after 1400 B.C.

The best evidence is to be seen from two groups at Minet el-Beida, Cave XIII (Syria XVII, 1936, p. 121, Fig. 13) and Deposit 213 (Ugaritica II, Figs. 52–53). Both groups are dated by the excavator to 1450–1365 B.C., but the homogeneous nature of Deposit 213 should place most of it at the end and not the beginning of the period. It will be seen that the trumpet-foot juglet is missing and that raised mouldings on jugs are replaced by painted lines, which appear for the most part to be more roughly applied than any from Duweir. It should be noted that the white paint is in no case applied with a multiple brush, and that all the jugs have lost the characteristic ridge at the junction of neck and body. The three jugs photographed opposite Fig. 53 from Cave XIII appear to be much closer to those in the Duweir series.

There can be no doubt that Lachish was strongly under Egyptian control during the reign of Amenhetep III, and scarabs of this king are the latest to be found in tombs which contained more than an odd Base-Ring vessel. It is thus quite clear that, while Syria was subject to Egyptian domination from 1450 to 1375 B.C., Base-Ring wares continued to reach Lachish in decreasing quantities. As soon as the security of the empire was seriously threatened, those trade contacts were lost. The latest and most decadent juglets, Types 864–867, at Lachish are not as poorly decorated as those which continued to be made in Syria. The notable Deposit 213 from Minet el-Beida illustrates that phase which ended in 1365 B.C. If the difference between the standard Base-Ring II jugs of Lachish and Minet el-Beida is not chronological, it may indicate that the former were derived from trade with Cyprus, while the latter were non-Cypriote products, as Sjöqvist suggests (PCBA, p. 81). The juglets, like Types 865 and 866, may well be derived from coastal emporia.

836	Minet el-Beida (*Ugaritica II*, Fig. 68: 16)	1450–1365 B.C.
837	Minet el-Beida (*Ugaritica II*, Fig. 52: 34) Dépôt 213	1450–1365 B.C.
839	Tell Abu Hawam (QDAP IV, Pl. XVII: 303)	Stratum V
841	Enkomi (SCE I, Pl. CXIII: 9) T. 3.280	LC II
842	Megiddo (MT, Pl. 50: 11) Tomb 1145B	LB I
	Enkomi (SCE I, p. 502, cf. PCBA, pp. 39, 104) T. 3.195	LC II
	Jericho (AAA XX, Pl. XXI: 1) Tomb 5d.1	1500–1450 B.C.
	Megiddo (M. II, Pl. 58: 20) T. 3018A	Stratum VIII
845	Megiddo (MT, Pl. 43: 8) Tomb 855	LB I
	Minet el-Beida (*Syria XVII*, 1936, p. 121, Fig. 13M)	XIVth century
	Tell Abu Hawam (QDAP IV, Pl. XVII: 258)	Stratum V
846	Enkomi (*Missions en Chypre*, p. 78, Fig. 32: 21) Tombe 3, couche sup.	XV–XIVth centuries
	Minet el-Beida (*Ugaritica II*, Fig. 52: 27) Dépôt 213	1450–1365 B.C.
	Jericho (AAA XXI, Pl. XXXIX: 2) M. III–V	XVth century
847	Minet el-Beida (*Ugaritica II*, Fig. 53A) Caveau XIII	XIVth century
	Minet el-Beida (*Syria XVII*, 1936, p. 121, Fig. 13L)	XIVth century
849	Minet el-Beida (*Ugaritica II*, Fig. 52: 20)	1450–1365 B.C.
	Megiddo (M. II, Pl. 58: 18) T. 3018B	Stratum VIII
857	Megiddo (MT, Pl. 50: 13) T. 1145 B	LB I
	Megiddo (MT, Pl. 43: 6, 7) Tomb 855	LB I
	Gurob (*Gurob*, Pl. XXII: 27) Tomb 27	Amenhetep I
	Sedment (*Sedment* II, Pl. LVII: 32) Group 254	Thothmes III
	Harageh (*Harageh*, Pl. XLV: 95 F) Tomb 601	Amenhetep II
	Enkomi (*Missions en Chypre*, p. 78, Fig. 32: 40, cf. PCBA, p. 102) Tombe 3, couche sup.	XV–XIVth centuries
	Tell Abu Hawam (QDAP IV, Pl. XVI: 262, 268)	Stratum V
858	Ras Shamra (*Ugaritica II*, Fig. 112: 11)	1450–1365 B.C.
	Jericho (AAA XXI, Pl. XXI: 2) Tomb 5c.12	1450–1425 B.C.
859	Ras Shamra (*Ugaritica II*, Fig. 112: 9)	1450–1365 B.C.
860	Megiddo (M. II, Pl. 51: 1) T. 3027	Stratum IX
	Megiddo (M. II, Pl. 58: 19) T.3005	Stratum VIII
863	Jericho (AAA XXI, Pl. XXXI: 1) M. I–Ia	XVth century
865	Minet el-Beida (*Ugaritica II*, Fig. 53: 7) Depot 213	1450–1365 B.C.
866	Minet el-Beida (*Syria XVII*, 1936, p. 121, Fig. 13J)	XIVth century
870	Minet el-Beida (*Syria XVII*, 1936, p. 121, Fig. 14L) Caveau XII	XIVth century
	Megiddo (M. II, Pl. 69: 8) S. 3158	Stratum VII A

871   Megiddo (M. II, Pl. 65: 24) W = 5023   Strata VII B–A
        Tell Abu Hawam (QDAP IV, p. 48: 298 and Pl. XVI: 257)   Stratum V
873   Minet el-Beida (*Syria XIII*, 1932, Pl. VI: 2, 2nd row)   1450–1365 B.C.
        Tell Abu Hawam (QDAP IV, p. 43: 267)   Stratum V

Imitation Imported Wares, Types Pls. 81–82

| Locus | Imitation Base-Ring | | | | | Imitation White Slip | Total |
	Jugs A	Jugs B	Jugs C	Other forms	Total		
502	880	—	—	—	1	—	—
508	—	890, 891, 892	—	—	3	—	—
556	—	—	—	908	1	—	—
557	—	—	—	906	1	—	—
4001	879	—	905	—	2	—	—
6016	884	—	—	—	1	910	1
559	880, 881, 882	—	—	907	4	—	—
532	882	893, 894, 895, 896	904, 905	—	7	913(2)	2
226	—	889(2), 890, 896(3)	—	—	6	—	—
539	884	—	—	—	1	—	—
561	883, 884	—	—	—	2	910	1
570	—	—	901	—	1	—	—
4013	884	888, 889, 891, 894, 895(4), 896(2)	900, 901	—	13	912, 913	2
4011	—	888, 895	902	—	3	—	—
4034	—	—	—	—	—	909	1
S. III	—	—	L. II: 284	—	1	—	—
221	—	899	903	—	2	—	—
527	—	888	—	—	1	—	—
536	—	—	904	—	1	—	—
542	—	—	900, 901, 904, 905	—	4	—	—
547	—	893	—	—	1	—	—
4019	878	886, 893, 898	—	—	4	—	—
1003	—	—	—	—	—	910, 911	2
548	—	—	904	—	1	—	—
554	—	—	901	—	1	—	—
555	—	885, 897	904	—	3	—	—
501	876, 877	—	—	—	2	—	—
216	—	886, 887, 894, 895	—	—	4	—	—
S. II	—	—	—	—	—	—	—
S. I	—	—	—	—	—	L. II: 153	1
Total	14	37	17	3	71	10	10

    The local manufacture of jugs imitating Base-Ring forms must have been taken up as true imports became scarce, and a great variety of plain and decorated jugs were produced (Types 876–905), though there is not much overlap except in the largest groups. Other shapes, bowls (Types 906–907), flasks (Type 908), were rarely made in local pottery, though the Base-Ring tankards (Types 850–853) may have been the originals for the series of mugs (Types 959–969, see p. 215).

    Other imitations are Types 909–913 based on White Slip milk-bowls.

Imitation Base-Ring Ware

The great majority of the Imitation Base-Ring wares are wheel-made jugs and they have therefore lost the characteristic tilt of their hand-made predecessors. The clay is reddish-brown containing some grits and the body is clumsy and very heavy. A pinkish-buff slip is usual, which sometimes becomes cream on later examples. Burnish is quite common, applied vertically on the neck with horizontal strokes around the body.

With one exception, the handles are applied and not inserted through the wall of the jug, and it is that Type 878 from Tomb 4019 which is indeed nearest to the original model. It retains painted white lines and scored incisions on the handle, but the coarse and heavy pink ware thrown on the wheel may compare with the newly discovered wheel-made Base-Ring bowls (ILN, 1949, 27 Aug. pp. 316–317, Fig. 2). The paint was lavishly applied with a five-point brush, though sets of four lines are more usual on real Base-Ring jugs. Type 879 retains the scored lines on the handle of the previous type though it is not inserted.

Red painted lines applied vertically or crossed diagonally on the body are the most usual decoration. Between them there are sometimes black, red or white zigzags and occasionally the ridge on the neck is emphasized or replaced by a painted band.

The jugs are divided into Classes A–C, as classified below, but the series is not sufficiently long to justify the working-out of a sequence and all three classes are contemporary.

Imitations of true Base-Ring wares become common once the imports have ceased, as comparison of the charts on p. 204 and p. 209 will show. The change took place no earlier than the reign of Amenhetep III, for the first tombs to contain imitation jugs are Tombs 216 and 501, both of which were in limited use during his reign. The small group 4019 contains a scarab of that king and four imitation jugs, though true Base-Ring ware was missing.

Though locally made jugs may have imitated Base-Ring forms somewhat earlier (see, for instance, the jugs in Tombs 221, 542 and 547 which were open during the occupation of Structure II), they cannot have been common as there is only one Class C jug from Structure III (L. II: 284).

Imitation Base-Ring jugs are present in Stratum C at Tell Beit Mirsim (AASOR XII, Pl. 47: 10 and sherds on Pl. 20). Grant and Wright note typical pitchers in Stratum IVa at 'Ain Shems (AS IV, Pl. LV: 8, 12; AS V, p. 115) and they compare a sherd (AS IV, Pl. XXXI: 10) with a pitcher from Tomb 5a.10 at Jericho (AAA XX, Pl. XXI: 7). Both comparisons appear more debased than the normal repertory at Duweir. The range of jugs from Tomb 4 layers a–c is, however, rather closer to our series (AAA XX, Pl. XI).

The northern sites of Megiddo and Tell Abu Hawam do not present any Imitation Base-Ring from city levels. Imitation Base-Ring jugs come from the Fosse Tombs at Tell Fara, but the majority are smaller and more debased than those in the Duweir series. The best comparison is with a jug of Class C from one of the earliest Fosse Tombs 905.

Imitation Base-Ring Jugs, Class A	Types, Pl. 81:
Tubular neck, ridged at junction with ovoid body; splayed base	876–881, 882 (Pl. 55: 62), 883, 884

A well-defined ridge at the base of the neck brings these jugs close to the Base-Ring prototype, like the scored lines on the handles of Type 878–879. Rising above the handle, the rims are usually moulded, and the bases are splayed in imitation of a ring base.

Jugs in Class A seldom preserve signs of slip or burnish, but this defect may be due to the condition of the surface. Type 883 with a palm branch below the handle is an exception which retains horizontal burnish on a buff-pink slip.

876 Jericho (AAA XX, Pl. IV: 15) Tomb 13a.20

Imitation Base-Ring jugs, Class B
Tubular neck, no ridge at base of neck, ovoid or globular body, splayed base

Types, Pl. 81–82:
885, 886 (Pl. 52: 39), 887 (Pl. 52: 43), 888, 889, 890 (Pl. 55: 11), 891 (Pl. 55: 10), 892 (Pl. 55: 9), 893 (Pl. 55: 58), 894 (Pl. 55: 56), 895 (Pl. 55: 61), 896 (Pl. 55: 57), 897–899.

Jugs of Class B have almost lost the ridge at the base of the neck, which is sometimes replaced by one or more bands of red paint. The plain ribbon handle is occasionally decorated with red, the rim is moulded and the bases are splayed though less well finished. Red diagonal lines in brush-applied groups of three or four are sometimes enlivened by the craftsman's own fancy; the design is painted on a buff surface, burnished with vertical strokes on the neck and horizontal lines around the body.

895   Jericho (AAA XX, Pl. XI: 4) Tomb 4b.7

Imitation Base-Ring jugs, Class C
Swollen neck, curved shoulder, ovoid or globular body, ring base

Types, Pl. 82:
900–903, 904 (Pl. 55: 59), 905 (Pl. 55: 60)

The tubular neck of Classes A–B is replaced in Class C by a curved one which bulges out opposite the point of attachment to the handle. The rim is usually moulded, but the base is less prominently formed. Decoration is poor and uncommon, consisting only of red lines diagonally applied in sets of three. With one exception there are traces of slip and burnish on all these jugs, which in their curved outline and small base appear furthest typologically from the Base-Ring original though chronologically they have an early trend.

905   Tell Fara (BP II, Pl. LXXXVII: 65 B³) Tomb 905   xixth dynasty

Imitation Base-Ring bowls and flask

Types, Pl. 82:
906–908

There is little to be said for the two bowls which reproduce wish-bone handles and other characteristics of Base-Ring shapes (cf. Type 871), beyond noting the addition of a red line on the rim. The handle of the flask 908 is attached at right angles to the body like the lentoid flasks (cf. Type 873).

For a tankard which may also be derived from Base-Ring models see Type 964 (under Mugs below).

Imitation White Slip   N.-E. Section, p. 53   Types, Pl. 82:
                                Level VI: 37   909–912, 913 (Pl. 55: 36)

Among the few imitations of White Slip wares, Types 910 and 911 from Tomb 1003 are perhaps the earliest and though small they retain the gourd-like shape. Types 909, 912 and 913 with a slightly everted rim could be at least a century later, like the fragment from Level VI.

909   Qrayé (BMB III, Pl. IX: g.1)   xviiith dynasty

Mycenaean

Pottery imported from the Aegean world to the Fosse Temple at Duweir was published in *Lachish II* and has been subsequently discussed by Dr. Hélène J. Kantor in her study on *The Aegean and the Orient in the Second Millennium B.C.* (AJA LI, 1947, pp. 17–108) and by Dr. Frank H. Stubbings in *Mycenaean Pottery from the Levant* (1951).

The fine one-handled kylix from the altar group of Structure I (L. II, Pl. XLIX: 257, Pl. LVIII: 5 and p. 83)

is reproduced by Stubbings (op. cit., Pl. XIV: 1) and he considers that the piece is "of undoubted Myc. II fabric. For the shape (F. 262) cf. 'Εφημερίς 'Αρχαιολογική (1399), Pl. 7: 19 (from Vapheio) and *Ch. Tombs*, Pl. XLI: 33 (from Mycenae); for the decoration, *Ch. Tombs, Pl. II.*" The same goblet "decorated with an intermittent wavy band and solid ivy leaves" is likewise assigned by Dr. Kantor to LH II (op. cit., p. 36).

She describes another kylix sherd from the Temple area "with the typical thick-rimmed spiral of LH I"

Mycenaean Imported Wares and Imitations, Types, Pls. 82–83

Locus	Mycenaean Imported	Imitation Pyxides	Imitation Piriform Jars	Total
Tell K. 16: 1031	949	—	—	1
Tell D/X	950	—	—	1
Tell J. 15: 1031	951	—	—	1
502	—	921	—	1
508	—	923	943	2
556	—	916	—	1
7017	—	*L. II*: 344	—	1
559	—	918, 930	—	2
532	—	927, 928, 929	944	4
539	—	926	—	1
561	—	917	—	1
571	947	—	—	1
4013	—	918, 919, 920, 922, 925, 926, 928, 929, *L. II*: 344	941	10
4011	—	924, 928	—	2
S. III	*L. II*: 219	*L. II*: 344, 345	—	3
221	—	*L. II*: 344	—	1
527	—	*L. II*: 345	—	1
536	946	—	—	1
542	946	922	—	2
547	—	927	—	1
1006	—	—	942	1
4002	948	923	—	2
4010	—	928, *L. II*: 344	—	2
4019	—	927	—	1
1003	—	—	—	—
524	—	914	—	1
555	945	—	940	2
501	—	—	941	1
216	945	915	—	2
S. II	—	—	—	—
S. I	*L. II*: 257	—	—	1
4004	—	923, 929	—	2
TOTAL	11	36	6	53

(op. cit., p. 36), while Stubbings considers that the same sherd, like the kylix of the altar group, is also Myc. II (MPL, p. 56).

While agreeing that all the other Mycenaean at Lachish belongs to Myc. III A or III B (cf. L. II, pp. 83 ff.), both Professor Blegen and Dr. Stubbings, who saw the assembled sherds at the Institute of Archaeology, decided that those of Mycenaean III B were more numerous.

All told, the collection is not large. There are few, if any, Mycenaean sherds from buildings or pits of Structure II (but see L. II, Pl. LXIII: 3). The upper part of a kylix decorated with an oblique murex motif and other sherds come from pits associated with Structure III (L. II, Pl. XLVI: 219, Pl. LXIII: 1, 4, 5) while

Pl. LXIII: 2, a piece from the shoulder of a stirrup-jar and 3, part of a kylix, were found in the Temple Area. All these are attributed by Stubbings (MPL, p. 85) to Myc. III B, which is usually dated 1300–1230 B.C. Schaeffer, on the other hand, would prefer a date about half a century earlier (*Stratigraphie*, p. 185).

Both the shallow bowl, Pl. LXIII: 1, and the potmark on Pl. LXIII: 4 appear to be of Cypro-Mycenaean type and though potmarks are common on Mycenaean pots from Cyprus, they are not, in Dr. Stubbings's view, clear proof of such origin (Letter, 12 Sept. 1949), though they are strong evidence in favour of it; cf. MPL, pp. 50–52. Possibly from that source is the pilgrim flask illustrated in L. II, Pl. LIV: 351, for this shape had a far greater popularity in Cyprus than in other Mycenaean areas (cf. PCBA, p. 69 and MPL, p. 100).

Mycenaean Wares from Tombs

Types, Pl. 83:
945 (Pl. 53: 23), 946–948

There are three piriform jars: from Tomb 216, Group 555 (Types 945) and Tomb 542 (Type 946). These appear to compare with Furumark's Levanto-Mycenaean piriform jar (Type 46, MP, p. 592, cf. MPL, p. 35), classified on typological grounds as Myc. III A: 2. In round figures, Furumark's date for the period is the fourteenth century (Furumark, CMP, p. 115) and typologically the first half of the century is indicated, a conclusion which would agree with the date of these tombs judged on Egyptian royal names, cf. the latest scarabs in Tomb 542 (Thothmes IV) and Tomb 216 (Amenhetep III).

Among the sherds in Jerusalem from Tomb 4013 (PM. 37.934) which Dr. Stubbings examined, he noted "fragments of a stirrup-jar, probably of piriform type, of which the top and some other sherds survive. . . . It is unusually large, the disc being some 6 cms. across and of fine buff clay with very well fired red paint. There are also fragments of another similar one" (MPL, p. 66 and Pl. XIV: 2). To judge from the style, he would think them "fairly early in Myc. III—perhaps as early as the Amarna finds" (Letter dated 12 Sept. 1949). Mid-fourteenth century would be about the earliest possible date for this group, which contained pottery of a later range than the previously mentioned tombs. There was a scarab of Horemheb, last king of the xviiith dynasty, and another of Rameses II, which must extend the range of the group into the thirteenth century.

Two other complete vessels are a pyxis or angular squat jar from Tomb 571 and a juglet or biconical jug from Tomb 4002. With regard to the pyxis, Type 947, the concave sides and convex bottom with two handles set low on the rather tall shoulder are typical of Sjöqvist's "Levanto-Helladic specific shape" No. 14 (PCBA, Fig. 18 and p. 68). (Furumark's Type 95, MP, p. 43, dated to III A: 2–B, 1375–1200 B.C.) The hand-made juglet, Type 948, corresponds roughly to Furumark's Type 126 (MP, p. 604 and Fig. 7), though, unlike most of the examples he lists, it is decorated with horizontal stripes like wheel-made Mycenaean. The torso of a terracotta figurine, Type 950, is comparable to Blegen's fourth and latest variety (*Prosymna II*, Fig. 612: 730, *type d* and I, pp. 358 ff.) or Furumark's Type Ψ, Fig. 1, which is generally datable to Myc. III B (CMP, pp. 86 ff.), 1300–1230 B.C.

Mycenaean and "Minyan" Wares from the
Tell, K. 16: 1031 (L. III, Pl. 115)

Types, Pl. 83:
949–951

The same open region which produced Lachish Bowl 3 and the fragments Nos. 4 and 5 with inscriptions in hieratic characters of the xixth or xxth dynasty (p. 132) also contributed sherds of two large and distinctive vessels.

Type 949. Enough remained to reconstruct the form of the neck and body, about 50 cms. wide, and the principal zone of decoration which consisted of a cuttlefish (Furumark, Motive 21) or octopus, whose tentacles fill most of the field. Made of light buff ware with a grey core containing many grits, the surface is covered with a thick and somewhat glossy buff slip. The design, the thick bands on rim, neck and belly, which recur near the base, are rather roughly applied in reddish-brown lustrous paint which has fired almost black in parts.

Among the sherds of "Mycenaean type" from Tell Beit Mirsim, Stratum C, Albright singles out one as different from the rest in not having lustrous (burnished) paint. The design is probably part of the loop of an octopus (AASOR XII, Pl. 15: 16 and §§ 60, 61).

213

POTTERY

Parallels for the shape do not appear in Furumark's study. Both the ware and the particular form of the cuttlefish motif place the pot outside the range of true Mycenaean wares, despite the obvious Mycenaean derivation of the ornament. A krater from Ras Shamra has the same general form (*Ugaritica I*, Fig. 96A), but a much closer parallel comes from Kokkinokremmos near Larnaca in Cyprus, dated to LC III (BSAA, *Annual Report*, 1951–1952, p. 48, Fig. 2). This painted amphora of exceptional size (diam. 73 cms.) is "presumably of local manufacture". Another very large piriform krater with stylised octopus ornament was among surface finds from the same settlement collected by Mr. Hector Catling in the following year (BSAA, *Annual Report*, 1952–1953, p. 57).[1]

Isolated sherds of a number of different vessels, all either kraters or bowls, were recovered from the same horizon. For the most part, the buff surface is matt and the brownish-red bands of paint are lustrous. Prominent in the collection are nearly a dozen sherds of a chariot vase of the Levanto-Mycenaean pictorial style. The principal decorative motifs are illustrated on Pl. 83.

Type 951. For the chariot wheel, see Furumark, Motive 39 (MP, Fig. 56). The drawing of the Duweir example suggests a date in Myc. III A.

Sherds from 'Ain Shems, Stratum IV B, were noted by Grant and Wright as being unusual for Palestine (AS V, pp. 49, 119–121 and AS IV, Pls. XXXIV: 4, XLIX: 1–2). The description of the ware resembles that of our fragments and the same can be said for the comparisons from Tell el-Ajjul, noted by Dr. Ben-Dor (AS V, p. 50 and AG IV, Pl. XLVI: 34–35). Other chariot vase fragments came from Tell Abu Hawam (QDAP IV, pp. 1–69, Pl. XX and MPL, p. 79 and Fig. 29) and Gezer (*Gezer III*, Pl. CLI: 3, 5, 8, 23 and MPL, p. 84, Fig. 30).

A magnificent hydria from Ras Shamra (*Ugaritica II*, Figs 89–90) decorated with a chariot scene in which the vehicle has a similar wheel to the Duweir sherd is attributed by Schaeffer to the period which ends in 1365 B.C., though he notes that an analogous fragment came from the following phase ending in 1200 B.C. (op. cit., Fig. 62: 24).

At Minet el-Beida and Ras Shamra, Schaeffer notes that fragments of a grey burnished pottery (very like the Minyan ware of Middle Helladic) were often found in association with Mycenaean pottery of the type dated by him between 1365 and 1200 B.C., and he illustrates a fine krater with bands of combed decoration (*Ugaritica II*, Fig. 60: 11, *Stratigraphie*, pp. 182 and 256). This ware, which is closely similar to the "Minyan" of Troy VI (*Troy III*, pp. 35 ff.), occurred with Late Helladic III fragments at Tell Abu Hawam (QDAP IV, Pl. XXII).

The same association is to be seen at Duweir on the surface of the Bronze Age city, with about a score of plain sherds fired to an even grey all through and containing few if any grits. The surface is horizontally wheel burnished, but it is difficult to tell how much the burning, which affected both Mycenaean and "Minyan" sherds in the region, has altered the character of the surface, when some pieces are reduced almost to slag. Four rim sections, each of a different pot, and a few pieces of wavy-combed decoration complete the tally of this ware (cf. L. II, Pl. LXIII: 8).

Imitation Pyxides

Types, Pl. 82
914, 915 (Pl. 53: 26), 916–922, 923 (Pl. 55: 7), 924–926, 927 (Pl. 55: 42), 928 (Pl. 55: 41), 929 (Pl. 55: 49), 930; *L. II*: 344, 345

Type 947, the only complete import among the pyxoid forms, was discussed above on p. 213. It had the concave sides and convex base with handles set low which are more typical of "Levanto-Helladic" shapes. It will be seen that the pyxoid jars in local ware illustrated on Pl. 82 are either cylindrical with flat bottoms or

[1] Similar kraters are numerous in the Heracleion Museum, Crete. Mr. V. Karageorghis, to whom I am indebted for the comparison, describes the ware as coarse and gritty and states that the shape never occurs in Mycenaean fabrics. In his opinion, therefore, Type 949 and its parallels from Cyprus derive from Crete, and date from Late Minoan III. Type 949 provides the first example of this period recovered from Syria–Palestine.

distinctly splayed with quite deep round bases, more reminiscent of alabastron shapes. The necks are often splayed, and all but Types 918–919 have two opposite horizontal handles, which are, in Furumark's opinion,

Types, Pls. 82, 84–85

Locus	Spouted Vessels	Pilgrim Flasks	Mugs	Miniature Pithoi	Kraters
503	—	—	963	—	—
508	—	—	969	—	—
523	—	958	—	977, 983, 984	—
556	—	953	—	—	—
557	—	—	966	—	—
6001	—	—	963	—	—
6007	—	957	—	—	991
7017	—	—	—	984	—
559	—	—	962	—	—
532	—	955	963	—	—
561	—	957	967	—	—
570	—	958	967	985	—
571	—	—	—	984	990(2), 992
4013	—	954	961, 962	976, 981, 982, L. III: 425	989
4003	—	L. II: 349	—	—	—
4034	—	956; L. II: 349	—	—	—
S. III	—	L. II: 349, 351	—	L. II: 342, 343	—
527	—	—	963	—	—
536	—	L. II: 349	—	—	—
541	—	958	961	—	L II: 248
542	—	954	—	—	—
543	—	—	968	—	—
547	—	954	962	977, 983	986
1006	939	—	—	—	—
4019	934	—	—	—	—
1003	938	—	960	974, 975, 980	—
548	—	958	—	—	—
555	932, 933, 936	952	—	978	—
564	—	—	—	981	—
501	—	—	961	—	—
216	937	—	959, 964, 965	979	987, 988
S. II	—	—	—	—	—
S. I	—	—	—	L. II: 244	—
4004	935	—	—	977, 984	—
1548	—	—	—	972	—
129	—	—	—	970	—
4022	—	—	—	971	—
153	—	—	—	973	—
1504	931	—	—	—	—
Total	9	18	19	27	9

signs of a specifically Helladic character (Furumark, MP, pp. 42, 83, 89). Apart from Type 918 from Tomb 4013, which reproduces hatched decoration on the shoulder and a spiral on the base, the decoration is of two kinds: horizontal bands in red and black on the splayed forms, and vertical lines with zigzags between on those shapes which tend to be cylindrical. The ware is brown with a few grits, medium fired, and there is horizontal hand burnish from neck to keel on most of the decorated examples.

215

No pyxoid jars were found in Structures I and II, but there were two incomplete examples from Structure III. The only considerable group of pyxoid forms came from Tomb 4013, the use of which extends into the reign of Rameses II.

At Tell Fara, pyxoid jars occur in the first four Fosse Tombs 920, 905, 902 and 914 (CPP Types 55 S^4, 55 S^5 and 55 M^6), with one later occurrence in Tomb 935 (BP II, Pl. LX).

Pyxides in local ware are also to be found among the latest elements in the top layer of Tombs 4 and 13 at Jericho (AAA XX, Pl. XXXII).

924	Megiddo (M. II, Pl. 64: 6)	Strata VII B–VI
L. II: 344	Tell Beit Mirsim (AASOR XII, Pl. 44: 3)	Stratum C

Imitation Piriform Jars	N.-E. Section, p. 53	Types, Pl. 82:
	Level VI: 20	940–942, 943 (Pl. 55: 8),
		944 (Pl. 55: 53)

The shape of the imported piriform jars, Types 945 and 946, is reproduced rather closely in Type 942 from Tomb 1006, which may well be the earliest of the series, since Tombs 555 and 501 have a long range of use. Type 941 attempts to reproduce the characteristic surface by application of a cream slip, and each imitation shows some effort at decoration.

The top layer of Tomb 13 at Jericho produced piriform jars described as among the latest elements in the tomb, which appear analogous to the Duweir examples; the same layer contributed an imitation pyxis (AAA XX, Pl. XXXII).

943 Jericho (AAA XX, Pl. IV: 2) Tomb 13a. 19

SPOUTED VESSELS

Types, Pl. 82:
931–936, 937 (Pl. 53: 17), 938,
939 (Pl. 51: 56)

The inspiration for some small spouted vessels is perhaps derived from the similar form of White Painted V (Type 825) or from an EB prototype, such as Pl. 58: 109 (p. 170).

The undecorated shapes have wide mouths on a bulgy body, rounded at the base. A tubular spout is inserted in the side and opposite there is a loop handle. Except for Type 935 from Tomb 4004, where the handle is horizontally attached just below the rim, all are vertically applied, though the handle is never poked through. Like the White Painted V imports, the base of Type 937 is scraped. The ware is buff or brown with some grits, fairly well fired.

Of four decorated shapes, two have a ring base, and it is likely that Types 931 and 933 were similarly supplied, though that feature is now missing. The ware tends to be pink rather than buff or brown, with an unburnished cream slip or surface. The only exception is Type 932 which was smoothly polished before the application of red paint. The designs consist of simple bands and zigzags.

The range at Tell ed-Duweir of both plain and decorated forms is confined to LB I and the first half-century of LB II. The shape is uncommon and only fragments were found in the pottery of the Fosse Temple. They are no doubt the latest versions of a type which goes back to Stratum XI at Megiddo.

934	Megiddo (M. II, Pl. 34: 5)	Stratum XI
	Megiddo (MT, Pl. 40: 16) Tomb 38	LB I
936	Megiddo (M. II, Pl. 59: 9)	Strata X–VIII

PILGRIM FLASKS

Compare L. II: 349–351   N.-E. Section, p. 53.   Types, Pl. 84:
                                  Level VI: 21, 22   952–954, 955 (Pl. 55: 52), 956 (Pl. 49: 11), 957, 958; *L. II*: 349

Three pilgrim flasks from the Fosse Temple were associated with Structure III. It is clear that the form was just coming into fashion towards the end of the fourteenth century and that the best decorated examples are contemporary with the rise of flared bowls after 1300 B.C.

The later history of pilgrim flasks is traced in Lachish III (Pl. 92 and pp. 307 ff.), and among those forms Type 430 from Pit 102 (not 120 as stated in the description) should perhaps be with the earlier Bronze Age series.

The smaller flasks are made of brown or buff ware with a buff or cream-slipped surface.

Type 952 is distinguished by the use of a pink wash on a reddish body, and it may belong to the final burials in Pit 555.

Type 953 from Tomb 556 equates both in the burnished ware and the unusual decoration of black circles outlined in red with a flask from Structure III (L. II: 351), and both are possibly imported. Similar in shape is a pilgrim flask from Megiddo, Stratum VII B, though it is only decorated in red.

Type 956 from the potter's workshop is especially significant, for it compares with an almost complete vessel from Level VI of the Section. The underlying buff ware of both pieces is covered with a thick cream slip, and both are elaborately decorated. Albright has noted that lentoid flasks with this painted decoration are not common (AASOR XII, § 85), and though the pieces from Stratum B at Tell Beit Mirsim are comparable in design to Type 956, they lack the thick cream slip, like the fine flask from Stratum VII A at Megiddo.

Types 957, 958 and L. II: 349 are of normal pink clay under a brownish burnished slip; though the decoration is crude, these examples appear to be contemporary with Type 956.

With the exception of Type 953, it will be seen that the handles of all flasks spring archwise from the point of attachment to the neck, a feature which Albright considers is characteristic of these flasks in Stratum C at Tell Beit Mirsim (AASOR XII, § 57).

952	Megiddo (M. II, Pl. 74: 14)	Strata VII–VI
	Tell el-Ajjul (AG III, Pl. XI: 65) Governor's Tomb	xviiith–xixth dynasties
953	Qrayé (BMB III, Pl. IX: b)	xviiith dynasty
954	Tell Abu Hawam (QDAP IV, p. 42: 255)	Stratum V
955	Tell Yehudiyeh (*Mound of the Jew*, Pl. XV: 13 and p. 46)	xxth dynasty
958	Tell Beit Mirsim (AASOR XII, Pl. 14: 2)	Stratum C
L. II: 351	Megiddo (M. II, Pl. 67: 1)	Stratum VII B

MUGS

Types, Pl. 84:
959 (Pl. 53: 28), 960–963, 964 (Pl. 53: 71), 965 (Pl. 53: 20), 966–968, 969 (Pl. 55: 6)

The decorated mugs, Types 959–963, usually made of a brownish ware, are treated with a cream or buff slip, burnished at least as far as the carination. The large mug, Type 963, exhibits opposed triangles of red and black with intervening metopes of crossed diagonals. Compare in this respect the decoration on the krater from the burning of Level VI (p. 53) and a large mug from Stratum VII B at Megiddo. Small versions of the same theme are Types 959–960, while Types 961 and 962 are more crudely made and decorated.

The plainer mugs, Types 964–966, of brownish-buff ware, are covered with a pink or red slip and show traces of burnish. Type 964, which is excellently finished, is a clear reflection of a Base-Ring tankard, Pl. 80: 850–853. Tomb 216 also provided Type 965. Types 967–969 without slip or decoration are much less elegant.

POTTERY

Both plain and decorated mugs are rare in the Fosse Temple, but compare the sherd from that area, L. II, Pl. LXIV: 6. Neither are they common at other sites. The range for these mugs should be chiefly in the thirteenth century, though Types 964, 965 and the decorated mugs Types 959–961 come from groups which are in the main earlier.

963 Megiddo (M. II, Pl. 63: 3) 2131
  Tell Fara (BP II, Pl. LXXXIV: 37 J¹) Tomb 978
964 Jericho (AAA XX, Pl. XXI: 3) Tomb 5d.20

Strata VII B–VII A
xix–xxth dynasties
1500–1450 B.C.

MINIATURE PITHOI

Compare
L. II, Pl. LIV: 334, 342–3

N.-E. Section, p. 53
Level VI: 13

Types, Pl. 85:
970, 971 (Pl. 51: 29 and Fig. 15: 5), 972–978, 979 (Pl. 53: 24), 980–985; *L. III*: 425

Single examples of small pithoi in various stages of development are scattered throughout the tombs at Duweir. They are not found in sufficient quantity to establish a good chronological series.

Types 970–973 are made of wares ranging from brick-red to pink or buff. Types 970 and 972 are finished with buff or cream slip vertically burnished. Three out of four examples have a small flattened base, like the contemporary storage jars (Class B) and all have round mouths and vertical loop handles on the shoulder. A date in late MB II or early III may be suggested for Types 970–973, while an incomplete and unburnished form from Structure I was compared to an amphora from Palace Store-room 44 at Jericho (L. II, Pl. LIV: 334 and AAA XXI, Pl. XXIII: 13).

Type 974 and 975 both come from Tomb 1003. They are about half the height of Types 970–973; the bodies are rotund, bearing rough decoration in red, and the necks are ridged. Both are made of coarse brown ware finished with a buff slip.

It is worth considering the relationship between these vessels and similar forms from Beisan (see AAA XX, Pl. X: 7–8) with, on the one hand, the flat-based painted vessels of Tomb 5, layers a–e, at Jericho (AAA XX, Pls. XXII, XXV), an example of which was also recovered from the "Streak" (AAA XXI, Pl. XXIV: 6, Pl. XXVII: 15 and p. 107) and, on the other hand, with the flat-based undecorated forms of Structure III (L. II: 342–343).

The absence from Duweir of the variety, which was characteristic of Tomb 5 at Jericho, may suggest that its zenith of popularity fell after the destruction of City Level VI, no earlier than the reign of Amenhetep II. In this connexion, compare Professor Garstang's estimate for the range of the type in question at Jericho from about 1575 to 1425 B.C. (AAA XXI, p. 107). Types 974 and 975 could in that case fall into place quite reasonably at the end of the series dating from about 1400 B.C., before the reoccupation of Structure III.

The priority of decorated over undecorated forms is also demonstrated by Type 976 from Tomb 4013, a group which contained a scarab of Rameses II of the xixth dynasty.

Type 977 should no doubt belong to the latest use of Tomb 4004, for it equates with the lower part of a flask from Level VI (NE 33/13 on p. 53). Both are decorated with lines and zigzags in dark-red paint on a thick cream slip and both have stump bases. There are good parallels both for decoration and shape from the Ramesside Tombs at Tell Fara, where small jugs, CPP Type 59 T (Duweir Type 725) are also similar in ware and surface treatment.

A flask like Type 977 occurs in the xxth dynasty tumuli graves at Tell Yehudiyeh (*Mound of the Jew*, Pl. XV: 12 and p. 46). With it were long-necked pithoi of the same general shape as Types 984–985.

Grant and Wright note the presence of a similar jar in Tomb 11 at Bethshemesh (AS V, p. 45, note 19, and BS, p. 173, second register, third jar from left), and they compare it with one from the Tomb of Tutankhamen (CTT III, Pl. L: A and B). They remark on the non-Palestinian nature of the high neck and mention two more examples from Tomb 552 at Tell Fara (CPP Types 44 R¹ and R² and BP II, Pl. XXIV). The long neck of a vessel covered with white-wash outside and decorated in red came from Stratum VII A at Megiddo (M. II, Pl. 67: 19).

In the Fosse Tombs at Tell Fara part of a large vessel not unlike Type 984 (BP II, Pl. LXXXVII: 55 W¹) from Tomb 934 also has a knob base, though the forms quoted above from Tomb 552 at the same site, which was in use during the Philistine domination, are smaller and have round bases.

971	Jericho (AAA XX, Pl. X: 5) Tomb 4b.23	
	Megiddo (M. II, Pl. 42: 5)	Stratum X
975	Beisan (AAA XX, Pl. X: 7–8)	Thothmes III
977	Sedment (*Sedment* II, Pl. LIX: 2) Tomb 33	xixth dynasty

KRATERS

Compare	N.-E. Section, pp. 53–55	Types, Pl. 85:
L. II, Pls. XLVIII, XLIX	Level VI: 2, 5, 8 (?), 14, 15, 32, 33, 34, 43	986, 987 (Pl. 53: 25), 988 (Pl. 53:
	Level VII: 58, 59, 60, 73, 76	18), 989–992
	Level VIII: 112, 113	

The evolution of decorated kraters can be traced back in a general way to the bichrome forms of LB I (cf. L. II: 256 and such local versions and imitations as L. II: 253–255). During the use of Structures II–III these large-keeled or biconical vessels exhibit considerable latitude in detail and design which makes comparison difficult.

The splayed and inturned rim, which is a feature of kraters and large bowls with handles, is very common in Levels VII–VI, though it is not always possible to decide whether the pieces come from bowls or kraters. Among those which may belong to large bowls are Nos. 14, 15 (cf. L. II: 149) and 32 (L. II: 70).

Among the incomplete forms from the Fosse Temple, it is often uncertain whether or not they were provided with handles, but Type 986 had one handle at least, and the small forms, Types 987–989, were certainly handleless. Types 987 and 988 are decorated in black and red.

Types 990 and 991 from Tomb 571 are both well painted, though it is unusual to find decoration on an unburnished surface. The single lotus flower on both examples of Type 990 is a motif which occurs in an xviiith dynasty context at Tell Yehudiyeh (HIC, Pl. XV). The corrugated neck of Type 992 can be matched in L. II, Types 241–2 and 247 from Structures II–III.

MISCELLANEOUS

Plate 86	*Locus*	
993 (Pl. 51: 15)	119	Pointed dipper with wide round mouth
994 (Pl. 51: 14)	119	Handleless flask
995	1504	Dipper with trefoil lip. Cf. Ras Shamra (*Ugaritica II*, Fig. 106: 12). See pp. 192 f.
996 (Pl. 53: 19)	216	Decorated flask with two handles
997	1003	Miniature lamp. *Other exs.* 4004(2)
998	559	Spoon-mouth flask with lug handles. Cf. Megiddo (M. II, Pl. 74: 16) Strata VI B–VI A; Beisan (B–S II, Pt. II, Pl. XLVII: 28) "Rameses II" level
999	523	Decorated strainer vase with basket handle. Cf. Megiddo (M. II, Pl. 63: 8) Stratum VII B
1000	561	Small krater. *Other ex.* 4013.
1001	4010	Decorated flask with two handles
1002	4034	Miniature jar with lug handles
1003 (Pl. 49: 7)	4034	Jar
1004	7008	Drainpipe with two loop handles. Cf. Megiddo (M. II, Pl. 256: 3) Stratum VII B
1005 (Pl. 48: 5, 7–9)	7013	Anthropomorphic jar, p. 89.

POTTERY
STORAGE JARS

Types, Pl. 87

Locus	A	B	C	D	E	Total
6001	—	—	—	1021	—	1
532	—	—	—	1020, 1021	—	2
539	—	—	—	—	1025	1
570	—	—	—	1018	—	1
571	—	—	—	1018	—	1
4011	—	—	—	—	1025	1
S. III	—	—	—	L. II: 389	—	1
1003	—	—	—	—	1023, 1024	2
501	—	—	—	1019	—	1
564	—	—	1017	—	—	1
216	—	1011	—	1018(4)	1022(2), 1023	8
S. II	—	—	—	L. II: 389	L. II: 393	2
S. I	—	L. II: 386(2), 387, 392	L. II: 390, 391	L. II: 389	—	7
1005	—	—	1015	—	—	1
7011	—	1008	—	—	—	1
4004	—	—	—	—	—	—
6002	1006(3)	1010(3)	1014(2)	—	—	8
1539	—	—	1016(2)	—	—	2
1546	—	1011	—	—	—	1
1548	1006	1010, 1011(2)	—	—	—	4
1542	—	1010	—	—	—	1
7003	—	1009	1013	—	—	2
7014	—	1008	—	—	—	1
129	1007	1010(2), 1012	—	—	—	4
115	—	1011	—	—	—	1
1552	—	1011	—	—	—	1
1502	1007	1010	—	—	—	2
119	1006(3), 1007	1010(3), 1011(2)	—	—	—	9
1505	—	1011(2), 1012	—	—	—	3
153	—	1008, 1010, 1011	—	—	.	3
187	—	1011	—	—	—	1
Total	10	34	9	13	8	74

The cleavage between the shape of storage jars of the last phases of the Early Bronze Age and these of comparable size in the following period is almost complete. That it should affect such large vessels, which could not be easily moved and which must have been made locally, suggests a gap in ceramic tradition which is indeed apparent at Duweir in the relative poverty of the corresponding layers NE 11–14 in the Section (p. 57).

That a rounded base, which now appears so impracticable, should replace the flat-based jar, suggests a change in function, which may mark the arrival of a wine-drinking instead of a beer-drinking community.

An ovoid body with a round or slightly flattened base, topped by a tall neck and a moulded rim, was already established as the standard shape when the earliest MB tombs were occupied at Duweir. The few jars without handles retain something of an earlier tradition in fine wheelmarks on the surface and they are much larger than the average MB storage jar.

The addition of one or two handles, and their position on the jar, together with small changes in the rim, give some means of classification in a form which preserved its main features for many centuries. By the middle of the fifteenth century, the slightly flattened base gave place to a pointed convex end which persisted to at least 1200 B.C.

Storage Jars in MB Glacis Fill (pp. 45, 55, 57)

Fragments of storage jars, covered in white lime-wash and decorated with blue, black and red bands and/or wavy lines, were found in the upper part of the glacis fill (NE 22/125, 21/133, 20/143, 19/161). No jars similarly decorated were found in the tombs.

Pieces of the same distinctive pottery were mostly ascribed to Strata G–F at Tell Beit Mirsim (AASOR XIII, § 18, Pl. 4: 13, 15–16; Pl. 22: 1–6, 8–10). Part of a stand originally ascribed to Stratum D (AASOR XII, Pl. 44: 14 and § 42) was allocated in the final publication to Strata G–F (AASOR XVII, p. 24). It can best be compared to the group of stands from Megiddo (M. II, Pl. 47: 10, 11, 13, 16) all of which came from an open area attributed to Stratum X, though the true horizon of the group could well be earlier. See the only other examples from Megiddo (M. II, Pl. 28: 1 in Stratum XII; Pl. 34: 17, Stratum XI and Pl. 43: 2, Stratum X).

Storage Jars, Class A	Types, Pl. 87:
	1006 (Pl. 50: 34), 1007

The storage jars without handles are between 70–80 cms. in height. They alone compare with those of the Early Bronze Age in size and they are among the finest products of the wheel. In Tomb 6002 three examples of Type 1006 occurred with jars of Classes B and C, so they all appear to have been in contemporary use, though typologically the jars of Class A are clearly earlier. It is doubtful if they were still being made at the end of the MB period.

For Albright's discussion on comparisons for these jars found in Stratum D at Tell Beit Mirsim see AASOR XII, § 29. They are in any case rarely published owing to their size and the difficulties of reconstruction.

At Jericho the Palace Store-rooms contain incomplete jars some of which may have been of this class and many of them were over a metre in height (AAA XXI, Pl. XVI).

1006	Tell Fara (BP I, Pl. XV: 43 A²) Tomb 550	MB II
1007	Tell Fara (BP I, Pl. XV: 43 A³) Tomb 550	MB II

Storage Jars, Class B	N.-E. Section, p. 55	Types, Pl. 87:
Compare	MB Fill: 147, 166, 167, 181	1008, 1009, 1010 (Pl. 50: 35), 1011
L. II, Pl. LVII: 386–388		(Pl. 50: 33), 1012

There is little to justify a division between Classes B and C, ranging from about 1750–1450 BC, except for the tall necks of Types 1008 and 1009 and the everted rim moulding. Types 1010 and 1011 have the same rim profile on a shorter neck attached to an elongated body. Nearly all the jars in Classes B–C have a small flat base.

The sherds of such jars from the Fosse Temple come from the spread of rubbish in or below the foundation level of Structure I.

1010–11	Jericho (AAA XIX, Pl. XXXIII: 4) Tomb 9a.11	
	Jericho (AAA XXI, Pl. XVIII: 22) Palace Store-room, "Kiln 1"	City B, MB II
	Tell Fara (BP I, Pl. XV: 43 E⁴) Tomb 550	MB II

Storage Jars, Class C	N.-E. Section, pp. 53–55	Types, Pl. 87:
Compare	Level VII: 57, 95	1013–1017
L. II, Pl. LVII: 390, 391	MB Fill: 117, 207, 223	

Jars of Class C survive from an earlier tradition. Type 1016 retains a rim ridge hardly visible on that drawing but which is clearer on the drawings of sherds from the glacis fill.

It was rims of this kind which Albright considered typical of Strata G–F at Tell Beit Mirsim (AASOR XII, Pl. 5: 24, Stratum H; XIII, Pl. 22: 20–22, Stratum G and § 18; XVII, § 33), but Ben-Dor found them throughout the occupation of the MB temple at Nahariya (QDAP XIV, p. 28).

The comparative scarcity of Class C jars in relation to Class B in the tombs and their absence from the large

CLASSES

LOCUS	A	B	C	D	E	F	G	H	J
TOMB 559			1 1	5 (1)	1 1	6	1	20	6
TOMB 532		(3)	2 (2)	3 (1)	2	4	3	21	26
TOMB 570		(1) (3)	1		(1)	1	1 1	2	2
TOMB 571		1 (3)	2 (1)		1	1		3	1
TOMB 4013		(4)	1 (1)	(4)	3 3 2	9	11 3	40	6
TOMB 4011		(3)	1	1	1 1	5	1	15	2
CAVE 4034		2	2					4	16
STRUCTURE III		7 2 (1)	11 (4)	(1)	8 24	14 12	30 7	373	147
TOMB 1003	(1)	5	1 6	2 4	7 11		6	15	14
TOMB 501	(2)	2	1 (4)	3 (1)	4 7		3	8	7
TOMB 216	2	5 (1)	1 2 3 (7)	2 4 (3)	5 17 2		7 1	42	15
STRUCTURE II	11 (14)	(2) (1)	7 4 (3)	1 15 (4)	13 34	3	26	(65)	76

STRUCTURE I

TOMB 4004

GROUP 1555

TOMB 129

TOMB 1552

TOMB 1502

TOMB 119

PIT 4022

BILOBATE TOMB 153

GRAVE 157

GRAVE 173

GRAVE 145

KEY {
BOWLS
LAMPS
JUGS
JUGLETS
DIPPERS
}

groups may be accounted for by the fact that they were on the wane at the period when the Duweir tombs were most in use. Compare also L. II: 390, 391, of which shards came from the spread of rubbish in and below the foundation level of Structure I.

1013	Tell Fara (BP I, Pl. XV: 43 E⁵) Tombs 551, 569	MB II
	Megiddo (M. II, Pl. 52: 1)	Strata X–IX
1014	Tell Fara (BP I, Pl. XV: 43 D⁴) Tomb 550	MB II
1015	Jericho (AAA XXI, Pl. XVII: 20) J. 31, City Burials 3	
1017	Megiddo (M. II, Pl. 21: 1)	Strata XIII–XII

Storage Jars, Class D	N.-E. Section, p. 53	Types, Pl. 87:
Compare	Level VI: 23, 45	1018 (Pl. 52: 48), 1019, 1020, 1021
L. II, Pl. LVII: 389	Level VII: 52, 70, 71, 89	

A heavy rim moulding to a straighter collar neck is typical of Class D, where the bodies are long and waspish, ending in a convex point. Type 1018 is equivalent to L. II: 389, which is represented in each of the three buildings of the Fosse Temple. In the Section fragments of the same type occur in Level VII, while in Level VI the rim becomes the common shape with stump bases to match.

Types 1019, 1020 and 1021 are coarsely and clumsily made. While Type 1019 came from Tomb 501, which came to an end later than Structure II, the last two jar types are confined to Tomb 532 and there are also comparable sherds from the LB house 6001, p. 294.

The deposit of eighty jars at Minet el-Beida are of Type 1019 and the form is also found at Qrayé in Syria made in light-coloured but heavy clay, with White Slip and Shaved wares. Furumark has noted that this form of storage jar is not Mycenaean, though examples with Minoan characters incised on the handles before firing have been found on the Greek mainland. He suggests Syria or Southern Anatolian rather than Egypt as the place of origin of pithos Type 13a (Furumark, MP, pp. 75–76).

1018	'Ain Shems (AS IV, Pl. LXIX: 1; V, p. 116)	Stratum IVa
1019	Minet el-Beida (*Ugaritica II*, Fig. 86: 7)	1450–1365 B.C.
	Megiddo (M. II, Pl. 59: 12)	Strata VIII–VII B
	Qrayé (BMB III, Pl. XI: g)	
1020	Tell Fara (BP II, Pl. LXXXVI: 43 P⁶) Tomb 905	xixth–xxth dynasties
1021	Tell Fara (BP II, Pl. LXXXVI: 43 H²) Tomb 949	xixth–xxth dynasties

Storage Jars, Class E	N.-E. Section, pp. 53–55	Types, Pl. 87:
Compare	Level VI: 3, 11	1022 (Pl. 52: 46), 1023 (Pl. 52: 42),
L. II, Pl. LVII: 393	Level VII: 53, 72	1024, 1025
	Pit A: 91	
	Level VIII: 109	

Jars with stepped rim moulding are not found in the MB tombs at Duweir, though they are considered by Albright as "very characteristic of E–D as well as C" (AASOR XII, § 28, where numerous references to sherds are given. For E examples see AASOR XIII, § 28).

Examples in the Section begin in Level VIII and are associated with the destruction of Level VII. In Pit A there is a neck sherd with red and black decoration, No. 91. The same rim with red and black or red and white lines on the body and diagonal red crosses on the handles is characteristic of Stratum C at Tell Beit Mirsim and persists into Stratum B, though the sherds in each case cannot be assigned to a particular phase (AASOR XII, Pl. 19: 1–3; Pl. 24: 35–36; XIII, Pl. 27: 14–16, 23–30).

Types 1002–1024 come from Tombs 216, 1003, and have decorated handles, though this detail is lacking in Type 1025 from Tomb 4011, which may date to the end of the xviiith dynasty. Even more elaborate in profile and decoration is the upper part of a jar from the burning of Level VI which should date to the Ramesside period.

1024	'Ain Shems (BS, p. 153: 805 and AS V, p. 44, note 18) T.11	xixth–xxth dynasties

PART IV
CEMETERIES

CHAPTER 11
AREAS 100, 200, 500, 1000
AREAS 100, 200

(*Lachish III*, Pls. 1: 1; 108; Plan on Pl. 125)

A GENERAL account of these crowded cemeteries was given in *Lachish III*, p. 178. Placed as they were on the lower slopes of the mound, the tombs were often re-used, and few among them were undisturbed. Significant MB II–III groups in the vicinity are those near bed-rock on the scarp which formed the basis of the mound, e.g. Graves 173, 145 and 157 (Plan on Pl. 90).

About the same time, or a little earlier, the row of Tombs 129, 115, 153 and 119 was begun and they appear to be spaced at fairly regular intervals at an equal distance from the mound. The ground between seems to have been clear, either for a roadway or for earthworks in connexion with the fosse.

The greater number of tombs were farther away and lower down the slope and many of them were disturbed or re-used by Iron Age people. On the whole, it was fortunate to find almost as many tombs with predominantly Late Bronze Age deposits.

101 Collapsed cavern in Grid Square D.5 (L. III, Pl. 3: 1)

A general description is given in L. III, pp. 178–179. The extensive use of the cavern as a quarry in Roman times was not confined to the roof and walls, for the even strokes of the late stone-cutters were also clear in the lower levels. The deposits are therefore disturbed and untrustworthy. Late Bronze Age sherds were common in the small area of floor which was exposed, and no earlier sherds were recorded. Though the apparent absence of Middle Bronze Age sherds in so restricted an area is inconclusive, the position of the cavern, intersecting the presumed line of the MB fosse where it should have turned the north-west corner of the mound, suggests one of two things: either the cavern was part of the essential drainage system which filled with rubbish soon after the fosse was abandoned as a defence, or it was constructed in the scarp, which presented an easily accessible source of good stone. If the second alternative is acceptable, it would clearly be a grave weakness in the defence if a large cave existed under the vulnerable north-west corner, unless it were originally an enemy mine.

See also notes on the Fosse, p. 46.

107 Tomb in Grid Square A.6, re-used as an ossuary adjoining and above Tomb 120 — MB bilobate chamber / Burials *c.* 900 B.C. (?) / Bone deposits 700–600 B.C.

No contents of Bronze Age. See L. III, pp. 187–188. For shape cf. Tomb 153, where the entrance shaft is on the north side.

108 Tomb in Grid Square A.6, re-used as an ossuary, adjoining and interconnected with Tombs 107 and 120 — MB bilobate chamber. / LB deposits. / Bone deposits 700–600 B.C.

The roof had partly collapsed. The two halves of the pit were divided by a stepped pilaster of original rock left uncut in the middle of the east wall (L. III, Pl. 4: 1). This two-lobed or "kidney" shape first appears at the end of the Caliciform Culture, see Tomb 2100/2101 on Pl. 93. Tomb 107 is one of several of this shape which were re-used in later times (L. III, p. 171). The original entry no longer exists.

It would appear that the thick lime plastersurface on the walls was applied in the Late Bronze Age, and numerous fragments of alabaster and stone vases were of the same period (see L. III, Pl. 4: 2). They indicate a rich burial which was cleared away to make room for the bone deposits of the Iron Age (L. III, p. 188).

Objects: Calcite vase fragments: Pl. 27: 1, see p. 86.

111 Pit in Grid Square B.8   MB III, *c.* 1675–1625 B.C.

Rubbish pit containing three vessels and the base of a storage jar.

Pottery: Bowls: carinate A 507   Jug: B 677   Juglet: F 771

115 Tomb in Grid Square B.9   Oblong chamber Shaft entry MB III, *c.* 1700 B.C.

The entrance from the western shaft to the chamber was blocked with two large vertically placed slabs, while a third one on the left side of the door had been replaced by small stones to close the gap through which robbers had removed the contents in patriarchal times. Some broken jars, ostrich-shell fragments and a bronze togglepin remained under the hard mud which filled the tomb.

Pottery: Bowls: carinate A 501; B 531; E 561
         Jugs: A 671; B 676 (2), 677; E 717
         Juglet: C 748   Storage Jar: B 1011

Objects: Metal: Togglepin: Pl. 24: 9
         Ostrich shell fragments. NP

The contents should fall within the range of Tomb 129, just before or contemporary with the *terre pisée* defences. The togglepin, Type 3, finds comparisons in Grave 145 and Tomb 129 (p. 81).

119 Tomb in Grid Square B.7 (see Chart on pp. 60–61)   Oval chamber Shaft entry MB III, *c.* 1700–1600 B.C.

Though the entrance shaft on the north was still blocked with stones, it was found necessary to remove all the roof before the chamber could be safely cleared. It was nearly filled with mud, and no bodies were recorded. Storage jars and smaller vessels formed part of a group which had been disturbed by the action of water (Pl. 5: 7). Toolmarks of those who cut the tomb are well preserved near the entrance (Pl. 5: 6).

Pottery   *Photographs on Pls. 50–51

Bowls: carinate A 500,* 501,* 512,* 513,* 514,* 515;* B 526,* 527,* 531
       plain G 584*(2), 585*
Lamps: A 643(2), 644*   Jugs: B 674;* D 695
Juglets: E 752, 763*   Dippers: A 781*(6)
Miscellaneous: 993,* 994*
Storage Jars: A 1006*(3), 1007; B 1010*(3), 1011*(2)

Objects

Metal: Daggers: Pl. 22:17, 18*   Togglepins: Pl. 24: 6–8*
Bone: Inlay Pl. 28: 2, 3
Bead: Pl. 29: 6 (1 cn.)
Scarabs: Pl. 30: 27–32

Date and Comparisons

The bowls are mostly flared carinate Class A, and piriform juglets are missing, and there are two examples of cylindrical juglets, Class E, with well-rounded bases. There are comparisons with sherds within the glacis fill (NE 17/184, 22/119, p. 55).

The daggers, Types 27 and 27a, are the normal forms in the series, and the two togglepins (Type 8a) are matched in Tomb 1542, and in Tomb 565 (BF I, Pl. IX: 63) at Tell Fara, and that type occurs in the lowest level of Tomb 5 at Jericho, where goblets are most common.

Tomb 119 seems to overlap with Tomb 129, which was closed a few decades earlier.

121 Tomb in Grid Square B.8   Round chamber. Shaft entry
                                                       MB III and later

Another tomb west of Tomb 119 may have been constructed in the same period. Three broken pots and part of a bronze togglepin with some bone inlay were found, but the tomb had been enlarged and used as a dwelling in later times and stairs leading to it had been cut in the rock.

Pottery: Bowl: curved H 605 Dipper: C L III: 282

Objects: Metal: Togglepin: Pl. 24: 23
               Bone: Inlay: Pl. 28: 17
               Bead: Pl. 29: 7 (1 bone)

122 Pit in Grid Square B.7   ?

An unfinished tomb shaft which was re-used as a grain or storage pit. It was lined with rough blocks of limestone resting on the earth filling of the shaft. No contents.

123 House and pits in Grid Square B.7   LB

Rock cuttings, wall traces and stone pavements, with three rubbish pits, the remains perhaps of a Late Bronze Age house. No contents.

124 Pit in Grid Square B.8   ?

Rubbish or grain pit. No contents.

125 Well shaft in Grid Square C.7   ?

Circular shaft, 4·5 m. in diameter, with rock-cut steps leading down to unfinished cutting. It contained Late Bronze Age sherds in the filling. Cf. shaft in Grid Square B.13.

127 Pit in Grid Square C.7   LB

One of several rubbish pits associated with the houses nearby. See Pits 128, 130.

128 Pit in Grid Square C.7   LB

One of several domestic rubbish pits. See Pits 127, 130.

129 Tomb in Grid Square C.6   MB II–III, *c.* 1800–1625 B.C.

The entrance shaft on the north was still blocked by stones, and it was necessary to remove the roof before the chamber could be safely cleared. More or less round in plan, it was 3·5 m. in diameter, and contained a valuable group of pottery, all of which was stacked on the east side (Pl. 5: 5). Its somewhat isolated position in the middle of a space devoid of rock cuttings may indicate special sanctity. The tomb lies due north from Tomb 119 at an equal distance from the line of the MB fosse.

Pottery

Bowls: carinate A 502, 503, 504, 505, 516, 517, 518, 519; B 527, 529, 530; C 537, 544(3), 545, 546(4), 547(2),
                     548; E 561; F 580
         curved H 593, 594(2), 595, 596, 597, 605

Lamps: A 645; E *L. II*: 195   Jug: E 716
Juglets: B 730, 733(4), 734; C 745(2) 746(2), 747; E 753(2), 754; F 764
Dippers: A 781(8)   Potstand: 812   Imported Wares: 813
Miniature Pithos: 970
Storage Jars: A 1007; B 1010(2), 1012

Objects

Metal: Daggers: Pl. 22: 19, 20   Togglepins: Pl. 24: 10, 11
Stone: Tripod bowl and pounders: Pl. 26: 19, 21–23   Vase: Pl. 26: 20
Beads: Pl. 29: 2 (4 qu.), 5 (2 paste), 6 (1 Ag.)
Scarabs: Pl. 30: 35–59

Date and Comparisons

There are comparisons with the sherds of the North-East Section within the glacis fill (NE 17/183, 184, p. 55) and a slightly longer range than that of Tomb 119 is suggested by the pottery. The bowls, for instance, are chiefly of Classes A–C, with Class C in the majority. The juglets are mostly piriform and there are more cylindrical shapes than in Tomb 119. Especially important is a complete White Painted IV juglet which equates with Strata XI–XII at Megiddo (see under *Imported Wares*, p. 198). A fragment of this ware was in the glacis fill, NE 18/174, and it also occurs at Tell Beit Mirsim, Strata G–F.

Both daggers are of Type 27a and there is a plain and a twisted togglepin (Types 3, 7).

The scarabs show some comparisons with those of Cemetery 500 at Tell Fara. On Rowe's attributions, Egyptian parallels would cover the xiiith–xvith dynasties.

In plan and section, Tomb 129 compares with Tombs 9 and 4 at Jericho (AAA XIX, Pls. XXIX and XX, Pl. VIII).

130 Pit in Grid Square C.7   LB

One of several domestic rubbish pits. No contents. See Pits 127, 128.

145 Grave in Grid Square D.7 (Plan on Pl. 90; See Chart on pp. 60–61)   MB III, 1750–1700 B.C.

Part of the oval grave was denuded, for it was only a few metres from the jagged scarp of the mound where it drops steeply from 234 to 232 m. near the north-west corner. The grave floor was at 234·13 m. The body was missing, but three juglets and a pin constituted a group which may have once contained other pieces.

Pottery: Juglets: A 727; C 746   Dipper: A 781

Objects: Metal: Togglepin: Pl. 24: 1

Date and Comparisons

Grave 145 should be considered with Graves 173 and 157, for all three were on the edge of the scarp, and were presumably covered by the fill of the plastered *terre pisée* defence.

Type 727 provides a good parallel with Jericho Tomb 9, layer d, and with Megiddo Stratum XI. The togglepin finds comparisons in Strata XII–X at Megiddo and in Tomb 1409 of the Courtyard Cemetery at Ajjul.

153   Bilobate chamber in Grid Square B.9 (see Chart on pp. 60–61)   MB III, *c.* 1700–1675 B.C.

The shaft to the north was blocked with small stones. It led to a chamber 3·5 m. across, divided into equal parts by a projection of rock opposite the entrance. The bodies were disturbed, but the group of pottery and scarabs is small enough to be a contemporary deposit with some heirlooms, perhaps, among the scarabs.

Pottery: Bowls: carinate B 528; C 540; plain G 587(2)
curved H 594, 598

Lamps: B 648(2)   Juglets: B 730, 737; E 760(2)
Dipper: A 781(3)   Miniature Pithos: 973
Storage Jars: B 1008, 1010, 1011

Objects: Metal: Togglepins NP
Faience kohl pots: Pl. 26: 15–17
Scarabs: Pl. 32: 104–125

Palestine Museum Nos.: PM 34.2931–34.2976

Date and Comparisons

Tomb 153 is a clear example of a bilobate chamber with the entrance shaft to the north like those of Cemetery 500 at Tell Fara (BP I, Pl. LXIV), where the faience kohl pot, four of the scarabs and most of the pottery can also be matched. Similar kohl pots are discussed on p. 83.

Comparisons with sherds of the North-East Section are found at NE 20/147 and NE 27/80, pp. 53–55.

On Rowe's attributions of the scarabs, they are concentrated in the xiiith–xvith dynasties. Pl. 33: 104 (RES 21) bears a title which he suggests may read, "treasurer of the work of the spelt(?)". 108, 111, 120 and 125 provide strong contact with Megiddo Stratum XI. A late comparison for No. 120 is a scarab from an early xviiith-dynasty grave at Gurob.

157 Grave in Grid Square D.7 (Plan on Pl. 90; see Chart on pp. 60–61)   MB III, 1750–1700 B.C.

Part of the grave was denuded, for it was only a few metres from the jagged edge of the mound where it drops steeply near the north-west corner. The shape and position of the shaft is therefore unknown. See Graves 145 and 173.

Pottery: Bowls: carinate B 528; C 543; plain G 583(2)
Juglets: B 730, 734(2); C 739, 740; D 750; E 751

Objects: Metal: Dagger: Pl. 23: 2
Stone: Macehead: Pl. 26: 4
Scarabs: Pl. 32: 90–103

Palestine Museum Nos.: PM 34.2977–34.3001

Date and Comparisons

The pottery covers much the same range as that in Tomb 153, though there are no bowls of Class H, and the high proportion of piriform juglets indicates a date early in the series. Though there are none with pricked pattern, there is the large cylindrical juglet, Type 750, with a band of pricked chevrons round the body, pp. 33, 189 f.

The dagger is the larger of two examples with one rivet hole in the tang, Type 27, p. 77.

The macehead, Pl. 26: 4, is not closely paralleled elsewhere, p. 72.

According to Rowe's attributions, the scarabs, which are all in Jerusalem, range from Dyn. xiii or later to Dyn. xv and "Hyksos". Pl. 33: 91 bears the title "Treasurer of the King of Lower Egypt", above the royal name *Neferewy-āa*. Pl. 33: 93 may be a defective or simplified version of a name, p. 96. For a full discussion of the scarabs see p. 109.

168 Quarry in Grid Square B.11

A quarry over 2 m. deep, with pick-dressed sides. A circular drum and some detached blocks remained on the floor.

Pottery: Bowl: carinate E 575

Objects: Scarabs: Pl. 32: 126

Date and Comparisons

It is indeed unfortunate that this cutting or quarry, isolated from tombs and other constructions on the western edge of the excavations, is not a sealed deposit. It contained a bronze (?) arrowhead (NP), a small and very late carinate bowl, and neither piece is likely to be associated with the scarab of Senusert I, which was the earliest Egyptian royal name to be found at Duweir. Scarabs of this king introduce a period of Egyptian contacts at many Palestinian and Syrian sites (see pp. 32, 94).

171 Pit in Grid Square C.11 (L. II, Pl. LXXIII)   ?

On the evidence of some fragments of a bichrome krater, the pit was somewhat doubtfully ascribed to Structure I (L. II, p. 90), but the straight-sided basin (p. 147) with inturned rim on Pl. 57 would appear to belong to an earlier horizon. See SAOC 10, Chart Column 1, Megiddo, Stages IV–I, and PPEB, Form III.

Pottery: Open bowl: 73

173 Grave in Grid Square E.7 (Plan on Pl. 90 and see Chart on pp. 60–61)   MB III, *c*. 1750–1700 B.C.

The small oval grave with contents undisturbed is the most important of a group of three cut in the rock on the slopes above the north-west corner. Whereas Graves 145 and 157 were partially denuded and not clearly sealed by the packing of the Middle Bronze Age glacis, Grave 173 was well covered by limestone chips which formed the constructional core of that defence (Pl. 5: 4).

The burial was that of a child, with head to the north and the limbs contracted in the narrow space (Pl. 5: 3). The five pots with the body were all different and distinctive types. As Starkey wrote at the time of discovery, "the position of the grave and its relationship to the layers of thrown limestone debris from the excavation of the fosse below leave no shadow of doubt that these forms precede this engineering work by some years".

Pottery   *Photographs on Pl. 20: 17–21

Bowls: carinate B 524;* C 537*
Jugs: A 669;* B 672*   Juglet: C 738*
Palestine Museum Nos.: PM 34.3005–3006, 34.7680–34.7682

Date and Comparisons

Four out of five pots in the group are wheel-burnished, a technique which is otherwise unusual at Duweir. The presence of both rounded and angular carinate bowls in this burial shows that both were being made at the same time. The jug 672, with its shoulder handle and flat base, and the piriform juglet, Type 738, would be equivalent to Stratum XI at Megiddo, while the bag-shaped jug, Type 669, is best matched in Stratum E at Tell Beit Mirsim, and the same form unburnished occurs in City C at Jericho.

187 Locus in Grid Square E.7 (Pl. 91)   MB III

The number marks the position of a large jar which was close to bed-rock on a line with Grave 173 near the north-west corner. It was covered by soil with limestone chips above, which was probably fill of the MB *terre pisée* defence.

Pottery: Storage Jar: B 1011

216 Tomb in Grid Square A.6 (Fig. 9)   Plastered pit.
                                                                             LB II–III, *c*. 1450–1300 B.C.

The circular pit, some 3 m. in diameter, was originally entered from a shaft on the west side; most of this entry and the roof had collapsed. To a depth of about 2 m. the walls were faced with thick lime plaster and the floor was similarly treated.

The pit had contained many burials, but they were much disturbed and only three skulls were worth preservation. More than 200 vessels were stacked around the walls.

Pottery *Photographs on Pls. 52–54

Bowls: carinate A *L. II*: 114(2); C 554;* E 564,* 565,* 566,* 567, 572*
plain G 584, 585, 589,* 592; *L. II*: 7, 25, 29
curved H 603,* 604; *L. II*: 20(14), 21(10), 38,* 45(3), 46, 50*(3), 51(5), 52, 137(2), 146
flared J 615,* 616*(2), 617(2), 618, 618A; *L. II*: 4, 28, 30, 81, 83, 91, 93, 95
miscellaneous 624*

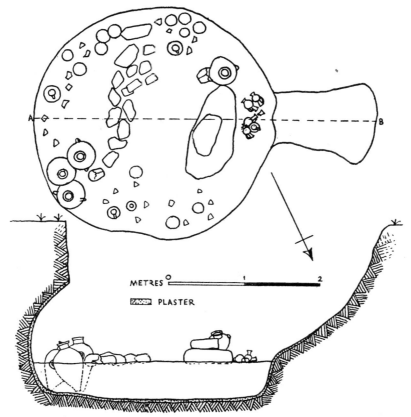

FIG. 9. Tomb 216

Censer and Chalice: 633,* 636
Lamps: C 656, 659;* D *L. II*: 193*(2); E *L. II*: 195*(13), 197, 199(2), 202*; G 666
Jugs: B 680,* 681,* 682,* 686(2); C 688, 691,* 694; D 697,* 700,* 701,* 713; E 720,* 721
Dippers: A *L. II*: 295;* B 786;* C 797*(3); *L. II*: 306*(2), 311;* *L. III*: 288;* D 798*(2), 799*
Imported Wares: 817,* 818, 819*(2), 820*(2), 821,* 824;* 825*(4), 826,* 828*(2), 829,* 831*(2), 832,* 833,* 834*
Base-Ring Ware: 836,* 838,* 839,* 842*(5), 843,* 844*(8), 845*(6), 846,* 848,* 849,* 850,* 851,* 852,* 853,* 854, 856,* 857*(11), 858*(2), 859*(2), 860,* 861,* 862,* 863*(2), 864*(2), 865*(2), 867*(4), 868,* 870, 871,* 872* (2), 873*(2)
Imitation Base-Ring: 886,* 887,* 894,* 895*
Mycenaean Imitation: 915*   Spouted Vessel: 937*
Mycenaean Imported: 945*   Mugs: 959,* 964,* 965*
Miniature Pithos: 979*   Kraters: 987,* 988*
Miscellaneous: 996*
Storage Jars: B 1011; D 1018*(4); E 1022*(2), 1023*

Objects

Metal: Dagger, spearhead and knives: Pl. 23: 3–9*
Togglepin: Pl. 24: 22*   Arrowheads: Pl. 25: 19–22*
Kohl stick: Pl. 25: 23*   Pendant: Pl. 25: 24*
Rivet: Pl. 25: 25*   Ear-ring: Pl. 54: 28*
Stone: Vases and bowls: Pl. 26: 35–39,* 41*   Spindlewhorl: Pl. 26: 40
Bone: Spacer: Pl. 28:6*   Wand: Pl. 28: 7*   Inlay: Pl. 28: 8,* 10–12*
Spindlewhorl: Pl. 28: 9*   Spindles?: Pl. 28: 13, 14

Beads:

Pl. 29:	2	4	5	6	14	15	16	19	21	25	27	32	35	37	47	48
Paste	4	88	—	—	10	—	—	3	1	5	19	1	2	16	—	—
Glass	6	—	61	—	2	—	14	1	—	—	—	—	—	—	1	1
Stone	2 lmst.	—	—	49 cn. 1 qu.	—	3 cn. 1 sard.	—	—	2 lmst. 1 dior. 1 onyx.	—	—	—	—	—	—	—

Amulets: Pl. 29: 59(3)
Scarabs and seals: Pl. 38: 298–310*
Paste: Playing pieces: Pl. 54: 6*
Palestine Museum Nos.: PM 36.1487–1490; 36.2237–2241

Date and Comparisons

The round chamber may well have been constructed for the burials which it actually contained. It is among the earliest of a group with lime-plastered walls, a detail which may be typical of Late Bronze Age tombs at Duweir.

The pottery is well preserved and abundant and the tomb contains the bulk of imported wares, White Shaved, White Painted V, Monochrome and White Slip, with Base-Ring I–II and four local imitations of jugs of Class B. For the general discussion on imported wares see pp. 196–208.

It will be seen that there is no evidence to show that Base-Ring wares were diffused from their source before 1550 B.C. (p. 207) and Petrie's suggestion that they spread in the wake of the northern campaigns of Thothmes III is supported yet once again by three scarabs of this king in Tomb 216. A scarab of Thothmes IV with two of Amenhetep III extend the range of the group to about 1375 B.C.

Sherd comparisons with the North-East Section are found between 27–32 ft. and in Pit A. There is little or no contact with the pottery of Structure I, but it is exceptionally strong for Structures II–III.

Lamps of Class E predominate in the tomb and they find parallels in Stratum C at Tell Beit Mirsim and in Layers VIII–VII B at Megiddo. Otherwise, the contacts with these two sites are not as numerous as one would expect. Base-Ring wares with white painted decoration are typical of Stratum C (AASOR XII, Pl. 16; XIII, Pl. 25), but White Shaved, White Painted V and Monochrome appear to be missing. The later and coarser White Slip bowls, Types 831–834, are also matched in Stratum C (AASOR XII, Pl. 17–18; XIII, Pls. 25 and 26).

At Megiddo the picture is very different. Only the undecorated Base-Ring I jug 842 and juglets 859 and 860 can be matched in Strata IX–VIII, where there is no sign of White Painted wares. The bowls, Types 870 and 871, on the other hand, survive in Stratum VII A. There is also a comparison for White Slip II bowl Type 834, which appears in Tomb 216 and is found in Structures II–III (L. II: 166).

Jericho provides contacts with Tomb 4, layers a–c.

The local imitations of Base-Ring jugs all belong to Class B and are among the latest types in the tomb.

The close progression of the common pottery forms in Tomb 216 suggests a uniform rate of burial from about 1450 to 1375 B.C., but a number of comparisons would extend its range into the period of Structure III.

Tomb 216 was exceptionally rich in metal (p. 78). It contained a dagger of Type 27a and the knives with recurved tips and ends fashioned in the shape of a horse's hoof (Pl. 23: 4–6). There were also two cutting-out knives (Pl. 23: 7–8).

The stone vase on Pl. 26: 39 is like one found in the Maket Tomb at Kahun, which is dated to the reign of Thothmes III.

The chalice 633 or censer is reproduced on Pl. 45. It compares in form with L. II: 217 found in Structure III; Type 636, on the other hand, is like the chalices of Structure II (L. II, Pl. XLVI). For the inscribed lid, see p. 128.

221 Tomb in Grid Square B.4 LB II, *c.* 1400–1350 B.C.

The tomb chamber was close to a quarry worked in Roman times (L. III, p. 210), which had not quite broken through to the earlier chamber. Later cuttings have obscured the original shape of the tomb. The Bronze Age deposit rested on bed-rock in the north-west corner.

Pottery: Bowls: curved H *L. II*: 24, 38
      Imported Wares: 826 Base-Ring Ware: 871
      Imitation Base-Ring: 899, 903
      Mycenaean Imitation: *L. II*: 344

Objects: Metal: Dagger: Pl. 23: 17 Arrowheads: Pl. 25: 54–57
           Togglepins: Pl. 24: 29, 30
      Scarab and plaque: Pl. 39: 376, 377

Palestine Museum Nos.: PM 36.1498–36.1513; 36.1514; 36.2269, 2270

Date and Comparisons

The group is contemporary with Structure II on the evidence of the two exclusive bowl forms and the White Painted V "teapot", cf. L. II: 282. The Base-Ring bowl Type 871 tends to be later than the jugs and it is a developed form. The splayed pyxoid, L. II: 344, compares with one from Structure III and the Class A and C Imitation Base-Ring jugs set an early limit for these shapes and suggest that little can be learned from the variety in form.

The dagger is incomplete, but it appears closest to Type 28a (Pl. 23: 16). The arrowheads are equivalent to the common forms in Tombs 4004 and 501. Togglepins, Types 8c(a), 8b, appear to be confined to *c.* 1600–1350 B.C.

The scarab and the finely cut plaque both bear the name of the god Ptah, and on the obverse of the latter it is combined with the name of Amen-Ra.

226 Tomb in Grid Square A.4 LB III, *c.* 1350–1300 B.C.

Partly covered and destroyed by an ancient terrace wall, Tomb 226 would appear to have had a shaft entry on the west side. It contained a group of broken pots.

Pottery: Bowls: carinate E 577; curved H 598; *L. II*: 21, 24, 30, 144, 145(2); flared J *L. II*: 91
      Lamps: G *L. II*: 204 Jug: C 694
      Imitation Base-Ring: 889(2), 890, 896(3)

Date and Comparisons

Seven out of nine bowls in the group are curved, with many comparisons in Structure III, and there is one flared bowl which is also exclusive to that last phase. The imitation Base-Ring jugs are all of Class B.

CEMETERIES

AREA 500
(Pls. 88–89; L. III, Pl. 7: 1–2; Plan on Pl. 126)

The relation of Area 500 to the other cemeteries around the tell may be seen in this volume on Pl. 88. A general description of this ground, which has always provided the best means of access to the city, was given in *Lachish III*, p. 219. Use of the approaches and of the roads did not encourage soil accumulation and after the desertion of the city the exposed position of the area still caught the full force of every wind. For the thin layer of soil over the denuded tombs see Pl. 9: 5.

501 Pit in Grid Square C.23   LB II–III, *c.* 1425–1275 B.C.

An open, oval pit, 4×3 m., of which the roof and upper part was missing. The burials and offerings were disturbed and scattered through denudation.

Pottery

Bowls: carinate C 541; E 567, 568, 569, 575; plain G 589; *L. II*: 7(2); curved H 598, 599; *L. II*: 20, 21(3), 24, 51; flared J 618; *L. II*: 30(4), 82, 94; miscellaneous 626
Chalices: 634, 635
Lamps: D *L. II*: 193(3); E *L. II*: 195(6), 199
Jugs: B 680, 683
Dippers: A *L. II*: 295(2); C 797(4); D *L. III*: 302
Imported Wares: 820, 825, 828, 833(2)
Base-Ring Ware: 842, 844(5), 845(2), 847, 849, 853, 857(3), 861(2), 865, 870, 871, 873, 874(3), 875; Bull Fig. 8: 8
Imitation Base-Ring: 876, 877   Mycenaean Imitation: 941
Mug: 961   Storage Jar: D 1019

Objects

Metal: Togglepin: Pl. 24: 24   Arrowheads: Pl. 25: 26, 27
       Ring: Pl. 25: 28   Ear-ring: Pl. 25: 29
Ivory: Wand: Pl. 28: 15   Comb: Pl. 28: 16
Beads:

Pl. 29:	1	2	4	5	6	16	21	36	37
Paste	—	8	1	—	—	—	—	1	1
Glass	—	—	—	1	2	1	2	—	1
Stone	—	—	—	1 stea.	1 cn.	—	—	—	—
Bone	1	—	—	—	—	—	—	—	—

Scarabs and seals: Pl. 38: 311–314

Date and Comparisons

Among the bowls, the bias is strongly contemporary with Structure II and the presence of chalices 634–635, which are characteristic of the second building, is also interesting.

The common pottery forms cover the same range as those in Tomb 216. The same may be said of the imported and Base-Ring wares, though they are much less numerous. A slightly later trend is clearly expressed in the Base-Ring Chart on p. 204, where Base-Ring I forms have decreased more noticeably than those of Base-Ring II. Local imitations are represented by two jugs of Class A and by a piriform jar, Type 941, far removed from the Mycenaean original (pp. 209, 212).

A leaf-shaped arrowhead with a blunt-tipped one find comparisons at Megiddo between Strata VIII–VII A.

The togglepin is of Type 8c(a), p. 80, which appears to be confined to *c.* 1600–1350 B.C.

The scarabs include a very late version of the figure and flower motif, No. 311, with an eye-backed and a semi-cylindrical seal giving the name of Amenhetep III, Nos. 313–314.

236

502 Tomb in Grid Square D.24   Bench tomb? LB III, *c.* 1300–1200 B.C.

A sloping passage from the north-east led to one or more rectangular chambers or alcoves cut in the rock. Both roof and walls were damaged by work in the adjoining quarry 504, but in the recess farthest from it a square-cut rock bench remained, on which there was a small but contemporary group of offerings.

Pottery: Bowls: curved H *L. II*: 30, 50, 145; *L. III*: 20
       Imitation Base-Ring: 880   Mycenaean Imitation: 921

Objects: Metal: Bracelet: Pl. 25: 42
       Pottery: Rattle: Pl. 28: 26
       Beads:

Pl. 29:	2	4	5	6	21	47
Paste	5	—	—	3	—	—
Glass	10	2	3	3	2	3

       Amulet: Pl. 29: 62
       Scarab: Pl. 39: 337

Date and Comparisons

The bowls are all curved forms typical of Structure III or later, but the imitations of Base-Ring and pyxoid forms are comparatively good. The amulet and scarab are probably Ramesside, and the group may well date from that period.

503 Pit in Grid Square B.22   LB III, *c.* 1275–1225 B.C.

The pit contained Iron Age and Roman sherds, see L. III, p. 219. The Bronze Age forms were close to the rock floor. The pottery is contemporary with the last phase of Structure III.

Pottery: Bowl: flared J *L. II*: 94 Lamp: E *L. II*: 199
       Jug: D 715 Dipper: C *L. III*: 300 Mug: 963

508 Tomb in Grid Square C.22   LB III, *c.* 1275–1225 B.C.

A passage from the south led to an irregular heart-shaped chamber, into which the roof had collapsed. Hard mizzi boulders in a matrix of softer limestone had prevented the construction of a regularly shaped tomb (Pl. 9: 4). Large rocks fallen from the roof had disturbed and broken the skeletons, but at least four skulls were intact (*Appendix B*).

Pottery   *Photographs on Pl. 55: 1–16

Bowls: curved H *L. II*: 51,* 145;* flared J *L. II*: 30*(2)
Lamps: F *L. II*: 203* Jugs: D 712,* 714,* 715*
Imitation Base-Ring: 890,* 891,* 892*
Mycenaean Imitation: 923,* 943* Mug: 969*

Objects

Stone: Pilgrim flask: Pl. 26: 47*

Beads:*

Pl. 29:	1	2	4	5	6	7	12	15	16	21	32	42	48
Paste	1	57	10	1	2	1	—	—	—	—	1	1	—
Glass	1	29	2	3	—	1	1	—	1	6	—	—	2
Stone	—	25 stea.	—	2	2	—	—	1 sard.	—	1 qu.	—	—	—

Scarabs: Pl. 39: 373–375

Date and Comparisons

The pottery is consistent and belongs to the last phase of burials in the Late Bronze Age; the local imitations of Base-Ring jugs fall into Class C, while the pyxoid and piriform jars are extremely debased.

The presence of two scarabs inscribed with the name Amen-Ra suggests that the group is no earlier than the reinstatement of the official cult in the latter part of the fourteenth century. The pilgrim flask is a xixth-dynasty form, p. 85.

510 Grave in Grid Square B.22   LB I, *c.* 1600–1450 B.C.

Oval grave containing sherds (NP).

511 Group in Grid Square E.26   MB III and EI

Two lines of stones parallel to the edge of the slope down to the Wadi Ghafr, probably part of a retaining wall (L. III, p. 221), denuded almost to bed-rock.

Objects: Metal: Arrowhead NP
         Scarabs: Pl. 32: 129–132
         Potmark: Pl. 18: 20

Date and Comparisons

The four scarabs (not five as stated in *Lachish III*) range in date from the xivth–xviiith dynasties or later; the first three appear from the style to be contemporary. For No. 129 there is a parallel from the unpublished Tomb 43 at Jericho, quoted by Rowe, and for No. 131 there is a comparison from Strata E–D at Tell Beit Mirsim.

512 Tomb in Grid Square B.22   LB

A sloping passage from the north-west led to an irregular ovoid chamber, which only contained a dipper, as L. II: 305, and a corroded bronze togglepin.

514 Cave in Grid Square B.22   EB

The tomb or cave-dwelling was empty except for the jar illustrated on Pl. 62: 287, which is unique at Duweir (p. 170), a jar neck with an incomplete potmark, Pl. 57: 72 and part of a pushed-up ledge handle.

515 Cave in Grid Square AA.23   *c.* 2000 B.C., in frequent use until 100 B.C.

An irregularly shaped cavern constructed as a dwelling in the Early Bronze Age. The entrance was still sealed with stones and earth, though the roof had partially collapsed. The contents are published in L. III, p. 221.

516 Cave in Grid Square B.24   EB and later

Though it was probably a cave-dwelling originally, this large cutting only contained sherds of mixed date.

523 Cave in Grid Square B.23   Construction date unknown. In use *c.* 1300–1000 B.C.

An artificial cavern of irregular shape, entered from the west. Various depressions in the floor suggest that at one time it was used for domestic or industrial purposes. The pottery included two burnished bowls (see L. III, B. 2, type 28 and B. 10, type 102), though the group is otherwise comparable to the last phase of burials in tombs of Cemetery 500.

Pottery: Bowls: carinate C 555   Pilgrim Flask: 958
         Miniature Pithoi: 977, 983, 984   Miscellaneous: 999

524 Pit in Grid Square AA.23   LB II and later, *c.* 1450–1350 B.C.

A rectangular pit or cave with partly cobbled floor, probably used as a dwelling. The Base-Ring sherds and the curious imitation pyxoid may not be contemporary; there was also part of a spouted jug (L. III: 364).

Pottery: Base-Ring Ware 842, 865, 869
        Mycenaean Imitation: 914

527 Tomb in Grid Square A.24   LB II–III, *c.* 1400–1300 B.C.

An oval chamber with plastered walls, probably constructed in the Late Bronze Age. The entrance way and the roof were missing through denudation (Pl. 9: 5).

Pottery: Bowls: carinate B *L. II*: 125; C 555
               curved H. *L. II*: 14, 30, 144; flared J 619; *L. II*: 91
        Dipper: B 790   Base-Ring Ware: 866
        Imitation Base-Ring: 888
        Mycenaean Imitation: *L. II*: 345   Mug: 963
Palestine Museum Nos.: PM 35.2945–2955; 38.126

Date and Comparisons

The small group of pottery appears to be contemporary with Structures II–III in the Fosse Temple. The bowl with the white lime inscription belongs to a type found in Structure II (L. II: 14) and the Base-Ring juglet is comparable to a form in Tomb 1003, but the imitations of imported wares fall more naturally into the period of Structure III. The inscription is discussed by Dr. Diringer on p. 129. (Pls. 43–44).

528 Pit in Grid Square AA.22   LB II and later, *c.* 1450–1350 B.C.

An oval pit, probably entered from the north-east, most of passage and roof missing. Five blocks of stone resting directly on rock divided the pit from east to west, but it is not clear whether they had fallen from the roof or were part of a wall.

Pottery: Imported Ware: 835   Base-Ring Ware: 845, 865

Date and Comparisons

The Base-Ring jug and juglet are neither of them early in the series of that ware, and the White Slip bowl is the most debased of its kind. A date during the occupation of Structures II–III would suit the pottery and there were also some Iron Age sherds.

532 Tomb in Grid Square A.24   LB III, *c.* 1225–1200 B.C.

The roof and walls were missing, but a row of unhewn blocks edged the pit on the south and east sides. Bones and pottery were much disturbed and scattered, though a group of pots, including two almost intact storage vessels, were standing on the west side (Pl. 9: 6).

Pottery   *Photographs on Pl. 55

Bowls: carinate E 576,* 577*
        curved H 610*(3); *L. II*: 20*(2), 21,* 48(3), 52*(3), 137(2), 143*(6), 145*
        flared J 618, 620,* 621* (2), 622;* *L. II*: 30*(19), 95(2)
Goblets: 640,* 641*
Lamps: F 664; *L. II*: 200*(3); G 665,* 668*(2)
Jugs: C 693,* 694;* D 712, 713, 714*
Dippers: B 794;* D *L. II*: 308*

Cooking-Pot: 801*   Imported Wares: 820,* 822,* 835*
Imitation Base-Ring: 882,* 893,* 894,* 895,* 896,* 904,* 905*
Imitation Imported: 913*(2), 927,* 928,* 929,* 944*
Pilgrim Flask: 955*   Mug: 963
Storage Jars: D 1020, 1021

Objects

Metal: Togglepin: Pl. 24: 31   Arrowheads: Pl. 25: 58–62*
Beads: Pl. 29: 2 (3 paste, 1 bone), 4 (1 paste), 6 (2 glass), 9 (1 paste)

Date and Comparisons

The common pottery forms in the group include more flared than curved bowls, and the lamps belong to the latest classes. True Base-Ring ware is missing, but all three kinds of imitation jugs are present, with an emphasis on Class B. Of imported wares, there are only a debased White Slip bowl and two White Shaved dippers, but there is a good range of imitation wares in pyxoid and milk-bowl forms. The Mycenaean Imitation piriform was almost at surface level. Nos. 640 and especially 641 are clearly related to the *tazze* or ribbed bowls, sometimes with stand attached, as seen in FFSV, Pl. XXXIII and QDAP XI, p. 105–106 (pp. 86, 184).

Apart from a few arrowheads and a small togglepin of Type 3, there were no small finds of value or interest.

The group as a whole is photographed on Pl. 55 to represent the latest burial phase in Cemetery 500, about contemporary with the end of Structure III.

Contacts with other sites are limited to lamps of Class F–G at Tell Beit Mirsim, Strata C–B, Megiddo, Strata VIII–VI, and Jericho, Tombs 13a, 4c and M building.

533 Locus in Grid Square AB.23   LB

A depression in the rock, containing stones, a bowl and a lamp, NK.

536 Tomb in Grid Square AB.23   LB II–III, *c.* 1375–1325 B.C.

A long chamber entered from the narrow north end, with two recesses on each side. It is possible that the shape, which is unusual for the period, was the result of quarrying or adaptation for later burials. The remaining pottery was much broken.

Pottery: Bowls: curved H *L. II*: 143(2); flared J *L. II*: 30
   Lamp: E *L. II*: 199   Imported Wares: 821, 822, 830
   Base-Ring Ware: 871   Imitation Base-Ring: 904
   Mycenaean Imported: 946   Pilgrim Flask: *L. II*: 349

Objects: Metal: Ring: Pl. 25: 49
   Stone: Spindlewhorl NP
   Beads: Pl. 29: 6 (1 cn.), 16 (1 cn.)

Date and Comparisons

The common forms are not in themselves numerous enough to allow a close dating for the group, which covers the period of Structures II–III. Imports are more common than local imitations, which are confined to Type 904, of which one example was found in Structure III. On the whole, the group is best regarded as contemporary with the foundation of the last building.

537, 538 Pits in Grid Squares D.23 and 24   LB III, *c.* 1250–1200 B.C.

Near the presumed position of the Middle Bronze Age fosse, which should be under the roadways of the Iron Age cities, there was a cluster of badly damaged pits. In each case, the roof and walls were completely denuded. Pit 537–538 was originally, perhaps, a cave dwelling, but it had been cut into by the adjoining round pit 570, which, with 571 to the south-east, lay on the edge of a slope which may be the counter-scarp of the fosse. It seems that the daggers and spears scarabs and beads from the broken tomb group 570 were collected and stored in Cave 537, within a rough enclosure of stones marked 538.

537

Objects: Metal: Knife: Pl. 23: 19
Beads: Pl. 29: 1 (6 glass), 4 (3 paste), 23 (1 glass)

538

Pottery: Bowl: miscellaneous 627

Objects: Metal: Daggers: Pl. 23: 18, 20, 2_   Ring: Pl. 25: 50
Vase: Pl. 25: 51
Stone: Pounder: Pl. 26: 45   Vase: Pl. 26: 46
Bone, Ivory, Shell: Pl. 28: 19–22
Beads:

Pl. 29:	2	4	5	6	7	8	16	23
Paste	7	3	1	—	—	—	—	—
Glass	—	—	3	—	—	1	—	—
Stone	—	—	—	1 cn.	11 cn.	—	3 cn.	1 am.
Metal	—	—	1 Au	—	—	—	—	—

Scarabs: Pl. 39: 370–372

Date and Comparisons

The small painted bowl with a raised cone inside has comparisons in Tombs 547 and 4013. The type is uncommon, but is reminiscent of metal bowls used in Arab times (p. 182).

The blade of the dagger, Type 27a, is not much more than half the length of MB examples of the same form, and the tang (now broken) was probably much longer. The knife is also incomplete.

The scarabs include a good example of linked scrolls in a gold setting, probably an heirloom, and one of three gods which is matched in other tombs and at Stratum VII at Megiddo.

539 Tomb in Grid Square AB.23   LB III, *c.* 1350–1250 B.C.

At some period of its occupation, stone blocks had been piled up on rock to support the roof, and all but a metre of that construction was denuded like the roof and the surrounding walls. The bowls and lamps were stacked close to the central pillar.

The group should be contemporary with the use of Structure III of the Fosse Temple, and has contacts with Tombs 4011 and 4013.

Pottery: Bowls: carinate B 534; curved H 609; *L. II*: 14, 21, 30; flared J *L. II*: 30, 118
Lamps: E *L. II*: 199(5); F 664; *L. III*: 144
Dipper: C 797   Imitation Base-Ring: 884
Mycenaean Imitation: 926   Storage Jar: E 1025

541 Pit in Grid Square AB.24   LB III, *c.* 1400–1350 B.C.

The walls of the circular pit had been plastered, but they were denuded to less than half a metre from the floor. The small group of pottery which remained would seem to fall late in the occupation of Structure II.

Pottery: Bowl: flared J *L. II*: 30   Base-Ring Ware: 865
Pilgrim Flask: 958   Mug: 961   Krater: *L. II*: 248

542 Pit in Grid Square A.25   LB II–III, *c.* 1400–1300 B.C.

The floor of the circular pit was plastered like its denuded walls, and two blocks of stone from the roof had fallen on the pottery.

The common pottery forms belong chiefly to Structure III; the lamps and dippers show strong contacts with Tombs 4011 and 4013, though an earlier trend is apparent in the scarab of Thothmes IV and in the presence of a Base-Ring juglet. The Mycenaean piriform 946 would also appear to belong to an early burial in the tomb. The Imitation Base-Ring jugs are all of Class C.

Pottery

Bowls: carinate A 522; E 562
            curved H *L. II*: 30(3), 48(2), 137, 144(2)
            miscellaneous: 625
Lamps: F *L. II*: 203   Dippers: B 787, 788, 789
Imported Wares: 820   Base-Ring Ware: 865
Imitation Base-Ring: 900, 901, 904, 905
Imitation Imported: 922   Mycenaean Imported: 946
Pilgrim Flask: 954

Objects

Metal: Arrowhead: Pl. 25: 43   Fibula and ear-rings: Pl. 25: 44–46
Beads:

Pl. 29:	4	6	11	21	22	37
Paste	1	—	—	—	—	1
Glass	—	1	—	1	2	—
Metal	—	—	1 Au	—	—	—

Amulets: Pl. 25: 65; 29: 63; 1 (Bes) NP
Scarabs: Pl. 39: 344–346

543 Pit in Grid Square A.24   LB II, *c.* 1400–1350 B.C.

A Bronze Age tomb under the walls of a later building (L. III, p. 227). The pottery and objects listed below come from high up in the filling and could well be contemporary with the reign of Amenhetep III, whose scarab was found with that of an unplaced king of the previous centuries.

Pottery: Bowl: flared J 623   Base-Ring Ware: 845   Mug: 968

Objects: Metal: Spearhead: Pl. 23: 16   Arrowhead: Pl. 25: 66
            Amulet: Pl. 25: 65
            Scarabs: Pl. 32: 127, 128

Palestine Museum Nos.: PM 35.2979–2981; 36.1484; 36.1818–1820

547 Pit in Grid Square AA.25   LB II, *c.* 1425–1400 B.C. and later

An irregular pit with plastered walls which were mostly denuded. The pottery was much broken, and some of the sherds were burnt almost to melting-point.

242

Pottery

Bowls: carinate C 555; E 575, 577; curved H *L. II*: 24
      miscellaneous 626, 627, 628 (*L. III*: 104 Iron Age)
Jugs: D 704; E 719 (*L. III*: 190 Iron Age)
Dippers: A *L. II*: 295 (*L. III*: 316 Iron Age)
Imported Wares: 825, 830, 831, 835
Base-Ring Ware: 842, 845, 865, 866, 869, 871, 874
Imitation Base-Ring: 893   Mycenaean Imitation: 927
Pilgrim Flasks: 954 (*L. III*: 430 Iron Age)   Mug: 962
Miniature Pithoi: 977, 983   Krater 986

Objects

Metal: Togglepin: Pl. 24: 28   Arrowheads: Pl. 25: 32, 35
      Ear-ring and bracelet: Pl. 25: 33, 34
Stone: Mortar, and fragments of *tazze*, see p. 86.
Bone: Spindlewhorl NP
Beads: Pl. 29: 6 (2 glass), 13 (1 microcline), 49 (1 glass)
Scarabs and seal: Pl. 39: 331–336

Date and Comparisons

The common pottery, of which there is not much in this large group, equates with Structures I–II and with Tombs 216, 501, 1003 and 4004. Most of the sherds are Imported and Base-Ring wares covering their main range. Imitations are limited to the jug 893 and the pyxoid jar 927. The double bowl 626 is one of the few from tomb groups. Examples are found in Structure II, but they become more common in Structure III and are associated with the destruction of the city (p. 53 and NE 36–34/1). There is a close comparison for the miniature pithos 977 from an xviiith-dynasty tomb at Sedment. The frog- and lion-backed seals are also found in Egypt at that time. Scarab 331 compares with one from Stratum IX at Megiddo.

The small metal objects include a togglepin of Type 3 which does not normally survive the end of Structure I. There were also a few Iron Age sherds of the eleventh–tenth century and later.

548 Pit in Grid Square AB.24   LB II, *c.* 1400–1350 B.C.

A circular pit with plastered walls, which were denuded. The sherds in the group cover part of the occupation of Structures II and III. The Base-Ring jug 844 is equivalent to L. II: 279 of which there are fragments in the two last periods, while the imitation is of Class C.

Pottery: Bowls: curved H *L. II*: 52   Base-Ring Ware: 844, 869
     Imitation Base-Ring: 904   Pilgrim Flask: 958

549 Cave in Grid Square A.25   LB III, *c.* 1300–1225 B.C.

Western half of a large cave; for eastern half see 569

Pottery: Bowls: carinate C 556; flared J *L. II*: 120

550 Locus in Grid Square AB.24   MB?

Objects: Stone: Loomweight NP   Sickle-flint NP

551 Pit in Grid Square AC.24   LB

A circular pit with plastered floor which was almost at modern ground level through the complete denudation of the roof and walls. No contents.

552 Pit in Grid Square AA.23

A round pit with plastered walls. It contained some sherds NK.

554 Locus in Grid Square A.26   LB I–III, *c.* 1500–1300 B.C.

A group of bowls and sherds probably thrown out from Pit 555 nearby, see below.

Pottery: Bowls: carinate B *L. II*: 125; curved H 598, 601; *L. II*: 14(2)
　　　　Base-Ring Ware: 842(2), 859, 869(2), 871
　　　　Imitation Base-Ring: 901

Objects: Stone: *Tazze*: Pl. 26: 32, see p. 86.

555 Pit in Grid Square A.25–26   LB I–III, *c.* 1500–1300 B.C.

A pit of irregular shape, containing an important group of pottery and objects. On the edges of the pit to east and west were deposits of pottery 554 and 564 which were presumably thrown out to make way for later burials. Of the three groups, 564 may contain the earlier material, but all are closely contemporary and will be discussed together.

Pottery

Bowls: carinate A *L. II*: 114; *L. III*: 9; C 555; E 564, 570
　　　　plain G 584, 588(2); *L. II*: 7, 29
　　　　curved H *L. II*: 20(3), 21(5), 30(5), 51(3), 52(2), 143(5), 146; *L. III*: 8
　　　　flared J *L. II*: 30, 78, 95, 120
Lamps: C 655, 656; D 661(8), 662(4); *L. II*: 193; E 663; *L. II*: 195(12), 197, 199(13); F *L. II*: 203; G 665, 666, 667
Jugs: B 680; D 699　Juglets: J 777(2)
Dippers: A 781; *L. II*: 295(2); B 784, 785, 787; C 795, 797
Imported Wares: 815, 825(2), 828
Base-Ring Ware: 839, 844, 849(4), 857(7), 860(3), 865(2), 869, 871, 875
Imitation Base-Ring: 885, 897, 904
Mycenaean Imitation: 940　Mycenaean Imported: 945
Spouted Vessels: 932, 933, 936　Pilgrim Flask: 952
Miniature Pithos: 978

Objects

Metal: Daggers and spearhead (?): Pl. 23: 13–15　Ear-ring: Pl. 25: 16
　　　　Arrowheads: Pl. 25: 17, 18
Stone: Vase: Pl. 26: 34
Bone: Inlay and bead: Pl. 28: 4, 5　Ivory leopard's head: Pl. 48: 4
Beads:

Pl. 29:	1	2	4	5	6	7	8	9	21	25	27	28	32	37	45
Paste	—	1	6	20	3	4	—	—	1	—	5	—	1	1	—
Glass	2	—	—	—	—	—	1	—	—	—	—	5	—	—	—
Stone	—	1 cn. 1 stea.	1 cn.	—	—	—	—	1 beryl 1 cn.	—	1 stea.	—	—	—	—	—
Shell	—	—	—	—	—	—	—	—	—	—	—	—	—	—	1

Amulet: Pl. 29: 56
Scarabs and seal: Pl. 38: 295–297
Palestine Museum Nos.: PM 35.2982–3067; 35.3072; 36.1821–1827; 36.2272

Date and Comparisons

The common pottery in the three groups, 554, 555 and 564, falls between that of Tombs 4004 and 216. Pit 555 was used for burials during the period of all three Structures, but particularly in that of Structure II; most of the lamps, for instance, belong to Classes D and E which are dominant in that Structure.

Among the early imports are parts of two Red Lustrous jugs, Type 815, which are matched near the altar of Structure I (L. II: 273). There is a Monochrome bowl equivalent to L. II: 167 from Structures I and II, and White Painted V "teapots" which are certainly comparable to those in Structure II (L. II: 282).

Base-Ring wares are well represented with a strong emphasis on those of Base-Ring I, while there are only three imitation jugs. The Mycenaean piriform Type 945 occurs with a very poor imitation Type 940. Fragments of an unusually large stirrup-jar, now in the Palestine Museum, are published by Stubbings (*Mycenean Pottery from the Levant*, Pl. XIV: 2 and p. 66). To judge from the style, he would date this jar and fragments of a similar one "fairly early in Myc. III—perhaps as early as the Amarna finds" (see p. 213). The three spouted vessels are peculiar to the group, though they have family resemblances in Types 931–939, all of which appear to belong to the earlier part of the xviiith dynasty (p. 215).

556 Pit in Grid Square A.24   LB III, *c.* 1250–1200 B.C.

A pit of irregular shape, partly under the later building 546 (L. III, p. 227).

Pottery: Bowls: curved H *L. II*: 14, 145; *L. III*: 20
Lamps: E *L. II*: 195; G 668   Dippers: B 787(2)
Imitation Base-Ring: 908   Imitation Imported: 916
Pilgrim Flask: 953

Objects: Metal: Ear-rings and bracelet: Pl. 25: 38–41
Stone: Hone: Pl. 26: 42   Double Spoon: Pl. 26: 43
Bone: Inlay: Pl. 28: 18
Beads:

Pl. 29:	1	2	4	5	6	7	9	16	21	29	32	33	34	35	37	42
Paste	1	48	4	—	9	1	5	1	—	2	1	1	1	4	4	1
Glass	1	—	—	2	9	—	—	1	—	—	—	—	—	—	—	—
Stone	—	—	—	—	1	—	1 cn.	—	1 cn.	—	—	—	—	—	—	—

Amulet: Pl. 29: 61
Scarabs: Pl. 39: 347–350

Date and Comparisons

The common pottery forms equate more closely with Structure III than with Structure II. The most interesting piece is the imported pilgrim flask, Type 953, which is somewhat closely paralleled by L. II: 351. A comparison from Tomb 922 at Tell Fara, also in imported ware, comes from the group which contained the scarabs with couchant sphinxes (BP II, Pl. L: 52–55), of which there is an example in Tomb 559. There is also a poor imitation lentoid flask and a pyxoid jar.

The fine scarab 347, set in gold, may bear the name of Senusert I, *Rā-kheper-kā*, though the first sign as written is not circular. For a rather similar variant of the name, see PSC, Pl. XII: 10 with *nub* below, and compare RES 6, and also RES 5 (or Pl. 33: 126 in this volume), which shows a similar central sign. The scarab 347 can be matched at Megiddo, Stratum X, and in both cases it was probably an heirloom. The three other scarabs include a poor version of Amen-Ra and a winged animal, more in keeping with the period of the group.

557 Pit in Grid Square A.25   LB III, *c.* 1250–1200 B.C.

A pit of irregular shape, under 546 (L. III, p. 227). The dipper is typed to an Iron Age form, the imitation Base-Ring bowl is far from the original and the mug is small and poorly decorated. The glass cylinder seal is described on p. 112. On the whole, the group is one of the latest of the Bronze Age series.

Pottery: Dipper: C *L. III*: 288   Imitation Base-Ring: 906
　　　　　Mug: 966

Objects: Beads: Pl. 29: 6 (1 glass), 21 (1 glass), 31 (2 paste)
　　　　　Cylinder seal: Pl. 38: 323

559 Cave in Grid Square AA.26 (see Chart on pp. 60–61)   LB III and later, *c.* 1250–1150 B.C.

The entrance to the cave was on the north side of an irregular chamber, with many boulders on the floor and some traces of dividing walls. The funerary deposits were much disturbed.

Pottery

Bowls: curved H *L. II*: 14, 30(4), 45, 48(3), 137, 143(4), 145; *L. III* 8, 20(3), 25
　　　　flared J *L. II*: 30(3), 93, 95, 120
　　　　miscellaneous 626, 629
Lamps: C 656; E *L. II*: 199; F *L. II*: 200, 203; *L. III*: 144(4); G *L. II*: 204
Jugs: D 702, 708, 709, 710, 711
Dippers: B 790, 792, 794; C 796; *L. III*: 282; D *L. II*: 309
Imitation Base-Ring: 880, 881, 882, 907   Mycenaean Imitation: 913, 930
Mug: 962   Miscellaneous: 998

Objects

Metal: Spearhead: Pl. 23: 12   Kohl stick: Pl. 25: 53
Beads: Pl. 29: 2 (1 paste), 6 (20 paste, 4 glass), 7 (7 paste), 16 (5 glass)
Scarabs: Pl. 39: 339–343

Date and Comparisons

This group may survive Structure III, both in lamp and jug classes. There are also contacts with the Iron Age in some of the common pottery forms.

Two Imitation Base-Ring jugs are decorated like the pyxoid jar, Type 918, which shows quite an elaborate design on a burnished surface. Type 930, on the other hand, is only to be matched by an Iron Age form (L. III: 415 and p. 305). The mug is quite well decorated. The spoon-mouth vessel is especially valuable for its links with Megiddo VI B–A, Beisan "Rameses III" level, and, whatever date may be accepted for them, all are agreed that these levels must be dated after and not before 1200 B.C.

The scarabs in the group are illuminating. Nos. 339 and 343 can be matched at Megiddo, Stratum VII, and both designs are typical of Cemetery 900 at Tell Fara (BP II). The design of a couchant sphinx with uraeus and *maat* is on the reverse of a plaque of Rameses III (PSC, Pl. XLV: 12) and is possibly typical of his reign.

561 Tomb in Grid Square B–C.25   LB III and later, *c.* 1200–1150 B.C.

A pit of irregular shape with walls and roof denuded. It lay under the ruined walls of building 560 (Pl. 9: 3). The common pottery of the group is closely akin to Tomb 559, which has, on the evidence of the lamps, a somewhat longer range on the early side. It is interesting to note that the Imitation Base-Ring jugs which were decorated in white in Tomb 559 are painted in red in Tomb 561.

Pottery

Bowls: carinate A *L. III*: 9; plain G 592; curved H *L. II*: 30, 38, 51(2), 137, 143(3); *L. III*: 20; flared J 621; *L. II*: 30, 78, 94

Lamps: F *L. III*: 144(4); G 666, 668(2)   Jug: D 709

Dippers: B 793 PM. 36.1485; C *L. II*: 311; D *L. II*: 308; *L. III*: 302

Imitation Base-Ring: 883, 884   Imitation Imported: 910, 917

Pilgrim Flask: 957   Mug: 967   Miscellaneous: 1000

Objects

Metal: Arrowhead NP

563 Stone-lined pit in Grid Square A.26   MB–LB?

The upper part of the construction is denuded, but the signs of burning in and around the pit suggest that it was an oven or kiln. The second alternative is supported by the presence of a basalt socket for a turntable in the vicinity, which is complementary to a tenon like that found in the cave workshop 4034 (Pl. 49: 12 and pp. 90 f.). The upper half of a storage jar, inverted, was set in the ground beside the edge of the pit (see 565).

Object: Basalt base for turntable: Pl. 21: 1

564 Locus in Grid Square A.26   LB I–III, *c.* 1500–1300 B.C.

A group of pottery and objects, probably thrown out from Pit 555, which see for date and comparisons.

Pottery

Bowls: carinate A 521; E 573; plain G 590; *L. II*: 2, 15(2)
     curved H 600; *L. II*: 20; flared J 614; *L. II*: 28, 93

Lamps: B 648, 649(4); C 657, 658; D *L. II*: 192; E *L. II*: 195

Juglet: J 778 PM. 36.1486   Dippers: A 782; C *L. II*: 306

Imported Wares: 825, 827   Base-Ring Ware: 842, 850, 861

Miniature Pithos: 981   Storage Jar: C 1017

Sherds: Fig. 8: 10, 13, on p. 204

Objects

Stone: Tripod bowl: Pl. 26: 33   Hone NP

565 Oblong oven or furnace in Grid Square A.26   ?

This oblong construction cut in the rock appears to be one of a series placed at almost equal intervals along the scarp of the area; see 566 to the south-east and 545 and 544 to the north-west. All three were attributed to the Iron Age (L. III, pp. 226–228) and 565 should most probably be contemporary. For a similar construction cf. the oblong furnace from 'Ain Shems (AS III, Map III, southern half), which is ascribed to Stratum IVb, 1425–1200 B.C. (AS V, p. 39). Land snail shells were also found on the mound in a post-exilic context (L. III, p. 155).

Objects: Land snail shells (*Helix cincta* Müller)

567 Quarry in Grid Square B.25–26   LB I–II

A roofless area about 13 m. square. The listed sherds came from a recess which lies below the kiln 568, and they appear to be the remaining contents of a tomb, mostly destroyed by the quarry. Among the sherds was the neck of a Red-on-Black painted jug (NP), and the bowl comparisons make the group contemporary with Structure II of the Fosse Temple.

Pottery: Bowls: carinate C 548; *L. II*: 139; curved H *L. II*: 41
      Jug: D 697

568 Pit in Grid Square B.25

Circular stone-edged pit, diameter 3 m., probably associated with the cave or quarry 567. It contained one poorly turned bowl base (NP).

569 Cave in Grid Square B.25   LB III, *c.* 1300–1225 B.C.

Eastern half of a large cave (see also 549), probably used as a burial place towards the end of the Late Bronze Age during the occupation of Structure III. It was also in use during the early part of the Iron Age and objects attributed to that period are published in L. III, p. 228.

Pottery: Bowl: plain G 586
      Sherds typed to L. II: 125 and L. II: 250

570 Cave in Grid Square D.23 (see Chart on pp. 60–61 and L. III, p. 219)   LB III and later, *c.* 1225–1175 B.C.

North of Pits 537 and 538 was another cave, over 12 metres in diameter, which was apparently a later construction. It was among the largest to show traces of a plastered floor and walls.

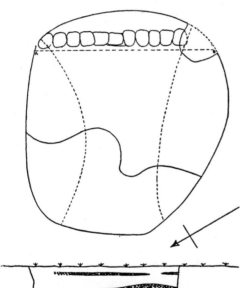

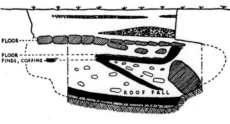

FIG. 10. Tomb 570

Above a thin deposit of grey silt there was a band of black earth some 50 cms. thick, which contained the broken funerary deposits, including fragments of at least two pottery coffins. Some teeth were the only recognisable human remains. Falls from the roof at one or more periods added to the confusion and part of the eastern wall with some of the contents had slipped down a steep slope which might prove to be the outer edge of the Middle Bronze Age fosse. Entry may have been from the fosse, like the Tell Fara tombs in Cemetery 900 (BP II, Pl. LX), or from a vertical shaft above, like Tomb 1 at Bethshemesh (BS, p. 179).

Pottery: Bowls: carinate C 555; F 581; curved H *L. II*: 48(2)
               flared J *L. II*: 91(2); miscellaneous 626
      Lamp: G 665   Jug: E 725   Dippers: B 787, 788(2)
      Imitation Base-Ring: 901   Pilgrim Flask: 958
      Mug: 967   Miniature Pithos: 985
      Storage Jar: D 1018

Objects: Metal: Ear-ring: Pl. 25: 63
      Beads: Pl. 29: 2 (1 paste), 4 (3 cn.), 21 (1 glass, 1 cn.)
      Amulets: Pl. 29: 67, 68
      Scarabs: Pl. 39: 384–387; 40: 393 (PM 39.796)
      Pottery Coffin and Lids: Pl. 45: 1–3; Pl. 46 (PM 38.767)

Date and Comparisons

The pottery shows more variety in form than usual, but the group is not large enough to cover a long space of time. It cannot be far removed from the period of the Fosse Temple, for there was a palm

248

and zigzag carinate bowl (cf. L. II: 117 from Structure II and 125 from Structure III). This style of decoration is also seen in the Section (NE 32/17) just before the final burning of the Late Bronze Age city. Seven pieces of a similar bowl were found in a silo at Tell Beit Mirsim attributed to Strata B 2–3, though the silo was abandoned before the end of that period (AASOR XII, Pl. 29: 13 and § 85).

Another valuable form is jug 725, covered in a thick white slip and bands of dark-red paint with thinner lines between. For ware and decoration the jug compares with Type 985 in the same group, which has an exceptionally long neck. For this feature and for general resemblances see under Tomb 571.

Three out of the five scarabs are well matched in Tombs 562, 934 and 984 at Tell Fara. The best uninscribed scarab is set in gold ornamented by granular triangles (Pl. 40: 393), and another in a plain gold mount bears signs which are not readable as a royal name in Egyptian hieroglyphs. The *kheper* emblem flanked by uraei on either side of the cartouche is frequent in groups of the Ramesside period.

Anthropoid coffins (Pls. 45 : 1–3; 46 and pp. 131 f.)

Conspicuous among the pottery from this tomb there were innumerable fragments of thick coarse ware with a greyish-black core. They proved to be parts of at least two cylindrical coffins, tapering towards the feet. The base is provisionally shown flattened in the reconstruction on Pl. 46. One coffin was inscribed in red paint down the centre panel. The surface over that area had been prepared by application of a slip and burnish of the same colour and technique as on the Duweir Ewer. Also in fragments were two lids with representations of the deceaseds' features in relief. Both chins are bearded and the hair is shown over the forehead and in locks on either side of the face. Short podgy arms are shown bent across the chest, and knobs are provided for easy removal of the lid, which was clearly sliced out of the coffin after it had been formed, as Griffiths notes in describing a coffin from Yehudiyeh (cf. *Mound of the Jew*, p. 45). Round holes had been pierced at head and foot in the latter, and vent holes are also seen in the front and side of the Duweir coffin (Pl. 46).

Anthropoid clay coffins of this class have been discussed in detail by Albright (AJA, 2nd Series, Vol. XXVI, 1932, pp. 295–306). In his summary of the comparative evidence he would prefer to see in them imitations of Egyptian models of the xviii–xixth dynasties, dating, as far as the Palestine material is concerned, from the thirteenth to the tenth centuries.

Accepting these broad limits for the class, the best comparisons for our lids come from Tombs 552 and 562 at Tell Fara (BP I, Pl. XXIV).

In Egyptian territory there is a parallel in a built tomb 17 at Nebesheh (*Tanis II*, Pl. I), though there is no knob and the fingers are more detailed. With the burial were a bronze and an iron spearhead (op. cit., p. 21 and Pl. III).

The work of Naville and Griffiths at Tell el Yehudiyeh in the tumuli graves of the desert, where painted pottery coffins were commonly enclosed in a bricked arch, established that they centred on the xxth dynasty (*Mound of the Jew*, p. 48). Pithoi found with them (Pl. XIV: 5 and XV: 12) are reminiscent of such types as 977 and 984–985, p. 218. Relevant scarabs are those of Rameses III, his father Set-nakht, and possibly also Rameses VI (AJA, op. cit., p. 304).

One of the best illustrations is the pottery coffin of Men at Yehudiyeh, found by Petrie and assigned by him to the middle of the xviiith dynasty (HIC, pp. 16 ff. and Pls. XIV–XV). It is of special interest in this connexion for the poorly written hieroglyphs, not unlike those of the central panel on the Duweir coffin, and for the figures of Isis and Nebthys on the side panels.

571 Cave in Grid Square D.24 (see L. III, p. 219)　　　　　　　　　LB III and later, *c.* 1225–1175 B.C.

Like Cave 570, this rock-cut tomb was probably entered from above or from the counterscarp of the Middle Bronze Age fosse. The circular chamber was about 3 m. in diameter; the burials were disturbed and the contents broken.

Pottery

Bowls: curved H *L. II*: 21, 52; *L. III*: 20; flared J 620; miscellaneous 630

Lamps: B 648; F *L. III*: 144 (*L. III*: 151 Iron Age)
Base-Ring Ware: 858, 867   Mycenaean Imported: 947
Miniature Pithos: 984   Kraters: 990(2) PM. 39.797, 992
Storage Jar: D 1018

Objects

Metal: Ring: Pl. 25: 64
Amulets: Pl. 29: 65, 66
Pottery: Bowl frags., inscribed (?): Pl. 47: 5
     Figurine of Astarte: Pl. 49: 1

Date and Comparisons

In common with Tomb 570 there is a palm and zigzag bowl and a storage jar of Type 1018. There is also a long-necked pithos, Type 984, which compares in form with Type 985, though the brownish-red surface is burnished. Late xviii–xxth dynasty comparisons are discussed on p. 218. The decorated kraters, Types 990 and 992, are not closely matched elsewhere, p. 219.

With these exotic wares there is one good quality imported pyxis, Type 947, and two very poor imported Base-Ring juglets which are both towards the end of the series.

The figurine compares with those of local make from the potter's workshop, though it is not from the same mould. See p. 90.

The bowl fragments, possibly inscribed in red paint, are mentioned by Dr. Diringer on p. 130.

AREA 1000

(Pls. 88–89)

The number designates the upper terrace of nari limestone, the eastern limits of which are represented by contour line 249 on the map published in *Lachish III*, Pl. 106, and p. 228. Plans of the caves are to be found in the same volume on Pl. 127.

1003   Tomb in Grid Square E.30 (see Chart on pp. 60–61)   LB II, *c.* 1425–1400 B.C.

The position of the cave, near the broken edge of the plateau, made it especially vulnerable to denudation, and as usual the roof had collapsed. Under the fallen blocks and rubble there was a rich deposit of pottery in a thick and jumbled mass (Pl. 9: 1, 2). This state of chaos may have been caused by the clearance of the eastern half of the same two-lobed chamber (Tomb 1004) to make room for Iron Age burials (L. III, pp. 236–238). The earlier contents of Tomb 1004 were then dumped in the western half over contemporary deposits. One bowl of White Slip II had been thrown out on to the scarp and few small objects of worth remained in the tomb. A partition of stone blocks between the two halves was damaged by a determined but unsuccessful attempt to cut through the mizzi boulders.

Pottery

Bowls: carinate E 562, 570(2), 571(2), 572, 573
     plain G 583(2), 592; *L. II*: 7(3)
     curved H 606; *L. II*: 19(3), 20, 21(4), 24(3), 30, 37; *L. III*: 21
     flared J 617, 618(3), 618A; *L. II*: 30, 42, 78(2), 83(4), 94
     miscellaneous 631(2)
Chalices: 637, 638
Lamps: C 659; D *L. II*: 193(2); E *L. II*: 195(4), 197(2), 199(5)

Jugs: B 684, 685, 686(2), 687; C 692; D 702(2), 703, 715
Dippers: A *L. II*: 295; C 797(6)
Imported Wares: 820, 825, 830(2), 831
Base-Ring Ware: 840, 844, 845(2), 847, 855, 857, 859(2), 866, 867, 869, 873
Imitation Imported: 910, 911   Spouted Vessel: 938
Mug: 960   Miniature Pithoi: 974, 975, 980
Miscellaneous: 997(2)   Storage Jars: E 1023, 1024

Objects

Metal: Togglepins: Pl. 24: 25–27   Arrowhead: Pl. 25: 30
     Ear-ring: Pl. 25: 31   Ring NP
Pottery: Rattles: Pl. 28: 24, 25
Stone: Spindlewhorl NP
Beads:

Pl. 29:	1	2	5	6	9	16	17	21	27	28	37	40	44	48
Paste	6	28	9	1	2	—	—	1	19	2	1	1	—	—
Glass	—	4	19	8	1	17	—	3	—	—	—	—	—	1
Stone	—	2 stea.	87 cn.	4 cn. / 1 lmst.	—	1 cn.	1 cn.	—	—	—	—	—	—	—
Shell	—	—	—	—	—	—	—	—	—	—	—	—	1	—

Scarabs: Pl. 39: 324–330
Ivory: Duck's head: Pl. 48: 6   Shell NP
Playing Pieces as Pl. 54: 6

Date and Comparisons

Among the carinate bowls, only those of the latest, most degraded Class E were found, and on balance the plain, curved and flared bowls have most in common with Structure II. The chalices 637 and 638, which are rare enough in the tombs, are also characteristic of that building (L. II, Pl. XLVI). The lamps, too, fall into place with those of Tombs 216 and 501, though the series ends with the best represented Class E.

A reduction in quantity and quality of Base-Ring wares, as noted in Tomb 501, becomes more marked, but Imitation Base-Ring jugs are missing, which provides an important pointer for the beginning of this class.

The miniature pithoi 974 and 975 are interesting in that they provide the best comparison which the site can offer to the decorated two-handled jars from Tomb 5 at Jericho (AAA XX, Pl. XXII: 5–13), but those are flat-based, p. 218. For form see also *Lachish II*, Types 342–343 from Structure III, which are undecorated.

The storage jars are both decorated pieces of Class E.

The togglepins belong to Types 8b and 8c(a) which seem to belong to the xviiith dynasty and are found with Base-Ring ware, p. 81.

The scarabs, Nos. 325–326, show kneeling figures on the *neb* sign, one of which can be matched in Stratum D at Tell Beit Mirsim. No. 324 is a scarab of Thothmes IV, who reigned in the last quarter of the fifteenth century. It is surprising that in such a large group there are no scarabs of his great predecessor Thothmes III, and the tomb can hardly have been used during the reign of his successor Amenhetep III, for scarabs of both great conquerors are most common at Duweir. The scarab evidence therefore suggests that the cave contained secondary burials contemporary with the reign of Thothmes IV, and this finding agrees with the indications of the pottery, which should be compared with that of Tombs 216 and 501. The first tomb at least has a longer range, both earlier and later than Tomb 1003, and Tomb 501 includes one scarab of Amenhetep III.

The contents of Tomb 1003 should be associated with Level VII at 29 feet in the North-East Section, which contained a scarab of the immediate predecessor of Thothmes IV, Amenhetep II, whose reign covered the third quarter of the fifteenth century.

1005 Tomb in Grid Square E.31   LB I, c. 1550–1450 B.C.

A damaged and denuded tomb near the edge of the nari-capped plateau. The common pottery forms in the group are well matched in Structure I: Type 521 is like L. II: 74, Type 590 like L. II: 6 and two Black Lustrous juglets, Type 776, correspond to L. II: 276. The storage jar 1015 with a very flat base compares with L. II: 387 and 388. Given this agreement for five out of six forms, the beaker-shaped jar 807 may well be contemporary, which conclusion is supported by the ware and decoration which has much in common with Bichrome pottery (p. 196).

Pottery: Bowls: carinate A 521; plain G 590
   Juglets: J 776(2)   Potter's Jar: 807, PM. 36.1602
   Storage Jar: C 1015

1006 Pit in Grid Square D.27   LB II, c. 1425–1375 B.C.

A damaged and denuded pit with plastered walls and floor, near the edge of the nari-capped plateau. The contents were disturbed and fragmentary.

This small but varied group is photographed almost in full on Pl. 51. The bowls are ordinary forms which could come from Structures I–III, like the White Slip II bowl. The chalice and lamp are as found in Structure II. With two well-made Base-Ring jugs, there is the exceptional piece, Type 841, which probably had a shovel neck. It was found in fragments at the bottom of the pit, and it may not be contemporary with the imitation piriform jar which was the topmost vessel in the group. The large bronze scoop was almost intact, but it was found with a smaller metal bowl which was completely crushed (NP).

Pottery   *Photographs on Pl. 51: 47–61

Bowls: plain G 591;* *L. II*: 7*(3); curved H 606; *L. II*: 30*
   flared J *L. II*: 93*
Chalice: 636*   Lamps: E *L. II*: 195   Jugs: D 705,* 706*
Imported Wares: 831*   Base-Ring Ware: 841,* 844,* 845,* 871*
Spouted Vessel: 939*   Mycenaean Imitation: 942*

Objects

Metal: Bowl: Pl. 42: 1*
Stone: Stopper: Pl. 26: 44*
Beads: Pl. 29: 41 (1 paste)

1008 Pit in Grid Square D.29   ?

A partially excavated pit containing part of a limestone pear-shaped macehead.

CHAPTER 12
AREAS 1500, 2000
AREA 1500, THE NORTH-WEST SETTLEMENT
(Pls. 88–89, 94–95)

THE physical aspect of the ground and its significance as the site of a Chalcolithic and Early Bronze Age settlement is discussed on pp. 39–43. Views and photographs of certain caves are to be found on Pls. 2–4. Used and re-used as dwelling- and burial-places at different times in the long history of the site, the caves and their contents are listed below in numerical order.

All those groups which contained Chalcolithic and Early Bronze Age sherds are followed by a list of comparisons, as well as by the usual note on the range of the group. The pottery is broken and disturbed, but some classification is attempted on pp. 144–155.

Three large groups and one smaller burial in a cave give a very clear progression through successive phases of the Early Bronze Age. Their contents have been classified and are treated in detail in Chapter 9. In chronological order they are Caves 1535, 1519, Burial 1556 and Cave 1513.

I am much indebted to Dr. B. S. J. Isserlin, who has made diligent search throughout the relevant books and who has taken a large share in drafting these notes. Between us, we have been through the collection at the Institute of Archaeology from the southern Tell Fara settlements (BP II) and have agreed on the comparisons with the relevant sherds in hand.

Some pottery and certain objects, numbered 1500, from the surface of that area, are of special interest. Unassociated with each other or with a particular group, they include the cup or crucible with textile impression on Pl. 13: 93–94, p. 72; the rough castings on Pl. 21: 11–15, p. 75, and the stone fragments on Pl. 21: 2–4 and Pl. 26: 9–11, pp. 71 f.

A number of caves had been used for burials during MB II and III, with slight indications of occupation during MB I.

Some graves oriented east and west are planned on Pls. 94–95; they were mostly empty, but see 1533 for beads and 1549 which contained a body. They appear to be post-exilic in date.

1501 Grave in Grid Square XII: J.9   EB II–III

A partly denuded burial in a rectangular grave.

Pottery: Jars with ledge handles: 174, 175
          Jar with loop handles: 124   Amphoriskoi: 127, 130
          Juglets: narrow-necked 125, 129; pointed 126
          Unclassified: 128

Date and Comparisons

With the miniature juglet 126 and the jar 124 which is a better developed version of a kind found in Jericho Tomb A (AAA XIX, Pl. VI: 15), this group should last into EB III. Of the two amphoriskoi, Type 127 is small and debased and compares with Type 117 from Cave 1535, while the better-made Type 130 is like 113 from the same group. The pottery as a whole falls within the period of Tomb 1535.

Pl. 58; 124   Lebe‘a (BMB I, 1937, Fig. 10: 2nd row, right) Tomb 6   2400–2100 B.C.
Pl. 58: 127   Jericho (AAA XXIII, Pl. XXXVI: 3)   Layer VI

1502 Tomb in Grid Square XII: K.8–9 (see Chart on pp. 60–61).   MB III, *c.* 1700–1650 B.C.

Size, shape and the location of the shaft entry to the north of the roundish chamber are similar to the plan of Tomb 129. As usual, the contents were much disturbed owing to the fall of the roof.

Pottery: Bowls: carinate A 514; B 528; C 542, 543(2)
              curved H 596
      Lamps: A 643; D 660   Juglet: E 751
      Dippers: A 780(2)   Storage Jars: A 1007; B 1010

Objects: Metal: Daggers: Pl. 22: 14, 15   Togglepin: Pl. 24: 5
      Stone: Tripod mortar: Pl. 26: 18
      Scarabs: Pl. 30: 23–25
      Ostrich shell fragments. NP
Palestine Museum Nos.: PM 34.2773–2794

Date and Comparisons

The date of the group is of some importance owing to the presence of an inscribed dagger which is discussed in detail by Dr. Diringer on p. 128. The pottery, however, consists of the most normal MB types, carinate bowls, lamps and dippers, with two storage jars, all of which would not be out of place anywhere within the range of our series, though the absence of piriform juglets suggests a date rather after than before 1700 B.C.

The engraved signs on the dagger are enlarged to double size on Pl. 42, to the left of the full-scale photograph. The dagger is one of two examples, both belonging to the same Type 27a which is the common one of the period, though the tang of the engraved dagger is long in proportion to the blade.

The tripod mortar and fragments of ostrich shell are often met with in this period.

Rowe ascribes scarab No. 23 to Neferhetep II of dynasty xiii (cf. No. 26 from Tomb 1542) and Nos. 24–25 he dates from about then to Hyksos times. No. 25 compares with a scarab from Megiddo, Stratum XI, and from Tell Fara, Tomb 594, but neither piece is as good in detail. The togglepin is like one from Tomb 1542.

The normal dippers and cylindrical juglets are matched in Tomb 9 at Jericho and in the Palace Stores.

1503 House in Grid Square XII: K.8–9   Chalc.–EB

Part of a poorly built house, most of which had collapsed and fallen into the valley. The plan was incomplete and the remaining walls stood to a maximum height of 30 cms. If there were once earth floors, they have long since been destroyed by the plough. The attribution of the sherds listed below to the period of the house is uncertain.

Pottery

Sherds photographed on Pl. 13: 70–72   Drawings on Pl. 56: 26–31
Other fragments as Pl. 57: 41; Pl. 62: 279

Objects

Basalt mortar: Pl. 26: 7   Flint blades, Appendix C.

Date and Comparisons

Ledge handles of Forms 5, 6 and 8 (pp. 149 ff.) indicate a start at the transition from the Chalcolithic and ranging well into the EB period. Other finds are consistent though they are stronger for the earlier phases of EB and for Fara H. The jar Type 26, the bowl 30 and the jug with multiple handle, Type 27, can all be paralleled. The grooved handle (Pl. 13: 72) also occurs at Fara and elsewhere and it is seen on a ledge-handled jug now in the Department of Egyptology of University College, dated between S.D. 43–70. The shape of the jug, which comes from Gerzeh, is in the published volume, but the ledge handles are broken and the detail of the groove is not shown (p. 155).

Pl. 13: 71	Gezer (*Gezer* III, Pl. XXII: 19) Cave 15 I	EB I
	For EB I date of these "troglodyte" caves, see Wright, PEQ, Jan. 1937, p. 73	
Pl. 13: 72	Megiddo (SAOC 10, Chart Column 9E)	Stage III
	Jericho (AAA XXII, Pl. XXXVI: 20) Strip 2, 9·11 m.	Layers VII–VI
	Tell Fara (BP II, Pl. XXXVII: bottom right) Site H, surface	
	Tell Fara (I. of A. ref.: E. IV. 2079) Site H, Pit 1	
	Gerzeh (LGM, Pl. XI: 2c; also in PEC, Pl. XXVIII)	S.D. 43–70
	Gezer (*Gezer* II, p. 153, Fig. 316: 19 and p. 154) Cave 2 I	EB I
	For date see PEQ, Jan. 1937, p. 73 (*Gezer* III, Pl. 19: 5) Cave 11 II	EB I
Pl. 56: 26	Tell Fara (BP II, Pl. XL: 47) Site H, 6·5–7 ft.	
Pl. 56: 30	Tell Fara (I. of A. ref.: E. IV. 2025) Site H, D.2, 6·5–7 ft.	

1504 Locus in Grid Square XII: E.20 — MB I or later

Of the seven pieces listed as from this deposit in a rock cavity, where there were no signs of a burial, only Types 550 and 995 are complete. The first is well matched in Stratum XV at Megiddo, and dipper 995 is of a kind which appears at Ras Shamra but is not closely dated (see pp. 192 f.). The sherds are perhaps intrusive.

Pottery: Bowls: carinate A 510; C 550; plain G *L. II*: 35
      curved H 601; *L. II*: 30
Spouted Vessel: 931   Miscellaneous: 995

1505 Cave in Grid Square XII: F. 20 — EB and MB

A square-cut cave dwelling filled with debris from the fallen roof to the depth of a metre and a half. In the floor there were various cupmarks and a pit on the north side. There were no contents apart from fragmentary storage jars and dippers, flint blades and stones used in domestic life.

Pottery: Dippers: A 781(2)   Storage Jars: B 1011(2), 1012

Objects: Stone: Flint flakes (4) NP   Mortar NP   Whetstone NP

1506 Bin in Grid Square XII: K/L.9 — EB–MB II

Rectangular bin or trough, about 4×2·5 m. square and 1·65 m. deep, lined with horizontal courses of small stones set in mud mortar. It was cut in the grey debris of the Early Bronze Age settlement. It contained a mortar and whetstone with four long sickle flakes (NP).

1507 Locus in Grid Square XII: K.9 — LB

One plain bowl of Class G and some sherds were found in a rock cavity. There was no burial.

1508 Locus in Grid Square XII. K.10 — MB III, *c.* 1750–1675 B.C.

Though the group of twelve pots was disturbed and unassociated with a burial, it appears to be homogeneous, and it contains a majority of piriform juglets. On the whole, it appears to fall within the earlier part of the series, contemporary with the construction of the *terre pisée* defences.

Pottery: Bowls: carinate A 516; B 531; curved H 594
    Lamps: A 644
    Juglets: B 730, 732; C 744, 746, 748; E 752, 753
    Dipper: A 781

1509 Cave dwelling in Grid Square XII: D/E.20   Upper Chalc., EB I–II

A long and irregular natural cave used as a dwelling. Various depressions were cut in the floor and there was a wall of stones at the west end over a metre in height; at the opposite end, the floor of the cave was more than two metres below rock surface level.

Pottery

Sherds photographed on Pl. 13: 66–69; other fragments as Pl. 11: 7
Drawings Pl. 56: 18–25; other fragments as Pl. 57: 38, 53

Objects

Stone: Flint sickle blades: Pl. 19: 4–6   Grindstone NP

Date and Comparisons

This group covers the end of the Chalcolithic period and continues into EB I–II. Links with Fara H are the bowl (Pl. 56: 25) and the ledge handles, Form 5 (Pl. 13: 66). Form 6 (Pl. 13: 68) somewhat recalls the series illustrated in BP II, Pl. XXXVI, though on examination of the actual specimens it proves to be different, especially where thickness in section is concerned. Associations of Forms 4 (Pl. 13: 69) and 10 (p. 154) suggest a medium range of EB I–II. The bowl on Pl. 56: 24 would agree with that date, while the juglet on Pl. 56: 18 would be later still.

Pl. 13: 66	Tell Fara (I. of A. ref.: E. IV. 2069) Site H, Pit 8	
	Et-Tell (*Ay*, Pl. XLVII: 2240) Fouille H, Ch. 116, sous parquet B	EB I–II?
	Megiddo (SAOC 10, Chart Column 14ʙ)	Stages IV–I
Pl. 13: 67	Megiddo (M. II, Pl. 98: 25)	Stratum XIX
	Jericho (AAA XXII, Pl. XXXV: 7) Strip 4, 10·80 m.	Layers V–IV
	(PEQ, 1952, p. 77, Fig. 5: 33–35) Upper midden against 2nd wall	EB II?
	Et-Tell (*Ay*, Pl. XLVII: 1766), Fouille V. 2, Ch. 198	EB II
	Beisan (MJ XXIV, 1935, Pl. IX: 21)	Level XII
Pl. 13: 68	Tell eṣ Ṣafi (BM, Pl. 26: 12)	"Early pre-Israelite"
Pl. 13: 69	Tell el Farʿah (RB LIV, 1947, p. 415, Fig. 5: 26)	EB I
	(RB LIV, 1947, p. 419, Fig. 7: 25)	EB II
Pl. 56: 25	Tell Fara (I. of A. ref.: E. IV. 2078) Site H, 6–7 ft.	

1510 Pit in Grid Square XII: K.10   Caliciform

The sherds in this domestic rubbish pit are analogous to those in Group 1529 (Pl. 66).

1511 Locus in Grid Square XII: F.20   EB

A collection of ten flint flakes were found together. They were probably derived from Cave 1505. See Appendix C.

1512 House in Grid Square XII: F.19   Caliciform?

Part of the denuded western flank of a large straggling building with central court. For east wing see House 1551. No contents.

1513 Cave in Grid Square XII: D.19   EB III–IV and later

A large natural cave with the roof partially intact. Many pits and cup-marks had been cut in the floor which was 3·55 m. below present ground surface.

The lower filling of the cave was strewn with human bones, but no undisturbed bodies were recorded. Above the main deposit were three isolated groups cf pottery which were largely of MB I date, but Group 2 included a jar of the Caliciform Culture (Pl. 59: 180) which is the only intact vessel of its kind from the North-West Settlement, while Group 3 produced a jug, Type 688, which compares with a fragment of undoubted Stratum H provenance at Tell Beit Mirsim (p. 188).

Pottery   *Photographs on Pl. 17

Group 1: Bowl: carinate C 553   Plain Jar: 805
Group 2: Bowl: carinate C 552
       Cup: 139*   Unclassified: 163,* 165*(2)
       Jar, flared neck (Caliciform): 180*
Group 3: Bowls: carinate C 551; D 557, 558; curved H 602
       Jugs: C 688, 689, 690
       Bowl: plain rim 135*   Unclassified: 157*
Group 4, Main Deposit
       Plain Jars: 802, 803, 804
       Bowls: flanged rim 142;* plain 136,* 137,* 138,* 141,* 143, 144, 145,* 146,* 147,* 148,* 149*
           with lugs 154,* 155;* string-cut 150, 151, 152;* 153*
       Cup: 140*
       Jars or Jugs with ledge handles: 172,* 174,* 175,* 176,* 177,* 178,* 179
       Jars: with loop handles 171;* narrow-necked 168,* 169, 170*
           with lugs 173*
       Juglets: wide-necked 161, 162;* pointed 158*(2), 159,* 160,* 166*(2)
       Unclassified: 156,* 164,* 167*
       Potmarks: Pl. 18: 19, 35, 67, 73

Objects

Metal: Dagger: Pl. 22: 7*   Ear-rings NP
Beads:

Pl. 29:	1	2	6	16	21	23	25	44
Paste	2	62	157	30	127	5	—	—
Stone	1	1	2	4	7	5	13	—
	qu.	qu.	gar.	cn.	stea.	cn.	stea.	
		5	5		14			
		cn.	cn.		cn.			
		2	9					
		gar.	stea.					
		3						
		stea.						
Metal	—	—	—	—	—	—	2	—
							cu.	
Shell	—	—	—	—	—	—	—	81

Date and Comparisons

The analogies for the main burial group in this tomb are chiefly with the final stages of EB III and perhaps the transition to EB IV. Parallels occur only in the latest deposits of Tomb A at Jericho and the cup, Type 140, can be matched at Bab ed-Dra. Red slip and burnish is a much less frequent feature in this tomb than in Tomb 1519. This may also be a sign of comparative lateness and development towards EB IV and the Caliciform Culture.

After the period of the Early Bronze Age burials, some later pots were left in wall niches, including the jar, Type 180, and carinated bowls and plain jars which can be matched at Ras el-Ain and Megiddo XIV–XIII. The three plain jars 802–804 were found with the main deposit.

Pl. 59: 135	Byblos (B. I, p. 369, Fig. 288: 5405) Bâtiment XXVII, Salle C	EB
Pl. 59: 140	Bab ed-Dra (BASOR 95, 1944, Pl. 1: 42)	EB
Pl. 59: 141	Jericho (AAA XIX, Pl. III: 3) Tomb A1.17c	EB III
Pl. 59: 146	Et-Tell (Ay, Pl. LXXV: 1390) Fouille H, Ch. 122	
Pl. 59: 152	Et-Tell (Ay, Pl. LXV: 9.1525 and 13.893) Fouille H, Ch. 116	
	Megiddo (MT, Pl. 5: 16) Tomb 1128 fill	Stages IV–I
Pl. 59: 159	Jericho (AAA XIX, Pl. II: 18) Tomb A0·5e	EB III
Pl. 59: 162	Jericho (AAA XIX, Pl. V: 12) Tomb A0·4m	EB III
Pl. 59: 164	Megiddo (SAOC 10, Chart Column 8B)	Stage II
Pl. 59: 167	Lebeʿa (BMB I, 1937, Fig. 10: top left, inset) Tomb 6	2400–2100 B.C.
Pl. 59: 170	Tell Beit Mirsim (AASOR XIII, Pl. 20: 25)	Stratum J
	Et-Tell (Ay, Pl. LXXV: 1282) Fouille V, Ch. 93	EB I?

1514 Pit in Grid Square XII: F.19   EB I–II

Sunken depression in the southern corner of cave-dwelling 1523 (q.v.)

Pottery: Sloping-necked Jar: 132   Amphoriskos: 134
       Juglets: narrow-necked 133; wide-necked 131

Objects: Flint flakes (5), Appendix C

Date and Comparisons

The character of the group is EB I–II since the amphoriskos, Type 134, can be matched at Tell en-Naṣbeh and Ay, while the juglets, Types 131 and 133, should be EB II if no later. They are similar to vases in Tomb A at Jericho but are less flabby in outline and likely to be earlier.

Pl. 58: 134	Tell en-Naṣbeh (TN II, Pl. 12: 213) Tomb 66	
	Et-Tell (Ay, Pl. LXXI: 774) Tombe G	EB I–III

1515 Grave in Grid Square XII: K.11   Post-exilic

No contents.

1516 Locus in Grid Square XII: K.11   EB II–III

Single burial in settlement debris. The analogies for this group lie in EB II and III. Perhaps it will therefore be best to place it near the transition between these two periods.

Pottery: Bowls: upright rim 260; plain rim 258, 259
       Jar: plain 233   Unclassified: 261
       Potmark: Pl. 18: 66

Comparisons

Pl. 60: 233	Lebeʿa (BMB I, 1937, Fig. 10: bottom left) Tomb 6	2400–2100 B.C.
Pl. 61: 258	Jericho (AAA XIX, Pl. III: 1) Tomb A2.18g	EB III
	Jericho (AAA XXII, Pl. XXXI: 28) Strip 1, 10·77 m.	Layers V–IV
	Megiddo (M. II, Pl. 6: 12)	Stratum XVI
Pl. 61: 260	Jericho (AAA XXII, Pl. XXX: 19) Room 129, 10·87 m.	EB II
	Megiddo (SAOC 10, Chart Column 22B)	Stages IV–III
	El Husn (APEF VI, 1953, Fig. 1: 6)	EB II

AREA 1500, THE NORTH-WEST SETTLEMENT

Ras el Ain (QDAP V, p. 121, Fig. 66)
Beisan (MJ XXIV, 1935, Pl. V: 21 and p. 14)
Megiddo (SAOC 17, Pl. 13: 8 and Chart XVIII: 21)
Et-Tell (*Ay*, Pl. LXXVI: 1739) Fouille Z, Ch. 151

EB
Levels XIV and XII
Strata XVII–XVI

1517 Cave in Grid Square XII: K.11 — Upper Chalc.

The northern half of a natural cave enlarged for use as a dwelling. See also Cave 1532. The roof was missing through denudation and the remaining walls of the cave were near present surface level. On the east side, the lower part of the original entrance was in position, flanked by stone door jambs.

Pottery: Sherds photographed on Pl. 11: 1–6; drawings on Pl. 56: 1–8

Date and Comparisons

Outstanding points are the indented edges on bowls, Pl. 11: 3, the sherd with rope moulding, Pl. 11: 2, and the ledge handles, Forms 1 and 5 (p. 149). Such an assembly is not very different from the Upper Chalcolithic at Umm Hamad Sherqi (AASOR XXV–XXVIII, Pt. II, pp. 505–508), where indented rims, rope moulding and the indented form of ledge handle are all typical. A tendency to produce a pushed-up ledge handle (Form 5) is also represented at Beisan XVI with which Umm Hamad Sherqi is contemporary (cf. Glueck, BASOR 97, 1945, p. 13). The less oblong, though probably more developed, form of the Duweir handles seems to agree with Beisan XVI rather than with those of Glueck's site. Kinship with material from the Jordan Valley is perhaps not complete, for the more elaborate indented rims found at Beisan, Umm Hamad Sherqi, Ghassul, etc., are absent from Duweir. On the other hand, links are evident for the southern Tell Fara, where parallels exist both in Site H and in the earlier Site O. Associations with the northern Tell el Far'ah (Énéolithique Moyen) may also be on the early side (cf. Albright, AJA LIII, 1949, p. 214; BASOR 114, 1949, p. 18), though there are also parallels to EB pottery.

The contents of Cave 1517 seem mainly centred in the Upper Chalcolithic period at a date corresponding to Beisan XVI or just after, XV (EB I), though a somewhat wider margin both ways is possible.

Pl. 11: 2	Megiddo (M. II, Pl. 95: 2)	Stratum XX
	Tell el Far'ah (RB LIV, 1947, Pl. XIV: 12)	Énéolithique Moyen B
	Tell Umm Hamad Sherqi (AASOR XXV–XXVIII, Pt. II, Pl. 99: 9)	Upper Chalcolithic
Pl. 11: 3	Tell Fara (BP II, Pl. XXXV: 6th row from top, 2nd on right) Site O	
	Tell el Far'ah (RB LIV, Pl. XIV: 8)	Énéolithique Moyen B
	Tell en-Naṣbeh (TN II, Pl. 85: 4th row, middle)	EB
	Tell Umm Hamad Sherqi (AASOR XXV–XXVIII, Pt. II, Pl. 104: 4)	Upper Chalcolithic
Pl. 11: 5	Beisan (MJ XXIV, 1935, Pl. II: 3 and p. 10)	Levels XVI and XV
	Megiddo (M. II, Pl. 103: 20)	Stratum XVIII
	'Ain Shems (AS IV, Pl. XXIII: 7)	Stratum VI
	Tell Umm Hamad Sherqi (AASOR XXV–XXVIII, Pt. II, Pl. 102: 9)	Upper Chalcolithic
Pl. 11: 6	Beisan (MJ XXIV, 1935, Pl. IX: 22)	Level XII
	Tell en-Naṣbeh (TN II, Pl. 11: 181) Room 17	Level II
	Tell Fara (I. of A. ref.: E. IV. 2068) Site H, D1, 5–6 ft.	
	Et-Tell (*Ay*, Pl. XLVII: 2480a) Tombe 12	EB II?
	Megiddo (SAOC 10, Chart Column 14G)	Stages VII–IV
Pl. 56: 5	Megiddo (SAOC 10, Chart Column 12B)	Stages III–I
	Affuleh (PEQ, 1936, pp. 150 ff., Pl. I: 9)	

1518 Cave in Grid Square XII: J.10 — Caliciform

A natural cave, enlarged perhaps for use as a dwelling and occupied by the incoming people at the end of the Bronze Age. The pottery is mostly analogous to that in Group 1529 (see p. 42).

Pottery: Bowl: inturned rim 401   Beakers: 402, 405
Flasks: 417(3), 419   Jars: 420, 424, 425, 426

1519 Cave in Grid Square XII: E.18   EB II–III

A cave-dwelling with vertically dressed sides, angular corners and a flat floor in which there were some pits and depressions. The upper levels contained many vessels associated for the most part with the cave's second period of use as a burial chamber. Among those which belong to an earlier horizon are the lightly baked jar fragments 279, 280 (p. 170).

Pottery   *Photographs on Pl. 16*

Group 1: Bowls: flanged rim 142;* plain rim 135(4); string-cut 152(7)
        Cups: 190,* 193* Funnels: 186,* 188*
        Jars: with ledge handles: 175
            with loop handles: 217, 218*
            plain or with lugs 220*(2), 221,* 230,* 233*
        Juglets: narrow-necked 204;* pointed 213,* 216*
        Unclassified: 199,* 210*
Group 2: Bowls: upright rim 198;* inturned rim 196;* flanged rim 142;* plain rim 189;* with lugs 195;*
            string-cut 152(4), 153
        Cups: 190;* 191,* 192* Crucible: 183* Jar: plain 229*
        Juglets: narrow-necked 206;* wide-necked 203*
        Unclassified: 208,* 211*
Group 3: Bowl: flanged rim 142* Crucible: 181*
        Jars: with loop handles 222;* 223*
            plain or with lugs 225;* 227,* 232*
        Jug and juglets: narrow-necked 228;* wide-necked 202;* pointed 209*
        Unclassified: 215,* 224*
Group 4: Crucible: 182 Cup: 191 Juglet: pointed 205*
Group 5, Floor Level
        Bowls: plain 135(2), 194;* with lugs 197;* string-cut 152(3)
        Crucible: 184 Funnels: 185;* 187*
        Jug with ledge handles: 226*
        Jars: with loop handles: 219;* plain 231*
        Juglets: wide-necked 200,* 201,* 202,* 203;* pointed 207,* 212,* 214*
        Unclassified: 279, 280
        Potmark: Pl. 18: 76

Objects from Floor

Stone: Macehead: Pl. 26: 3 Flint flakes (11) NP
Palestine Museum Nos.: PM 34.2795–2889; 34.7667–7676

Date and Comparisons

As comparisons show, the main part of this group lies in the later stages of EB III The pointed miniature juglets 209 and 216 and the funnels 185–188 are particularly clear indications. Analogies with Jericho, Tomb A, are especially well developed. The group seems, however, to be a result of burials over some prolonged time, on the evidence of such items as juglets Types 204 and 228 and Type 215. The great frequency of technically well-executed red burnish also separates the group from Tomb 1513 while it helps to link it with the preceding period of EB II.

Pl. 59: 135	Byblos (B. I, p. 369, Fig. 288: 54C5) Bâtiment XXVII, Salle C	EB I
Pl. 59: 152	Megiddo (MT, Pl. 5: 16) Tomb 1128 Fill	Stages IV–I
	Et-Tell (*Ay*, Pl. LXV: 9.1525 and 13. 893) Fouille H, Ch. 116	EB II or III
Pl. 60: 184	Et-Tell (*Ay*, Pl. LXXVIII: 3566) Fouille H, Ch. 116	EB II or III
Pl. 60: 186	Jericho (AAA XIX, Pl. VII:15) Tomb A3.7c	EB III
	Ras el Ain (QDAP V, p. 120, Fig. 20)	EB
Pl. 60: 187	Jericho (AAA XIX, Pl. IV: 6) Tomb A3.28b	EB III
	Megiddo (MT, Pl. 6: 22) Tomb 1101B lower	Stages I–O
Pl. 60: 198	Affuleh (JPOS XXI, Pl. VI: 40) Pit E	
Pl. 60: 199	Beisan (MJ XXIV, 1935, Pl. X: 15 near and p. 17)	Levels XII and XI
Pl. 60: 204	Jericho (AAA XXII, Pl. XXXI: 8) Strip 5, 10.31 m.	Layers V–IV
	Gezer (*Gezer* II, p. 139, Fig. 309: 2nd left) Cave II 28. See PEQ, Jan. 1937, p. 74, note 35	EB II
Pl. 60: 205	Jericho (AAA XIX, Pl. V: 1) Tomb A2.8f	EB III
	Jericho (AAA XXII, Pl. XXXI: 22) Room 129, 11·15 m.	Layers V–IV
Pl. 60: 208	Jericho (AAA XIX, Pl. XXVII: 12) Tomb A4.m.10	EB III
Pl. 60: 209	Megiddo (M. II, Pl. 5: 2)	Stratum XVII
Pl. 60: 215	Jericho (AAA XIX, Pl. XXVII 13) Tomb A4.y3	EB III
Pl. 60: 216	Jericho (AAA XIX, Pl. III: 16) Tomb A1.6d	EB III
Pl. 60: 220	Jericho (AAA XIX, Pl. VIII: 17) Tomb A2.16f	EB III
Pl. 60: 221	Tell Beit Mirsim (AASOR XIII, Pl. 1: 8 and p. 62, § 5)	Stratum J
Pl. 60: 222	Jericho (AAA XIX, Pl. VI: 17) Tomb A1.16f	EB III
	Et-Tell (*Ay*, Pl. LXVII: 20.691 for outline only) Tombe C	
Pl. 60: 223	Megiddo (SAOC 10, Chart Column 11c) for form only: Megiddo example is metallic ware, Duweir example has red bur.	Stages III–I
Pl. 60: 226	Jericho (SW, Pl. 21, C. 1)	Canaanite
Pl. 60: 228	Saqqara (*Tomb of Hemaka*, Pls. XXVI and XXVII, Type 12)	ist dynasty
	Jericho (AAA XIX, Pl. VIII: 16) Tomb A1.28g	EB III
	Tell el Farʿah (RB LIV, 1947, Fig. 7: 29)	EB II
Pl. 60: 230–231	Megiddo (SAOC 10, Chart Column 5B and p. 8, Fig. 3, with trickle paint)	Stages III–I
Pl. 60: 233	Lebeʿa (BMB I, 1937, Fig. 10: bottom left) Tomb 6	EB

1520 Cave in Grid Square XII: E.17/18   Upper Chalc., EB

A natural cave adapted for use as a dwelling. The northern half was divided from the main cave by a wall of stones based at 246·37 m. on debris 55 cms. above the floor. With the exception of amphoriskos Type 113 all the vessels were found together in a group.

Pottery: Photographs on Pl. 13: 73–80
            Drawings on Pl. 57: 44–48; other fragments as Pl. 58: 113

Date and Comparisons

While this group still shows some Chalcolithic analogies, it is essentially of developed Early Bronze character, e.g. ledge handle Form 5 (Pl. 13: 79), and it even reaches to an advanced stage in this period (cf. Form 6, Pl. 13: 74; Form 9, Pl. 13: 79). Some affinities exist with Fara Site H.

Pl. 13: 73, 74, 80 for white wash and red stripes	Ophel (I. of A. ref.: 1946/25.84)	
	Tell Beit Mirsim (AASOR XII, Pl. 2: 16)	Stratum J
	Jericho (AAA XXII, Pl. XXXVII: 1) Strip 2, 10·20 m.	Levels V–IV
	Tell Fara (I. of A. ref.: E. IV. 2059) Site H, Pit XIII	
	Tell el Farʿah (RB LIV, 1947, Pl. XV: 6, 7)	Énéolithique Supérieur
Pl. 13: 79	Megiddo (SAOC 10, Chart Column 14B)	Stages IV–I
Pl. 57: 46	Tell Fara (BP II, Pl. XL: 49) Site H	

1521 Single grave in Grid Square XII: K.11   Post-exilic?

A semicircular grave with diameter on an east–west axis. The body was disturbed and only two beads were found (NP).

1522 Cup-mark in Grid Square XII: F. 17   **EB**
1523 Cave in Grid Square XII: F. 18   Middle Chalc.–EB I and later

A natural cave adapted for use as a dwelling. The roof and much of the walls were missing, especially on the east side, where the entrance was most likely to have been (Pl. 3: 1).

Starkey wrote as follows at the time of discovery:

"Here we see a large rectangular room excavated down in the rock, utilising the pre-existing caverns with a slight dressing back of the rock to straighten the alinement of the walls, the upper strata being left to span the room thus formed. Various natural holes provided very necessary ventilation and light for the occupants below. In the floor are sunk some circular pits, bee-hive shape in section, which gave storage accommodation, probably for cereals. Towards the north-west end of the chamber a mortar in hard mizzi limestone had been carefully set into the floor of soft white howr limestone, in just the position where the modern coffee *grn* would be found in the home of today. (Pl. 3: 5.) In the south corner is a large sunken depression (No. 1514) a feature which is common to the majority of these dwellings, and I think should be looked on as the communal bed. It is probable that these dwellings were roofed where necessary with thatch. The absence of mud from the filling of these chambers seems to preclude the possibility of its being used to any extent in roof construction. It is indeed remarkable how clean and light the debris usually is."

For a similar mortar set in the floor, cf. *Ay* (Pl. XXXV: 1) Fouille V 5, Ch. 211.

The three stones in the foreground of Pl. 3: 1 are the remains of a wall founded on earlier settlement debris, to be associated with a later phase of house construction. In all probability the western limits of the large building in Grid Square XII: 18/19 covered part of Cave 1523 and of the adjoining Caves 1527–1529, which would account for the absence of contemporary occupation in them. See the alinement of walls in House 1512 northwards.

The numerous pits contained sherds as listed below, while the scrapers (Pl. 19: 2, 3) and a plain copper pin were found on the floor of the cave (for analysis, see p. 328).

Pottery

Drawings on Pl. 57: 38–41; other fragments as Pl. 11: 3; Pl. 13: 80; Pl. 56: 30(3), 35; Pl. 57: 43, 50(4), 58(2);
     Pl. 60: 183(2); Pl. 62: 279
Sherd with basket impression: Pl. 13: 92
Ledge handles, Forms 1–3, 4, 5, 6, 8 (pp. 149–153)

Objects

Bone point: Pl. 13: 96   Basalt ring: Pl. 13: 97
Flint scrapers: Pl. 19: 2, 3

Date and Comparisons

From the upper levels of debris there were parts of a cooking pot, Type 39, while other pieces came from Pit D. The vase, Pl. 57: 40, might be comparable to a form at Chassul, though it has no lugs. No. 41 can be paralleled at Fara Site H and both forms are reasonably complete.

The pits A–E mostly contain many fragments of crucibles like Types 35, 43, 50 and 58 with a larger handmade bowl like Type 30. These are common in the nearby kiln 1525, and it is reasonable to suppose that the potter who used it was living or working in the cave. An interned holemouth rim, Type 38, from Pit A could be EB I or earlier.

Pl. 57: 38	Tell el-Far'ah (RB LV, 1948, p. 561, Fig. 6: 6)	EB I
Pl. 57: 40	Teleilat Ghassul (TG II, Pl. 78: 10)	Niveau IV
Pl. 57: 41	Tell Fara (BP II, Pl. XXXI: bottom, 2nd from right) Site H	

1524 Single grave in Grid Square XII: K.11   Post-exilic

Oriented east–west. Body undisturbed, position extended, head to west, face south. No contents.

1525 Kiln in Grid Square XII: E/F.20 (Fig. 11)   Lower Chalc.–EB I

Less than a metre below the surface, the lower part of an elaborate construction was excavated, which appeared to be the remains of an oven or kiln (Pl. 2: 6). The ground plan consisted of a rectangular depression with the long axis oriented north and south. Three flues or channels radiated from the central part southwards,

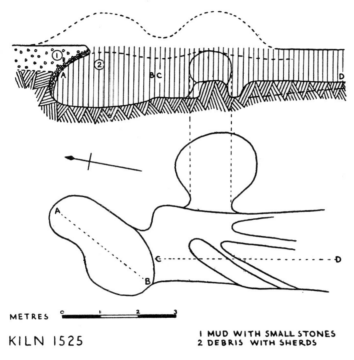

METRES

KILN 1525

1 MUD WITH SMALL STONES
2 DEBRIS WITH SHERDS

Fig. 11

and the east and north sides opened into round enclosed pits 2 metres in diameter, lined with small stones set and covered in mud plaster.

The debris which filled and covered the flues contained much hand-made pottery, including many sherds of crucibles.

Pottery: Drawings on Pl. 57: 60–64; other fragments as Pl. 56: 30, 35; Pl. 57: 58

Date and Comparisons

Associations range from Lower Chalcolithic to EB I, while the bowl 30 compares with Fara Site H. The middle part of the full range might be preferable. See also Cave 1523.

Pl. 57: 61	Tell en-Naṣbeh (TN II, Pl. 85: 3rd row, left)	EB
	Jericho (AAA XXIII, Pl. XXXII: 23B)	Layer VIII
Pl. 57: 62	Megiddo (SAOC 10, Chart Column 12G)	Stages VII–IV
Pl. 57: 63	Megiddo (M. II, Pl. 102: 5)	Stratum XVIII
	Beisan (MJ XXIV, 1935, Pl. IV: 4)	Level XIV
	Tell el Far'ah (RB LIV, 1947, p. 411, Fig. 3: 5)	EB I
	Teleilat Ghassul (TG II, Pl. 82: 19)	Niveau IV A

1526 Single grave in Grid Square XII: L.11 Mixed and post-exilic

Oriented east–west. Body undisturbed, position extended on right side, head to west, face south. The bowls and sherds of mixed date recorded as from Grave 1526 are from a small pit below, and are not associated with the burial to which the beads belong.

Pottery: Drawings on Pl. 57: 42, 43

Objects: Beads NP (Beck classifications: I.B.1.b (4 ex.), I.C.1.b. (18 ex.), I.D.1.b. (4 ex.), I.D.2.b. (5 ex.). Red, green and blue paste, white and blue glass)

Date and Comparisons

The crucibles include one with associations at Fara Site H. There are besides sherds which compare with those from Group 1529 (Pl. 66).

Pl. 57: 43   Tell Fara (BP II, Pl. XL: 43) Site H

1527–1528 Cave in Grid Square XII: F.18 Chalc. or EB I and later

The nari stratum of the roof was practically intact, and the cave formed one of a group with 1523 and 1529. Probably associated with an EB I occupation are the vessels and crucibles on Pl. 57: 49–54 and possibly the bead.

Late in the Early Bronze Age, with many other caves in the vicinity, the place was taken over by the incoming people of the Caliciform Culture, and sherds like those in Group 1529 (Pl. 66) belong to this phase.

Pottery: Drawings on Pl. 57: 49–54; other fragments as Pl. 66: 401, 407, 424

Objects: Bead: Pl. 29: 21   Flint blades, Appendix C

Comparisons

Pl. 57: 50	El Husn (APEF VI, Fig. 1: 4)	EB I
Pl. 57: 53	Megiddo (MT, Pl. 3: 2) Tomb 903 Upper	Stages VII–IV
	Jericho (AAA XXIII, Pl. XXXVI: 13)	Layer VII

1529 Cave in Grid Square XII: F.18 Caliciform

The most easterly of a cluster of dwellings which included Caves 1523 and 1527–1528, Cave 1529 lay directly under the probable alinement of the west side of the building in Grid Square G.18/19. The roof had collapsed, and much domestic pottery had been dumped in the consequent depression. It was closely packed together and no human remains were found.

The sherds shown in photographs and drawings are only a small selection from a great quantity; they include Ledge Handle Form 11. The date and comparisons for this important group are discussed on pp. 42, 171, 178 f.

Pottery: Sherds photographed on Pl. 13: 81–89
      Drawings on Pl. 66: 394–424
Palestine Museum Nos.: PM. 34.7750–7751

1531 Cave in Grid Square XII: F.18 Lower-Upper Chalc.

Denuded cave-dwelling. The basin would perhaps be best placed in the Upper Chalcolithic period, but the references below to an indented edge cover the full range of that age. The basin illustrated by Glueck in AASOR XXV–XXVIII, Pt. II, Pl. 129: 10 from Sibya and attributed to MB I is technically different and is more closely akin to that illustrated on Pl. 66: 449.

Pottery: Pl. 56: 9

Comparisons

Pl. 56: 9	Tell Fara (BP II, Pl. XXXII: top middle) Site E	
	(BP II, Pl. XXXV: 3rd on right) Site O	
	Jericho (AAA XXII, Pl. XXXV: 5) Strip 3, 9·62 m.	Layers VII–VI
	Megiddo (SAOC 10, Chart Column 14G)	Stages VII–IV
	Megiddo (M. II, Pl. 98: 23)	Stratum XIX
	Tell el Far'ah (RB LIV, 1947, Fig. 2: 18 and p. 401)	Énéolithique Supérieur

1532 Cave in Grid Square XII: K.11   Upper Chalc. ?

The southern half of a natural cave enlarged for use as a dwelling and partitioned by walls of stone. See also Cave 1517.

1533 Single grave in Grid Square XII: K.12   Post-exilic ?

Oriented east–west. Body undisturbed, extended position on right side, head to west, face south. In the same grave was a child's body with which the following beads were associated: Beck classifications: I.B.1.b. (1 red glaze, 3 glass, 2 cn.); I.B.2.b. (1 cn.); I.D.1.e (1 cn., 5 glass, 1 onyx); Group XVII, A.2.a. (2 au); Group XIX, A.1 (1 glass); Group XXVII, A.3 (8 shell). There were two gold beads for which there is no Beck classification.

1534 Cave in Grid Square XII: H.12   Middle-Upper Chalc.

A natural cave adapted for use as a dwelling, with pits and depressions in the floor.

Pottery: Sherds photographed on Pl. 12: 33–52
        Drawings on Pl. 56: 10–17; other fragments as Pl. 56: 2; Pl. 57: 45, 61
        Holemouth rims as NE 2/374, NE 4/362, NE 5/347, NE 9/247 (see pp. 164 f.)
        Ledge handles, Forms 1–3, 5, 8 (pp. 148 f.)

Date and Comparisons

This group includes a few rather early items. The most important of these is the pottery ladle, Type 10, Pl. 12: 34, with analogies at Fara Site D, Ghassul, Tell el Far'ah (Énéolithique Moyen) and elsewhere both in Palestine and outside (cf. V. G. Childe, *New Light*, pp. 38 and 39, Fig. 14; *Dawn*, pp. 17, 124, 128, 135, 280, 315). Other items could be attributed to stages equal to Fara Site M (Pl. 12: 46), Fara A (Pl. 12: 52) and Ghassul (Pl. 12: 48), though these might also be dated later. The bulk of the material seems, however, to come from the Middle to Upper Chalcolithic. The pierced handle (Pl. 12: 35) is comparable to specimens at Beisan XVIII (though also at Fara Site O). Ledge handles include Forms 4 and 5 (Pl. 12: 47, 49, 50 and p. 149). The tilted-up form can be matched at Umm Hamad Sherqi attributed by Glueck to the same age as Beisan XVI, where the same tendency occurs. Several analogies to Fara Site H include the multiple handles (Pl. 12: 42, 43) and the indented edge (Pl. 12: 40). Contacts for periods later than the Upper Chalcolithic are not outstanding and the cave may not have been much occupied in the Early Bronze Age. Parallels for the less bulbous holemouth rims are to be found in the North-East Section.

Pl. 12: 33	Jericho (I. of A. ref.: PB 3.20–21)	
Pl. 12: 34	Tell Fara (BP II, Pl. XXII: 2, right; Pl. XXVIII: 22) Site D	
and	Teleilat Ghassul (TG I, Pl. 44: 58)	Niveau IV
Pl. 56: 10	Megiddo (M. II, Pl. 255: 3)	Stratum XVIII
	Tell el Far'ah (RB LV, 1948, p. 546, Fig. 1: 4)	Énéolithique Moyen
	Gezer (*Gezer* III, Pl. XXII, No. 20a, b) Cave 15 I. For date see PEQ, Jan. 1937, p. 73	EB I
Pl. 12: 35	Beisan (MJ XXIV, 1935, Pl. II: 16)	Level XVIII
	Tell Fara (BP II, Pl. XXIX: middle) Site O	

Pl. 12: 36	Tell Fara (I. of A. ref.: E. IV. 2048) Site H, D2, 6·5–7 ft.	
Pl. 12: 39	Tell Fara (I. of A. ref.: E. IV. 2072) Site H, surface	
	Gezer (*Gezer* III, Pl. XXII: 3) Cave 15 I. For date see PEQ, Jan. 1937, p. 73	EB I
Pl. 12: 40	Tell el Far'ah (RB LIV, 1947, p. 409, Fig. 2: 4)	Énéolithique Supérieur
	Tell Fara (BP II, Pl. XXXV: 7th row, right) Site O	
	(BP II, Pl. XXXVII: 4th row, 3rd from right) Site H	
	Tell Hammam (TG I, p. 102, Fig. 52: 6)	Niveau IV
Pl. 12: 41	Jericho (I. of A. ref.: PB 3.20–21)	
Pl. 12: 42	Tell Fara (BP II, XXXI: bottom middle) Site H, 7–7·5 ft.	
	Jericho (AAA XXII, Pl. XXXVI: 15 for triple handle) Strip 2, 9·21 m.	Layers VII–VI
Pl. 12: 43	Tell Fara (BP II, Pl. XXXVII: 3rd from bottom, right) Site H, 6–7 ft.	
Pl. 12: 45	Ophel (I. of A. ref.: E. XXXIV 7/3 489/47)	
Pl. 12: 46	Tell Fara (BP II, Pl. XXXIII: 3rd row, centre) Site M	
	Tell Iktanu (AASOR XXV–XXVIII, Pt. II, Pl. 82: 1, drawn on Pl. 151: 1)	Chalcolithic
Pl. 12: 48	Teleilat Ghassul (TG II, Pl. 86: 7, 19)	Niveau IV B
Pl. 12: 49	Tell en-Naṣbeh (TN II, Pl. 11: 179) City Wall, V layer	
	Jericho (AAA XXII, Pl. XXXV: 5) Strip 3, 9·62 m.	Layers VII–VI
	Tell Fara (I. of A. ref.: E. IV. 2069) Site H, Pit 8	
Pl. 12: 50	Tell Umm Hamad Sherqi (AASOR XXV–XXVIII, Pt. II, Pl. 102: 5)	Upper Chalcolithic
Pl. 12: 51	Beisan (MJ XXIV, 1935, Pl. II: 24)	Pits and Level XVIII
	Tell el Far'ah (RB LIV, 1947, p. 407, Fig. 1:17)	Énéolithique Moyen
	(RB LIV, 1947, p. 415, Fig. 5: 19)	EB I
Pl. 12: 52	Tell Fara (I. of A. ref.: E. III. 2045) Site A	
	Beisan (MJ XXIV, 1935, Pl. I: 25 with raised band)	Level XVIII
Pl. 56: 11	Teleilat Ghassul (TG II, Pl. 78: 9)	Niveau IV
Pl. 56: 14	Et-Tell (*Ay*, Pl. LXX: 666) Tombe C	EB II?

1535 Cave in Grid Square XII: F.18 — EB I–III

Probably one of the best-preserved dwellings on the site, Cave 1535 was strengthened by the addition of stone walls to support the roof, so that it was more than usually intact (Pl. 2: 5). In the floor there was a pit lined with stone slabs, very similar in character to those in Caves 1558 and 6005 (Pl. 3: 2).

After the cavern was abandoned as a home, numerous burials were made in the filling of the chamber, and it is to that second phase of occupation that most of the pottery belonged.

Pottery

Bowls: upright rim 198; flanged rim (rounded top) 86, 87, 90, 91, 92
        inturned rim 83; plain rim 75–80, 84, 135, 145
        with lugs 88, 89(2); string-cut 85
Crucibles: 33, 183   Cups: 81, 82
Spouted bowls: 106, 107, 108(2)
Jars: with ledge handles 121; with loop handles 118
Amphoriskoi: 110, 111(3), 112–117
Juglets: narrow-necked 93, 98, 99, 100; wide-necked 18, 94–97 202
        pointed 101(2), 102, 103
Unclassified: 104(2), 105, 109, 119, 120, 122, 123, 128
Potmarks: Pl. 18: 64, 70, 71, 72, 77
Ledge handles: Forms 7, 8, 10 (pp. 152 f.)

Objects

Flint blades, Appendix C

Beads:

Pl. 29:	2	6	7	9	16	17	21	25	44	45
Paste	80	13	—	2	22	—	2	5	—	—
Stone	—	1 cn.	1 s:ea.	—	—	—	—	—	—	—
Metal	—	—	—	—	—	1 au	—	—	—	—
Shell	—	—	—	—	—	—	—	—	4	1

Date and Comparisons

Some parallels show that this cave was in use during EB I (cf. especially such forms as the amphoriskoi 110–117). EB II is likewise represented. There are also a number of vases attributable to EB III, more especially to Jericho Tomb A and these include items such as the miniature juglet 102. However, the main history of the tomb ended before that of Tomb 1519, while Tomb 1513 was even later. Foreign parallels for objects in the tomb include a reasonably close comparison for amphoriskos Type 113 at Protodynastic Abusir el Meleq and for Type 105 (unclassified) at Qau and Badari dated to dynasty ix. This would be very late but need not disturb us in view of the difference in fabric between the red-slipped and burnished Palestinian vase and the buff Egyptian ware, for this difference may well correspond to a considerable stretch of time.

Pl. 58: 75	Jericho (AAA XXII, Pl. XXXI: 28) Room 129, 10·77 m.	Layers V–IV
Pl. 58: 77	Jericho (AAA XXIII, Pl. XXXVI: 5)	Layer VI
	Et-Tell (*Ay*, Pl. LXXIX: 773) Tombe G	EB II–III
Pl. 58: 79	Byblos (B. I, p. 369, Fig. 288: 5403) Bâtiment XXVII, Salle C, see also	EB I
	Byblos (RB LIX, 1952, Pl. III: 3rd row, centre)	EB I
Pl. 58: 85	Megiddo (SAOC 10, Chart Column 2)	Stages IV–I
Pl. 58: 86	Jericho (AAA XXII, Pl. XXX: 14) Room 126, 10·74 m.	Layers V–IV
Pl. 58: 87	Jericho (AAA XIX, Pl. IV: 12) Tomb A2.34b	EB III
Pl. 58: 88	Et-Tell (*Ay*, Pl. LXXXV: 1569 fourth row) Fouille H, Ch. 144, assise 2	
	Et-Tell (*Ay*, Pl. LXVII: 22.635) Tombe C	EB II?
	Beisan (MJ XXIV, 1935, Pl. V: 18 and p. 16)	Levels XIII and XII
	Tell el Far'ah (RB LIV, 1947, p. 417 Fig. 6: 2 and p. 419, Fig. 7: 36)	EB II
	Jericho (PEQ, 1952, p. 77, Fig. 5: 35) Upper midden against 2nd wall	EB II?
Pl. 58: 89	Jericho (AAA XXII, Pl. XXX: 20—without lugs—cf. AAA XXIII, p. 93) Room 126, 10·74 m.	Layers V–III
	Jericho (AAA XXIII, Pl. XXXVII: 10)	Layer III
	Ras el Ain (QDAP V, Pl. LXIV: 11)	EB III
	Jericho (PEQ, 1952, p. 77, Fig. 5: 36) Upper midden against 2nd wall	EB II?
Pl. 58: 90	Jericho (AAA XIX, Pl. IV: 23) Tomb A2.40	EB III
Pl. 58: 91	Jericho (AAA XIX, Pl. IV: 18) Tomb A2.35	EB III
	Megiddo (MT, Pl. 4: 5) Tomb 910a Fill	Stages IV–III
Pl. 58: 94	Jericho (AAA XIX, Pl. VI: 5) Tomb A2.28c	EB III
Pl. 58: 96	Jericho (AAA XIX, p. 39, Fig. 8: 10) Tomb 24	EB I
Pl. 58: 100	Tell el Far'ah (RB LVI, 1949, p. 120, Fig. 6: 34) Tomb 2	EB I
Pl. 58: 101	Jericho (AAA XIX, Pl. V: 1) Tomb A2.8f	EB III
	Jericho (SW, Pl. 21: E3)	Canaanite
Pl. 58: 102	Jericho (AAA XIX, Pl. II: 5) Tomb A2.22b	EB III
Pl. 58: 103	Jericho (AAA XIX, Pl. II: 7) Tomb A3.31a	EB III
Pl. 58: 105	Qau and Badari (QB II, Pl. LXXXX: 15B) Tomb 1746	Dyn. ix
Pl. 58: 108	Tell Beit Mirsim (AASOR XII, p. 6; Pl. 2: 14)	Stratum J
	Gezer (*Gezer* I, p. 91, Fig. 31) Cave 15 I	
Pl. 58: 113	Abusir el Meleq (Pl. 13: 59 for shape only)	
Pl. 58: 115	Tell en-Naṣbeh (TN I, p. 73; II, Pl. 12: 209) Tomb 67	EB I–II
Pl. 58: 116	Gezer (PEQ, Jan. 1935, Pl. IV: top row, 2nd from right)	EB I–II

Pl. 58: 122	Tell en-Naṣbeh (TN II, Pl. 9: 143) Cave 193c	EB I–II
Pl. 58: 123	Megiddo (M. II, Pl. 3: 2)	Stratum XIX
	Beisan (MJ XXIV, 1935, Pl. IV: 14)	Level XIV
Pl. 60: 198	Affuleh (JPOS XXI, Pl. VI: 40) Pit E	
	Jericho (PEQ, 1952, pp. 62 ff., Fig. 6: 7) Construction of 3rd wall	

1536 Locus in Grid Square XII: G.17   Caliciform

One distorted cup, like Pl. 66: 409

1537 Cave in Grid Square XII: K.12   Lower and Upper Chalc.

Part of the cutting on the east side was denuded owing to its position near the edge of the scarp. This cave may have been occupied in both the Lower and Upper Chalcolithic stages. For the earlier period see comparisons for Pl. 11:10 and ledge handle Form 3 (p. 149). The ledge handles of Form 5 with their tendency to become slightly pushed up are better placed at a stage corresponding to Beisan XVI (cf. Glueck, BASOR 97, Feb. 1945, p. 13). As our specimens seem more developed than the published Beisan handles, they should be somewhat later. It might indeed be possible to compress the whole of the material from this cave strictly into the Upper Chalcolithic, but, in view of the multiplicity of associations from the earlier stages, it is perhaps inadvisable.

Pottery: Photographs on Pl. 11: 7–15

Comparisons

Pl. 11: 10	Tell Fara (I. of A. ref.: E. III. 2027) Site A	
	Tell Fara (BP II, Pl. XXXIII: 4th row, middle) Site B	
	(BP II, Pl. XXXV: 7th row, right) Site O	
	(BP II, Pl. XXXVII: 4th row, middle) Site H	
	Jericho (AAA XXII, Pl. XLIII: 17) Tomb 355	
	ʿAin Shems (AS IV, Pl. XXIII: 16)	Stratum VI
	Teleilat Ghassul (TG II, Pl. 81: 20, 21)	Niveau IV B
Pl. 11: 14	Tell Fara (BP II, Pl. XXXVI: top left) Site H, D2, 7·5–8 ﬔ	

1538 Cave in Grid Square XII: F/G.16   Chalc. and later

A large cave-dwelling in which the roof had collapsed except in the north-east corner. The floor was strewn with boulders and pitted with many cup-marks and contained one partially stone-lined pit.

Probably to be associated with the dwelling phase are:

Pottery: Sherds photographed on Pl. 11: 16–32

Objects: Stone from Pit A: Maceheads: Pl. 26: 1, 2 (see p. 71)
                 Flint blades, Appendix C
    Bone: Bead: Pl. 29: 21

Vessels which probably belonged to burials in EB II–III:

Pottery: Crucible: 262   Cup: 263   Spouted Bowl: 264
        Amphoriskoi: 265, 266, 267
        Juglets: wide-necked 268–271; narrow-necked 272

Date and Comparisons

The dwelling phase of occupation possesses well-developed affinities with Fara Site H. Ledge handles Form 2 (p. 149) link it with Megiddo XIX, Beisan XVII and Tell el Farʿah (Énéolithique Supérieur), Form 5 equates with Beisan XVI and Umm Hamad Sherci, while Form 7 extends into Beisan Level XIII. Only one or two forms seem to belong to an earlier context (Sub or Lower Chalcolithic). Neither is the extension of this early group into Early Bronze very significant. There are, however, items which should be attributed to repeated use of the cave. Some, like the amphoriskoi 265–267, might find their place in EB II if not before; others, like the spouted bowl 264 and juglet 269, are attributable to EB III.

Pl. 11: 20   Tell Fara (I. of A. ref.: E. IV. 2052) Site H, Pit 6
             Tell Fara (BP II, Pl. XXXII: 3rd row, left, for decoration only) Site O
Pl. 11: 21   Tell Fara (I. of A. ref.: E. IV. 2048) Site H, Pit XI
Pl. 11: 23   Tell Fara (BP II, Pl. XL: 67) Site H
Pl. 11: 24   Tell Fara (BP II, Pl. XXX: 7) Site D
Pl. 11: 25   Et-Tell (*Ay*, Pl. LVIII: centre) Fouille Z, ch. 207   Niveau II
Pl. 11: 26   Tell Fara (I. of A. ref.: E. III. 2027) Site A
Pl. 11: 27   Megiddo (SAOC 10, Chart Column 14D)   Stages V–III
             Beisan (MJ XXIV, 1935, Pl. VI: 8)   Level XIII
             Jericho (AAA XXII, Pl. XXXV: 12) Strip 3, 9·67 m.   Layers VII–VI
             Jericho (AAA XXII, Pl. XLIII: 17) Tomb 355
             Affuleh (JPOS XXI, 1948, Pl. VII: 15) Pit A–B surface
             Tell el Far'ah (RB LIV, 1947, p. 407, Fig. 1: 31)   Énéolithique Moyen
                           (RB LIV, 1947, p. 409, Fig. 2: 21)   Énéolithique Supérieur
             Tell ed-Dhiyabeh (AASOR XXV–XXVIII, Pt. II, Pl. 57. 4)   EB I
             Tell Fara (BP II, Pl. XXXIII: 4th row, middle) Site B
                       (BP II, Pl. XXXV: 7th row, right) Site O
                       (BP II, Pl. XXXVII: 4th row, middle) Site H
             'Ain Shems (AS IV, Pl. XXIII: 16)   Stratum VI
             Teleilat Ghassul (TG II, Pl. 86: 20, 21)   Niveau IV B
             'Ameidat (AASOR XXV–XXVIII, Pt. II, Pl. 1: 2)   EB I–II
Pl. 11: 28   Et-Tell (*Ay*, Pl. LXXXVI: 1445) Fouille H, Ch. 138, sous mur   EB I–II?
             Eastern Palestine (AASOR XVIII–XIX, p. 54, Fig. 29)   EB IV A
Pl. 11: 31   Megiddo (M. II, Pl. 98: 23)   Stratum XIX
             Beisan (MJ XXIV, 1935, Pl. II: 8)   Level XVII
             Tell el Far'ah (RB LIV, 1947, p. 409, Fig. 2: 18)   Énéolithique Supérieur
             Tell Umm Hamad Sherqi (AASOR XXV–XXVIII, Pt. II, Pl. 102: 9)   Late (Upper) Chalcolithic
             Tell Fara (BP II, Pl. XXXVI: top left) Site H, D2
Pl. 11: 32   Beisan (MJ XXIV, 1935, Pl. II: 3 and p. 12)   Levels XVI–XIV
             Jericho (PEQ, 1952, p. 77, Fig. 5: 4) Below first town wall   EB Ib?
             Megiddo (SAOC 10, Chart Column 14G)   Stages VII–IV
             Jerusalem (JST, Pl. VII: 13) Galerie III
Pl. 61: 269 Gezer (*Gezer* III, Pl. CXLIII: 10)   "First Semitic"

1539 Tomb in Grid Square XII: G.17   MB III, *c.* 1750–1700 B.C.

A cave or tomb, possibly of bilobate character but partially denuded, which contained a small group of pottery. There are fragments in the MB Glacis fill of the North-East Section of storage jars like Type 1016.

Pottery: Bowls: carinate C 543(2), 544; flared J 612
        Juglet: C 748   Dipper: A 781
        Storage Jars: C 1016(2)

1540 Locus in Grid Square XII: G.16   Chalc.—EB

A group of pottery near the entrance to Cave 1538 and possibly associated with it. The sloping-necked jar can be matched at Ghassul but the family is also represented by fragments at Fara Site H. The whole group could probably be placed at the transition from Chalcolithic to EB.

Pottery: Drawings on Pl. 57: 55–59; other fragments as Pl. 57: 50

Comparison

Pl. 57: 59   Teleilat Ghassul (TG II, Pl. 77: 7)   Niveau IV

1541 Tomb in Grid Square XII: J.13   Caliciform

Irregular-shaped cave or tomb containing sherds comparable to those in Group 1529 (Pl. 66).

1542 Cave in Grid Square XII: H.14   MB III, *c.* 1750–1700 B.C.

One of several probably re-used EB caves, close in position and date to each other. The contents appeared to consist of normal burial offerings. There are contacts with Jericho Tomb 9 and with the Palace Stores, also with Tell Beit Mirsim Stratum E and Megiddo Strata XII–X.

The scarab may bear a variant of the sun name of Neferhetep II (cf. No. 23 from Tomb 1502).

Comparisons for the togglepin Pl. 24: 3 are from Tomb 556 (BP I, Pl. IX: 43) and Tomb 1021 (BP II, Pl. XLIII: 3) at Tell Fara, and in Tomb 1702 at Ajjul (AG IV, Pl. XXXII: 496). Cf. also Pl. 24: 4 with 5 from Tomb 1502.

Pottery: Bowls: carinate B 525, 526; C 540, 541
      Jug: B 673   Juglets: C 742, 743(2)
      Dipper: A 781   Storage Jar: B 1010

Objects: Metal: Togglepins: Pl. 24: 3, 4
      Scarab: Pl. 30: 26
Palestine Museum Nos.: PM 34.2891–2902, 34.3094

1543 Cup-marks in Grid Square XII: K.13   EB?

Group of four holes or "cup-marks" (Pl. 2: 3). See p. 39.

1544 Cup-marks in Grid Square XII: F.17   EB?

Group of eight holes or "cup-marks". See p. 39.

1545 Pit in Grid Square XII: J.13   MB I–II?

Square pit with apsidal northern end lined with stones, dimensions 3·50 × 2·50 × 1·45 m. in depth.

1546 Cave or tomb in Grid Square XII: H.13/14   MB III, *c.* 1700–1650 B.C.

Though partially denuded, the tomb contained pottery analogous to that from other nearby tombs, 1547 and 1552.

Contacts are good with Jericho Tomb 9, layers b and c, and Tomb 4, layer c. The faience kohl pot is matched in Tomb 31. Connexions with Strata E and D at Tell Beit Mirsim are about equal.

Pottery: Bowls: carinate C 540, 541(2), 543(6); E 562(2)
      Lamps: A 644   Jugs: B 674; E 717
      Juglets: E 751, 753(3), 756, 757, 758; F 765
      Dippers: A 780, 781   Storage Jar: B 1011

Objects: Faience kohl pots: Pl. 26: 13, 14
      Bead: Pl. 29: 37 (1 paste)

1547 Cave in Grid Square XII: J.14   MB III, *c.* 1700–1650 B.C.

The eastern part of Cave 1552 contained offerings which were perhaps later than those in the western half. The pottery resembles that of Tomb 550 at Tell Fara, while the togglepin on Pl. 24: 14 is matched in Tomb 551 (BP I, Pl. VI: 6) and in Tomb 1026 (BP II, Pl. XLIV: 63). Tombs 4 and 5 at Jericho are represented.

Pottery: Bowls: carinate C 543; E 563
          Lamps: A 643; B 650; C 657
          Juglets: E 756, 757, 758, 759; F 765(3), 766, 767, 768, 769
          Dippers: A 780, 781(2)

Objects: Metal: Togglepins: Pl. 24: 13–15
         Scarab, amethyst, uninscribed NP

1548 Cave in Grid Square XII: J.14   MB III, *c.* 1675–1625 B.C.

A small part of the large cave-dwelling 1553 was divided by a partition wall of stone to make room for later burials which were, however, much disturbed and broken.

Pottery: Bowls: carinate A 514, 520; B 532; C 546
          Lamp: A 645   Jugs: D 697(2), 698
          Juglets: F 764, 770   Dippers: A 781(4)
          Miniature Pithos: 972
          Storage Jars: A 1006; B 1010, 1011(2)

Objects: Flint blades, Appendix C

1549 Single grave in Grid Square XII: G.20   Post-exilic

One of a series of more than twenty graves, cf. the east–west series described in *Lachish III*, p. 174. Usually the body had disappeared and there were no offerings, but in this case it was undisturbed, with position extended, head to the west and face south.

1550 Pit in Grid Square XII: G.20   Chalc.–EB

Irregular-shaped pit containing sherds and crude hand-made cups or crucibles. A dating at the transition from Chalcolithic to Early Bronze seems indicated.

Pottery: Drawings on Pl. 56: 32–35
          Ledge handles: Forms 1–3, 5

1551 House in Grid Square XII: G.19   Caliciform Culture? *c.* 2100 B.C.

The walls of this room seem to form the eastern flank of a much larger, straggling building; see Room 1512 in a corresponding position on the west side. The remains are in both cases preserved to a height of about 60 cms. All the rest has been lost through continuous use of the plough. Two beakers, one of which is comparable to Type 441 in Cemetery 2000 (Pl. 66), suggest that the contemporary house represents an early attempt at settlement by the people of the Caliciform Culture. The same kind of poorly planned houses were built over the ashes of the Early Bronze Age city at Jericho (PEQ, 1952, p. 90).

Dr. Waechter's report on the flints from the room shows that, with many new changes in ceramic technique introduced by these people, there was also a difference in the sickle blades, which are coarser, while end-scrapers and burins also appear (Appendix C). Part of a copper casting like the piece illustrated on Pl. 21: 11 may suggest the date for the other examples on that plate which come from surface areas (p. 75, and Appendix D).

Pottery: Drawings on Pl. 56: 36, 37

Objects: Metal: Rough casting NP
Flint sickle blades: Pl. 19: 8–15

1552 Cave in Grid Square XII: J.14

MB II–III, *c.* 1800–1675 B.C.

The northern and larger part of a cave which is connected with 1547. The burials and offerings were disturbed.

Photographs on Pl. 50

Pottery

Bowls: carinate A 510*(3), 516,* 519, 520*(2); B 523,* 528;* C 539,* 542;* F 578,* 579*
curved H 595*(2); flared J 611*
Lamps: D 660*(3)   Jug: A 670*
Juglets: A 728,* 729;* B 731,* 734;* C 741;* E 751*(2), 753, 756*(2)
Dippers: A 779,* 780,* 781*; *L. II*: 295*
Storage Jar: B 1011*

Objects

Metal: Daggers: Pl. 22: 11–13*   Togglepins NP
Stone: Vase: Pl. 26: 25*
Beads: Pl. 29: 2 (3 paste), 5 (2 paste, 2 cn., 1 am.), 6 (6 paste, 3 qu.), 16 (3 paste, 1 cn.), 21 (1 cn.), 24 (1 microcline)
Amulet: Pl. 29: 51
Scarabs: Pl. 30: 1–22
Ostrich shell frags. NP

Date and Comparisons

The range of the group extends through Strata E–D at Tell Beit Mirsim and from Strata XIV–IX at Megiddo, in fact through much of MB II–III, and there are parallels in Tombs 5 and 9 at Jericho.

Three daggers are all of Type 27a, p. 77, and No. 11 compares closely with No. 14 from Tomb 1502. No. 12 was the subject of a metallurgical report, see Appendix D, p. 331.

The scarabs include early pieces attributed by Rowe to the xiiith–xivth dynasties and there are besides several links with tombs of Cemetery 500 at Tell Fara (BP I). Possible contractions of royal names (*Ra-kheper*) appear on Nos. 1, 2 and 4. This contraction is also found at Jericho in Tombs 19 and 5 (AAA XX, Pl. XXVI: Tomb 19: 2, Tomb 5: 4).

1553 Cave in Grid Square XII: J.14

Upper Chalc.–EB II

A large cave-dwelling which had been divided from its southern annexe by a partition wall of stones. That part, numbered 1548, was re-used for burials in the Middle Bronze Age.

Pottery: Sherds photographed on Pl. 12: 53–56
Drawings on Pl. 57: 65–68; other fragments as Pl. 13: 78; Pl. 56: 11; Pl. 57: 45(2)

Objects: Stone: Sickle blade: Pl. 19: 1
Bone: Point: Pl. 13: 96; Ox-bone: Pl. 21: 5

Date and Comparisons

Ledge handles comprise Forms 4, 5 and 7 (pp. 149 ff.). The little crucible with handle (Pl. 12: 54 and Pl. 57: 66) can be matched at Tell Hammam and would thus be dated to EB I. Pl. 57: 65 recurs at Fara H. A dating within the range from Upper Chalcolithic to EB II would probably fit the remaining objects, and thus the range of the group might equal Megiddo Stages V–III.

Comparisons for the ox-bone on Pl. 21: 5, discussed in more detail on pp. 72 f., date from the Chalcolithic period to the end of the Early Bronze Age, and the same limits would include the bone point on Pl. 13: 96.

Pl. 12: 54	Tell Hammam (TG I, Pl. 61: 5)	EB I
Pl. 57: 65	Tell Fara (I. of A. ref.: E. IV. 2026) Site H, Pit XI	

1554 Single grave in Grid Square XII: G.20   Post-exilic

One of a series of more than twenty graves, oriented east and west. See for example 1549. The body was undisturbed, position extended on right side, head to the south and facing west.

1555 Locus in Grid Square XII: K.9 (see Chart on pp. 60–61)   LB I, 1600–1450 B.C.

This comparatively small group was possibly thrown out from cavity 1507. It is anyhow of special interest as the elements are varied enough in a group which is not too large to show an unusual phase of LB I.

The bowls and jugs are small and debased in relation to their predecessors. Of three lamps, one belongs to Class B which was so common in Tomb 4004 and two belong to Class C which superseded it in Structure I.

The last cylindrical bodies occur on juglets Types 772 and 773, while the latter has a neck and smooth finish identical with those of Types 775 and 776, both of Black Lustrous ware (Class J). There is also a White Shaved dipper and a Base-Ring I juglet with handles inserted.

Pottery   *Photographs on Pl. 51

Bowls: carinate A 510*(2); plain G 586*; flared J 613*
Lamps: B 653;* C 654*(2) Jugs: B 678;* E 718*
Juglets: G 772;* H 773;* J 775;* 776*(2)
Dippers: A 782*(2) Imported Ware: 821 Base-Ring Ware: 860*

1556 Burial in Cave 1558, Grid Square XII: H.14   EB III

A single male burial near the entrance to Cave 1558 (Pl. 3: 6, 7). The bones, which were scattered and disturbed, rested on the earlier filling of the cave, and much fine pottery and a copper dagger formed part of the group.

"In one of the cave-dwellings", Starkey wrote at the time, "we have discovered a collection of pottery in association with a disturbed burial of a man, and close to the skull was a fine copper dagger, one of the best specimens I have seen from this early period. . . . The group of pottery consists of a pithos, 83 cms. in height, finished with a combed surface and bearing a mark incised by the potter before firing; two hand-burnished pots with ledge handles; one spouted bowl and several small shallow bowls, similarly burnished. With these more important pieces were a number of miniature vessels. This group . . . forms a connecting link between the sherds found in the lower levels of our Tell section, just above bed-rock, and the period of our N.W. Settlement, when these cave-dwellings were being used as burial places, which we consider to represent the second phase of the settlement's history." (Field Report, December 1934.)

Pottery   *Photographs on Pl. 14

Bowls: plain rim 234,* 235,* 236,* 237,* 238,* 242, 243*
     with lugs: 244,* string-cut 241*
Cup: 239* Spouted bowls: 250,* 252* Pithos: 296*
Jars and Jugs with ledge handles: 251,* 255,* 256*
Jars: narrow-necked 254*; with lugs 257*
Amphoriskos: 245* Juglets: pointed 246,* 247,* 248,* 249*
Unclassified: 240,* 253*
Potmarks: Pl. 18: 2, 6, 10, 24

Objects

Metal: Dagger: Pl. 22: 6,* for analysis see Appendix D
Flint Implements Appendix C   Pitch NP

Date and Comparisons

Internal comparison shows many types in common with Cave 1513 and a corresponding decrease in slip and burnish, in sharp contrast to Caves 1519 and 1535, which each provide only one duplicate. This result agrees with external evidence, showing more contact with EB III than EB II. The pithos 296 is comparable to the uncombed Type 303 and others from the caverns in Area 5000, and it is also linked to jars in the North-East Section, Nos. 358 and 241 on pp. 57–59.

The dagger is definitely associated with the skeleton (Pl. 3: 6), but its association with the pottery is less clear. However, it is earlier in type than the daggers in the Caliform Cemetery 2000 and in the "Copper" Age Cemeteries at Ajjul; therefore there is no reason to separate it from the main group. It compares with a dagger from Tomb 351 at Jericho, attributed by Wright to EB IV (PPEE, p. 108).

Pl. 61: 244	Et-Tell (*Ay*, Pl. LXXVII: 2013) Fouille H, Ch. 116	EB II or III
Pl. 61: 251	Jericho (AAA XIX, Pl. VI: 13 with wider neck) Tomb A1.2c	EB III
Pl. 61: 254	Tell el Hesi (MMC, Pl. 3: 84) City Sub I or I	Amorite
Pl. 62: 296	Megiddo (M. II, Pl. 6: 7 for lugs)	Stratum XVI
	Gezer (*Gezer* II, p. 138, Fig. 308 for outline) Crematorium, see PEQ, 1937, p. 70	EB I
	Abydos (RT II, Pl. V: 18) incised drawing on stone fragment	Dyn. i?

1557 Cave in Grid Square XII: G.15 — EB I–II

A cave-dwelling with denuded roof. The door-sill and well-worn socket were in position on the north-east side, flanked by two upright door jambs (Pl. 3: 4). There were numerous pits and depressions in the floor.

One sherd analogous to Pl. 56: 25 is paralleled at Fara Site H. Ledge handles, Forms 1–3, 5 (p. 149), range from Megiddo VII–I, so that an equation somewhere near the middle of that range seems best for the whole assembly. Part of a Ghassulian cornet is a stray object from an earlier period.

Pottery: As Pl. 56: 25; Ledge handles, Forms 1–3, 5

Objects: Trachyte Mortar: Pl. 26: 6   Sickle flints and pitch NP
Pitted stone, as Pl. 21: 2–3

1558 Cave in Grid Square XII: H.14. Fig. 12 — Chalc.–EB

The cave was entered from a narrow passage on the north side, but most of it, like the roof, had disappeared through denudation. To the south of the main chamber there was a raised alcove which compares in position with the sunken pits in Cave 1523, No. 1514, and elsewhere, which Starkey considered were communal beds.

Sunk in the floor were two circular pits lined with flat stone slabs rising for more than half their height above floor level (Pl. 3: 3). Similar lined pits were found in Caves 1535 and 1005.

About a metre above floor level was a single male burial which is described under No. 1556 above.

Pottery: Sherds photographed on Pl. 12: 57–65
Drawing on Pl. 57: 74; other fragments as Pl. 56: 25; 6/319 on p. 59.

Date and Comparisons

This appears to be a somewhat heterogeneous assembly. The red polished sherd (Pl. 12: 65 and Type 74) is probably near enough to Egyptian Polished Red Ware, particularly if the grass-wiped inner surface is examined, to assume a direct relationship (p. 72). The shape cannot be matched exactly among the pottery in the Department of Egyptology, University of London, but the nearest for ware and technique is PEC, Pl. XIII, Type P.68 B

(U.C. 4161) from Naqada, dated to S.D. 34. Another comparable piece came from Diospolis Parva, Type 46 K (U.C. 10828), S.D. 70.

The handles (Pl. 12: 60, 61), with their widened attachments could on general grounds be attributed to

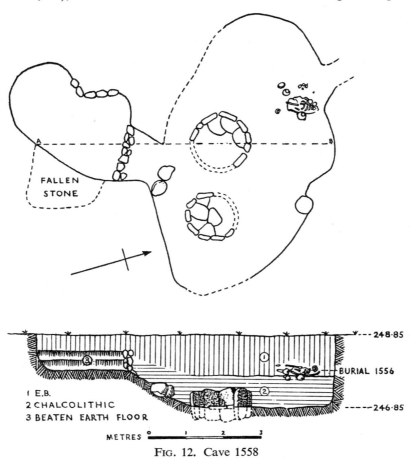

FIG. 12. Cave 1558

Wright's Middle Chalcolithic, but somewhat similar specimens from Fara H, covered with red slip, are also to be found in the collection of the Institute of Archaeology in London. The sherd on Pl. 12: 64, on the other hand, might be dated to EB II.

Pl. 12: 57, 58   Tell Fara (I. of A. ref.: E. IV. 2025) Site H, D1, 4–5 ft.?

Pl. 12: 59, 62   Tell Fara (BP II, Pl. XXXVI: 2) Site H

Pl. 12: 60, 61   Teleilat Ghassul (TG I, Pl. 92)   Niveau IV

Pl. 12: 61   Tell el Farʿah (RB LIV, 1947, p. 407, Fig. 1: 17)   Énéolithique Moyen

Pl. 12: 63   Jericho (AAA XXII, Pl. XXXII: 1) Strip 3, 11·34 m.   Layers V–IV

                Et-Tell (*Ay*, Pl. LXXXII: 2197) Fouille H, Ch. 116, parquet B   EB II?

Pl. 12: 64   Jericho (AAA XXIII, Pl. XXXVII: 2) 8·60 m.   Layer IV

CEMETERY 2000

(Pls. 88–89; 93)

Owing to the uniformity of the tombs in this cemetery of the Caliciform pottery period and the few objects found in them, all the available information is tabulated below. Numbers omitted from the list are those of tombs and quarries which were empty. For the tomb shapes, Fig. 13: Shape O, square shaft and chamber (1 ex.);

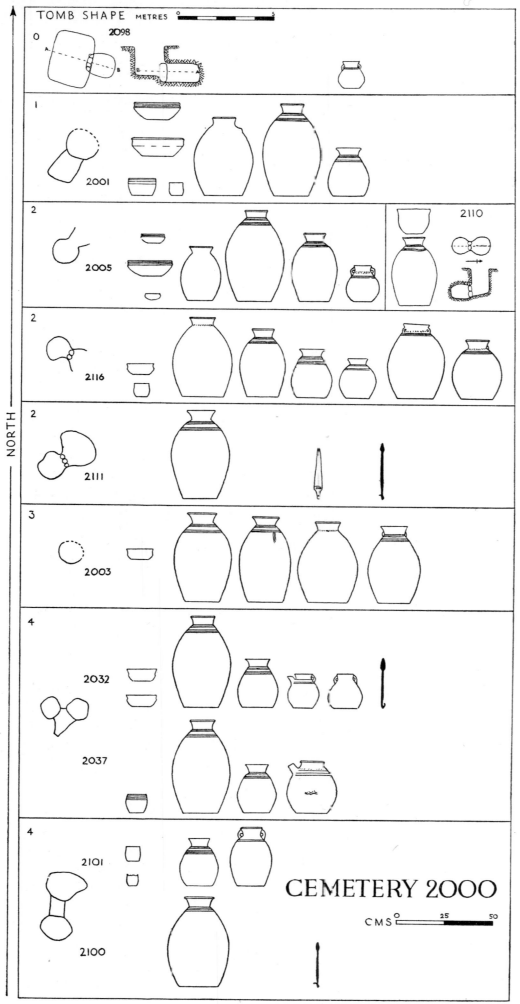

TOMB SHAPE METRES

2098

2001

2005

2110

2116

2111

2003

2032

2037

2101

2100

CEMETERY 2000

CMS

NORTH

FIG. 13

Shape 1, square shaft, rounded chamber (9 ex.); Shape 2, rounded shaft and chamber (37 ex.); Shape 3, no shaft, round or oval chamber (34 ex.); Shape 4, bilobate chamber (8 ex.); Shape 5, irregular and unclassified (15 ex.). Tombs marked in the list with an asterisk are illustrated on the chart. For the pottery, see Pls. 20, 66 and 67; type specimens drawn on these plates are italicized in the list below, where plate references for other objects are also given. For discussions of pottery forms and analogies from other sites, see pp. 171–175.

Grid Ref. on Pl. 93	Tomb	Tomb shape	Contents
Area 2000	—	—	"Teapot" 486, Squat Jar 497(2)
N.6	*2001	1	Bowls 430 (photograph on Pl. 20: 5), 437 (photograph on Pl. 20: 6), Beakers 439 (photograph on Pl. 20: 7), 441 (photograph on Pl. 20: 8), Jars 462, 468(2), 477
N.6	2002	4	"Teapot" 452, Jar 468
N.6	*2003	3	Bowl 432, Jars 469, 470, 472, 484
N.6	2004	3	Jars 463, 474, Squat Jar 495
N.6	*2005	3	Jar 477
N.7	2006	2	"Teapot" 453, Jars 474(2), 477, Squat Jar 491
N.6	2007	3	Jar 480, Squat Jar 489
N.6	2008	3	Jar 457
N.6	2009	3	Jars 468, 469, 477; Pike Pl. 21: 6; 22: 9
N.6	2010	5	Jar 469
O.6	2011	Quarry	Unguentarium, as L. III, Pl. 90: 376
N.6	2012	3	Jar 477
N.5	2013	3	Jar 457
N.5	2014	3	Jar 474
N.6	2015	2	Bowls 429, 430, Funnel 450, Jars 464(2), 468, 474(2), Squat Jar 490. Group in situ, Pl. 4: 3
N.7	2016	5	Jar 476
N.7	2017	1	Jar 457
N.7	2018	3	Lamp 448 (photograph on Pl. 20: 16), Jar 464, Squat Jar 496
N.7	2019	5	Jar 468
O.8	2021	3	Jars 461, 462
N.7	2022	3	Jar 474
N.7	2023	5	Jar 477
O.8	2024	5	Jars 462, 468, 474
N.7	2025	2	Jar 472
N.7	2026	5	Jars 465, 474
N.7	2027	2	Squat Jar 493
O.8	2028	2	Jars 476, 480
O.8	2029	5	Beaker 441, Squat Jar 490
O.8	2030	5	Bowl 428 (photograph on Pl. 20: 2), "Teapot" 454 (photograph on Pl. 20: 3), Jar 455 (photograph on Pl. 20: 1). PM 34.2903–2905
O.9	2031	2	Jars, 472, 481
O.9	2032	4	Bowls 433, 435, Jars 477, 493, "Teapot" 487. Javelin, Pls. 21: 7 and 22: 2
O.9	2033	3	Jar 476
O.9	2034	1	Jar 457, Squat Jar 492
O.9	2035	3	Bowl 436, Jars 464, 472, Squat Jar 497
O.8	2036	3	Jars 476(2), 477, Squat Jar 493. Bone Point NP
O.9	*2037	4	Beaker 440, Jars 456, 468, 476
O.9	2039	2	Jar 476
O.9	2041	3	Copper point, Pl. 22: 10
O.8	2042	3	Jar 475
N.8	2043	3	Jars 466, 472
N.8	2045	3	Jar 469
O.10	2046	3	Beaker 440, Jars 465, 476, 484
O.9	2047	3	"Teapot" 485. PM 34.7679
N.8	2048	3	Jar 476, Squat Jars 497, 498

CEMETERIES

Grid Ref. on Pl. 93	Tomb	Tomb shape	Contents
O.10	2049	5	Jar 484. Dagger, Pls. 21: 8 and 22: 5
O.9	2050	2	Jar 480
O.10	2051	2	Bowl 431, Jars 465(2), 483
O.10	2052	3	Bowl 427, Beaker 441
O.10	2053	1	Jar 469(2)
N.8	2054	2	Squat Jar 497
O.10	2055	3	Jar 464
O.10	2056	3	Squat Jar 497
O.10	2057	3	Jar 476
O.10	2058	3	Jars 476(2), Squat Jar 497
O.10	2059	4	Bowl 434, Beaker 443, Jars 469, 478, 482. PM 34.2906–2909
O.11	2060	5	Squat Jar 497
O.10	2061	1	Lamp 448, Jar 470. PM 34.2911–2912
O.9	2062	1	Squat Jar 493
O.9	2063	2	Jar 477
O.10	2065	3	Bowl 435, Squat Jar 497
O.10	2066	2	Jars 469, 478(2), Squat Jar 497
O.10	2067	3	Jar 465
O.11	2072	5	Bowl 438, Jar 463. PM 34.2913–2914
O.11	2073	2	Squat Jar 497
O.10	2074	2	Jars 464(2), "Teapot" 487
O.11	2075	4	Jar 467, Squat Jar 488. PM 34.2915–2916
O.11	2076	3	Jars 465, 478
O.11	2077	2	Squat Jar 493
O.11	2079	2	Jar 472
O.11	2080	2	Basin 449. PM 34.2917
O.11	2081	2	Jar 465, Squat Jar 497
O.10	2083	2	Beaker 440, Jar 466, Squat Jar 488
O.11	2084	3	Jars 461, 469
O.11	2085	3	Jar 468, Squat Jars 493, 497
P.11	2087	4	Jars 463, 477
O.11	2088	1	Jars 465, 473
P.11	2089	1	Beaker 441
O.11	2090	2	Bowl 431, Beaker 442, Jar 474
P.10	2091	2	Jar 469
O.11	2092	3	Jars 459, 461, 464
O.11	2094	3	Jar 465
O.11	2095	2	Squat Jar 490. Tomb shaft, see Pl. 4: 4
P.11	2097	2	Jar 469, Squat Jar 497
O.11	*2098	0	Squat Jar 497
P.11	2099	2	Jars 469, 478
P.11	*2100	4	Jar 471. Javelin Pl. 22: 3. PM 34.2918–2919
P.11	*2101	4	Beakers 441, 447. Jars 476, 481
O.11	2102	5	Jars 468, 472
O.11	2103	2	Jar 482, Squat Jar 491
P.11	2104	2	Beaker 441, Jar 464
O.11	2105	2	Bowl 432, Jar 482, Squat Jar 496
O.11	2106	2	Jar 460 (photograph on Pl. 20: 4)
P.11	2107	2	Squat Jar 497. PM 34.2920
P.11	2108	2	Pot 446, Squat Jars 490, 497
O.11	2109	2	Jars 465, 477
P.11	*2110	2	Beaker 445, Jar 474
O.11	*2111	2	Jar 469. Dagger, Pls. 21: 10 and 22: 4; Javelin, Pls. 21: 9 and 22: 1
P.11	2112	5	Beaker 444, 493. PM 34.2921–2922

Grid Ref. on Pl. 93	Tomb	Tomb shape	Contents
O.11	2114	2	Bowl 431, Funnel *451*, Jars 464, 470, 473(3)
O.11	*2116	2	Bowl 432 (photograph on Pl. 20: 15), Beaker 441 (photograph on Pl. 20: 14), Jars 472, 474, 477 *479*, 482, 483 (photographs on Pl. 20: 9–13).
O.11	2117	5	Bowl 433, Lamp 448
O.12	2118	1	Squat Jar *494*
O.12	2119	5	Squat Jar 497
O.12	2120	2	Jar *458*. Potmark Pl. 18: 69
O.12	2121	2	Jar 479
O.12	2122	—	Chamber or grave, see Pl. 4: 6 and p. 42

CHAPTER 13
AREA 4000, POTTER'S WORKSHOP 4034,
AREAS 6000, 7000

AREA 4000, NORTH-EAST CORNER

(Pls. 88–89; L. III, Pl. 128)

FOR a general description see *Lachish III*, p. 239 and Pl. 128, where the tomb plans of all periods are shown. On these convenient lower slopes of the mound, where traces of the earliest occupation occur in the adjoining Area 6000 (L. III, Pl. 129), natural caves were enlarged and re-used time and again for all manner of purposes.

As they are somewhat less congested than the Caverns 6000, it is easier to compare contemporary cuttings. Especially noticeable are Caves 4020, 4009, 4004 and 4012. They were probably cut first for industrial purposes at roughly equal distances from each other and from the mound. Olive stones in the vats and on the floor of Cave 4020 leave little doubt of their use and it is perhaps to the Early Bronze Age rather than Roman times that the construction of Cave 4012 belonged (*Lachish III*, p. 242 and Pl. 9: 4, 5).

Roughly in line from south to north are Caves 4023, 4013, 4016, 4005 and 4002. 4019 should also be included in this group. All these compare in shape with the circular tombs surrounded by loculi which were a feature of the horse burials at Tell el Ajjul (e.g. AG I, Pl. LVII), a stage which is otherwise poorly represented at Duweir. In the cases of Caves 4013 and 4019 at least, the original entry may have been through a hole in the roof, blocked by a stone; see the central sump in Cave 4019 and the great stone on the floor of Cave 4013 (Pl. 7: 5). It is also significant that where these caves had been re-used in the Late Bronze Age for burials, the floors had been plastered.

4001 Grave in Grid Square T.1   LB III, *c.* 1250–1200 B.C.

A rectangular depression in the rock, which was probably the site of a grave, denuded nearly to the floor. No human bones were recorded. The burial was probably contemporary with Structure III.

Pottery: Bowls: curved H *L. II*: 45; *L. III*: 20
         Jug: B 683   Imitation Base-Ring: 879, 905

4002–3 Cave, artificially enlarged, in Grid Square S.1. (See L. III, Fig. 28 on p. 239)   Circular chamber with five loculi, *c.* 2000–900 B.C.
LB II–III burials, *c.* 1400–1200 B.C.

It is possible that the original adaptation of the cave for burials was made in the Middle Bronze Age (see L. III, Pl. 9: 1 and p. 241 and general note above). An equine mandible and the bowls 532–533 may perhaps belong to this phase. The former type compares with one from Tell Beit Mirsim, Stratum E.

Probably at a later stage, part of the floor was plastered and the pottery which remained in the brown earth above falls between Structures II and III.

The juglet 948 is dated to Mycenaean III B. This and an imitation pyxoid jar 923 would both be in place towards the middle of the thirteenth century.

The beads are an interesting group with small and large segmented shapes (Nos. 27, 28) and others are notched and gadrooned (Nos. 33, 35, 37). The disk 42 is especially characteristic of the Tell el Amarna necklace (L. II, Pl. XIV) from the shrine of Structure III.

The amulets and the scarabs find comparisons at Tell Fara in Tomb 934 and Nos. 365, 367, 368 and 369 are clearly Ramesside. No. 364 is certainly an heirloom with its well-made scrolls and No. 366 is a variant of the kneeling figure which was popular at the turn of the Middle–Late Bronze Age.

Apart from deposits attributed to the Iron Age (L. III, p. 240), above the black layer which may indicate the destruction of the city, the contents of the cave cover a century or more at the end of the Bronze Age, ending perhaps with the reign of Rameses III.

4002

Pottery: Bowls: carinate B 532, 533; flared J *L. II*: 78
Lamps: E *L. II*: 199, 202
Mycenaean Imitation: 923   Mycenaean Imported: 948

Objects: Beads:

Pl. 29:	2	4	5	6	7	9	21	23
Paste	15	10	8	1	—	—	3	—
Stone	—	—	1 haem.	—	—	1 cn.	—	1 cn.
Metal	—	—	—	—	2 Au	—	—	—

also the following paste beads: Pl. 29: 26(1), 27(3), 28(1), 33(1), 35(1), 37(1), 42(10), 43(3)
Amulets: Pl. 29: 52–55
Scarabs: Pl. 39: 364–369
Pottery bird, head and wings missing NP

4003

Pottery: Pilgrim Flask: *L. II*: 349

4004 Cave in Grid Square T.1 (Fig. 14)

MB III–LB III, *c.* 1600–1370 B.C.
Re-used *c.* 1220 B.C.

All three chambers were cut in soft howr limestone and the roof was less damaged than is usual when it consists of the top nari stratum. However, the roof had fallen near the two entrances on the east side, where rock-hewn steps appear to be the later means of entry (Pl. 7: 3).

The main chamber was a rectangle, 5×2·5 m., with well-cut corners and a flat floor. Divided from it by raised sills on the west and south sides were two cave-like recesses with floors a few centimetres lower than the main chamber (Pl. 7: 6).

Early in the clearance, a thick, black, sooty deposit was observed which impregnated the filling of layers 2 and 3 in all three chambers and had discoloured the roof. On the floor was a consolidated mass of blackened, broken bones, and all the large pottery vessels were smashed and scattered. In fact, nearly everything was concentrated in the deposit, layer 3, which covered the floor to an even depth of about 30 cms.

The only things found above the main deposit were a few bronze arrowheads, one of the kohl pots, and the cylinder seal, Pl. 34: 164. Apart from sherds, including the palm and panelled zigzag bowl of Structure III, L. II: 125, and part of a goblet, Pl. 72: 639, which is also analogous to forms in the same structure (L. II: 233, 235), there was little pottery among the stones and black earth of layer 2. The thin streak of yellow clay, layer 4, under the main deposit, only produced three glass beads.

At the time it was thought that the burials had been burnt to an unusual degree, but doubts arose when the sooty deposit was examined under the microscope. Professor A. Reifenberg reported that "in all probability the black stuff does not represent a burnt layer, but consists of decayed organic material" (L. III, p. 246).

It must therefore be accepted that the sooty deposits were the result of chemical action set up by a concentration of saturated and decayed matter in a confined space with little air or drainage.

The amount and variety of the funerary equipment and the concentration of the shattered offerings into a depth of only 30 cms. suggests that the cave was used as a charnel house. The offerings were not necessarily exceptional among the community at Lachish, but conditions have conspired to preserve them in tenacious mud within a deep and sheltered cave.

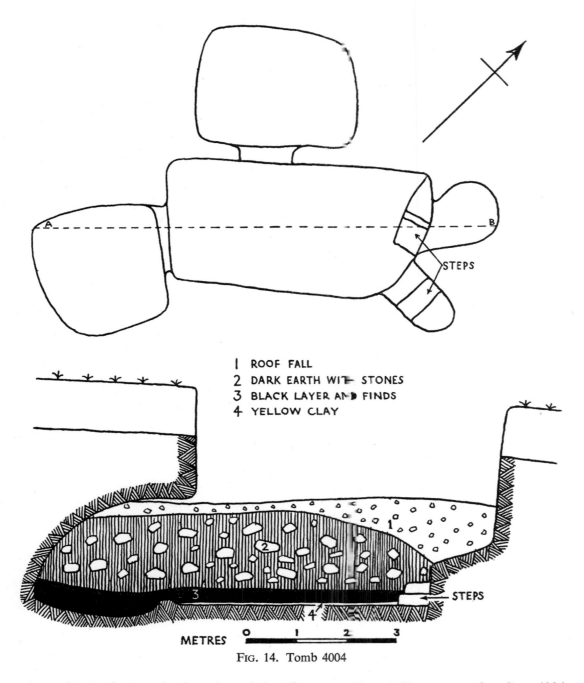

1 ROOF FALL
2 DARK EARTH WITH STONES
3 BLACK LAYER AND FINDS
4 YELLOW CLAY

METRES

FIG. 14. Tomb 4004

Comparison with the form and orientation of the olive press, Cave 4020, suggests that Cave 4004 may have originally been cut for the same purpose, for it does not conform to the normal tomb shapes of the Middle Bronze Age.

Pottery

Bowls: carinate A 516(2); *L. II*: 114; B *L II*: 125; C 537, 543(6), 545; E 572; plain G 587; *L. II*: 7(2)
curved H 593, 596, 602; *L. II*: 19, 30(4), 36, 41, 46, 51, 137, 145
flared J 617, 620; *L. II*: 90; miscellaneous *L. II*: 158
Goblet: 639
Lamps: A 644(6); B 648(2), 649(9), 651(3), 652(4), 653(27); C 654(2), 655; E *L. II*: 197(9); F *L. II*: 203(2)
Jug: B 679   Juglets: E 756, 761, 762; J 777(17), 778(42)
Dippers: A 781(3); *L. II*: 290, 292(13), 295; B 784
Imported Wares: 816, 819, 823, 825, 827(2), 830(2); *L. II*: 167, 168
Base-Ring Ware: 837, 857, 862, 863(3), 865(2)
Mycenaean Imitation: 923, 929   Spouted Vessel: 935
Miniature Pithoi: 977, 984   Miscellaneous: 997(2)

Objects

Metal: Spearhead: Pl. 23: 11   Togglepins: Pl. 24: 17–21
Arrowheads: Pl. 25: 1–6   Tweezers: Pl. 25: 7
Rings, Pendant and Ear-rings: Pl. 25: 8–12, 15
End of Head-band Pl. 25: 13   Crescent amulet: Pl. 25: 14
Stone: Vases and kohl tube: Pl. 26: 26–31
Bone, etc.: Inlay, spindlewhorls, shells, ostrich shell NP
Glass: Spacers: Pls. 27: 3, 28: 23, 27   Figurine: Pl. 27: 2
Beads: Photographs on Pl. 27: 4–9

Pl. 29:	1	2	3	4	5	6	9	15	16	18	20	21	25	26	27
Paste	5	196	—	54	62	11	27	—	—	—	1	4	3	1	14
Glass	—	41	4	—	180	29	8	—	16	—	—	3	—	—	—
Stone	—	8	—	9	11	10	—	3	2	2	—	7	—	5	—
		stea.		cn.	cn.	cn.		sard.	am.	cn.		cn.		cn.	
					5	1									
					onyx	stea.									
					6										
					am.										
Bone	—	—	—	—	—	—	—	—	—	—	—	—	5	—	—
Metal	—	—	—	—	—	1	—	—	—	—	—	—	—	—	—
						cu.									

Pl. 29:	28	29	30	31	32	33	35	37	38	39	40	41	44	45	46	47	49	50
Paste	—	—	—	2	4	2	38	14	1	3	2	1	—	—	1	—	—	2
Glass	3	—	—	3	—	—	—	—	—	—	—	—	—	—	3	11	1	—
Stone	—	—	1	—	—	—	—	—	—	—	—	—	—	—	1	—	—	—
			cn.												haem.			
Bone	—	1	—	1	—	—	—	—	—	—	—	—	—	—	—	—	—	—
Shell	—	—	—	—	—	—	—	—	—	—	—	—	1	4	—	—	—	—

Amulets: Pl. 29: 57, 58
Scarabs and seals: Pls. 34, 35, 36, 37, 38: 140–294
Palestine Museum Nos.: PM 37.710–728; 38.52–68

Date and comparisons

The greater part of the pottery in the tomb bridges the gap between the Middle and Late Bronze Ages. It retains affinities with the past in the bowls, lamps and dippers, but cylindrical juglets are uncommon. In their place are Black (or Grey) Lustrous juglets, Class J, with early imports of Red-on-Black(?), White Painted V, Monochrome and Base-Ring wares.

During the occupation of Structure III, and about the time of the fall of the Bronze Age city, as seen near the surface of the North-East Section (p. 53), some further use was made of the tomb.

The Main Deposit

The bowls are of forms which could occur in any of the three structures, but the lamps, Class B with inturned rim, are most distinctive, and at Duweir they are exclusive to this tomb and a few contemporary deposits. They far outnumber the lamps of other classes and, already by the time of Structure I, the inturned rim had given place to the high-prowed lamp of Class C. The same short range applies to the Black Lustrous juglets, Class J, and study of the chart on p. 6 will show how they take over from the cylindrical forms.

The ubiquitous dipper of MB groups, Type 781, is soon replaced in Tomb 4004 by those with a squat body, though the early preference for a pointed base is still retained.

A concentration of Monochrome bowls in Tomb 4004 and succeeding groups and in Structure I preceded the development of Base-Ring bowls which appear to be their true descendant. Comparatively few vessels of Base-Ring are found in Tomb 4004 and in Structure I representing, on the whole, the earlier forms.

Lamps of Class B were prominent, which are especially characteristic of Tell Beit Mirsim, Strata E–D, and Tombs 550, 551 and 569 at Tell Fara. There are several connexions with the central layers of Tombs 4, 9, 13 and 19 at Jericho. At Megiddo, common forms range between Strata XII and IX with emphasis on the last level; the same can be said of the personal ornaments and scarabs.

The togglepins on Pl. 24: 17, 18 are matched in Cemetery 500 at Tell Fara (BP I, Pl. XI: 69; Pl. IX: 62), while those on Pl. 24: 19 —Type 8c(a)— and 21 —Type 8b— carry on into the fifteenth century (see Pls. 24: 22, 24, 26, 27, 29 and 25, 30).

Sections of a glass necklace or bracelet are photographed on Pl. 27 and drawn on Pl. 28: 23. They are closely matched at Megiddo, where similar pieces in faience were found in position on the neck of a burial attributed to Stratum IX (M. II, Fig. 343 and Pl. 211).

The fine mould-pressed glass figure of Astarte, also photographed on Pl. 27, is discussed on p. 83.

The stone vases on Pl. 26: 26–27 find parallels respectively in Stratum D at Tell Beit Mirsim, and a tomb group from Gurob dated to the reign of Amenhetep I, mid-sixteenth century.

Scarabs and Seals

Out of nearly 400 drawn scarabs from the site, over 150 came from Tomb 4004, and there were besides ten uninscribed scarabs of quartz and amethyst and many others of glass and paste.

In a group of this size, standing midway between the last two main phases of the Bronze Age, it is inevitable to find that every motif and style of our series is represented, and a better appreciation of their range is reached through a study of the other groups.

Among possible royal names of obscure kings before the xviith dynasty are Nos. 140–141 and 196 and some simplified or defective versions, Nos. 145, 188, 189 (see p. 96). The scarab of Pepy, No. 140, is common elsewhere and the name is placed by Weill towards the end of the Hyksos period. See also the scarab of an unknown king from Tomb 551 at Tell Fara (BP I, Pl. VII: 11) for a scroll border, though the bird above the name has lost its legs.

There are no royal scarabs of the early xviiith dynasty at Duweir, and indeed few are found anywhere in Palestine until the reign of Thothmes III. He and his immediate successors are all represented in Tomb 4004 (Nos. 281–294). Scarabs which appear late in style include Nos. 240–244 and Nos. 269–275, which find parallels in the Ramesside cemeteries of Tell Fara.

The three cylinder seals 163–165 are described and dated on p. 111 f. They are attributed to the very end of the Bronze Age; cylinder 164 was one of the few objects found above the main deposit, so that all three should perhaps equate with the latest pottery in the group.

Summary

Taking the deposit as a whole, it would seem that the earliest pottery dates from the end of the Middle Bronze Age, showing more contact with Tell Beit Mirsim D than with E and closer affinity with Stratum IX at Megiddo than with any earlier level, though connexions go back in some instances to Stratum XII. The range of the contents is still considerable, for the main weight of deposit antedates Structure I, and the presence of scarabs of Thothmes III and his immediate successors down to and including Amenhetep III brings us at least to 1400 B.C. Indeed, there is strong indication that the tomb was open and re-used (layer 2) about the time that Level VI and Structure III were burnt.

The lack of Aegean imports and of lamps in Class D does suggest that little use was made of the tomb during the earlier occupation of Structure III.

Late elements in the pottery forms are to be found in the bowls carinate (Class B, *L. II*: 125; Class E, 572) flared (*L. II*: 90 and 620) the goblet 639, and lamps (Classes E–F). The imitation pyxoid jars 923 and 929 and the decorated pithoi 977 and 984 also belong to this phase, while the Bucchero jug 830 was among the topmost vessels in the western chamber.

Among the objects which should be associated are the bronze spearhead, Pl. 23: 11, the kohl tube, Pl. 26: 29, possibly the crescent amulet on Pl. 25: 14 and the cylinder seals on Pl. 34.

4008 Hole in Grid Square U.2   MB III, *c.* 1700–1600 B.C.

A natural hole in the rock filled with soil. Lying on top there were four skeletons with a small group of pottery vessels. With the small and poorly made carinate bowls, and the high-prowed lamps, the group may extend to an early phase of Structure I.

Pottery: Bowls: carinate A 508; E 560
              Lamps: C 655, 657   Juglets: B 730(2); E 757(2)
              Dippers: A 780(2), 781(2)

Objects: Metal: Togglepin NP
              Beads: Pl. 29: 6 (1 cn.), 15 (1 glass), 21 (1 paste)

4009 Cave in Grid Square U.3   LB I, *c.* 1550 B.C.

The cave somewhat resembled 4004 in dimension and rectangular shape, but it was damaged through proximity to Tomb chamber 4010, with which it was connected by a doorway. The meagre contents of Cave 4009 were deposited at the same time as the bulk of the pottery in Tomb 4004 and the cave chosen was the central one of a series which were probably cut at a much earlier period.

Pottery: Lamps: A 643(2)   Juglets: J 777(7)
              Dipper: A *L. II*: 292

Objects: Metal: Knife Pl. 23: 10

4010 Tomb chamber in Grid Square U.2   *c.* 2000–1000 B.C. Re-used *c.* 900–
                                                      600 B.C.

The original shape of the tomb was much obscured by the later enlargements, but it was apparently circular with raised benches all round except where the stepped entrance occupied the north side.

Some Iron Age dippers and bowls (L. III, p. 242) were found high in the filling, but many Bronze Age sherds established an earlier origin for the tomb. Some types, of which fragments were found, are listed below but are not entered on the plate descriptions.

The cave was in use for primary or more possibly secondary burials during the occupation of Structures II–III.

Pottery: Bowl: plain G *L. II*: 12   Mycenaean Imitation: 928
　　　　　Miscellaneous: 1001; *L. II*: 268, 344
　　Also: Bowls: curved *L. II*: 149; flared *L. II*: 100, 123, 135; miscellaneous *L. II*: 177
　　　　　Jugs: *L. II*: 279, 284   Dippers: *L. II*: 301, 309
　　　　　Pilgrim Flask: *L. II*: 351

4011 Tomb in Grid Square U.3 (see Chart on pp. 60–61)   LB III, *c.* 1350–1300 B.C.

The rock-cut cavity, 3 m. in diameter, contained fourteen skulls and other bones with over thirty pottery vessels.

Pottery

Bowls: carinate E 570; curved H *L. II*: 20(2), 30(3), 45, 46, 48, 50(4); *L. III*: 8(3); flared J 619; *L. II*: 30
Lamps: F *L. II*: 203 (5)　Jug: D 707
Dippers: B 788, 791, 793　Imported Wares: 820
Imitation Base-Ring: 888, 895, 902　Mycenean Imitation: 924, 928
Storage Jar: E 1025

Objects

Beads:

Pl. 29:	2	3	6	16	21	25	33	37
Paste	9	1	9	2	2	1	1	1
Glass	—	—	4	—	—	—	—	—
Stone	—	—	3	—	—	—	—	—
			cn.					

Amulet, eye NP
Scarabs and seals: Pl. 39: 351–356
Palestine Museum Nos.: PM 37.730–752; 38.72–85; 38.122

Date and Comparisons

Most of the bowls in the group are curved and there are only two flared examples. Some have a thin red line on the rim. Though many of the bowls could come from Structure II, the absence of all lamps but those of Class F should preclude attributions to a date before the foundation of Structure III. The fact that both lamps and dippers are concentrated in one class suggests that the group is homogeneous, and the lack of true imports, except for a White Shaved dipper, is another point of interest.

The scarabs also appear to be consistent. They include a commemorative issue of Thothmes III, and a scarab of Ay, the usurper who reigned for about a decade in the latter half of the fourteenth century.

4013 Pit in Grid Square T.3   *c.* 1320–1250 B.C.

The plastered floor, some 6 m. in diameter, with a sump or depression in the centre (cf. Tomb 4019) was well preserved in an otherwise denuded tomb (Pl. 7: 5). It is suggested that the large store in the picture was used to seal the original entrance through the roof, but at some time in the occupation of the tomb steps were cut leading to it from the south.

There were raised benches or alcoves round the north and west sides. Human remains were disturbed and fragmentary.

Pottery

Bowls: carinate E 564, 574; *L. III*: 56
　　　　plain G 592; *L. II*: 10(2), 13(8)
　　　　curved H 602, 607, 608; *L. II*: 14(2), 21(3), 30(6), 50(5), 52, 137(3), 143(16); *L. III*: 20
　　　　flared J 620(5); *L. II*: 95; miscellaneous 628

Lamps: E *L. II*: 195(3); F *L. II*: 203(9); G *L. II*: 204(3)
Jugs: C 691; E 722, 723
Dippers: B 787, 788, 792, 793; C *L. III*: 300; D 800; *L. III*: 301(3)
Imported Wares: 830
Base-Ring Ware: 875
Imitation Base-Ring: 884, 888, 889, 891, 894, 895(4), 896(2), 900, 901
Imitation Imported: 912, 913, 918, 919, 920, 922, 925, 926, 928, 929, 941; *L. II*: 344
Pilgrim Flask: 954   Mugs: 961, 962
Miniature Pithoi: 976, 981, 982; *L. III*: 425
Krater: 989   Miscellaneous: 1000

Objects

Metal: Arrowhead: Pl. 25: 52
Beads:

Pl. 29:	2	4	6	9	16	21	24	25	27	29	33	35	37	43	45
Paste	47	11	39	1	17	7	—	4	3	1	2	1	1	—	—
Glass	—	—	3	—	3	—	—	—	—	—	—	—	—	—	—
Stone	—	—	2 cn.	—	1 cn.	—	1 cn.	—	—	—	—	—	—	1 cn.	—
Shell	—	—	—	—	—	—	—	—	—	—	—	—	—	—	2

Amulet: Pl. 29: 64
Scarabs and seal: Pl. 39: 357–363
Palestine Museum Nos.: PM 37.753–828; 38.86–121; 38.134, 135, 138, 139

Date and Comparisons

The range of the group, which is larger than the previous 4011, is also longer, particularly on the late side, as the jugs and dippers show. Two bowls and four dippers are typed to Iron Age shapes.

Among earlier pieces is the Base-Ring lentoid flask, but most of the jugs are imitation Base-Ring of Class B and there are nine imitation pyxoid jars.

The scarabs are most informative. They include one of the rarely named last king of the xviiith dynasty, Horemheb, the immediate successor of Ay, who reigned for only a few years. In keeping with the range of the pottery is the well-cut scarab of Rameses II, third Pharaoh of the xixth dynasty, who began to reign in the first decade of the thirteenth century. A commemorative issue of Aahmes is matched in the Ramesside tombs of Tell Fara, where scarabs like No. 361 bearing the name of the reinstated god, Amen-Ra, are common.

Cut perhaps early in the xviiith dynasty or even before, the deposits recovered from the floor probably belong to the latter half of the dynasty and extend at least into the early years of the reign of Rameses II.

4014 Hole in Grid Square T.2   ?

The rock-cut cavity, 2 m. in diameter, only contained some sherds.

4018 Locus in Grid Square U.3   EB–LB

A stone wall was built across the eastern end of Cave 4020 after it had filled with soil. In the resulting triangle above the steps leading down into the cave there were some pots of mixed date. A hand-made lug-handled pot (NP) may belong to the original occupation of Cave 4020.

Pottery: Bowls: curved H *L. II*: 146   Juglet: F 769

4019 Pit in Grid Square T.2   LB II, *c.* 1400–1350 B.C. Re-used
c. 900–600 B.C.

A circular pit, 4 m. across, with plastered floor and four alcoves for burials. At a later date a rough line of stones was built dividing the main space into unequal parts. While the larger northern half contained only some Iron Age sherds (L. III, p. 243), the Bronze Age pottery was behind the wall which may have been built for its protection. Like Tomb 4013, there was a sump or depression in the floor.

Pottery: Bowl: curved H *L. III*: 20   Lamps: E *L. II*: 197(3), 202(2)
Jugs: C 691, 694   Dipper: C *L. II*: 311
Imported Ware: 830   Imitation Base-Ring: 878, 886, 893, 898
Mycenaean Imitation: 927   Spouted Vessel: 934

Objects: Metal: Arrowhead: Pl. 25: 36   Bracelet: Pl. 25: 37
Togglepin NP
Beads: Pl. 29: 2 (3 paste, 2 stea.), 4 (2 paste), 6 (1 glass), 7 (1 cn.)
Amulet: Pl. 29: 60
Scarab: Pl. 39: 338

Date and Comparisons

The pottery behind the wall dates from the xviiith dynasty, extending, perhaps, to the early occupation of Structure III. True Base-Ring is missing and imitation jugs are common. Among imported forms there is a Bucchero jug which can be matched in Structure III (L. II: 285), like the scarab of Amenhetep III (L. II, Pl. XXXII B: 36–38).

4020 Cave in Grid Square U.3   **EB**

The pottery from Locus 4018 in the top filling shows that the cave was no longer used for its primary purpose in the Middle Bronze Age. Numbers of olive stones in the vats and on the floor leave no doubt as to its function; at the same time it was probably used as a dwelling before the roof collapsed. Compare Cave 4004, which may have been cut for the same purpose, though the details of the installation were obscured by its later use as a burial-place.

Cut in the plastered floor there were vats and depressions of uncertain use, and in the west end of the inner recess there was a niche, perhaps to take the press beam; five pierced stones are to be seen against the south wall of the chamber (Pl. 7: 4).

For an olive or wine press attributed to Roman times, but which may be older, see Cave 4012 (L. III, p. 242).

Objects: Beads: Pl. 29: 2 (1 paste), 7 (1 cn.)

4022 Pit in Grid Square V.3 (Plan and section, Fig. 15)   EB I–II deposits
MB III burials, *c.* 1725–1675 B.C.

Near the south-western limits of excavation, a square water cistern of Byzantine date indicated ground level in late Roman times (see unnumbered construction, L. III, Pl. 12E, Grid V.3). Close to that building and sloping beneath it, the depth of soil increases as the rock dips below the alluvium of the valley.

Cut in the limestone at this point there was a curious deep pit. The surface debris contained sherds of Iron Age bowls and a whole storage jar comparable to L. III: 475. In the dark earth of layer 1 there was the pottery illustrated on Fig. 15: 1–8, with the remains of at least five skeletons. From the vessels, the scarabs and the personal ornaments it seemed to be a normal burial group.

Below in layer 2 of dark clay there was a mixture of Early and Middle Bronze Age sherds (NP), two flint borers not datable, and an end-scraper which is undoubted but isolated evidence of Natufian contact (Appendix C). During that phase a plaster floor was constructed which sealed in part of the deposits below (Pl. 7: 1),

Layer 3 filled the lower part of the pit to a depth of a metre and a half. It contained the sherds, Fig. 15: 9–16, for which there are comparisons near bed-rock in the North-East Section. This refuse from the tell probably dates from EB I–II, a period which is otherwise poorly represented in the pottery from Duweir.

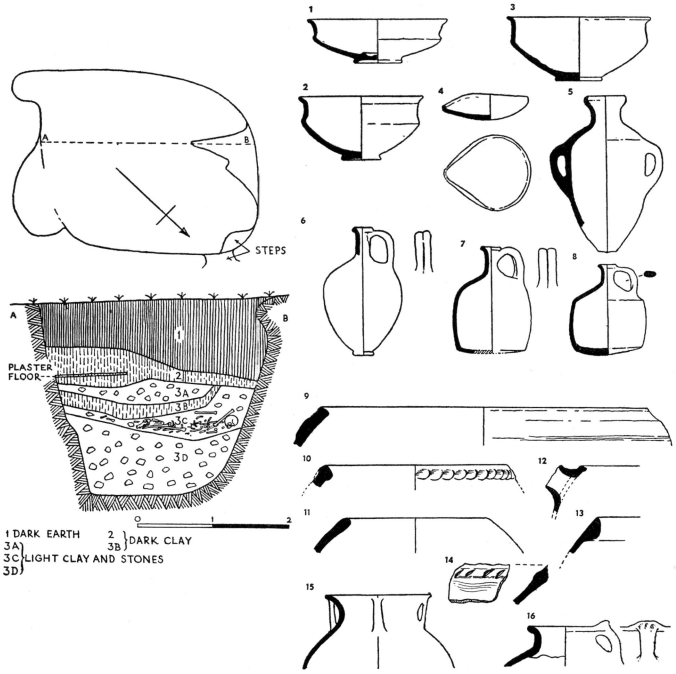

FIG. 15. Pit 4022: Plan, Section and Pottery

Among a tangled mass of bones (layer 3c), three human skulls were discovered, and on top of the pile there was the almost intact skeleton of a dog (Pl. 7: 2). See Appendix B for a report by the late Miss D. M. A. Bate on these and other animal bones from the pit, which were presented by the Trustees to the British Museum (Natural History), South Kensington.

Pottery (*Layer 1*): Fig. 15   *Photographs on Pl. 51

1–3 Bowls: carinate A 509,* 520;* C 537*   4 Lamp: B 649*
5 Miniature Pithos: 971*   6–8 Juglets: B 736;* E 760;* F 770*
Not illustrated on Fig.: Lamp: B 648; Jug: B 680

Objects (*Layer 1*)

Metal: Togglepin: Pl. 24: 16   Scarabs: Pl. 30: 63–66

Sherds (*Layer 3*)

  9 Holemouth rim. Lt. bn., grits^2; S; hand-made. 2 ex., 1 burnt. Cf. NE 1/397   6060c
 10 Holemouth rim. Bn., gy. core, grits^1; M; hand-made. Cf. *Ay*, Pl. LXXXII: 1748, Fouille V, ch.   6060g
     198, niv. I–III EB II
 11 Holemouth rim. Gy., grits^2; M; hand-made, burnt gy. 2 ex. Cf. NE 5/347   6060b
 12 Spouted bowl. Bn., grits^2; M; greenish surface out., rough in., hand-made. Cf. Tell el-Far'ah   6060k
     (RB LIV, 1947, p. 411: 6) EB I
 13 Holemouth rim. Bn., gy. core, grits and mica^2; M; hand-made. Cf. NE 6/319; *Ay*, Pl. LXXXIV: 6060d
     2149D, Fouille H, ch. 136–137 EB II
 14 Raised band, rope moulding, notched. Pk.; S; rough in., combed out., traces limewash. Cf.   6060h
     Type 294
 15 Jug neck, 2 handles, oval section. Bn., grits^3; M; hand-made; coarse oatmeal surface in. and out.   6060j
 16 Jug neck and handle, oval section. Bn., grits^2; M; hand-made; smoothed in. and out., "grain"   6060i
     wash out., bn. under bk.

Date and Comparisons

   The burial group in layer 1 is roughly contemporary with Tomb 153 and with the lower layers of Jericho Tombs 4 and 13. The sherds in layer 3 correspond with deposits just above bed-rock in the N.E. Section.

   The togglepin is of the simplest kind, Type 3, p. 80. The scarabs are: No. 63, a royal name, enclosed in a cartouche which is not yet identified; No. 64 shows a seated figure dressed in a toga-like garment, with name and attributes disposed around the high-backed chair. No. 65 bears the royal emblems of North and South of which many examples occur in Tomb 153, p. 98.

4023 Pit in Grid Square T.3   *c.* 1500–1200 B.C. Re-used 900–600 B.C.

   A round plastered pit about 6 m. in diameter. There were no human remains, and only a few sherds of Late Bronze and Iron Age date (L. III, p. 243).

4024 Pit in Grid Square T.3   *c.* 1500–1200 B.C. Re-used later

   An oval plastered pit about 4 m. in diameter. There were no traces of burials and the only contents were some sherds of Late Bronze and Iron Age date (L. III, p. 243).

4030 Entrance to Cave 4034 in Grid Square R.4   *c.* 1200 B.C. and later?

   See House 4033, Cave 4034 and L. III, p. 244.

4033 House in Grid Square S.4 (Pl. 91)   *c.* 1250–1050 B.C.

   Part of a house built over Cave 4034. The remaining traces of stone walls continued under the unexcavated ground both to south and east, so that the plan is incomplete.

The thick wall from east to west, shown in *Lachish III* on Pl. 128, belongs to the cave below and was probably built to support the roof, though it did not prevent an extensive collapse in the eastern half.

It is probable that the house was associated with the cave in its main phase of use as a potter's workshop, for there were at least two lime plaster floors below the latest cobbled surface. A few sherds of Early Iron Age date suggest that the house was still occupied when the cave was used as a stable.

POTTER'S WORKSHOP

Cave 4034 in Grid Square R.4 (Pls. 8, 92 and L. III, Pl. 128)   LB III–Iron I, 1300–1050 B.C.

On the upward course of the Wadi Ghafr towards Hebron, the natural line of approach skirts Tell ed-Duweir at the north-east corner. Near this point, where travellers would first reach the city, excavations early in 1937 exposed a sloping passage leading to a large cave which differed in the manner of construction from that of an ordinary tomb (Pl. 8: 3).

Slag and unbaked sherds in the entrance passage were early signs of a long-wished-for discovery, and as work developed in the following season the full equipment of the potter's craft left no doubt that a workshop had been found.

Cut in soft limestone under the harder layer which formed the roof, its condition was so unsafe 10 metres from the entrance that nothing could be done beyond that limit without a surface clearance. A considerable space, however, 10 by 9 metres square, was exposed down to the rock floor in the main cave, besides the whole extent of a long narrow annexe to the west, which was apparently blocked on the outer side by stones (Pl. 8: 5).

Inside the cave, at least six layers of deposit (Pl. 92) summarize the history of its occupation from the thirteenth century B.C. until the entrance was blocked by water-laid mud some centuries later. A Neolithic or Chalcolithic arrowhead in the mud at the bottom of Pit B may indicate an earlier occupation (see p. 327).

Layer 1

The narrow entry was filled with light earth and stones. Within the cave some ribbed Roman sherds, a dipper (as L. III: 296) and pieces of a pilgrim flask (as L. III: 436) were exceptional in a filling which otherwise contained sherds comparable to those from Structure III of the Fosse Temple.

Layer 2

Dark earth or mud partially blocked entry to the cave and penetrated to the limits of excavation within. It contained horse bones and an iron arrowhead.

Layer 3

Under the mud and some light earth, a dark streak observed near the entrance resembled the effects of burning in appearance, but the result of an analysis applied to samples of a sooty deposit over other groups near the north-east corner is a warning that it was not necessarily caused by fire (L. III, p. 246). Below an intervening layer of light earth, a lime plaster floor was still intact over nearly half the cave and all the western chamber.

Layer 4

About 2 metres in from the entrance, between the plaster floor 3 and a lower plaster floor 5, there was an even deposit of dark earth, and that filling contained many sherds, some of which were discoloured as if by fire. Just above floor 5 there were several pieces of a bowl painted with palms and zigzags (as L. II: 117, 125), and other vessels represented in the filling were storage jars with red painted bands, and pilgrim flasks with burnished cream slip and painted spirals. Seven pieces of Iron Age hand burnish on red slip are typical of an early stage in that technique.

Objects: Mortars and stone frags. NP   Knucklebones NP
        Seal: Pl. 39: 383

Layer 5

The shaded stones on the sketch-plan are all to be associated with the adaptation of the cave for use as a sheep-fold. Inge wrote in a field report, "A small square space enclosed by a low stone wall and adjoining a double row of rough masonry was recognised at once by one of our workers as a pen and manger still quite fit for use". Some of the sherds from layer 4 should belong to this phase of occupation.

Layer 6

Forming only a thin deposit of compact clay over the cave floor, layer 6 contained quantities of unbaked sherds which were much less common near the entrance. Though the potter's kilns were not found, their possible position may be indicated by a widening streak of greenish earth and slag, layer 6A, which was most clearly defined in the farthest recesses of the cave.

Pits

Pits and depressions in the cave were either formed through continuous use over a long period, or were made deliberately to meet a practical need. The irregular Pit C, for instance, about a metre deep, was probably caused by use of the stone seat or slab set in the wall, on which the potter sat (Pl. 8: 1, 2). Above the seat to the right there was a light or air vent which is visible in the picture. Both Pits C and D (Pl. 8: 4) were possible emplacements for the potter's wheel. Compare the maximum width of the tenons (Pl. 49: 12, 20 cms.; Pl. 49: 13, 16 cms.) with the breadth of the lower hole in Pit D, 30 cms.

On the other hand, Pit A was over 2 metres in depth, and its mouth was still open when the sheep-fold was in use. The drainage channels leading to it from the pen were perhaps cut at that time. Floor 5 was broken away above this pit and its main filling—comparable to that of layer 6—was directly covered by layer 4. This observation is confirmed by the discovery of half a pottery figure in layer 4, while the missing part was 50 cms. down in the filling of Pit A. Among many large stones and quantities of unbaked sherds was another incomplete figure of the Great Goddess and part of a mould. The lower part of a similar plaque of unbaked clay is satisfactory evidence of local origin (Pl. 49: 2–5 and p. 90).

Though some sherds from Pits A and B were found to be parts of the same vessel, diligent search failed to reassemble all the fragments, which is not surprising when many may yet lie under the fallen roof.

The contents of Pit A were largely broken trial pieces and the vessels and tools needed in the potter's craft. In Pit B more finished bowls of various kinds were found. Both pits and floor produced heaps of raw material, clay, crushed lime and shells, charcoal, and lumps of red and yellow ochre (pp. 91, 140).

Contents of Pit A

Pottery: Bowl: carinate B 536 (Potmark: Pl. 18: 78)
        Potter's Jars: 808, 809, 810, 811 (Pl. 49: 6)
        Sherds NK: Bowl: *L. II*: 158   Krater: *L. II*: 250
                Cooking-Pots: *L. II*: 364, 366, 370, 371
                Storage Jars: 1009, 1018, 1025
        Sherd with red ochre: Pl. 49: 10

Objects: Pottery figurines and mould: Pl. 49: 2–5
        Pottery templates, worn: Pl. 49: 15
        Stone Mortar: Pl. 49: 14   Pebbles: Pl. 49: 15
        Bone Point: Pl. 49: 15   Stone tenons: Pl. 49: 12–13

Pit B

Through a hole cut at floor level in the main cave, rock steps led down to Pit B, which measured about 5·80 × 3·60 metres (Pl. 8: 6). It seems to have served as a drying room and storage chamber, for much of the potter's stock-in-trade was still piled on the floor. Almost every shape was already familiar from the contents of the latest structure of the Fosse Temple, and it appears most probable that much of the pottery found in Structure III derived from this convenient source.

Like Pit A, access to Pit B was still possible at a later time, which would account for the presence of a few Philistine and some Iron Age sherds. Four bodies had been buried in the wet clay above the pottery, but there was nothing with them to provide a date.

Contents of Pit B   *Photographs on Pl. 49

Pottery

Bowls: carinate B 535; C 555, 556; E 576;* plain G *L.II*: 2
       curved H *L. II*: 30, 48, 52, 137*
       flared J 618; *L. II*: 90(3), 91*(5), 94(5), 95, 120
       miscellaneous: 626*(6), 632; *L. II*: 66*
Lamp: E *L. II*: 195   Potstand: Pl. 49: 9, as *L. II*: 330
Imitation Imported: 909   Pilgrim Flasks: 956; *L. II*: 349*
Miscellaneous: 1002(2), 1003*

Objects

Scarabs: Pl. 39: 382, 383
Palestine Museum Nos.: PM 39.800–809, 834

Date and Comparisons

Lack of Base-Ring fragments, of White Slip and Aegean wares suggests that the workshop was not in use until late in the occupation of Structure III, or, alternatively, it would support the likelihood that they were true imports. Anyhow, the contents recovered from the pits and floor would represent the refuse of the last months of work, and this indeed does seem to be the case. Above 32 feet in the North-East Section, Base-Ring and White Slip wares are absent, while the flared and double bowls appear. The bent bowl of Structure III, also found in the workshop, occurs like the double bowls in Stratum VII at Megiddo. The complete pilgrim flask 956 compares closely with NE 32/21, which is also represented in Stratum VII A at Megiddo and in pits of Stratum B at Tell Beit Mirsim (AASOR XII, Pl. 30: 2, 4, 5).

It is worth noting a few sherds of Imitation Base-Ring jugs and a copy of a White Slip bowl which is the only one of its kind (see AASOR XIII, Pl. 27: 18–21, Stratum C). See p. 209.

The presence of a few Philistine sherds in Pit B reopens the question of their origin and range. The ware is red and gritty, showing pronounced wheelmarks inside. The exterior is thickly covered with white lime, but the painted arcs and bands in black and red were faint and worn. These pieces belonged to jugs or flasks, but there were also two bowl fragments without a lime wash, painted in black and red.

On comparative grounds we have seen that the workshop was in use up to the time of the ruin of town and temple, after which there was probably little or no market for the potter's wares. We can equate the contents with Stratum C² or even B¹ at Tell Beit Mirsim and with Stratum VII at Megiddo. The few Philistine sherds suggest that Pit B was not completely filled before the middle of the twelfth century. About a dozen pieces of Iron Age burnish from layer 4 and from Pits A and B suggest that these two convenient openings continued to receive the sweepings of the cave floor and were not finally closed until the eleventh or tenth century.

AREA 6000, EAST SIDE AND NORTH-EAST CORNER
Pls. 88–89 (*Lachish III*, Pl. 129)

Except for the space in Grid Square V.19 (Houses 6001) no excavation was attempted on the lower slopes of the east side, and the remains proved too close to the modern ground surface to repay extensive excavation.

Conditions on the congested north-east corner were described in *Lachish III*, p. 246, and by the end of the Middle Bronze Age every available space had been used and re-used, though it did not prevent some later clearance for burials of the Iron Age.

6001 Houses in Grid Square V.19 (Pl. 91)   LB III, *c.* 1250–1200 B.C.

During the first season, a space about 13 metres square was examined close to the south-east corner of the mound. At that point, the slopes were not as steep as they were at the opposite corner near the Fosse Temple, but they were much encumbered with masonry (Pl. 10: 5-6).

A few hours' work exposed the foundations of brick dwellings on stone foundations, provided with ovens for breadmaking and containing many large jars set in the floor.

From the nature of the ground, it seems that the sheltered eastern side of the tell was occupied by a congested quarter of small houses, which skirted the slopes and spread to the edge of the Wadi Ghafr.

Four of the six rooms cleared were empty. Sherds from the other two compare with wares of the last structure of the Fosse Temple. Near a wall foundation were fragments of a large bronze fluted bowl, and with it there was a bronze feather, overlaid with gold leaf (Pl. 40: 392). It represents the conventional ostrich plume, the Egyptian symbol of truth and justice. The feather had been wrapped in linen cloth, of which traces are preserved from its contact with the bronze core. It measures 14 cms. from the tip to the broken end of the quill, and both sides are similarly engraved with a conventional rendering of the barbs.

Sherds (NK)

Bowls: carinate C 555; plain G 587; curved H *L. II*: 19, 48, 137
     flared J 620(2); *L. II*: 95
Jugs: D 702, 715   Cooking-Pot: 801   Base-Ring Ware: 845   Mug: 963   Storage Jar: 1021

Objects

Bronze: Feather: Pl. 40: 392   PM 34, 131 Bowl, broken and corroded NP

Date and Comparisons

Nearly all the sherds are compatible with the occupation of Structure III and with contemporary tomb groups. The bowl with palm and zigzag design is represented, which recurs near the surface of the North-East Section (p. 53), and in the filling of the potter's workshop. From the presence of domestic, industrial and religious establishments at widely separated points on the lower slopes, there is good reason to believe that the city had expanded beyond any city walls which then existed. There is no sign that the house was burnt like Structure III, and deliberate destruction of this poor quarter would hardly have been worth while. The feather, wrapped and hidden at the base of a wall, was probably a poor man's loot when the city fell.

6002 Cave in Grid Square U.4   MB III, *c.* 1675 B.C.

An ovoid cave cut in the rock with roof intact. Besides the remains of three bodies, it contained eight large storage jars and an assortment of other vessels which appear to constitute an homogeneous group, though no order was discernible in the jumbled mass. Entrance to the tomb was gained through a small opening cut in the terrace floor outside Cave 6013.

Pottery: Bowls: carinate A 499, 506, 511; B 529(2); C 538, 540, 544
              plain G *L. II*: 3; curved H 600
        Lamps: A 642; D 660(2)
        Dippers: A 780, 781(4)
        Storage Jars: A 1006(3); B 1010(3); C 1014(2)

Objects: Metal: Dagger: Pl. 22: 16   Togglepin NP
        Scarabs: Pl. 30: 33, 34; amethyst (3), uninscribed: NP

Date and Comparisons

Contemporary with the earlier main tombs in the MB series, this burial group contains a liberal supply of storage jars, but no juglets. The dagger is of Type 27a, but it is smaller and less well formed than usual. The scarab 33 provides contact with Tomb 574 at Tell Fara and with Tomb 1410B at Tell el-Ajjul.

6005 Cave in Grid Square U.5   EB I–II and later

The masons who cut court 6022 (L. III, p. 250) only escaped breaking through the rock to the early Cave 6005 (Fig. 16) below by a margin of 15 cms. The cave spread out beneath the court in all directions and was accessible from 6031 and from 6024. There were two pits in the rock floors, 60 and 80 cms. deep respectively, lined with upright stone slabs as in Caves 1535 and 1558. Both pits were covered and sealed in by a plaster floor which should probably be dated to the period of Iron Age occupation of Cave 6024 above.

Pottery

Platters: upright rim 306
        flanged rim, concave top 309; rounded top 307, 308
        plain rim 304
Bowls: flanged rim 310; string-cut 305
Vats: 275, 311, 313
Holemouth Jars: thin rims 315, 318; bulbous rims as NE 1/398, 3/375, 4/362
Pithoi: 291, 292(2)   Juglet: wide-necked 312
Unclassified: 314, 316, 317, 319
Potmarks: Pl. 18: 11, 41, 43, 75, 79

Date and Comparisons

Comparisons are chiefly found in the Section below 7 feet.

The best outside analogies for the group come from Jericho, Layers V–IV, covering the period EB I–II. Comparable pieces of the same date were found at Beisan and Ay. Pithoi rims from Ay have the same narrow necks, though the incisions on the moulded bands are differently treated (*Ay*, Pl. XLIX. 1: 899).

Pieces which are apparently later in context, possibly as late as EB IV, are the juglet, comparing with one from Level XII at Beisan and from T. 351 at Jericho, the platter 304, and possibly the jugs 316 and 319. There are no ledge handles from this cave, and there is little to suggest that it was much occupied in EB III.

Pl. 63: 305	Jericho (AAA XXII, Pl. XXVIII: 34 for stripes on rim) Strip 2, 11·53 m.	Layers V–IV
	(AAA XXII, Pl. XXXIII: 14) Strip 3, 11·53 m.	Layers V–IV
Pl. 63: 306	Tell el Hesi (TH, Pl. VI: 66)	"Amorite"
	Beisan (MJ XXIV, 1935, Pl. V: 20 and p. 16)	Levels XIII and XII
	Et-Tell (*Ay*, Pl. LXXXI: 1177 II) Fouille V, Ch. 78, assise 3	EB I
	(*Ay*, Pl. LXXVII: 2023) Fouille H, Ch. 116, parquet A	EB I–II
Pl. 63: 312	Beisan (MJ XXIV, 1935, Pl. X: 12)	Level XII
	Jericho (AAA XXII, Pl. XXXIV: 4) Tomb 351	EB IV
Pl. 63: 314	Jericho (AAA XXII, Pl. XXVIII: 3) Strip 2, 11·53 m.	Layers V–IV

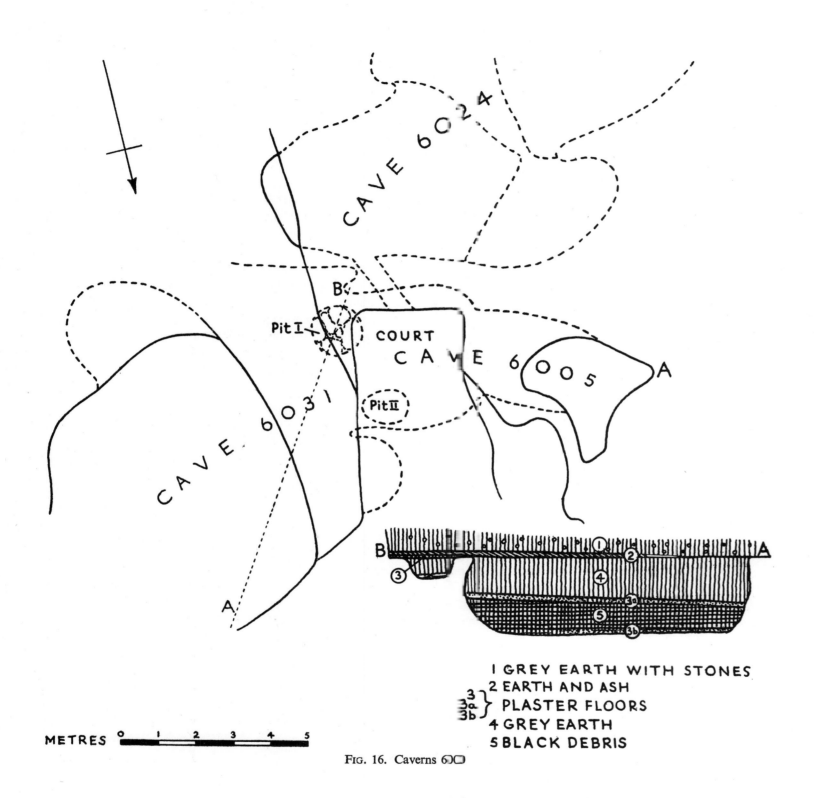

CAVE 6024

CAVE 6005

B

COURT

CAVE 6031

Pit I

Pit II

A

A

A

B

1
2
3a
4
3b
5

1 GREY EARTH WITH STONES
2 EARTH AND ASH
3
3a } PLASTER FLOORS
3b
4 GREY EARTH
5 BLACK DEBRIS

METRES 0 1 2 3 4 5

FIG. 16. Caverns 60

296

6007 Cave in Grid Square U.4   LB III, *c.* 1250–1200 B.C.

An oval cave approached by steps on the east side. It contained a single burial with five pots, all of which were broken and disturbed. The group belongs to the end of the Bronze Age.

Pottery: Bowls: curved H *L. II*: 36; flared J 620; *L. II*: 91
   Pilgrim Flask: 957   Krater: 991

6008 House in Grid Square V.4   LB

A room or court in a building; part of the south wall remained with three stone-lined pits. See 6014.

6009 Cave in Grid Square U.4   EB

The entry to this tomb, still blocked by stones, like that of Cave 6013 near by, was cut in the side of the same open terrace. Inside, there was just room for three bodies in a row, placed with heads to the south-east, each in the same partially contracted position. (See Appendix B).

Objects: Paste (?) bead as Pl. 29: 5

6010 Cave in Grid Square U.4   Cut before 2000 B.C. In continuous use as a dwelling

The roof and upper part of the cave had been removed. The floor was covered by loose grey earth and stones to a depth of over a metre, and the filling contained Early Bronze Age pottery. Above the earth and stones a plaster floor had been made, associated perhaps with the stone building 6023 (L. III, p. 250).

Pottery: Bowl: string-cut 369   Juglet: wide-necked 391A

6011 Cave in Grid Square U.4   EB

A large rectangular cave originally cut or enlarged in the Early Bronze Age, when it was used as a dwelling. The entrance was from the north. Subsequently the cave filled with debris, and during the Iron Age some burials were put in the south-east corner (L. III, p. 249). Some Early Bronze Age sherds came from a depression in the floor (NP).

6012 Areas in Grid Square U.4   Cut before 2000 B.C. Intermittent use thereafter.

An open terrace to the east of Cave 6013 in which the entrance was cut. Beside it there was a pile of Early Bronze Age sherds, presumably cleared from that large cave (L. III, p. 249). Flint blades, Appendix C.

6013 Cavern in Grid Square U.4 (Fig. 17)   EB I, II, III

The most impressive and extensive cave-dwelling so far excavated at Duweir was approached through a small entrance blocked by stones (Pl. 10: 2).

At the time of discovery it seemed certain that the cavern had not been entered since the Early Bronze Age, and three contracted burials had already been found near by (Cave 6009). Early Bronze Age sherds were piled near the entrance, which was cut in the rock face of the open terrace 6012. It was subsequently shown that the pottery was cleared from the cave, as pieces of the same pot were found in both places.

Just inside the blocking of the doorway, on top of water-laid mud, there were two bodies, also lying on their sides with knees drawn up and hands in front of the face. Both burials were somewhat disturbed from the inflow of water and a partial fall of stone. Farther in, on a rock bench skirting the east wall, there were four more burials, similarly disposed, and other unattached skulls were found elsewhere in the outer part of the cave. The bones and skulls were in exceptionally good condition (see Appendix B). Bodies of an adult and a child came from debris underlying mud which had penetrated from the entrance.

Apart from numerous alcoves and irregularities, the cave when cleared measured 15 × 7 metres with one rough pillar to support the roof (Pl. 10: 3). From time to time it had been enlarged by the cutting of new bays in a

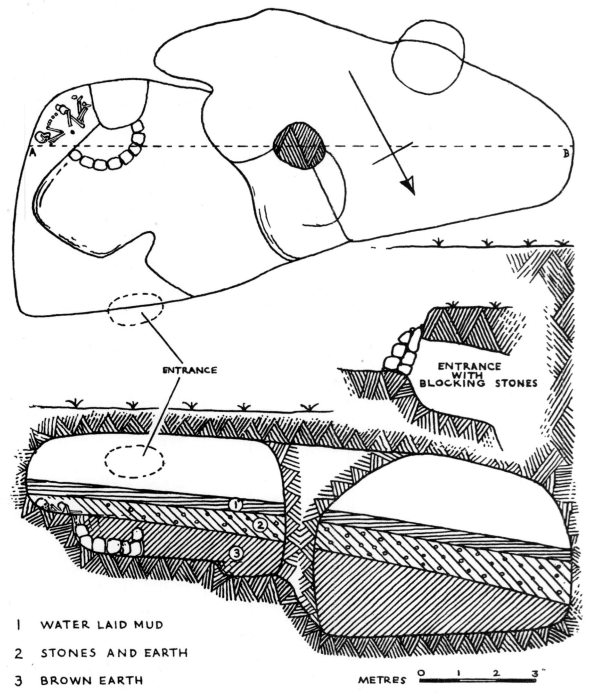

ENTRANCE

ENTRANCE
WITH
BLOCKING STONES

1 WATER LAID MUD

2 STONES AND EARTH

3 BROWN EARTH

METRES 0 1 2 3

Fig. 17. Cave 6013

haphazard manner. Indeed, the toolmarks on the roof and on those parts of the walls which were free from mud were as clear as if they were newly cut. The marks were almost certainly made by a stone adze about 4 cms. across the cutting edge (Pl. 10: 4).

298

Although the roof was not seriously discoloured by smoke, it seems likely that the cave was first used as a dwelling. Traces of that occupation are collapsed remains of stone-lined pits or silos and the magnificent jar (Pl. 62: 289) which was standing on the rock in the farthest recess of the cave. It was not until the floor was covered with brown earth to a depth of 2 metres that any use was made of the cave as a burial place; some of the bodies in a layer of earth and stones had been raised by water seepage to the mud level, which effectively sealed this group.

Pottery: *Photographs on Pl. 15: 4–5

Platters: inverted rim 344
       flanged rim: concave top 350; rounded top 348
            flattened top 347
       inturned rim 349; plain rim 277(2), 278 (Layer 2), 341
Bowls: flanged rim, rounded top 346
      plain rim 145, 147, 337, 342, 343
      with lugs 345; string-cut 338, 339, 340
Vats: 274, 275, 276, 290,* 353   Spouted Bowls: as NE 7/299; 351, 358
Holemouth Jars: bulbous rim 289*(2), 354; miscellaneous as NE 4/362; 355, 356
Pithoi: 283, 284, 293, 297, 298, 299(2), 300, 301(2)
Jar, with notched decoration: 361
Jars or Jugs with ledge handles: 251, 288(9)
Ledge Handles, Form 8 (p. 153): 364(25)
Unclassified: as NE 4/371; 6/323, 340; 8/272(2), 275; 9/255; 352, 357, 359, 360, 362(3), 363
Sherd as Pl. 13: 80   Base of cornet NP
Potmarks: Pl. 18: 3, 5, 14, 17, 21, 30–33, 40, 47–54, 57, 60, 61, 63
Iron Age Sherds: L. III, Pl. 105: 5, 12, 14

Objects

Flint blades, Appendix C   Chalk pierced stone NP
Palestine Museum Nos.: PM 38.732–741; 39.791; 39.837–839

Date and Comparisons

Though a small piece of a cornet base suggests a very early start for the use of this cave, it was certainly occupied in the first two phases of the Early Bronze Age, having contacts with Beisan XIV and Ay, and also with Layers V–IV at Jericho and the debris of the 1952 Second wall.

A slightly later trend than that of Cave 6005 is suggested by the contacts in the Section ranging from 4 to 9 feet.

Pl. 61: 251	Jericho (AAA XIX, Pl. VI: 13 with wider neck) Tomb A 1. 22c	EB III
Pl. 62: 277	Megiddo (M. II, Pl. 5: 19) 5203	Stratum XVII
Pl. 62: 278	Megiddo (M. II, Pl. 5: 18)	Stratum XVII
Pl. 62: 289	Et-Tell (*Ay*, Pl. LXXVIII: 2543) Fouille H, Ch. 116, sous parquet B	EB I?
	(*Ay*, Pl. LXXXIV: 619) Fouille D, Ch. 34	
Pl. 62: 290	Tell el-Hesi (MMC, Pl. 3: 85) City I and Sub I	"Amorite"
	Et-Tell (*Ay*, Pl. LXXVII: 2082) Fouille V¹, Ch. 229, niv. 1	EB III?
Pl. 64: 337	Jericho (AAA XXII, Pl. XXVIII: 13) Strip 2, 11·53 m.	Layers V–IV
Pl. 64: 346	Tell el Farʿah (RB LIV, 1947, p. 405, Fig. 5: 2)	EB I
	Jericho (AAA XXII, Pl. XXVIII: 38) Strip 2, 11·53 m.	Layers V–IV
Pl. 64: 348	Jericho (PEQ, 1952, p. 77, Fig. 5: 39) Upper midden against 2nd wall	EB II?
Pl. 64: 354	Jericho (PEQ, 1952, p. 77, Fig. 5: 11) Construction of 2nd wall	EB II?
Pl. 64: 357	Beisan (MJ XXIV, 1935, Pl. IV: 20; VIII: 22).	Levels XIV, XI
	Tell Beit Mirsim (AASOR XII, p. 6, Fig. 1: bottom right)	Stratum J

Pl. 64: 358	Megiddo (MT, Pl. 6: 29) Tomb 1101B lower	Stages O–I
Pl. 64: 360	Et-Tell (*Ay*, Pl. LXXXIV: 457) Fouille D, Ch. 25	
Pl. 64: 361	Megiddo (M. II, Pl. 101: 31)	Stratum XVIII

6014 House in Grid Square V.4 — LB II

A room or court in a building with no traceable floors. A circular stone-lined pit, similar to those in the adjoining area 6008, contained Base-Ring and fragments of painted storage jars.

6015 Area in Grid Square U.4 — ?

A wall built across a rock cavity was probably associated with the buildings 6008, 6014. No contents.

6016 Cave in Grid Square U.4 — EB III and LB III, *c.* 1250–1200 B.C.

The small cavity contained a disturbed burial placed there during the Late Bronze Age in a consistent and uniform fill of grey earth; much of the roof was missing. Pushed-up ledge handles, raised rope moulding and comb-faced ware represent an earlier phase of occupation.

Pottery: Bowls: curved H 609; *L. II*: 137; *L. III*: 20
Lamp: B 653   Imitation Base-Ring: 884
Imitation Imported: 910

Objects: Metal: Arrowheads: Pl. 25: 47, 48

6017 Court in Grid Square U.3 — MB III, *c.* 1675–1625 B.C.

A stone-lined enclosure near the entrance of Tomb 6006 (L. III, p. 247).

Pottery: Bowl: carinate C 546   Juglet: E 753

6018 Cave in Grid Square U.4 — ?

The entrance was blocked by stones, but the roof was missing and the back wall was cut almost to the floor, which rested partly on the grey soil filling Tomb 6019. There were some bone fragments and sherds of mixed date.

6019 Cave in Grid Square U.4 — Neolithic, EB III and later

Farther down the tell slope below the terrace outside the great cavern 6013 there was another cave, completely denuded of its roof. The remaining lower half was filled with six layers of debris containing characteristic sherds of EB III, sealed in by the well-prepared clay floor of House 6008. A bronze hook (Pl. 25: 67) and some tweezers should be associated with it. A painted sherd was the only one of Neolithic type from the site (pp. 6, 29, 44).

Pottery: As Pl. 60: 229 and NE 16/203

Objects: Bronze hook: Pl. 25: 67; tweezers NP
Flint Implements, Appendix C

6022 Court in Grid Square U.5 — EB and later

A square court or platform leading through a narrow passage to the dwelling and workshop 6024, q.v. Under the court was Cave 6005, mainly occupied in EB I–II. A tabular flint scraper found on the court is associated with this earlier period (see Appendix C).

Objects: Flint tabular scraper: Pl. 19: 7   Alabaster fragment NP

6024 Dwelling and workshop in Grid Square U.5 (*Lachish III*, pp. 250–252) EB and later

A large partly denuded cave, with irregular chambers or recesses, used as a dwelling in the Early Bronze Age. The lower fill of black debris is of that period (Fig. 16).

6025 Wall in Grid Square V.4 ?

Part of a wall which presumably continues beyond the limits of the excavation. Its purpose was to retain the soil and house foundations on the slopes at the edge of the Wadi Ghafr, and its position suggests that the course of the river bed has not altered appreciably since the Late Bronze Age. The wall was covered with a black layer, possibly the sooty deposit so noticeable in the area, rather than the effects of fire.

Objects: Flint sickle blades: Pl. 19: 16–22

6026 Cave in Grid Square V.4 EB III

The roof was missing and the cave contained pushed-up ledge handles, matt and burnished bowls and combed fragments, besides a complete jug.

On the east side, the deposits in the upper part had been disturbed by the construction of Tomb 6027 above.

Pottery: Jug, ledge-handled: Pl. 62: 288 and Pl. 15: 3

Pl. 62: 288	Tell el-Judeideh (BM, Pl. 23: 2J)	"Early Pre-Israelite"
	Et-Tell (*Ay*, Pl. LXV: 11.1565) Fouille H, Ch. 141, sanctuaire. Cf. *Syria XVI*, 1935, Pl. LVI	EB III?

6027 Cave in Grid Square V.4 MB III, *c.* 1700–1650 B.C.

Close to the eastern limit, and at the lowest point of excavation, yet another cave was examined. The entrance was sealed with stones, and, unlike the majority of caves in the vicinity, the roof was almost intact. The burials and offerings were in and on a layer of light earth which was never more than 50 cms. in depth, and the black sooty deposit was very noticeable on the surface of the fill, the sides of the tomb, and on all exposed vessels and bones (see L. III, p. 246).

The human remains were poorly preserved owing to the position of the tomb, low on the slopes near the normal course of rain-water to the valley. Thirteen adults were buried in the cave with one child. Eleven skulls were piled together on the west side, and two more were near the east wall (see Appendix B).

Pottery

Bowls: carinate A 506(2), 520; C 540(2), 543(6); curved H 596(2)
Lamps: A 644, 646, 647; B 648(2); C 657; D 660(3); F *L. III*: 144
Jugs: B 675; D 696
Juglets: B 733, 734; C 738; E 753(10), 755, 756, 758, 760
Dippers: A 780(3), 781

Objects

Metal: Togglepin: Pl. 24: 12   Ear-ring NP
Stone: Hone: Pl. 26: 24
Beads: Pl. 29: 5 (8 paste, 4 cn.), 6 (1 paste, 1 qu.), 21 (1 cn.)
Scarabs: Pl. 32: 67–89; amethyst (2), quartz (1), carnelian (1), uninscribed NP
Palestine Museum Nos.: PM 38.752–754

Date and Comparisons

The group may go back earlier than Tomb 6028, and both pottery and scarabs show some affinity with the tombs below the MB defences. The popularity of red crowns and emblems of North and South on scarabs compares with the motifs of Tomb 153, and Cemetery 500 at Tell Fara also provides several connexions.

6028 Cave in Grid Square V.4   MB III, *c.* 1675–1625 B.C.

South of Cave 6027 at a higher level on the slope was a burial chamber of only half the size. It contained the scattered bones of seven adults and one child (see Appendix B) with pottery and scarabs. The mould was probably a surface find.

Pottery: Bowls: carinate B 532; C 540, 543(2)
        Lamps: A 644; D 660   Juglets: E 759; F 767(2), 759
        Dippers: A 780; B 783

Objects: Metal: Togglepins NP   Bone: Inlay: Pl. 28: 1
        Scarabs: Pl. 30: 60–62   Mould: Pl. 47: 6–7

Date and Comparisons

With half the number of burials, Cave 6028 overlaps in part with the previous tomb, though it shows a slightly later tendency. The bone inlay is comparable to sets from Megiddo beginning in Stratum XII, and the birds without eyes are closest to those at the end of the range in Stratum IX. The scarabs compare with Stratum D at Tell Beit Mirsim, and with the Structural Tombs of Stratum XI at Megiddo.

6029 Cave in Grid Square U.4   Chalc. and EB

The clay floor of House 6008 in the upper fill of Cave 6019 covered the entrance to Cave 6029, which contained a uniform filling of light earth. The bones of a single burial were disturbed and poorly preserved. The two cups were side by side in the fill, and like the pithos they are most common in the last phases of the Early Bronze Age. Dr. Waechter found that the bulk of the flints belonged to the same period, though there was one Chalcolithic blade (Appendix C, p. 326).

Pottery: Cups: 392, 393   Pithos: 302

Objects: Sickle Flints

Comparison

Pl. 65: 393   Et-Tell (*Ay*, Pl. LXV: 8.1528) Fouille H, Ch. 133, près de l'autel   EB II

6030 Cave in Grid Square U.4   Chiefly EB III

The cave deposit was partially covered by a section of Late Bronze Age wall which appears to be a continuation of the retaining wall 6025, and of the diagonal section in the same alinement beyond building 6023.

The accumulation in Cave 6030 consisted of one uniform fill of earth and ash to a depth of 6 metres, in which there were flint blades, fragments of bronze or copper, and burnished sherds.

Pottery

Platters: upright rim 322
        flanged rim, rounded top as NE 5/345; 325, 327(4)
        inturned rim 324(2); plain rim 320(5), 321, 323
Bowls: plain 326, 329, 332; string-cut 328
Vats: 273 (2)   Spouted Bowls: 331, 333, 335
Pithoi: 294, 303 (and Pl. 15: 1, 2)
Jars or Jugs with ledge handles: 285(5), 286(3)
Ledge Handles: 330(14)   Unclassified: 336(2)
Reptile: Pl. 13: 95
Potmarks: Pl. 18: 9, 16, 26, 28, 34, 45, 58, 65, 68
Palestine Museum Nos.: PM 38. 759–761

Date and Comparisons

Apart from a few Chalcolithic and EB I sherds, the bulk of the material in the cave equates with EB III at Ay and with Megiddo Stages IV–I, pushed-up ledge handles being extremely common. The two comparisons from Megiddo Stratum XVIII are not very significant as they came from disturbed areas. Parallels in the Section range from 6 feet upwards.

Pl. 62: 303	Et-Tell (*Ay*, Pl. XLIX: 2)	EB III
Pl. 63: 321	Megiddo (M. II, Pl. 102: 27) E = 4033	Stratum XVIII
Pl. 63: 322	Tell el-Hesi (TH, Pl. VI: 66)	"Amorite"
	Et-Tell (*Ay*, Pl. LXXVII: 2023) Fouille H, Ch. 116, parquet A	EB III
Pl. 63: 323	Et-Tell (*Ay*, Pl. LXXVII: 2004) Fouille H, Ch. 116, parquet A	EB III
Pl. 63: 324	Megiddo (SAOC 10, Chart Column 1D)	Stages IV–I
	Megiddo (M. II, Pl. 102: 37) = 4045	Stratum XVIII
Pl. 63: 330	Megiddo (SAOC 10, Chart Column 14B)	Stages IV–I

6031 Cave and quarry in Grid Square U.5   **EB III and earlier**

Originally a dwelling in Early Bronze Age times, the cave was much destroyed by quarrying, and some parts remain undug beyond the limits of excavation (Pl. 10: 1).

Several occupational phases are distinguishable in the deposits which adjoin, and are connected with, Cave 6005 (Fig. 16).

Pottery

Platters: flanged rim, concave top 379; rounded top 375, 376, 377; flattened top 378
        inturned rim 373; plain rim 370
Bowls: flanged rim, rounded top as NE 6/313
        plain rim 136, 145, 148, 365(2), 366, 367, 368 (layer 3), 371, 372
        with lugs 374; string-cut 369
Crucible: 45   Vats: as NE 9/250; 275(4), 290(6)
Spouted Bowls: 108, 381
Holemouth Jars: bulbous rim 387, 390; miscellaneous 384, 388
Pithoi: as NE 9/254; 281, 282, 295
Jars with notched decoration: 386, 389
Jug with ledge handles: 385   Ledge Handles, Form 8, p. 153: 382(34)
Jars: with loop handles: 118; with lugs 220
Juglet: pointed 383   Unclassified: 380, 391(7)
Potmarks: Pl. 18: 1, 4, 7, 8, 15, 22, 25, 27, 29, 36, 37, 39, 42, 44, 46, 55, 56, 59, 62

Objects

Copper Point: Pl. 22: 8   Flint implements, Appendix C

Date and Comparisons

The contents of Cave 6031 are again predominantly EB III in character, if the long range of holemouth jar rims is allowed for. Comparisons in the Section are from 7 to 9 feet and others link it to Jericho Tomb A2.

Pl. 58: 108	Tell Beit Mirsim (AASOR XII, Pl. 2: 14 and p. 6)	Stratum J
Pl. 60: 220	Jericho (AAA XIX, Pl. 8: 17) Tomb A2.16f.	EB III
Pl. 62: 290	Et-Tell (*Ay*, Pl. LXXVII: 2082) Fouille V¹, Ch. 229, niv. 1	EB III?
Pl. 65: 365	Jericho (AAA XXII, Pl. XXVII: 9) Strip 2, 11·53 m.	Layers V–IV
Pl. 65: 378	Jericho (AAA XIX, Pl. IV: 23) Tomb A2.40	EB III
Pl. 65: 379	Et-Tell (*Ay*, Pl. LXXXI: 1437) Fouille H, Ch. 125, assise 2 du mur nord	
Pl. 65: 383	Jericho (AAA XIX, Pl. III: 15) Tomb A2	EB III

Pl. 65: 387	Et-Tell (*Ay*, Pl. LXXXIV: 226) Fouille G, Ch. 3	EB III
Pl. 65: 389	Tell en-Naṣbeh (TN II, Pl. 10: 151) Tomb 61	
	Megiddo (SAOC 10, Chart Column 10)	Stages IV–I
Pl. 65: 390	Megiddo (SAOC 10, Chart Column 12D)	Stages VII–III
	Megiddo (M. II, Pl. 97: 11) S = 4047	Stratum XIX
	Jericho (AAA XXII, Pl. XXVIII: 28) Strip 2, 11·53 m.	Layers IV–III
	Tell Beit Mirsim (AASOR XII, Pl. I: 18)	Stratum J
	Tell el Farʿah (RB LV, 1947, p. 419, Fig. 7: 12)	EB II
	Et-Tell (*Ay*, Pl. LXXXIV: 357 row 4) Fouille G, Ch. 3	EB III?

6032 Pit in Grid Square U.5   *c.* 1200 B.C.

A small open pit blocked on the east side by four courses of stone, possibly part of the Late Bronze Age retaining wall observed in 6025 and 6030. Washed alluvial soil in the pit suggests that the Wadi in spate was the reason for the construction of the wall. The pit only contained some bronze and fragments of pottery coffins, like those from Pit 570.

6033 Wall and pit in Grid Square U.5   ?

Though it was not in alinement with the retaining walls 6025, 6030 and 6032, the small section preserved in this area probably fulfilled a similar purpose. Near by, a stone-lined pit was only partially excavated.

AREA 7000, AT HEAD OF SOUTHERN VALLEY
(L. III, Pl. 130)

A general account of the approaches leading to the city gate is given in *Lachish III*, p. 253. It described the probable traces of three roads or tracks, the earliest of which, road (c), is attributed to the second millennium.

7003 Locus in Grid Square G.26   MB III, *c.* 1800–1750 B.C.

Some 30 centimetres below a stone-paved section of this road, broken pottery was found which provides a *terminus ante quem* for the construction of the road (c). The position of the group in Grid G.26 suggests that it is probably on or near the line of the MB fosse which may have been seen in Grids D.34, 24 (see Tombs 570, 571; cf. the plan in *Lachish II*, Pl. LXXII).

Pottery: Bowls: carinate A 506; C 537, 549; E 559
       Jug: B 675   Juglets: B 732, 735
       Storage Jars: B 1009; C 1013

Date and Comparisons

The group is quite early in the Duweir series, having several vessels which are not matched in tombs. Its best contacts are with 7014 and with 6027. This accords with parallels from other sites, beginning at Megiddo in XIII A, Tell Beit Mirsim E and Jericho Tomb 13c and Tomb 5g.

7004 Road in Grid Square H.27   ?

Section of paved road. Beyond this point to the south all traces of the road had disappeared.

7005 Pit (not marked on L. III, Pl. 130)   LB III and later, *c.* 1300 B.C.

The pit was near the eastern limit of excavation. It was partly damaged and the contents were disturbed. The walls were plastered. Two bronze armour scales and a ring were published in L. III, Pl. 58: 3–5 and p. 253.

Pottery: Bowl: curved H *L. II*: 50   Jug: E 726

7008 Cistern in Grid Square J.28   LB III, *c.* 1300–1200 B.C.

A roughly hewn cistern, plaster-lined and straight-sided (L. III, p. 254). Sections of drainpipes, about 20 cms. in diameter, were made to fit into each other, and they were also supplied with loop handles. Compare the drainpipes from the Residency (L. III, Pl. 90: 390). See also those associated with Strata VIII–VII B at Megiddo (M. II, Pl. 256: 2–5). For the use of similar pipes at Knossos, see *Technology*, Fig. 349.

Pottery: Bowl: carinate F 582   Drainpipes: 1004

7009 House in Grid Square J.28   ?

Part of a house, most of which lies under the unexcavated eastern scarp. There was a clay oven in the north-west corner and pot holes in the floor.

7011 Oval grave in Grid Square K.26   LB I, *c.* 1550 B.C.

Oriented north-east to south-west, the isolated grave only contained pots; the body was missing. The Black or Grey Lustrous juglets, so common in Tomb 4004, occur in the grave with a Black Slip III juglet. It is unique at Duweir and not too common in the Cypriote repertory (p. 199). The dipper is like those of Structure I and the form of the storage jar is comparable to L. II: 386, also from the first Fosse Temple building.

Pottery: Juglets: J 774, 777   Dippers: A *L. II*: 292
        Imported Ware: 814   Storage Jar: B 1008
Palestine Museum Nos.: PM 38.762–765; 39.793, 794

7012 Cave in Grid Square J.26   LB III, *c.* 1300–1200 B.C.

A rectangular cave near the northern limit of excavation, where the rock drops sharply to the eastern valley. All the east side was missing. Among the contents was part of a moulded female figurine which may be compared to those from the potter's workshop 4034 (Pl. 49).

Pottery: Dipper: A *L. II*: 292

Objects: Astarte figurine frag. NP   Sickle flints NP

7013 Area in Grid Square K.26   LB I–III

An open area on the rock where many sherds were found, some of which may have come from Cave 7012. Scattered fragments of burnished and painted pottery were reconstructed to form a unique anthropomorphic vessel (Pl. 48). Two Iron Age forms are published in L. III, p. 254.

Of the fragments listed below, the chalice and the krater belong to the period of Structure II, while the baking plate could be found in Structure I or in groups of the following century. The date of the painted vessel cannot be fixed with certainty, but the style and colour of the burnish and paint suggest a date contemporary with Structure III (p. 89).

The togglepin, Type 8c(b), may belong to the earlier part of LB I (p. 80).

Pottery: Jug: E 724

        Anthropomorphic Jar: 1005 and Pl. 48: 5, 7–9 (PM. 39. 795)
        also Chalice: *L. II*: 206; Krater *L. II*: 243
            Baking Plate: *L. II*: 338

Objects: Metal: Togglepin: Pl. 24: 32

7014 Cave in Grid Square J.26   MB III, *c.* 1725–1675 B.C.

A large cave with angular corners was complete except for the missing south side. No human remains were recorded. The pottery equates with Megiddo XIII–X, with Tombs 5, 9 and 13 at Jericho and with Strata E–D at Tell Beit Mirsim. The dagger (Type 27a), the togglepin (Type 3), and the faience juglet matched in Tomb 1013 at Fara and a group of the xvith dynasty at Sedment, complete this interesting collection.

Pottery: Bowls: carinate A 520; B 528; C 537; plain G *L. II*: 35
              Lamps: A 644(2)   Juglets: B 732, 733; C 745(2); E 751, 753
              Dippers: A 781(2)   Storage Jar: B 1008

Objects: Metal: Dagger: Pl. 23: 1   Togglepin: Pl. 24: 2
             Faience Juglet: Pl. 26: 12
             Beads: Pl. 29: 6 (1 qu.), 15 (1 am.)

7015 Alcove in Grid Square J.26   LB I, *c.* 1550 B.C.

An alcove or recess in the north-west wall of Cave 7012, just below floor level. It contained a baby's skull with a lamp and a dipper, both of which are Structure I forms.

Pottery: Lamp: C 655   Dipper: A *L. II*: 292

7016 Road in Grid Square K.27   ?

Section of stone paving, probably part of road surface leading up from the eastern valley. See Area 7000, 7004.

7017 Wall in Grid Square K.27   LB III, *c.* 1300–1225 B.C.

Part of a wall; sherds and three scarabs were found in the vicinity. The latter are Ramesside in style.

Pottery: Dipper: D *L. II*: 308   Imitation Imported: *L. II*: 344
             Miniature Pithos: 984

Objects: Beads: Pl. 29: 7 (1 cn.), 21 (1 glass)
             Scarabs: Pl. 39: 379–381

7018 Area in Grid Square K.27   ?

A patch of ash and burnt earth containing sherds similarly affected by fire.

APPENDICES

APPENDIX A

PLANT ECONOMY IN ANCIENT LACHISH

By HANS HELBAEK

IN spite of their modest extent, the deposits of carbonized plants recovered from Lachish (Tell ed-Duweir) in Palestine have by their nature thrown an unexpectedly comprehensive light on the plant husbandry and vegetable food-gathering of the Palestinians of the Early Bronze Age and the Iron Age (Pl. 15).

It appears that many-sided agricultural activity was displayed in both periods illustrated by our finds. Two products stand out as particularly important: cereals and Olive. The universal and abundant occurrence of the remains of olives as compared with the other foodstuffs suggests production for more than home consumption. At both times wheat was an important food: while the Early Bronze Age specimens were supplemented by smaller amounts of barley, wheat was the only cereal in the Iron Age grain sample. This is most probably fortuitous since barley was an important Iron Age crop in the Near East and elsewhere. However, in the course of the second millennium, which is not represented in the plant deposits, the species of wheat changed, in that Emmer, which was the main bread corn in the Bronze Age, was replaced almost completely by Club or Bread wheat. This development was also observed in the contemporary material from Hama[1] in Syria and may be connected with the introduction of Iron Age influence.

Grape pips, also, are present in all the mixed samples of both periods, and we may take it that the vine was commonly grown and that grapes were consumed with the daily meals. An outstanding feature of our plant list is the numerous species of the Pea family represented. It is, however, characteristic of Mediterranean finds of ancient plant remains that they normally consist of a much higher percentage of these seeds as compared with the grain, than in finds from more northerly regions. Even today Mediterranean peoples consume the seeds of leguminous plants to a larger extent than we do in northern Europe. The principal difference between cereals and leguminous seeds is the much higher content of protein in the latter.

There seems to be no reason to suggest that Hawthorn and Pistachio were cultivated in the Bronze Age. When we find their fruit stones with the seeds of cultivated plants it must, however, mean that they were utilized in the food, and we may conclude that these fruits were gathered on the hillside. In Hawthorn it was the fruit flesh that was consumed, whereas it would be the fat and palatable seed of the Pistachio nut which attracted the ancient peasants. This species has no edible fruit flesh.

Only two species may be considered as pure weeds, unintentionally present in the food, viz. Darnel and Caterpillar. Both these field weeds are widely distributed in the Mediterranean region today, just as they must have been in prehistoric times.

In the plant list below, the Bronze Age specimens are all of the third millennium B.C. They are tabulated under headings which give their position in feet above bed-rock in the North-East section cut through the city deposits. Thus specimens under heading "2" were found 2 feet above bed-rock and so on. (For the section drawing see Pl. 96.) Other samples come from three different localities and periods in the Iron Age: (*a*) dwelling and workshop 6024, in use in the Early Bronze Age and reoccupied about 1000 B.C. (L. III, p. 250); (*b*) a room attributed to Level III, destroyed in 700 B.C. (L. III, p. 113, H. 15: 1035); (*c*) a heap of burnt matter lying on the road inside the gate of Level II, which was probably deposited soon after the destruction of 586 B.C. (L. III, Pl. 113, heap marked "burning").

It has not been possible to account for the proportions of the various species by quoting exact figures as the general state of preservation is unusually poor in all the specimens. Therefore, in the plant list the principal components are denoted by "× × ×", less frequent occurrence by "× ×", while "×" means that only one or a few specimens were present.[2]

309

	Early Bronze Age					Iron Age		
	N.-E. Section: feet above bed-rock					Sample number		
	2	3	5	6	8	A	B	C
1. Vine	×	×	×	×	—	—	×	—
2. Pistachio (butm) . .	×	×	×	×	—	—	—	—
3. Fenugreek (ḥilbah) . .	—	—	—	—	—	—	×	—
4. Caterpillar (sillaykah) .	×	—	×	—	—	—	—	—
5. Chickpea (ḥummuṣ) . .	×	×	×	—	—	—	×	—
6. Vetch (fûl) . . .	×	—	×	—	—	—	×	—
7. Horsebean? (fûl-baladi) .	—	—	—	—	—	—	×	—
8. Lentil (àdas) . . .	×	×	×	×	—	—	—	—
9. Grass Pea (jilbân) . .	×	—	—	—	—	—	—	—
10. Hawthorn (za'rûr) . .	×	—	—	—	—	—	—	—
11. Olive (zaytûn) . . .	× × ×	× × ×	× × ×	× × ×	× × ×	× × ×	—	× × ×
12. Eincorn	—	—	×	—	—	—	×	—
13. Emmer	× × ×	× × ×	× × ×	× × ×	—	—	×	—
14. Club or Bread Wheat .	—	—	—	—	—	—	× × ×	—
15. Darnel (zûwan) . . .	×	—	×	×	—	—	× ×	—
16. Hulled Barley . . .	× × ×	× × ×	× × ×	× ×	—	—	—	—
Amount in cubic cms. . .	30	8	35	30	1	200	90	10

(Arrangement of plant list according to Post 1932; Arabic names in Italics (brackets) after Guest 1933 and Post 1932).

1. Grape: *Vitis vinifera* L.

All mixed samples, irrespective of period, contained whole or broken grape pips. These seeds are oblique and roughly pear-shaped, with two furrows framing a solid ridge on the ventral side, and the domed dorsal side is characterized by a round or oval shield-like figure.

The complete seeds are too few for statistical considerations, but it may be noted that the Bronze Age specimens are larger than the Iron Age ones. One perfect Bronze Age pip is 5·67 mm. long, 4·39 mm. wide and 3·66 mm. thick; another, defective one, was evidently still larger. The smallest one is 4·76 mm. long, 2·93 mm. wide and 2·56 mm. thick. On the other hand, the Iron Age pips are 4·58 to 4·94 mm. long, 3·66 to 3·84 mm. wide and 3·29 mm. thick. (Pl. 15. EB, fig. c, IA fig. e, left.)

In the pottery from Hama in Syria the writer has identified a consecutive series of imprints of grape pips, starting in the Early Bronze Age stratum L, and attaining in the Iron Age a far greater frequency than cereal imprints. It seems as if the Iron Age potters were eating fresh or dried grapes while doing the pot turning, spitting out the pips upon the lathe, or on the floor, where the raw clay was deposited.[3]

The importance of viticulture is well known from the earliest literature, and there are representations of the plant, the grapes, and their treatment in early Semitic and Egyptian iconography. However, what we usually find is the description of wine, its production and social function, but in the present context it is raisins, the other product of the vine, which we are dealing with. The refuse from wine production would not be found in food, but raisins were used together with cereals and other farinaceous food, and the pips would remain after carbonization, while the succulent flesh usually disappeared. The writer has, however, identified many whole carbonized raisins in unpublished Early Bronze Age material from Palestine, showing unmistakable evidence of having been dried before burning.

Wild vine species are distributed in the Near East. In the Subboreal period, mountainous central and southern Europe was a natural habitat of the Forest Vine. Today it is only to be found in scattered localities along the Danube and the Rhine. The utilisation of grapes undoubtedly started before agriculture, and Neolithic and Bronze Age finds of pips occur in Italy and central Europe, even as far north as Brandenburg in north-eastern

Germany.[4] However, the actual cultivation of the plant most probably started in the Near East, spreading from there eventually with sea trade to Greece, France and Italy.

2. Pistachio: *Pistacia atlantica* Desf.

Whole or fragmentary shells of a small nut were found in all the Early Bronze Age grain specimens (Pl. 15: b). No. 2 contained two practically whole shells, one of which is 5·9 mm. long and 4·3 × 3·7 mm. wide, with a worm hole of 0·9 mm. The other is 3·9 mm. long and 3·5 mm. wide. The base is flat and thickened with a conspicuous duct in or near the centre (cf. Pl. 15: b, left).

These stones correspond to the fruit of Pistachio stripped of its fruit flesh. Eleven species are described, distributed in the subtropical-temperate zone throughout the world. Five species are mentioned for Palestine today, of which, considering the size and non-oblique shape, our fruits seem to conform with *Pistacia atlantica*, allowing for carbonisation shrinkage and lack of fruit flesh. It is distributed north and south along the Mediterranean and the Near East (except Sinai and Egypt) to Afghanistan.[5]

Certain species of this genus are being cultivated, or exploited in the wild state. Their sap is used for turpentine, resin (Mastix), and gum, as well as for tanning mediums and incense, and their oleaginous seeds are also used in baking and confectionery.

Our find would suggest the use of the seeds in the food.

3. Fenugreek: *Trigonella graecum* L.

Six Fenugreek seeds were encountered in the Iron Age Specimen B. They are 3·84–4·21 mm. long and 1·83–2·20 mm. wide. They are of a characteristic angular shape with the radicle appressed to the cotyledons, up to two-thirds of the length of the seed (Pl. 15: e, top).

Seeds of this species have been reported from Tell Halaf, about 4000 B.C.,[6] and Meadi in Egypt of about 3000 B.C.[7]

Fenugreek is cultivated extensively in India and the Near East and Egypt, for fodder and food. Like many others of that genus it has a strong coumarin smell. Since antiquity the seeds have been used medicinally, for stomach complaints and as an antipyretic.[8] Their occurrence in the Iron Age food may be accidental, but the possibility of the seeds having been used as a spice cannot be rejected.

4. Caterpillar: *Scorpiurus subvillosa* L.

In each of the Early Bronze Age specimens Nos. 2 and 5 two small leguminous seeds were found which were of a peculiar shape. They are reniform and bluntly pointed at both ends, 2·75 to 2·93 mm. long, and 2·0 mm. wide. This shape indicates a curved pod, constricted between the seeds, such as that of the genus *Scorpiurus*. An experiment showed that seeds of *S. subvillosa*, 3·30 mm. long in the fresh state, shrank to 2·93 and 3·10 mm. when carbonized, and the end of the germ puffed up in a bubble, exactly as in the ancient specimens. Other species of the genus which might come into discussion for Palestine have seeds too long and slender to conform with those from Lachish.

This species of Caterpillar is commonly found in fields and sandy places in the Mediterranean coastlands and the Near East. It does not seem to be cultivated, but it is a most valuable grazing plant. At Lachish it was undoubtedly a weed.

5. Chickpea: *Cicer arietinum* L.

The Bronze Age specimens Nos. 2, 3 and 5, and the Iron Age Specimen B, contained a few fragmented or almost whole seeds of Chickpea. They are normally bluntly angular with the germ drawn out in a point. Our seeds have lost most of these characteristics, by puffing and wear, but they are still characteristically different from all other leguminous seeds, and the broken point at one end places them safely enough. They vary in length from about 3·5 to 5 mm., in width from 3·3 to 4·5 mm. They are depicted to the right of the grape pips in Pl. 15: e.

Chickpeas are widely cultivated and highly esteemed in southern Europe and the Near East. They are used for fodder and food, and their seeds are very nutritious and quite palatable. They may be eaten in soup or in the roasted state (ar. *kudâmi*), and they are also used in baking and confectionery. The young shoots are cooked like spinach, and the immature pods are consumed as a potherb.[9]

This plant, unknown in the wild state, occurs in many cultivated varieties bearing much larger seeds than these ancient ones. It seems to be one of the first leguminous plants to be cultivated, judging by seeds occurring in very early plant deposits from Palestine and Iraq, examined but not yet published by the present writer.

6. Vetch: *Vicia sp.*

In samples from both periods a few round seeds of leguminous plants were present. In none of them the seed coat or hilum was preserved, so no more exact identification can be attempted. Very many species of this genus occur in this region.

7. Horsebean?: *Vicia faba* L., f. *celtica* Heer.

One much damaged cotyledon of a leguminous plant with the mark of the germ at one end was found in Specimen B. The edges being much worn, its width of 5·3 mm. represents a seed originally somewhat larger, probably some 6–7 mm. The only leguminous seed of this size occurring in finds from these tracts would be that of the Horsebean, and since the plant was grown in the Mediterranean countries and southern and central Europe from Neolithic times, there is nothing improbable about its occurrence in Iron Age Lachish[10] (Pl. 15: e, lower right).

8. Lentil: *Lens esculenta* Moench.

All the Bronze Age grain samples contained Lentils, from two to seven more or less whole, in addition to some fragments. Nine specimens could be measured. On the average they are 3·44 mm. wide (2·56–4·76 mm.), and 2·0 mm. thick (1·10–2·20 mm.). They have retained much of their lenticular shape and the keeled edge in spite of some puffing, but the seed coat and the hilum have disappeared (Pl. 15: a).

Practically all plant deposits of the Bronze and Iron Ages from the Middle East contain Lentils. In Egypt also the cultivation of this plant is of very great antiquity, the seeds having been found in predynastic tombs.[11] It was a highly important food plant, and from its propounded centre of origin, the Anatolian-Caucasian region, it spread to Europe at an early date. Thus it is already found in Hungary, Switzerland and Germany in Neolithic times.[12] Today it is cultivated extensively in Central and Western Asia, on the Mediterranean coast and in southern Europe.

9. Grass Pea: *Lathyrus sativus* L.

One slightly damaged seed of Grass Pea was identified among the grain of the Bronze Age sample No. 2. It is squat and wedge-shaped, approximately 5·5 mm. long, and 4·0 mm. wide. The hilum, placed at the top of the wedge, has disappeared with the seed coat.

The Grass Pea (or Blue Vetchling) occurs as a weed in fields of winter crops, and cultivated varieties are grown all over western Asia, Egypt, and southern Europe, as food and fodder plants. It was grown by the ancient Egyptians and Greeks, and its seeds were found among plant remains at Bronze Age Troy,[13] as well as in Neolithic plant deposits in Hungary.[14] The writer has identified it among Field peas from Neolithic Switzerland, and in burial offerings in Late Iron Age graves in Rome; also in Early Neolithic deposits from Iraq, and Late Neolithic graves in Egypt.

10. Hawthorn: *Crataegus sp.*

The Bronze Age sample, No. 2, contained a fruit stone (pyrene) of Hawthorn. It is roughly hemispherical, the domed dorsal side is faintly grooved longitudinally, the flat ventral side has a conspicuous suture ending in a little pit one-third from the apex. The shell is extremely thick, especially along the flanks. The stone is 7·7 mm. long, 7·5 mm. wide and 5·3 mm. thick. The seed occupies a cavity only 4·9 mm. long and 3·1 mm. wide, approximately circular in cross-section.

Three species may be considered in our district, the pyrenes of which are principally alike, but vary greatly according to the number developed in the fruit (up to five). Although this specimen may well belong to the very common *C. monogyna* Jacq., the writer does not offer any definite opinion.

Regarding the occurrence of this stone among food remains it is interesting to note a remark by Evan Guest referring to present-day Iraq, where Hawthorn trees are sometimes grown in gardens in Baqubah, where the berries are said to fetch a good price in the local market.[15]

11. Olive: *Olea europaea* L.

Except for Specimen B, all Bronze and Iron Age samples contained or consisted of olive stones. The fruit flesh has disappeared in all but one stone which was covered by a thin wrinkled coat which was probably the shrivelled flesh. The heat has evidently been so strong that the oleaginous flesh could not be expected to leave traces. Many shrivelled seeds show that the stones were not cracked before the burning, and there was no trace of animal attack.

These stones are approximately round in cross-section, about twice as long as thick, with a rounded base and pointed apex. The shell is fairly thick and its surface is coarsely grooved longitudinally, especially near the base. The Lachish stones are extremely fragile; only a few have remained whole; most of them have been crushed or, at best, split in half.

Early Bronze Age (20 stones)				Iron Age (25 stones)			
	av.	min.	max.		av.	min.	max.
L. mm.	11·2	9·0	13·2	L. mm.	10·1	8·2	12·6
T. mm.	5·7	5·0	6·2	T. mm.	5·7	5·1	6·4
T:L index per cent.	51·8	44	67	T:L index per cent.	57	48	67

The table shows the dimensions of the stones. They do not differ very much, but a typical decrease of length to the same thickness is notable in the Iron Age specimens. Whether this feature has any bearing on the stage of artificial breeding is uncertain.

The obvious importance of Olive cultivation at Lachish is not surprising. The natural habitat of the tree is a fairly dry, warm mountain side, not irrigated land. In antiquity it was not grown in the Nile Valley proper or in Mesopotamia. Egypt had to import the bulk of olive-oil supplies from higher land in the Fayum and the Libyan oases—and also presumably from districts like Lachish. In Palestine, Syria, Asia Minor and the Aegean Islands cultivation of olives started very early, radiating to the Greek mainland probably during the second millennium, and reaching Italy and France some time in the first millennium B.C. Olive stones found in Early Bronze Age Spain are interpreted as those of the wild tree.[16] The fruit was eaten, and the oil was used in cooking, ointments and temple offerings, and as fuel in lamps.

The wild olive tree is distributed from Baluchistan along the northern Mediterranean countries, to Spain and western North Africa. At present the most important olive-producing countries are those mentioned west of the Aegean. The tree is grown for oil in Upper Iraq, but it does not yield fruit in the river basin.

12. Eincorn: *Triticum monococcum* L.

13. Emmer: *Triticum dicoccum* Schübl.

All the Bronze Age grain samples seem to contain more wheat than barley. In No. 6 the wheat even amounts to some 80 per cent. of the grain. No spikelet parts were found, but judging by the proportions of the kernels the bulk may be referred to Emmer, with minor quantities of Eincorn admixed, Pl. 15: d.

The discrimination between the grains of these two primitive wheats must be based upon their thickness-breadth index. In fresh material this is fairly simple, but in the carbonised material the distortion sometimes blurs the distinctive details. In Eincorn the width is practically always less than the thickness (dimension from ventral to dorsal side), as opposed to the Emmer grain, in which the thickness is less than, or at the most equal to, the width. In the process of carbonisation both thickness and width increase, the width usually more than the thickness. In this way the Eincorn grain will attain a greater width as compared to the thickness, or, in other words, a lower transversal index. It may even reach equality in the two dimensions and thus pass into the maximum index group for Emmer.[17] This especially applies to the grains of the two-grained variety of Eincorn, in which the kernels are wider than in the one-grained one.[18] In the fifty grains measured from our samples, almost one-quarter show a thickness–breadth index of 95 to 100, and in this group some Eincorn grains are probably concealed. Only two kernels are of an index of more than 100, viz. 108 and 118 (L: 5.49, B: 2·38 and 2·01, T: 2·56 and 2·38 mm.). These may safely be identified as Eincorn. Thus it may be concluded that the material contains a minor proportion of Eincorn, presumably of the two-grained type.

Dimensions of 50 Eincorn and Emmer Grains

	av.	min.	max.
L. mm.	5·45	3·34	6·77
B. mm.	2·63	1·33	2·93
T. mm.	2·35	1·33	2·93
T:B index per cent.	89	71	118

At the end of the third millennium Emmer seems to have been the most important wheat everywhere, except perhaps Asia Minor, where Eincorn also was much grown,[19] and in Switzerland, where Club wheat was quite common.[20] Club or Bread wheat did occur in most places, but obviously not as the staple wheat species. Eincorn is usually found in varying quantities admixed with Emmer in prehistoric deposits, except in Egypt.[21]

Neither Eincorn nor Emmer is grown in Palestine today.

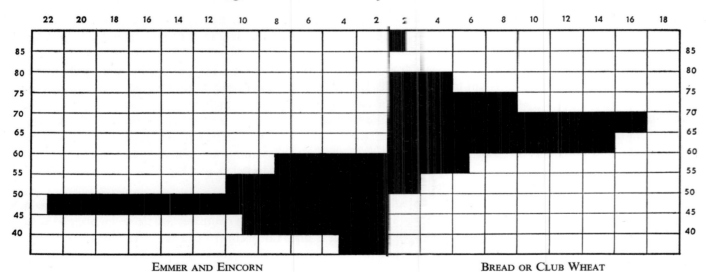

EMMER AND EINCORN   BREAD OR CLUB WHEAT

Horizontal figures: number of grains; vertical figures: B:L indices, per cent.

DIAGRAM: The difference between Lachish wheat grains expressed by their breadth–length indices

14. Club or Bread Wheat: *Triticum compactum* Host., or *T. vulgare* Vill.

While in the Bronze Age deposits there was no trace of this cereal, the Iron Age sample B was almost exclusively composed of wheat (Pl. 15: d, three lower rows). Less than 1 per cent. of Emmer was found, and only one grain of Eincorn.

As opposed to the pointed and slender grains in Emmer and Eincorn, the kernels of Club and Bread wheat are squat and rounded. They are shorter but broader than Emmer, as it appears from the above diagram, expressing the relation of width to length in these two species. The average B:L index of Emmer in our material is just under 50, whereas the Club or Bread wheat reaches an average of almost 70.

The expression "Club or Bread" wheat is used because these two varieties of the hexaploid Naked wheat have grains of principally the same shape, and when dealing with ancient material we have usually no standard by which to segregate them. That is because the only means of exact discrimination are the internodes and pales, and these cereals being easily threshable without drying, these details are rarely preserved in the carbonised deposits.

Dimensions of 50 Club or Bread Wheat Grains

	av.	min.	max.
L. mm.	4·76	3·66	5·86
B. mm.	3·18	2·56	3·66
T. mm.	2·56	2·20	3·29
B:L index per cent.	67	52	86
T:B index per cent.	82	68	100

The present concept of the emergence of these varieties is rather confused. A short-grained wheat appears quite early in Near Eastern finds, but we know of no actual deposit or profuse occurrence. Not until the Iron Age does it seem to have gained importance. In Europe, on the other hand, a very definite type of Club wheat, differing from all recent types, has been found repeatedly in Pile Dwellings in Italy and Switzerland, dated to the Neolithic and Bronze Ages.[22] Even whole spikes with internodes and pales easily definable were found there. Already in the earliest Danish agricultural communities a short-grained wheat was grown, and in one case it has been possible to identify a piece of a rachis with dimensions unmistakably conforming with Club or Bread wheat.[23] It seems, however, as if these species were of more sporadic occurrence in the Emmer–Eincorn fields of northern Europe until, in the Early Iron Age, the old crops were replaced by new species,[24] exactly as it seems to have happened in Lachish.

15. Darnel: *Lolium temulentum* L.

Except for Specimen No. 3, all grain samples contained the fruits of Darnel. In the Iron Age wheat they were fairly numerous, viz. 22 grains. These fruits are squat and strong with the robust ventral pale frequently preserved, or represented by remains of sturdy veins (Pl. 15: h).

Dimensions of 12 Darnel Grains

	av.	min.	max.
L. mm.	3·92	3·48	4·58
B. mm.	1·94	1·65	2·20
T. mm.	1·33	1·10	1·83

The Darnel (or Poisonous Ryegrass) occurs in abundance with ancient Egyptian grain,[25] it has been found in prehistoric grain deposits from Italy and Hungary,[26] and it is of common occurrence in Near Eastern finds.

The grass is a very common weed in cornfields all over the Mediterranean and Near Eastern region, and it may be found, though more sporadically, in north and western Europe. Its poisonous properties are derived from a fungus, normally attached to the inside of the seed coat.[27]

16. Hulled barley: *Hordeum sp.*

Barley was present in the Bronze Age grain samples, but not in the Iron Age specimen. Most of the grains are more or less defective, the radicle point lacking in all but a few, and the surface usually being wholly or partly worn off. Only eleven specimens, with the radicle point preserved, could be measured (Pl. 15: g).

APPENDIX A

Dimensions of Eleven Barley Grains

	av.	min.	max.
L. mm.	6·33	5·67	7·50
B. mm.	2·75	2·01	3·29
T. mm.	2·09	1·65	2·38

Compared with other Mediterranean prehistoric barley these grains are rather large, and the maximum size is rarely surpassed elsewhere. All specimens not completely ruined show evidence of pales, either by actual remains, or by the faint longitudinal ridges and grooves, and an angular cross-section, which is caused by the pressure of the pales on the maturing fruit. In no case is there the slightest indication of the naked variety. That is, however, all that can be concluded from the material.

Thus it was not possible to establish the spike type, whether two- or six-rowed. For the identification of this detail the preservation of the internodes or pale bases is necessary, and even then it may be difficult to prove the two-rowed type with certainty if no lateral florets are preserved. Very often a certain twist in the grain is visible in carbonised material, indicating the six-rowed spike, but not even that can be pointed out with certainty. Since in Neolithic Iraq and Syria the two-rowed barley was common,[28] this species might well be expected in Lachish, but, on the other hand, there is no doubt that six-rowed barleys were distributed all over the Orient at that time.

The absence of barley from the Iron Age sample is fortuitous. It is improbable that the cereal was not grown then at Lachish, since it is commonly found in contemporary deposits from all over the Near East.

Conclusion

The picture of the plant economy as seen in our plant list shows amazingly little change in tastes and agricultural practice at Lachish. Time and again, Palestine was overrun by foreign peoples in the course of many centuries; but always the land gave, it never received. The ecological circumstances of the country governed the choice of crops and vegetable food. A new species of wheat was introduced, but that does not seem to have given rise to new culinary inventions. The additions to the farinaceous food were still the same, grapes, Olive, and leguminous seeds, in the remote past as they are today. So frugal a diet seemed rich to the invading nomads, and in their eyes Palestine was a land of plenty.

REFERENCES

1. The carbonised material from Hama was examined by the writer, but is not yet published.
2. For distribution, etc., of plants, cf. the following handbooks:
   L. H. BAILEY (1949), *Manual of Cultivated Plants*. New York.
   GUSTAV HEGI (1931), *Illustrierte Flora von Mitteleuropa*. Munich.
   EVAN GUEST (1933), *Notes on Plants and Plant Products with their Colloquial Names in Iraq*. Baghdad.
   GEORGE E. POST (1932), *Flora of Syria, Palestine and Sinai*. II Ed. Beirut.
   VIVI LAURENT TÄCKHOLM and M. DRAR, *Flora of Egypt*, Vol. I 1941, Vol. II 1950. Cairo.
   M. ZOHARY (1950), *Flora of Iraq and its Phytogeographical Subdivision*. Baghdad.
3. Only the Iron Age imprints are published; cf. Hans Helbaek (1948), "Les empreintes de céréales", Appendix II in P. J. Riis (1948), "Hama". *Fouilles et recherches de la Fondation Carlsberg II*, 3. Copenhagen.
4. E. SCHIEMANN (1953), "Vitis im Neolithicum der Mark Brandenburg". *Der Züchter* 23. Berlin.
5. M. ZOHARY (1952), "A Monographical Study of the Genus Pistacia." *Palestine Journal of Botany*. Jerusalem.
   The present writer wishes to acknowledge his gratitude to Prof. M. Zohary, for kind co-operation, and for supplying him with samples of the fruits of Palestinian species of Pistacia.
6. E. NEUWEILER (1935), "Nachträge Vorgeschichtlicher Pflanzen I", p. 22. *Viert.-jahrschr. Naturforsch. Ges. Zürich*.
7. E. NEUWEILER (1946), "Nachträge Vorgeschichtlicher Pflanzen II", p. 136. ibid.
8. EVAN GUEST (1933), op. cit., p. 101.
9. Ibid., p. 22.

10. E. NEUWEILER (1905), "Die prähistorischen Pflanzenreste Mitteleuropas", p. 104. *Botanische Exkursionen etc.*, Zürich.
GEORG BUSCHAN (1895), *Vorgeschichtliche Botanik*, p. 109. Breslau.

11. G. BRUNTON (1948), *Matmar*. Brit. Exp. to Middle Egypt, 1929–1931. London.
J.-P. LAUER, V. LAURENT TÄCKHOLM et E. ÅBERG (1950), "Les Plantes découvertes dans les souterrains de l'enceinte du Roi Zoser à Saqqarah (IIIe dynastie)". *Bulletin de l'Institut d'Égypte*, T. XXXII. Cairo. (Identification of non-cereal seeds by Vivi Täckholm.)

12. E. NEUWEILER (1905), op. cit., p. 88; 1946, p. 130.
G. BUSCHAN (1895), op. cit., p. 203.

13. Loc. cit., p. 208.

14. E. NEUWEILER (1905), op. cit., p. 88.

15. EVAN GUEST (1933), op. cit., p. 26.

16. GEORG BUSCHAN (1895), op. cit., p. 134.

17. HANS HELBAEK (1952), "Spelt, Triticum spelta, in Bronze Age Denmark". *Acta Archaeologica*. Copenhagen.

18. E. SCHIEMANN (1940), "Die Getreidefunde der neolithischen Siedlung Trebus, Kr. Lebus/Mark". *Ber. Deut. Bot. Ges.* Berlin.

19. E. SCHIEMANN (1951), "Emmer in Troja". *Ber. Deut. Bot. Ges.*, pp. 155–169. Berlin.

20. OSWALD HEER (1865), "Die Pflanzen der Pfahlbauten". *Mitt. Antiq. Ges.* Zürich.

21. HANS HELBAEK (1953), "Queen Ichetis' Wheat". *Dan. Biol. Medd.* 21, 8. Copenhagen.
HANS HELBAEK (1956), "Ancient Egyptian Wheat". *Proc. Preh. Soc.* (Childe *Festschrift*) Cambridge.

22. OSWALD HEER (1865), op. cit.
E. NEUWEILER (1935), op. cit., p. 104.
E. NEUWEILER (1946), op. cit., p. 126.

23. HANS HELBAEK (1954), "Store Valby, Introduction of Cereal Husbandry in Denmark". *Aarbøger for nordisk Oldkyndighed* 1954, pp. 202 ff.

24. KNUD JESSEN and HANS HELBAEK (1944), "Cereals in Great Britain and Ireland in Prehistoric and Early Historic Times". *Kgl. Dan. Vid. Selsk. Biol. Skrift. III, 2.* Copenhagen.
HANS HELBAEK (1952), "Early Crops in Southern England". *Proc. Preh. Soc.* Cambridge.

25. VIVI LAURENT TÄCKHOLM (1950), op. cit., p. 145.
G. SCHWEINFURTH (1908), "Über die Pflanzenreste aus den Gräbern des Mittleren Reiches zu Abusir", in H. Schäfer (1908), *Priestergräber von Totentempel des Ne-user-re.* Leipzig.

26. HANS HELBAEK (1956), "Vegetables in the Funeral Meals of Pre-Urban Rome", in: EINAR GJERSTAD, *Early Rome*, II, 1956, pp. 287 ff. (*Skrifter utgivna av Svenska Institutet i Rom*, 4°, XVII, 2). Lund.

27. G. LINDAU (1904), "Über das Vorkommen des Pilzes des Taumellolchs in altägyptischen Samen". *Sitzber. Königl. Preuß. Akad. d. Wiss.* 92.

28. HANS HELBAEK (1953), "Archaeology and Agricultural Botany". *Ann. Rep. Inst. Arch. London Univ.*

317

APPENDIX B

THE HUMAN AND ANIMAL REMAINS

THE CRANIA

By MADELEINE GILES. M.A., F.R.A.I.

(From the Duckworth Laboratory, University Museum of Archaeology and Ethnology, Cambridge)

Introduction

THE series of Bronze Age crania and mandibles under discussion comprises twenty-seven individuals, from Caves 6009 and 6013 (of Early Bronze Age date, with five individuals represented), 6027 and 6028 (of Middle Bronze Age date with fourteen individuals represented), and 508, 501 and 4011 (of Late Bronze Age date, with eight individuals represented). The object of the present analysis is to ascertain whether, from a study of this series, it can be inferred that any change of physical type took place in the population of Lachish between the Bronze and the Iron Ages. With such a purpose in view, it is proposed to compare the Bronze Age series with the very large Iron Age series previously discussed by Commander D. L. Risdon (1939).

The age distribution of the Bronze Age series was estimated by reference to the closure of the basal suture and the three principal calvarial sutures (the coronal, sagittal and lambdoid). There is a surprisingly high proportion of immature persons (eleven individuals, or 40·8 per cent. of the total). Four of these have the palate missing, so cannot be aged approximately on the basis of dentition; from their size it might be judged that they were adolescent. Of the remaining seven juveniles, two are females aged between twelve and fifteen, and one is an adolescent male approaching maturity. The four sub-adolescent crania seem to have belonged to persons between six and nine years of age. Anatomical sexing of the adults indicates the presence of seven males and nine females. Mandibles are associated with the crania of three males (Nos. 805, 806 and 815), two females (Nos. 825 and 833) and one juvenile (No. 840). The average age of the male specimens seems to lie between thirty and forty, and that of the female between twenty and thirty. The high proportion of juveniles and the low average age of the adults would suggest that no valid comparison can be made between this series and a normal graveyard population. It is not possible, however, to reach any definite conclusion regarding the cause of death, since none of the skulls shows signs of disease or of injury received before death.

Anomalies

Although, as has just been stated, no pathological conditions were observed, one of the male skulls (No. 809) is of unusual size, but quite normally proportioned, with well-marked sexual characteristics. A female skull (No. 832) has a complete metopic or persistent frontal suture, accompanied by a bulging of the bone in the supraglabellar region, at the bregma, and in the planum occipitale. It was not considered necessary to exclude this specimen from the calculation of the means. Remnants of a metopic suture occur in Nos. 825 and 826 (both female). Ossicles of lambda, associated with Wormian bones in the lambdoid suture, are present in three of the female skulls (Nos. 824, 830 and 835). One of the male skulls (No. 806) has an epipteric bone on both sides, and two of the female skulls (Nos. 826 and 831) have one on the left side. Several of the skulls are calcined (Nos. 810, 812 and 816, male, and No. 820, female). Eight of the adult specimens have carious teeth. No. 806 had lost three teeth, all on the right side, before death, and the right M^2 and the left M^1 are badly decayed. Nos. 811 and 816 (both male) and Nos. 821, 824, 830, 831 and 833 (all female) also exhibit advanced carious conditions of the teeth or have teeth missing *ante mortem*.

318

TABLE I

Constants of Bronze Age (Giles) and Iron Age (Risdon) Crania from Lachish*

	Males			Females		
	Bronze Age	Iron Age		Bronze Age	Iron Age	
Character	$\bar{x}$	μ	σ	$\bar{x}$	μ	σ
Glabello-occipital length (L) . .	182·8 (6)	184·5 (322)	5·88	177·9 (9)	176·8 (259)	5·09
Maximum biparietal breadth (B) . .	137·6 (7)	136·8 (327)	5·10	134·1 (9)	133·3 (261)	4·55
Minimum frontal breadth (B') . .	94·9 (5)	95·5 (319)	4·26	93·7 (9)	92·2 (245)	4·37
Basi-bregmatic height (H') . . .	137·9 (6)	133·8 (268)	5·00	130·6 (7)	128·4 (213)	5·05
Auriculo-apical height (OH) . .	114·9 (4)	115·1 (108)	3·69	109·8 (8)	109·4 (89)	4·22
Frontal chord (S_1')	112·9 (5)	112·9 (299)	4·51	107·9 (9)	108·7 (248)	4·11
Parietal chord (S_2') . . .	114·9 (7)	116·0 (323)	5·88	112·4 (9)	112·1 (251)	5·48
Occipital chord (S_3') . . .	96·7 (5)	96·3 (280)	4·73	96·2 (5)	94·0 (216)	4·52
Frontal arc (S_1)	126·6 (5)	129·2 (296)	6·01	123·8 (9)	124·7 (248)	5·75
Parietal arc (S_2)	128·6 (7)	129·9 (321)	7·25	126·0 (9)	124·9 (249)	7·16
Occipital arc (S_3) . . .	117·6 (5)	116·9 (279)	6·98	113·2 (5)	113·3 (215)	6·68
Total sagittal arc (S) . . .	372·7 (5)	375·5 (255)	12·73	363·3 (5)	363·0 (212)	11·48
Transverse bregmatic arc (T') . .	313·3 (6)	308·6 (306)	9·60	300·6 (9)	297·8 (234)	9·31
Maximum horizontal perimeter (U) .	511·5 (6)	518·1 (304)	13·51	500·6 (9)	500·4 (214)	12·48
Foraminal length (FL) . . .	37·8 (4)	37·0 (247)	2·52	36·3 (5)	35·8 (193)	2·14
Foraminal breadth (FB) . . .	31·0 (3)	30·4 (244)	2·16	29·3 (7)	28·9 (192)	1·99
Basi-nasal length (LB) . . .	102·7 (5)	100·7 (243)	3·82	99·1 (7)	96·4 (206)	4·24
Basi-alveolar length (GL) . .	94·3 (5)	94·3 (89)	4·71	92·2 (7)	90·6 (76)	4·65
Upper facial height ($G'H$) . .	70·3 (5)	70·1 (98)	4·36	67·8 (8)	66·9 (87)	3·94
Bimaxillary breadth (GB) . .	97·9 (4)	94·4 (107)	4·81	93·2 (6)	91·8 (81)	4·04
Bizygomatic breadth (J) . . .	136·9 (3)	128·4 (49)	4·97	124·2 (5)	121·3 (40)	4·28
Nasal height (NH)	51·6 (5)	51·4 (136)	2·64	49·9 (8)	48·9 (116)	2·70
Nasal breadth (NB)	24·6 (4)	25·2 (123)	1·74	24·0 (4)	24·5 (88)	1·73
Orbital breadth (O_1) . . .	41·2 (4)	41·5 (148)	1·64	40·9 (8)	40·6 (111)	1·65
Orbital height (O_2) . . .	32·3 (5)	32·9 (152)	2·05	32·7 (8)	33·2 (112)	2·01
Palatal length (G_1') . . .	44·5 (4)	46·7 (100)	2·79	45·5 (6)	44·8 (90)	3·00
Palatal breadth (G_2) . . .	42·9 (3)	40·3 (57)	2·29	38·3 (4)	39·2 (68)	2·28
100 B/L	75·6 (6)	74·3 (310)	3·08	75·2 (9)	75·5 (252)	2·99
100 H'/L	75·5 (6)	72·7 (257)	2·93	73·5 (7)	72·7 (209)	2·92
100 B/H'	100·1 (6)	102·4 (256)	4·72	101·8 (7)	103·8 (206)	5·11
100 $(B-H')/L$	0·1 (6)	1·7 (246)	3·25	1·3 (7)	2·8 (202)	3·52
Oc. I.	58·9 (6)	59·5 (278)	2·59	62·2 (6)	60·0 (215)	2·48
100 FB/FL	80·3 (3)	82·7 (222)	5·82	81·5 (5)	81·4 (167)	5·31
100 $G'H/GB$	72·7 (4)	74·6 (63)	4·64	72·3 (6)	72·9 (59)	5·14
100 NB/NH	48·7 (4)	49·4 (114)	4·00	48·7 (4)	50·2 (84)	3·81
100 O_2/O_1	78·2 (4)	79·4 (141)	4·96	80·2 (8)	82·0 (100)	4·50
100 G_2/G_1'	92·8 (2)	85·9 (44)	4·95	84·5 (3)	86·9 (55)	5·73
$N\angle$	63·3° (5)	64·0° (89)	3·43°	63·9° (7)	64·5° (75)	3·79°
$A\angle$	75·6° (5)	73·9° (89)	2·83°	74·9° (7)	73·7° (75)	3·50°
$B\angle$	41·7° (5)	42·0° (89)	2·77°	41·3° (7)	41·8° (75)	2·90°

* The sample size is given in parentheses after each mean. Only one male Bronze Age skull was sufficiently intact for its capacity (C) to be determined. This is 1316 c.c. The mean capacity of seven female skulls is 1270·4 c.c. The values of NH, O_1, O_2,, and the indices of which they are components are for characters measured on the *left* side. With the exception of the occipital index (*Oc. I.*), viz. 100 $S_3/S_3'\sqrt{\{S_3/24(S_3-S_3')\}}$, the indices need no explanation. The angles $N\angle$, $A\angle$ and $B\angle$ are subtended by the sides GL, LB and $G'H$, respectively, of the upper facial triangle.

Metrical Characters

The measurements of the crania and mandibles were in greater part taken by Dr. I. G. Cunnison, the writer being responsible for the rest. The biometric technique is adopted throughout, apart from cranial capacity (*C*), to determine which Breitinger's method has been used (Breitinger, 1936; Tildesley and Datta-Majumder, 1944). Definitions follow those of the writer's discussion of the Iron Age skulls from Lachish (Giles, 1953).* The means of the Bronze Age series are given, together with the means and standard deviations of Risdon's Iron Age series, in Table I. As the number of mandibles is very small, no means have been found for them. The individual measurements follow those of the crania in Table III.

Discussion

The very small size of the Lachish Bronze Age samples imposes considerable restriction on the use of statistical procedures in comparing their means with those of the much larger Iron Age series studied by Risdon. Fifteen

TABLE II

Differences between Means of Bronze Age (Giles) and Iron Age (Risdon) Crania from Lachish*

Character	Male			Female			Character	Male			Female			Character	Male			Female		
	d	e_d	d/e_d	d	e_d	d/e_d		d	e_d	d/e_d	d	e_d	d/e_d		d	e_d	d/e_d	d	e_d	d/e_d
L	1·7	2·40	0·7	1·1	1·70	0·6	U	6·6	5·52	1·2	0·2	4·16	0·0	100 B/L	1·3	1·26	1·0	0·3	1·00	0·3
B	0·8	1·93	0·4	0·8	1·52	0·5	LB	2·0	1·71	1·2	2·7	1·60	1·7	100 H'/L	2·8	1·20	*2·3*	0·8	1·10	0·7
B'	0·6	1·91	0·3	1·5	1·46	1·0	G'H	0·2	1·95	0·1	0·9	1·39	0·6	100 B/H'	2·3	1·93	1·2	2·0	1·93	1·0
H'	4·1	2·04	*2·0*	2·2	1·91	1·2	NH	0·2	1·18	0·2	1·0	0·95	1·1	100 (B−H')/L	1·6	1·33	1·2	1·5	1·33	1·1
T'	4·7	3·92	1·2	2·8	3·10	0·9	O₂	0·6	0·92	0·7	0·5	0·71	0·7	Oc.I.	0·6	1·06	0·6	2·2	1·01	*2·2*

*Differences which are statistically significant are shown in *italics*.

characters were selected from the total of forty in Table I, comparison being restricted to the means based on at least five observations for each sex. The method used is the same as that adopted in the writer's treatment of the slightly larger Iron Age series from Lachish. It has again been assumed that the values of the means and standard deviations of Risdon's male and female samples are equivalent to the parameters of the Lachish Iron Age population instead of being estimates of them.

If *n* is the number of observations on which the mean value of any cranial character $\bar{x}$ for one sex in the Lachish Bronze Age series is based, μ and σ are the respective values of the mean and standard deviation of the same character in the corresponding Lachish Iron Age population, and *d* is the difference between $\bar{x}$ and μ irrespective of sign, then $\sigma\sqrt{(1/n)}$ is the standard error e_d of that difference *d*, and d/e_d is the value of *d* in terms of its standard error, or the so-called "critical ratio".

Table II gives for male and female crania, in the first place, the difference between the two means (either $\bar{x}-\mu$, or $\mu-\bar{x}$); secondly, the standard error of the difference e_d; and thirdly the difference divided by the standard error d/e_d, i.e. the critical ratio. The value of d/e_d is taken to be statistically significant if it is 2·0 or more, at the 5 per cent. probability level. At this level it may be expected that one result in twenty will differ significantly from zero. It will be seen that, in the case of the males, of the fifteen characters compared, the differences between two (*H'* and 100 *H'/L*) are significant, but it should be noted that *H'* or the basi-bregmatic height is a component of the index 100 *H'/L*. In the case of the females, only one value for d/e_d is significant (*Oc. I*). This result, together with the close association of the characters showing significant differences for the male skulls, would suggest that, on the available evidence, the Bronze Age series cannot be said to differ appreciably from the Iron Age population of Lachish. It is not possible, however, to make any definite statement on the basis of data drawn

* Two errors appear s.v. "Mandible" in the definitions, however, and should be amended to read as follows: "*RB*, minimum radial breadth (in any direction, left)" and "*C_rH*, projective height of coronoid process (left)". The headings of the eleventh and fourteenth columns at the foot of Table III should read "*C_pL*" and "*C_rH*", respectively.

TABLE III

Individual Measurements of Adult Bronze Age Skulls from Lachish

No.	Sex	C	L	B	B'	H'	OH	S₁'	S₂'	S₃'	S₁	S₂	S₃	S	T'	U
805	♂	1316	183·5	139·5	97	140·5	112	110·5	107	97	126·5	118·5	121	366	307	514
806	,,	—	175	134	89·5	134	116	106·5	119	—	118·5	133·5	—	—	305	495
809	,,	—	201·5	145·5	97	147·5	—	128·5	116	104	143	128	128·5	400	335	550
810	,,	—	182	140·5	—	133	—	—	117	101·5	—	132·5	124·5	—	—	509
811	,,	—	—	135	—	—	—	—	118·5	91	133	108	—	318	—	
812	,,	—	176	139	96	140	117·5	114	112·5	—	128·5	125·5	—	318	506	
816	,,	—	178·5	130	95	132·5	114	105	115	90	116·5	129	106	352	301	495
821	♀	1117	175	134	89	128·5	111	108·5	110	100	121·5	124	118·5	363	295	486
824	,,	—	168·5	131	90	126	108	103·5	102	—	118·5	114·5	—	—	292	477
825	,,	1269	173	141	97	—	112	110	108·5	—	128·5	121·5	—	—	307	502
826	,,	1277	179	136	95·5	131	112·5	105·5	115	92	120·5	129	106·5	356	304	501
830	,,	1273	176·5	131·5	92·5	130	111	106·5	110	92·5	120·5	125·5	109	355	292	495
831	,,	1309	174·5	132	92·5	133·5	103·5	110·5	109·5	97	127	126	111·5	365	296	494
832	,,	1438	183	140	100·5	134	112	107·5	120	99·5	125·5	131	120·5	378	317	517
833	,,	1210	187·5	125	94	131	108·5	112	112	—	128	124·5	—	—	296	505
835	,,	—	184	137	91·5	—	—	107	124·5	—	124·5	138·5	—	—	307	518

No.	Sex	FL	FB	LB	GL	G'H	GB	J	NH	NB	O₁	O₂	G₁'	G₂
805	♂	34·9	30·7	110	99	74·5	100	135	55·2	—	42·1	33·1	46·2	42·4
806	,,	—	—	94	91	63·5	95·5	130·5	46·8	23·4	37·0	30·0	41·9	39·3
809	,,	40·9	31·4	111·5	105	77	105·5	145	52·9	27·8	43·7	33·9	—	47·0
810	,,	34·9	—	—	—	—	—	—	—	—	—	—	—	—
811	,,	—	—	—	—	—	—	—	—	—	—	—	—	—
812	,,	—	—	94·5	81·5	66·5	—	—	52·2	24·5	—	32·8	44·0	—
816	,,	40·7	31·0	103·5	95	70	91	—	51·0	23·1	41·9	31·6	45·7	—
821	♀	34·0	27·7	94·5	90	65	95	—	47·4	24·2	38·3	29·9	—	36·9
824	,,	—	28·5	96	90	63	92	—	48·2	—	39·6	30·9	43·9	35·0
825	,,	—	—	—	—	68	89·5	124	47·9	23·0	40·1	34·9	45·3	—
826	,,	34·9	28·3	103·5	97	69	95·5	127	51·0	24·3	42·1	32·7	48·0	41·2
830	,,	38·8	27·9	100	91·5	67	—	—	46·9	—	42·6	33·0	—	—
831	,,	37·0	32·5	100	89·5	72	—	122·5	51·4	24·6	40·1	33·0	45·5	40·0
832	,,	36·9	31·4	95	82	64·5	86	120·5	53·9	—	40·7	34·3	40·7	—
833	,,	—	29·2	105	105·5	74	101	127	52·0	—	43·8	33·6	49·6	—
835	,,	—	—	—	—	—	—	—	—	—	—	—	—	—

No.	Sex	100 B/L	100 H'/L	100 B/H'	100 (B−H')/L	Oc.I.	100 FB/FL	100 G'H/GB	100 NB/NH	100 O₂/O₁	100 G₂/G₁'	N∠	A∠	B∠
805	♂	76·0	76·6	99·3	−0·5	57·2	87·9	74·5	—	78·6	91·8	62°	77·5°	41·5°
806	,,	76·6	76·6	100	0·0	—	—	66·5	50	81·1	93·8	68°	72°	40°
809	,,	72·2	73·2	98·6	−0·9	57·7	76·8	73·0	52·5	77·6	—	65°	73·5°	42·5°
810	,,	77·2	73·1	105·3	4·1	58·2	—	—	—	—	—	—	—	—
811	,,	—	—	—	—	61·0	—	—	—	—	—	—	—	—
812	,,	79·0	79·5	99·3	−0·6	—	—	—	46·9	—	—	58°	79°	43·5°
816	,,	72·8	74·2	98·1	−1·4	61·9	76·2	76·9	45·3	75·4	—	63·5°	76°	41°
821	♀	76·6	73·4	104·3	3·1	—	81·5	68·4	51·1	78·1	—	66°	73°	41°
824	,,	77·7	74·8	103·9	2·9	61·9	—	68·5	—	78·0	79·7	65·5°	75°	39·5°
825	,,	81·5	—	—	—	61·2	—	76·0	48·0	87·0	—	—	—	—
826	,,	76·0	73·2	103·8	2·8	—	81·1	72·3	47·6	77·7	85·8	65°	75°	40°
830	,,	74·5	73·7	101·2	0·8	—	71·9	—	—	77·5	—	63°	76·5°	41°
831	,,	75·6	76·5	98·9	0·9	63·9	87·8	—	47·9	82·3	87·9	60°	75·5°	44·5°
832	,,	76·5	73·2	104·5	3·3	61·9	85·1	75·0	—	84·3	—	58·5°	80°	42°
833	,,	66·7	69·9	95·4	3·2	65·1	—	73·3	—	76·7	—	70°	69°	41°
835	,,	74·5	—	—	—	59·2	—	—	—	—	—	—	—	—

TABLE III (cont.)

No.	Sex	G_0G_0	C_rC_r	W_1	C_yL	RB'	M_2P_1	ZZ	H_1	C_pL	RL	ML	C_rH	M_2H	$M\angle$	$R\angle$
805	♂	—	—	—	—	36·6 (R)	28·0 (R)	—	—	—	63·4 (R)	—	70·5 (R)	29·0 (R)	118·0° (R)	74·5° (R)
806	,,	—	—	—	19·9 (R)	31·9 (R)	25·7 (R)	46·0	33·6	67·0	54·5 (R)	—	60·4 (R)	25·5 (R)	130·5°	—
816	,,	86·3	90·4	114·4	—	32·9	29·0 (R)	41·2	31·3	74·4	70·7	101·1	73·6	28·1 (R)	111·0°	78·5°
825	♀	—	—	104·2	18·8	31·4	28·8	45·8	34·0	73·2	62·6	105·5	63·6	28·7	126·0°	67·0°
833	,,	80·5	—	120·5	20·3	36·1	—	44·0	36·0	78·2	52·6	110·3	57·2 (R)	—	133·0°	66·5° (R)

from such small samples, and with more extensive data the view expressed above might well be either substantiated or modified. It may only be suggested that the material under discussion does not provide sufficient reason for stating that the population of Lachish changed in any major respect between the Bronze and Iron Ages.

Acknowledgements

The writer is indebted to the authorities of the British Museum (Natural History) for permission to bring the Lachish Bronze Age series on loan from London to Cambridge, to Dr. J. C. Trevor, Director of the Duckworth Laboratory of Physical Anthropology, Cambridge, for entrusting the material to her for study, and to the Trustees of the Estate of the late Sir Henry Wellcome, F.R.S , for their financial support of the research.

REFERENCES

BREITINGER, EMIL (1936). "Zur Messung der Schädelkapazität mit Senfkörnen." *Anthrop. Anz.* XIII.

GILES, MADELEINE (1953). "The Crania" in *Lachish III*: *The Iron Age* (Oxford, 1953).

RISDON, D. L. (1939). "A study of the cranial and other human remains from Palestine excavated at Tell Duweir (Lachish) by the Wellcome-Marston Archaeological Research Expedition." *Biometrika* XXXI.

TILDESLEY, M. L., and DATTA-MAJUMDER, N. (1944). "Cranial capacity; comparative data on the techniques of Macdonell and Breitinger. *Amer. J. Phys. Anthrop.*, N.S., II.

ANIMAL BONES

By DOROTHEA M. A. BATE

About half the specimens from Pit 4022 (Pl. 7: 1 and Fig. 15) are fragmentary, but it seems evident that no species are present other than those which have been identified and it is thought that the bulk of the fragments represent a small equine. Only three species have been recognised, and they seem undoubtedly to represent domesticated races:

Canis sp.   Domestic Dog
Sheep or Goat
Equus sp.   Domestic Donkey

Canis sp.: Domestic Dog (Pl. 7: 2)

Over fifty specimens represent a domestic dog, and these are of great interest, since they include an almost complete associated skull and skeleton preserved in the matrix, two nearly perfect skulls, portions of two others, and eight mandibular rami, several with the full dentition present. There are, besides, two rami of small puppies, and also a number of limb bones. Although there is some variation in the size of the dog skulls, this is not sufficient to suggest the presence of more than one race, particularly since they are all of a single type. A similar type of skull is seen in a few specimens from the Iron Age (cf. L. III, p. 410).

The Early Bronze Age dog skulls are small, with rather short muzzles and with the supra-orbital air sinuses considerably developed. The three complete skulls have the following total lengths: 16 cms. (with skeleton), 18 cms. and 19·5 cms. This shows that only the largest was equal in size to that of a small wolf. A few measurements of the total lengths of the bones of the fore limb which forms part of the skeleton are compared below with those of a recent Afghan greyhound and a Slughi:

	Tell Duweir dog	Afghan Greyhound	Slughi
Total lengths in a straight line:	cms.	cms.	cms.
Scapula	12	14	16
Humerus	15	18	18
Ulna	18	21·5	21
Metacarpus	6	—	—

The above measurements show clearly that the Tell Duweir dog was not specialised for coursing like the modern Afghan greyhound or the Slughi, and this is borne out by the shape of the skulls. For instance, a recent Slughi skull has a length of 19 cms., but it is very much narrower than the Early Bronze Age skulls and has a compressed muzzle, with the teeth, especially the pre-molars, small and weak. Mr. Starkey was very probably correct in referring to the Tell Duweir skeleton as being of "seluki" type (PEQ, October 1937, p. 8), but it was very far from having attained the highly specialised character of the modern breed. These Early Bronze Age dogs may have been used for chasing hares and other small game, but were probably kept primarily as watchdogs.

The Tell Duweir skulls are very different from that of the Natufian domestic dog from Mugharet el-Wad (*The Stone Age of Mount Carmel*, I, p. 176), being smaller, with weaker dentition and a shorter and narrower muzzle; also the frontal air sinuses are noticeably more developed in the Early Bronze Age specimens than in the older skull.

Sheep or Goat

A sheep or goat is represented by a single cheek tooth and by two metapodials.

Equus, cf. *asinus*: Domestic Donkey

The greater number of the bones from the Early Bronze Age level are those of a small equine, believed to be the domestic donkey. Most of the bones are those of adult animals, though there is a small proportion of limb bones of young. A number of complete foot bones proved to be most helpful for comparison and identification, and these show considerable differences from the corresponding bones of the Kiang. While there is a closer resemblance to those of a wild ass (*A. africanus*), the very small terminal phalanges seem to make it certain that the remains are those of a domestic ass. This is not surprising, since donkeys were possessed by the Hebrews in Abraham's time, and in Egypt were known as early as the Gerzean period before the first Egyptian kings.

The total lengths of four complete metatarsals range from 22 cms. to 24 cms., while two complete metacarpals give a measurement of 18·5 cms.

SHELLS

By D. F. W. BADEN-POWELL

The shells have been compared with various collections and books in the University Museum, Oxford, and are identified as follows:

Cave 1557—EB I–II

A *Planaxis*, perhaps *Planaxis mollis*. This is a tropical shell and probably comes from the Red Sea.

Cave 1535—EB I–III

This broken shell is probably *Nassa circumcincta*, which has varieties living in both the Mediterranean and the Red Sea. Derivation might be from either direction.

Cave 1513—EB III–IV and later

One *Nerita*, probably *yoldii* (Red Sea).
One *Purpura* Sp. (no derivation definite).
A large number of shells with the tops rubbed away, probably *Ancilla ovalis*, derived from the Red Sea.

North-East Section—EB III–IV

NE 2   The shell fragments cannot be identified, except that they include a *Pectunculus* Sp.
NE 3   A snail shell, not identified. Two individuals of *Planaxis* cf. *mollis*, probably from the Red Sea.
NE 5   Five or six individuals of *Planaxis* Sp., probably from the Red Sea. Two individuals (? *Pupa* Sp.)
NE 6   Seven individuals of *Planaxis* Sp.
NE 8   One *Planaxis* Sp.
NE 10   One *Pectunculus* Sp., not definitely identifiable but might be a Mediterranean type.

Tomb 4004—MB III–LB III

One shell *Pectunculus* Sp.
One shell and several fragments of *Planaxis* Sp.
One shell of ? *Potamides* Sp.
One shell, probably *Pleurotama sacra*, showing the brown or orange bands. This may be from the Red Sea, but derivation is not definite by comparison with the material at my disposal.
One cowrie, probably *Cypraea annulus*. It could be from the Red Sea.
One *Conus* Sp. with top rubbed away. I cannot tell definitely whether it is from the Mediterranean or the Red Sea.
Four shells which are difficult to identify as their mouths appear to be rubbed, but they resemble a tropical shell, *Mitra oniscina*. This identification is by no means certain.

Tomb 216—LB II–III

Nerita yoldii (or possibly *Nerita polita*). One individual, very worn and bleached. Probably derived from the Red Sea area, and, as far as is known, not from the Mediterranean.

Tomb 4002—LB II–III

Two individuals of *Cypraea annulus*, one of which shows part of the characteristic yellow ring on its surface. These shells are almost certainly from the Red Sea.
There is also a circular object which is probably worn down from the operculum of a large shell. No derivation can be suggested in this case.

Tomb 4019—LB II

Shell of *Pectunculus* Sp., too water-worn for identification. No derivation can be suggested.

Conclusions

The shells from these samples include some species which prove derivation from the Red Sea area, but additional derivation from the Mediterranean has not been proved or disproved.

APPENDIX C

FLINT IMPLEMENTS

By JOHN WAECHTER, PH.D., F.S.A.

THE flint implements at Tell ed-Duweir are derived from three main sources: the mound, the caves in the North-West Settlement, and the surface of that area. By far the largest quantity comes from the surface (Area 1500). It is, of course, mixed, and ranges from the Middle Aurignacian through the intervening periods to gun flints of the eighteenth and nineteenth centuries. The greater proportion is, however, datable to the Early Bronze Age, and consists mostly of simple sickle blades of Cananean type (Pl. 19: 1) and tabular scrapers (Pl. 19: 2, 3 and 7). In view of the mixture of this material, no useful purpose can be gained by describing it in detail, and this report will concentrate on the material with pottery associations.

In describing the remaining material, it must be remembered that the flint implements of the Bronze Age cannot be fitted accurately into the existing pottery sub-divisions. This is partly due to the fact that our knowledge of the flint industries concerned is by no means exact, and also because these industries do not always follow the changing fashions of the pottery. For these two reasons we are only able to use the terms Early, Middle and Late Bronze Age rather loosely, and the possibility of the flint industries continuing from one period into another must not be overlooked.

Apart from the material from Area 1500 to which reference has already been made, the main group is that from the caves in the North-West Settlement; it is derived from various localities and is for the most part associated with datable pottery. Few of these caves have produced much flint material, and for this reason three groups have been taken as representing the three main stages of the Bronze Age, partly because each group is typical of the stage to which it belongs, and also because each contains a reasonable amount of material.

Early Bronze Age

By far the greater part of the collection represents this period. As we have already said, it is not possible to divide it into the threefold divisions which are in general use for the pottery. As is to be expected, the range of tool types in these later periods is becoming much more restricted, partly because the change to agriculture from hunting meant that fewer tool types were required, and partly because, as the Bronze Age advanced, metal was used in increasing quantities. As a result, most of our dating depends on only one or two tool types. The characteristic implements of the Early Bronze Age are the Cananean blades and the tabular scrapers. The former are simple blades which often reach a considerable length and all have the central ridge removed; this occurs occasionally in other industries, but here it is a very definite feature. The edges are generally not retouched, but nearly always show marked signs of use. When used as sickle blades the ends are snapped off, leaving the centre section, which is usually about 5 cms. long. Lustre is present on all the sickle blades, sometimes on both edges, indicating that the blade was reversed when blunt.

The second characteristic implement is the tabular scraper. These range in shape from the true fan scraper to those which are almost circular. They are not struck from a core in the ordinary sense, but were detached from a large block of tabular flint, the block often being left *in situ*. As these flakes are obtained by hitting the edge of the block just under the upper face, the original cortex of the block remains on the upper face of the resultant flake. The retouch is confined to the edges, in some cases not round the whole of the margin, and often the bulb of percussion is chipped away and the platform is prepared. The shape of these scrapers is largely governed by the technique, as the fracture lines tend to fan out from the point of impact, and as the block is much bigger than the flake being removed this also causes the hinge fracture which all these scrapers have on the end.

In addition to the normal Cananean blades, which are usually rather wide, there is a narrower series.

These are also generally longer, but as they have corn lustre on the edges they were obviously used as sickles as well (Pl. 19: 4, 5 and 6).

The best examples of this Early Bronze Age material come from Cave 1509. This group contains the typical Cananean blades and the narrow type, but there were no tabular scrapers; there are, however, several specimens from Cave 1523: Pits, and Cave 1538, associated in both cases with Cananean blades. Cave 1553 is classed, as far as the pottery is concerned, as Chalcolithic and Early Bronze Age; unfortunately, the flint industry is rather scappy: there are two fragments of tabular scrapers and part of a Cananean blade section, but there are no definite Chalcolithic elements. In Cave 6029 the bulk of the material is Early Bronze Age, with Cananean blade sections, but there is also a sickle blade of earlier type which has flat controlled flaking in from the edges but not extending over the whole of the upper face. This type is characteristic of the Chalcolithic levels of Jericho. Another group which shows differences is Group 4022, where in addition to blade flakes of normal Early Bronze Age type there is an end-scraper which is undoubtedly Natufian.

Early Bronze Age flints were found in the following groups: 1501, 1503, 1505, 1509, 1511, 1514, 1523, 1528, 1534, 1535, 1538, 1548, 1553, 1556, 1557, 1558, 4022, 4034, 6012, 6013, 6019, 6022, 6029, 6030 and 6031. In addition, eleven flakes came from Cave 1519 but have not been examined as they are in the Palestine Museum, Jerusalem (PM 34.2878–2888).

Caliciform Culture (Intermediate EB–MB)

This period shows a change in the sickle blades, though the tabular scrapers are still present. Whether these continue throughout the period is not clear, but it is unlikely, since they were absent in the Middle Bronze Age levels at Jericho.

Group 1551 has been chosen as an example of this stage. The sickle blades are thicker and not so neat as in the previous period, and they generally have blunting retouch on the back, either up the whole or part of it (Pl. 19: 8–15). The tabular scrapers are the same as before. Included in the material from Group 1551 are two end-scrapers and two burins. The burins are simple, single-blow type, made down the edge of a blade section; one of the end-scrapers is neatly made on the end of a blade and may possibly be earlier, the other is rather rough and not very typical.

The indications that there is a transition period between the Early and Middle Bronze Ages are supported by the material from Cemetery 2000. Some of the blades from the surface in this area are of the ordinary narrow type of the Early Bronze Age, but there are three blades of Cananean type, though with the ends squared, and another with retouch up the back. This last example might suggest some mixture, but the squared blades made on an earlier form might well indicate a change of technique on an earlier type.

Middle Bronze Age

No flints were found in the tomb groups of the Middle Bronze Age. The only flints which can be assigned to this period are from the relevant levels in the North-East Section (21–25 ft.) and these appear to be identical with the sickle blades of Group 1551.

Late Bronze Age

A good group of sickle blades representing this stage comes from Wall 6025, the Late Bronze Age retaining wall of the Wadi Ghafr. These blades are much squarer than those of the preceding periods, and the majority of them have retouch across the ends as well as along the back (Pl. 19: 16–22). Some, such as No. 9, are pointed and were used at the end of the sickle.

Flints belonging to this period also come from Groups 4006 (see L. III, pp. 241–242), 6008, 6014, 6025, L. 13: 1063 (see L. III, p. 118), and L. 15: 54 (see L. III, p. 153). In some localities there is evidence of more than one period being present: Cave 6031 is a case in point. The material has been described as coming from a late quarry cut into an Early Bronze Age dwelling, and the implements clearly show this double element, being partly

Cananean and partly Late Bronze Age blades. In addition to Late Bronze Age flints in Cave 4034, Pit B contained Early Bronze Age blades in Level 2, and part of an arrowhead of Chalcolithic or Neolithic type in the mud at the bottom of the pit, Level 3.

None of the material so far described has come from the mound. There is, however, a small collection from the North-East Section. These flints are very few in number, and most levels only produced one or two. In spite of their scarcity, these flints are interesting because they represent the whole range of the main cutting. As is to be expected, they show the same types as those from other localities. From 13 feet come two very typical Early Bronze Age blades of the narrow type; from 20 feet comes a short narrow blade, squared at one end, whose exact date is uncertain; from 21–25 feet the material is of Middle Bronze Age type, a blade from 21 feet being very typical, and from 32–36 feet the material is either Late Bronze Age or later.

There is also a small series from the West Section (L. III, pp. 71–76), which equates with the upper levels of the North-East Section and is similar in character to the flints from the Late Bronze Age levels, 32–36 feet.

Conclusion

The Early Bronze Age material is well authenticated from other sites, particularly from the Early Bronze Age levels of Jericho, where the association of Cananean blades and tabular scrapers is clear. This association also occurs at Père de Vaux's site at Tell el-Far'ah, near Nablus, in the level which he calls Énéolithique Supérieur (RB LIV) and equates with Beisan, Level XVI (M.J. XXIV). Another obvious site for comparison is Tell Fara, Site H (BP II). The material from the Early Bronze Age at Tell ed-Duweir and at Site H is very similar and has the tabular scraper and the narrow blades in common, but at Site H, the Cananean blade, though occurring spasmodically, is not very characteristic. In spite of these slight differences, which may well be due to different raw material, the material cannot be considered as fundamentally different, and it suggests that these two sites, as far as the flint industries are concerned, can be considered closely related. Whether the material from Site H is to be considered as Early Bronze Age or belonging to the period of the Caliciform Culture is for the pottery experts to decide. The attribution of the coarser blades to that stage has some support from Jericho, where similar blades post-date the Early Bronze Age material. As far as Tell ed-Duweir is concerned, it is not possible to be very precise, but there is little doubt that these coarse blades also post-date the Early Bronze Age material from Tell Fara, Site H (see p. 30).

For comparison with the Late Bronze Age, there is the well-known material from Petrie's site at Tell Jemmeh (*Gerar*, Pl. XVI; for revised dating, see AJA, 1939, p. 460). The implements from this site are identical with those from Tell ed-Duweir, but again it must be emphasised that the exact duration of these implements is not yet clear, and there are some indications that they may well have continued into the Iron Age.

The range of periods at Tell el-Far'ah, near Nablus, suggests that when the flint industries are fully published we shall have a much clearer picture, though whether the northern material will equate exactly with that of the south remains to be seen. There is a possibility that the Cananean blade occurs earlier in the north, as it does, of course, in Iraq.

APPENDIX D
METAL ANALYSES
I. ANALYSES BY THE NATIONAL PHYSICAL LABORATORY

Objects from Areas 2000 and 1500

Object	Plate No.	Locus	Copper	Lead	Iron	Arsenic	Nickel	Sulphur	Field No.	Period
Pike . .	21: 6	2009	95·1	—	0·5	trace	—	—	2303	
Javelin . .	21: 7	2032	96·0	—	0·7	trace	—	—	2349	CALICIFORM
Javelin . .	21: 9	2111	93·7	—	2·6	trace	—	—	2482	CULTURE
Dagger . .	21: 10	2111	96·8	—	1·2	trace	—	—	2481	
Rough Casting	21: 14	1500	94·26	2·32	2·28	—	0·07	—	2272	
Dagger . .	22·6	1556	98·5	—	1·2	—	—	faint trace	4067	EARLY BRONZE
Dagger .	22: 7	1513	96·9	—	0·5	trace	0·07	—	1831	AGE
Pin . .	pp. 75, 262	1523	99·8	—	—	faint trace	faint trace	faint trace	1965	

Notes

The analyses presented above were prepared under the auspices of the Sumerian Committee on Ancient Metals, by the Staff of the National Physical Laboratory working under the supervision of Dr. C. H. Desch, F.R.S.

It will be seen from the tabulation that the pin and the two daggers which are oldest in archaeological context (EB III–IV or earlier) contain the highest proportion of copper. When the analyses were made, Dr. Desch commented that even 99·8 per cent. for the pin was too low "as there was a little sandy matter included. Only very faint traces of nickel, arsenic and sulphur could be detected, less than that which we usually return as a trace."

The rough casting cannot be dated, for it was one of a group of cast implements without pottery from a surface area (p. 75), though the analysis itself would place it with the later rather than the earlier group, and it is the only specimen to contain lead.

The weapons from graves of the Caliciform Culture (p. 75) which intervenes between the Early and Middle Bronze Ages and may even overlap with them in part, show as pure copper with iron and trace of arsenic, though nickel and sulphur were absent, which did occur in the Early Bronze Age specimens.

II. METALLURGICAL REPORT ON A DAGGER OF THE CALICIFORM CULTURE COMPARED WITH MIDDLE AND LATE BRONZE AGE SPECIMENS

By PROFESSOR F. C. THOMPSON, D.MET., M.SC., F.I.M.

Spectrograms were obtained from each of the samples after the corrosion product had been removed, see Fig. A. From the Fig. it will be seen that the specimen from Area 00 (cf. Pl. 23: 3) is clearly a bronze, but probably of not very high tin content. This conclusion is in accord with the microstructure, which will be described later. The other two examples are "copper", and from a comparison of exposure 6, for good, present-day commercial copper, are of reasonable purity, the specimen from Cemetery 2000 (Pl. 22: 5) being somewhat less pure than that from the Middle Bronze Age tomb (Pl. 22: 12).

Fig. A. Spectrogram: comparison of Bronze Age weapons with modern metals.

1. Late Bronze Age dagger from Area 100 — Bronze
2. Middle Bronze Age dagger from Tomb 1552 — Copper
3. Dagger of the Caliciform Culture from Tomb 2049 — Copper
4. Pure Zinc
5. Pure Tin
6. Good commercial copper
7. Carbon arc

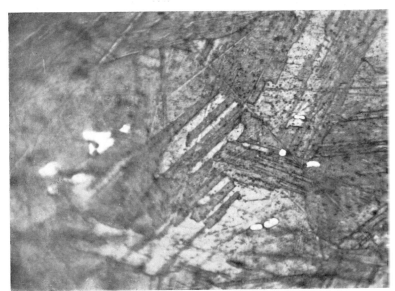

FIG. B. Microstructure near the edge of a dagger of
the Caliciform Culture from Tomb 2049. × 1000
diams.
The white areas are oxide

FIG. C. Microstructure near the surface of a dagger
of the Late Bronze Age from Area 100. × 400
diams.
Dark—corrosion product
Light—copper-tin alloy

FIG. D. Microstructure of Late Bronze Age dagger
(see Fig. C) showing cored and twinned structure of
uncorroded bronze. × 400 diams.

Microstructures. Sections, both transverse and lengthwise, were cut from each dagger, polished and etched with ferric chloride acidified with hydrochloric acid.

On examination under the microscope the following facts emerged:

Dagger of the Caliciform Culture (Pl. 22: 5 from Tomb 2049)

The cored structure was completely absent from this sample, which would be consistent with the dagger having been cast and then fully annealed, or alternatively, and perhaps more probably, having been very slowly cooled after casting, say in a hot mould. At the centre there were a few strain markings but no twins. Near the edge, on the other hand, undeformed twins were present in quantity (Fig. B) together with more frequent strain markings than at the centre. The method of production would, therefore, appear to have been to cast the dagger roughly to shape and hammer the edges while the metal was hot; a final, quite light, hammering of the edges completing the process.

Middle Bronze Age Dagger (Pl. 22: 12 from Tomb 1552)

Although the sample appeared to be solid metal it proved, in fact, to be mainly corrosion products cementing together residual particles of copper. These particles were markedly flattened, and it is reasonable, therefore, to assume that the sample had been heavily hammered. In these unchanged areas clear evidence of a deformed twinned structure could be seen. There was, further, distinct evidence of the cored structure.

These facts are consistent with the view that this dagger was produced from a cast bar or slab which had been quickly cooled. This was then reheated, hammered, reheated and hammered again; the sequence of reheatings and hammerings may have been even longer. The final hammering was clearly done while the metal was cold or nearly so.

Late Bronze Age Dagger (Pl. 23: 3 from Area 100)

This sample, like the Middle Bronze Age one, showed appreciable corrosion almost to the core, and Fig. C illustrates the intergranular nature of this penetration. In the small amount of solid metal remaining there was very clear evidence of a highly deformed core structure, together with equally clear indications of undeformed twins, Fig. D. The structure consisted entirely of the α phase, the $\alpha\delta$ eutectoid being completely absent. The dagger, therefore, was cast and heavily worked whilst still hot. The absence of the $\alpha\delta$ eutectoid suggests that the tin content could not be very high, and the severity of the working would be consistent with the view that after casting (whether to shape or as a slab cannot be determined) the material was heated and hammered, this being probably repeated several times. There is no evidence that after the final hot hammering operation any further cold work was done, though since the extreme edge has been lost due to corrosion, this statement must be accepted with some hesitation.

Further spectrographic examination showed that the only trace element clearly present was iron, which occurred in each of the three samples. Nickel, zinc, bismuth, antimony, tin, arsenic, lead and silver were absent so far as plates taken on the Hilger medium spectrograph show. It is possible that on the large Hilger instrument some of these might show up, but to all intents and purposes they were absent. It is clear that the copper from which these speciments were made was of high purity apart from the iron.

APPENDIX E
OBJECTS IN THE PALESTINE ARCHAEOLOGICAL MUSEUM, JERUSALEM

Museum No.	Field No.	Plate No.	Museum No.	Field No.	Plate No.
33.1952	717	NP	34.2803	1857	59: 152
33.1953	718	24: 10	34.2804	1858	59: 135
33.1954	727	30: 37	34.2805	1859	60: 218 and 16: 38
33.1955	728	30: 52	34.2806	1861	59: 175
33.1956	740	30: 41	34.2807	1862	60: 193 and 16: 12
33.2072	1389	NP	34.2808	1863	60: 199 and 16: 18
33.2073	1390	NP	34.2809	1864	59: 152
33.2074	1399	NP	34.2810	1865	59: 152
33.2096	1436	NP cf. RES 713	34.2811	1866	60: 190 and 16: 9
34.111	441	NP	34.2812	1867	59: 152
34.112	442	27: 1	34.2813	1868	60: 220
34.131	1458	40: 392	34.2814	1869	60: 213 and 16: 33
34.2773	1708	69: 542*	34.2815	1870	60: 210 and 16: 30
34.2774	1709	68: 514	34:2816	1871	60: 221 and 16: 41
34.2775	1710	68: 528	34.2817	1872	60: 217
34.2776	1711	87: 1007	34.2818	1873	59: 142
34.2777	1712	87: 1010	34.2819	1874	59: 135
34.2778	1713	69: 543	34.2820	1875	59: 152
34.2779	1714	NP	34.2821	1876	59: 152
34.2780	1715	72: 643	34.2822	1877	60: 216 and 16: 29
34.2781	1716	73: 660	34.2823	1878	59: 152
34.2782	1717	70: 596	34.2824	1880	59: 152
34.2783	1718	69: 543	34.2825	1881	59: 152
34.2784	1719	78: 780	34.2826	1882	59: 152
34.2785	1720	78: 780	34.2827	1883	60: 190
34.2786	1721	77: 751	34.2828	1884	60: 183 and 16: 2
34.2787	1722	30: 25	34.2829	1885	60: 229 and 16: 47
34.2788	1723	30: 23	34.2830	1886	60: 195 and 16: 14
34.2789	1724	30: 24	34.2831	1887	60: 206 and 16: 25
34.2790	1725	22: 14	34.2832	1888	60: 189 and 16: 8
34.2791	1726	22: 15 and 44: 1	34.2833	1889	60: 192 and 16: 11
34.2792	1727	24: 5	34.2834	1890	60: 211 and 16: 31
34:2793	1728	26: 18	34.2835	1892	60: 203 and 16: 22
34:2794	1729	NP	34.2836	1893	60: 196 and 16: 15
34.2795	1849	60: 230 and 16: 48	34.2837	1894	60: 191 and 16: 10
34.2796	1850	60: 233 and 16: 51	34.2838	1895	59: 142 and 16: 7
34.2797	1851	59: 135	34.2839	1896	60: 198 and 16: 17
34.2798	1852	59: 135	34.2840	1900	60: 224 and 16: 42
34.2799	1853	60: 186 and 16: 4	34.2841	1901	60: 232 and 16: 50
34.2800	1854	60: 188 and 16: 6	34.2842	1903	60: 209 and 16: 28
34.2801	1855	60: 220 and 16: 40	34.2843	1904	60: 181 and 16: 1
34.2802	1856	59: 152	34.2844	1905	59: 142

* Underlined numbers indicate type specimens.

Museum No.	Field No.	Plate No.	Museum No.	Field No.	Plate No.
34.2845	1906	60: 223 and 16: 37	34.2905	2341	67: 454 and 20: 3
34.2846	1907	60: 202 and 16: 21	34.2906	2397	67: 478
34.2847	1908	60: 228 and 16: 46	34.2907	2398	67: 282
34.2848	1909	NP	34.2908	2399	67: 469
34.2849	1910	NP	34.2909	2400	66: 434
34.2850	1911	60: 182	34.2911	2403	67: 470
34.2851	1912	60: 191	34.2912	2404	66: 448
34.2852	1913	NP	34.2913	2414	67: 463
34.2853	1914	60: 205 and 16: 24	34.2914	2415	66: 438
34.2854	1915	59: 135	34.2915	2420	67: 488
34.2855	1916	59: 152	34.2916	2420a	67: 467
34.2856	1917	59: 152	34.2917	2425	66: 449
34.2857	1918	60: 231 and 16: 49	34.2918	2455	67: 471
34.2858	1919a	NP	34.2919	2456	22: 3
34.2859	1920	60: 202	34.2920	2472	67: 497
34.2860	1921	60: 184	34.2921	2483	66: 444
34.2861	1922	NP	34.2922	2484	67: 493
34.2862	1923	62: 279	34.2931	2583	87: 1008
34.2863	1924	62: 280	34.2932	2584	77: 760
34.2864	1927	60: 214 and 16: 34	34.2933	2585	78: 781
34.2865	1928	60: 185 and 16: 3	34.2934	2586	68: 528
34.2866	1929	60: 212 and 16: 32	34.2935	2587	70: 587
34.2867	1930	60: 194 and 16: 13	34.2936	2588	87: 1011
34.2868	1931	59: 152	34.2937	2589	69: 540
34.2869	1932	60: 187 and 16: 5	34.2938	2590	70: 587
34.2870	1933	60: 197 and 16: 16	34.2939	2591	70: 598
34.2871	1934	59: 135	34.2940	2592	73: 648
34.2872	1935	NP	34.2941	2593	77: 760
34.2873	1936	60: 207 and 16: 26	34.2942	2594	73: 648
34.2874	1937	60: 203	34.2943	2595	85: 973
34.2875	1938	60: 200 and 16: 19	34.2944	2596	77: 730
34.2876	1939	NP	34.2945	2598	70: 594
34.2877	1940	NP	34.2946	2599	26: 17
34.2878–2888	1941	NP	34.2947	2600	26: 16
34.2889	1879	59: 153	34.2948	2601	26: 15
34.2890	1961	NP	34.2949	2602	32: 107
34.2891	2078	87: 1010	34.2950	2602a	NP
34.2892	2079	74: 673	34.2951	2603	32: 104
34.2893	2080	68: 526	34.2952	2604	32: 105
34.2894	2081	78: 781	34.2953	2605	32: 120
34.2895	2082	68: 525	34.2954	2606	32: 112
34.2896	2083	69: 541	34.2955	2607	32: 118
34.2897	2084	77: 742	34.2956	2608	32: 111
34.2898	2085	77: 743	34.2957	2609	32: 108
34.2899	2086	77: 743	34.2958	2610	32: 110
34.2900	2087	69: 540	34.2959	2611	32: 116
34.2901	2088	24: 4	34.2960	2612	32: 123
34.2902	2089	24: 3	34.2961	2613	32: 115
34.2903	2339	67: 455 and 20: 1	34.2962	2614	32: 122
34.2904	2340	66: 428 and 20: 2	34.2963	2615	32: 117

Museum No.	Field No.	Plate No.	Museum No.	Field No.	Plate No.
34.2964	2616	32: 106	34.7667	1860	60: <u>204</u> and 16: 23
34.2965	2617	32: 114	34.7668	1891	60: <u>208</u> and 16: 27
34.2966	2618	32: 124	34.7669	1897	60: <u>227</u> and 16: 45
34.2967	2619	32: 109	34.7670	1898	60: <u>222</u> and 16: 36
34.2968	2620	32: 113	34.7671	1899	60: <u>225</u> and 16: 43
34.2969	2621	32: 121	34.7672	1902	60: <u>215</u> and 16: 35
34.2970	2622	32: 125	34.7673	1919	60: <u>201</u> and 16: 20
34.2971	2623	32: 119	34.7674	1925	60: <u>226</u> and 16: 44
34.2972	2624	NP cf. RES 425	34.7675	1926	60: <u>219</u> and 16: 39
34.2973	2625	NP cf. RES 424	34.7676	1942	26: 3
34.2974	2626	NP cf. RES 428	34.7677	2268	21: 15.
34.2975	2627	NP cf. RES 427	34.7678	2269	21: 12
34.2976	2627a	NP	34.7679	2376	67: <u>485</u>
34.2977	2638	77: <u>730</u>	34.7680	2684	74: <u>672</u> and 20: 21
34.2978	2639	77: <u>739</u>	34.7681	2687	74: <u>669</u> and 20: 20
34.2979	2640	77: <u>750</u>	34.7682	2688	77: <u>738</u> and 20: 19
34.2980	2641	70: <u>583</u>	34.7750, 7751	1977a	66: <u>408</u>
34.2981	2642	70: 583	35.2945	3577	78: <u>790</u>
34.2982	2643	77: <u>740</u>	35.2946	3578	71: <u>619</u>
34.2983	2644	NP	35.2947	3579	81: <u>888</u>
34.2984	2645	26: 4	35.2948	3580	72: *L. II*: 91
34.2985	2646	23: 2	35.2949	3582	71: *L. II*: 30
34.2986	2647	32: 94	35.2950	3583	69: <u>555</u>
34.2987	2648	32: 98	35.2951	3584	68: *L. II*: 125
34.2988	2649	32: 97	35.2952	3585	82: *L. II*: 345
34.2989	2650	32: 95	35.2953	3586	80: 866
34.2990	2651	32: 91	35.2954	3587	84: 963
34.2991	2652	32: 96	35.2955	3588	NP
34.2992	2653	32: 93	35.2979	3733	80: 845
34.2993	2654	32: 99	35.2980	3734	84: <u>968</u>
34.2994	2655	32: 100	35.2981	3736	25: 66
34.2995	2656	32: 92	35.2982	3770	81: <u>885</u>
34.2996	2657	32: 90	35.2983	3771	82: <u>940</u>
34.2997	2658	32: 101	35.2984	3772	75: <u>699</u>
34.2998	2659	32: 102	35.2985	3773	85: <u>978</u>
34.2999	2660	32: 103	35.2986	3774	82: <u>932</u>
34.3000	2661	NP	35.2987	3775	82: <u>936</u>
34.3001	2662	NP	35.2988	3776	79: 825
34.3002	2678	NP	35.2989	3777	84: <u>952</u>
34.3003	2679	32: 126	35.2990, 2991	3779	80: 849
34.3004	2680	NP	35.2992–2996	3780	80: 857
34.3005	2685	68: <u>524</u> and 20:18	35.2997	3781	80: 865
34.3006	2686	69: <u>537</u> and 20: 17	35.2998, 2999	3782	80: 860
34.3088	3053	NP	35.3000, 3001	3783	77: <u>777</u>
34.3089	3051	38: 322	35.3002	3784	81: 875
34.3090	3060	NP	35.3003	3785	83: 945
34.3091	3062	NP	35.3004	3786	82: <u>897</u>
34.3092	3082	NP	35.3005	3782	80: 860
34.3093	3084	NP	35.3006	3787	78: 781
34.3094	2090	30: 26	35.3007	3788	78: <u>784</u>

Museum No.	Field No.	Plate No.	Museum No.	Field No.	Plate No.
35.3008	3789	81: 869	35.3065	3842	28: 4
35.3009	3790	79: 828	35.3066	3843	28: 5
35.3010	3791	82: 933	35.3067	3840	25: 17
35.3011	3792	79: 825	35.3072	3807	70: 584
35.3012, 3013	3793	73: L. II: 195	36.1484	4349	32: 128
35.3014	3794	73: L. II: 199	36.1485	4367	78: 793
35.3015, 3016	3795	73: L. II: 195	36.1486	4400	77: 778
35.3017-3019	3796	73: 662	36.1487	4456	74: 681 and 52: 34
35.3020–3022	3797	73: 661	36.1488	4496	75: 701 and 52: 41
35.3023	3798	73: 655	36.1489	4572	80: 851 and 53: 70
35.3024	3799	73: L. II: 203	36.1490	4600	79: 824
35.3025	3800	73: L. II: 193	36.1498	4882	79: 826
35.3026	3801	73: 665	36.1499	4883	82: 899
35.3027	3802	73: L. II: 197	36.1500	4884	81: 871
35.3028	3803	73: 666	36.1501	4885	82: L. II: 344
35.3029	3804	73: 663	36.1502	4886	82: 903
35.3030	3805	73: 656	36:1503	4887	71: L. II: 24
35.3031	3806	73: 667	36.1504	4888	71: L. II: 38
35.3032	3808	70: 588	36.1505	4889	NP
35.3033	3809	71: L. II: 20	36.1506	4890	39: 376
35.3034	3810	71: L. II: 30	36.1507	4892	23: 17
35.3035	3811	72: L. II: 95	36.1508	4893	25: 55
35.3036	3812	72: L. II: 78	36.1509–1511	4894	25: 54
35.3037	3813	71: L. II: 20	36.1512	4895	25: 56
35.3038	3814	71: L. II: 51	36.1513	4896	25: 57
35.3039	3815	71: L. II: 146	36.1514	4898	24: 29
35.3040	3816	71: L. II: 21	36.1602	5194	79: 807
35.3041	3817	70: L. II: 29	36.1813	3470	32: 131
35.3042	3818	71: L. II: 30	36.1818	3735	23: 16
35.3043	3819	68: L. III: 9	36.1819	3737	25: 65
35.3044	3820	70: L. II: 7	36.1820	3738	32: 127
35.3045	3821	71: L. III: 8	36.1821	3837	23: 15
35.3046	3822	71: L. II: 52	36.1822	3841	25: 16
35.3047	3823	71: L. II: 30	36.1823	3844	38: 297
35.3048	3824	72: L. II: 120	36.1824	3845	29: 56
35.3049	3825	71: L. II: 143	36.1825	3846	38: 295
35.3050	3826	71: L. II: 52	36.1826	3847	48: 4
35.3051	3827	69: 570	36.1827	3848	29: 1, 4, 5, 6, 7, 9, 25, 28, 32, 37
35.3052	3828	68: L. II: 114			
35.3053	3829	69: 564	36.1829	4041	NP
35.3054	3830	NP	36.2237	4476	80: 838 and 53: 41
35.3055	3831	78: 795	36.2238	4523	79: 829 and 53: 40
35.3056	3832	78: 785	36.2239	4607	80: 852 and 53: 72
35.3057	3833	NP	36.2240	4609	80: 856 and 53: 44
35.3058	3834	NP	36.2241	4636	23: 7 and 54: 46
35.3059	3835	26: 34	36.2269	4891	39: 377
35.3060	3836	23: 14	36.2270	4897	24: 30
35.3061	3838	23: 13	36.2272	3778	79: 815
35.3062, 3063	3839	25: 18	37.710	5548	73: 653
35.3064	3840	25: 17			73: 649

Museum No.	Field No.	Plate No.	Museum No.	Field No.	Plate No.
37.711, 712	5551	73: *L. II*: 197	37.799, 800	5962	78: 788
37.713, 714	5553	73: *L. II*: 203	37.801	5964	78: 800
37.715	5556	78: *L. II*: 292	37.802	5965	82: 900
37.716	5561	77: 762	37.803–805	5966	81: 895
37.717	5567	77: 777	37.806	5967	81: 896
37.718	5582	70: 593	37.807	5969	81: 884
37.720, 721	5588	71: *L. II*: 30	37.808	5970	82: 901
37.722	5591	71: *L. II*: 51	37.809	5971	81: 888
37.723	5592	69: 543	37.810	5972	81: 891
37.727	5612	25: 2	37.811	5973	81: 894
37.728	5613	25: 3	37.812	5975	76: 722
37.730	5900	76: 707	37.813	5976	79: 830
37.731	5901	87:1025	37.814	5977	84: 961
37.732, 733	5902	73: *L. II*: 203	37.815	5981	82: 919
37.734	5903	71: *L. II*: 30	37.816, 817	5983	82: 926
37.735	5904	82: 902	37.818	5986	82: 929
37.736, 737	5906	71: *L. II*: 20	37.819	5987	82: 922
37.738	5907	71: *L. II*: 30	37.820	5988	82: 925
37.739	5909	71. *L. III*: 8	37.821	5991	85: *L. III*: 425
37.740	5911	78: 788	37.822	5993	85: 982
37.741	5913	81: 895	37.823	5995	85: 976
37.742	5914	71: 619	37.824	5996	82: 941
37.743–746	5917	71: *L. II*: 50	37.825	5997	NP
37.747	5918	71: *L. II*: 45	37.826	6005	29: 64
37.748	5920	71: *L. II*: 48	37.827	6006	NP
37.749	5921	71: *L. II*: 46	37.828	6007	25: 52
37.750	5922	NP	38.52	5617	24: 17
37.751	5928	NP	38.53	5649	38: 250
37.752	5929	NP	38.54	5656	34: 165
37.753–761	5931	71: *L. II*: 30	38.55	5664	34: 164
37.762–768	5932	71: *L. II*: 143	38.56	5665	34: 163
37.769–772	5933	71: *L. II*: 50	38.57	5670	38: 251
37.773, 774	5934	71: *L. II*: 137	38.58	5674	34: 190
37.775	5935	71: *L. II*: 137	38.59	5718	38: 288
37.776	5936	70: 592	38.60	5724	36: 246
37.777–779	5937	771: 620	38.61	5726	34: 188
37.780–782	5938	71: *L. II*: 21	38.62	5727	34: 189
37.783	5939	72: *L. II*: 95	38.63	5728	36: 239
37.784	5940	71: *L. II*: 52	38.64	5739	36: 235
37.785	5947	69: 574	38.65	5741	36: 210
37.786	5949	70: 602	38.66	5746	34: 161
37.787	5950	71: *L. II*: 14	38.67	5772	34: 174
37.788	5951	71: *L. II*: 14	38.68	5775	34: 149
37.789	5952	70: *L. II*: 10	38.69	5788	NP
37.790	5954	73: *L. II*: 204	38.70	5792	NP
37.791–793	5955	73: *L. II*: 203	38.72	5902	73: *L. II*: 203
37.794	5956	73: *L. II*: 195	38.73	5905	81: 888
37.795	5957	73: *L. II*: 204	38.74	5908	79: 820
37.796	5959	78: 787	38.75	5910	78: 793
37.798	5961	78: *L. III*: 301	38.76	5912	78: 791

Museum No.	Field No.	Plate No.	Museum No.	Field No.	Plate No.
38.77	5915	82: 928	38.122	5927a	39: 356
38.78	5916	82: 924	38.126	3581	71: *L. II*: 14 and 43: 1
38.79	5917	71: *L. II*: 50	38.134	5995a	75: 691
38.80	5919	69: 570	38.135	5996a	NP
38.81	5923	39: 351	38.138	5998	39: 360
38.82	5924	39: 352	38.139	5999	39: 363
38.83	5925	39: 353	38.720	6241	83: 949
38.84	5926	39: 354	38.721	6243	NP
38.85	5927	39: 355	38.723	6257	47: 4
38.86	5931	70: *L. II*: 13	38.724	6259	47: 3
38.87	5933	71: *L. II*: 50	38.732–741	6544	18: 3, 5, 14, 17, 21, 30,
38.88	5941	71: *L. III*: 20			31, 32, 33, 40, 47–52,
38.89	5942	82: 912			54, 57, 60, 61, 63
38.90	5943	70: 608	38.752	6604	68: 506
38.91	5944	72: 628	38.753	6611	77: 753
38.92	5945	69: 564	38.754	6653	32: 70
38.93	5946	69: *L. III*: 56	38.755	6673	30: 60
38.94	5947	70: *L. II*: 10	38.756–758	6676	28: 1
38.95	5948	70: 607	38.759	6680	62: 303 and 15: 1, 2
38.96	5953	82: 913	38.760, 761	6682	18: 9, 16, 26, 28, 34, 45,
38.97	5955	73: *L. II*: 203			58, 65, 68
38.98	5956	73: *L. II*: 195	38.762	6688	73: *L. II*: 292
38.99	5958	78: 793	38.763	6689	NP
38.100	5960	78: 792	38.764	6691	77: 777
38.101	5963	78: *L. III*: 300	38.765	6693	NP
38.102	5966	81: 895	38.767	6733	46; and 45: 3
38.103	5967	81: 896	38.772	6928	NP
38.104	5968	81: 889	38.883	6930	NP
38.105	5974	76: 723	39.791	6542	62: 290 and 15: 4
38.106	5978	85: *L. III*: 425	39.793	6690	79: 814
38.107	5979	84: 962	39.794	6692	77: 774
38.108	5980	85: 989	39.795	6697	86: 1005
38.109	5982	82: 918			48: 6, 7–9
38.110	5984	82: 928	39.796	6736	40: 393
38.111	5985	82: *L. II*: 344	39.797	6747	85: 990
38.112	5989	84: 954	39.800	6956	79: 811 and 49: 6
38.113	5990	81: 875	39.801	6986	49: 7
38.114	5992	85: 981			86: 1003
38.115	5994	82: 920	39.802	6992	49: 3
38.116	5997	NP	39.803–806	6997	49: 15
38.117	6000	39: 362	39.807	6998	NP
38.118	6001	39: 358	39.808	7000	39: 382
38.119	6002	39: 357	39.809	7001	39: 383
38.120	6003	39: 359	39.834	6994	49: 13
38.121	6004	39: 361	39.837–839	6544	See 38.732–741

INDEX

PRINTED IN
GREAT BRITAIN
AT THE
UNIVERSITY PRESS
OXFORD
BY
CHARLES BATEY
PRINTER
TO THE
UNIVERSITY